# MACRO—
# ECONOMICS

# MACRO-ECONOMICS

## Third Edition

# ROGER N. WAUD

**University of North Carolina, Chapel Hill**

1817

**HARPER & ROW, PUBLISHERS, New York**
Cambridge, Philadelphia, San Francisco,
London, Mexico City, São Paulo, Singapore, Sydney

Photo credits: Smith, p. 14, Culver Pictures; Keynes, p. 188, Brown Brothers; Friedman, p. 329, The University of Chicago; Malthus, p. 418, Brown Brothers; Ricardo, p. 445, Brown Brothers; Marx, p. 497, THE GRANGER COLLECTION, New York.

Sponsoring Editor: John Greenman
Project Editor: Ellen Meek Tweedy
Text Design Adaptation: North 7 Atelier Ltd.
Cover Design: DanielsDesign Inc.
Text Art: Vantage Art, Inc.
Production: Debra Forrest
Compositor: Donnelley/ROCAPPI Inc.
Printer and Binder: R. R. Donnelley & Sons Company

**MACROECONOMICS,** Third Edition

**Library of Congress Cataloging-in-Publication Data**
Waud, Roger N., 1938–
  Macroeconomics.
  Includes index.
  1. Macroeconomics.   I. Title.
HB172.5.W38   1986          339          85–21993
ISBN 0–06–046946–3

85 86 87 88  9 8 7 6 5 4 3 2 1

**To Myra**

# Brief Contents

# Detailed Contents

**FOUR**
# Inflation, Unemployment, Economic Stability, and Growth          **345**

**15** Monetary and Fiscal Policy and Budget Deficits          347

# Preface

Since its inception, this book's primary objective has been to demonstrate how principles of economics are used to analyze real-world events and problems. To meet this objective in a new way, a major feature has been added to the third edition—a series of discussions about contemporary economic problems and policies for dealing with them. Each chapter has from one to four such sections, called "Policy Perspectives." They are directly related to the chapter's content and, because they deal with real-world situations, they enhance students' understanding of important economic issues.

Ultimately, a basic education in economics should attempt to develop a facility, indeed a habit, for disentangling and making sense of important economic issues encountered daily in the popular press and on television. The third edition's Policy Perspectives demonstrate how to do this, while at the same time exploring matters of concern to most citizens. As a chapter unfolds, the Policy Perspectives provide effective vehicles for showing beginning students *why* the study of economics is useful.

The third edition contains a number of significant substantive changes. In addition, all related data and graphs have been updated and, in a number of instances, new statistical information and graphs have been added. Every chapter has been reexamined with an eye to improving exposition and presentation, and no chapter has remained unchanged as a result of this process.

## MACROECONOMICS: MAJOR CHANGES

A major difference between the second and the third editions is that aggregate demand and supply are now developed and presented graphically with the aggregate price level on the vertical axis and total output on the horizontal axis, a change requested by many second edition users. In addition, the sequence of some chapters has been changed, several were rewritten, and three are almost entirely new. The following lists the macro chapters that have been substantially revised, or are new, together with an accounting of the changes from the second edition.

**Chapter 5,** "Macroeconomic Concepts," is a new chapter that introduces the macro section of the book by discussing the circular flow of income and product, explaining the meaning of GNP and the distinction between real and nominal GNP, and giving a brief introduction to aggregate demand and supply. In the previous edition, Chapter 5 covered national income accounting.

**Chapter 6,** "Economic Fluctuations, Unemployment, and Inflation," covers essentially the same material as in the second edition. However, a discussion of changes in the composition of unemployment during business cycle peaks and troughs and a more extensive discussion of cost-of-living allowance clauses (COLAs) in union contracts have been added. The discussion of the accelerator principle now appears in an appendix.

**Chapter 7,** "Measuring National Income and Product," is now a short chapter on national income accounting that is completely different from the second edition's Chapter 7.

**Chapter 8,** "Aggregate Demand and Supply: The Income-Expenditure View," combines material from Chapters 7 and 8 of the second edition in rewritten form. It begins with a brief discussion of the classical theory of income and employment determination, represented in terms of a vertical aggregate supply curve and a downward-sloping aggregate demand curve (price level on vertical axis, output on the horizontal). The chapter then develops Keynesian income-expenditure theory, initially presenting it in terms of a horizontal aggregate supply curve and downward-sloping aggregate demand curve in order to contrast the assumptions of wage and price rigidity with the classical assumptions of perfect wage and price flexibility. Finally, the chapter develops the consumption, saving, and investment schedules and presents the determination of equilibrium income and expenditure in the Keynesian 45-degree diagram.

**Chapter 10,** "Government Spending, Taxation, and Fiscal Policy," covers all of the material previously covered in Chapter 10 of the second edition *except* that the section on the implications of supply-side economics for fiscal policy has now been moved to the next chapter.

**Chapter 11,** "Aggregate Demand and Supply: Inflation and Supply-Side Economics," is a completely new chapter. It begins by showing how the downward-sloping aggregate demand curve (price level on vertical axis, output on the horizontal) may be derived from the total expenditure schedule of the Keynesian 45-degree diagram. The chapter then develops in greater depth the aggregate supply curve (briefly introduced previously, along with the aggregate demand curve, in Chapters 5 and 8). The aggregate demand-aggregate supply framework is then used to discuss demand-pull and cost-push inflation, stagflation, and supply-side economics and their implications for fiscal policy.

**Chapter 13,** "Banks, Money Creation, and the Role of the Federal Reserve System," is a revision of Chapter 12 of the second edition. The section on the monopoly bank has been removed, as recommended by some second edition users. This chapter now discusses the development of the demand for money and explains how money demand and supply interact to determine the equilibrium level of the interest rate in the money market. (Both of these topics appeared in the chapter immediately following this one in the second edition.)

**Chapter 14,** "The Role of Money in Income Determination," is a revision of Chapter 13 of the second edition. The material on money supply and demand and the determination of the interest rate has been removed and placed in the previous chapter, as already noted. Instead, the monetarist view of the way money affects the economy is developed, in addition to the Keynesian view, which was the only view presented in the second edition's version of this chapter. The way in which money affects aggregate demand and the price level is also examined using the aggregate demand and supply analysis developed earlier in Chapters 5 and 11.

**Chapter 15,** "Monetary and Fiscal Policy and Budget Deficits," combines some of the information from Chapters 14 and 15 of the second edition. This chapter begins by explaining the differences between Keynesian and monetarist views on the extent to which fiscal policy actions affect real GNP and the price level. It then explains the different effects on the economy of pure fiscal policy actions as distinguished from those accompanied by money supply changes, a distinction that is very important to understanding the effects of government deficits on the economy. The difficulties of coordinating monetary and fiscal policy, particularly in the presence of large government deficits, are then examined.

**Chapter 16,** "The Inflation-Unemployment Trade-off: Supply-Side, Accelerationist, and New Classical Views," is such a substantial revision of Chapter 15 of the second edition that it is essentially a new chapter. It begins by examining the Phillips curve, first in terms of the role of supply-side shocks of the 1970s vis-à-vis the aggregate demand and supply analysis developed in Chapters 5 and 11. Then the natural rate is defined and the inflation-unemployment trade-off is analyzed, first from the perspective of the accelerationist view, and then in terms of the new classical view based on rational expectations. Finally, this chapter examines the implications of the changing nature of unemployment for the inflation-unemployment trade-off.

**Chapter 17,** "Guidelines, Controls, Indexing, and Jobs," is essentially an updated revision of Chapter 16 of the previous edition. Of particular note is a discussion of the Job Training Partnership Act (put into effect in 1983) and the results realized to date under that program, as compared to job-training programs implemented by the federal government in previous years.

## Government Budget Deficits

This important subject receives extensive treatment in this edition. It is first discussed in the text of Chapter 10 and in two of the Policy Perspectives in that chapter. Two of the Policy Perspectives in Chapter 11 also focus on aspects of deficits, including what has contributed to their dramatic increase in recent years. Chapter 15 explicitly treats implications for the economy of how government budget deficits are financed. Too often current texts do not give sufficient attention to these implications. They relate directly to the issue of crowding out and the effectiveness of fiscal and monetary policy as discussed in Chapter 15. These implications are also quite relevant to the discussion of contemporary problems of fiscal and monetary policy and to the inflation-unemployment trade-off discussed in Chapter 16.

## On Explaining Things

It may seem an odd pitch to make about a textbook, but this book places an emphasis on explanation. In recent years many economics principles texts seem to put a premium on being terse—even to the point of being "slick." But there is a trade-off between brevity and explanation. Given the need to explain, the ideal is to be as brief as possible but not briefer than necessary. As a practical matter, books typically and unavoidably end up somewhat to one side or the other of the ideal. I have decided that if I am condemned to err, I would opt for explaining too much rather than too little. Every effort has been taken to make the book as understandable as possible. Numerous examples are provided to give concreteness to difficult concepts.

## MORE ABOUT THE POLICY PERSPECTIVES

Each Policy Perspective has been selected because it illustrates an economic problem and concept directly related to the economic principles developed in a particular chapter. A Policy Perspective typically has two questions at the end that are intended to challenge the student to think (and hopefully encourage discussion) about the problems and issues raised. In addition to engaging the student's attention in a relevant way, the Policy Perspectives show how and why economic analysis is a powerful and useful tool. The following lists the Policy Perspective titles and page numbers.

- "What GNP Does Not Measure," Chapter 5, p. 108
- "Dating Business Cycle Peaks and Troughs—When Do They Occur?," Chapter 6, p. 120
- The Consumer Price Index—Does It Measure the Cost of Living or What?," Chapter 6, p. 135
- "Wage-Price Controls—A Difficult Way to Curb Inflation," Chapter 6, p. 137
- "The Great Depression—Attempts to Explain a Paradox," Chapter 8, p. 176
- "A Common Misconception About the Saving-Investment Process—The Role of Banks," Chapter 9, p. 189
- "The Variety of Taxes and Their Effects on Spending," Chapter 10, p. 212
- "Discretionary Versus Nondiscretionary Expenditures," Chapter 10, p. 217
- "The Deficit Problem—Crowding Out Capital Formation," Chapter 10, p. 223
- "Deficits and the Growing Government Debt—Facing Up to a Problem," Chapter 10, p. 227
- "Tax Evasion and the Underground Economy—Another Source of Deficit Growth," Chapter 11, p. 246
- "Where Are We on the Laffer Curve?" Chapter 11, p. 248
- "Indexing Income Taxes—Putting the Brakes on Rising Tax Rates," Chapter 11, p. 250
- "The Reagan Deficits—The Result of Supply-Side Economics or What?," Chapter 11, p. 252
- "Money and Prices—Two Cases of Hyperinflation," Chapter 12, p. 267
- "The Bank Panic Problem Returns Again," Chapter 12, p. 280
- "Bank Failure and Deposit Contraction—How Serious Is the Threat?," Chapter 13, p. 297
- "Ideological Differences Between Keynesians and Monetarists," Chapter 14, p. 326
- "Monetarist Experiment?—How the Fed Under Volcker Slowed Inflation," Chapter 14, p. 338
- "The Politics of Coordinating Fiscal and Monetary Policy," Chapter 15, p. 353
- "Why Have Real Interest Rates Been So High?," Chapter 15, p. 359
- "Viewpoints on the Costs of Reducing Inflation," Chapter 16, p. 376
- "Our Most Recent Experience with Wage-Price Controls," Chapter 17, p. 393
- "Indexing and the Fight Against Inflation," Chapter 17, p. 398
- "How Serious Are the Limits to Growth?," Chapter 18, p. 426
- "How We Keep Running Out of Energy—The Role of the Market," Chapter 18, p. 428
- "Protection and Trade Policy—The Two-Way Street," Chapter 19, p. 457
- "How Can the Dollar Be So Strong When the Trade Deficit Is So Large?," Chapter 20, p. 485

## OTHER PEDAGOGICAL FEATURES

### Checkpoints

Checkpoints appear in every chapter, generally at the ends of major sections. At each Checkpoint the student is signaled to stop and answer a series of questions about concepts just presented—to stop and check on his or her progress and grasp of the material. Questions and problems placed at the ends of chapters are too often easily ignored, like so much litter at the back of a closet that one is rarely forced to face. The Checkpoints are intended to surmount this problem by helping the student reconsider what has just been read—to assure the student's understanding of concepts as they are encountered. Answers to the Checkpoints appear at the back of the book to provide immediate feedback for the student who uses the Checkpoints. Frequently, the Checkpoints also provide grist for class discussion.

### Learning Objectives

Learning objectives are listed and set off from the main text at the beginning of each chapter. They outline a plan of study for the chapter, as well as provide an overview of what's to be done. After completing the chapter, the student can also use the list of learning objectives as a quick check to see whether he or she has mastered the material in the chapter.

## Economic Thinkers

Economic Thinkers essays are not so much personal biographies as studies in the history of economic thought. Their major purpose is to highlight the development of economic thinking on major problems and concerns while indicating the significant role that particular individuals have played in this development.

## Key Terms and Concepts

Terminology is unavoidably abundant in economics. In addition, words that have several meanings in common everyday usage often have a more precise meaning when used in economics. Such words, along with other important economic terms, appear in boldface type when they are first introduced and defined in the text. The "Key Terms and Concepts" list at the end of each chapter highlights the new terminology presented in the chapter. These terms and concepts are defined again in the glossary at the back of the book.

## Summaries

The summaries at the end of each chapter are fairly comprehensive. They tie together the main concepts developed in the chapter as well as alert the student to areas that may require rereading.

## Questions and Problems

Questions and problems are also located at the end of each chapter. They are generally more complex and extended than the questions found in the Checkpoints. Some are almost case studies. Many may be readily used for class discussion. Answers to all end-of-chapter questions and problems are provided in the *Instructor's Manual*. The Checkpoints together with the end-of-chapter questions and problems and Policy Perspective questions provide significantly more in-text questions and problems than are offered by most other economic principles texts currently available.

## Figures, Graphs, and Tables

Liberal use of real-world data is made in tables and figures throughout the book. Quite often, tables containing hypothetical data are used to illustrate particularly difficult concepts. The captions describing each graph and figure generally begin with a brief summary statement followed by a reasonably complete description of what is portrayed.

## SUPPLEMENTS AND TEACHING AIDS

The text is supplemented by the following learning and teaching aids: a student study guide, an instructor's manual, transparency masters, and an expanded computerized test bank designed and constructed along lines recommended by the Joint Council on Economic Education.

## Study Guide

The student *Study Guide* was written by Professor John E. Weiler of the University of Dayton. Each chapter in the study guide corresponds to a chapter in the textbook. At the beginning of each study guide chapter there is a summary of the corresponding chapter in the textbook. Then a set of basic problems follows with at least one problem for each basic concept developed in the textbook chapter. The problems are aimed at helping the student use the economic principles developed in the text to quantitatively analyze a specific issue. The basic problem set is followed by a set of multiple-choice questions, a set of true-false questions, and a set of problems, questions, and exercises on matching terms. Each of the sets of problems, questions, and exercises is designed to give complete coverage to each major concept developed in the textbook chapter. The answers to all problems, questions, and exercises are given at the back of the study guide.

## Instructor's Manual

Three suggested outlines for a one-semester course appear at the beginning of the *Instructor's Manual.* Each chapter of the manual first gives a summary of the corresponding textbook chapter along with a discussion of important chapter concepts and learning objectives. The manual contains answers to all the end-of-chapter textbook questions and problems.

## Test Bank

The test bank has been expanded for the third edition. The test bank contains over 2,000 questions. The test bank is also available on MICROTEST, Harper & Row's computerized testing service. Contact your local Harper & Row representative for further information about the MICROTEST system for PCs.

The test bank, designed in accordance with guidelines suggested by the Joint Council on Economic Education, contains questions constructed to provide a balanced coverage, both by concepts and by the levels at which each concept might be tested. This is done in the following systematic way. In each test bank chapter, a table identifies, for each question, the principal concept which that question tests and the level at which the concept is tested. The concepts tested are closely coordinated with the learning objectives listed at the beginning of each textbook chapter. *A real effort has been made to include questions that test the student's ability to use a concept in a variety of settings.* Questions at the level of application are typically underrepresented in other test banks. This is not true of this test bank. Many of the questions in the test bank have been used at the University of North Carolina, Chapel Hill, where they have been subjected to statistical test item analysis.

## Transparency Masters

All important graphs, roughly 90 in number, are available to adopters as a set of transparency masters.

## ACKNOWLEDGMENTS

Many people have provided helpful comments and contributions to this book throughout the course of its development. I would like especially to thank the reviewers of the third edition of the book (starred names), as well as those of the earlier editions:

* Phillip Allman,
    University of the Pacific
* Fred M. Arnold,
    Madison Area Technical
    College
Alan Batchelder,
    Kenyon College
Arthur Benavie,
    University of North
    Carolina, Chapel Hill
Charles A. Bennett,
    Gannon University
Dennis M. Byrne,
    University of Akron
H. Richard Call,
    American River College
Anthony J. Campolo,
    Columbus Technical
    Institute
Robert C. Dauffenbach,
    Oklahoma State University
David Denslow,
    University of Florida
Richard Froyen,
    University of North
    Carolina, Chapel Hill
* Philip Gilbert,
    Mira Costa College
Jack B. Goddard,
    Northeastern State
    University

Roger S. Hewett,
    Drake University
* Robert Jerome,
    James Madison University
* William E. Kamps,
    South Dakota State
    University
David B. Lawrence,
    Drake University
* Patrick M. Lenihan,
    Eastern Illinois University
John L. Lewis,
    Northern Illinois
    University
* Patrick Litzinger,
    Robert Morris College
John G. Marcis,
    Kansas State University
* Ken McCormick,
    University of Northern
    Iowa
* Robert K. Miller,
    Pennsylvania State
    University, Beaver
    Campus
* Walt Mitchell,
    College of the Mainland
Henry K. Nishimoto,
    Fresno City College
Martin Oettinger,
    University of California at
    Davis

John Rapp,
    University of Dayton
* R.K. Russell, Southwestern
    Oklahoma State University
* Timothy P. Ryan,
    University of New Orleans
Michael Salemi,
    University of North
    Carolina, Chapel Hill
James A. Skurla,
    University of Minnesota at
    Duluth
* John A. Sondey,
    University of Idaho
Izumi Taniguchi,
    California State University,
    Fresno
Helen Tauchen,
    University of North
    Carolina, Chapel Hill
* Robert Turner,
    Colgate University
* Lawrence A. Waldman,
    College of St. Benedict
Samuel Williamson,
    University of Iowa
Edgar W. Wood,
    University of Mississippi
* Allan Harris Zeman,
    Robert Morris College

ROGER N. WAUD

# To the Student

You don't have to have had a course in economics to be aware of economic problems. Newspapers, radio, and television bombard you with them daily. You no doubt are well aware of inflation, unemployment, and budget deficits. Paying tuition bills, finding a job, and just getting a few bucks to spend on a favorite pastime already have given you experience at economic problem solving. In short, you're not a novice to the subject of economics in the same way you might be to college physics. Nonetheless, economics is a rigorous subject. It should be studied in the same way that you would study a course in one of the sciences—a little bit every day.

Before reading a chapter, always look at the learning objectives that are set out at the beginning. They will give you a brief outline of what you are about to read and of the author's aims. At various points in the chapter your attention will be drawn to a Policy Perspective (a discussion of some economic problem or policy) where basic economic principles are developed to enable you to understand such topics. You will find that the economic way of thinking, which at times may seem somewhat abstract, is a powerful tool for analyzing real-world problems. Also, after completing a chapter, you should go back and see how well you have accomplished the learning objectives set out at the beginning. Doing so will provide a self-check on your grasp of the concepts and principles developed in the chapter.

When reading this book, read for understanding, not speed. Each chapter is broken into major sections that focus on important concepts. At the end of a major section, you will encounter a Checkpoint—a brief series of questions that enable you to test your understanding of what you have just read. You should always stop and measure your progress by trying to answer the questions in these Checkpoints. The answers to the Checkpoint questions appear at the back of the book to give you feedback as you study.

Economics is a problem-analyzing discipline. In order to give you more practice, further questions are provided at the end of each chapter. Try your hand at these as well. Discuss them with fellow students and your instructor whenever you feel unsure about the answers. Further problems and questions designed to supplement this book are contained in John E. Weiler's *Study Guide*. The *Study Guide* will give you considerable practice at economic problem solving and aid your understanding of important economic principles.

Finally, bear in mind that the concepts and principles studied in each chapter are typically used again and again in subsequent chapters. Mastering the material as you go makes the chapters that follow that much easier.

I wish you success in your study of economics.

ROGER N. WAUD

# MACRO-ECONOMICS

# ONE

## Introduction

# 1

# Economics and Economic Issues

════════

**AFTER READING THIS CHAPTER, YOU WILL BE ABLE TO:**

1. Define the terms *economy* and *economics*.

2. List and define the basic economic terms used most often in economic discussions.

3. Distinguish between and give examples of positive and normative statements.

4. Identify the basic elements that make up any economic theory.

5. Construct a simple graph from data given in a table.

6. Define the terms *macroeconomics* and *microeconomics*.

7. Define and give examples of the three major fallacies that may be found in statements of economic theory or analysis.

8. Explain the role of economic theory and analysis in economic policymaking.

**I**t has been said that there are three kinds of people: those who make things happen, those who watch things happen, and those who wonder what happened. If you sometimes find yourself among the last group, the study of economics is for you.

How can the study of economics help you? Most importantly, a knowledge of economics will help you to analyze economic issues that are reported daily in the press and on television. Although the laws of economics may not be as absolute as the law of gravity, they will help you deal with facts and opinions about economic issues. As a result, you will be able to come to intelligent, informed conclusions when faced with both day-to-day problems and questions of national policy.

## ECONOMY AND ECONOMICS

The word **economy** typically brings to mind ideas of efficiency, thrift, and the avoidance of waste by careful planning and use of resources. We might say that some job was done with an "economy of motion," meaning that there was no unnecessary effort expended. The word comes from the Greek *oikonemia*, which means the management of a household or state. In this sense, we often speak of the U.S. or the Chinese economy; of a capitalist, socialist, free-market, or planned economy; or of industrialized and underdeveloped economies. We use the term in this last sense when we refer to *a particular system of organization for the production, distribution, and consumption of all things people use to achieve a certain standard of living.*

The term **economics**, on the other hand, is not so simple. It covers such a broad range of meaning that any brief definition is likely to leave out some important aspect of the subject. Most economists would agree, however, that economics is a social science concerned with the study of economies and the relationships among them. *Economics is the study of how people and society choose to employ scarce productive resources to produce goods and services and distribute them among various persons and groups in society.* This definition touches upon several important concepts—choice, scarcity, resources, production, and distribution—with which we will be concerned both in this chapter and throughout the book.

Before reading any further you should understand that, whatever it is, economics is not primarily a vocational subject such as accounting, marketing, or management. Nor is it primarily intended to teach you how to make money, though it may help. Economics studies problems from society's point of view rather than from the individual's. Nevertheless, it is likely you will find the study of economics helpful in whatever career you choose. Moreover, it should make you a more knowledgeable and able citizen.

## THE LANGUAGE OF ECONOMICS

As is the case with many subjects, the words used in economics often seem strange to the beginner. Physicists talk about neutrons, quarks, and hysteresis; football coaches talk about fly patterns, look-in patterns, and flex defenses. To make sense of a typical news item about economic issues you must be familiar with the language of economics. Economists frequently use common words to mean something more precise than is generally expected in everyday conversation. For instance, when you say someone has a lot of money, common usage suggests that you mean a person who owns a lot of things such as cars, houses, buildings, bonds, stocks, cash, and so on. In economics, however, we generally accept that "money" means one's holdings of currency and demand deposits at a commercial bank. When we mean something else, we always spell out exactly what other items we mean to include in our definition of money. Certain basic terms, such as money, will come up again and again throughout this book. The following definitions will help you to understand and use them correctly.

## Economic Goods

An economic good is any item that is desired and scarce. In general, economic goods may be classified as either commodities or services. Commodities are tangible items such as food or clothing. (*Tangible* means, quite literally, able to be touched.) Commodities do not have to be consumed when they are produced; that is, they may be stored. Services are intangibles (that is, nontouchables) such as shoeshines or haircuts. They cannot be stored or transferred. For example, I cannot give you my haircut (a service), but I can give you my coat (a commodity). Such distinctions are not always clear-cut. For example, the economic good electricity might be called a service by some who say it is intangible and a commodity by those who note that it can be stored in a battery. Most often, an economic good is simply referred to as a good. You may have heard of the output of the economy referred to as "goods and services." This is done largely to remind us of the existence of services.

Whether they are commodities or services, all economic goods share the quality of being **scarce**. That is, there is not enough of them to supply everyone's needs and desires. As a result, people have to pay to obtain them. What they have to pay is called the **price** of the good. As we will see in Chapter 4, price is determined to a large extent by the number of people who desire and are able to pay for a particular good, together with what it costs producers to provide it.

People desire economic goods because these goods provide some form of satisfaction. A refrigerator provides satisfaction by keeping food cold. A stereo system provides satisfaction by giving us entertainment. Because an economic good gives us satisfaction, we say that it is useful to us. As a result, economists sometimes refer to the satisfaction a good yields as its utility. The creation of goods that have utility is called production. Production is carried out through the use of economic resources.

## Economic Resources

*Economic resources,* also called the factors of production, are all the natural, man-made, and human resources that are used in the production of goods. These resources may be broken down into two broad categories, non-human resources (capital and land) and human resources (labor).

### Capital

*Capital* is an example of a term that is used to mean one thing in everyday conversation and another in economics. We often speak of capital when referring to money, especially when we are talking about the purchase of equipment, machinery, and other productive facilities. It is more accurate to call the money used to make the purchase financial capital. An economist would refer to this purchase as investment. An economist uses the term capital to mean all the man-made aids used in production. Sometimes called investment goods, capital consists of machinery, tools, buildings, transportation and distribution facilities, and inventories of unfinished goods. A basic characteristic of capital goods is that they are used to produce other goods. For example, electricity is produced with capital goods consisting of boilers, turbines, fuel storage facilities, poles, and miles of wire. Capital is scarce relative to the desire for the output of goods and services made with the use of capital.

### Land

To an economist, *land* is all natural resources that are used in production. Such resources include water, forests, oil, gas, mineral deposits, and so forth. These resources are scarce and, in many cases, are rapidly becoming more scarce.

### Labor

*Labor* is a very broad term that covers all the different capabilities and skills possessed by human beings. Labor is scarce relative to the desire for the output of goods and services made with the help of labor. Labor consists of welders, carpenters, masons, hod carriers, dentists, scientists, teachers, managers, and so forth. The term *manager* embraces a host of skills related to the planning, administration, and coordination of production. A manager may also be an entrepreneur (or enterpriser). This is the person who comes up with the ideas and takes the risks that are necessary to start a successful business. The founders of companies are entrepreneurs, while those running them are more accurately called managers.

### The Firm

These economic resources of land, capital, and labor are brought together in a production unit that is referred to as a business or a *firm*. The firm uses these resources to produce goods, which are then sold. The money obtained from the sale of these goods is used to pay for the economic resources. Payments to those providing labor services are called wages. Payments to those providing buildings, land, and equipment leased to the firm are called rent. Payments to those providing financial capital (those who own stocks and bonds) are called dividends and interest.

### Gross National Product

The total dollar value of all the final goods (as distinguished from goods still in the process of production) produced by all the firms in the economy is called the *gross national product* (GNP). In order to make meaningful comparisons of the GNP for various years, economists often use real GNP—GNP adjusted so that it only reflects changes in quantity of output, not changes in prices. When the real GNP goes down, we say the economy is in a state of recession. A severe recession is called a depression, although there is no general agreement as to how to decide exactly when a recession becomes a depression.

### Inflation and Unemployment

The economic health of the nation, of which GNP is one measure, is directly affected by two other important factors, *inflation* and *unemployment*. Inflation is an ongoing general rise in prices. The steeper this rise, the faster the decline of a dollar's purchasing power. The unemployment rate measures the percentage of the total number of workers in the labor force who are actively seeking employment but are unable to find jobs. The higher the unemployment rate, the more the economy is wasting labor resources by allowing them to stand idle. However, it is generally believed that a decrease in the unemployment rate will lead to an increase in inflation, all other things remaining the same. ("All other things remaining the same" is an important phrase in economics that we will look into later in this chapter.)

### Positive and Normative Statements

Intelligent discussion of economic issues requires that we distinguish between positive and normative statements. In the previous paragraph we made the statement that "a decrease in the unemployment rate will lead to an increase in inflation." This is a statement of fact that may be supported or refuted by examining data. As such, we can say it is a **positive statement**. *Positive statements tell us what is, what was, or what will be. Any disputes about a positive statement can be settled by looking at the facts.* "It rained last Thursday" and "the sun will rise in the east tomorrow" are positive statements.

But now let's change our statement about inflation and unemployment slightly. Let's say that "it is *better* to decrease unemployment and live with the resulting increase in inflation than to allow a large number of people to go without jobs." This is a **normative**

**statement**—*an opinion or value judgment.* Those of you who are looking for jobs would probably tend to agree with this statement. But your grandparents who are retired and living on fixed incomes would be likely to disagree. Since they are not seeking employment, an increase in the number of jobs available would in no way compensate them for a rise in prices. As far as they are concerned, it would probably be better to slow the rise in prices. This, of course, would lead to an increase in unemployment, which would make all job-seekers very unhappy. The dispute between these two groups cannot be settled by facts alone.

Normative statements tell us what should be (*normative* means establishing a norm or standard). *Although normative statements often have their origin in positive statements, they cannot be proven true or false by referring to objective data.* For example, I may make the normative statement, "You shouldn't drink and drive." This statement has its origin in the positive statement, "Drinking alcoholic beverages slows down one's ability to react." We could disagree forever over the first statement, but statistical studies could be brought to bear on any dispute over the second.

In any discussion about economic issues, as soon as voices rise you can almost be certain that the discussion has shifted from logic and fact to value judgment and opinion. However, don't forget that value judgments and opinion often parade in the clothes of logic and fact.

---

*CHECKPOINT\* 1-1*
**Pick out a short news item in today's paper and make a list of all the positive statements and a list of all the normative statements. Examine the normative statements and try to determine what kinds of positive statements they may be based on.**

\*Answers to all Checkpoints can be found at the back of the text.

---

# ECONOMIC REALITY AND ECONOMIC THEORY

*Economic reality*—making a living, paying the rent, shopping for food, paying taxes, and so forth—forces us to deal with a large and confusing swarm of facts, figures, and events. The activities of households, firms, and federal, state, and local governments all have a direct effect on our economic lives. In order to make some sense out of the world around us we all have formulated some economic theories, even without being aware of doing so.

How to hold down inflation is a topic about which practically everyone has a theory. One individual, having just filled out an income tax return, might say, "If we don't curb all this government spending, inflation will get worse." The owner of a small business, on the other hand, feels that "if something isn't done to break up the big unions and big corporations, we'll never bring inflation under control." Based on observations of the way certain groups, organizations, and institutions function, each individual has focused on the relationship that appears to be most relevant to an explanation of inflation. From these examples, we can say that *an* **economic theory** *is an attempt to describe reality by abstracting and generalizing its basic characteristics. Economists often refer to an economic theory as a law, principle, or model. Each of these terms may be taken to mean the same thing.*

## Observations and Predictions: The Scientific Method

The inflation-control theories of the individuals above share two common features: (1) each is based on observation of facts or events, and (2) each makes a prediction about the consequences of certain events. We can now add to our definition of an economic theory by saying that *an economic theory provides an explanation of observed phenomena that may be judged by its ability to predict the consequences of certain events.*

Although economics is not a science like chemistry or physics, it does make use of the scientific method in arriving at and testing theories. The aspects of the **scientific method** that we are most concerned with here are induction and deduction. **Induction** *is the process of formulating a theory from a set of observations.* **Deduction** *is the process of predicting future events by means of a theory.* The predictions made by deduction are then tested by once again observing facts or events to see if what was predicted actually takes place. If not, the theory will have to be changed to conform with reality, and the whole process begins again. For example, suppose there is an increase in government spending, the crucial event in the first individual's theory, but we do not observe the predicted increase in inflation. Following the scientific method, we must either modify or discard the theory because of its failure to predict correctly. The process of induction and deduction is never-ending, since all theories must be continually retested in light of new facts and events.

## Constructing a Theory

Our income-tax payer and our small-business owner, needless to say, did not really use the scientific method in drawing up their theories. But now let's see how an economist would go about formulating a theory. As an example, we will analyze the law of demand, a theory that will be referred to many times throughout this book.

### Elements of Economic Theory

Every formal statement of a theory has four basic elements:

1. a statement of specific variables;
2. a set of assumptions about other variables that may be relevant;
3. a hypothesis about the way the specific variables are related;
4. one or more predictions.

The law of demand states that the quantity of a good demanded per unit of time will increase as the price of the good decreases, all other things remaining the same. Let's break this statement down into the four elements listed above.

*Variables.* The law of demand is concerned with two variables, price and quantity demanded. We call these variables because they can vary, that is, they are subject to change. As we noted in our discussion of the language of economics, price is the amount that must be paid to obtain a good. Quantity demanded is the amount of that good that people want and can pay for per unit of time.

*Assumptions.* The law of demand makes the assumption that, except for price, all other variables that might influence demand will remain the same. This assumption, which is a feature of all economic theories, is often referred to as **ceteris paribus**. Logically enough, that's Latin for "all other things remaining the same." This assumption is important when we come to the point of testing our theory. Real-world events may not turn out as the theory says they should. We must be sure to find out whether this is because the theory is wrong or because something other than just price has changed, thus violating the *ceteris paribus* assumption.

*Hypothesis.* A hypothesis is a statement of the way we think the variables in question relate to each other. Our hypothesis in the law of demand is that as price decreases, quantity demanded will increase. This is known as an **inverse relationship**, since the variables are changing in opposite ways. If the variables change in the same way (an increase in one leads to an increase in the other), we say they have a **direct relationship**.

*Prediction.* Here we move directly into the realm of the real world. Armed with our theory, what can we say will likely happen if the manager of our local clothing store reduces the price of Irish knit sweaters from $45 to $35? While customers might not break down the doors to get in, our theory tells us that we can safely bet that the number of sweaters they want to buy will increase. Historically, the development of the automobile is a good example of the validity of the law of demand. The original cars, which were made on an individual basis, were so expensive that only the rich could afford them. Then Henry Ford developed the assembly-line method of production, which made cars less costly to produce. As a result of using this method, he was able to reduce prices. The quantity demanded soared.

## How Exact Is Economic Theory?

Since economic theory tries to explain and predict human behavior, you probably wonder how it is possible to be very exact. Economic theory cannot be as exact as Newton's three laws of motion. But economic behavior is on average more predictable than the behavior of many subatomic particles currently studied in high energy physics. If economic behavior weren't predictable, stores wouldn't hold sales, banks wouldn't need vaults and security guards, and traffic tickets wouldn't carry fines. If you don't think economic behavior is predictable, drop a pail of quarters in a public swimming pool some summer afternoon. Make a practice of this and see if you notice a predictable pattern of behavior.

The law of demand is a good predictor because people's behavior on average is such that they will buy more of a good the lower its price is. True, there is the occasional person who will buy more of a good the higher its price because of "snob appeal." But this is unusual. When we look at the behavior of a large group of individuals, the on-average similarity of the behavior of the majority of them dominates the unusual behavior of the few.

*CHECKPOINT 1-2*
**During the Arab oil embargo of 1973–1974, people waited in long lines to fill up their gas tanks. What does the law of demand suggest to you about a** **way in which those lines could have been shortened?**

## Theories into Graphs

So far, we have been using words to explain how the law of demand works. But when we come to the point of relating the theory to data obtained through research, it is time to use pictures. In economics, the pictures we use take the form of graphs. Let's construct a graph from data about electricity use.

### Basic Elements of a Graph

An ordinary graph starts out with two lines, which are called axes. One of the lines is drawn vertically, the other horizontally. The point at which they meet is called the origin and has a value of zero (see Figure 1–1). The value along each axis increases as we move

**FIGURE 1-1   Basic Elements of a Graph**

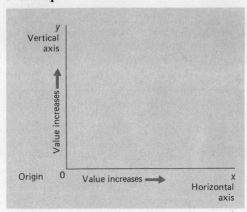

Every graph starts out with two lines. One is called the vertical (or *y*) axis. The other is called the horizontal (or *x*) axis. The point at which they meet is called the origin and has a value of 0. The value of the variable being measured on each axis increases as you move farther away from the origin. This means moving up along the vertical axis and to the right along the horizontal axis.

away from the origin. This means moving up along the vertical axis and to the right along the horizontal axis.

In the case of the law of demand, we noted that we would be looking at two variables, price and quantity demanded. In economics, it is customary to use the vertical axis to measure price. Quantity demanded, therefore, is measured along the horizontal axis. What does this mean in terms of our investigation into the demand for electricity? We now have to find out what numbers to use on each axis. In other words, we must determine how much electricity is demanded at various prices. Let's suppose that our research into electricity demand in one city comes up with the data given in Table 1-1.

### Constructing a Graph

Returning to our graph, we can now label the vertical axis "Price per kilowatt-hour" and the horizontal axis "Kilowatt-hours demanded (in millions per month)," as shown in Figure 1-2. (These labels correspond to the column headings in Table 1-1.) We di-

vide the vertical axis evenly into units representing $.01 increases in price. We divide the horizontal axis evenly into units representing 10-million kilowatt-hour increases in quantity demanded. Our next task is to find the points on the graph corresponding to the quantity demanded per hour figure and the price per kilowatt-hour figure for each of the six pairs of numbers given in Table 1-1. (We have labeled these pairs of numbers a, b, c, d, e, and f in our table.)

For combination a, we first move right along the horizontal axis to a point equal to 15 million kilowatt-hours. We then move directly upward from that point until we are opposite the point on the vertical axis that represents a price of $.06. We label the point at which we have arrived a, since it corresponds to combination a on our table. We use the same procedure to locate points b, c, d, e, and f. Our graph now looks like Figure 1-2.

If we draw a line connecting points a through f, we have what is called a demand curve. Our graph now looks like Figure 1-3. In this case, we see that the demand curve slopes downward and to the right. This tells us that as price decreases (moves down along the vertical axis), quantity demanded increases (moves right along the horizontal axis).

Thinking back to our discussion of the elements of a theory (pp. 8–9), you will remember that we called this type of relationship between two variables an inverse relationship. All inverse relationships (one variable increasing while the other is decreasing) produce this type of downward, rightward-sloping curve. It is one of the major purposes of a graph to show us, without our even having to read the specific numbers involved, what the relationship between the variables is. When we compare the picture of demand provided by our graph with our theory, we see that the theory is consistent with the facts. The downward, rightward slope of the demand curve shows us that as price decreases, quantity demanded increases.

Finally, it should be emphasized that an

**TABLE 1-1 Demand for Electricity at Different Prices** (Hypothetical Data)

| | Price per Kilowatt-Hour | Kilowatt-Hours Demanded (in Millions per Month) |
|---|---|---|
| (a) | $.06 | 15 |
| (b) | .05 | 17 |
| (c) | .04 | 20 |
| (d) | .03 | 25 |
| (e) | .02 | 35 |
| (f) | .01 | 50 |

This table tells us how much electricity will be demanded per month at various prices. If the price is $.06 per kilowatt-hour, the quantity demanded will be 15 million kilowatt-hours per month (combination a). If the price is $.03 per kilowatt-hour, the quantity demanded will be 25 million kilowatt-hours (combination d).

**FIGURE 1-2** **Demand for Electricity at Various Prices**

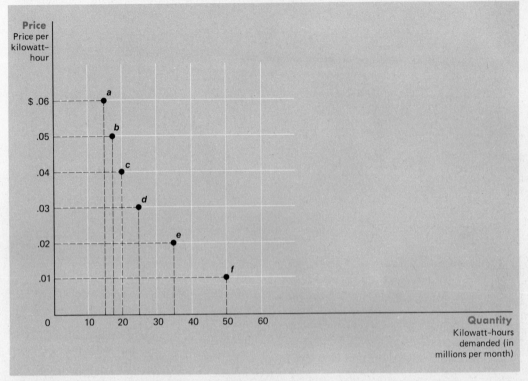

Using the data obtained from Table 1–1, we are able to locate points on the graph that represent the various price-quantity demanded combinations for electricity. To locate combination c, for example, we move right along the horizontal axis until we come to 20 million kilowatt-hours. We then move directly upward from this point until we are opposite the $.04 mark on the vertical axis. The same procedure is used to find the other combinations listed in Table 1–1.

economic theory can be (1) stated in words, (2) represented in a table (Table 1-1), and (3) illustrated in the form of a graph (Figure 1-3).

*CHECKPOINT 1-3*
**Suppose that utility companies say they are finding it difficult to produce all the electricity their customers are demanding. Keeping in mind the graph in Figure 1-3, let us suppose we were able to obtain information on electricity demand in another city. In this case, let us suppose that the data indicate that the demand in this other city is less sensitive to changes in price than the demand in the city we've been looking at so far. What sort of shape do you think the demand curve for electricity would have compared with the one shown in Figure 1-3? In which city would an increase in price most relieve the strain on the utility companies? Why?**

**FIGURE 1-3 Demand Curve for Electricity**

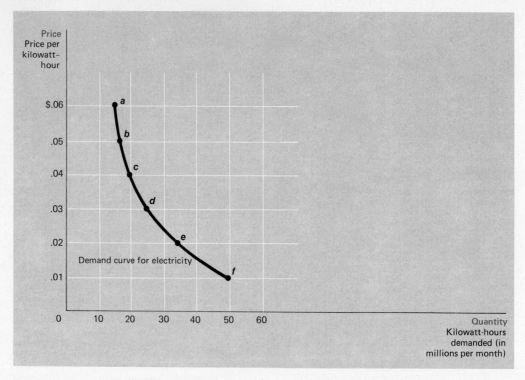

After we have located all the points that correspond to the price-quantity demanded combinations in Table 1–1, we draw a line connecting them. This line is called the demand curve. In this case, because the relationship between price and quantity demanded is an inverse relationship, the curve slopes downward and to the right.

## MACROECONOMICS VERSUS MICROECONOMICS

Economists often use the terms *macroeconomics* and *microeconomics* to distinguish between different levels of economic analysis.

In **macroeconomics** we are concerned with the workings of the whole economy or large sectors of it. These sectors include government, business, and households. For the purposes of analysis, the smaller groups that make up these large sectors are often lumped together and treated as one unit. For example, the consumer sector may be treated as though it were one large household. The

business sector might be considered to be one large business. Macroeconomics deals with such issues as economic growth, unemployment, recession, inflation, stagflation, and monetary and fiscal policy.

**Microeconomics,** on the other hand, focuses on the individual units that make up the whole of the economy. Here we are interested in how households and businesses behave as individual units, not as parts of a larger whole. Microeconomics studies how a household spends its money. It also studies the way in which a business determines how much of a product to produce, how to make best use of the factors of production, what pricing strategy to use, and so on. Microeconomics also studies how individual markets and industries are organized, what patterns of competition they follow, and how these patterns affect economic efficiency and welfare.

## ECONOMIC REASONING: COMMON PITFALLS

In order to analyze an economic issue or problem correctly, we must avoid certain common pitfalls of economic reasoning. One of the most common fallacies arises from the difficulty of distinguishing between cause and effect. Another is commonly known as the fallacy of composition.

### Cause and Effect

As we have seen in our analysis of the law of demand, a key interest of economics is to determine how events in the real world can be explained and even predicted. In other words, we are looking for causes. We want to be able to say with reasonable certainty that if A happens, B will be the result. Having analyzed the law of demand, we are able to say that if price is decreased, quantity demanded will increase, all other things remaining the same. Unfortunately, it is not always easy to tell if some event was the cause of another event or if it just preceded it in time. The situation is especially tricky when event B regularly follows event A.

In economics there are many times when it is very difficult to tell whether A caused B or B caused A. Perhaps there is no causal relationship between B and A at all, but both occur together because event C always causes both A and B to happen. A fire causes smoke and light, but smoke doesn't cause light and light doesn't cause smoke. People in high-income brackets tend to have better health and more education than people in low-income brackets. Possibly they were born with a hardier constitution and more than the average amount of energy. These factors would enable such people to attend school more

regularly and have a greater capacity for work. If so, it is possible that high income and education are no more causally related than smoke and light, but that being born with a hardy constitution causes both. On the other hand, it may be that higher education causes higher income, which makes it possible to afford a better diet and better medical care.

*The rather common fallacy of concluding that A caused B simply because A occurred before B is known as the* **fallacy of false cause.**

### Fallacy of Composition

Common sense will tell you that if you find yourself in a burning building, you should get out as fast as you can. However, if the burning building is a crowded movie theater and each individual in it tries to get through the door at the same time, the results are likely to be tragic. What is good advice for you as an individual is not good advice for the group as a whole. *The false assumption that what is true for a particular part of the whole is also true for the whole itself is called the* **fallacy of composition**. (The whole is made up, or composed, of two or more individual parts.)

We can see how this fallacy works on an economic level if we consider the following example. If you are unemployed and have a mortgage on your house, you might be wise to sell the house. You can use the money obtained from the sale to pay off the mortgage and buy a cheaper house. In this way you can eliminate the burden of monthly mortgage payments. But if everyone on your block decides to do the same thing, the glut of houses on the market may drive prices down so low that you may not be able to get enough money to pay off the mortgage and buy a new house. What makes good economic sense for the individual does not necessarily make good economic sense for the whole economy. We will see other examples in this book where what is true at the microeconomic level is not necessarily true at the macroeconomic level.

## ECONOMIC THINKERS

### Adam Smith — 1723–1790

Adam Smith is often thought of as the father of modern economics, although his great work, *An Inquiry into the Nature and Causes of the Wealth of Nations* (1776), would not look very much like a modern economics textbook to today's reader.

One of Smith's most significant contributions to economic thought was his explanation of the importance of the division of labor and its relationship to the development of the economy. In his famous description of operations in a pin factory, Smith shows how output can be greatly increased by dividing tasks into small segments, each performed by specialists who require little training.

Smith's central theme was the value of enlightened self-interest, and he preached the doctrine of laissez faire. In Smith's view, the role of government should be minimized, in contrast with the power governments had exercised over all types of commerce in the past. Beyond maintaining national security, preserving internal order, and undertaking a few tasks such as public education, government was, according to Smith, to exercise little power. An advocate of economic freedom, Smith generally accepted the idea of "natural order" taught by the Scottish philosopher Francis Hutcheson, which implied the removal of restrictions of all kinds. Such a theory well suited the rising commercial class in Western Europe, particularly in England, which found government regulations irksome. Freedom allowed the natural instincts provided by a wise providence (in other words, self-interest) to prevail and provide the drive to turn the wheels of trade and commerce.

As Smith saw it, it would be foolish to assume that people satisfy the needs of others simply as a result of feelings of altruism. On the contrary, the baker, the brewer, and the candlestick maker each undertakes to satisfy the needs of others as a means of satisfying his or her own needs. By seeking to fulfill personal needs, each individual is helping to increase the wealth of society:

*He generally, indeed, neither intends to promote the public interest nor knows how much he is promoting it. By preferring the support of domestic to that of foreign industry, he intends only his own security; and by directing that industry in such a manner as its produce may be of the greatest value, he intends only his own gain; and he is in this, as in many other cases, led by an invisible hand to promote an end which was no part of his intention.*

FOR FURTHER READING

Clark, John J., and others. *Adam Smith, 1776–1926.* University of Chicago Press, 1928.

Smith, Adam. *An Inquiry into the Nature and Causes of the Wealth of Nations.* Modern Library ed. New York: Random House, 1937.

In judging what is true for the whole of society, we must not go to the opposite extreme and assume that what is true for the whole is also true for the individual parts. Such an assumption is known as the **fallacy of division**. For example, while it is true that society as a whole may benefit from a highly competitive marketplace, some individual firms with weak management skills may go bankrupt.

## CHECKPOINT 1-4

**Think of some examples where confusions about cause and effect might arise. Can you think of a fallacy**

**of composition that frequently occurs when a crowd watches a football game?**

## ECONOMIC POLICY

Economic theories have by and large evolved as responses to problems. In other words, necessity has been the mother of invention. But theory is only a tool, a way of looking at economic reality. It does not provide ready-made solutions to problems. John Maynard Keynes, a highly regarded policymaker as well as theorist, put it this way:

> The theory of economics does not furnish a body of settled conclusions immediately applicable to policy. It is a method rather than a doctrine, an apparatus of the mind, a technique of thinking, which helps its possessor to draw correct conclusions.

**Economic policy** *is concerned with finding solutions to economic problems.* While policymakers use economic theory to help them, they must go beyond it as well. They must consider the cultural, social, legal, and political aspects of an issue if they are to formulate a successful policy. In the end, making economic policy involves making value judgments such as those we explored when we looked at the conflict between unemployment and inflation. And an economist has no special claim over anybody else to making these judgments.

### Economic Analysis and Economic Policymaking

While economic theory and analysis may not always be able to tell policymakers what they should do, it usually can tell them what they shouldn't do. An understanding of economic principles can keep us from both pursuing unwise policies and chasing conflicting goals. A few examples will illustrate how this is so.

### An Unwise Policy

The printing of money by a government in order to finance its expenditures has long been considered by economists to be an unwise move. Despite their warnings, however, history is a graveyard of fallen governments that have yielded to this temptation. Somehow it always seems easier to turn on the printing press than to raise taxes. After World War I, the German government printed money at such a clip that the rate of inflation reached several thousand percent per week! At this point the deutsche mark ceased to have any value at all as a medium of exchange. No one would accept it in payment for goods or services. Faith in the government's ability to manage was seriously shaken. The resulting political instability probably contributed in some degree to the rise of Adolf Hitler and the Nazi party.

### Conflicting Goals

In the conflicting goals category, an election year is often marked by talk of achieving full employment and reducing inflation—both at the same time. Full employment today is usually defined as an unemployment rate of roughly 6 percent. Almost everyone would agree that a 1 percent rate of inflation is low. But almost any economist will tell you that these two goals conflict with each other. A 6 percent unemployment rate goal is probably not compatible with a 1 percent inflation rate goal. Research findings, while not final or always clear-cut, might indicate that a 6 percent unemployment rate is possible only if we are willing to accept a 9 percent inflation rate. On the other hand, in order to cut inflation to 1 percent, we might have to live with an unemployment rate of 10 percent. This serves to remind us that an economy's behavior can only be modified within limits. (You can't expect a large bus to take corners like a sports car, or a sports car to carry 50 passengers.) Economic analysis can help us to form realistic policy objectives that don't conflict with one another.

The conflict between goals can be illustrated further by looking at the case of a retail clothier. Suppose the clothier stocked a large number of winter coats—the goal, to make money from their sale. But suppose the winter season is drawing to a close and the clothier still has a large number of winter coats on hand. The clothier has another goal—to make room for new spring fashions. Economic analysis, in particular the law of demand, tells the clothier to lower prices, in other words, to have a sale. But this may mean that the coats will have to be sold for less than what they cost the clothier. As a policymaker, the clothier has to choose between making money on winter coats and making room for the new fashions.

## Economic Policy, Special Interests, and the Role of the Economist

Making economic policy forces us to choose among alternatives that have different consequences for different groups. Each of us is a member of one or more special interest groups. As students and educators, we might find it in our interest to pay special attention to any proposed legislation that affects education and institutions of learning. Similarly, labor unions are concerned about legislation on right-to-work laws and the powers and rights of unions to help one another enforce strikes and deal with strikebreakers. Business interests are also concerned with labor legislation, but their stands on such matters are usually opposed to those of labor. Farmers and consumers are both concerned with agricultural policy, but once again their interests are often in conflict. Resolution of these conflicts typically involves choices such as those we have discussed in connection with the inflation-unemployment trade-off. That is, we must make choices that are matters of value judgment. As we have noted, economists have no special calling to make subjective judgments as to what particular group should gain at another's expense. Economists probably do their greatest service to policymaking when they take the goals of all parties concerned as given and confine themselves to exploring and explaining which goals are compatible and which conflict, and what economic consequences will result from different policy actions.

## Major Economic Policy Goals in the United States

A list of economic policy goals that most economists, policymakers, and citizens feel are important in the United States would probably look like this:

1. *Price stability:* in recent years this has meant checking inflation.
2. *Full employment:* in recent years most economists would take this to mean keeping the unemployment rate down around 6 to 6.5 percent.
3. *Economic growth:* continued growth in the standard of living for the average citizen.
4. *Environmental standards:* more control over the pollution and wastes that our production processes produce and impose on the environment.
5. *Economic security:* provision of an adequate standard of living for those who are unable to work either because of age, illness, and other handicaps beyond their control or because there are simply not enough jobs for all who want them.
6. *An equitable tax burden:* people, especially the middle-income groups, have shown increasing concern that our tax system favors those, typically in higher income brackets, who are in a position to take advantage of various loopholes in our tax laws to avoid or greatly reduce their "fair share" of the tax burden.
7. *Economic freedom:* the idea that businesses, consumers, and workers should be given much freedom in their economic activities.

We have already pointed out how economic experience has suggested that goals 1 and 2 may not be compatible, and that there seems to be a trade-off between the achievement of one at the expense of the other. The same may be true of goals 3 and 4 and of

## POLICY PERSPECTIVE

### Why Economists Disagree—The Role of Ideology

Put two economists in the same room and what do you get? An argument, or so it would seem to most people. Why do economists seem to disagree so much? How can the Nobel prize be awarded in economics and how can economics be regarded as a science if different economists can come up with such dissimilar answers when confronted with the same policy issue? The problem is that economics, unlike chemistry and physics for example, deals with human beings, the societies they live in, and the questions of who shall get what and how. Such questions invariably raise issues of value judgment about what is a "good" and "just" society, that is, issues of political ideology. The way different economists view an issue and the nature of their policy recommendations are usually colored by their particular ideological orientation. At the risk of oversimplification, there are three broadly recognizable political ideologies that provide different viewpoints on almost any economic issue. These different viewpoints may be termed conservative, liberal, and radical.

### The Conservative View

Modern conservative ideology is rooted in two basic propositions. First, individual rights and the freedom of consenting parties to enter into private contracts (such as between buyer and seller) must be preserved to the greatest extent possible. Second, a competitive market system is central to the proper organization of society. Conservatives oppose any "unnatural" interference in the marketplace, and view the growth of big government as the greatest threat to economic progress and individual freedom. The government's proper role is: to maintain law and order;

to define and preserve property rights; to see that contracts are enforced; to provide a legal system to settle disputes; to promote competition by preventing the growth of monopoly power; to provide services not naturally provided by the market, such as national defense; to deal with problems not naturally solved by markets alone, such as environmental pollution; and to supplement private charity and the family to aid children and others handicapped for reasons beyond their control. In short, conservatives believe that government, the ultimate monopoly, should not do for people what they are capable of doing for themselves. Where government goes beyond these bounds, not only is individual freedom threatened, but otherwise well-intended government policies can cause or worsen economic problems. For example, conservatives would claim that minimum wage laws intended to improve the lot of low-paid workers actually hurt them in general. Conservatives argue that a government-enforced minimum wage higher than that otherwise determined by the market provides greater income for some workers but reduces the quantity demanded of those workers who are poorest, typically the unskilled and disadvantaged.

### The Liberal View

A national opinion poll has suggested that Americans tend to associate the word "liberal" with big government, labor unions, and welfare. However, compared to conservatives and radicals, liberals are somewhat more difficult to pin down to a representative position. The liberal spectrum on public policy positions ranges from those who favor a moderate level of government intervention to those who advocate broad government planning of the economy. While liberals are defenders of the principle of private property and private enterprise, they do not view these as endowed with categorical rights to the extent conservatives do. Compared to conservatives, liberals are more prone to believe that individual property rights and the right to act freely in the marketplace must be constrained by concern for the general social welfare. Hence, government intervention in the economy, and even occasional direct regulation of certain industries and markets, is more acceptable to liberals than to conservatives. Liberals would argue that the benefits to the whole society of such intervention outweigh the infringements on individual liberties and property rights which government action might entail. Liberal economists and conservative economists both rely on the same tools of supply-and-demand analysis to explain markets and the behavior of the economy. They don't always differ so much on how to describe what is happening as they differ over how and whether government should intervene to affect the outcome.

### The Radical View

To understand the representative radical position it is necessary to recognize the central role played by Marxist analysis (though there are some radicals who would reject a close association with Marxism). While it is impossible to do justice to the Marxist critique of capitalism in this short space, in brief, Marx essentially viewed capitalism as a system by which those who own the means of production, the capitalist class, are able to dominate and exploit the working class. According to Marx, the dominant capitalist class shaped private values, religion, the family, the educational system, and

political structures all for the purpose of production for private profit. Marxist analysis does not separate economics from politics and society's value system. The bourgeois democracies of the Western world are viewed as simply the tools for the dominant capitalist interests. For a Marxist, the problem with the capitalist system is the system itself, and no resolution of the problem is possible without changing the system. Coupled with this Marxist heritage, modern radicals are motivated by what they see as the failings of present-day liberalism. Liberal pursuit of policies for general social improvement are viewed as attempts to protect only some interest groups. And those who *really* benefit under liberal programs are seen as being those who have always gained. Corporate power continues to grow and the same elitist groups rule who have always ruled. Furthermore, liberal goals to improve the national well-being are also perceived as contributing to the exploitation of less-developed nations, continuing the cold war, and increasing the militarization of the economy.

When considering any economist's analysis of an economic issue it is always helpful to know his or her ideological orientation—to know "where he or she is coming from."

### Questions

1. What do you think a Marxist would say about the conservative view of minimum wage laws?

2. Among the seven major economic policy goals, how do you think conservatives and liberals would differ in the relative importance they would attach to achieving those goals that we argued tend to conflict with one another?

goals 4 and 7. Goals 2, 3, and 5 all seem compatible in the sense that if we achieve 2 and 3, we will very likely enhance economic security, goal 5. With respect to goal 6, some would argue that certain of the so-called loopholes are important as a spur to risky business ventures and that without the tax breaks for these activities there would be less of the sort of enterprising activity essential to economic growth and full employment, goals 2 and 3. They would contend that goal 6, therefore, may not be compatible with goals 2 and 3.

### Economic Analysis and the Economist

The examples we have considered illustrate why economic analysis is useful in formulating economic policy. In sum, economic analysis (1) helps to predict what the consequences of any policy action are likely to be, (2) indicates from among several ways to achieve a given goal which ones are most efficient in that their side effects are least detrimental, or possibly even helpful, to the achievement of other goals, (3) suggests which goals are compatible with one another and which are not, and (4) indicates what the likely trade-offs are between goals that are not mutually compatible.

If economic analysis does nothing else but keep policymakers from pursuing foolhardy policies, this alone is justification for its use as a policy tool. When economists go beyond the exercise of economic analysis summarized by points 1 to 4, they join the ranks of the various parties to any policy dispute. Their opinions and programs are then properly treated as those of a special interest group. Since economists, just like everyone else, usually do have opinions on matters of value judgment, they often use their economic expertise in support of a cause. In the end, therefore, the burden of separating objective economic analysis from value judgment must rest with you, the citizen. This fact alone should justify the time you devote to the study of economics.

## SUMMARY

**1.** Economics is a social science concerned with the study of how society chooses to use its scarce resources to satisfy its unlimited wants. Economics studies the many issues and problems associated with this process from an overall point of view.

**2.** Goods are produced by using economic resources. Economic resources are of two basic kinds—human resources (labor) and non-human resources (capital and land). Economic resources are also referred to as the factors of production.

**3.** Discussions of economic issues make use of two kinds of statements. Positive statements are statements of fact. Normative statements, which may be based on positive statements, are statements of opinion.

**4.** In an effort to explain "how things work," economic analysis makes use of the scientific method. This method uses induction to formulate a theory from observation of facts and events. The theory is then used to predict future events (deduction).

**5.** Every economic theory has four basic elements: (1) a statement of variables, (2) a set of assumptions, (3) a hypothesis, and (4) one or more predictions about future happenings. Economic theories may also be called economic laws, principles, or models. Economic theory is exact to the extent that economic behavior is predictable.

**6.** Economic theories, such as the law of demand, may be represented graphically.

**7.** Economic analysis has been divided into two broad areas. Macroeconomics is concerned with the functioning of the whole economy or large sectors within it. Microeconomics focuses on individual units such as households and firms.

**8.** In economics, it is important to determine whether one event is the cause of another event or simply preceded it in time.

**9.** The assumption that what is true of the parts is true of the whole is known as the fallacy of composition. The assumption that what is true of the whole is true of the parts is known as the fallacy of division.

**10.** Economic policymakers use economic theory and analysis to help them formulate ways in which to solve the problems posed by economic reality. In most cases, the solution to these problems involves resolving a conflict between special interest groups. Such a resolution usually depends upon value judgments, and economists are no more qualified than anyone else to make such judgments. Economic analysis is most useful in determining the possible consequences of various policies.

## KEY TERMS AND CONCEPTS

*ceteris paribus*
deduction
direct relationship
economic policy
economics
economic theory
economy
fallacy of composition
fallacy of division
fallacy of false cause
induction
inverse relationship
macroeconomics
microeconomics
normative statement
positive statement
price
scarce
scientific method

## QUESTIONS AND PROBLEMS

**1.** Why is economics called a social science instead of a social study?

**2.** Why is it that economists, who supposedly use scientific methods when analyzing economic issues, are so often in disagreement?

**3.** Pick out a story from the financial and business section of today's newspaper and find instances in which a concept or subject is mentioned or discussed that is related to one or more of the economic terms introduced in this chapter.

**4.** Open today's newspaper to the financial and business section. Pick a story at random and calculate the ratio of positive statements to the total number of statements in the story. Now go to the financial and business *editorial* section and do the same.

**5.** *Think* about the following experiment. Suppose you were to run an ad in your local paper this week stating that you own a vacant 1-acre lot and that somewhere on the lot is buried a metal box containing $10. You state that any and all are welcome to come dig for it and that you will give the $10 to whomever finds it during the coming week. How many people do you think will show up to dig? Suppose, instead, you had said the box contained $30 instead of $10. How many diggers do you think would show up during the same week? Estimate how many would show up during the same week if the reward were $60, $120, or $150. Now construct a graph that measures dollars of reward on the vertical axis and number of diggers on the horizontal axis. Find the points representing each combination of dollars and diggers and draw a line connecting them.

a. Is the relationship you observe between the size of the dollar reward and the number of diggers an inverse relationship or a direct relationship?

b. What led you to hypothesize the relationship you did between the size of the dollar reward and the number of diggers?

c. If you actually ran the ads over the course of a year and tabulated the number of diggers who showed up for each reward, plotted the results, and found a relationship opposite to the one you had predicted, what would you conclude about your theory? Might the season of the year during which you ran each ad have had something to do with the difference between your theory and what actually happened? Suppose when you ran the $150 reward ad it rained for the whole week the offer was good. Suppose when you ran the $120 reward ad it was sunny the first day of the week and rained the next six. Suppose for the $90 reward ad it was sunny for the first two days and rained the next five. Suppose for the $60 reward ad it was sunny for the first three days and rained the next four. Suppose for the $30 reward ad it was sunny the first five days and rained the next two. Finally, for the $10 reward ad suppose it was sunny the whole week. How do you think the curve obtained by plotting the combinations of dollar reward and number of diggers might look now? Looking back at the first curve you drew, how important do you think your "other things remaining the same" assumption was?

d. Suppose your original curve was based on the assumption that it was always sunny. If instead it was always raining, where would the curve be—to the left or to the right of the original curve?

e. What would you predict would happen if you raised the amount of the reward money to $1,000?

f. Can you, as my economic policy advisor, recommend how I might clear off and dig up a 1-acre lot that I own in town?

g. Can you, as my economic policy advisor, tell me how to deal with the racial tensions that might arise between the people who show up to dig on my lot?

h. Do you think people respond to economic incentives?

i. Do you think human behavior is predictable?

**6.** The following item appeared in the *Wall Street Journal* of September 14, 1976:

Election Returns: Who holds the presidency "has an effect on the workers' ability to organize into unions," the AFL-CIO argues in its analysis of the past 16 years. It cites figures showing that in the Kennedy-Johnson years 57 percent of workers voted for unions in NLRB [National Labor Relations Board] elections, while only 44 percent favored unions in the Nixon-Ford years.

a. What do you think of the merits of this cause-and-effect argument?

b. Are there other explanations that might be offered for these facts?

# 2

# Scarcity, Choice, and the Economic Problem

**AFTER READING THIS CHAPTER, YOU WILL BE ABLE TO:**

1. Explain why the combination of scarce resources and unlimited wants makes choice necessary.

2. Define the term *economic efficiency* and distinguish between unemployment and underemployment of resources.

3. Explain the concept of the production possibilities frontier and show why when an economy is on the frontier, it can have more of one good only by giving up some of another.

4. Demonstrate why the selection of an output combination on today's production possibilities frontier affects the location of tomorrow's frontier.

5. Formulate the basic questions posed by the fundamental economic problem that every economy must answer.

6. Distinguish among pure market economies and command economies.

**I**n this chapter we will focus on the basic economic problem that has always confronted human beings and the fundamental questions it poses. Then we will look into the ways economies may be organized to answer these questions. The answers are related to the fundamental issues of how well people live, how hard they work, and how choices about these matters are to be made.

## THE ECONOMIC PROBLEM

*The basic* **economic problem** *that underlies all economic issues is the combined existence of scarce resources and unlimited wants.* Ben Franklin put it this way: "The poor have little,—beggars none; the rich too much,—enough not one." As we noted in Chapter 1, the economic resources of land, labor, and capital exist only in limited amounts. Consequently, there is a limit to the quantity of economic goods that can be produced with these scarce resources. But unfortunately, people's desires for goods are really unlimited for all intents and purposes of economic analysis. While in theory it may be possible to attain a level of abundance that would satisfy everybody's appetites for all things, no such state has ever existed. And at this time, the prospects of achieving such a state seem remote to nonexistent. One only has to consider the standard of living in the world's richest nation, the United States, to realize that there is hardly a person who couldn't draw up a list of wanted goods that far exceeds his or her means to obtain them. Ask yourself, or anyone else, what you would do with an additional hundred dollars. If you felt completely without want, you might say that you would give it to a charity. But why does charity exist? Because some other group or person has unsatisfied wants.

### Opportunity Cost and Choice: A Simple Example

*Scarcity and unlimited wants force us to make choices.* Let's consider a simple example.

Suppose a settler named Clyde lives alone in the wilds of Alaska. Clyde has to be self-sufficient. He produces only two goods: corn (for food) and wood (for heat). Clyde's scarce resources are his own stamina and his ability to grow corn and cut wood. Clyde will always try to produce the most he can with his scarce resources. He only has a fixed amount of resources and so he will try not to waste them.

### *The Production Possibilities Frontier*

The nature of Clyde's economic problem can be illustrated by the use of a **production possibilities frontier.** *A production possibilities frontier is a curve representing the maximum possible output combinations of goods that can be produced with a fixed quantity of resources.*

Suppose Clyde's production possibilities frontier is the downward-sloping straight line in Figure 2–1. It shows the *maximum possible* combinations of quantities of corn and wood that Clyde can *choose* to produce in a year if he *fully utilizes* his fixed resources in the *most efficient* way he knows. By maximum we mean that Clyde cannot produce any combination of corn and wood represented by points lying to the right of or above his production possibilities frontier, the line from *a* to *e* in Figure 2–1. For example, he cannot choose to produce a combination of 27 bushels of corn and 15 cords of wood, point *f* in Figure 2–1. He simply doesn't have enough resources. On the other hand, Clyde can produce any combination lying to the left or below the frontier—for example, a combination consisting of 15 bushels of corn and 5 cords of wood, point *g*. But he would not want to do so because that would be an inefficient use of his fixed resources. Efficient resource utilization will always enable him to produce more of both goods than he gets at a point such as *g*.

### *Opportunity Cost*

Clyde will always choose to produce a combination of goods represented by a point on

**FIGURE 2-1    Clyde's Production Possibilities Frontier**

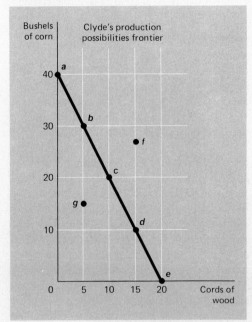

Clyde's production possibilities frontier is represented by the downward-sloping straight line *ae*. Each point on the frontier represents some maximum-output combination of bushels of corn and cords of wood that Clyde can choose to produce annually if he fully utilizes his fixed resources as efficiently as possible.

Clyde cannot produce any combinations represented by points to the right or above the frontier, such as *f*. He simply doesn't have enough resources—stamina and ability to grow corn and chop wood. Clyde can produce any combination represented by points to the left or below the frontier, such as *g*. But he wouldn't want to because that would entail an inefficient ultilization of his resources.

his production possibilities frontier. (Later we will see that the frontier may not be a straight line.) Five of these possible combinations are indicated by points *a*, *b*, *c*, *d*, and *e*. For example, if Clyde chooses combination *b*, he will grow 30 bushels of corn and chop 5 cords of wood during the coming year. Alternatively, he may choose combination *c*, consisting of 20 bushels of corn and 10 cords of wood. All he has to do is devote less of his fixed resources to corn growing and use the resources released from that activity to chop more wood. If Clyde chooses to produce combination *c* instead of *b*, he has to give up 10 bushels of corn (the difference between 30 and 20). However, he gains 5 cords of wood (the difference between 10 and 5). Conversely, if he chooses combination *b* instead of *c*, he gives up 5 cords of wood and gains 10 bushels of corn.

In general, if Clyde wants to produce more of one kind of good, he must of necessity produce less of the other. We say he must pay an **opportunity cost.** *The opportunity cost equals the amount of one good that must be given up in order to have more of another.* We see from Clyde's production possibilities frontier in Figure 2–1 that he has to *give up* 2 bushels of corn in order to get an additional cord of wood (a move downward along his production possibilities frontier). Conversely, he has to *give up* half a cord of wood in order to get an additional bushel of corn (a move upward along his production possibilities frontier). Hence the opportunity cost of a cord of wood is 2 bushels of corn. The opportunity cost of a bushel of corn is half a cord of wood.

### Choice

When Clyde uses his fixed resources efficiently, he can choose to produce any output combination on his production possibilities frontier. Whenever he considers the choice between one combination and another along the frontier, however, he is always forced to choose between a combination with more wood and less corn and a combination with less wood and more corn. If he could have more of both or more of one without having to sacrifice any of the other, there would be no "hard" choice because nothing would have to be given up. Unfortunately, Clyde's limited or scarce resources always force him to give up something—to pay an opportunity cost—whenever he makes a choice. A choice requires that one opportunity be given up to gain another.

The concept of a production possibilities frontier, the existence of opportunity costs, and the need for choice are just as relevant for an entire economy as they are for Clyde. Let's see why.

## Scarcity, Production, and Efficiency

*Given that resources are limited and people's wants are unlimited, the problem that faces any economy is how to use scarce resources and organize production so as to satisfy to the greatest extent possible society's unlimited wants.* This means that the available resources must be used as efficiently as possible. In other words, the maximum output must be obtained from the resources at hand.

There are two major problems that can prevent a society from achieving **economic efficiency**. These are **unemployment** and **underemployment,** or **resource misallocation**.

### Unemployment

*Maximum economic efficiency cannot be achieved if available resources are not fully used.* This holds true for both human and nonhuman resources. As long as there are workers looking for work and unable to find it, or if plant capacity remains unused, maximum economic efficiency cannot be achieved. Notice that we stress that in order to have economic efficiency all *available* resources must be employed. Some parts of the population may not seek employment. By custom and law some people, such as children and the aged, may be prevented from working. Certain kinds of land are prohibited by law from use for certain types of productive activity. However, whenever there are available resources standing idle, there are fewer inputs into the economy's productive process. As a result, there is a lower output of goods to satisfy society's wants.

### Underemployment, or Resource Misallocation

*If certain available resources are used to do jobs for which other available resources are better suited, there is underemployment, or misallocation of resources.* For example, if cabinetmakers were employed to make dresses and seamstresses were employed to make cabinets, the total amount of cabinets and dresses produced would be less than if each group were employed in the activity for which it was trained. Similarly, if Florida's orange groves were planted with wheat while Minnesota's farms were planted with orange trees, the same total land area would provide the country with substantially less of both crops than is the case with the conventional arrangement. Resource underemployment also results whenever the best available technology is not used in a production process. A house painter painting with a toothbrush and a farmer harvesting wheat with a pocketknife are both underemployed. A 10-ton bulldozer is underemployed when used to clear a half-acre yard once a week. *Whenever there is resource underemployment, or misallocation, a reallocation of resources to productive activities for which they are better suited will result in a larger output of some or all goods and no reduction in the output of any.*

## Production Possibilities Trade-off

When an economy's available resources are fully employed (that is, there is no unemployment or underemployment), we say that economy is producing its maximum possible output of goods. Given that resources are limited, the maximum possible output level is, of course, limited too. Therefore, as in Clyde's world, producing more of one kind of good will of necessity mean producing less of another. Again, the amount of reduction in the production of one good that is necessary in order to produce more of another is called *opportunity cost*.

Let us illustrate this concept by focusing

on the issue of the cost of cleaning up environmental pollution. Suppose that the output of an economy may be divided into two categories—scrubbers and bundles of all other goods. (A scrubber is an antipollution device that removes pollutants from factory smokestack emissions.) One bundle will contain one of each and every good produced in the economy *except* a scrubber. A bundle may be thought of as a good—the composite good. The issue to be illustrated here is of more than academic interest. If we are to have a cleaner environment, we will need to use scrubbers in many production processes that cause pollution. How do we measure the cost to society of providing these devices?

### Production and Choice

In answering this question we will make certain assumptions, as follows:

1. The existing state of technology will remain unchanged for the period in which we are examining this issue.
2. The total available supply of resources (land, labor, and capital) will remain the same. However, these resources may be shifted from producing scrubbers to producing bundles of all other goods and vice versa.
3. All available resources are fully employed (there is no unemployment or underemployment in the economy).

Given the existing supply of resources and level of technology, society must make choices. Should its fully employed resources be devoted entirely to the production of bundles of all other goods? Or should it reduce its output of bundles and use the factors of production released from that activity to produce scrubbers? If so, what combinations of bundles and scrubbers can it produce, given that its resources are fully employed? Clearly, the more scrubbers the economy produces, the more resources will have to be devoted to their production. Fewer resources

will then be available for the production of bundles. Given that resources are fully employed, whatever combination of bundles and scrubbers the economy might think of producing, any other combination will necessarily contain more of one and less of the other. If the economy wants to produce more scrubbers, it will have to give up a certain number of bundles. If it wants to produce more bundles, it will have to give up a certain number of scrubbers.

Just as in Clyde's world, something must be given up in order to gain something. In short, you can't get something for nothing. You have to pay an opportunity cost.

### Choices for Pollution Control

Some of the possible combinations of bundles and scrubbers that the economy we have been considering can produce per year when all resources are fully employed are listed in Table 2–1. If this economy were to devote all of its resources to producing bundles of all other goods, it would be able to produce 80 million bundles per year and no scrubbers (combination *A*). Although it seems very unrealistic and highly unlikely, the economy could devote all of its fully employed resources to producing scrubbers and go without all other goods (combination *E*). Such a choice would certainly carry environmental considerations to the extreme, in the sense that the cost would amount to giving up the production of all other goods. However, at the other extreme, combination *A* would probably not be very desirable either. With this combination, the economy would not be doing anything at all about pollution. If it were deemed desirable to do something about pollution, the economy could be moved away from point *A* toward point *E*. *To do this, resources would have to be shifted out of the production of bundles and into the production of scrubbers.* How much of a shift in this direction society chooses to make will depend upon the degree of concern about pollution. A cleaner environment will cost

**TABLE 2-1 Possible Combinations of Scrubbers and Bundles of All Other Goods That May Be Produced in a Full-Employment Economy** (Hypothetical Data)

| Product | Production Possibilities (Output per Year) | | | | |
| --- | --- | --- | --- | --- | --- |
| | A | B | C | D | E |
| Scrubbers (in thousands) | 0 | 50 | 80 | 100 | 110 |
| Bundles of all other goods (in millions) | 80 | 60 | 40 | 20 | 0 |

something. Suppose society's concern is such that it chooses to produce combination B instead of combination A. The cost of the 50,000 scrubbers it will now have is the 20 million bundles of all other goods it must give up to achieve this combination. If society has an even greater concern about pollution, combination C or even combination D could be chosen. However, to have the greater quantities of scrubbers associated with combination C or combination D requires that society forgo the production of more bundles of all other goods.

### The Opportunity Cost of Choice

In summary, because economic resources are scarce, a full-employment economy cannot have more of both bundles and scrubbers. To have more of one, it must give up some of the other. The cost of having more of one is the opportunity cost, or the amount of the other, that must be given up. By choosing combination B in Table 2-1 *instead* of combination A, society must forgo the opportunity of having 20 million bundles of all other goods (the difference between 80 million and 60 million). The opportunity cost of the 50,000 scrubbers is therefore 20 million bundles. The opportunity cost of choosing combination C *instead* of combination B, or the opportunity cost of having an additional 30,000 scrubbers, is another 20 million bundles. The opportunity cost of choosing C *instead* of A, or the opportunity cost of having

80,000 scrubbers, is 40 million bundles, the difference between the number of bundles associated with combination A and the number associated with combination C.

*Whenever scarcity forces us to make a choice, we must pay an opportunity cost. This cost is measured in terms of forgone alternatives.* All costs are opportunity costs (often simply referred to as costs). If you buy a note pad for a dollar, you forgo the opportunity of spending that dollar on something else. Since the pad cost you a dollar, you now have a dollar less to spend on all other goods, unless you have an infinite supply of money, which is impossible. There is no free lunch.

### CHECKPOINT* 2-1

**What is the opportunity cost to Clyde of choosing combination *d* instead of combination *c* in Figure 2-1? Of choosing combination *b* instead of combination *d*? Of choosing combination *d* instead of combination *b*?**

*Answers to all Checkpoints can be found at the back of the text.

### The Economy's Production Possibilities Frontier

To derive our hypothetical economy's production possibilities frontier, let's plot the data from Table 2-1 on a graph. On the horizontal axis we measure the number of scrubbers. On the vertical axis we measure the number of bundles. As we did in Chapter 1, we now locate all the points on the graph that represent the possible scrubbers-bundles combinations listed in our table. If we draw a line connecting the points, the result looks like Figure 2-2. The curve slopes downward because when the available resources are fully employed, more scrubbers can be produced only by producing fewer bundles.

### On and Off the Frontier

The curve we have drawn by connecting all the points on the graph is our hypothetical

**FIGURE 2-2   The Production Possibilities Frontier**

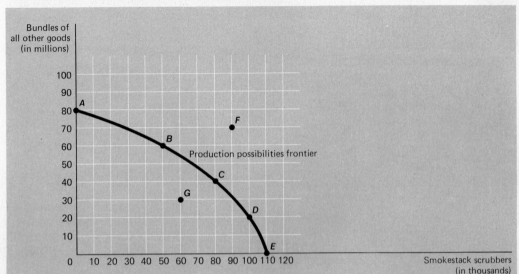

Each point on the downward-sloping curve represents some maximum-output combination for an economy whose available resources are fully employed. In this case, the output consists of scrubbers and bundles. Because no combination to the right or above the curve is possible, it is called the production possibilities frontier.

Point *G* represents a combination of scrubbers and bundles produced when the economy is operating inefficiently. Unemployment or underemployment of economic resources has resulted in a smaller output than is actually possible. Point *F*, on the other hand, represents a combination that cannot be produced given available resources and technology. This point can only be achieved if the production possibilities curve shifts outward as a result of economic growth.

economy's production possibilities frontier. *Each point on a production possibilities frontier represents a maximum output combination for an economy whose available resources are fully employed.* The term *frontier* is used because it is not possible for the economy to produce any combination of scrubbers and bundles represented by a point above or to the right of the curve. For example, a combination of quantities of scrubbers and bundles represented by the point *F* in Figure 2–2 is not possible.

What if the economy's available resources are not being used efficiently (they are either unemployed or underemployed)? Then the economy cannot produce any combination of scrubbers and bundles represented by any point on its production possibilities frontier. It will only be able to produce output combinations represented by points inside the frontier, such as point *G*.

### The Law of Increasing Costs

Figure 2–2 illustrates how graphs plotted from economic data can make the relationship between two economic variables immediately obvious. In Figure 2–2 we are struck at once by the change in the trade-off between bundles and scrubbers as we move from combination *A* to *B* to *C* and so on to *E*. When we move from *A* to *B*, a sacrifice (or cost) of 20 million bundles allows us to have 50,000 scrubbers. However, a move from *B* to *C*, which costs another 20 million bundles, allows us to have only an additional 30,000 scrubbers. The additional quantity of scrubbers obtained for each succeeding sacrifice of 20 million bundles continues to get smaller as we move from *C* to *D* to *E*. The reason for the deteriorating trade-off is that economic resources are more adaptable to some production processes than others. As more and more resources are shifted from the production of bundles into the production of scrubbers, we are forced to use factors of production whose productivity at making scrubbers is lower and lower relative to their productivity at making bundles. For example, when we move from *A* to *B*, a large number of engineers and scientists might be moved from bundle production to the highly technical production of scrubbers. As we continue moving from *B* to *E*, it becomes harder and harder to find labor resources of this nature. When moving from *D* to *E*, only the labor least suited for producing scrubbers will be left—poets, hod carriers, and so forth.

The decrease in the number of additional scrubbers obtained for each additional sacrifice of 20 million bundles as we move from *A* to *E* is a common economic phenomenon. It is sometimes called the **law of increasing costs**. To illustrate this law more clearly, divide the number of bundles that must be sacrificed by the additional number of scrubbers obtained by moving from one combination to the next. In the move from *A* to *B*, it costs 20 million bundles to obtain 50,000 scrubbers, or 400 bundles per scrubber. In the move from *B* to *C*, it costs 20 million bundles to obtain 30,000 scrubbers, or 666.6 bundles per scrubber. The move from *C* to *D* costs 1,000 bundles per scrubber. The move from *D* to *E* costs 2,000 bundles per scrubber. We are accustomed to measuring costs in dollars—so many dollars per unit of some good. Since dollars merely stand for the amounts of other goods they can buy, we have simply represented the cost of scrubbers in terms of bundles of other goods. *The law of increasing costs says that when moving along the production possibilities frontier, the*

*cost per additional good obtained measured in terms of the good sacrificed rises due to the difference in productivity of resources when used in different production processes.*

### Economic Growth

The production possibilities frontier in Figure 2–2 is based on a given state of technology and a fixed quantity of resources (land, labor, and capital). What happens if there is a change in technology or in the quantity of resources? The potential total output of the economy will change. Hence the production possibilities frontier will shift position.

The economy's population and labor force tend to grow over time. So too does its stock of capital—the quantities of machines, buildings, highways, factories, and so forth. In addition there are advances in the state of technology. *The growth in the economy's resources and improvements in technological know-how cause* **economic growth,** *an increase in the economy's ability to produce output.* This shifts the economy's production possibilities frontier outward (up and to the right) as shown in Figure 2–3. As a result the economy can produce more of both scrubbers and bundles when its available resources are fully employed.

### Ecology's Price Tag

Some people are wondering whether the cost of protecting the environment is outrunning the benefits of doing so. The production possibilities frontier shows us the nature of the choices and the associated costs that must be considered when answering this question. The economist can objectively say that society would be making an inefficient use of resources if it decided to produce a combination of goods inside the frontier. Similarly, an economist can objectively say that a combination above or to the right of the frontier is not possible. But the following also needs to be said. In an economy such as that summarized in Table 2–1, it must be pointed out to those who would like to produce 80,000 scrubbers that they cannot produce 80 mil-

**FIGURE 2-3   Economic Growth Means That
the Production Possibilities Frontier Shifts Outward**

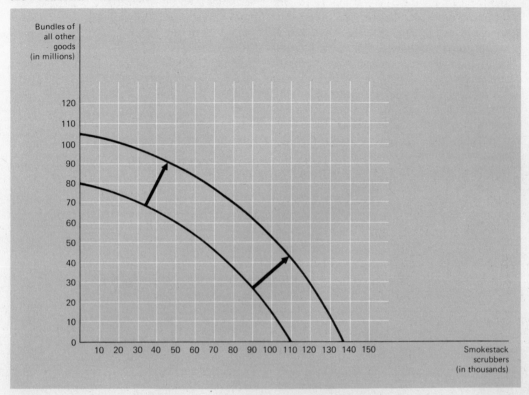

Growth in the economy's available resources and technological know-how shifts the
production possibilities frontier outward. This allows the economy to produce more of
both scrubbers and bundles—to have economic growth.

lion bundles as well. Almost everyone is for
God, mother, and country—and environmental protection. The question is, How
much are we willing to pay for it, *in terms of
other goods and services not produced?*

## Choice of Product Combination:
## Present Versus Future

We are all aware that choices made today are
an important determinant of the choices
available to us tomorrow. Therefore it
should not surprise us that *an economy's pre-*

*sent choice of a point on its production possi-
bilities frontier influences the future location of
that frontier.*

To demonstrate why this is so, suppose we
divide the total output of an economy into
two categories—consumption goods and
capital goods. Consumption goods are such
things as food, clothing, movies, tennis balls,
records, and so forth. Capital goods are such
things as machinery, tools, and factories;
they enable us to produce other goods, including machinery, tools, and factories. An
increase in the quantity and quality of capital
goods contributes to economic growth, the
expansion of the economy's capacity to pro-

duce all goods. Suppose the production possibilities frontier for our economy in 1986 is as shown in Figure 2–4—capital goods are measured on the horizontal axis, consumption goods are measured on the vertical axis.

If the economy chooses point *a* on its 1986 frontier, it will produce an output combination consisting mostly of consumption goods. Alternatively, if it chooses point *b* on the frontier, the economy will produce a combination predominantly made up of capital goods. All other things remaining the same, we can expect the economy's future (1990) production possibilities frontier to be farther

out if it chooses point *b* on its 1986 frontier than if it chooses point *a*. That is, the choice of point *a* on the 1986 frontier will give rise to 1990 frontier *a*, whereas choosing point *b* will give rise to 1990 frontier *b*. The reason is that choice *b* produces more capital goods, the kind of goods that contribute to economic growth, whereas choice *a* produces fewer of such goods. We hasten to add, however, that this does not mean *b* is a better choice than *a*. After all, remember that choice *b* means having fewer consumption goods to enjoy in 1986 relative to the number resulting from choice *a*.

**FIGURE 2-4   Present Choices Affect Future Production Possibilities Frontiers**

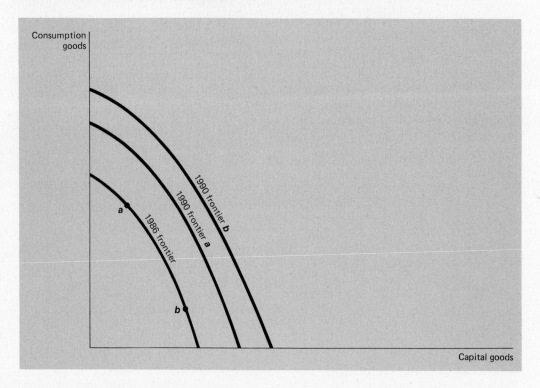

If the economy chooses point *a* on its 1986 frontier, it emphasizes consumption goods production; if it chooses point *b*, it favors capital goods production. Therefore choice *a* gives rise to less economic growth or a smaller outward shift in the frontier (to 1990 frontier *a*) than does choice *b* (to 1990 frontier *b*).

CHECKPOINT 2-2
**In Table 2–1 what is the opportunity cost of choosing combination *C* instead of *D*; *B* instead of *C*; or *A* instead of *D*? Consider the movement from *E* to *A* in Figure 2–2 and represent the law of increasing cost measured in terms of scrubbers.**

## BASIC PROBLEMS FOR ANY ECONOMY

Given an economy's available resources and technology, we have seen how the production possibilities from which it may choose can be characterized by a production possibilities frontier. A frontier can be determined for any economy, whatever its form of government. A knowledge of what is possible is necessary in order to answer a number of important questions or problems that any economy, be it that of the Soviet Union or the United States or Pakistan, must solve. These questions confront socialist, communist, and capitalist countries, developed and underdeveloped economies alike. These questions are:

(1) What and how much to produce?
(2) How should production be organized?
(3) For whom should goods be produced?

### What and How Much to Produce

We could draw up an incredibly large list of goods that could be produced in the United States, including everything from needles and thread to space vehicles and kidney dialysis machines. Some of the goods on the list, while possible to produce, might not be desired by anybody. Other goods, such as various kinds of food, might be desired by nearly everyone. If we were to draw up a list of goods that could be produced by one of the less developed countries in the world, it

would probably be considerably shorter. Nevertheless, given its respective list, each country would have to decide what goods and how much of each to produce.

In the economy summarized in Table 2–1, the answer to the question, "What to produce?" was scrubbers and bundles of all other goods. The question, "How much?" really asks what point on the production possibilities frontier would be selected. The answer to this question must be decided by society's tastes and priorities. The answer is thus a value judgment. As we noted in Chapter 1, an economist's value judgment has no superior claim over anyone else's. It may be that a relatively underdeveloped country seeking rapid economic growth and industrialization would feel little concern about the environmental impact of these processes. It might not want to divert resources to producing scrubbers. However, a country such as the United States, having experienced growth and industrialization, might be more aware of their adverse environmental impact. It therefore might be more willing to divert a larger share of resources to producing scrubbers. Whether the cost of protecting the environment is outrunning the benefits will depend on who is assessing the benefits.

Who makes the decisions about what and how much to produce? The answer to this question varies greatly from one economy to another. In countries such as the Soviet Union or Communist China, these decisions are made by a central planning bureau of the government. In the United States, Canada, and Western Europe, a large portion of the decisions about the allocation of resources is made by the pricing system, or market mechanism. However, the political process has legislated government intervention in some decisions. In the United States, for example, electric utility companies set rates subject to approval by government regulatory agencies. Similarly, decisions about pollution control have to a considerable degree been made through congressional action. Government intervention seems desirable in certain cases because society has decided that

## POLICY PERSPECTIVE

### Defense Spending—How Much Does It Cost?

In recent years there has been an increasingly heated debate about whether or not the United States is spending enough on defense. An important aspect of this debate is the cost of national defense.

As with any good or service, we can only have more defense goods and services (more guns, missiles, and the services of soldiers) by giving up nondefense goods and services (such as automobiles, golf carts, and the services of house painters). The opportunity cost of more defense is measured by the amount of the necessary sacrifice of nondefense goods and services. This is illustrated by the economy's hypothetical production possibilities frontier in Figure P2-1 which shows the maximum-output combinations of defense and nondefense goods and services the economy can choose to produce when available resources are fully employed. If point $A$ is chosen the economy would produce the quantities OD for defense (horizontal axis) and ON for nondefense (vertical axis). However if policymakers decide that more defense is needed, say an additional amount equal to $DD'$, then it will be necessary for the economy to move to point $B$ by giving up a quantity of nondefense goods and services equal to $NN'$—that is the (opportunity) cost of the increased defense. *The additional cost $NN'$ is the additional "spending" on increased defense.*

Some perspective on the actual cost of national defense in the United States is provided by measuring defense spending as the percentage of GNP (gross national product), the economy's total annual output of final goods and services. Such a percentage tells us what portion of the dollar value of total output is given over to the production of defense goods and services. In terms of opportunity cost, it is the portion of total output that otherwise could have gone into the production of nondefense products—the goods and services given up in order to produce defense products. In 1960, defense spending amounted to 9.7 percent of GNP (on a fiscal year basis). By 1970 it had declined slightly to 8.4 percent and, due largely to the ending of the Vietnam War, it declined more noticeably to 5.2 percent by 1980. Since 1980 defense spending has increased to an estimated 6.7 percent of GNP in 1984 and has been projected to rise further to around 7.6 to 7.8 percent by 1989.

Here we have focused on the economic way to measure the cost of national defense. How much national defense we should have depends on one's views of international tensions and their implications for war and peace, and thus the potential

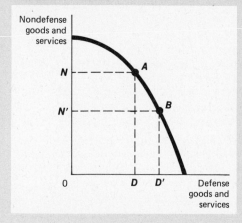

FIGURE P2-1 **Production Possibilities Frontier for Defense and Nondefense Goods**

benefits of national defense. But that is a different, and more controversial, issue.

### Questions

1. What would the opportunity cost be of choosing point *A* instead of point *B* in Figure P2–1?

2. Why might it be said that economic growth would reduce the intensity of the debate between those who want more defense spending and those who don't?

the resource allocations made by free markets have been unsatisfactory in some areas. Pollution control is one of these. National defense is another.

## How Should Production Be Organized?

In discussing the production possibilities frontier, we emphasized that to be on the frontier it is necessary to use economic resources in the most efficient way. Once society has determined what goods to produce, the amount of each of those goods it will be able to produce will depend on how available resources are allocated to various productive activities. If we try to grow oranges in Minnesota and raise wheat in Florida, we are not going to have as much of either as we would if those land resources were used the other way around. In addition, even when resources are allocated to their most productive activities, the most efficient known productive processes must be used. Harvesting wheat in Minnesota with pinking shears and making orange juice in Florida by squeezing the oranges by hand is still not going to give us as much wheat or orange juice as is technologically possible. Ideally, *society should allocate available resources to productive activities and use known productive techniques in such a way that no reallocation of resources or change of technique could yield more of any good without yielding less of another. This is true of any combination of goods represented by any point on the production possibilities frontier.*

This ideal is easy enough to understand and describe. But it may have struck you by now as a little like being told that the way to make money on the stock market is to buy low and sell high. You can understand that perfectly and wouldn't disagree a bit. But only a moment's reflection will lead you to ask the inevitable question: "Yes, but how do I *know* when a stock is at its low and when it is at its high?" Similarly, an economy doesn't have a big television screen up in the sky with a picture of its production possibilities frontier and a white dot that can be moved around by turning knobs until society has got itself right at the desired spot on the frontier. Society can't "see" the economy's production possibilities frontier, nor is it a simple matter of turning a few control knobs to "move" onto it. So how should an economy go about organizing its available resources in order to use them most efficiently? How will the most efficient production techniques be determined? What regulating mechanisms or management techniques can be used to ensure that the appropriate kinds and necessary amounts of resources will be directed to industries producing desired goods? Any economy, be it centrally planned or completely market oriented, wants to be on its production possibilities frontier. The question is, How does it get there?

## For Whom to Produce

For whom should the output of the economy be produced? Put another way, how should the economy's total output be distributed among the individual members of the economy? Should it be distributed to individuals according to their productive contribution to the making of that output? Or should we take from each according to his or her ability and give to each according to his or her need? If people receive strictly according to their productive contribution, it's clear some people are going to be terribly poor. On the other hand, if there is no relationship between an individual's productive contribution and the reward received for it, what will be the incentive for hard work? If the able and productive members of society do not have incentives to work hard, the total output of the economy will not be as large. If the total pie is smaller, there simply will be less to go around. All societies must wrestle with this problem. They must decide how to distribute output in such a way as to encourage the productive members to work up to their ability and at the same time try to maintain a minimum standard of living for all. In short, they must decide what degree of income inequality can be tolerated given these conflicting goals. The range of opinion on this is wide indeed and can fire the most heated debates. It is a matter of politics, cultural values, and moral issues.

In addition to solving this problem, all economies must decide how much of the total output should go to government, how much to business, and how much to households. This, of course, raises questions about how taxes should be levied and who should pay them. It raises questions about how much of the decision-making process for allocation of resources should be in the hands of the government rather than of the private sector (households and businesses). In wartime, any society is likely to give to the government whatever portion of output it needs to ensure survival. In peacetime, without the pressure of such a common goal, decisions about how to distribute total output are not usually made with such a consensus.

## Full Utilization of Resources

In our discussion of economic efficiency and the problem of how to organize production, we emphasized that *an economy can fall short of its production possibilities frontier if resources are misallocated or if the best-known production techniques are not used. Another kind of economic inefficiency, also noted earlier, occurs whenever available resources are allowed to stand idle. This kind of inefficiency will also keep an economy from operating on its production possibilities frontier.*

In twentieth-century capitalist economies, such as that of the United States, there have been frequent periods of recession, which means that significant amounts of labor and other available resources have been idle, or unemployed. During the depression of the 1930s, the measured unemployment rate was around 25 percent. Economists estimate that the actual rate of unemployment may have been considerably higher than this. (The reason is that some of the unemployed were not reported.) In capitalist economies we often refer to the recurring pattern of increasing and decreasing unemployment associated with decreasing and increasing output as **business fluctuations** or **business cycles**. Centrally planned economies such as those of the Soviet Union, Communist China, and the Eastern European nations are not free from the problem of fluctuations in their production of output. The underlying reasons why they have these difficulties are different, and for ideological reasons they describe the problem differently. An economist visiting the United States from the central planning bureau of an Eastern European country was asked if they experienced anything like our business fluctuations. He said, "Oh, no." The question was then rephrased, "Well, don't you ever experience fluctuations in production?" He responded, "Oh, you mean 'technical cycles'!"

In the industrialized economies of the

Western world, the problem of eliminating or reducing unemployment of labor and other available resources is a high priority of economic policy. In the United States, Congress passed the Employment Act of 1946, declaring that it shall be the continuing policy and responsibility of the federal government "to promote maximum employment, production, and purchasing power."

Unemployment of economic resources is similar in its effects to the underemployment of economic resources that results from their misallocation to inappropriate activities or when the best-known techniques of production are not used. Both unemployment and underemployment cause the economy to produce at a point inside its production possibility frontier. However, the appropriate ways to deal with these two problems are quite different. *The underemployment problem requires an answer to the question of how to organize production.* Remedies there require establishing ways to see to it that Minnesota is planted with wheat and not oranges, and that harvesting machines instead of pinking shears are used to cut it. These kinds of problems are generally studied in microeconomics.

*Remedies for the unemployment problem generally take the form of ensuring that there is enough demand for goods and services to require the full utilization of all available resources to meet that demand.* You might think it strange that resources could be idle at all, and that it could be due to a low demand for goods. After all, don't people work in order to earn income to buy goods? Unfortunately, in a money-using economy producing many kinds of goods, a person's offer of labor services in one place is quite removed from his or her desired purchase of goods in another. A line of unemployed job-seekers at a steel mill's gate does not mean that each wants to work in direct exchange for a ton of cold-rolled steel to be carried home at the end of the day. The mill manager's plans to produce steel and hire workers are affected quite differently by a line of job-seeking, unemployed steelworkers than they are by a line of customers wanting to place orders. It is not obvious that if workers were employed in the back, customers would materialize out front to purchase their output. This is true even though the workers would most likely use their earned money to buy a multitude of items requiring steel. All firms in the economy producing all kinds of goods are in the same situation as the steel mill. Clearly when there are unemployed laborers and other resources in the whole economy, it is a result of the totality of these situations. The remedies for this sort of problem are studied in macroeconomics.

## Change, Stability, and Growth

All economies are subject to change. The underlying causes of change are sometimes quite predictable. Population growth and the increase of technological know-how are a main impetus to economic growth. These kinds of change are fairly steady and ongoing. Population growth in underdeveloped countries is typically higher than in more industrialized countries. It is so high, in fact, that it poses a problem for those economies. Namely, it makes it very difficult to increase the standard of living. The growth in the number of people to be fed makes it difficult to divert resources from agricultural production to the capital formation needed for industrialization. This applies not just to the formation of physical capital but to the investment in human capital needed to provide the level of literacy and know-how required of the labor force in an industrialized economy. In other countries, such as Australia, it is felt that the rate of population growth is too low to spur the kind of economic growth desired. Depending on the particular economy, the level of population growth can pose a problem by being either too high or too low. In India, birth control measures are a primary policy concern. In Australia, population policy has been aimed at creating incentives to encourage immigration from abroad and the settlement of the vast interior of the continent.

Other kinds of change are often less predictable and pose severe problems for maintaining stable economic processes in a country. The abrupt onset of the energy shortage in the United States in 1973 and 1974 was not widely predicted or anticipated. It is felt by most economists that it was a major contributing factor to the recession that began in late 1973 and lasted through the first quarter of 1975. At that time this was the severest recession in the United States since the depression of the 1930s.

Often, drastic institutional and political changes, even when well intended, can cause severe economic problems for an economy. After the Communists took over in China in 1949, they instituted a new agricultural and industrialization program. This program increased grain production from 108 million tons in 1949 to 182 million tons in 1956 and steel production from 360,000 tons in 1950 to 3.32 million tons by 1956. Then in 1958 the Chinese leadership attempted to institute what they called the Great Leap Forward. They constructed backyard steel furnaces throughout the country, mandated 18-hour workdays, and transferred half a billion peasants into giant communes. All this, combined with three years of bad weather, proved to be too much change for the economy to adapt to. In some places, there was near starvation for the first time since the Communist takeover. Production dropped sharply and economic progress may have been set back by as much as a decade.

A major cause of instability in industrialized Western economies in recent years has been increases in the general levels of prices. This phenomenon is more commonly referred to as inflation. Since World War II, the general direction of prices in the United States has been continually upward. But during the 1970s the rate of increase of prices rose considerably. Perhaps of equal concern from the standpoint of stability has been the variation in the rate of increase. For example, during the recession lasting from November 1973 through March 1975, the consumer index rose at a compound annual rate of 10.9 percent. During the subsequent year of recovery, it rose at a compound annual rate of 6.1 percent. In 1980 the inflation rate peaked at 13.5 percent and then declined during the largely recessionary years of the early 1980s, falling to a 3.2 percent rate by 1983. This kind of variation creates uncertainty among consumers and businesses. Consumers often become more cautious about making major purchases, such as of housing and automobiles. Businesses and labor unions spend more time haggling about cost-of-living clauses in contracts. Economists are in broad agreement that price instability is a most undesirable source of change in the economy.

Every economy has to contend with various kinds of change at one time or another. Some are thought to be desirable, such as the growth in technological knowledge. In industrialized economies of the West, change in consumer tastes and an economy's ability to adapt to meet those changes is generally considered desirable. Other kinds of change, including inflation, recession, and external shocks to the economy, such as that caused by the Arab oil embargo, are on everybody's bad list. About some forms of change we have mixed feelings. A prime example in the United States in recent years is economic growth. We like it to the extent that it provides employment and an increase in goods and services. On the other hand, we don't like the accompanying increase in pollution, congestion in urban areas and on highways, and what many feel is a growing rootlessness and depersonalization of our way of life.

*A major problem to be solved by an economy is how to adapt to various kinds of change so as to maximize the benefits derived from the desirable aspects of change and minimize the losses caused by the undesirable.*

## CHECKPOINT 2-3

**Do you think the questions of what to produce and for whom to produce it are of a normative or a positive nature? Why?**

## THE VARIETY OF ECONOMIC SYSTEMS

There is a wide variety of ways of organizing an economy to answer the basic questions we have discussed in this chapter. How an economy deals with the basic problem of scarcity—the questions it poses—is also an expression of its vision of the relationship between the individual and society. The way in which a society chooses to organize its economy is therefore to a large extent a reflection of its cultural values and political **ideology**. It was in recognition of this fact that the subject of economics was originally called political economy. Almost any debate over the relative merits of various types of economic systems cannot avoid dealing with the different political ideologies on which they are based. In this section we will consider two basic types of economic systems without dwelling at any length on their political and ideological implications. Nonetheless, it should be kept in mind that these implications are usually regarded as matters of considerable importance.

### Pure Market Economy, Laissez Faire Capitalism

**Laissez faire** is a French expression that means "let [people] do [as they choose]." Especially in matters of economics, it means allowing people to do as they please without governmental regulations and controls. *The ideological basis of such an economic system is the belief that if each economic unit is allowed to make free choices in pursuit of its own best interests, the interests of all will be best served.*

What are the main features of a **pure market economy** based on laissez faire **capitalism**? The means of production are privately owned by private citizens and private institutions. Private property is the rule. Government ownership is generally limited to public buildings and other facilities needed by the government in order to provide such things as national defense, a judicial system, police and fire protection, and public schools and roads. There is freedom of choice for consumers, businesses, and all resource suppliers. Consumers may purchase what they want subject to the limits of their money incomes—there is consumer sovereignty. Businesses are free to purchase and utilize resources to produce whatever products they desire and sell them in markets of their choice—there is free enterprise. Suppliers of resources such as labor, land, and financial capital are likewise free to sell them in whatever markets they please. The major constraint on businesses and resource suppliers is imposed by the marketplace, where consumer sovereignty decides what goods and services can and cannot be produced and sold profitably. Freedom of choice and all market activities are subject to the broadest legal limits consistent with maintaining law and order and with enforcing contracts freely entered into by consenting parties.

### The Market Mechanism

The mechanism that serves to coordinate the activities of consumers, businesses, and all suppliers of resources is the market. A **market** is defined as an area within which buyers and sellers of a particular good are in such close communication that the price of that good tends to be the same everywhere in the area. The answers to the questions of what and how much to produce are determined by the signals communicated between buyers and sellers via the interacting network of markets and prices. The potential buyers of a good make contact with the sellers or suppliers in the market. Then a price must be determined such that suppliers will provide just the quantity of the good that buyers wish to purchase. On the buyers' (demand) side of the market, the level of the price determines who will buy the good and how much will be bought. On the suppliers' side of the market, the price level determines who will supply the good and how much will be supplied. If buyers want more than is being supplied at the prevailing price, they will signal their desires for more by bidding up the price. Suppliers will then respond by providing more of the good. If at the prevailing price sellers are providing a larger quantity of the good than buyers demand, prices will be bid down. This will be a signal to sellers to reduce the quantity of the good they supply to the market. In this way prices serve as the communicating link between buyers and sellers in a market economy.

### Markets Determine What, How, for Whom

The markets for different goods are interrelated because the alternative to using one good is to use another. If the price of beef were felt to be too high, one alternative would be to buy poultry. And if the price of poultry were likewise thought to be too high, another alternative might be to buy ham. Hence the amounts of these goods buyers will demand will depend on the price of beef relative to the price of poultry and ham. Similarly, suppliers will be induced to supply those goods that are selling for the highest prices relative to the prices of other goods. Changes in the price in one market will set up a chain reaction of adjustments in quantities demanded and supplied in related markets. For example, other things being equal, an increase in demand for new housing will cause an increase in the price (wages) of architects, bricklayers, carpenters, furniture sales personnel, and so on. This will induce labor resources to move from other activities into those that now appear relatively more rewarding. All markets in the economy are interrelated with one another to varying extents in this way. It is the "invisible hand" of the marketplace that determines the allocation of resources, *what* goods will be produced, and *how much* of each.

Competition among suppliers of goods and labor services will ensure that the most efficient and productive will charge the lowest price for any good and thus make the sale to shopping buyers. Hence the forces of the marketplace will cause labor and other resources to flow into those occupations and

uses for which they are best suited. This is the way a market economy determines *how production should be organized*.

*For whom* are goods produced in a market economy? Obviously, for whomever is able to pay the price for them. And who are these people? Those who are able to sell their labor services and any other resources they own that can be used in the production of other goods. The emphasis is on competition and a reward structure oriented toward the most efficient and productive. The vision of the individual's relation to society that underlies pure market, laissez faire capitalism has sometimes been characterized as an ideology of the survival of the fittest. All are free to go into any line of work or business they choose, to take any risks at making as much or losing as much money as they care to. The individual is entitled to all the rewards of good decisions and must bear the full consequences of bad ones.

### Resource Utilization

How fully do pure market systems utilize their available resources? This is difficult to evaluate, because history provides few, if any, examples of a pure market economy without any form of government intervention. However, many of the industrialized economies of the Western world have a significant portion of their economic decisions determined by market forces. This was even more so in the nineteenth century and the twentieth century prior to World War II. The Great Depression, which afflicted these nations during the 1930s, together with the record of previous decades, suggests that pure market economies have difficulty keeping their available resources fully employed all the time.

### Change, Stability, and Growth

As to change, stability, and growth, economies that most closely approximate pure market, laissez faire capitalism have achieved some of the highest standards of living in the world. Such systems seem particularly well suited to responding to the changing tastes of consumers. They are also able to develop new products and bring new technologies to the everyday use of the masses. From the standpoint of stability, fluctuations in economic activity as measured by GNP, employment, and the behavior of prices have always been a source of concern in such economies.

Obviously, one would be hard pressed to find a pure form of this type of economy today. In the late eighteenth century at the beginning of the Industrial Revolution, England and the United States came pretty close. Nonetheless, there are still many economies today where markets play a dominant role. Moreover, *the concept of pure market, laissez faire capitalism may be viewed as one extreme on a spectrum of ways of organizing an economy.*

## The Command Economy

In the **command economy,** also called the planned economy, the government answers the questions of how to organize production, what and how much to produce, and for whom. These answers take the form of plans that may extend for as far as 10 to 20 years into the future. In such a planned economy, the government literally commands that these plans be carried out.

### Government Domination

Typically, the government owns the means of production, as in the Soviet Union or Communist China, but this is not always so. In Nazi Germany the government controlled and planned the economy, but ownership remained largely in private hands. *In economies where planning is the most centralized and complete, the government must be very authoritarian. Therefore, it is often a totalitarian regime—ideologically committed to communism or to fascism.* Even in these economies the government may allow markets to operate in certain areas of the economy if it is consistent with, or helpful to, the achievement of other planning objectives. The Soviet Union allows this to some extent in its agricultural sector, for example. In a command economy all forms of labor, including management, are essentially government employees. The state is the company store, the only company.

### Planning What, How, and for Whom

*The underlying rationale for a command economy is that the government knows best what is most beneficial for the entire economy and for its individual parts.* In a command economy there are differences between what consumers may want and what the planners have decided to produce. If planners do not want to devote resources to television sets, consumers simply will go without. Once the plan for the entire economy has been drawn up, each producing unit in the economy is told *what* and *how much* it must produce of various goods to fulfill its part of the plan. This determines each unit's need for labor, capital equipment, and other inputs. Obviously it is not easy to centrally coordinate all the component parts of the plan to ensure that the right kinds and amounts of labor, capital, and other inputs are available to each producing unit so that each may satisfy its individual plan. *How to organize production* is quite a task for central planners overseeing the economy of an entire nation. Managing General Motors, AT&T, or IBM pales in comparison.

For *whom* is output produced? Centrally planned economies typically provide for all citizens regardless of their productive contribution to the output of the economy. However, planners cannot avoid the fact that human nature does respond to material incentives. As a result, government-determined wage scales vary from one occupation or profession to the next, depending on where planners feel there are shortages or surpluses of needed labor skills. This, of course, depends on how authoritarian the government wants to be in allowing people to pick and choose their occupation or profession. For example, it appears that Communist China is more authoritarian in this regard than some of the Eastern European countries.

### Resource Utilization

*Full utilization* of available resources presumably does not pose a problem in a command economy. Remember that by full utilization we mean that there are no available resources standing idle. This is a different issue from whether or not resources may be underemployed due to poor planning. In the Soviet Union planners seem to have continual difficulty in meeting their agricultural goals. If they think their goals are reasonable, their relatively frequent shortfalls from these goals suggest that the resources devoted to agriculture may not be as efficiently employed as possible, even allowing for setbacks caused by bad weather.

### Change, Stability, and Growth

How do planned economies deal with *change* and *growth?* Obviously, in a planned economy growth and many kinds of change can be engineered by the central planning bureau to a large extent. If the government wants more economic growth, the central planning agency will draw up plans devoting a larger share of the economy's resources to the production of capital goods. On the other hand, critics argue that authoritarian control, large bureaucratic structure, and centrally dictated goals put a damper on individual initiative and innovation. Because of this it is argued that technological discovery and change are inhibited. This is considered a major factor in economic growth, a factor that critics feel is weak in planned economies. The *stability* of planned economies depends on how well the government is able to set realistic goals and structure the appropriate plans to attain them. If goals are too ambitious, and if the amount of reorganization in the economy is too great for the time allowed, the loss of economic stability can be severe. This was the case with Communist China's ill-fated Great Leap Forward discussed earlier.

### Summing Up

*The planned, or command, economy may be viewed as representing the other extreme on the spectrum of economic organization from that of pure market, laissez faire capitalism.* No two economies in the world are exactly alike, but each may be thought of as lying somewhere on the spectrum between the two extremes we have described. Most fall under the very broad category of the **mixed economy,** which represents all the in-betweens. All economies have to grapple with the economic problem posed by scarcity, unlimited wants, and the consequent need for choice. In the next chapter we will examine the nature of the mixed economy.

### CHECKPOINT 2-4

**Describe the likely process of selecting a point on the production possibilities frontier of Figure 2–2 (that is, the combination of scrubbers and bundles) for a pure market economy and a planned, or command, economy. For each of these two kinds of economies, what difference do you think it makes, in terms of the point chosen on the frontier, if they are industrially underdeveloped as compared to the likely outcome if they are industrially advanced?**

### SUMMARY

**1.** While available economic resources are limited, human wants are virtually unlimited. This creates the fundamental problem of scarcity, which makes it necessary to make choices.

**2.** Economic efficiency requires that there be no unemployment or underemployment of resources. Unemployment exists whenever some available resources are idle. Underemployment (or resource misallocation) exists if certain available resources are employed to do jobs for which other available resources are better suited. It also exists whenever the best available technology is not used in a production process.

**3.** When there is no unemployment or underemployment of available resources, an economy is able to produce the maximum amount of goods possible. When producing this maximum, the economy is said to be on its production possibilities frontier. This frontier is a curve connecting the maximum possible output combinations of goods for a fully employed economy. In this situation, the production of more of one kind of good is possible only if the economy produces less of another. The cost of having more of one good is the amount of the other that must be given up. This cost is often called the opportunity cost of a good.

**4.** Economic growth occurs when an economy's available supply of resources is increased or when there is an increase in technological know-how. As a result, the production possibilities frontier expands outward. The output combination chosen on today's frontier affects the amount of capital goods that will be available tomorrow. Therefore, today's choice will affect the location of tomorrow's production possibilities frontier.

**5.** Any economy, whatever its political ideology, must answer certain questions that arise because of the basic economic problem of scarcity. Every economy must decide what goods to produce, how much to produce, how to organize production, and for whom output is to be produced. The answer to the question of what to produce determines the nature and location of the production possibilities frontier. The answer to the question of how much to produce determines the point chosen on the frontier. How to organize production determines whether the chosen point on the frontier will be reached. For whom to produce is largely determined by ideological orientation as to the proper mix of free markets, government regulation, and central planning.

**6.** Every economy must concern itself with maintaining full employment of its resources (avoiding unemployment). This has frequently been a problem for the industrialized economies of the West. Every economy must also deal with change. The stability of an economy depends very much on how well it is able to adjust to change. An important kind of change is economic growth, and economies are often judged on how well they promote economic growth.

**7.** There are two basic kinds of economies, or ways of organizing the process of deciding what and how much, how, and for whom to produce. Each kind presumes a particular relationship between the individual and the state. They are basically distinguished by the amount of government intervention they permit in the decision-making process of the economy.

a. *Pure market, laissez faire capitalism.* Individual economic units are given free choice in all economic decisions, which are completely decentralized. There is no interference by government in the form of regulations or controls. Markets and prices are the sole coordinating mechanisms for allocating resources and organizing production.

b. *Command, or planned, economy.* An authoritarian government decides what and how much, how, and for whom to produce. Government typically owns the means of production, plans economic activities, and commands that these plans be carried out. The underlying rationale is that the government knows best what is most beneficial for the entire economy and its individual parts.

## KEY TERMS AND CONCEPTS

business cycles
business fluctuations
capitalism
command economy
economic efficiency
economic growth
economic problem

ideology
laissez faire
law of increasing costs
market
mixed economy
opportunity cost
production possibilities frontier
pure market economy
resource misallocation
underemployment
unemployment

## QUESTIONS AND PROBLEMS

**1.** Think about the following situation in terms of the concept of opportunity cost. If you choose not to go to college, suppose your best alternative is to drive a truck for $12,000 per year. If you choose to go to college, suppose that you must pay a tuition fee of $2,000 per year and buy books and other school supplies amounting to $400 per year. Suppose that your other living expenses are the same regardless of which choice you make. Suppose you choose to go to college. What is the opportunity cost of your college diploma?

**2.** The following is a production possibilities table for computers and jet airplanes:

| Product | Production Possibilities | | | | |
| --- | --- | --- | --- | --- | --- |
| | A | B | C | D | E |
| Computers (in thousands) | 0 | 25 | 40 | 50 | 55 |
| Jet airplanes (in thousands) | 40 | 30 | 20 | 10 | 0 |

a. Plot the production possibilities frontier for the economy characterized by this table.

b. Demonstrate the law of increasing costs using the data in this table.

c. Suppose technological progress doubles the productivity of the process for making computers and also of that for making jet airplanes. What would the numbers in the production possibilities table look like in that case? Plot the new production possibilities frontier.

d. Suppose technological progress doubles the productivity of the process for making computers but there is no change in the process for making jet airplanes. What would the numbers in the production possibilities table be now? Plot the new production possibilities frontier.

e. Suppose technological progress doubles the productivity of the process for making jet airplanes but there is no change in the process for making computers. What would the numbers in the production possibilities frontier be now? Plot the new production possibilities frontier. Why is it that, despite the fact that there is no change in the productivity of producing computers, it is now possible at any given level of production of jet airplanes to have more computers?

**3.** Consider a production possibilities frontier for consumer goods and capital goods. How would the choice of a point on that frontier affect the position of tomorrow's frontier? Choose three different points on today's production possibilities frontier and indicate the possible location of tomorrow's frontier that is associated with each.

**4.** Construct your own production possibilities frontier by putting a grade point scale on the vertical axis to measure a grade in your economics course and the number of waking hours in a typical day (say 16) on the horizontal axis. Out of those 16 hours per day, how many do you think you would have to give up to get a D? a C? a B? an A? Plot the frontier determined by these combinations.

**5.** Compare and contrast the ways in which the two types of economies we have discussed deal with the five basic questions or problems any economy faces.

# 3

# The Nature of
# the Mixed Economy

## AFTER READING THIS CHAPTER, YOU WILL BE ABLE TO:

1. Explain why markets exist.

2. Explain how money makes trading much easier and therefore promotes specialization and trade.

3. Define *normal profit*.

4. Define the role of profit in the creation and allocation of capital.

5. State the nature and rationale of government intervention in a mixed economy.

*In a mixed economy the answers to the questions what and how much to produce, how to organize production, and for whom to produce are determined by a mixture of government intervention, regulation, and control in some areas of the economy, coupled with private enterprise and a reliance on markets in other areas.*

In some mixed economies, government intervention extends even to the ownership of certain industries—such industries are called **nationalized industries.** In Great Britain, for example, the steel, the airline, and the railroad industries are nationalized. The public by and large felt that these industries would operate better under complete government control than under private ownership subject to varying degrees of government regulation, as is the case with the railroads and airlines in the United States. Hence, *a mixed economy may involve not only a mixture of private and public decision making but a mixture of private and public ownership as well.*

The role of government varies from one mixed economy to the next, reflecting the varying opinions on this issue in different countries. Nonetheless, there are certain characteristics common to all. They all have markets where the exchange of goods and services takes place using money as the medium of exchange. They all have had a strong tradition of capitalism stemming from their history of economic development, particularly the fact that they experienced the Industrial Revolution.[1] They all have felt the need to modify capitalism and the workings of free markets through government intervention.

In this chapter we will get a brief overview of some of the main characteristics of mixed economies like our own. Much of the analysis in the rest of this book will focus on mixed economies. This chapter will also briefly explore the role of markets, money, profits, and government in such an economic

[1] Countries that most commonly come to mind are the United States, Great Britain, Canada, the Scandinavian countries, France, West Germany, Italy, Australia, New Zealand, and Japan.

system. Of course a good deal of what we say about each of these subjects is true whether or not we are speaking of a mixed economy.

## MARKETS AND MONEY

Specialization gives rise to the need for trade, and trade creates markets. Money makes trade easier and therefore encourages specialization and a more extensive development of markets. Let's consider the truth of each of these statements in turn.

### Specialization and Markets

Why do markets exist in the first place? Why are goods traded? What is it that leads people to go to market? The answer lies in the fact that each of us is better at doing some things than at doing others. We often refer to our best skill as "my thing," "my bag," or my "long suit." We tend to specialize in that thing we are best at. We "trade on it." Have you ever heard it said of movie stars that "they trade on their good looks"?

When each of us specializes in that particular thing he or she is best at, the whole economy is able to produce more of everything than if each of us tries to be self-sufficient. Of course when each specializes in producing one thing, each is dependent on others for the production of everything else. *With specialization most of what one produces is a surplus that must be traded for the other things that one wants. Hence the more **specialization of labor** there is in an economy, the greater is the need for trade.* And as trade becomes more important to the functioning of an economy, markets in all kinds of goods and services become more commonplace.

### The Role of Money

A prominent characteristic of markets with which you are familiar is that goods are traded for money. *In a* **barter economy** *goods are traded for goods.* The more an economy is characterized by specialization of labor, the less likely it is that we will observe goods being traded directly for goods. What led people to start using money in the first place? The fundamental reason for the invention and existence of money is that it makes specialization and trade much easier. This is most obvious if we consider the difficulties of trade in a barter economy.

### Trade in a Barter Economy

Suppose you are a member of an economy in which each individual specializes in the production of a particular good. Like everyone else, you produce more of your particular good than you need for yourself and trade the surplus for other goods. Suppose you specialize in chopping wood and today you decide to go shopping for a pair of sandals. Lugging your wood on your back, you go in search of a sandal maker. Finding one at last, you are disappointed to find that the sandal maker has no need for chopped wood. No trade takes place, and so with aching back and sore feet you continue on your quest. Your problem is twofold. You must first find someone who has sandals to trade. Second, while you may encounter several such people, you must find among them one who wants to acquire chopped wood. In other words, you are looking for an individual who coincidentally has sandals to trade *and* also wants chopped wood. In order to have a trade, it is necessary to have a **coincidence of wants**.

At this point you might ask, is it not possible that someone who has sandals to trade, but no need for chopped wood, might accept the wood and then trade it for something he or she does want? Yes, it is possible, but very inconvenient. If that person accepts the wood, the problem of finding a coincidence of wants has really just been transferred from you to him or her.

In sum, *the difficulties involved in finding a coincidence of wants tend to discourage specialization and trade in a barter economy.* Given the effort and time that must be spent just to find a coincidence of wants, many individuals in a barter economy would find it easier to be more self-sufficient and produce more items for their own consumption. To this extent, the gains from specialization and trade cannot be fully realized.

### Money as a Medium of Exchange

How does the use of money allow us to get around these difficulties? *Money eliminates the need for the coincidence of wants.* If the economy uses money to carry on trade, you can sell your chopped wood to whomever wants it and accept money in exchange. Whether the purchaser makes something you want is now irrelevant. As long as you can use the money received to buy what you want you are satisfied. You can use the money to buy a pair of sandals or whatever. Similarly, the sandal maker will accept your money even though he or she may have no need for your chopped wood. We say money serves as the medium of exchange.

At different times and in different societies, the medium of exchange used as money has taken many forms—from hounds' teeth to precious stones to gold coin to currency, checks, and credit cards. Whatever its form, *money's common characteristic is that it must be acceptable to people because they know they can use it as buyers. Because money eliminates the need for coincidence of wants, it promotes specialization and trade and thereby makes possible the gains that stem from specialization and trade. The incentive for societies to use money in exchange derives from these gains. The introduction of money into a barter economy essentially causes that economy's production possibilities frontier to be shifted outward.*

---

### CHECKPOINT* 3-1

**Suppose there are three people, A, B, and C, and that A specializes in growing corn, B in catching fish, and C in growing wheat. A has a surplus of corn, B a surplus of fish, and C a surplus of wheat. Suppose A would like to get some wheat from C, but C doesn't have any desire for A's corn. Suppose that C would like to get some**

fish from B, but B doesn't want any of C's wheat. And suppose that B would like to get some corn from A, but A doesn't want any of B's fish. Each wants something from one of the others, but has nothing to offer in exchange. What is lacking here? Further, suppose each lives alone on an island 20 miles from each of the others and that each has a boat. Describe how trade would have to be carried on under a barter system, if it were carried on at all. By comparison, describe how trade would be carried on if A, B, and C used money.

*Answers to all Checkpoints can be found at the back of the text.

## MARKETS AND PROFITS

A money-using economy with extensive markets fosters specialization among workers and in the methods of production. This specialization leads to the development of more sophisticated production processes, which typically require large amounts of investment in capital goods. In a capitalistic economy where the productive units or firms are privately owned either by those who run them or by shareholders, sizeable amounts of funds, or financial capital, must be raised by the owners in order to acquire the capital goods. Whether or not it is worthwhile to commit funds to such investments depends on that controversial thing called profit. And the amount of profit is determined by the markets where the goods produced by the capital goods are sold. Another key role played by profit in a capitalistic economy is to provide an incentive for entrepreneurial activity. The entrepreneur described in Chapter 1 is a key factor in the creation and organizing of new production techniques and the founding of firms that employ these techniques to satisfy the demands of new and continually changing markets.

## What Is a Normal Profit?

Profit is one of the most controversial and least understood concepts in economics. For some people the mere mention of the word conjures up images of exploitation and robber barons carving out their pound of flesh from the downtrodden. But what is a "reasonable" profit, or what economists call a **normal profit**? When we say that a firm is earning a normal profit, what must be the relationship between its total sales revenue and its total costs?

In order to answer these questions, recall that we emphasized in the previous chapter that all costs are opportunity costs due to the fact that resources are scarce and have alternative uses. Our discussion of the production possibilities frontier indicated that if resources are used to produce one good, they are not available to produce other goods. The cost of the one good is thus the alternative goods that must be forgone in order to produce it. This notion of cost is directly applicable to the individual firm. All the resources, including financial capital and entrepreneurial skills, that a firm needs in order to produce its product have alternative uses in the production of other products by other firms. Hence *the costs of production for a firm are all those payments it must make to all resource suppliers in order to bid resources away from use in the production of alternative goods. When the firm's total sales revenue is just sufficient to cover these costs, all resources employed by the firm are just earning their opportunity costs.* In particular, *the financial capital and the entrepreneurial skills used by the firm are being compensated just enough to keep them from leaving and going into some other line of productive activity. That amount of compensation is called a normal profit.*

## Profit and the Allocation of Resources

Changes in the level of profits that are earned in different markets play an important role in the efficient allocation of resources in a dynamic, changing economy. Suppose that a market for a new product develops or that there is a sudden increase in demand for an existing product. Firms already in the market or those first to enter will find they can earn more than normal profits or above-normal profits. This happens because demand so exceeds the existing capacity to meet it that prices considerably in excess of cost can be charged. Above-normal profits serve as a signal to entrepreneurial skills and financial capital in other areas of the economy that they can earn more by moving into the new and expanding markets. Resources will continue to move into these areas so long as above-normal profits exist. Eventually, enough resources will have moved into these markets and increased capacity sufficiently that above-normal profits will no longer exist. In this way *above-normal profits serve to allocate resources to those areas of the economy where they are most in demand. Similarly, of course, below-normal profits in one area of the economy will cause entrepreneurial skills and financial capital to move out of that line of productive activity and into those where they can earn their opportunity cost.*

## Controversy About the Role of Profit

Anytime you read something or hear a discussion about profit, you should ask yourself how the term is being used. There is a good deal of misunderstanding about the nature of profit in mixed economies.

### Early Views on Profit

Suspicion of profit is an ancient theme in Western culture. A sixteenth-century French thinker, Michel de Montaigne, wrote an essay entitled "The Profit of One Man Is the Damage of Another." His thesis was that "man should condemn all manner of gain." However, with the dawn of the era of capitalism two centuries ago, the profit motive found an able defender in Adam Smith—the renowned author of *The Wealth of Nations*. In this book, published in 1776, Smith argued that profits are the legitimate return for risk and effort. He put forward the notion that the "invisible hand" of market forces turns private greed into productive activity, which provides goods for the benefit of all. A century later, Karl Marx argued the opposite view. He maintained that labor, not capital, was the ingredient that added value to goods or raw materials in the production process. He asserted that profit was the "surplus value" that the capitalist unjustifiably added on to the real worth of the product.

### Twentieth-Century Views on Profit

In the early part of the twentieth century, the Fabian socialists argued that profits should be "taxed into oblivion" to create a new socialist order. If they meant above-normal profit, they might have a good case in certain circumstances. In the mixed economy of the United States, public policy has recognized that due to the technology of producing certain kinds of goods and due to the size and nature of certain kinds of markets, one firm can become dominant and exclude any others from the market. In that case, the monopoly position of the firm allows it to charge high prices and earn above-normal profit because consumers who want the product have no alternative but to buy it from that firm. Electric power companies, telephone companies, and gas companies are examples. Without some type of government intervention, such firms could go on earning above-normal profits until technological innovation provided some substitute good not yet existent. Because of this, utility companies are subject to government regulation of the prices they can charge. In this way, profit in excess of normal profit, frequently called monopoly profit, is supposed to be taxed into oblivion. Most economists, policymakers, and the general public feel this procedure is justified in such "natural" monopoly situations. In practice such regulation has not always been able to achieve the desired goal.

Suppose the Fabians' expressed desire to tax profits into oblivion were meant to apply to normal profits. This would effectively remove any return to financial capital and entrepreneurial skill. It would, therefore, remove the incentive for anybody to provide the financial capital necessary for the creation of physical capital goods or the innovative effort necessary to create new technology and supply new markets. When an economy ceases to build capital goods, the growth in its capacity to produce other goods stops. If the Fabians meant by profits normal profits, taxing profits out of existence would certainly be an extreme position. There would definitely be a new social order.

The taxation of profits will undoubtedly always be a much debated issue in mixed capitalistic economies. Unfortunately, much of the debate is often the result of misunderstanding over the meaning or meanings of the word profit.

### Profit in Today's Economy

Today the average individual directly or indirectly owns a sizeable portion of the shares (or stock) of corporations in the United States. The dividends paid on these shares derive directly from the profits of the corporations. Nearly half of all corporate shares, measured in dollar value, are owned by institutions such as pension funds, insurance companies, college endowments, and churches. Hence, for millions of Americans such things as the assurance of a retirement income, the soundness of an insurance policy, and the availability of a college scholarship are heavily dependent on the continued profitability of U.S. corporations. When profits go down or turn into losses, the average person in the street often has as much cause for concern as the corporate board of directors. It should be said, however, that above-normal profits derived from situations where competition in the marketplace is nonexistent or inhibited are generally considered not to be in the economy's best interest.

**CHECKPOINT 3-2**

**Samuel Gompers (1850–1924) was an American labor leader. He was the first president of the American Federation of Labor, a position he held from 1886 until his death (except for one year, 1895). He once said, "The worst crime against working people is a company which fails to operate at a profit." What do you suppose he meant by this? Like Gompers, Marx championed the working class. How do their views on profit seem to differ?**

## GOVERNMENT'S ROLE IN THE MIXED ECONOMY

As with profits, there is always a good deal of controversy over the appropriate role of government versus that of markets in determining what, how, and for whom to produce. "Be thankful you don't get all the government you pay for" say some who are skeptical of what government does and how efficiently it does it. A critic of the market system once said, "Competition in the marketplace brings out the best in products and the worst in people."

Government, whether it is local, state, or federal, performs four main functions in a mixed economy: (1) it provides the legal and institutional structure in which markets operate; (2) it intervenes in the allocation of resources in areas of the economy where public policy deems it beneficial to do so; (3) it redistributes income; and (4) it seeks to provide stability in prices, economic growth, and economic conditions generally. Of course, government actions in any one of these spheres almost invariably have implications for the others.

### Legal and Institutional Structure for Markets

Even in pure market, laissez faire capitalism, the government must provide for legal definition and enforcement of contracts, property rights, and ownership. It must also establish the legal status of different forms of business organizations, from the owner-operated small business to the large corporation. It must provide a judicial system so that disputed claims between parties arising in the course of business can be settled. Government also provides for the supply and regulation of the money supply, the maintenance of a system of measurement standards, and the maintenance of a police force to keep order and protect property.

You will find little disagreement anywhere as to the need for government to provide this basic legal and institutional structure. Since the turn of the century, however, the legal sanctions and constraints on the functioning of markets and the economic relationships between business, labor, and consumers have become more complex. In the United States the government has taken an active role in trying to maintain competition in markets. We have already noted how government regulates pricing activities in the utilities industries, where technological and market conditions do not naturally encourage competition. In an attempt to maintain competitive conditions in all markets, Congress has enacted a number of antitrust laws, which are essentially aimed at preventing market domination by one or a small number of large firms. Starting with the Sherman Act of 1890, these laws also make it illegal for firms in any particular market to collude in setting prices or conspire to restrict competition. Legislation such as the Taft-Hartley Act of 1947 was enacted to impose legal constraints on the way unions are organized and run and on collective bargaining procedures. These laws also prescribe how strikes that threaten the general well-being of the nation are to be handled. Government intervention to protect consumers has been the subject of legislation throughout the twentieth century, starting with the Pure Food and Drug Act of 1906. More recently the government has actively intervened in the area of pollution control. In 1969 Congress established the Environmental Protection Agency in order to develop quality standards for air and water with the assistance of state and local governments.

Government intervention in the marketplace through creation and change of certain aspects of the legal and institutional structure has often proved beneficial. In other instances, it has not. One of the most disastrous examples was the Volstead Act passed in Congress in 1919. It prohibited the production and sale of alcoholic beverages. The act became so unpopular that Congress repealed it in 1933. Many observers feel that it provided a tremendous economic windfall to the underworld, which did a thriving business in the illicit production and sale of the liquor that a thirsty public would not do without. This is felt to have laid the foundation for modern organized crime as a big business.

## Resource Allocation

Government affects resource allocation in our economy through its spending activities, its tax policies, and its own production of certain goods and services.

### Government Spending

In the United States about 70 percent of all output is produced and sold in markets. The quantity and variety of goods and services represented by this 70 percent of total output is the result of decisions made by numerous firms and consumers—the private sector of our economy. The other 30 percent of the economy's output is the result of government (public sector) expenditure decisions. This includes all levels of government—state, federal, and local. Though much of this output of goods and services is produced by private businesses, it is done under government contract and reflects government decisions about what to produce and for whom—highways for motorists, schools, and military hardware for national defense are just a few examples.

## POLICY PERSPECTIVE

### Should Profit Be the Only Objective of Business?

Do businesses have obligations to society beyond making profit? There is considerable disagreement over the appropriate answer to this question. On one side of the issue it is argued that the *only* responsibility of business is to make profits because by pursuing that goal alone society's interests are best served. Alternatively, the other side of the issue holds that businesses should act according to higher moral principles to prevent damage to society that might otherwise result from a single-minded pursuit of profit. In the extreme, this view holds that it amounts to "murder for profit" when businesses produce and advertise cigarettes, market automobiles that are not "adequately crash-proof," and dump toxic wastes in rivers. Are there not moral principles that should inhibit such behavior even at the cost of forgone profit opportunities?

#### The "Only Profits" View

The view that profit should be the sole objective of business points out that corporate managers in today's world are responsible to the corporation's stockholders (the owners) who expect them to do everything within the law to earn the owners a maximum return (profit) on their investment. The "only profits" view argues that if a corporate executive takes an action that the executive feels is "socially responsible" and that action reduces profit, then the executive has spent (in effect, stolen) the owners' money. This violates a fundamental tenet of our political-economic system that no individual shall be deprived of property without his or her permission. Corporate executives who want to take socially responsible actions should use their own money, supporting special interest groups, charities, or political parties and causes that promote the social actions they desire. However, to the extent that executives sacrifice profit to such actions, they effectively deprive stockholders of the right to spend the sacrificed higher profits (which otherwise belong to stockholders) on social actions of the stockholders' choosing, and on anything else for that matter. If corporate executives and stockholders choose to spend their *own* money to support (in whatever way) social actions to regulate business behavior, so be it.

#### The "Profits Plus Other Concerns" View

The point of view that business should not pursue profit to the complete exclusion of other social concerns argues that the sole pursuit of profit tends to give rise to immoral, if not illegal, business behavior. According to this view business firms do have a moral responsibility not to design products or engage in behavior (for example, deceptive advertising) that they have reason to believe will seriously injure or possibly kill people. Business's willingness to do what is clearly immoral for the sake of profit conflicts with an old moral precept (going back at least to Aristotle) that money is a means to an end, in itself not the sort of end that justifies acting immorally to get it. The "profits plus other concerns" view also argues that if profit is the sole objective of business then the associated abuses and immoral behavior that result will lead the public to impose greater government regulation on business activity. Increased government intrusion in the private sector will cause economic inefficiency as well as pose potential threats to individual freedoms. Therefore, it is argued, it is in the long run in the best interest of business (and all of us) to pay heed to moral principles while pursuing profit. Otherwise society will increasingly use the government and political processes to correct perceived abuses.

### How Do You Get Socially Responsible Business Behavior?

Is it really possible for firms to be "socially responsible" and survive in a competitive market? Firms that incur additional costs to make a safer product or avoid polluting the environment, say, may put themselves at a competitive disadvantage vis-a-vis less socially responsible rival firms. Will the more socially responsible firms not be driven out of business, leaving only those motivated solely by profit, thus making the greater government regulation predicted by the "profits plus other concerns" view inevitable? It depends on the nature of the socially responsible behavior firms engage in. Firms that make products that get a reputation for being unsafe, for example, will lose sales to the safer products of rivals—they will be disciplined by the market while the more socially responsible firms will be rewarded.

On the other hand, socially responsible firms that voluntarily incur costs to prevent environmental pollution are likely to lose out to less socially responsible rivals because pollution control efforts don't show up in product quality where they will be rewarded by the market. Therefore government regulation to protect the environment may be the only solution to pollution control problems, while the discipline of the market may be a more reliable and efficient way to enforce product safety. Even on the issue of product safety however, the question is "how many injuries and lost lives does it take for the market to react against an unsafe product?" Where the public has answered "too many," government regulation has been called for, giving rise to such regulatory bodies as the Food and Drug Administration and the National Transportation Safety Board.

### The Role of Human Nature

What if human nature is such that it is only realistic to expect that the main objective of business *is* profit, as Adam Smith believed (see Adam Smith, p. 14)? Then the relevant questions are: (1) What kinds of socially irresponsible business behavior will be curbed by the discipline of the market, and what kinds will not? (2) Where market discipline is of questionable effectiveness, are the costs of government regulation (in terms of increased threat to individual freedom as well as increased tax cost) less than the costs (such as injury and loss of life) that trigger market discipline?

Some perspective on answers to the last question is provided by the following examples. Despite the fact that lower speed limits are known to reduce highway fatalities, there is no public outcry for lower speed limits. The public values reduced travel time more than reduced fatalities. (People do put a price on life!) Similarly, there is a limit to what people will pay for a "crash-proof" car. A business that tried to produce them, out of a sense of social responsibility, would probably go bankrupt because only a few people would be willing to pay a price that would cover the cost of making them. If the public is unwilling to pay for such a level of product safety, it would hardly seem justifiable to many citizens for the government to impose it by subsidizing production of such cars with taxpayers' money. It would also be misleading to assume the absence of such cars is due to automakers' lack of social conscience and singular pursuit of profit.

### Questions

1. In some states motorcyclists are required to wear crash helmets. Why might you expect a helmet manufacturer to differ from a motorcycle company on the two views about profit in this case?

2. In the United States it is legal to sell alcoholic beverages but not marijuana. How *might* this distinction be justified?

---

### Taxation

Another way in which the government affects the allocation of resources is through its power to levy taxes. For example, we have already noted how changes in profit affect the incentive to create new capital goods. From our discussion of the production possibilities frontier in the previous chapter, we know that there is a trade-off between producing capital goods and producing goods for present consumption. In order to produce more of one kind of good, it is necessary to obtain the resources to do so by cutting back on production of the other. That is, it is necessary to reallocate resources from one line of productive activity to another. By changing the rate of taxation of profit, the government changes the incentive to produce capital goods relative to the incentive to produce goods for current consumption. For instance, suppose the government increased taxes on profits. This would discourage the production of capital goods relative to consumer goods. Some resources would therefore be reallocated from capital goods production to consumer goods production. This is but one example of the way in which the government can affect the allocation of resources through tax policy.

### Government Production of Goods and Services

Another way that the government affects resource allocation is by producing goods and services itself. There are certain kinds of goods and services that would not be produced at all if the choice were left up to the market mechanism, even though it might be acknowledged by everybody that such goods provide benefits for all. Such goods are **public goods**.

*An essential feature of a public good is that it cannot be provided to one person without providing it to others.* If the government provides a dam to protect your property from floods, the benefits accrue to your neighbor as well. Public goods are *not* subject to the so-called **exclusion principle**. *Any good whose benefits accrue only to those who purchase it is said to be subject to the exclusion principle.* Those who do not buy the good are excluded from its benefits. The exclusion principle almost invariably applies to goods produced and sold in a market economy. When producers cannot prevent those who don't pay for the good from having it, the exclusion principle does not hold for that good. If one can have a good without paying for it, then there is no way for producers to charge and receive a price to cover the costs of producing it. Hence there will be no incentive for firms to produce it in a market economy. If I build a lighthouse, there is no way I can exclude any ship at sea from benefiting from its beacon. Hence there is no way I can charge ships at sea for its service, so I won't build it, despite the fact that shipping companies all agree that it cuts down their economic losses due to shipwrecks. Similarly, it is difficult to privately produce and sell the services of a dam, national defense, cloud seeding, and clean air.

*Another feature of a public good is that once it is provided for one citizen, there is no additional cost to providing it for others.* This is really just another aspect of the fact that when a public good provides benefits to one, it unavoidably provides them to others. It costs no more to protect one ship at sea than to protect several with the same lighthouse.

Of course, there are many goods that are not by nature public goods that the government provides anyway. Examples of goods and services that can be privately produced and sold in markets but are provided by state, local, or federal government are education, police and fire protection, certain kinds of preventive medical treatment, sewage treatment, garbage collection, bridges, toll roads, and air shows financed by the government through the Defense Department. In most of these cases, it is usually argued that there are substantial social benefits, and that if their provision were left strictly to private producers and markets, less of these goods would be produced than is desirable.

## Income Redistribution

In virtually all modern, industrialized, mixed economies there are specific government policies aimed at alleviating the hardships of poverty. If people cannot earn some minimal standard of living in the marketplace, it is generally agreed that they should be given economic assistance in some form. Whatever form it takes, this assistance makes it necessary to redistribute income from those judged to have enough to those who do not. One obvious way to do this is for the government simply to levy heavier income taxes on people in higher income brackets and transfer the money collected to those in lower brackets.

Many government transfers of income and wealth between citizens do not necessarily redistribute from the rich to the poor. Social security payments to retired persons are financed by social security taxes paid by all those citizens presently working as well as by their employers. Any retired citizen over 62 years of age, even a multimillionaire, is eligible for these benefits. And even the lowest-paid worker is obliged to pay the social security taxes used to finance these benefits.

Government has played a growing role in income redistribution since World War II. This is illustrated in Figure 3–1, which shows that an increased share of federal government outlays takes the form of payments to individuals. The payments to individuals are transfer payments in the form of Medicare and social security benefits to retired workers and the disabled, unemployment benefits, and payments to those eligible for various welfare and special assistance programs. The payments to individuals are often referred to as income maintenance programs because they effectively maintain minimum income levels for the recipients. They represent an income redistribution from taxpayers to those receiving the payments. The share of total federal government outlays accounted for by payments to individuals grew from 12.3 percent in 1953 to 41.5 percent in 1983.

A good deal of the transfer of income and wealth among citizens takes the form of government provision of goods and services at zero or below cost to the citizens who use them. These are not included in "payments to individuals." The costs of providing such goods and services are covered by tax revenue, much of which is collected from citizens who may not themselves use these governmentally provided goods and services. Public education, parks and recreation areas, public libraries, and a partially subsidized postal service are but a few examples. Again, a wealthy person might choose to use these facilities while someone with a much lower income might use them little or not at all, even though he or she pays taxes used to subsidize the government provision of such goods and services.

Another way in which the government affects income distribution is by direct intervention in the marketplace. Well-known examples of this are governmentally enforced

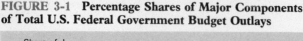

**FIGURE 3-1  Percentage Shares of Major Components
of Total U.S. Federal Government Budget Outlays**

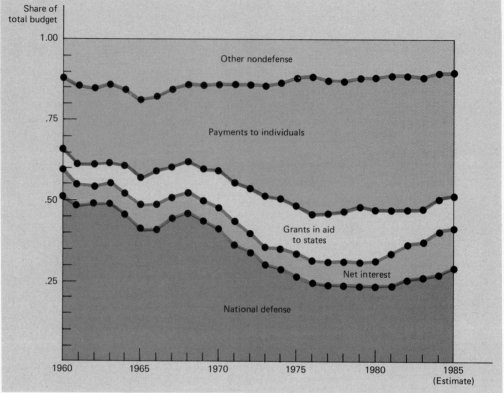

Federal budget outlays reflect increased emphasis on income redistribution in the form of payments to individuals.

price supports in agricultural markets and minimum-wage laws in labor markets. Farm price supports reflect a desire to maintain the income levels of farmers. Minimum-wage laws supposedly reflect a desire to see to it that laborers' wage levels ensure some minimum standard of living. In the case of agriculture such direct market intervention has been criticized for unjustly favoring special interests and distorting resource allocation. It has also been charged that minimum-wage laws aggravate unemployment and contribute to poverty rather than alleviate it. Some argue that minimum-wage laws reflect the desire of skilled or unionized workers to di-

minish the competition they face from low-wage workers.

## Economic Stabilization

In the previous chapter we noted the difficulties that market-oriented economies have avoiding recessions in economic activity, fluctuations in employment and GNP, and unacceptable levels of inflation. In most capitalistic, mixed economies, we observed that a good deal of responsibility for avoiding these difficulties has been vested in the government—witness the Employment Act of 1946 in the United States. Governmental efforts to carry out the spirit of that act are an example of how the exercise of a government responsibility in one area invariably affects other areas. Fiscal policy—government expenditure and tax changes aimed at smoothing out fluctuations in economic activity—unavoidably affects resource allocation, income distribution, and even the competitive market structure of industries in which the government buys goods and lets contracts for public projects. By changing the levels of interest rates, monetary policy has similar effects on resource allocation and income distribution.

## Controversy About the Role of Government

In recent years there has been a growing skepticism about the ability of government to provide services to the public, direction to the economy, and solutions to a number of social problems. This has led to a critical examination of how government functions in our economy, a search for the reasons why once-optimistic expectations about the government's role have often not been fulfilled.

### Efficiency in Government

Many critics point out that government bureaucracies by their very nature do not have the built-in incentives for efficiency that exist in the typical business firm. The reward of profit and the threat of loss are absent. Moreover, it is typically difficult to measure either output or performance. It is often impossible for a government bureaucrat to show how and where he or she has saved the taxpayers money. How can one tell how efficiently the Department of the Interior, the local library, or a city school system is being operated? If efficient performance is hard to demonstrate, it is likely to be unrecognized and unrewarded, so why try so hard? Similarly, an inefficient performance is equally hard to detect. Neither the carrot nor the stick is much in evidence under these circumstances. In short, because the relationship between taxpayer dollars and benefits produced is hard to

establish, the incentives for efficiency are weak.

### Special Interest Legislation

Special interest groups often push hard for legislation that provides special benefits for them and possibly little or no benefit for anyone else. Special interest groups often get their way even when it may not serve the broader public interest. Why?

Suppose some special interest group presses for a program that will cost each individual taxpayer only a dollar. The total cost of the program may be tens of millions of dollars. But as far as the individual taxpayer is concerned the extra dollar of taxes will hardly be noticed. For the individual taxpayer it is scarcely worth the effort to become informed about the program. However, those in the special interest group may stand to benefit substantially, so that they have very strong feelings about whether the program is approved or not. Consequently a politician who doesn't vote for the special interest group's program stands to lose the group's vote in the next election and quite likely a helpful financial contribution to his or her campaign as well. On the other hand, a vote for the program will probably cost the politician few if any votes among the other largely uninformed voters. Consequently the politician votes for the special interest group's program, even though it may not be in the broader public interest.

For example, you are a member of Congress from a district where a large company dumps toxic wastes into a river. Downstream the river runs through heavily populated areas, creating a health hazard and requiring costly water treatment plants. Suppose the citizens downstream are ill-informed about the source of their dirty water. An antipollution law is proposed in Congress that would require offending companies, such as the one in your district, to clean up their toxic wastes. The company and its employees, who fear a loss of jobs, are a special interest group on this issue. You can't afford to lose their vote and so you vote against the legislation, to the detriment of the larger but ill-informed public downstream.

## Consumer Preferences and the Bundle Problem

When you buy goods in the marketplace, you shop for them on an item-by-item basis. You are able to be very selective. Your selection of governmentally provided goods and services is much more limited because you must select them through an intermediary, the candidate for political office. Each candidate really represents a bundle of public goods and services, the ones that the candidate will support and vote for if he or she is elected. Your choice of bundles is limited by the number of candidates running for an office. Each candidate may have certain goods and services in his or her bundle that you want and others that you don't want. You vote for the candidate whose bundle most closely matches your preferences. Even then you are forced to take some public goods and services you don't want in order to get those that you do want.

For example, you choose to vote for candidate A because A supports the construction of a dam that you want very much. The candidate may also be in favor of price supports for wheat and corn, which you don't want, but you don't feel as concerned about price supports as you do about the dam. Candidate B is against the price supports but does not favor the dam either. You vote for A instead of B. Even though A's bundle of goods and services doesn't match your preferences perfectly, it comes closer than the alternative bundle represented by B.

## Bias Toward Current Benefit, Hidden Cost Projects

Because politicians must worry about getting reelected, there is a natural tendency for them to favor projects and programs that have immediate, highly visible benefits and less visible costs. An objective economic analysis of project A might show it to be more worthwhile than a number of other projects. But suppose project A's benefits are spread over a distant future, while tax increases will be required to cover its immediate costs. Project A is therefore likely to lack support, while other economically less worthwhile projects that have more immediate benefits and less visible costs will be pushed forward.

It should be emphasized that none of these criticisms of the way government functions to provide goods and services is a criticism of politicians and government bureaucrats. They respond to rewards and incentives just like people in other walks of life. Given that, these criticisms are directed at the ways in which the reward and incentive structures of our political and governmental institutions are not always geared to provide goods and services in the most economically efficient manner.

## Resource Utilization

How good are mixed economies at maintaining a *full utilization of their available resources?* The Great Depression of the 1930s, which plagued the industrialized economies of the West, led these countries to call for more government intervention in the future. In this way, these economies hoped to avoid another episode of such dramatic underemployment of resources. The ideas put forward at that time by the British economist John Maynard Keynes provided a rationale for how government intervention could prevent such a calamity. Income tax reductions and stepped-up government expenditures to offset the fall in expenditures by businesses and consumers were among the recommended measures to be used. Most economists today are of the opinion that such government intervention would be appropriate and effective in averting another Great Depression. However, there is considerable debate and skepticism among economists as to whether such intervention has been either practicable or effective in alleviating the recessions that have occurred in the United States since World War II.

### Change, Stability, and Growth

Mixed economies justify government intervention, at least in part, as a means of promoting stability and growth and those kinds of change that are considered desirable. How well mixed economies have succeeded is a matter of continual debate among economists.

In the United States some economists think that the antitrust activities of the government on the whole have helped to prevent the growth of monopoly and thereby promoted competition in some areas of the economy. It is felt that more competition better serves changing consumer tastes and leads to more innovation in products, which is a spur to economic growth. On the other hand, the government has intervened to save large faltering corporations from bankruptcy, as in the case of Chrysler. Many critics feel that this interferes with the beneficial working of the marketplace, which serves to weed out inefficient producers, a form of change felt to be desirable. Furthermore, they ask, why should the government prop up certain large failing corporations when many smaller businesses fail every day because they are unable to meet the rigors of the marketplace?

With regard to economic growth and stability, many economists argue that in the United States greater growth and stability have been promoted by government intervention. Others say, not so, that the increasing growth of government has stifled the private sector with heavy personal income and corporate profits taxes. In addition, they argue that government policies have been a major cause of inflation. The reply to these criticisms is often "Well, even if there is some truth to that, at least we have not had another Great Depression." Debates over the pros and cons of mixed economies and the

appropriateness or folly of government intervention in different areas of the economy are unending. We will encounter these issues again and again throughout this book.

---

**CHECKPOINT 3-3**
**Explain how the government's power to enforce contracts contributes to the development of markets. Is the postal service a public good or not? Why or why not? Is the military draft a form of government transfer of income or wealth? Why or why not? It appears that sometimes when a government agency isn't working very efficiently, its budget is increased. What happens when a private business doesn't operate very efficiently? In order to eliminate some of our present political system's shortcomings for providing governmentally produced goods and services, it has been suggested that limits should be placed on the number of terms that politicians can remain in office. Explain why you think this might or might not help.**

---

### SUMMARY

**1.** Individuals have different abilities for performing different tasks. Because of this, individuals have an incentive to specialize in production and to trade the surplus of their output in excess of their own need for the other goods they want but don't produce themselves. This incentive stems from the fact that specialization and trade make possible a larger output of goods and services than is possible if each individual tries to be self-sufficient—that is, if there is no specialization and trade.

**2.** There is an incentive to use money as a medium of exchange because it eliminates the need for the coincidence of wants, which is necessary for trade to take place in a barter economy. Because of this, money promotes specialization and trade and hence makes possible a larger output of goods and services than is possible within the context of a barter system of trade.

**3.** A firm's costs are all those payments it must make to all resource suppliers in order to bid resources away from use in alternative lines of production of goods. Among the resources used by the firm are financial capital and entrepreneurial skills. When they are being compensated just enough to keep them from leaving and going into some other line of productive activity, we say they are earning a normal profit.

**4.** Above-normal profits will draw resources to those areas of the economy where they are most in demand. Below-normal profits in one area of the economy will cause entrepreneurial skills and financial capital to move out of that line of productive activity and into those where they can earn their opportunity cost.

**5.** At minimum in any economy, government typically has basic responsibility for maintaining law and order, providing for the nation's money supply, its national defense, the judicial system, and a uniform standard of time, weight, and measurement. In mixed economies government: reallocates resources in instances where it is felt the market mechanism gives unacceptable or undesirable outcomes; often strives to maintain competitive conditions in markets not naturally conducive to them; redistributes income in accordance with some norm of equity and concern for those who can't work or earn a minimally adequate income; and attempts to maintain economic stability with reasonably full employment of resources.

**6.** There are several reasons why the government is not a very efficient producer of goods and services. Government bureaucracies have a weak incentive structure due to the difficulty of measuring their output and judging their performance. Politicians often support special interest legislation because it wins them votes from special interest groups without losing the votes of an often ill-informed public. A voting citizen must choose from a limited number of candidates, each representing a particular bundle of goods and services that typically does not accurately match the voter's preferences. Politicians are subject to an incentive structure biased toward the adoption of projects and programs with highly visible immediate benefits and well-hidden costs.

**7.** Government policies are likely to be effective in preventing another Great Depression. There is less agreement as to how effective government policies are at avoiding the periodic bouts of unemployment associated with post-World War II recessions. Controversy also surrounds the government's intervention in the marketplace, which is sometimes intended to promote competition through antitrust policy and occasionally to rescue large corporations from bankruptcy. There is also ongoing debate about the government's effect on economic growth and inflation.

## KEY TERMS AND CONCEPTS

barter economy
coincidence of wants
exclusion principle
nationalized industries
normal profit
public goods
specialization of labor

## QUESTIONS AND PROBLEMS

**1.** We have discussed specialization in terms of its economic advantages. From the laborer's standpoint, what are some of the disadvantages of specialization often heard about in the modern industrialized world?

2. We have noted that it might be possible that someone who has sandals to trade, but no need for chopped wood, might nonetheless accept the chopped wood and trade it for something else. In a situation such as this, where there is a lack of coincidence of wants, do you think the sandal maker would be more, or less, willing to accept strawberries than chopped wood (given that the sandal maker wants neither and must trade them for something he or she does want)? Why? Compared to a situation where there is a coincidence of wants between woodchopper and sandal maker, how do you think the terms of the exchange (the amount of wood needed to purchase a pair of sandals) would be different if the woodchopper wanted sandals but the sandal maker didn't want chopped wood?

3. Elaborate on the following statement: "Profits can, of course, be immoral—if they are exploitive, for example, or result from price-fixing schemes or monopolies. But most profits . . . are an essential and beneficial ingredient in the workings of a free-market economy."

4. Describe the nature of the role of profit that the author of the following statement must have in mind. "Today profits, far from being too high, are still too low to ensure the nation's continued economic health. Among the top 20 industrialized countries, the United States in recent years has fared badly in terms of new industrial investment per capita. . . ."

5. A perhaps overly cynical view of government is that the function of government is to distribute money, that the effectiveness of government is measured by the sums dispensed, and that the worth of politicians is weighted by how much they are able to get the federal government to spend in their districts. It is illegal for a politician to slip a derelict $5 for a vote, but a politician can buy office by legislating billions of dollars. As a result of this situation, a number of critics of Congress claim there is much more government spending than can be justified on objective economic grounds.

One suggested way of dealing with this problem is to require that Congress establish some sort of total spending ceiling at the beginning of each new term.

   a. Why might this force members of Congress to make more economic choices?

   b. Why might this curb the "you vote for my pet project and I'll vote for yours" type of logrolling among members of Congress? Why is it such logrolling leads to ever higher levels of government spending?

# 4

# Demand, Supply, and Price Determination

**AFTER READING THIS CHAPTER, YOU WILL BE ABLE TO:**

1. Formulate and explain the law of demand and construct its graphical representation, the demand curve.

2. Enumerate the determinants of demand.

3. Demonstrate the significance of, and recognize the difference between, shifts in the position of a demand curve and movements along a fixed demand curve.

4. Formulate and explain the law of supply and construct its graphical representation, the supply curve.

5. Enumerate the determinants of supply.

6. Show how demand and supply interact to mutually determine equilibrium price and quantity (also called market equilibrium).

7. Demonstrate how changes in the determinants of demand and supply disturb the existing market equilibrium and result in the establishment of a new market equilibrium.

**I**n this chapter we will focus on the laws of demand and supply. We will examine in some detail the notion of the demand curve and the supply curve. And we will consider how demand and supply interact to determine the equilibrium price at which the quantity of a good or resource supplied is just sufficient to satisfy demand for it. We will see how all of this is necessary for a better understanding of how markets work and how prices function to allocate resources.

## DEMAND AND DEMAND CURVES

You have already met the notion of demand and its graphical representation, called the demand curve, in Chapter 1. There it was presented as an example of an economic theory or law. Here we want to examine in more detail the law of demand and how the demand curve is determined. We will see how individual demand curves can be combined to give the aggregate demand curve representing the entire market demand for a particular product, resource, or service. Finally, we will examine the very important distinction between shifts in the position of a demand curve and movements along it.

### Law of Demand

As we saw in Chapter 1, the **law of demand** is a theory about the relationship between the amount of a good a buyer both desires and is able to purchase per unit of time and the price charged for it. Notice that we emphasize the ability to pay for the good as well as the desire to have it. Your ability to pay is as important as your desire for the good, because in economics we are interested in explaining and predicting actual behavior in the marketplace. Your *unlimited* desires for goods can never be observed in the marketplace because you can't buy more than you are *able* to pay for. At a given price for a good, we are only interested in the buyer's

demand for that good which can effectively be backed by a purchase.

*The law of demand hypothesized that the lower the price charged for a product, resource, or service, the larger will be the quantity demanded per unit of time. Conversely, the higher the price charged, the smaller will be the quantity demanded per unit of time—all other things remaining the same.* For example, the law of demand predicts that the lower the price of steak, the more steak you will desire and be able to purchase per year—all other things remaining the same. As we noted in Chapter 1, the law of demand is confirmed again and again by observed behavior in the marketplace. Businesses have sales (cut prices), and the amount of goods they sell per period increases. If the price of steak goes up, the amount purchased per unit of time decreases. Why is this? For most goods there are other goods that may be used to satisfy very nearly the same desires. When the price of steak goes up, if the prices of pork chops, lamb chops, and hamburger remain unchanged, then all these kinds of meats are now relatively cheaper compared to steak. Hence, buyers will purchase more of them and less of steak. These kinds of meats are *substitutes* for steak. Although not exactly the same as steak, they are another kind of meat that will do.

### Individual Demand

The inverse relationship between the price of a good and the quantity of the good demanded per unit of time can be depicted graphically as we demonstrated in Chapter 1. Suppose we consider an individual's demand for hamburger. Table 4–1 shows the number of pounds of hamburger that the individual will demand per month at each of several different prices. Note that the higher the price, the smaller the quantity demanded per month. Conversely, the lower the price, the greater the quantity that will be demanded per month. Why? Again, because the higher the price of hamburger, the greater the incentive to cut back on consumption of it and

**TABLE 4-1 An Individual's Demand for Hamburger** (Hypothetical Data)

| Price per Pound | Quantity Demanded (Number of Pounds per Month) |
|---|---|
| $5 | 1.0 |
| 4 | 2.0 |
| 3 | 3.0 |
| 2 | 4.5 |
| 1 | 6.5 |

eat other kinds of meat instead—assuming their prices and all other things remain the same. *Relative* to hamburger, other kinds of meat simply become cheaper to eat as the price of hamburger rises. Conversely, more hamburger will be demanded when successively lower prices are charged for it because it will become less and less expensive relative to other kinds of meat.

If we plot the price and quantity combinations listed in Table 4-1 on a graph, we obtain the **demand curve** *DD* shown in Figure 4-1. (If you need to brush up on how to plot data on a graph, refer back to pp. 9-10.) Economists almost always represent the demand for a good, resource, or service by use of a demand curve. Verbal descriptions or tabular descriptions such as Table 4-1, while useful, are not typically as readily understood. This is an instance where a picture is worth a thousand words.

**FIGURE 4-1 An Individual's Demand Curve for Hamburger**

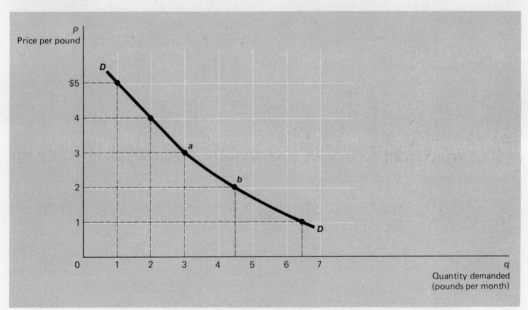

The individual's demand curve for hamburger is plotted here using the data from Table 4-1. It slopes downward from left to right reflecting the inverse relationship between the quantity demanded and the price of the good. It illustrates the law of demand, which says that individuals will demand more of a good the lower is its price. A change in the price of the good causes a change in the quantity demanded, and is represented by a movement along the demand curve. For example, if price changes from $3 per pound to $2 per pound, the quantity demanded increases from 3 to 4.5 pounds per month. This is represented by the movement from *a* to *b* along the demand curve *DD*.

## Demand Determinants: The Other Things That Remain the Same

When we draw a demand curve such as that in Figure 4-1, we emphasize the way in which the price charged for a good determines the quantity of it demanded. The price of the good is thereby singled out as the determining factor, and all other things are said to be equal, or remain the same. (If you prefer Latin, you may say *ceteris paribus*.) The important point is that *movement along the demand curve means that only the price of the good and the quantity of it demanded change. All other things are assumed to be constant or unchanged.* What are these other things? They are (1) the prices of all other goods, (2) the individual's income, (3) the individual's expectations about the future, and (4) the individual's tastes. A change in one or more of these other things will change the data in Table 4-1. Therefore the position of the demand curve in Figure 4-1 will be shifted. Such a shift in the demand curve is called a *change in demand*. A movement along a fixed demand curve is referred to as a *change in the quantity demanded*.

### Prices of All Other Goods

We may classify all other goods according to their relationship to the good for which the demand curve is drawn, say good X. Other goods are either substitutes for X, complements of X, or basically unrelated to X.

**Substitute good**: *A good is a substitute for X to the extent that it can satisfy similar needs or desires as X.* Different substitute goods will, of course, vary in the extent to which they satisfy the needs or desires that X does. T-bone steak is a closer substitute for sirloin steak than are lamb chops, although both T-bone steak and lamb chops typically would be regarded as substitutes for sirloin steak. *When the price of a substitute good for good X rises, the demand curve for good X will shift rightward.* This is so because when the price of the substitute *rises*, it becomes cheaper to use X instead of the substitute good.

For example, suppose initially the demand curve for hamburger is $DD$ in Figure 4-2. Now suppose the price of a substitute, chicken, rises. This will cause the individual's demand curve to shift rightward from $DD$ to $D_1D_1$. This means that at *any* given price of hamburger (measured on the vertical axis of Figure 4-2), the quantity of hamburger demanded (measured on the horizontal axis) will now be larger as a result of the increase in the price of chicken.

The opposite of the above is also true— *when the price of a substitute for good X falls, the demand curve for good X will shift leftward.* This happens because when the price of the substitute *falls*, it becomes relatively more expensive to use X instead of the substitute good. For example, a fall in the price of chicken causes a leftward shift of the demand curve in Figure 4-2, such as from $DD$ to $D_2D_2$.

**Complementary good**: *A good is a complement, or complementary good, to good X to the extent it is used jointly with good X.* For example, gasoline and tires are complements to each other. So are football shoes and football helmets, records and phonographs, and salad dressing and lettuce. *When the price of a good that is a complement to good X falls, the demand curve for good X will shift rightward.* This happens because the complementary good is now less expensive to use and therefore more of it will be demanded. More of good X will be demanded as well, because it is used jointly with the complement. For example, a complementary good to hamburger is hamburger buns. If the price of the buns falls, the cost of a hamburger in a bun will be less. This will cause the demand curve $DD$ for hamburger to shift to the right in Figure 4-2—to a position such as $D_1D_1$ for instance. At *any* given price of hamburger, the quantity of hamburger demanded will be greater.

The opposite is also true. *When the price of a good that is complementary to good X rises, the demand curve for good X will shift leftward.* The complementary good is now more expensive to use and therefore less of it will be demanded. Less of good X will be demanded because, again, it is used jointly with

**FIGURE 4-2** **Shifts in an Individual's Demand for Hamburger**

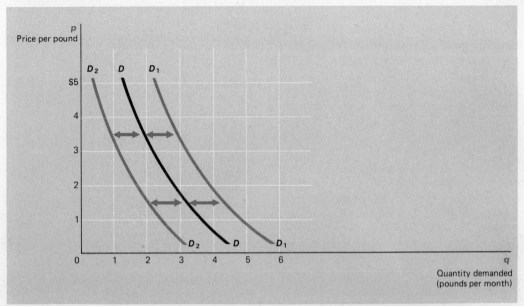

The position of the demand curve is given by the determinants of demand. These are the prices of all other goods, the individual's money income, the individual's expectations about the future, and the individual's tastes. Changes in any of these will cause a change in demand, which is represented by a shift in the demand curve either rightward or leftward. A shift of the demand curve to the right represents an increase in demand. A shift of the demand curve to the left represents a decrease in demand. *Warning:* Do not confuse the concept of a *change in demand*, represented by a shift in the demand curve, with the concept of a *change in the quantity demanded*, represented by movement along a fixed demand curve such as that described by the movement from *a* to *b* in Figure 4–1.

the complement. In Figure 4–2 a rise in the price of hamburger buns will cause *DD* to shift leftward to a position such as $D_2D_2$.

Finally, some goods are basically *unrelated* to good X in that it would be very difficult to classify them as either substitutes or complements for X. In this sense toothpaste seems basically unrelated to garden clippers, or pears to combs, or tennis balls to ball-point pens.

### Income

Another thing assumed equal or constant when we move along an individual's demand curve is the individual's money income.

How does a change in the individual's in-come affect the individual's demand curve for a particular good? The answer depends on the nature of the good. Basically we may distinguish between two types of goods in this respect: normal goods and inferior goods.

**Normal good:** A normal good is one that most people typically want more of as their income goes up. Such things as food, cloth-ing, and medical services are examples. *An individual's demand curve for a normal good will shift rightward when the individual's in-come rises. Conversely, when the individual's income falls, the demand curve will shift left-ward.*

**Inferior good:** An inferior good is one that an individual will want more of at lower income levels than at higher income levels. For example, it has been observed that poor people tend to eat more potatoes and bread than do people in higher income brackets. Evidence suggests that people tend to cut back on their consumption of such foods as their income rises above a certain level. *An individual's demand curve for an inferior good will shift rightward as income rises only at very low levels of income, and then shift leftward as income rises to higher levels.* Conversely, as an individual's income falls, the individual's demand curve for an inferior good will shift rightward until income reaches some low level of income at which point a further fall in income will cause the demand curve to shift leftward.

Suppose the individual in Figure 4–2 is a student and that hamburger is a normal good. If the student's income were to rise as a result of an increase in a scholarship stipend, the student's demand curve for hamburger would rise from $DD$ to $D_1D_1$.

### Expectations

Among the other things assumed equal or constant when we move along an individual's demand curve are the individual's expectations about all things relevant to his or her economic situation. For example, suppose there is suddenly an upward revision of what the individual expects the price of hamburger to be in the future and the individual therefore wants to buy more now to avoid paying a higher price for it later. As a result the demand curve $DD$ shifts rightward to a position such as $D_1D_1$ in Figure 4–2.

### Tastes

Tastes are another thing assumed equal or constant when we move along an individual's demand curve. If a person suddenly develops a sweet tooth, that person's tastes have changed. This will be reflected in a rightward shift in that person's demand curve for candy. Conversely, several painful sessions at the dentist might cause you to lose your taste for candy. In that event your demand curve for candy would shift leftward.

## Market Demand: The Sum of Individual Demands

The **market demand curve** for a good is obtained by summing up all the individual demand curves for that good. To illustrate in the simplest possible case, suppose there are only two individuals who have a demand for hamburger. The first individual's demand is that given in Table 4–1. These numbers are repeated in Table 4–2, along with the second individual's demand for hamburger at each of the five prices listed. The market demand, or total demand, for hamburger is the sum of the quantities demanded by each individual at every price. The sums obtained in this way at each of five of these prices are shown in the last column of Table 4–2. Using the data from Table 4–2, we construct the individual demand curves in Figure 4–3, along with the market demand curve, which is the summation of these individual demand curves.

Because market demand curves are the sum of individual demand curves, they are subject to the same determinants and are affected in the same way by changes in those determinants as the individual curves. There is one additional determinant of a market demand curve, however, and that is the number of individual demand curves or buyers that enter into the summation. *An increase in the number of buyers in the market will cause the market demand curve to shift rightward. Conversely, a decrease will cause it to shift leftward.* In sum, the other things that are assumed to remain the same as we move along a market demand curve are (1) prices of all other goods, (2) money income, (3) expectations, (4) tastes, and (5) the number of buyers.

## Changes in Quantity Demanded Versus Shifts in Demand

*Warning:* One of the most common areas of confusion in economics concerns the distinction between movement along a demand curve versus shifts in the position of the demand curve.

*Movement along a demand curve represents*

TABLE 4-2 **The Market Demand for Hamburger:**
**Two Individual Buyers** (Hypothetical Data)

| Price per Pound | Quantity Demanded per Month | | | | | |
|---|---|---|---|---|---|---|
| | First Individual's Demand (Pounds per Month) | | Second Individual's Demand (Pounds per Month) | | Total Market Demand (Pounds per Month) | |
| $5 | 1.0 | + | .5 | = | 1.5 | |
| 4 | 2.0 | + | 1.5 | = | 3.5 | |
| 3 | 3.0 | + | 2.5 | = | 5.5 | |
| 2 | 4.5 | + | 3.5 | = | 8.0 | |
| 1 | 6.5 | + | 4.5 | = | 11.0 | |

*a change in the price of the good under consideration and the associated change in the quantity of the good demanded, and nothing else. All other determinants of demand are assumed to remain the same.* For example, when the price of hamburger is changed from $3 to $2 per pound in Figure 4–1, the quantity of hamburger demanded increases from 3 pounds to 4.5 pounds per month. This is represented by the movement from point *a* to point *b* along the demand curve *DD*. By convention, when we simply refer to *a change in the quantity of a good demanded,* we mean *a movement along a fixed demand curve,* such as

that from *a* to *b* in Figure 4–1, unless we say otherwise.

In contrast, a change in one or more of the five determinants of demand discussed above will cause the position of the demand curve to change in the manner shown in Figure 4–2. By convention, when we simply refer to *a change in demand* we mean a *shift in the position of the demand curve,* unless we say otherwise. *When the demand curve for a good shifts rightward, more of that good will be demanded at every possible price. When the demand for a good shifts leftward, less of that good will be demanded at every possible price.*

FIGURE 4-3 **The Sum of the Individual Demand Curves Gives the Market Demand Curve**

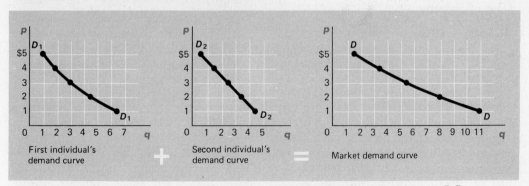

The first individual's demand curve $D_1D_1$ and the second individual's demand curve $D_2D_2$ are constructed from their individual demand data in Table 4–2. The market demand curve *DD* is equal to the sum of the individual demand curves and is constructed from the total market demand data in Table 4–2.

*A change in demand results from a change in one or more of the five determinants of demand.*

---

### CHECKPOINT* 4-1

**If the price of peas were to rise, what do you think this would do to the demand curve for lima beans? If the price of pretzels were to fall, what do you think this would do to the demand curve for beer? What would it do to the demand curve for pretzels? Would we say there is a change in the demand for pretzels or a change in the quantity of pretzels demanded? If the price of hamburger buns went up, what do you think this would do to the demand curve for hamburgers?**

*Answers to all Checkpoints can be found at the back of the text.

---

## SUPPLY AND SUPPLY CURVES

Given that there are demands for goods, what is the nature of the process that determines how those demands will be met? To answer this question we must have an understanding of the law of supply and the concept of a supply curve and its determinants.

### Law of Supply

The law of supply is a statement about the relationship between the amount of a good a supplier is willing and able to supply and offer for sale per unit of time and each of the different possible prices at which that good might be sold. That is, if we said to the supplier, "Suppose the good can be sold at a price of such and such dollars per unit. How many units of the good would you be willing and able to produce and offer for sale per unit of time?" We write down the answer along with the price we quoted to the supplier. Then we repeat the question exactly *except* that now we quote a somewhat higher price. We observe that the higher the price, the larger the quantity the supplier is willing and able to supply for sale per unit of time. And, of course, the lower the price, the smaller the quantity that is offered. This observed relationship is the **law of supply**, which *says that suppliers will supply larger quantities of a good at higher prices than at lower prices.*

### The Supply Curve

Suppose the supplier whom we have been questioning produces hamburger. Table 4–3 lists some of the answers that the supplier gave in response to our questions. If we plot the data of Table 4–3 on a graph, we obtain this supplier's supply curve. As in Figure 4–1, we measure the price per unit (a pound) on the vertical axis and the number of units (pounds) on the horizontal axis. The resulting curve *SS* is shown in Figure 4–4. We have plotted only the five price-quantity combinations. At all the possible prices in between, we presumably could have filled in the whole curve as shown by the solid line connecting the five plotted points. You may view the **supply curve** in different ways. *It indicates the amount of the good the supplier is willing to provide per unit of time at different possible prices.* Or alternatively, you may say *it shows what prices are necessary in order to give the supplier the incentive to provide various quantities of the good per unit of time.*

The shape of the supply curve clearly shows that as the price of the good rises the supplier supplies more of the good; as the price falls the supplier supplies less of the good. Why is this? Just as with a demand curve, *such movement along a supply curve always assumes that all other things will remain the same.* Among other things, the prices of all other resources and goods are assumed to remain the same, including the prices of the inputs used by the supplier. Thus the profit that can be earned from producing a good will almost certainly increase as the price of the good rises. The supplier has a greater incentive to produce more of the good. This is one basic reason why a supply curve slopes upward to the right. An-

**TABLE 4-3  An Individual Producer's
Supply of Hamburger** (Hypothetical Data)

| Price per Pound | Quantity Supplied (Number of Pounds per Month) |
|---|---|
| $5 | 1,200 |
| 4 | 1,100 |
| 3 | 900 |
| 2 | 600 |
| 1 | 200 |

other is the fact that beyond some point most production processes run into increasing production costs per unit of output. This is because certain inputs such as plants and equipment cannot be increased in a short period of time. Hence as the producer increases output by using more of the readily variable inputs,

such as labor and materials, fixed plant and equipment capacity causes congestion and bottlenecks. Productive efficiency drops, and the cost of additional units of output rises. Therefore producers must receive a higher price to produce these additional units.

Consider the individual producer's supply curve for hamburger shown in Figure 4–4. Assuming the prices of all other resources and goods are constant, if the price per pound is raised from $1 to $2, it becomes relatively more profitable to produce hamburger. In this instance, the price increase is just sufficient to make it worthwhile to employ the additional resources necessary to increase production from 200 pounds per month to 600 pounds per month. This is indicated by the move from point *a* to point *b* on the supply curve. Similarly, successively

**FIGURE 4-4  An Individual Producer's Supply
of Hamburger**

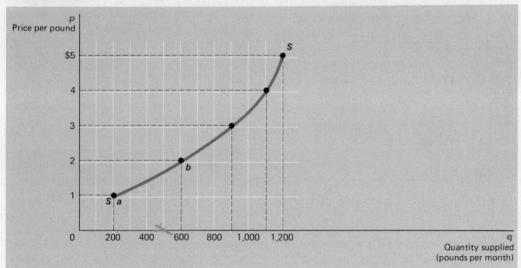

An individual producer's supply curve for hamburger is plotted here using the data from Table 4–3. It slopes upward from left to right reflecting a direct relationship between the quantity of the good supplied and the price of the good. It illustrates the law of supply, which says that suppliers will supply more of a good the higher is its price. A change in the price of the good causes a change in the quantity supplied and is represented by a movement along the supply curve. For example, if price changes from $1 per pound to $2 per pound, the quantity supplied increases from 200 pounds per month to 600 pounds per month. This is represented by the movement from *a* to *b* along the supply curve *SS*.

higher prices make it even more profitable to produce hamburger, and the supply of hamburger will be even larger.

Suppose that there are 100 producers of hamburger, each of whom has a supply curve identical to that of Figure 4–4. At each price per pound listed in Table 4–3, the quantity of hamburger supplied by the sum of all producers is simply 100 times the amount supplied by one producer. Using these data, Figure 4–5 shows the market or industry supply curve $SS$ for hamburger. Note that the units on the horizontal axis of Figure 4–5 are a hundred times larger than those on the horizontal axis of Figure 4–4.

## Supply Determinants: The Other Things That Remain the Same

When we draw a supply curve such as $SS$ in Figure 4–5, we emphasize the way in which the price of the good determines the quantity of it supplied. As with a demand curve, the price of the good is singled out as the determining factor and all other things are assumed to be unchanging. These other things are (1) the prices of resources and other factors of production, (2) technology, (3) the prices of other goods, (4) the number of suppliers, and (5) the suppliers' expectations. If one or more of these things change, the supply curve will shift.

### 1. Prices of Resources

As we saw in Chapter 1, all production processes require inputs of labor services, raw materials, fuels, and other resources and goods. These inputs to a production process are frequently referred to as the **factors of production**. The supplier of a good has to purchase these factors in order to produce the good.

Suppose now that the price of one or more of the factors of production should fall—that is, one or more of the input prices that were assumed to be constant when we drew $SS$

now changes to a lower level. Hence at each possible price of the good suppliers will find it profitable to produce a larger amount of the good than they were previously willing to supply. The supply curve will therefore shift rightward to a position such as $S_1S_1$ in Figure 4–5. Conversely, if one or more of the input prices should rise, the cost of production will now be higher and producers will not be willing to supply as much at each possible price of the good. The supply curve will therefore shift leftward to a position such as $S_2S_2$ in Figure 4–5.

For example, if producers could sell hamburger for $2 a pound, they would be willing to supply 60,000 pounds of hamburger per month. This price-supply combination is represented by point $a$ on the market supply curve $SS$ in Figure 4–5. Suppose that the price of one or more inputs falls so that the market supply curve shifts rightward to $S_1S_1$. Now a price of $1.50 per pound is sufficient to induce suppliers to produce 60,000 pounds of hamburger per month, as indicated by point $d$ on $S_1S_1$. Because they are receiving $2 per pound, however, they are encouraged to expand output even more until they have moved up the supply curve $S_1S_1$ from point $d$ to point $b$. Here they are producing 80,000 pounds per month. At point $b$, the price of $2 per pound is just sufficient to induce producers to supply this quantity of hamburger per month.

Alternatively, suppose the price of one or more inputs should rise so that the supply curve shifts leftward from $SS$ to $S_2S_2$. Now a price of $2.80 per pound is sufficient to induce suppliers to produce 60,000 pounds of hamburger per month, as indicated by point $e$ on $S_2S_2$. However, if they are receiving only $2 per pound, they will reduce output until they have moved back down the supply curve $S_2S_2$ from point $e$ to point $c$, where they will produce 30,000 pounds per month. Once again, at point $c$ the price of $2 per pound is just sufficient to induce suppliers to produce this level of output and no more.

**FIGURE 4-5  Shifts in the Market Supply Curve for Hamburger**

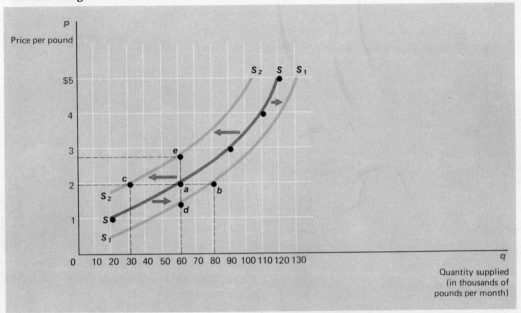

The position of the supply curve is established by the determinants of supply. These are the prices of factors of production, technology, the prices of other goods, the number of suppliers, and the suppliers' expectations about the future. Changes in any of these will cause a change in supply, which is represented by a rightward or leftward shift in the supply curve. A rightward shift represents an increase in supply. A leftward shift represents a decrease in supply. *Warning:* Do not confuse the concept of a *change in supply,* represented by a shift in the supply curve, with the concept of a *change in the quantity supplied,* represented by movement along a fixed supply curve such as that described by the movement from *a* to *b* in Figure 4–4.

## 2. Prices of Other Goods

Along a fixed supply curve, it is also assumed that the prices of other goods are unchanged. Why do we distinguish between the prices of other goods and the prices of factors of production? The prices of factors of production refer only to the goods used in the production of the good for which the supply curve is drawn. The prices of other goods we now refer to are all the other goods not used in the production of the good for which the supply curve is drawn.

Factors of production are attracted to those production activities where they are paid the highest prices. The higher the price the producer gets for the good produced with those inputs, the greater his or her willingness to pay high prices for those factors. Hence, if the price of milk rises relative to the price of hamburger, farmers will use less of their pastureland for grazing beef cattle in order to make it available for grazing dairy cattle. The opportunity cost of using pasture to produce the beef used in hamburger has effectively risen because the value of that pasture in its alternative use of producing milk has risen. Factors must be paid their opportunity cost if they are to be used in a particular productive activity. That is, the price that must be paid a factor input must be at least as high as what it could earn in an alternative activity. Since the price of pastureland will go up because of its increased value in milk production, the cost of using it in beef production will rise. The supply curve for hamburger will then shift leftward, such as from $SS$ to $S_2S_2$ in Figure 4-5. To induce hamburger producers to supply any given quantity of hamburger, the price of a pound of hamburger will have to be higher. Why? To cover the increased cost of pastureland, which is now more expensive to use because of its increased value in milk production due to the rise in the price of milk. Again we are reminded that the economic problem is how to allocate scarce resources to alternative uses.

### 3. Technology

Any production process uses some form of technology, whether it involves tending a rice paddy with a handmade sickle in Southeast Asia or making synthetic fibers in a large plant in Wilmington, Delaware. The term **technology** *refers to the production methods used to combine resources of all kinds, including labor, to produce goods and services.* The history of the human race is in no small way a history of the advancement of technology.

This advancement has been characterized by an increase in the ability of humans to produce goods and services—that is, by an increase in productivity. Often productivity is measured as output produced per labor hour used in the production process. Increases in productivity are then taken to mean increases in output per labor hour. *Because technological advance increases productivity, it lowers the cost of producing goods.* Suppose, for example, that there is a technological advance in the technique used to produce hamburger—such as the development of electric meat grinders. This lowers the cost of producing hamburger. Suppose the position of the supply curve in Figure 4-5 is

at $SS$ before the technological advance. The advance will cause the supply curve to shift rightward to a position such as $S_1S_1$. At every level of output the price necessary to induce suppliers to produce that output level will now be lower, because costs will be lower.

Circumstances that reduce productivity can arise as well. A drought will reduce the productivity of land and cause crop yields to be less. Such adverse developments essentially require the application of additional production techniques if output levels are to be maintained—the construction of irrigation ditches, for example. But these new techniques add to the cost of production. If the crop were corn, a rise in the cost of production would cause the supply curve for corn to shift leftward.

A news item on rising farm prices might note that "the weather in much of the farm belt was bad for crops this summer." Bad weather tends to decrease the productivity of the land. For example, the grass on pastureland will grow less rapidly, and so fewer cattle can be raised per acre. Since the output per unit of input falls, the cost per head of beef cattle rises. This will raise the cost of producing hamburger, so that the supply curve of hamburger will shift leftward, such as from $SS$ to $S_2S_2$ in Figure 4-5. The price required to induce hamburger producers to supply any given quantity of hamburger will now be higher.

Remember that whenever we speak of movement along a fixed supply curve, the state of technology is assumed to be unchanged.

### 4. Number of Suppliers

When we constructed the market or industry supply curve $SS$ in Figure 4-5, we did it by assuming there were a hundred identical individual suppliers, each with a supply curve like that shown in Figure 4-4. Summing the individual supply curves horizontally gave us the market supply curve $SS$. If there had been more suppliers, the market supply curve would have been further to the right at a position such as $S_1S_1$. It follows from these observations that when more suppliers enter the industry, the aggregate supply curve will shift to the right. When suppliers leave the industry, it will shift to the left. When we speak of movement along an aggregate supply curve, it is assumed that the number of suppliers does not change.

### 5. Suppliers' Expectations

This term refers to the expectations suppliers have about anything that they think affects their economic situation. For example, if garment manufacturers expect a strike to stop their production in a few months, they may attempt to supply more now so that stores can build up their inventories to tide them over—the garment industry's supply curve would shift rightward. If suppliers of a good expect its price to be higher in a few months, they may hold back supply now in order to sell it at higher prices later—the industry's supply curve would shift leftward. Changes in expectations can cause the supply curve to shift in either direction depending on the particular situation. However, for any movement along a supply curve, expectations are assumed to remain unchanged.

In sum, the other things that are assumed to remain unchanged when we move along a supply curve are (1) the prices of resources and other factors of production, (2) the prices of other goods, (3) technology, (4) the number of suppliers, and (5) the suppliers' expectations. When one or more of these things change, the supply curve shifts.

### Changes in Quantity Supplied Versus Shifts in Supply

*Warning:* Along with our earlier warning about the demand curve, another common confusion in economics concerns the distinction between movement along a supply curve versus shifts in the supply curve.

Movement along a supply curve represents a change in the price of the good under con-

sideration and the associated change in the quantity of the good supplied. All other things are assumed to be unchanged. By convention, when we simply refer to a *change in the quantity of a good supplied,* we mean a *movement along a fixed supply curve,* such as that from *d* to *b* in Figure 4–5, unless we say otherwise.

A change in one or more of the five determinants of supply discussed above will cause the supply curve to shift in the manner shown in Figure 4–5. By contrast, movement along a fixed supply curve always assumes these five things remain unchanged. By convention, when we simply refer to *a change in supply,* we mean *a shift in the position of the supply curve,* unless we say otherwise. *When the supply curve for a good shifts rightward, more of that good will be supplied at every price. When the supply curve shifts leftward, less of that good will be supplied at every price. A change in supply results from a change in one or more of the five determinants of supply.*

---

### CHECKPOINT 4-2

**If wages go up, what effect will this have on the supply curve *SS* in Figure 4–5? If someone develops an improved process for fattening cattle to be used to make hamburger, what effect will this have on the supply curve *SS* in Figure 4–5? Suppose the price of lamb were to rise. Would we refer to the effect of this on *SS* in Figure 4–5 as a "change in the supply" or a "change in the quantity supplied" of hamburger? Explain the economic process by which farmland used to produce corn becomes converted into factory property for the production of CB radios.**

---

### MARKET EQUILIBRIUM: INTERACTION OF SUPPLY AND DEMAND

As any armchair economist knows, supply and demand are what economics is all about.

Like the blades of a scissors, supply and demand interact to determine the terms of trade between buyers and sellers. That is, supply and demand mutually determine the price at which sellers are willing to supply just the amount of a good that buyers want to buy. The market for every good has a demand curve and a supply curve that determine this price and quantity. When this price and quantity are established, the market is said to be in equilibrium. In equilibrium there is no tendency for price and quantity to change.

## Equilibrium Price and Quantity

In order to see how equilibrium price and quantity are determined in a market, consider again our hypothetical example of the market demand and supply for hamburger. Table 4-4 contains the market supply data (usually called the market **supply schedule**) on which the market supply curve *SS* of Figure 4-5 is based. It also contains the market demand data (usually called the market **demand schedule**) that determine the market demand curve for hamburger. In this case, the market demand schedule has been obtained by supposing that there are 20,000 individual buyers in the market. Each of these buyers is assumed to have an individual demand schedule like that given in Table 4-1.

(That table contained the data for the individual demand curve of Figure 4-1.) The market quantity demand data of Table 4-4 thus equals 20,000 times the individual quantity demand data given in Table 4-1.

## Market Adjustment When Price Is Above the Equilibrium Price

Observe in Table 4-4 that at a price of $5 per pound suppliers would supply the market 120,000 pounds of hamburger per month (column 2). Buyers, however, would only demand 20,000 pounds per month (column 3). At this price, there is an excess of supply over demand, or a *surplus* of 100,000 pounds of hamburger (column 4). A price of $5 per pound serves as a relatively strong incentive to suppliers on the one hand, and a relatively high barrier to buyers on the other. If suppliers should produce the 120,000 pounds, they will find they can sell only 20,000. They will be stuck with 100,000 pounds. This surplus will serve notice to suppliers that $5 per pound is too high a price to charge. They will realize that the price must be lowered if they want to sell more hamburger (column 5), as the law of demand would predict. If they continue to produce 120,000 pounds per month in the belief that they can sell that much for $5 per pound, unwanted invento-

**TABLE 4-4  Market Supply and Demand for Hamburger** (Hypothetical Data)

| (1) Price per Pound | (2) Total Number of Pounds Supplied per Month | − | (3) Total Number of Pounds Demanded per Month | = | (4) Surplus (+) or Shortage (−) | (5) Price Change Required to Establish Equilibrium |
|---|---|---|---|---|---|---|
| $5.00 | 120,000 | − | 20,000 | = | +100,000 | decrease |
| 4.00 | 110,000 | − | 40,000 | = | + 70,000 | decrease |
| 3.00 | 90,000 | − | 60,000 | = | + 30,000 | decrease |
| 2.50 | 78,000 | − | 78,000 | = | 0 | no change |
| 2.00 | 60,000 | − | 90,000 | = | − 30,000 | increase |
| 1.00 | 20,000 | − | 130,000 | = | −110,000 | increase |

ries will grow due to the continuing surplus. Competition among suppliers will cause the price to be bid down as each tries to underprice the others in order to sell their individual surpluses.

As a result of suppliers' attempts to correct this undesirable situation through competitive price cutting, the price eventually falls to $4 per pound. Now suppliers will produce a lower total quantity of hamburger, 110,000 pounds per month (column 2), and buyers will increase quantity demanded to 40,000 pounds per month (column 3). At this price, the quantity supplied will still exceed the quantity demanded, however. Though smaller, the surplus amounts to 70,000 pounds of hamburger per month (column 4). Again, if suppliers continue to produce 110,000 pounds per month in the belief that they can sell that much for $4 per pound, unwanted inventories will continue to grow due to the continuing surplus. This situation will cause individual suppliers to continue to try to underprice one another in their competitive attempts to get rid of their individual surpluses. The price in the market will therefore continue to fall (column 5).

At $3 per pound, the quantity supplied will still exceed the quantity demanded, but the surplus that cannot be sold will have fallen to 30,000 pounds of hamburger (column 4). Nonetheless, this will still signal that price must fall further (column 5). Only when price has been reduced to $2.50 per pound by the competition among suppliers will they be induced to produce and supply a quantity that is just equal to the quantity that will be demanded at that price, 78,000 pounds per month (columns 2 and 3). No unsold surplus will be produced (column 4), and there will be no incentive to change price any further (column 5). Market equilibrium will prevail. **Market equilibrium** *is established at the price where the quantity of the good buyers demand and purchase is just equal to the quantity suppliers supply and sell. The price and quantity at which this occurs are called the* **equilibrium price** *and* **equilibrium quantity**. In equilibrium the forces of

supply and demand are in balance. Price and quantity will have no tendency to change. They are at rest.

The process just described and the equilibrium achieved are readily visualized with the aid of a market demand curve and a market supply curve. Using the supply and demand schedule data given in Table 4–4, the market supply curve and demand curve for hamburger are constructed in Figure 4–6. This is done in exactly the same manner used to obtain the demand and supply curves drawn in the previous figures in this chapter. Indeed the supply curve SS in Figure 4–6 is the same one shown in Figure 4–5 as SS. Both the quantity demanded and the quantity supplied are measured on the horizontal axis in Figure 4–6. Equilibrium occurs at the point where the market demand and supply curves intersect. The equilibrium point corresponds to the equilibrium price of $2.50 and the equilibrium quantity of 78,000 pounds of hamburger bought and sold per month. It is readily apparent from the diagram that at prices above $2.50 supply exceeds demand. Competition among suppliers attempting to underprice one another in order to get rid of their surpluses will cause the price to be bid down. This price cutting will cease when the equilibrium price is reached—the price at which quantity demanded equals quantity supplied.

### Market Adjustment When Price Is Below the Equilibrium Price

Suppose that we consider an initial price below the equilibrium price, say $1 per pound. The situation in the market for hamburger is now reversed. The price inducement for suppliers to produce hamburger is relatively low, and so they produce relatively little. Because the price barrier to buyers is relatively low, the quantity demanded is relatively high. From Table 4–4 the total quantity supplied is 20,000 pounds per month (column 2), while the total quantity demanded is 130,000 pounds per month (column 3).

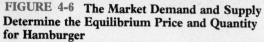

FIGURE 4-6 **The Market Demand and Supply Determine the Equilibrium Price and Quantity for Hamburger**

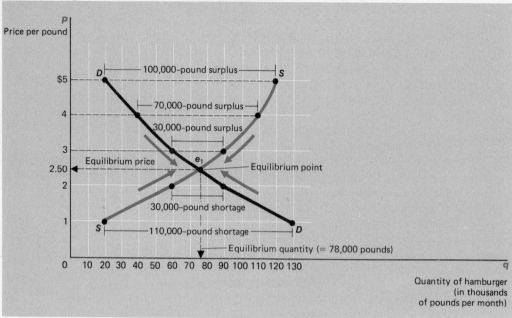

The determination of the equilibrium price and quantity is indicated by the intersection of the market demand curve DD and the market supply curve SS at $e_1$. The equilibrium price is $2.50 per pound and the equilibrium quantity is 78,000 pounds. At prices above the equilibrium price, there will be surpluses as indicated. These surpluses will cause a competitive bidding down of price, thereby reducing the quantity supplied and increasing the quantity demanded until they are equal and equilibrium is achieved. At prices below the equilibrium price, there will be shortages as indicated. These shortages will cause a competitive bidding up of price, thereby increasing the quantity supplied and decreasing the quantity demanded until they are equal and equilibrium is achieved.

Hence there is now an excess demand for hamburger. Buyers cannot purchase as much as they want at this price. The shortage amounts to 110,000 pounds (column 4).

There is not enough hamburger "to go around" at $1 per pound. Buyers begin to bid up price (column 5) as they compete with one another by letting suppliers know they are willing to pay more to get the inadequate supply increased. As the price of hamburger is bid up, suppliers are encouraged to devote more resources to the production of hamburger, in accordance with the law of supply.

At the same time, as price rises, buyers will begin to reduce the quantity of hamburger that they demand, in accordance with the law of demand. When price has risen to $2 per pound, suppliers will be encouraged to increase production to 60,000 pounds per month (column 2). The quantity demanded will be reduced to 90,000 pounds per month (column 3). The quantity demanded still exceeds the quantity supplied, but the shortage has been reduced considerably—to 30,000 pounds (column 4). Nonetheless, there is still a shortage. Buyers will continue to bid price up (column 5) as they compete with one another for a supply of output inadequate to satisfy demand. Only when price has been bid up to $2.50 per pound will the quantity demanded be equal to the quantity supplied—78,000 pounds per month (columns 2 and 3). Market equilibrium will prevail. The shortage has been eliminated. All buyers who demand hamburger at $2.50 per pound will be able to get it. All suppliers who are willing to supply it at $2.50 per pound will find they can sell exactly the quantity they desire to supply. There will be no further incentive for price to be changed.

This process of adjustment to equilibrium is illustrated in Figure 4–6. At prices below $2.50 per pound, quantity demanded clearly exceeds quantity supplied and a shortage will exist. Competitive bidding by buyers attempting to secure some of the inadequate supply will cause price to rise. As price rises suppliers are induced to buy more inputs and produce more hamburger. The quantity demanded, on the other hand, will fall as buyers are increasingly discouraged from purchasing hamburger as the price rises. Again, this process will eventually lead to the equilibrium point where the demand and supply curves intersect to determine the equilibrium price and quantity.

### The Nature of Market Equilibrium

Whether price is initially above or below the equilibrium level, market forces operate to cause adjustment to the same equilibrium point. If the process starts from above the equilibrium price level, we may envision buyers moving down the demand curve DD and suppliers moving down the supply curve SS as adjustment takes place. If the process starts from below the equilibrium price level, buyers move up DD and suppliers up SS. There is only one price at which the quantity supplied is equal to the quantity demanded. At that price every buyer will be able to buy exactly the quantity each demands, and every supplier will be able to sell exactly the quantity each desires to supply. *At the equilibrium price the demand intentions of buyers are consistent with the supply intentions of suppliers.* When these intentions are actually carried out in the form of buyers' bids to purchase and suppliers' offers to sell, they mesh perfectly. *In equilibrium, the decisions of buyers are not frustrated by shortages and the decisions of sellers are not frustrated by surpluses.* Since shortages lead to price rises and surpluses to price reductions, *the absence of shortage or surplus will mean price will neither rise nor fall.* The market is in equilibrium.

## Changes in Supply and Demand

Suppose the market for hamburger is initially in the equilibrium position depicted by the intersection of the demand and supply curves shown in Figure 4–6. These curves are reproduced as DD and SS in Figure 4–7. We know from our discussion of the determinants of supply and demand that any change in one or more of these determinants will cause either the supply curve or the demand curve or both to shift. Such a shift will undo the existing market equilibrium at $e_1$ and establish a new equilibrium position in the market.

### A Change in Demand

Consider first the effect of an expected decrease in beef supplies. Such an expectation would very likely cause people to change their expectations about the future price and availability of hamburger. In particular, people are now likely to expect that the future price of hamburger will be higher. Therefore, they will want to buy more hamburger now and "stock up" on it in order to avoid paying a higher price for it later. Hence the market demand curve for hamburger will shift rightward to $D_1D_1$ as shown in Figure 4–7. At every possible price the quantity demanded is now larger.

In particular, at the initial equilibrium price of $2.50 per pound the quantity demanded will increase from 78,000 to 120,000 pounds per month. At this price the quantity

**FIGURE 4-7** **An Increase in Demand for Hamburger**

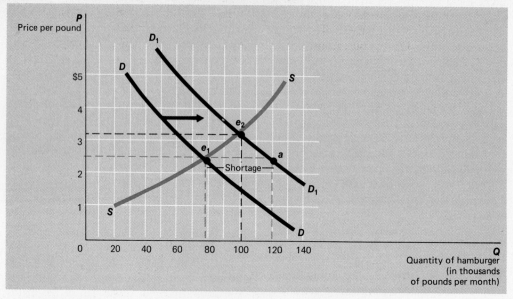

The market is initially in equilibrium where market demand curve *DD* intersects market supply curve *SS* at $e_1$. At this point, the equilibrium price is $2.50 per pound and the equilibrium quantity is 78,000 pounds. The increase in demand is indicated by the rightward shift of the market demand curve from *DD* to $D_1D_1$. This initially gives rise to the shortage of 42,000 pounds indicated. Competitive bidding among frustrated buyers pushes the price up until market equilibrium is established at $e_2$. The new equilibrium price is $3.30 per pound and the new equilibrium quantity is 100,000 pounds.

demanded will now exceed the quantity suppliers are willing to provide. Specifically, there is now a shortage amounting to 42,000 pounds of hamburger. This shortage is the difference between point *a* on $D_1D_1$ and the initial equilibrium point $e_1$ on the supply curve *SS* in Figure 4-7. As a result of this shortage, buyers will tell sellers they are willing to pay a higher price for hamburger in order to get some. When price is eventually bid up high enough, equilibrium will once again be established. Now equilibrium is found at point $e_2$ where the demand curve $D_1D_1$ intersects the supply curve *SS*. The new equilibrium price is $3.30 per pound, and the new equilibrium quantity bought and sold is 100,000 pounds per month. Hence an *increase in demand, represented by a rightward shift in the demand curve, will increase both price and quantity assuming other things remain the same.* (Supply is one of the things that remain unchanged, as represented by the unchanged position of the supply curve.)

It is interesting to note that the expectation of an increase in the price of hamburger is in fact sufficient to cause an actual price increase. Eventually price rises enough to ration or cut back the quantity demanded (a movement from *a* to $e_2$ along $D_1D_1$) while at the same time causing an increase in the quantity supplied (a movement from $e_1$ to $e_2$ along *SS*). This increase in quantity supplied is sufficient to restore equilibrium in the market and eliminate the shortage.

## A Change in Supply

For the moment set aside the effect of a change in expectations on the market. In our discussion of the determinants of the supply curve, we noted that adverse weather conditions cause the supply curve to shift leftward. In addition, we know from our earlier discussions that increases in the prices of inputs will also cause the supply curve to shift leftward. Again consider the initial equilibrium as shown in Figure 4–8. (The demand curve DD and the supply curve SS are in exactly the same position as DD and SS in Figure 4–7.) Suppose both the onset of bad weather and a rise in farmers' costs conspire to reduce

supply or shift the market supply curve leftward from SS to $S_1S_1$. At every possible price, suppliers will now reduce the quantity of hamburger they are willing to supply. In particular, at the initial equilibrium price of $2.50 per pound, they are now only willing to supply 50,000 pounds of hamburger per month. At this price buyers will continue to demand 78,000 pounds per month, however. The quantity demanded therefore exceeds the quantity supplied and there is now a shortage amounting to 28,000 pounds, represented by the distance between points b and $e_1$. Again this causes the price to be bid up. When the price reaches $3 per pound, the quantity demanded will again equal the

**FIGURE 4–8  A Decrease in the Supply of Hamburger**

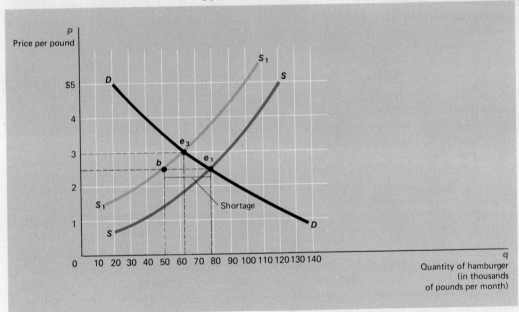

The market is initially in equilibrium where market demand curve DD intersects market supply curve SS at $e_1$. This gives an equilibrium price of $2.50 per pound and an equilibrium quantity of 78,000 pounds. The decrease in supply is indicated by the leftward shift of the market supply curve from SS to $S_1S_1$. This initially gives rise to the indicated shortage of 28,000 pounds, represented by the distance between points b and $e_1$. Competitive bidding among frustrated buyers pushes the price up until market equilibrium is established at $e_3$. The new equilibrium price is $3 per pound, and the new equilibrium quantity is 62,000 pounds per month.

quantity supplied. Equilibrium in the market will once more be restored. The equilibrium point is now at the intersection of $DD$ and $S_1S_1$ indicated by $e_3$. At the new equilibrium price of $3 per pound, the equilibrium quantity bought and sold is 62,000 pounds per month. Hence *a decrease in supply, represented by a leftward shift in the supply curve, will increase price and decrease quantity assuming other things remain the same.* (Demand is one of the things that remain the same, as represented by the unchanged position of the demand curve.)

### Both Supply and Demand Change

Suppose that in fact the expectations affecting hamburger demand and the events affecting hamburger supply have all occurred at about the same time. To analyze the consequences for the market for hamburger we must consider the rightward shift in the demand curve of Figure 4–7 together with the leftward shift in the supply curve of Figure 4–8. This combination of shifts is shown in Figure 4–9. Again the market supply curve $SS$ and the market demand curve $DD$ are the same as shown in Figures 4–7 and 4–8, and the initial equilibrium point determined by their intersection is again shown as $e_1$. The rightward shift in the demand curve from $DD$ to $D_1D_1$ caused by the changed expectations is exactly the same as that shown in Figure 4–7. The leftward shift in the supply curve from $SS$ to $S_1S_1$ caused by the bad weather and rising farmers' costs is exactly the same as that shown in Figure 4–8. At the initial equilibrium price of $2.50 per pound, the quantity demanded increases from 78,000 to 120,000 pounds per month. At the same time, the quantity suppliers are willing to supply falls from 78,000 to 50,000 pounds per month. The shortage now is equal to the sum of the shortages shown in Figures 4–7 and 4–8. Specifically, there is now a shortage amounting to 70,000 pounds of hamburger, the difference between point $a$ on $D_1D_1$ and point $b$ on $S_1S_1$. To restore equilibrium, price will have to be bid up until the quantity of hamburger demanded once again equals the quantity suppliers are willing to provide. This occurs where the demand curve $D_1D_1$ intersects the supply curve $S_1S_1$ at $e_4$. The new equilibrium price is $3.80 per pound, and the equilibrium quantity bought and sold is now 80,000 pounds of hamburger per month.

Note that when the leftward shift of the supply curve is considered together with the rightward shift of the demand curve in Figure 4–9, the resulting rise in price is greater than when either shift is considered alone, as in Figures 4–7 and 4–8. This is readily apparent from Figure 4–9. When only the demand shift was considered, the new equilibrium point was $e_2$. When just the supply shift was considered, the new equilibrium point was $e_3$. When the effect of both shifts is considered, the new equilibrium point is $e_4$, which occurs at a higher price than at either $e_2$ or $e_3$.

In general, when demand increases and supply decreases, as in Figure 4–9, it is possible for the new equilibrium quantity bought and sold to be either larger or smaller than that of the initial equilibrium position. Whether it is larger or smaller depends on the relative size of the shifts in the two curves. In the hypothetical example of Figure 4–9, the relative sizes of these shifts are such that the new equilibrium quantity associated with $e_4$ is slightly larger than the initial equilibrium quantity associated with $e_1$. If the leftward shift of the supply curve had been somewhat larger, or the rightward shift of the demand curve somewhat smaller, or both, the new equilibrium quantity might have been somewhat less than the initial equilibrium quantity.

### CHECKPOINT 4-3

**If the price of hot dogs should fall, what do you predict would happen to the equilibrium price and quantity of hamburger? If the price of hamburger buns falls and the wage rate that producers of hamburger must pay labor also falls, what do you predict would happen to the equilibrium price**

**FIGURE 4-9   Combined Effects of an Increase in Demand and a Decrease in Supply for Hamburger**

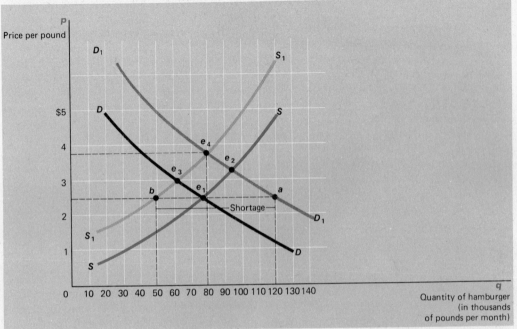

The combined effects of the increase in demand in Figure 4–7 and the decrease in supply in Figure 4–8 are shown here. Starting from the initial equilibrium determined by the intersection of DD and SS at $e_1$, the market demand curve shifts rightward to $D_1D_1$ while the market supply curve shifts leftward to $S_1S_1$. The initial shortage amounts to 70,000 pounds, the sum of the initial shortages indicated in Figures 4–7 and 4–8. Competitive bidding among frustrated buyers pushes the price up until market equilibrium is established at $e_4$. At that point, the new equilibrium price is $3.80 per pound, and the new equilibrium quantity is 80,000 pounds per month. Notice that the new equilibrium price is higher than that established when either the increase in demand or decrease in supply is considered separately, as in Figures 4–7 and 4–8. The new equilibrium quantity is larger given the relative sizes of the demand and supply curve shifts shown here. Had the leftward shift of the supply curve been larger or the rightward shift of the demand curve been smaller, or both, the new equilibrium quantity could have been smaller than the initial equilibrium quantity at $e_1$.

and quantity of hamburger? If the price of electricity rises and the rent rate for office space used by the producers of hamburger also rises, what do you predict would happen to the equilibrium price and quantity of hamburger? If someone told you that the price of hamburger had risen but gave you no other information, what would you be able to say about the quantity of it bought and sold? If you were told that the price of shoes had increased and the quantity bought and sold had decreased, what would you make of a newspaper story that claimed consumers' income was increasing? (*Hint:* What do you think an increase in consumers' income would do to shoe demand?)

## POLICY PERSPECTIVE

### Math and Science Teachers in Short Supply

In recent years over 40 states have reported shortages of math and physics teachers. Moreover, a survey by the National Science Teachers Association revealed that about a quarter of math and science teachers surveyed said they were planning to leave teaching for better paying jobs in industry. The shortage is aggravated by teachers unions' traditional opposition to pay differentials among teachers who teach different subjects.

The problem can be illustrated in terms of the hypothetical demand and supply curves for math teachers shown in Figure P4–1. Suppose teachers' unions prohibit schools from paying math teachers more than $20,000 per year. This annual wage (vertical axis) corresponds to point *a* on the demand curve *D* for math teachers. At point *a* schools demand the annual services of 2 million math teachers (horizontal axis). However only 1 million math teachers are willing to work for the schools at this wage, corresponding to

point *b* on the supply curve *S*. The shortage of math teachers equals the difference between points *a* and *b*, so that at an annual wage of $20,000 a million more math teachers are demanded than are supplied. If the union prohibition against paying math teachers a higher wage were lifted, schools would bid the wage of math teachers up to $30,000 corresponding to the intersection of the demand and supply curves at point *c*. Here the number of math teachers willing to teach, 1.5 million, would just equal the number schools want to hire. The shortage would be eliminated.

Why is it necessary to pay math and science teachers more than other teachers? Because those with math and science training can work for higher wages in other sectors of the economy. If schools want to eliminate the shortage of math and science teachers they will have to change their wage policies to recognize that in the marketplace society places different values on different kinds of labor skills, just as it places different values on different kinds of goods.

#### Questions

1. What is true of the opportunity cost of math and science teachers relative to the opportunity cost of other kinds of teachers?

2. How would an increase in scholarship aid to college students majoring in math and science affect Figure P4–1?

**FIGURE P4–1**   **Demand and Supply for Math Teachers**

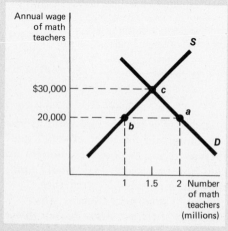

## POLICY PERSPECTIVE

### Energy Consumption and the Price of Energy—Adjusting to Energy Shocks

Throughout the 1950s and 1960s, the price of energy increased less rapidly than the prices of most other goods. This means that the *real* price of energy—its price in terms of other goods—was gradually falling. This pattern continued into the early 1970s. The falling real price of energy encouraged people to use more of it, as the law of demand would predict. Consumers bought ever more powerful gas-guzzling cars, and the per capita consumption of gasoline rose year after year. Electrical appliances were used increasingly to do household chores previously done by hand. Homes were heated to higher temperatures in winter and cooled to lower temperatures in summer. Natural

gas was so cheap that oil producers often burned it as a nuisance by-product of oil production.

#### The Era of Cheap Energy

The decline in the real price of energy and the rise in U.S. energy consumption from 1960 to 1973 can be explained in terms of changes in the demand and supply for energy, as illustrated in Figure P4-2, part a. The demand curve for energy was shifted rightward by increasing population and economic growth between 1960 and 1973. But over this period the supply curve for energy was shifted rightward an even greater amount by oil and natural gas discoveries, improved oil-

**FIGURE P4-2  Interaction of the Demand and Supply for Energy**

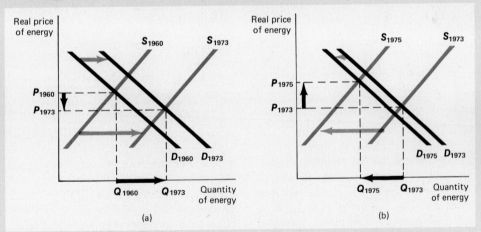

From 1960 to 1973 the demand curve for energy shifted rightward, but by a smaller amount than the rightward shift in the supply curve (part a). Consequently, the real price of energy fell while the quantity consumed increased.

From 1973 to 1975 the demand curve for energy shifted leftward, but by a smaller amount than the leftward shift in the supply curve (part b). Therefore, the real price of energy increased while the quantity consumed decreased.

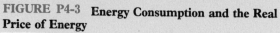

**FIGURE P4-3**  **Energy Consumption and the Real Price of Energy**

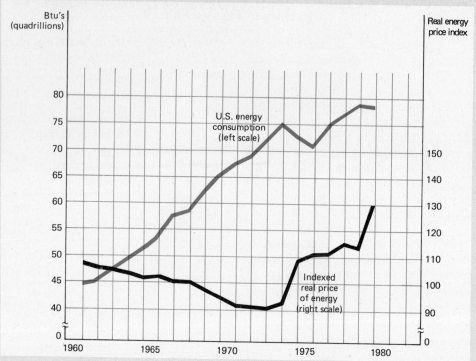

The gradual decline in the real price of energy until 1973 encouraged the steady increase in U.S. energy consumption. The Arab oil embargo of 1973 caused a sharp rise in the real price of energy, which led to a decline in energy consumption from 1973 through 1975. A similar episode, caused by the Iranian revolution in 1979, halted a similar, later rise in U.S. energy consumption.

SOURCE: U.S. Department of Labor, Bureau of Labor Statistics; U.S. Energy Information Administration, *Annual Report to Congress,* Vol. II.
a The real price of energy is a composite real price index that includes the prices of fuel oil, coal, bottled gas, piped natural gas, electricity, gasoline, motor oil, coolant, and so on.

drilling and natural gas pipeline technology, and increased efficiency in electric power generation. As a result the real price of energy fell from $P_{1960}$ to $P_{1973}$, and the quantity consumed increased from $Q_{1960}$ to $Q_{1973}$ in Figure P4–2, part a.

### The Arab Oil Embargo

The Arab oil embargo of 1973 abruptly reversed the downward trend in energy

prices. The real price of energy rose about 22 percent between 1973 and 1975, and energy consumption fell a bit more than 5 percent, as can be seen from Figure P4–3. This behavior can be explained in terms of the changes in demand and supply shown in Figure P4–2, part b. The demand curve for energy was shifted leftward during this period as the economy experienced the most severe recession since World War II. But the Arab oil embargo caused the supply curve to shift leftward by an even greater amount. The net result was that the quantity of energy consumed fell from $Q_{1973}$ to $Q_{1975}$ while the real price of energy rose from $P_{1973}$ to $P_{1975}$ in Figure P4–2, part b.

### The Iranian Revolution

From 1975 to 1978 the real price of energy rose only slightly (somewhat more than 3 percent), and U.S. energy consumption resumed its upward climb. However, consumption did not regain its 1973 level until 1976 (Figure P4–3). The Iranian revolution of 1979 abruptly interrupted world oil supplies once again. The real price of energy rose sharply (by about 12 percent) and again the upward climb in U.S. energy consumption ceased (Figure P4–3).

In sum, *experience shows the extent to which U.S. energy consumption is sensitive to the real price of energy.* The rise in the real price of energy has encouraged energy conservation—fuel-efficient cars, better-insulated houses, reuse (rather than dumping) of process heat by industry, and increased energy efficiency in appliances and heating and air-conditioning systems. It has also made feasible the development of alternative, but previously prohibitively expensive, sources of energy.

### Questions

1. What could you say about the change in the price of energy and the quantity of energy bought and sold if a major oil discovery occurred at the same time as a breakthrough in solar heating technology?

2. Similarly, what could you say about the change in price and quantity of energy if there were a severe winter coupled with another oil embargo?

## SUMMARY

**1.** The law of demand asserts that the lower (higher) the price charged for a good, the larger (smaller) will be the quantity demanded—all other things remaining the same. This law may be represented graphically by a demand curve that slopes downward left to right on a graph with price measured on the vertical axis and quantity measured on the horizontal. Any point on a demand curve tells us the quantity of a good buyers desire to purchase per some specified unit of time at the price associated with that point.

**2.** In addition to the price of the good for which the market demand curve is drawn, the other determinants of market demand are (1) the prices of all other goods, (2) money income, (3) expectations, (4) tastes, and (5) the number of buyers in the market. A change in one or more of these determinants will cause the market demand curve to shift either rightward (an increase in demand) or leftward (a decrease in demand). A shift in the demand curve is referred to as a change in demand. It is to be distinguished from a change in the quantity demanded, which refers to a movement along a fixed demand curve. The latter can only occur because of a change in the price of the good for which the demand curve is drawn.

**3.** The law of supply asserts that suppliers will supply larger quantities of a good at higher prices for that good than at lower prices—all other things remaining the same. This law may be represented graphically by a supply curve that slopes upward left to right on a graph with price measured on the vertical axis and quantity measured on the horizontal axis. Any point on a supply curve tells us the quantity of a good suppliers are willing to produce and desire to sell per some specified unit of time at the price associated with that point.

**4.** Along with the price of the good for which the supply curve is drawn, the other determinants of supply are (1) the prices of resources and other factors of production, (2) the prices of other goods, (3) technology, (4) the number of suppliers, and (5) the suppliers' expectations. A change in any of these determinants will cause the supply curve to shift either rightward (an increase in supply) or leftward (a decrease in supply). Such a change is called a change in supply. It is to be distinguished from a change in the quantity supplied, which is a movement along a fixed supply curve due to a change in the price of the good for which the supply curve is drawn.

**5.** Supply and demand interact to adjust price until that price is found where the quantity of the good demanded is just equal to the quantity supplied. This is the equilibrium price and quantity, which is determined by the intersection of the supply and demand curves. When this point of intersection is established, we have market equilibrium.

**6.** Changes in supply and demand, represented by shifts in the supply and demand curves, will upset equilibrium and cause either shortages or surpluses. This will set in motion competitive price bidding among buyers and sellers that will ultimately restore market equilibrium, most typically at new levels of equilibrium price and quantity.

**7.** An increase (decrease) in demand will lead to an increase (decrease) in equilibrium price and quantity—other things remaining the same. An increase (decrease) in supply will lead to a decrease (increase) in equilibrium price and an increase (decrease) in equilibrium quantity—other things remaining the same. When both supply and demand change, the effect on equilibrium price and quantity depends on the particular case.

## KEY TERMS AND CONCEPTS

complementary good
demand curve
demand schedule
equilibrium price
equilibrium quantity
factors of production
inferior good
law of demand
law of supply
market demand curve
market equilibrium
normal good
substitute good
supply curve
supply schedule
technology

## QUESTIONS AND PROBLEMS

**1.** Classify each of the following goods according to whether *in your opinion* it is a normal (essential) or inferior good: shoes, beer, leather gloves, life insurance, auto insurance, stereo equipment, pet dog, four-ply tires.

**2.** Classify each of the following pairs of goods according to whether you think they are substitutes, complements, or basically unrelated to each other: ham and eggs, meat and potatoes, Fords and Chevrolets, ice skates and swimsuits, coffee and tea, butter and margarine, apples and oranges, knives and forks, saltshakers and hats.

**3.** Suppose today's weather forecast states that chances are 9 out of 10 there will be rain all during the coming week. What effect do you think this will have on the demand curve for each of the following: umbrellas, baseball tickets, electricity, taxi rides, parking space in shopping centers, camping equipment, books, and aspirin?

**4.** What do you predict would happen to the market demand curve for oranges in the United States as a result of the following:

a. a rise in average income;

b. an increase in the birthrate;

c. an intensive advertising campaign that convinces most people of the importance of a daily quota of natural vitamin C;

d. a fall in the price of orange juice;

e. a fall in the price of grapefruit juice?

5. What will happen to the supply of cars if each of the following should occur? Explain your answers.

a. an increase in the price of trucks;

b. a fall in the price of steel;

c. introduction of a better assembly-line technique;

d. an increase in the desire of auto manufacturers to be highly esteemed by the nation rather than to earn as much money as possible;

e. an increase in the price of cars?

6. If goods are expensive because they are scarce, why aren't rotten eggs high priced?

7. What will be the effect on the supply curve of hogs of a fall in the price of corn? What will be the effect on the supply curve of corn of a fall in the price of hogs?

8. What effect do you think an advertising campaign for coffee would have on each of the following—other things remaining the same: the price of coffee, the price of tea, the quantity of sugar bought and sold, the price of doughnuts, the quantity of sleeping pills bought and sold, the price of television advertising time on the late show?

9. Suppose you read in the paper that the price of gasoline is rising along with increased sales of gasoline. Does this contradict the law of demand or not? Explain.

10. Suppose there is a strike in the steel industry. Other things remaining the same, what do you predict will happen to the price of steel, the price of automobiles, the quantity sold and the price of aluminum, the price of aluminum wire, the price and quantity of copper wire sold, and the price of electricity? At each step of this chain spell out your answer in terms of the relevant shift in a demand or supply curve. What do you think of the characterization of the economy as a chain of interconnected markets?

11. Suppose we were to look at some industry data on the buggy whip industry collected at about the time the automobile industry was rapidly moving out of its infancy. What would you make of the finding that many buggy whip manufacturers were getting out of the business, yet the price of buggy whips was not falling? Demonstrate your analysis diagrammatically.

12. During the energy crisis of late 1973 and early 1974 it was not uncommon to see automobiles lined up for blocks waiting to buy gas.

a. Demonstrate diagrammatically what happened in the gasoline market when the energy crisis hit.

b. Given the long lines of cars observed waiting to buy gas, do you think the equilibrium price of gas was established at that time?

c. If gasoline prices haven't risen that dramatically since early 1974, what would explain the disappearance of the lines of waiting motorists at gasoline stations since that time?

# TWO

## Aggregate Income, Employment, and Fiscal Policy

# 5

# Macroeconomic Concepts

**AFTER READING THIS CHAPTER, YOU WILL BE ABLE TO:**

1. Explain the interconnecting economic relationships between households, businesses, and government as characterized in flow diagrams.

2. Define the concept of GNP and list the kinds of economic transactions that are and are not included in this measure.

3. Explain the difference between current dollar or money GNP and constant dollar or real GNP.

4. State some of the deficiencies of GNP as a measure of the economy's welfare.

5. Define aggregate demand and supply and explain how they determine the economy's equilibrium price and total output levels.

This chapter begins our study of macroeconomics. Recall from Chapter 1 that macroeconomics is concerned with the performance of the economy as a whole or with large sectors of it, such as government, business, and households. Macroeconomics attempts to explain why the economy's total output of goods and services fluctuates over time, giving rise to the business cycle with its accompanying upward and downward movements in the unemployment rate and the rate of inflation. Macroeconomics is concerned with the potentially helpful as well as possibly harmful role that government plays in these events, including such issues as the government's ability to control inflation, the effectiveness of government policies aimed at smoothing the business cycle, and the size and effects of government budget deficits, an issue of much concern in recent years.

We will use flow diagrams in this chapter to develop a descriptive overview of the ways in which the major sectors of a capitalistic, mixed economy like that of the United States are linked together. We will then examine the important concept of gross national product, or GNP, the most commonly used measure of the economy's total output of goods and services. In Chapter 6 we will examine the historical record of the American economy in order to gain perspective and a feel for the way the economy behaves, the nature of the business cycle, and the closely related problems of inflation and unemployment. Chapter 7 will present the basics of national income accounting, the way we go about keeping track of the economy's performance. Chapters 8, 9, 10, and 11 will focus on explaining how the economy's total level of output is determined, the reasons why the economy does not always operate at full capacity (full employment), and the nature of public policies aimed at correcting this recurrent problem.

## THE CIRCULAR FLOW OF GOODS AND MONEY

In a capitalistic, mixed economy like that of the United States money is used by house-holds, businesses, and government to buy and sell goods and resources in markets, to pay and collect taxes, and to borrow and lend in financial markets. The flow of goods and resources in exchange for money, the flow of money to fulfill tax obligations to government and to redistribute income from one group to another, the flow of money from lenders to borrowers in exchange for borrowers' IOUs, and the expenditure of the borrowed funds on goods can all be envisioned schematically in a flow diagram.

### The Exchange Flow Between Households and Businesses

Consider first a flow diagram representing an economy in which there is no government intervention in economic activities. For the moment, we will also ignore the existence of financial markets and simply assume that businesses and households are the only two groups of decision makers. The relationship between these two groups is shown in Figure 5–1. The upper channel represents the flow of economic resources (land, labor, and financial capital) owned by households and supplied to businesses. The direction of this flow is indicated by the counterclockwise arrow running from households to businesses. In exchange for these services, businesses make money payments in the form of wages, rents, interest, and the distribution of profits. These payments constitute business demand for factors of production. The direction of this flow is indicated by the clockwise arrow running from businesses to households. All these exchanges take place at mutually agreeable money rates of exchange (or prices), determined by the functioning of markets for production inputs. *Wages* go to labor, *rents* to landowners, *interest* and *profits* to those supplying financial capital and entrepreneurial skills (a particular kind of labor service). All these money payments received by households constitute income.

The lower channel represents the flow of goods and services produced and supplied by businesses using all the inputs provided by the upper flow channel. This flow of goods

**FIGURE 5-1   The Exchange Flow Between Businesses and Households**

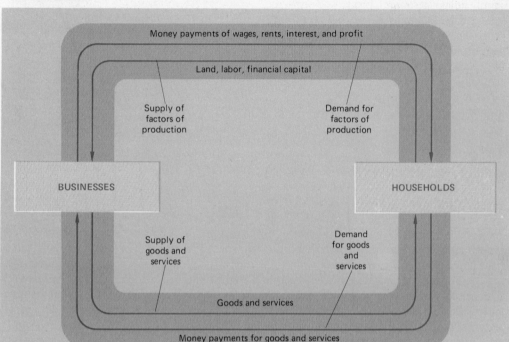

In a money-using economy, businesses obtain the resources (land, labor, and financial capital) necessary for production from households in exchange for money payments (wages, rents, interest, and profit) as indicated in the upper flow channel. These payments are income to the households, which spend it on goods and services produced by businesses. This is indicated by the money payments made to businesses in exchange for goods and services in the lower flow channel. Businesses use the money proceeds from sales to purchase the resources in the upper flow channel, thus completing the loop.

and services in the lower channel runs from businesses to households, as indicated by the counterclockwise arrow. The goods and services are demanded and purchased by the households with the money receipts (or income) obtained by selling the services of their resources, as indicated in the upper channel. The money payments made to businesses in exchange for goods and services are indicated in the lower channel by the arrow running clockwise from households to businesses. These exchanges also take place at mutually agreeable prices determined by the functioning of markets.

The money payments made by businesses in the upper channel are viewed as costs by them, while their receipt by households is viewed as income. The money payments received by businesses in the lower channel are viewed by them as sales revenue. For households these payments are the expenditures of the income they receive for supplying the resources that were used to produce the goods and services. Hence, in this money-using, pure market economy we have a clockwise flow of money payments made against a counterclockwise flow of resources, goods, and services. The clockwise circular flow of money expenditures may be thought of as the demand for the counterclockwise circular supply flow of resources, goods, and services, although both flows take place at the same time. These simultaneous flows reflect the ongoing and repetitive exchanges between buyers and sellers in the many markets of the economy.

## The Exchange Flows with Financial Markets

The exchange flows shown in Figure 5-1 are oversimplified in several respects. For one thing, businesses produce and sell goods to one another—capital equipment, for example. Similarly households buy from and sell labor services to one another, for example domestic services such as babysitting.

### Households and Businesses Save

We also know that households do not typically spend all their income on goods and services, nor do businesses pay out all their sales revenue for the current use of land, labor, and financial capital. *Households save part of their income, usually by putting it in banks and other financial institutions. Similarly, businesses save part of their sales revenue. Some of this saving takes the form of* **depreciation allowances.** *These allowances are funds that are set aside for the replacement of capital equipment when it wears out. The rest of their saving usually takes the form of* **retained earnings.** Like households, businesses put savings in banks and other financial institutions. Often they use their savings to purchase bonds and other forms of IOUs issued by parties that want to borrow money. Banks and other financial institutions perform the function of taking the savings of households and businesses and lending this money to borrowers who in turn use it to buy goods and services. When businesses, and sometimes households, use their savings to buy bonds and IOUs directly without the assistance of the intermediary role played by banks and other financial institutions, the effect is the same—savings are lent to borrowers.

### The Role of Financial Markets

*The markets that perform the function of taking the funds of savers and lending them to borrowers are called* **financial markets.** The households and businesses that lend their savings to borrowers through these financial markets receive compensation in the form of interest payments. Financial markets serve the function of taking the funds from the saving flows of businesses and households and lending them to borrowers at interest rates mutually agreeable to both lenders and borrowers. Who are the borrowers? Other businesses and households. What do they do with the borrowed funds? Spend them on goods and services. *In effect, financial markets take the savings, or the flow of funds provided by those businesses and households that do not want to spend them on goods and services, and put them in the hands of those that do want to spend them on goods and services.*

### Flow Diagram with Financial Markets and Savings

The role of financial markets can be represented in diagram form by making some changes in Figure 5-1. Figure 5-2 reproduces Figure 5-1 with the addition of savings flows and financial markets. Note now that not all of the sales revenue of businesses is immediately paid out in wages, rents, interest, and profit. Some is retained and saved, and it flows from businesses into the financial markets as indicated by the counterclockwise arrow labeled "Business saving." (It should be emphasized that these savings are still owned by the stockholders of the businesses who have provided financial capital.) Similarly, households do not spend all of their income on goods and services. That which is not spent is saved and flows into financial markets as indicated by the clockwise arrow labeled "Household saving."

The financial markets in the lower part of the diagram lend out the savings of businesses and households to other businesses and households that want to borrow funds. These borrowers do not borrow money and

**FIGURE 5-2  Exchange Flows with Savings and Financial Markets**

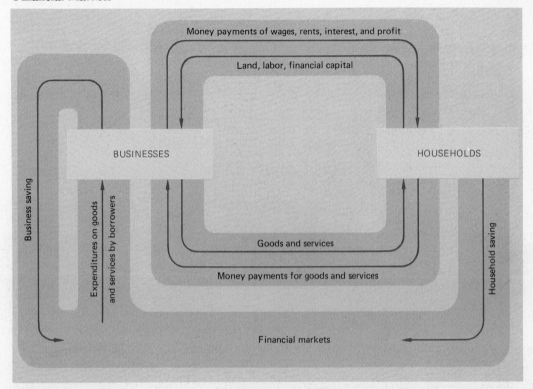

Money payments of wages, rents, interest, and profit

Land, labor, financial capital

BUSINESSES

HOUSEHOLDS

Business saving

Expenditures on goods and services by borrowers

Household saving

Goods and services

Money payments for goods and services

Financial markets

This diagram elaborates on Figure 5–1 by adding the savings flows from households and businesses. These feed into the financial markets, where they are loaned to borrowers at some mutually acceptable rate of interest. The borrowers then spend the funds on goods and services produced by businesses. The financial markets thus serve to redirect the savings money flows, otherwise diverted from expenditure on goods and services, back into the hands of those who will spend them on goods and services. Figure 5–2 may be viewed as representing a pure market, laissez faire capitalist economy.

make interest payments on their loans just for the privilege of holding the money. They use it to buy goods and services from businesses, as indicated by the upward-directed arrow labeled "Expenditures on goods and services by borrowers." These goods and services are part of the flow labeled "Goods and services," indicated by the counterclockwise arrow running from businesses to households. The business borrowers purchase goods and services from other businesses.

The main point is this: *The flow of money which is diverted away from further expenditure on goods and services by saving is redirected through the financial markets into the hands of those who will spend it on goods and services.* In performing this function financial markets play a crucial role in capitalistic, market-oriented economies. Because there is no government economic intervention indicated in Figure 5-2, it may be interpreted as representing an economic system of pure market, laissez faire capitalism.

## The Exchange Flows Between Businesses, Households, and Government

In order to characterize a capitalistic, mixed economy in a flow diagram it is necessary to bring government into the picture. This has been done in Figure 5-3. (The term *government* as used here includes federal, state, and local government.)

## Government Expenditures, Taxes, and Transfers

In order to carry out its functions, government must hire labor and other resources owned by households. This is indicated by the counterclockwise arrow running from households to government labeled "Labor and other resources." The money payments by government for these resources are indi-

**FIGURE 5-3  Exchange Flows with Savings and Financial Markets and Government**

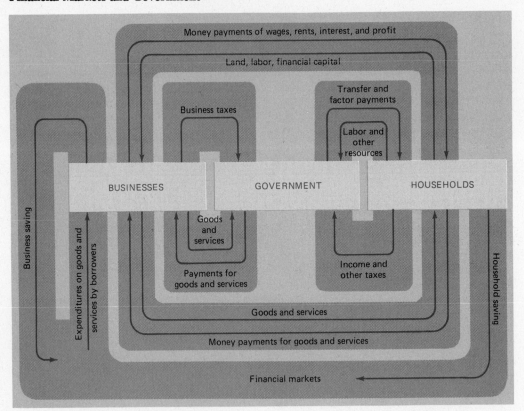

This diagram elaborates on Figure 5-2 by adding government, which is financed by taxes from businesses and households. Government uses tax proceeds to make transfer payments to households as well as to hire labor and purchase other resources from households. Government also uses tax revenue to purchase goods and services from businesses. In this way government reallocates resources and redistributes income. Also, by varying tax rates and the level of its expenditures, government can affect the size of the flows in the flow channels—that is, the level of economic activity. Figure 5-3 may be viewed as representing a capitalistic, mixed economy.

cated by the clockwise arrow running from government to households labeled "Transfer and factor payments." The factor payments are made to cover wage, rent, and interest payments to households in exchange for labor services, buildings and land rented to the government, and the financial capital provided through household holdings of government bonds. These factor payments are viewed as expenditures by the government and as income by the households. Transfer payments represent government payment to households of social security benefits and other benefits provided by public assistance programs. Transfers also include tax refunds. Transfer payments are viewed as income by the households receiving them.

In order to help finance its operations, the government must collect taxes from households in the form of income taxes, property taxes, and sales taxes. These tax payments by households to government are represented by the clockwise arrow running from households to government labeled "Income and other taxes." The government also collects taxes from businesses in the form of corporate profits taxes, property taxes, and sales taxes. These tax payments to government are represented by the clockwise arrow running from businesses to government labeled "Business taxes." There is yet one other way in which government can finance its operations. That is by issuing and selling new government bonds in the financial markets. The money proceeds from these sales can be used in the same ways as tax proceeds. (The flow channel between government and the financial markets is not shown in Figure 5-3.)

The government uses receipts from bond sales along with the tax receipts from businesses and households in part to make the transfer and factor payments to households already mentioned. The government also uses these receipts to purchase goods and services from businesses. These include anything from paper clips and staples to jet bombers, rockets, and the construction of dams, highways, and buildings by private contractors. The payments for these items are represented by the clockwise arrow running from government to businesses labeled "Payments for goods and services." The provision of goods and services in exchange for these payments is indicated by the counterclockwise arrow running from businesses to government labeled "Goods and services."

### Government Affects Resource Allocation and Income Distribution

The taxes paid by businesses must come out of their sales revenue, while those paid by households must come out of their income. By increasing or decreasing the amount of these taxes, government can divert a larger or smaller share of the sales revenue of businesses and the income receipts of households into activities determined by government expenditures, as opposed to the market activities determined by business and household expenditures. This is an obvious way in which government affects resource allocation. Similarly, it can be seen how the government affects income distribution through the redistribution of tax proceeds to households in the form of transfer payments.

### Government Affects the Level of Economic Activity

By changing its expenditure and tax policies, government can affect the level of overall economic activity as represented by the flows in Figure 5-3. Consider two extreme examples.

Suppose government increases income taxes on households but does not spend the increased tax proceeds. This obviously takes income from households that would otherwise have been spent on goods and services or saved and put in the financial markets, where it could have ultimately been used by some borrower to buy goods and services. Hence, the volume in the lower two flow channels of Figure 5-3 would be reduced. This would lead to a drop in sales by businesses and a consequent drop in some or all of the categories of business saving, business taxes, and income earned by households, as measured by businesses' money payments of wages, rent, interest, and profit in the upper flow channel of Figure 5-3.

Alternatively, suppose government increased expenditures on goods and services but did not raise taxes to finance these expenditures. Suppose, instead, that it financed them by simply printing money. The result would be that businesses would experience an increase in the dollar volume of sales. This would lead to an increase in some or all of the categories—business saving, business taxes, and income earned by households.

Changes in the expenditure plans of businesses and households can also lead to changes in economic activity as represented by the flows in Figure 5–3. Government stabilization policy is aimed at changing all or some combination of government expenditures, tax rates, and the money supply in such a way as to offset undesirable changes in the level of economic activity that may result from changes in business and household expenditure plans.

The flow diagrams are very simplified pictures of the economy. Much detail is omitted. Nonetheless, they give some idea of how the mixed economy's various decision-making units—business, households, and government—are linked together to form an interlocking, interdependent system.

---

*CHECKPOINT\* 5-1*
**How would the flow diagram in Figure 5-3 have to be changed if it were to describe an economy such as Great Britain, where the government nationalized (took over, owned, and operated) certain businesses?**

*\*Answers to all Checkpoints can be found at the back of the text.*

---

## WHAT IS GROSS NATIONAL PRODUCT (GNP)?

Probably the most cited measure of the economy's overall performance is its **gross national product (GNP)**. In short, *GNP is the market value of all final goods and services* *produced by the economy during a year.* GNP has several important characteristics. First, it is a flow concept. Second, it is measured in money terms. Third, it only includes goods and services bought for final use, not unfinished goods in the intermediate stages of production that are purchased for further processing and resale. Fourth, GNP has two sides—it may be viewed from the income side or from the expenditure side.

### GNP Is a Flow

*A* **flow** *is a quantity per unit of time,* such as so many gallons of water running through a pipe per minute. By contrast, a stock is a quantity measured without respect to time, such as the number of gallons of water in a tub. GNP is a flow measured as the quantity of final goods and services produced by the economy per year. It is a flow that is measured at an annual rate.

We could measure GNP by giving a complete listing of all final goods and services produced per year—the number of automobiles, haircuts, toothbrushes, car washes, and so forth. (We couldn't add the quantities of these different goods together to get one number—you can't add apples and shirts.) This obviously would be a rather cumbersome list, probably about the size of a large city's telephone directory, depending on how fine a breakdown of product description is desired. It is far easier and less awkward to simply summarize all this information by adding up the dollar values of all these goods. Hence the dollar value of GNP is given as the sum of the price of an automobile times the number of automobiles per year plus the price of a haircut times the number of haircuts per year plus the price of a toothbrush times the number of toothbrushes per year plus the price of a car wash times the number of car washes per year plus . . . , and so forth. *GNP may be viewed either as a flow of numbers of units of final goods and services produced per year or as a flow of the dollar value of these final goods and services produced per year.*

The importance of distinguishing between final goods and services produced this year and those produced in other years cannot be overemphasized. Only those produced this year are to be counted in this year's GNP. Those produced in other years are counted in GNP for the years in which they were produced.

The measurement of GNP requires that we add up all the market transactions representing the purchase and sale of final goods and services. Such transactions measure the dollar value of productive activity that actually went into the production of final goods and services this year. However, there are many market transactions in our economy that do not involve the purchase and sale of final goods and services produced this year. For the purpose of measuring GNP, these are nonproductive transactions, and care must be taken not to include them in the measurement of GNP. In addition, it should be recognized that some productive activities that should be included in GNP do not always show up as market transactions.

### Productive Versus Nonproductive Transactions

Many market transactions that occur in our economy do not represent the production of a good. Therefore, we don't want to count them in GNP.

The purchase and sale of *used goods* is an example of such a transaction. If A buys B's 2-year-old stereo set for $300, this transaction does not involve the purchase of a final good produced *this year*. When the set was purchased new 2 years ago, its purchase price was included in GNP for that year. What about a set produced and purchased in February of this year and then resold by the initial buyer a month later? The purchase of the set by the *initial* buyer would be included in GNP for this year because it was produced this year. However, it would not be correct to include the resale transaction in GNP because this would amount to counting the pro-

duction of the set more than once. *The resale of a used good is a transaction that merely represents the transfer of ownership of a previously produced good—it does not represent the production of a new good.* Always remember that GNP is a measure of productive activity. You and I could buy and sell the same car back and forth daily, but we have not produced any new cars.

There are also certain types of *financial transactions* in our economy that do not represent any productive activity that adds to the output of final goods and services. Therefore, they are not included in GNP. Such transactions include (1) the trading of stocks, bonds, and other kinds of securities in financial markets; and (2) private and public transfer payments.

1. The trading in stocks and bonds in financial markets amounts to several tens of trillions of dollars per year. None of this is counted in GNP, however, because it only represents the trading of paper assets. True, businesses and government often issue new stocks and bonds to raise funds to spend on currently produced final goods and services. But this only amounts to a minute fraction of the total yearly purchases and sales of securities. Funds raised and used to purchase final goods and services are included in GNP when they appear in business firms' accounts recording such sales.

2. Private and public **transfer payments** are transactions in which the recipient is neither expected nor required to make any contribution to GNP in return. The transfer of funds from one individual to another, either as a gift, a bequest, or a charitable donation, constitutes a private transfer payment not included in GNP. Also included under private transfer payments are payments out of private pension funds. Public transfer payments are made to some groups in the economy by the government. Such payments include social security, welfare, unemployment, and veterans' benefits. While these payments are not included in GNP, the national income accounts do keep a record of them, as we shall see.

### Productive Nonmarket Transactions

If GNP is to measure the economy's production of final goods and services, it is necessary to recognize that not all productive activities show up as market transactions on the business accounting statements used to construct an estimate of GNP. Therefore, it is necessary to impute a dollar value to productive activities not represented by a market transaction and to include this dollar value in the calculation of GNP.

For example, people who live in their own home do not write themselves a rent check every month. However, those who do not own their home must make such an explicit rent payment. Both groups receive a currently produced service—the shelter provided by their dwellings—yet only the payments made by renters to landlords show up as a market transaction. The rent on owner-occupied homes must be imputed as the rent payments the owners would have to make if they rented their homes from landlords. These payments could also be looked at as the amount of rent owners could receive if they were to rent their home to somebody else. Such an imputed rent on owner-occupied homes is included in GNP, along with the rent payments made to landlords. Similarly, the value of the food that farm families produce and consume themselves must be imputed and included in GNP.

However, there are a number of productive nonmarket transactions that are not included in GNP. The productive services of homemakers—cooking, laundering, housecleaning—are not included despite the fact that this constitutes a sizeable amount of productive activity. (If you're not convinced, just check the want ads to see what it would cost you to hire a cook and a housekeeper.) Many people repair and remodel their own homes, cars, and a host of other items. Yet the productive services of the do-it-yourselfers are not included in GNP, largely because it is so difficult to estimate and keep track of the total value of such activities in our economy.

### Value Added: Don't Double Count

We have stressed that GNP only includes goods and services bought for final use. It does not include the unfinished goods in the intermediate stages of production that are purchased by one firm from another for further processing and resale. The market value of a final good is the full value of the good in that it already includes the **value added** at each stage of the production process. If we also counted the purchases of the component parts of the good each time they were sold by a firm at one stage of the production process to a firm at the next stage, we would end up counting the market value of the final good more than once. For example, we don't want to count the sale of Firestone tires to the Ford Motor Company because the cost of the tires will be included in the price of the cars that Ford sells to final customers. If we did include the sale of tires from Firestone to Ford, the tires would be double counted in GNP.

These points are illustrated by the example in Table 5-1. Suppose it costs you $.50 to buy a pad of notebook paper in your local retail store. This pad is a final product since you intend to use the paper yourself, not to transform it into another product and resell it. The market value of the final product, $.50, equals the sum of the values added at each stage of the production process.

How does this work? Firm 5, the retail store that sells the pad of paper to you, must pay $.45 of the $.50 it receives (columns 3 and 4) to Firm 4, the paper manufacturer that provides Firm 5 with the paper. Firm 5 pays out the remaining $.05 in wages, rent, interest, and profit to the factors of production used by Firm 5 to provide the retailing service. This $.05 constitutes the value added (column 5) to the final product by Firm 5 through its provision of these services. Firm 4 must pay $.30 of the $.45 received from Firm 5 to Firm 3, the pulpwood mill, for the pulpwood Firm 4 processes into notebook paper. Firm 4 pays out the remaining $.15 in wages, rent, interest, and profit to the factors

**TABLE 5-1 Sale Receipts, Cost of Intermediate Products, and Value Added at Each Stage of Production of Notebook Paper** (Cents per Pad of Paper)

| | (1) | (2) | (3) | (4) | (5) |
|---|---|---|---|---|---|
| | Production Stage | Product | Sale Price of Product | Cost of Intermediate Product | Value Added (Wages, Interest, Rent, and Profit) |
| Firm 1 | Tree farm | Trees | $.15 | — $.00 = | $.15 |
| Firm 2 | Logging company | Logs | .20 | — .15 = | .05 |
| Firm 3 | Pulpwood mill | Pulpwood | .30 | — .20 = | .10 |
| Firm 4 | Paper manufacturer | Notebook paper | .45 | — .30 = | .15 |
| Firm 5 | Retail store | Retailing service | .50 | — .45 = | .05 |
| Final Sale | | | | | $.50 (Final sale price = sum of value added) |

of production it uses to process pulpwood into paper. This $.15 is the value added to the final product by the paper manufacturer. Proceeding back through each stage of production, the pulpwood mill adds value to the final product by processing the logs it buys from the logging company. And the logging company adds value to the final product by making logs out of the trees it buys from the tree farm.

*The value added to the final product at each stage of production is the difference between what the firm sells its product for and what it pays for the intermediate materials or good it processes at that production stage. This difference is paid out in wages, interest, rent, and profit to all the factors of production that provide the productive services which add value to the product at that stage of production. The sum of the values added at each stage of production equals the sale price of the final good or service.*

In the example of Table 5–1, the $.50 sale price of the final good, a pad of notebook paper, equals the sum of the value-added figures of column 5. If, instead, we added up the sales figures in column 3 we would get $1.60. This figure overstates the value of the final good because it counts the value added by Firm 1 five times, that by Firm 2 four times, Firm 3 three times, and Firm 4 two times. In order to avoid this double, or multiple, counting, it is necessary to subtract the purchase price of intermediate products to be processed at each stage of production, as indicated by the arrows. This leaves the value-added figures of column 5, the sum of which equals the correct value of the final product. For this reason that is the only figure we want to include in GNP. We do not add in the sales transactions between the first four firms.

*CHECKPOINT 5-2*

**While the purchase and sale of used cars are not included in GNP, the sales commissions earned by used-car dealers are. Similarly, the purchase and sale of stock on the New York Stock Exchange are not included in GNP, but the sales commissions earned by stockbrokers are. Why are the sales commissions generated from these activities included in GNP while the sales themselves are not? During the last 30 years or so the proportion of working wives in the labor force has increased considerably. What effect does this have on GNP? Construct a hypothetical value-added table like Table 5–1 for the production and sale of a loaf of bread.**

## MONEY GNP VERSUS REAL GNP

Money GNP is the economy's gross national product measured in terms of the prices at which final goods and services actually sell. Real GNP is money GNP adjusted to remove the effects of inflation. It is important to understand what this means.

### Adjusting GNP for Price Change: A Simple Example

Suppose, for simplicity, that the entire economy produced only one kind of good. Say that good is widgets. In any given year the economy's money GNP equals the *current* price of a widget multiplied by the number of widgets produced during the year. Any change in money GNP from one year to the next could therefore be due to a change in price or a change in quantity or both. However, we typically are only interested in GNP to the extent that it measures the quantity of output produced.

For instance, suppose the economy has a dollar GNP of $1,000 in 1988, which results from the production of 1,000 widgets that sell at a price of $1 per widget. It will be no better or worse off in 1998 with a dollar GNP of $2,000 if that GNP again results from the production and sale of 1,000 widgets, at a price of $2 per widget. When prices rise over time in this way we have **inflation**—a decrease in the purchasing power of a dollar. It takes $2 to buy one widget in 1998 that could have been purchased for $1 in 1988. Similarly, if prices decline over time we have **deflation**, an increase in the purchasing power of a dollar. The task is to somehow adjust the dollar GNP figure so that it only reflects changes in quantity of output produced and not price changes— not inflation or deflation.

Table 5–2 illustrates the way in which national income accountants would make this adjustment for our simple widget economy. Suppose that over a 5-year period the current price $p$ of widgets rises, as shown in column 2. Suppose also that the quantity $Q$ of widgets produced each year is increasing at a rate of 10 percent per year, as shown in column 3. The money GNP for each year equals the current price $p$ times $Q$, as shown in column 4. Clearly the increase in money GNP (or GNP in current prices) from year to year is much greater than the yearly increase in the physical quantity of widgets produced, due to the increases in the current price of widgets. Since these money GNP figures are inflated over time by the rising current price of widgets (column 2), it is necessary to adjust them so that they only reflect changes in quantities of output produced, and not price changes.

This adjustment is made by constructing a **price index**. A price index expresses the current price of widgets in each year as a ratio relative to the current price in some base, or benchmark, year. This base year may be chosen arbitrarily. In Table 5–2, the base year is the third year. The price index constructed in this way is shown in column 5.

**TABLE 5-2 Adjusting Money GNP for Price Level Changes to Obtain Real GNP: A Simple Example**

| (1) | (2) | (3) | (4) | (5) | (6) |
|---|---|---|---|---|---|
| Year | Price per Widget ($p$) | Number of Units (Widgets) of Output per Year ($Q$) | Money GNP or GNP in Current Prices *nominal* | Price Index | Real GNP or GNP in Constant Prices or Dollars |
| | | | $p \times Q = $ (2) $\times$ (3) | (2) $\div$ Price in year 3 | (4) $\div$ (5) |
| 1 | $ 2 | 1,000 | $ 2,000 | $2/5 = $ .40, or 40 percent | $5,000 |
| 2 | 3 | 1,100 | 3,300 | $3/5 = $ .60, or 60 percent | 5,500 |
| 3 = base year | 5 | 1,210 | 6,050 | $5/5 = 1.00$, or 100 percent | 6,050 |
| 4 | 7 | 1,331 | 9,317 | $7/5 = 1.40$, or 140 percent | 6,655 |
| 5 | 10 | 1,464 | 14,640 | $10/5 = 2.00$, or 200 percent | 7,320 |

$$NGNP \div PI = RGNP$$
$$\frac{NGNP}{PI} = RGNP \qquad NGNP = RGNP \times PI$$

For example, the price of a widget in year 1 is two-fifths, or 40 percent, of the price of a widget in year 3 ($2 ÷ $5). Hence, if we want to adjust the money GNP of year 1 (column 4) to obtain output in terms of year 3 prices, we must multiply the money GNP of year 1 by $5/2$ or, equivalently, divide it by .40, the value of the price index in year 1. Year 1 GNP expressed in year 3 prices is $5,000 (column 6). By the same procedure the money GNP of each of the other 4 years may be expressed in terms of year 3 prices to give real GNP, or GNP in constant dollars or prices (column 6). The GNP figures in column 6 are "real" in the sense that their year-to-year change accurately reflects the year-to-year change in the quantity of widgets produced in the economy (column 3). The figures in both columns increase at a rate of 10 percent per year. It also may be said that the GNP figures of column 6 are stated in constant dollars or prices in the sense that they are all expressed in terms of the year 3 price of widgets.

In sum, **money GNP**, *or GNP in current prices or dollars, measures the dollar value of final goods and services produced in a given*

*year at the prices at which they actually sold in that year.* **Real GNP**, *or GNP in constant prices or dollars, measures the dollar value of final goods and services sold in a given year in terms of the prices at which those goods sold in some base, or benchmark, year.*

### Money and Real GNP in the United States

Our widget economy example greatly over-simplifies the problem of transforming money GNP into real GNP, yet the basic principle of adjustment carries over to the real world. The essential difference, of course, is that a real world economy typically produces a multitude of different goods, not just widgets. This means there are many different prices that may change over time, so that the price index used must be constructed as an average (usually a weighted average) of all these prices.

Such a price index (called the GNP deflator) for the United States economy is shown for selected years in column 3 of Table 5-3. The base year is 1972. This column tells us, among other things, that the general

**TABLE 5-3 Money GNP and Real GNP in the United States, Selected Years** (in Billions of Dollars)

| (1) | (2) | (3) | (4) |
|---|---|---|---|
| Year | Money GNP (Current Dollars) | Price Index:[a] Base Year 1972 | Real GNP (Constant 1972 Dollars) |
| | | | (2) ÷ (3) |
| 1950 | $ 286 | .54 | $ 530 |
| 1955 | 400 | .61 | 656 |
| 1960 | 506 | .69 | 733 |
| 1965 | 691.1 | .74 | 934 |
| 1970 | 992.7 | .91 | 1,091 |
| 1972 | 1,185.9 | 1.00 | 1,186 |
| 1975 | 1,549.2 | 1.26 | 1,230 |
| 1980 | 2,626.1 | 1.77 | 1,484 |
| 1983 | 3,309.5 | 2.16 | 1,535 |

SOURCE: U.S. Department of Commerce.

[a] GNP deflator.

level of prices rose 116 percent from 1972 to 1983, that the general level of prices in 1950 was 54 percent of that prevailing in 1972, and that prices quadrupled between 1950 and 1983. Money GNP—GNP in current prices or dollars—is shown in column 2. Using exactly the same procedure as in Table 5-2, the money GNP figures in column 2 of Table 5-3 are divided by the price index for the corresponding year in column 3 to give real GNP in column 4. This real GNP is thus expressed in constant 1972 prices or dollars. The behavior of real GNP in column 4 indicates that the *quantity* of final goods and services produced by the economy increased roughly fivefold between 1950 and 1983. Column 2 indicates that money GNP, the quantity of final goods and services evaluated in current prices, increased somewhat more than elevenfold over this period. This reflects the fact that prices quadrupled, as indicated in column 3. Clearly, if we want a more accurate measure of the economy's productive performance, we must use real GNP—GNP measured in constant dollars (column 4).

The difference in the behavior of money GNP (GNP in current dollars) and real GNP for the years since 1960 is shown graphically in Figure 5-4. While GNP in current dollars rises continuously throughout these years, largely reflecting the inflation in prices during this period, GNP in constant (1972) dollars generally grows more slowly and even declines in some years (1970, 1974, 1975, 1980, and 1982). Figure 5-4 clearly indicates that whenever we talk, read, or write about GNP it is important to be clear whether it is money GNP or real GNP that is referred to. There is obviously a difference.

*CHECKPOINT 5-3*

**Using Table 5-2, calculate real GNP in terms of constant year 2 dollars. It is sometimes said that calculating real GNP "inflates" the money GNP data for years before the base year. In what sense is this so?**

**FIGURE 5-4   Gross National Product (GNP) in Current and Constant 1972 Dollars: 1960–1984**

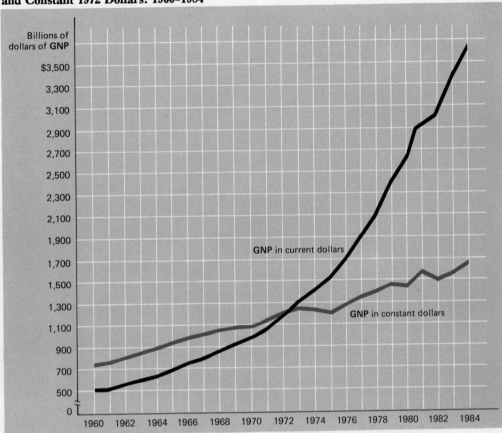

Since 1960, GNP in current dollars (money GNP) has grown continuously. However, GNP in constant 1972 dollars (real GNP) reveals that growth in the economy's production of final goods and services has not been as rapid or continuous. While real GNP declined in 1970, 1974, 1975, 1980, and 1982, GNP in current dollars increased, reflecting the general inflation in prices.

# INTRODUCTION TO AGGREGATE DEMAND AND AGGREGATE SUPPLY

Chapter 4 showed how demand and supply interact to determine price and output for a particular good or service. In a similar fashion we can envision an aggregate demand curve and an aggregate supply curve interacting to determine the economy's price level and its level of total output. The price level is a price index such as the GNP deflator and the economy's total output is represented by real GNP. Here we will introduce the basic elements of aggregate demand and supply which will be used and developed more fully in later chapters.

## POLICY PERSPECTIVE

# What GNP Does Not Measure

It is easy, and tempting, to look at GNP as a measure of society's well-being. Yet it was never intended to be a measure of social welfare. It is simply an accounting measure of economic activity. While there is certainly reason to believe that an economy is "better off" if it has a large real GNP—more goods and services for all—this is not *necessarily* so. On the other hand, a society may become better off in ways that GNP simply does not measure. Let's consider some of the "goods" and "bads" that GNP does not measure.

### Product Quality

A generation ago, even a multimillionaire couldn't buy the kinds of medicines commonly available to the person of average means today. Yesteryear's automobiles didn't have four-wheel brakes, automatic transmissions, and a host of safety features commonly built into today's cars. Suppose you were given a Sears catalog for 1950 and a copy of today's Sears catalog with the prices in each listed in the same constant dollars. From which one would you rather buy kitchen appliances, sports equipment, TV sets, adding machines (calculators), and air conditioners? *Because GNP is a quantitative rather than a qualitative measure, it does not measure product improvement and the development of new kinds of goods.* The GNP in 1950 did not include the kinds of goods that are included in today's GNP. But when their value is measured in dollars alone, yesterday's products are indistinguishable from today's.

### Costs Not Measured: Pollution

GNP does not measure many of the by-products associated with producing the goods and services that are measured by GNP. And many of these by-products are "bads"—smoke, noise, polluted rivers and lakes, garbage dumps, and junkyards. The costs of health problems (both physical and mental) caused by such environmental blight are either not measured at all or do not show up until years after the production of the GNP that caused them. These undesirable by-products tend to increase right along with growth in GNP. If the costs of these bads were subtracted from GNP, the resulting GNP would not appear as large or grow as fast. It would also be a more accurate measure of society's true well-being.

### Leisure and GNP

For most people a certain amount of leisure is desirable. When people take more of it, less working time is devoted to producing goods and services. This means GNP will be smaller than it otherwise might be. However, this increase in leisure must add to people's sense of well-being more than enough to offset the forgone output, or else people wouldn't have chosen to take it. Therefore it would be completely misleading to interpret the reduction in GNP that results from increased leisure as a reduction in society's well-being. For example, the length of the average workweek has been roughly cut in half over the last century. Workers have chosen to take more leisure, and as a result GNP is not as large as it would be if workers put in as many work hours as they typically did a hundred years ago. However, it would be erroneous to conclude that society is worse off because GNP is not as large as it could be. Why? Because more leisure has been chosen in *preference* to the additional output.

### Per Capita GNP and the Distribution of Output

If we divide up a side of beef among 5 people, each individual will certainly be better off than if we have to divide it up among 10 people. Similarly in order to assess how well off a nation is, we need to know more than just the size of its annual output, its real GNP. We also need to know how that output is divided among its citizens. If it were divided equally among them, then we would simply divide the nation's GNP by its population. This gives **per capita GNP**.

Figure P5-1 shows how real per capita GNP (in 1972 dollars) has grown since 1929 in the United States.

While there is in fact no economy where GNP is distributed equally among its citizens, per capita GNP gives a simple measure of how well off an economy would be *if* its GNP were divided up in this fashion. For example, in 1973 the GNP of Bangladesh was approximately $7.7 billion, while that of Chile was about $7.6 billion. However, Bangladesh had a population roughly eight times as large as Chile's. Consequently, per capita GNP in Bangladesh was about $100, while in Chile it was $777. Hence, despite the fact that both nations had about the same level of GNP, Chilean citizens would appear to be much better off than those of Bangladesh.

Because an economy's GNP is typically distributed unequally among its citizens, it is necessary to study this distribution in more detail in order to get a more accurate assessment than that provided by per capita GNP.

**FIGURE P5-1** **Growth of Real per Capita GNP in the United States** (1972 Dollars)

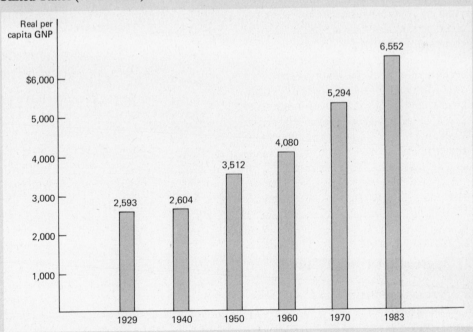

**FIGURE P5-2   The Changing Composition of GNP in the United States**

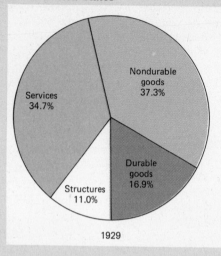

1929

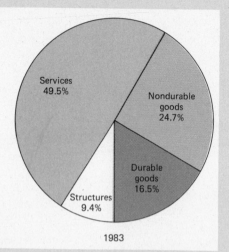

1983

### Composition of GNP

The kinds of goods produced by an economy are completely hidden from view by a GNP figure. One economy could have a $100 billion GNP composed entirely of weapons for war, and another could have a $100 billion GNP composed entirely of sports cars, steak dinners, and fine clothes. These economies would clearly have different kinds of living standards, though you could never tell it from GNP data. GNP alone tells nothing about the composition of the economy's output. For example, the composition of GNP in the United States has shifted more toward the production of services, as shown by the comparison of the composition of GNP in 1929 with that in 1983 in Figure P5–2.

### Questions

1. Suppose the portion of an economy's GNP spent on health care increases over time. What considerations would be important in deciding whether this represented an increase in society's well-being or not?

2. How do coffee breaks and sick leaves affect GNP? Which sort of time loss affects GNP in the same direction as societal well-being?

## The Aggregate Demand Curve

The **aggregate demand curve** *(AD) shows the relationship between the economy's total demand for output and the price level of that output.* The aggregate demand curve slopes downward left to right (is negatively sloped) as shown in Figure 5–5. Its shape indicates that *the lower the price level the larger the quantity of total output demanded, and the higher the price level the smaller the quantity demanded.*

## FIGURE 5-5 Aggregate Demand and Supply Determine the Economy's Equilibrium Price Level and Real GNP

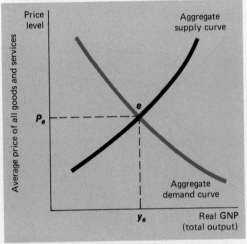

The aggregate demand curve is negatively sloped indicating that the lower the economy's price level the larger is the quantity of total output (real GNP) demanded. The economy's aggregate supply curve is positively sloped indicating that the economy's businesses will produce a larger quantity of total output (real GNP) the higher the economy's price level. The interaction of the aggregate demand and supply curves at point e determines the economy's equilibrium price level $p_e$ and total output $y_e$.

### Difference Between AD Curve and Individual Demand Curve

Though the shape of the *AD* curve looks like that of a market demand curve for an individual good, such as corn or gasoline, the reasons for its shape are not the same. Recall that movement along a market demand curve for a particular good corresponds to a change in the price of that good, the prices of all other goods assumed constant. The price of the particular good therefore changes *relative* to the prices of all other goods. The particular good becomes either cheaper or more expensive relative to all other goods, depending

on the direction of its price change. By contrast, movement along the *AD* curve corresponds to a change in *the economy's price level*, an average of the prices of *all* the goods and services that make up total output. So the reasons why the *AD* curve slopes downward left to right are different.

### Slope of the AD Curve

There are several reasons why the *AD* curve has a negative slope. For our purposes it is sufficient to focus on one, the effect of changes in the price level on consumer wealth. Much consumer wealth consists of fixed-dollar assets—assets whose values are fixed in terms of dollars. The most obvious example is money itself. Others are corporate and government bonds and savings accounts. Whenever the price level rises the real value or purchasing power of these fixed-dollar assets declines; that is, the amount of goods and services that can be purchased with them goes down. (For example, the quantity of goods that a 10-dollar bill will buy declines roughly 20 percent if there is a 20 percent increase in the price level.) Conversely, whenever the price level falls the purchasing power of fixed dollar assets goes up.

*Therefore, the aggregate demand curve has a negative slope because a higher price level, by reducing the purchasing power of consumer wealth, causes consumers to cut back on the quantity of goods and services they demand. A lower price level increases the purchasing power of consumer wealth and causes them to increase the quantity of goods and services they demand.*

### The Aggregate Supply Curve

*The* **aggregate supply curve** *(AS) shows the amount of total output that the economy's businesses will supply at different price levels.* The aggregate supply curve shown in Figure 5–5 is upward sloping left to right (positively sloped). In later chapters we will examine conditions that give rise to a vertical aggregate supply curve, as well as conditions that can cause the aggregate supply curve to be horizontal.

The positively sloped *AS* curve in Figure 5–5 reflects short-run conditions. In the short run, when the economy's price level (the average of all prices) rises the prices of firms' products tend to rise faster than firms' costs. Therefore firms' profits rise, encouraging them to expand output. Hence in the short run the higher the economy's price level the larger the quantity of total output supplied. We will examine the *AS* curve in greater detail in subsequent chapters.

## The Interaction of Aggregate Demand and Supply

The intersection of the aggregate demand and aggregate supply curves at point *e* in Figure 5–5 determines the economy's equilibrium price level $p_e$ and its equilibrium level of total output $y_e$. Again it should be emphasized that the economy's price level is an index or average of the prices of all the individual goods and services produced in the economy, an index such as the GNP deflator for example. The economy's total output is its real GNP—its GNP measured in constant dollars. If the economy were the simple one-good, widget economy of our earlier example, then its equilibrium real GNP or total output $y_e$ would be the total number of widgets produced and sold. Its equilibrium price level $p_e$ would be the price per widget.

In later chapters we will study why aggregate demand and supply curves shift, and how these shifts affect the economy's output, employment, and price level. We will find that there are different views on these matters and hence different schools of thought on how to deal with the problems of economic fluctuations (the business cycle), unemployment, and inflation—problems which will be described in the next chapter.

### CHECKPOINT 5-4
**Explain why the economy's aggregate demand curve is fundamentally different from a demand curve for a single good. Why is the aggregate demand curve negatively sloped?**

### SUMMARY

**1.** A mixed economy and the basic economic links between its three groups of decision-making units—businesses, households, and government—can be given a skeletal representation in a flow diagram. Such a diagram can show the flow of resources and of goods and services in exchange for money; flows of savings into the financial markets, where they are loaned to borrowers and spent on goods and services; and the flows of taxes, transfers, and expenditures linking the government to businesses and households.

**2.** Gross national product (GNP) is the market value of the economy's total output of final goods and services produced during a year.

**3.** GNP does not include so-called nonproductive transactions, such as the purchase and sale of used goods, the trading of stocks and bonds in financial markets, and private and public transfer payments. Certain productive nonmarket activities are included, such as the imputed rent on owner-occupied housing and the value of food produced and consumed by farm families. However, other activities are not included, such as the services performed by homemakers and the myriad tasks performed by do-it-yourselfers.

**4.** Money GNP, or GNP in current prices or dollars, measures the dollar value of GNP in a given year in terms of the prices at which final goods and services actually were sold in that year. Real GNP, or GNP in constant prices or dollars, measures the dollar value of GNP in a given year in terms of the prices at which final goods and services sold for in some base, or benchmark, year.

**5.** When calculating GNP, care must be taken to avoid double, or multiple, counting of intermediate goods.

**6.** GNP is an accounting measure and was never intended to be a welfare measure. GNP does not reflect changes in product quality or in the composition of output, nor does it take account of the costs of pollution or the benefits of leisure. Per capita GNP is a better indicator of an economy's welfare than GNP alone, but neither really tells us anything about the true distribution of any economy's output among its citizens.

**7.** The aggregate demand curve is negatively sloped and indicates that the economy's total demand for output is larger the lower the price level. The aggregate supply curve is positively sloped in the short run indicating that the economy's businesses will produce a larger quantity of total output the higher the price level. The intersection of the aggregate demand and supply curves determines the economy's equilibrium total output and price level.

## KEY TERMS AND CONCEPTS

aggregate demand curve
aggregate supply curve
deflation
depreciation allowance
financial markets
flow
gross national product (GNP)
inflation
money GNP
per capita GNP
price index
real GNP
retained earnings
transfer payments
value added

## QUESTIONS AND PROBLEMS

**1.** "Despite general agreement about the need for tremendous amounts of new capital, there is no consensus about how the money should be raised. Liberal economists generally favor more generous individual tax cuts . . . to stimulate consumer buying, which, in turn, creates heightened economic activity. Conservative economists . . . would prefer federal policies that would enable companies to keep more of their earnings either through higher depreciation allowances for the purchase of new equipment or a further lowering of the corporate tax rate."

In Figure 5–3, where would liberal economists' policies affect the flow diagram as contrasted with those of conservative economists?

**2.** Why is GNP a flow and inventory not a flow?

**3.** When we measure GNP, why is the problem of productive versus nonproductive transactions never an issue in the case of services (as distinct from goods)?

**4.** How is a transfer payment different from the purchase of a final good? Why is Christmas so "good for business" if gifts are merely private transfer payments?

**5.** Home milk delivery service used to be more common a generation ago than it is today, yet milk consumption per capita has not changed all that much in the meantime. What effect do you think the gradual decrease in home milk delivery has had on GNP and why?

**6.** For a number of years during the last third of the nineteenth century in the United States the general level of prices fell. Suppose you were told that GNP in current prices tripled over this period of time.

a. What would you be able to conjecture about the change in real GNP? (We do not in fact have GNP figures and price indices for this period that are of the quality of those constructed for the years since 1930.)

b. In 1870 the population of the United States was roughly 38.5 million, and by 1900 it was approximately 76 million. What would you be able to conjecture about the change in per capita real GNP over this period of time?

7. When measuring GNP, what similarity do you see between the problem of double, or multiple, counting and the problem of nonproductive market transactions?

8. It has been argued that the production of goods often gives rise to bad by-products, such as polluted rivers and air, whose costs to society are not included in the price of the final good. Suppose the average price of an automobile is $7,000. Suppose it would cost $1,000 to clean up the air and water pollution associated with the production of an automobile but that neither the auto company nor the buyer of the car has to pay the cost—the "mess" is simply not cleaned up. If the company were forced to clean up the mess, what would be the effect on money GNP? What would be the effect on real GNP? What do you think of the contention that GNP is such a "silly" measure that if allowance were made for the cost of bads, GNP actually would go up?

9. Indicate in Figure 5-3 where the various flows that constitute the economy's total demand for goods and services appear.

# 6

# Economic Fluctuations, Unemployment, and Inflation

**AFTER READING THIS CHAPTER, YOU WILL BE ABLE TO:**

1. Describe the way the economy moves over time.

2. Explain how the structure of the economy affects the business cycle.

3. Define the concepts of frictional, structural, and cyclical unemployment and the concept of full employment.

4. Describe the United States's recent experience with inflation.

5. Distinguish between anticipated and unanticipated inflation and explain who gains and who loses when inflation is unanticipated.

Economic fluctuations have been a major problem for our economy throughout its history, and unemployment and inflation are major costs associated with that problem. In this chapter we will concern ourselves with the nature of business cycles and the interrelated problems of unemployment and inflation. Much of our discussion in the following chapters will focus on trying to understand the causes of economic fluctuations, unemployment, and inflation. We will also look at various policies aimed at eliminating or at least reducing these problems.

## HOW THE ECONOMY MOVES

Even the most casual observer of our economy is aware that it seems to move by "fits and starts." Periods of rapid growth alternate with periods of slower growth or even contraction. These economic fluctuations, often referred to as business cycles, are most commonly recognized by their effects on unemployment, sales, and the behavior of prices—in particular the rate of inflation. Of course the business cycle is reflected in many other measures of economic activity as well.

### Growth and Fluctuations

Some idea of the way the economy moves is conveyed in part a of Figure 6–1 by the graph of real GNP (1972 dollars) since 1929. Two things are obvious. The economy grows over time, but there are irregular fluctuations in its rate of growth from one year to the next. The size of these fluctuations is further illustrated by the graph of the annual percentage changes in real GNP over this period of time, part b of Figure 6–1. Since World War II these fluctuations have been less violent than those of the 1930s or the 1940s. The size of the fluctuations during the 1930s was a reflection of unstable conditions resulting from the Great Depression. Those of the 1940s came about when the economy was converted to wartime during the first half of the decade and then reconverted to peacetime

during the second half. It is easy to see from part a of Figure 6–1 why one might describe the economy as "climbing a cliff and then resting on a plateau before climbing another cliff."

## The Business Cycle

The fluctuations in real GNP that are so clearly shown in part b of Figure 6–1 are often called **business cycles**. Comparing parts a and b of Figure 6–1, we can see that business cycles are a phenomenon quite separate from the growth trend in this aggregate measure of economic activity. The growth trend (of roughly 3.5 percent over this period) is represented by the horizontal broken line in the bottom graph. The business cycles during this period are represented by the irregular but recurrent up-and-down movement of the saw-toothed solid line about this trend. In general, *business cycles are irregular but recurrent patterns of fluctuations in economic activity. They are apparent in aggregate measures of sales, output, income, employment, and a host of other measures over a period of years, quite apart from any long-run trends in these series.*

### Phases of the Business Cycle

A hypothetical, idealized version of the business cycle, measured in terms of real GNP, is shown in Figure 6–2. The cycle may be viewed as having four phases: a peak, a recession, a trough, and an expansion. The **recession** phase corresponds to the contraction, or slowing down, of economic activity. During this phase unemployment rises while sales, income, and investment all fall. An unusually severe recession is sometimes called a **depression**, such as the Great Depression of the 1930s, which is so noticeable in Figure 6–1. The lower turning point of the business cycle is often called the **trough**. At this point economic conditions are at a low ebb. This is followed by an upturn in economic activity, or the **expansion** phase of the cycle. During this phase unemployment falls and sales, income, output, and capital formation all rise. This phase and the subsequent upper turning point or **peak** phase of the cycle are sometimes referred to as a "boom." Output, income, sales, and capital formation reach their highest levels while unemployment falls to its lowest level. Business and consumer optimism about the future typically rise throughout the expansion phase of the cycle and fall during the recession phase.

Comparison of the real world of Figure 6–1 with the hypothetical one of Figure 6–2 indicates that actual business cycles are not nearly as regular or periodic as the idealized picture presented in Figure 6–2. This is the reason real-world business cycles are often more accurately called business fluctuations—no two are ever quite alike. Furthermore, it is not always very clear when the economy is passing into another phase of the business cycle.

### Seasonal Variation

To get a clearer picture of business cycles, we have seen that it is helpful to abstract from any long-run trend that may be in the data. This is essentially what we did in part b of Figure 6–1. In addition, it is also helpful to adjust the data for **seasonal variation**. For example, general retail sales are typically high in December because of the Christmas holidays. On the other hand, sales of a particular good, air conditioners, are typically low at that time of the year but high during the summer months. From the standpoint of the business cycle we need to know how sales look after allowing for their typical seasonal behavior. "Raw" retail sales data typically rise from November to December in a given year. When we allow for the usual seasonal rise in these data at that time of year, we might find that retail sales have risen less than normally—for example, because the economy is in a recession.

How do statisticians adjust data to remove seasonal variation? Suppose past monthly sales data for air conditioners indicate that, on average, air conditioner sales in August are 1.9 times as high as average monthly sales

over the course of a year. Similarly, suppose air conditioner sales in February are only .7 times as large as average monthly sales over the course of a year. To remove the seasonal variation from the data, the statistician would divide the August sales figures by 1.9 and the February sales figures by .7. In similar fashion the sales figures for each month would be adjusted by such seasonal adjustment factors. The resulting sales figures are said to be *seasonally adjusted.*

One of the difficulties with seasonal adjustment is that seasonal variation patterns often change over time. Given that the seasonal adjustment factors are necessarily derived from past data, they are not able to account for these changes in the most recent data. Thus seasonal adjustment may not accurately remove the seasonal variation from these data.

### Duration of Cycles

The ups and downs of the U.S. economy have been traced by the National Bureau of Economic Research all the way back to 1854. From that date to the end of World War II, the National Bureau recognizes a total of 22 cycles. Characteristics of the duration of these cycles are summarized in Table 6–1. Measured from trough to trough the average duration was 49.5 months. The average length of the expansion phase was 28.9 months, and the average length of the recession phase was 20.6 months. On average the expansion phases of these cycles were about 1.5 times as long as the recession phases.

The eight cycles from the end of World War II up through 1983 had an average duration of 60 months. The average length of the expansion phase of these cycles was 44 months, and the average length of the recession phase was 11 months. The expansion phases of these cycles were four times as long as the recession phases on average.

While business cycles represent recurring patterns of expansion and recession, the sizeable differences shown in Table 6–1 between the shortest and longest indicate a significant degree of variability in their duration.

**FIGURE 6-1    Real GNP Fluctuates About a Long-Term Growth Trend**

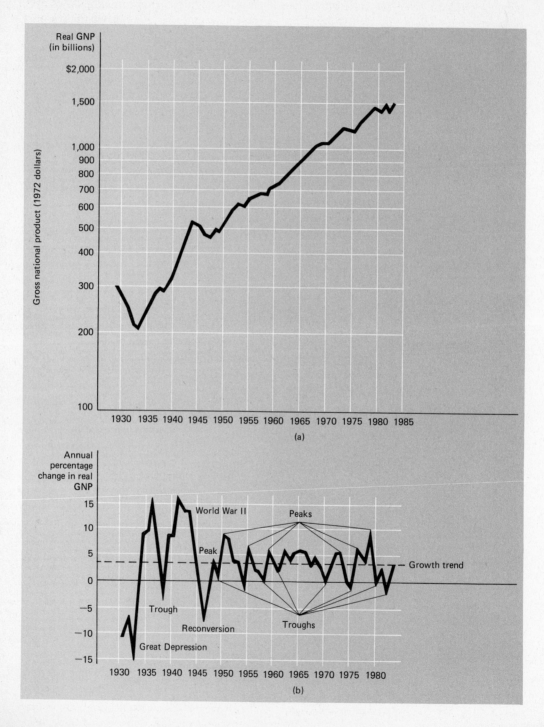

**FIGURE 6-2   Phases of the Business Cycle**

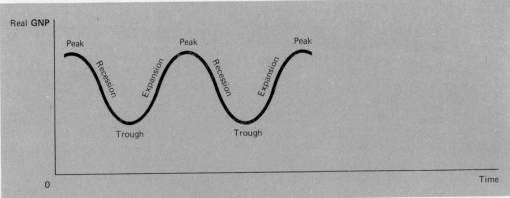

The two hypothetical business cycles shown here (measured in terms of real GNP) are idealizations. Actual business fluctuations are never quite this regular or periodic, and no two are ever quite this similar to each other.

The recession phase of the cycle corresponds to the contraction, or slowing down, of economic activity. During this phase unemployment rises while sales, income, output, and investment all fall, along with business and consumer optimism. The lower turning point is the trough of the cycle. Here economic activity is at its lowest ebb. In the ensuing expansion phase of the cycle sales, income, output, and investment all rise while unemployment falls. Business and consumer optimism are also on the rise throughout this phase. Finally the expansion loses steam at the upper turning point, or peak, and the cycle then repeats itself.

## CHECKPOINT* 6-1

**When we look at the graph in part a of Figure 6-1, it appears that the expansion phase of business cycles is a great deal longer than the recession phase. Would you agree with this assessment? Why or why not? What do you think the monthly seasonal adjustment factors for textbook sales would look like over the course of a year?**

*Answers to all Checkpoints can be found at the back of the text.

Part a shows real GNP (1972 dollars) since 1929. It fluctuates about a long-term growth trend.

Note that the vertical axis in part a is a logarithmic, or ratio, scale on which equal distances represent equal percentage changes. (Convince yourself by measuring that the distance from 600 to 900 equals that from 1,000 to 1,500.) If real GNP were plotted on an ordinary arithmetic scale, its plot would curve sharply upward because a given percentage change in a small number would be represented by a smaller distance than the same percentage change in a larger number.

The plot of the annual percentage changes in real GNP shown in part b gives a more vivid picture of the fluctuations in real GNP. These fluctuations are the so-called business cycles with their peaks and troughs. These fluctuations have been milder since the early 1950s by comparison with the 1930s and the turbulent war and postwar years of the 1940s.

## POLICY PERSPECTIVE

### Dating Business Cycle Peaks and Troughs—When Do They Occur?

How do we know when the expansion phase of a business cycle is over and a recession has begun, or when a recession is over and an expansion has begun? Such turning points in the business cycle become easier to recognize the more time passes after their occurrence. However there is an unavoidable arbitrariness in designating the dates of turning points because economic theory provides no hard and fast criteria.

Many economists and government officials are sympathetic to designations of turning points that focus on the behavior of real GNP. For example, a business cycle peak might be said to have occurred and the economy to be in a recession if real GNP does not grow for at least two quarters in a row. One might well ask why the criterion is not one quarter, or three

out of four, all of which points out the element of arbitrariness in any definition. Other important factors that economists often take into consideration are the behavior of the unemployment rate, the rate of investment spending on new plant and equipment, and the rate of capacity utilization in the manufacturing sector (that is, the degree to which the available stock of capital equipment is being used in production).

The National Bureau of Economic Research (NBER), a nonprofit organization, is recognized as the official designator of business cycle turning points. The NBER designates these dates by use of an elaborate system that takes account of the factors previously mentioned as well as numerous others. It defines a recession as three consecutive quarters of declining

**FIGURE P6-1    Real GNP and Officially Designated Peaks and Troughs in Business Cycles in the United States, 1976–1984** (Seasonally Adjusted Quarterly Data at Annual Rates)

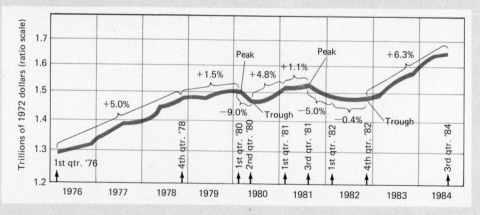

SOURCE: Federal Reserve Bank of St. Louis.

real GNP. Even the criteria used by the NBER have an element of arbitrariness, again reminding us that economic theory does not offer precise answers to the dating issue. The officially designated peaks and troughs associated with the two recessions of the early 1980s are shown along with real GNP in Figure P6–1.

### Questions

1. Some observers say that the two recessions of the early 1980s indicated in Figure P6–1 could really be viewed as just one larger recession. On the basis of the evidence in Figure P6–1 how would you defend this interpretation?

2. Consider the designated peaks and troughs in Figure P6–1. Does the location of any of them suggest that considerations other than the behavior of real GNP may have played prominently in making the designation? Why?

## Determinants of the Business Cycle

The characteristics of the business cycles of an economy will depend on the shocks that hit it and the way it is "put together"—the nature of its products, the structure of its markets, and the interconnecting relationships between its industries.

### Product Characteristics— Durables and Nondurables

Industries that produce durable goods— steel, machinery, motor vehicles, construction, consumer appliances, and so forth—experience much larger fluctuations in employment, production, and sales over the course

**TABLE 6-1 Average Duration of Business Cycles, Pre-World War II Period (1854–1945) and Postwar Period** (in Months)

|  | Pre–World War II 1854–1945 | Post–World War II 1945–1983 |
|---|---|---|
| Number of Cycles | 22 | 8 |
| Average Duration (Trough to Trough) | 49.5 | 56 |
| Length of Longest Cycle | 99 (1870–1879) | 118 (1961–1970) |
| Length of Shortest Cycle | 28 (1919–1921) | 28 (1980–1982) |
| Average Length of Expansions | 28.9 | 44 |
| Length of Shortest Expansion | 10 (1919–1920) | 12 (1980–1981) |
| Length of Longest Expansion | 80 (1938–1945) | 106 (1961–1969) |
| Average Length of Recessions | 20.6 | 11 |
| Length of Shortest Recession | 7 (1918–1919) | 6 (1980) |
| Length of Longest Recession | 65 (1873–1879) | 17 (1981–1982) |

of the business cycle than do industries that produce nondurable goods—textiles, food products, agricultural commodities, and so forth. The major reason for this lies precisely in the difference in the nature of durable and nondurable goods.

When the economy goes into a recession, unemployment rises. Businesses find themselves with idle productive capacity in the face of lagging sales as consumer and business optimism about the future declines. Consumers tend to make the old car or refrigerator last another year, particularly if they are unemployed or faced with increasing job uncertainty. Similarly, businesses make do with existing plant and equipment, especially since some of it is idled by the slowdown in sales and the accompanying buildup of unsold inventories. In short, when times are bad and a cloud of uncertainty shrouds the future, durable goods purchases will tend to be postponed. This is possible precisely because durable goods are durable. This, of course, means that a recession hits the durable goods industries especially hard.

By contrast, nondurable goods purchases cannot be put off nearly as long. People can't postpone eating, brushing their teeth, being sick, or heating their homes. They also seem very reluctant to cut back on smoking and other personal consumption habits. As a result history shows that during recessions nondurable goods industries do not experience nearly as severe a decline in employment, production, and sales as do the durable goods industries.

On the other hand, during business cycle expansions, durable goods purchases previously postponed are now carried out. Rising sales put increasing demands on productive capacity and businesses have a greater incentive to buy new equipment and expand plant size. Similarly, consumers have more job certainty, employment and paychecks rise, and more households are willing to replace the old car and refrigerator with new ones. As a result, durable goods purchases pick up at a faster rate than purchases of nondurables.

### Market Structure

Markets in which there are numerous firms competing with one another in the production and sale of a product tend to reduce prices more sharply in the face of declining demand than do markets dominated by a few large firms that have monopoly-type power. On the other hand, monopoly-type markets tend to reduce output and employment more sharply than do markets with numerous competing firms. In short, over the course of the business cycle, monopoly-type markets adjust to changing demand largely by changing production rather than by changing price. Highly competitive markets with numerous firms adjust largely by changing price rather than by changing output.

Monopoly-type market structures tend to prevail in durable goods industries such as steel, oil, electrical machinery, appliances, and automobiles. Each of these industries is dominated by less than 10 firms. (The auto industry is dominated by the well-known Big Three.) On the other hand, competitive market structures tend to prevail in nondurable goods industries such as agriculture and wearing apparel. There are literally tens of thousands of farmers, for example.

### Causes of Business Cycles

We have briefly examined a few of the important aspects of the economy's internal, or endogenous, structure that determine how it moves when it is subjected to external shocks. The nature of its products (durable versus nondurable), the structure of its markets (competitive versus monopolistic), and the interconnecting relationships between its industries are all important internal determinants of the economy's motion. In subsequent chapters we will examine other characteristics of the economy's internal structure that are also important determinants of the way it moves. These determinants affect the economy just as weight, size, and center of gravity affect the way a rocking horse moves when given a push.

Now we will briefly describe a few frequently cited explanatory factors underlying business cycles that are generally regarded as external, or exogenous, causes, like the push applied to a rocking horse. Among these factors are changes in population growth rates and migration trends; new inventions and technological developments; the discovery of new mineral deposits and energy sources; the opening up of new land frontiers; and political events and social upheavals, like wars.

Most of these factors are thought of as external to the workings of the economy—like the push given to the rocking horse. But it is often difficult to make a clear-cut distinction on this score. For example, increases in the population growth rate seem to be encouraged by economic expansion and dampened by recessions. However, this is a two-way street. Increases in the population growth rate tend to stimulate economic expansion, while decreases tend to slow down the growth of demand for goods and services. The same sort of two-way influences may exist for any of the so-called external factors listed above. Unstable economic conditions in post–World War I Germany may have contributed to the rise of Hitler and the advent of World War II, which in turn pulled the U.S. economy out of the depression years of the 1930s. On the other hand, the hike in oil prices by the Arab oil-exporting countries in 1973–1974 is viewed by many economists as an external shock to the U.S. economy that helped trigger the 1974–1975 recession—the second most severe recession in the postwar period.

Finally, the ebb and tide of optimism or confidence about the future—what Lord Keynes called "animal spirits"—is often cited as a crucial factor in the business cycle. For example, it is sometimes argued that optimism lost touch with reality in the late 1920s. This allegedly led to excessive speculation in land and stocks and to overinvestment in plant, equipment, and apartment and office buildings far beyond what demand warranted. When sober judgment finally set in, the economy was plunged into the deepest and longest depression in our history, and a mood of deep pessimism prevailed. At its depth in 1932 Franklin Roosevelt may have measured the main problem very well when he said, "The only thing we have to fear is fear itself."

---

**CHECKPOINT 6-2**

**Gardner Means did a study of the percentage drop in product price and the percentage drop in production in each of 10 industries during the onset and downturn of the Great Depression of the 1930s. These industries were textile products, agricultural implements, agricultural commodities, petroleum, motor vehicles, leather, cement, food products, iron and steel, and automobile tires. How do you think they ranked (1) in terms of the degree of price reduction he observed in each of them, and (2) in terms of the degree of output reduction?**

---

## UNEMPLOYMENT AND EMPLOYMENT

*The economy's* **labor force** *includes all persons over the age of 16 who are employed plus all those who are unemployed but actively looking for work.* The labor force in our economy amounts to more than half of the population over 16. While the labor force includes people in the military, unemployment is a problem that only afflicts the civilian labor force. Our discussion of unemployment and employment therefore focuses on the civilian labor force. In the discussion that follows, we will consider such questions as, Are there different types of unemployment? Is there such a thing as a normal level of unemployment, or what is full employment? What are the costs of unemployment?

## Types of Unemployment

A worker may become unemployed in basically three different ways. (1) The worker may quit his or her current job to look for a better job, giving rise to what is called *frictional unemployment*. (2) The worker's current job may be permanently eliminated—the plight of buggy whip makers at the turn of the century—possibly causing so-called *structural unemployment*. (3) The worker's current job may be temporarily eliminated by a recession, thus giving rise to *cyclical unemployment*. Let's look more closely at each of these types of unemployment.

### Frictional Unemployment

Many times, workers quit jobs to look for ones that pay better or are more attractive in some other way. In the meantime they are often unemployed for short periods of time while they are between jobs. Suppose, for example, that each worker in the labor force changed jobs once a year and was unemployed for a 2-week period while in transition. Suppose also that the number of workers changing jobs at any one time is spread evenly over the year. At any time during the year $2/52$, or 3.8 percent, of the labor force is thus unemployed, if there are no other causes of unemployment. If only half of the labor force switched jobs in this manner, the unemployment rate would be 1.9 percent.

Other forms of frictional unemployment are due to seasonal layoffs, such as those that affect farm workers and construction workers. New entrants into the labor force with marketable job skills are also frequently unemployed for a brief period of time before finding a job.

### Structural Unemployment

As the term *structural* implies, this kind of unemployment is due to fundamental changes in the structure of labor demand—specifically, the kinds of jobs that the economy offers. Technological change, the development of new industries and the demise of old ones, and the changing economic role of different regions in the country all mean that new kinds of jobs need to be done and that many old ones cease to exist. The new jobs often require different skills and educational backgrounds than the old ones and are frequently located in different geographic regions.

Workers often find themselves displaced by these structural changes. They may lack the required skills and training needed to gain employment in other areas of the economy. Often they are dismayed by the prospect of having to move away from old friends and familiar neighborhoods. As a result, they end up among the ranks of the long-term and hard-core unemployed. This is a particular problem among older workers, unskilled workers in declining economic regions such as Appalachia, and many unskilled, mostly black, youths trapped in decaying inner cities and depressed rural areas. In general, *the basic characteristic of the structurally unemployed is their lack of marketable skills*.

### Cyclical Unemployment

*Cyclical unemployment is caused by the business cycle.* When the economy's total demand for goods and services rises during the expansion phase of the cycle, employment rises and unemployment falls. During the recession phase of the cycle, total demand for goods and services falls, causing unemployment to rise and employment to fall. Cyclical unemployment looms large in the movement of the unemployment rate. This is illustrated in Figure 6–3 which compares the unemployment rates in peak years of the business cycle, 1973 and 1979, with the unemployment rates in the trough years, 1975 and 1982, following each peak. For each year the unemployment rate is broken into four components: job leavers—workers who quit their jobs voluntarily; new entrants—new workers just entering the labor force; reentrants—experienced workers who have dropped out of the labor force for some time but are again

**FIGURE 6-3  Cyclical Unemployment and the Unemployment Rate**

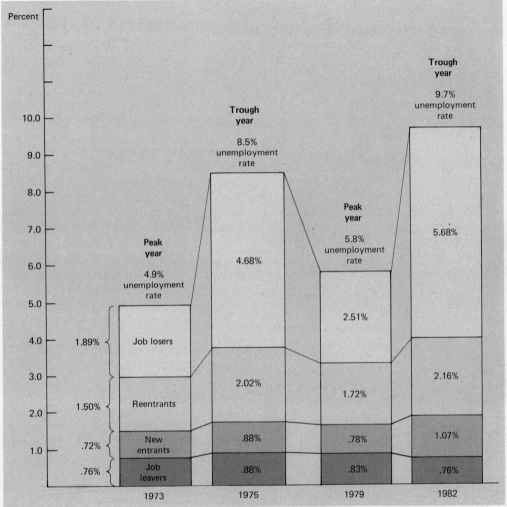

The change in the unemployment rate over the course of the business cycle from peak year to trough year is largely due to the change in the job losers component which reflects cyclical unemployment.

looking for work; and job losers—workers who are laid off or fired. The increase in the job loser category from peak year to trough year reflects cyclical unemployment and is clearly the major source of change in the overall unemployment rate over the course of the business cycle.

## Natural Rate of Unemployment— Or, What Is Full Employment?

It is clear from our discussion of frictional unemployment that full employment cannot mean that there is a zero rate of unemployment. *The general view among economists is that the existence of frictional unemployment and a certain amount of structural unemployment constitutes a natural rate of unemployment towards which the economy automatically gravitates in the absence of other disturbances.* Full employment is the level of employment associated with the natural rate of unemployment. In the early 1960s economists generally felt that full employment roughly corresponded to a 4 percent unemployment rate—what might be called the natural unemployment rate. Since that time the level of the natural unemployment rate has been revised upward. In recent years a number of economists have come to think that it may be somewhat more than 6 percent. Why is this? Should we be concerned? How we measure unemployment and the nature of the relationship between population growth and labor force growth have a lot to do with the answers to these questions.

### Measuring Unemployment

*The most commonly used definition of* **unemployment** *states that to be considered unemployed you must be out of work, looking for a job, and available to take one immediately.*

Some think this definition is too broad because it doesn't distinguish between those who need jobs to support themselves and their families and those who don't. Hence, critics say this measure overstates unemployment distress. They point out that a full-time student seeking part-time work or a job-seeking teenager living at home with two working parents counts just as much in this measure of unemployment as does a jobless head of household out of work for weeks. However, others argue that this measure understates unemployment because it doesn't include "discouraged" workers who have dropped out of the labor force after a prolonged, unsuccessful search for a job, nor does it include part-time workers who are looking for a full-time job.

### Population and Labor Force Growth

Longer-run changes in the size of the labor force relative to the size of the total popula-

tion have implications for the unemployment rate and the percent of the working-age population employed. So do longer-run changes in the age and sex makeup of the labor force.

If the size of the total population grows faster than the size of the labor force, the number of people demanding goods and services will grow faster than the number of people who want jobs. Other things remaining the same, this should tend to lower the unemployment rate. On the other hand, if the size of the labor force grows more rapidly than the size of the total population, the number of people wanting jobs increases faster than the number demanding goods and services. This will tend to increase the unemployment rate, other things remaining the same.

From the latter half of the 1960s up to the present, the U.S. economy has had to cope with a labor force that has grown faster than the total population—the labor force as a percentage of the total population has increased, as shown in Figure 6–4. In part this has been due to the maturing of the post-World War II "baby boom" generation, which has swelled the working-age population during these years. In addition, the proportion of working-age women who have moved into the labor force has increased dramatically. Whereas only about 33 percent of the country's population of adult females were in the labor force in the early years after World War II, somewhat more than 50 percent now work or are seeking work. Despite this, the economy has done quite well in providing jobs for these people. In the decade 1970–1980 total employment in the United States was up 23 percent while population was up 11.5 percent. In other words, total employment grew twice as fast as the total population. Job creation during the 1970–1980 decade resulted in a growth in employment nearly double that of the decade 1950–1960 and about 4 percentage points greater than that during the 1960–1970 decade. Employment increased 11.6 percent in 1950–1960, 19.5 percent in 1960–1970, and 23.4 percent in 1970–1980.

**FIGURE 6-4  Labor Force as Percentage of Total Population**

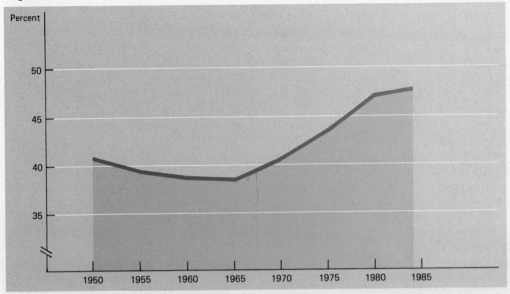

The labor force as a percentage of the total population has increased since the mid-1960s. This reflects the maturing "baby boom" generation entering the labor force, the increased participation of women in the labor force, and the decline in the birth rate since 1961.

On the negative side, many economists argue that the more rapid rate of growth of the labor force relative to that of the total population has contributed to a rise in the level of what should be considered the natural unemployment rate (the rate that corresponds to so-called full employment). They believe that the unusually large increase in the number of new job-seekers relative to the growth in the population pushes the level of frictional unemployment higher. Another possible factor in a higher natural unemployment rate is the increased flow into the public's pockets of nonpaycheck money—unemployment compensation, welfare money, and so on. This may well cause people who are really not trying very hard to get employed to list themselves as unemployed.

What is the meaning of all this for our interpretation of the unemployment rate? It is often assumed that an economy with an unemployment rate of 3 percent is healthier than one with an unemployment rate of 6 percent. Is this necessarily so? In 1953 the U.S. unemployment rate was only 2.9 percent while the percent of the working-age population (everyone over 16) employed was about 55 percent. In 1980 the unemployment rate was 7.1 percent, but the percent of the working-age population employed was 58.5. When the percent of the working-age population employed is considered along with the unemployment rate, the difference in the health of our economy (at least from the standpoint of jobs) between these two periods does not appear as great as when we compare the unemployment rates alone.

### The Costs of Unemployment

Labor is an essential factor of production in our economy. Consequently, the greater the total demand for goods and services, the higher is the level of employment and

**FIGURE 6-5** **The GNP Gap, the Unemployment Rate, and the Changing General Price Level Since 1952**

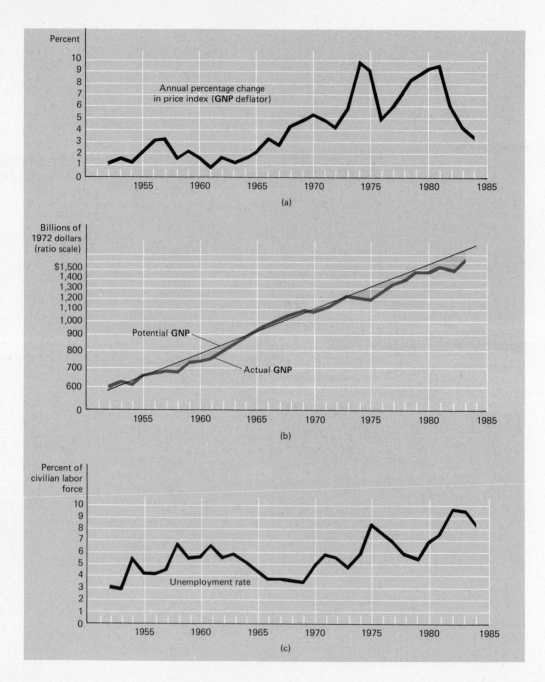

the lower the level of unemployment, given the available labor supply. Recall from Chapter 2 that unemployment exists whenever any available factors of production are idle. The term *available* is important. *Unemployment exists among laborers whenever there are laborers who make themselves available for work by actively looking for a job but are unable to find one.* For society as a whole, unemployment means fewer goods and services are produced, and a smaller pie means there is less available for all. This is the economic cost of unemployment. As a matter of public policy, unemployment is of particular concern because it also represents hardship for those unemployed. How might we measure these costs and hardships?

### Economic Cost: The GNP Gap

How can we measure the economic cost of unemployment to society? First we might estimate the economy's **potential GNP**, or what GNP would be if the economy were "fully" employed. We would then subtract actual GNP from potential GNP to get the GNP gap. *The **GNP gap** is the dollar value of final goods and services not produced because there is unemployment. The GNP gap is*

*therefore a measure of the cost of unemployment.*

Government economists have attempted to measure the GNP gap. Their measure (in constant 1972 dollars) of potential GNP and the associated GNP gap, equal to the difference between potential and actual GNP, is shown in Figure 6–5, part b. The unemployment rate is shown in Figure 6–5, part c. We can see by comparing the two graphs how the GNP gap widens when the unemployment rate rises and narrows when the unemployment rate falls. Indeed, during 1952 and 1953 (the Korean War years) and from 1966 through 1969 (the Vietnam War years) the unemployment rate was at its lowest levels and actual GNP exceeded potential GNP (the GNP gap was negative). This reflects the fact that the potential GNP does not represent the *maximum* GNP the economy can produce but rather that which it can produce at what is considered the normal level of unemployment. At the normal level of unemployment, the economy is considered to be operating at full employment. When the economy produces above its potential level, productive facilities are being utilized beyond their most efficient capacity levels and there is much overtime employment. The

---

The difference between potential and actual GNP since 1952 is the GNP gap shown in part b, expressed in constant 1972 dollars. This gap is a measure of the dollar value of final goods and services not produced because there is unemployment. In this sense it is a measure of the cost of unemployment.

Comparison of the behavior of the unemployment rate in part c with that of the GNP gap indicates how the unemployment rate rises when the GNP gap widens and falls when the GNP gap narrows. From 1966 through 1969, the Vietnam War years, the unemployment rate was at its lowest levels and actual GNP exceeded potential GNP (the GNP gap was negative). This reflects the fact that the potential GNP does not represent the maximum GNP the economy can produce but that which it can produce at some natural rate of unemployment.

Up through 1971 the annual percentage rise in the general price level (the GNP deflator), part a, tended to be larger when the GNP gap narrowed and the unemployment rate fell and smaller when the GNP gap widened and the unemployment rate rose. By contrast there was a dramatic jump in the percentage rise in the general price level in 1973, 1974, and 1975, accompanied by an unprecedented widening in the GNP gap. The pre-1971 pattern has since reemerged. In particular note the dramatic drop in the percentage change in the general price level that accompanied the widening GNP gap in the early 1980s.

unemployment rate is squeezed below what is considered its normal level.

The GNP gap for the years in which the economy operated below its potential is indicated by the shaded areas in Figure 6–5, part b. These areas represent the economic costs of unemployment, measured in constant 1972 dollars. For 1954 these costs amounted to $16 billion. For the years from 1955 through 1964 the cumulative GNP gap amounted to $237 billion. From 1970 through 1972 it amounted to $83.9 billion, from 1974 through 1980 to $500.5 billion, and from 1980 through 1983 it came to $496.6 billion. The large costs of the years since 1974 reflect the deepest recessions and highest unemployment rates of the postwar years.

### Other Costs of Unemployment

The burden of unemployment is obviously more severe if you happen to be one of the unemployed than if you are among the employed. And different groups in the labor force tend to have a higher incidence of unemployment than others. For example, in 1982, when our economy experienced its highest rate of unemployment since World War II, the overall unemployment rate for the civilian labor force was 9.7 percent. Yet among whites the unemployment rate was 8.6 percent, while among blacks it was 17.3 percent. Among those over 20 years of age the unemployment rate was roughly 8.5 percent, while among teenagers, the newest entrants to the labor force, it was a whopping 23.2 percent.

Aside from those aspects of unemployment that can be quantified, there is a social pathology associated with unemployment that is more difficult to measure. The unemployed worker often suffers a loss of self-esteem. Medical researchers have reported findings suggesting that anxiety among unemployed workers leads to health problems and family squabbles. Severely prolonged unemployment of family breadwinners often leads to broken homes and desertion. History

suggests that high unemployment rates tend to spawn political and social unrest, and that more than one social order has been upset for want of jobs. The high unemployment rates among black teenagers in our cities has had a lot to do with the sense of hopelessness, desperation, and anger that leads to high crime rates in city streets and occasionally to the looting and burning of whole neighborhoods.

### CHECKPOINT 6-3

**Comparing parts b and c of Figure 6–5, what appears to be the level of the natural unemployment rate on which the estimate of potential GNP, the full employment level of GNP, is based?**

## PRICE CHANGE AND INFLATION

The burden of unemployment falls most heavily and obviously on those who are unemployed. Inflation, while often more subtle, affects virtually everybody. This happens because **inflation** *is a pervasive rise in the general level of prices of all goods and services. Inflation, therefore, reduces the purchasing power of money.* The term inflation is not used when the prices of just a few goods rise. Rather, inflation refers to a situation in which the average of all prices rises. (Deflation is just the opposite of inflation—the average of all prices falls.) When we discussed the difference between money GNP and real GNP in the previous chapter, we saw that inflation means a dollar will purchase fewer goods tomorrow than it does today.

### Recent Experience with Inflation

The annual percentage change in a measure of the general price level (the GNP deflator) for the years since 1952 is shown in Figure 6–5, part a. Note that the general price level has gone up, though at different rates, in almost every year over this period.

It is interesting to compare the size of these percentage increases with the changes in the size of the GNP gap, Figure 6–5, part b, and the unemployment rate, Figure 6–5, part c. Roughly speaking, up through 1971 the percentage rise in the general price level tended to be smaller when the GNP gap widened and the unemployment rate rose—when the economy had more excess capacity. This has long been regarded as the conventional pattern in the relationship between inflation, the GNP gap, and the unemployment rate.

However, the dramatic jump in the percentage rise in the general price level in 1973, 1974, and 1975 was accompanied by an unprecedented degree of widening in the GNP gap. In other words, the economy experienced a severe period of inflation during a deep recession. This unconventional combination of events has given rise to the term *stagflation,* which means the occurrence of economic stagnation combined with high rates of inflation. Since 1976 the conventional relationship between inflation and the GNP gap appears to hold again. For example, note the decline in the percentage change in the general price level associated with the widening GNP gap in the early 1980s. In subsequent chapters we will examine explanations of the conventional pattern of the relationship between inflation and unemployment, as well as explanations of the pattern known as stagflation.

## Anticipated Versus Unanticipated Inflation

Inflation is sometimes said to be the most effective, continuously operating thief. It steals the purchasing power of your money whether you hold it in your hand, your wallet, your checking account, or even in the vault of a bank. People have an incentive to protect themselves from inflation just as they have an incentive to protect themselves from theft of any kind. And they will attempt to do so if they anticipate or expect inflation. It is when they fail to anticipate inflation that they are most often hurt by it.

## Anticipated Inflation and Contracts: Indexing

The terms of a great many economic transactions are stated in dollars and are spelled out in a contract to which all parties to the transaction agree. Labor unions and management agree to a labor contract stipulating the hourly wage rate to be paid, along with other conditions of employment—length of workweek, amount of paid vacation, and so on. Loan contracts set out the terms of loans mutually agreed to by borrowers and lenders. These terms include the amount of a loan, the interest rate to be paid by the borrower, and the rights of each party in the event of default. Pension plans, insurance policies, rent leases, construction contracts, and contracts to produce and deliver goods to a customer by a certain date at a certain price are all examples of such contracts.

When one or both parties anticipate inflation, they will attempt to account for it explicitly in the terms of the contract. If it is a labor contract and the union anticipates inflation, it may press to have a cost-of-living allowance (COLA) clause in the contract. Such a clause **indexes** wages to the rate of inflation by stipulating that if the general price level rises by $x$ percent, then the hourly wage rate must be increased by $x$ percent as well. Suppose the union fails to anticipate inflation and agrees to a $5 per hour money wage rate over the next 2 years. The onset of a 10 percent rate of inflation would mean that the real, or constant dollar, wage would fall to $4.50 by the end of the first year. In other words, the money wage of $5 would only have 90 percent of the purchasing power it had at the beginning of the contract. At the end of 2 years the money wage of $5 would only have roughly 81 percent of its original purchasing power. If the union had insisted on a cost-of-living clause in the contract, the money wage at the end of the first year would be $5.50. At the end of the second year it would be roughly $6.05. The real wage would then remain $5—5 constant dollars. Figure 6–6 shows that when the infla-

**FIGURE 6-6** **The Inflation Rate and the Percent of Unionized Workers Covered by Indexed Wages**

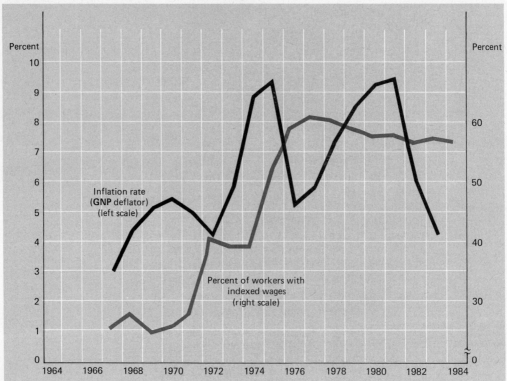

When the inflation rate increased in the late 1960s and early 1970s so did the percent of unionized workers with wages indexed to the inflation rate by cost-of-living allowance (COLAs) clauses in their collective bargaining agreements.

SOURCE: Various issues of the *Monthly Labor Review* (U.S. Department of Labor).

tion rate increased in the late 1960s and early 1970s unionized workers began to anticipate inflation by demanding and getting indexation of their wages to the inflation rate, in the form of cost-of-living allowance (COLA) clauses in their collective bargaining agreements.

In sum, *it is not only money (cash and checking accounts) that is robbed of purchasing power by inflation, but any contract that is stated in terms of dollars. If the inflation is anticipated, the terms of the contract can be set* *to protect its real value from the erosion of inflation.*

### Gainers and Losers from Unanticipated Inflation

We can see that if inflation is correctly anticipated, people can try to take steps to protect themselves against it. Unfortunately, the world is an uncertain place. What is anticipated is often different from what occurs. *The amount of inflation that occurs that is un-*

*expected is* **unanticipated inflation**. *Whenever there is unanticipated inflation, there are both gainers and losers.* Who are they?

1. *Creditors versus debtors.* Suppose A, the creditor or lender, lends $100 to B, the debtor or borrower, at a 10 percent rate of interest for 1 year. We will assume that A entered into this loan agreement anticipating that there would be no inflation over the year. This means that A, the creditor, was induced to lend $100 of purchasing power by the prospect of getting back $110 of purchasing power 1 year from now. Conversely, B, the debtor, is willing to agree to pay A $110 of purchasing power 1 year from now in order to get $100 of purchasing power today.

Suppose that over the course of the year there actually is a 20 percent rise in the general price level—a 20 percent rate of inflation—that was completely unanticipated by A. Now when B pays $110 at the end of the year, as stipulated by the loan agreement, this $110 has only about 90 percent of the purchasing power of the original $100 that A lent B. The 20 percent rate of inflation more than offsets the 10 percent rate of interest on the loan. As it turns out, A has given up more purchasing power than A actually gets back. Due to unanticipated inflation, A has suffered a loss. B, on the other hand, ends up paying back less purchasing power than was originally received. Because of unanticipated inflation, B has gained. B's gain in purchasing power is just equal to A's loss. A would never have entered into the loan agreement with B had A known that this was going to be the outcome. B in effect has ended up getting a loan on much more favorable terms than would have been possible had A correctly anticipated the inflation.

*Whenever there is unanticipated inflation, there is a redistribution of wealth from creditors to debtors that would not have occurred if the inflation had been anticipated.*

2. *Fixed-income groups.* We have noted how a labor union anticipating inflation would like to get a cost-of-living clause in its union contract. Indeed, all those anticipating inflation would want to ensure that their real income would not be reduced by inflation. For example, many retired people have found that their pension plans do not have a provision for this. The dollar incomes they receive do not rise with inflation and their real incomes therefore fall. The same thing can happen to any group of individuals in our economy who fail to anticipate inflation or who fail to anticipate it sufficiently. People with fixed-dollar incomes lose ground relative to those whose dollar incomes rise right along with any increase in the general price level. The fixed-dollar income group's claim on a share of the economy's total pie falls relative to those whose dollar incomes keep pace with inflation.

3. *Fixed-dollar versus variable-dollar assets.* We have seen that if you lend out money (enter into a loan contract) but fail to anticipate a rise in the general price level, you can end up getting back a smaller amount of purchasing power than you initially bargained for. There are a number of assets that have fixed-dollar values that give them this property.

If you put $100 into a savings account at your local bank, you can subsequently withdraw the $100 plus the initially stipulated rate of interest at any time. If in the meantime there is an unanticipated rate of inflation, you will not get back the amount of purchasing power you had counted on. There are several kinds of **fixed-dollar assets**—money, bonds, bank loans to businesses and consumers, and in general *any kind of asset that guarantees a repayment of the initial dollar amount invested plus some stipulated rate of interest* (zero in the case of money). Parties who make these kinds of investments without anticipating inflation end up recovering an amount of purchasing power less than they had bargained for.

On the other hand, there are many assets, **variable-dollar assets**, that *do not guarantee the owner any fixed-dollar value that may be recovered.* Such assets are also frequently called real assets. If you buy a piece of land, you can get rid of it any time, but only at what you can sell it for. The same is true of a share of stock in a corporation (an indirect ownership of a real asset), a painting, an automobile, a house, or an antique. When there is an inflation, these assets can frequently (but not always) be sold at prices that are higher than their original purchase price by an amount that reflects the increase in the general price level. People owning these kinds of assets do not necessarily lose purchasing power as do those holding fixed-dollar assets such as money, savings accounts, and bonds. Consequently *an unanticipated inflation will result in a loss of wealth on holdings of fixed-dollar assets and often in little or no loss of wealth on variable-dollar assets.* Fixed-dollar asset holders may thus lose relative to variable-dollar asset holders. Since many people own some of each kind, whether they are net gainers or losers will depend largely on the relative proportions of the total assets they hold in each.

### Unanticipated Inflation and Uncertainty

It is often argued that inflation isn't necessarily bad provided it occurs at a constant rate that everyone comes to anticipate. Then all parties can make their plans and enter into economic transactions on terms that fully take account of the inflation. There will be no gainers and losers, no unplanned redistributions of income and wealth such as occur when there is unanticipated inflation.

When there is uncertainty about what the rate of inflation may be, fear of the consequences of unanticipated inflation make it harder for businesses and consumers to make plans. This puts a damper on the economy's ability to operate at a full-employment level—to close the GNP gap. Thus, one of the major goals of economic policy is price stability.

In sum, *price stability is one of the major goals of economic policy because (1) it is necessary in order to avoid the arbitrary redistribu-* *tion of wealth that results from unanticipated inflation, and (2) by reducing uncertainty about inflation it enhances the economy's ability to operate at its full-employment potential.*

---

### CHECKPOINT 6-4
**Deflation is the opposite of inflation. Explain how an unanticipated deflation would affect the distribution of wealth between creditors and debtors, and between fixed-income groups and nonfixed-income groups. If inflation "steals" money, what does deflation do? When you look at parts a and b of Figure 6–5 for the years 1972–1976, can you think of a possible reason for the severity of the 1973–1974 recession based on inflationary considerations?**

---

### WHERE DO WE GO FROM HERE?

We noted at the outset that the business cycle, unemployment, and inflation are all more or less interrelated problems. In the following chapters, we will examine how modern economics attempts to analyze their causes. This will require that we become more familiar with the institutional structure of the economy as well as with some tools of economic analysis. Ultimately, we want to grapple with the following sorts of issues: How do government deficits affect the economy? Can monetary and fiscal policy effectively put a damper on business fluctuations? Is there a trade-off between inflation and unemployment? (That is, can we reduce the amount of one of them only if we are willing to have more of the other?) Why is it that during the 1970s our economy was plagued with recessions and their accompanying high unemployment while suffering from inflation at the same time—the so-called problem of stagflation (the simultaneous existence of stagnation and inflation)?

## POLICY PERSPECTIVE

### The Consumer Price Index— Does It Measure the Cost of Living or What?

Probably the most commonly used and widely publicized measure of the general level of prices in the economy is the **consumer price index** (CPI) compiled by the Department of Labor, Bureau of Labor Statistics (BLS). The rate of inflation is often measured as the percentage rate of change in the CPI. Very often the press, politicians, and people in general interpret the CPI as a measure of the "cost-of-living," and changes in the CPI as changes in the cost of living. However, examination of the way the CPI is constructed reveals that change in the CPI may be a misleading measure of the actual change in the cost of living.

#### The Market Basket

The CPI is a weighted average of the prices of a market basket of goods and services purchased by a typical urban worker's family. The weights are calculated as equal to the proportions of a typical worker's expenditures made on food, clothing, housing, medical care, and so on, based on a BLS survey of urban workers' families in 1972 and 1973.

One problem with viewing changes in the CPI as changes in the cost of living is immediately obvious. While construction of the CPI for any subsequent year (after 1973) uses the subsequent year's prices for each expenditure category, the weights used are still those for 1972–1973. However, we know that expenditure patterns change over time, a fact that the CPI ignores. How does this bias the CPI as a tool for measuring changes in the cost of living? When the prices of different goods change relative to one another consumers tend to spend more on goods that have become relatively cheaper, less on those

now relatively more expensive and, as shown in Figure P6–2, differences in the amount of price change between different kinds of goods and services have been substantial. By not changing the weights in the CPI to reflect this fact, over time the CPI increasingly overstates the importance of the relatively higher priced goods. Therefore the CPI, and change in the CPI, is biased upward.

#### Changing Composition and Quality of Market Basket

Another problem with the CPI is due to the fact that many items consumers buy today were not available in the 1972–1973 period and are therefore not represented at all in the calculation of today's CPI. A somewhat similar problem arises from the fact that the CPI does not take account of changes in the quality of goods and services. Typically, higher-quality items cost more. For example, a jet plane capable of carrying 120 passengers costs more than yesteryear's propeller-driven aircraft of the same capacity, though the jet aircraft may cut travel time in half. Hence, the price per constant-quality unit of a 120-passenger aircraft has not gone up nearly as much as the price of such a plane. Similarly today's medical care is much better than in the past (some drugs and cures weren't even available), and much more expensive as well. But again, the price per constant-quality unit of medical care has not gone up nearly as much (if at all) as the quality unadjusted price of medical care used in the CPI. The lack of adjustment for quality improvement in the goods and services represented in the CPI is another source of upward bias in that price index.

**FIGURE P6-2** **Percentage Increase in Prices of Major Expenditure Classes of the Consumer Price Index, 1972–1983**

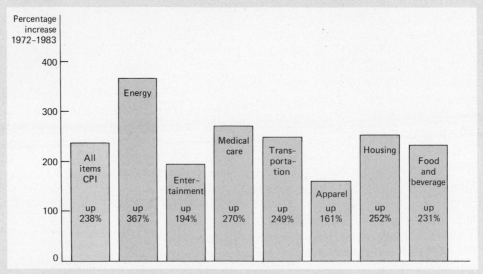

SOURCE: U.S. Department of Labor, Bureau of Labor Statistics.

### CPI Overstates Inflation

Because of the above considerations, as well as others, the evidence suggests that on balance the CPI overstates the rate of inflation. However, there has been opposition to altering the way the CPI is constructed. In particular, organized labor opposed any such change because labor tends to benefit from a high reported rate of inflation. Upward cost-of-living adjustments to wages are geared to cost-of-living clauses in union contracts. And these adjustments are typically tied to changes in the CPI. Organized labor also expressed opposition to construction of a broader index that would cover everyone in the economy, and not just urban wage earners and clerical workers. Again labor knew that a broader index would not show as high a rate of inflation, and cost-of-living clauses in union contracts tied to a broader index would not be as beneficial

to union wage increases. The BLS struck a compromise after pressure from organized labor and in 1977 started publishing two indexes. One is an updated version of the old CPI, covering urban wage earners and clerical workers. The new index is a more inclusive CPI covering all urban households.

### Questions

1. On the basis of the evidence in Figure P6–2 which expenditure class's price increase probably tends to cause the CPI to overstate the cost of living in the Sun Belt relative to the rest of the country?

2. On the basis of the evidence in Figure P6–2 which expenditure class's price behavior has been such as to most likely lead to an understatement of the importance of those goods in the market basket over time?

## POLICY PERSPECTIVE

### Wage-Price Controls—A Difficult Way to Curb Inflation

**Wage-price controls** are governmentally enforced limits on the rate at which wages and prices are allowed to increase. Buyers and sellers engaging in transactions at prices and wages higher than the limit are subject to prosecution under the law. While wage-price controls have often been used during wartime, the emergence of an accelerating inflation during the late 1960s and early 1970s led the Nixon administration to impose controls for the first time during peacetime (in the United States)—with varying degrees of enforcement effort and debatable results. Many other countries have also tried wage-price controls policies to deal with inflation since World War II. But despite their ready appeal—simply make inflation illegal—controls are difficult to enforce and can be evaded in ways that render them ineffective inflation fighters.

#### The Incentive to Evade

The basic reason why controls are hard to enforce is illustrated in Figure P6–3, which shows the demand curve $D$ and supply curve $S$ for a typical market in the economy. (You may want to review briefly the discussion of market demand and supply in Chapter 4.) If the market were allowed to operate freely, the equilibrium price and quantity would be $p_e$ and $Q_e$, respectively, corresponding to the intersection of the demand curve $D$ and the supply curve $S$ at point $e$. However, suppose price controls make it illegal for suppliers in this market to charge a price higher than $p_c$. At the price $p_c$ suppliers are only willing to supply the quantity $Q_s$, corresponding to point $c$ on $S$, while buyers will demand a quantity $Q_d$, corresponding to point $a$ on $D$. With the price held down to $p_c$, there will be a persistent shortage, equal to $Q_d$ minus $Q_s$, and frus-

trated buyers who cannot get as much of the good as they want. Since these buyers are willing to pay a higher price to get more of the good, there is an economic incentive for suppliers to evade the price controls, even though they run the risk of getting caught breaking the law. Obviously, the effectiveness of price controls

**FIGURE P6–3  The Economic Incentive to Evade Price Controls**

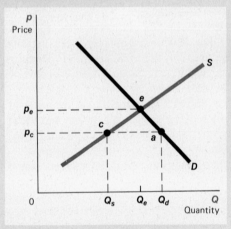

In a typical freely functioning market, the equilibrium price $p_e$ and quantity $Q_e$ are determined by the intersection of demand curve $D$ and supply curve $S$ at point $e$. The existence of price controls forbidding suppliers to sell their product at a price higher than $p_c$ would lead them to supply quantity $Q_s$ to the market, corresponding to point $c$ on $S$. Buyers would demand the larger amount $Q_d$, corresponding to point $a$ on $D$, resulting in a persistent shortage equal to $Q_d$ minus $Q_s$. The existence of frustrated buyers willing to pay a higher price for the good gives suppliers an economic incentive to evade price controls. Hence, the effectiveness of price controls depends on how intensively the government polices them to detect evasion.

will depend on how intensively the government polices them to detect evasion.

The same is true of wage controls. Suppose that employers' demand for labor in a particular labor market is represented by the demand curve $D$ in Figure P6–3, while $S$ is the supply curve of labor. If wage controls prohibit employers from paying a wage higher than $p_c$, there will be a shortage of labor equal to $Q_d$ minus $Q_s$. Frustrated employers will be tempted to evade the wage control and pay a higher wage in order to get more labor. And, of course, more workers will be induced to offer their services if they can get a higher wage.

### Enforcement and Evasion

The U.S. economy produces literally millions of different kinds of products varying in complexity from hairpins to 747 jets. To enforce price controls on every one of them would take an army of enforcement agents. We can get some idea of the magnitude of the problem of enforcing wage-price controls by considering a few examples of how such evasion can occur.

#### Price-Control Evasion Through Product Change

Producers can effectively evade controls by changing the product without changing the price. For example, the typical automobile contains around 15,000 different parts. If the price of automobiles is controlled, the producer can substitute a cheaper plastic part for a metal part here, use a little less or a cheaper grade fabric there, and so on. The outside of the car may look the same but the inside of the car can be changed in numerous ways. While the overall price of the car hasn't increased, the quality and durability of the car that is purchased at that price has been lessened. In a simple product such as a 10-cent pack of gum, the size of the gum sticks could be reduced. Whether the product is simple or complex, changes like these mean that consumers are getting less for their money—and that's inflation, controls or no controls. Such changes mean that reported price data for the consumer price index (CPI) may not rise above control limits. Hence, the rate of inflation measured by the rise in the CPI will appear to slow down as a result of the controls, but product quality changes spurred by the controls make this a false impression. The rate of decline in what you are getting for your money may not have slowed down at all. In truth, properly measured, the upward trend in inflation may be unaffected by controls.

#### Wage-Control Evasion— Reducing Actual Work Hours

Evasion of wage controls can take place in a similar fashion. An enforcement agent who periodically inspects company payrolls may find that hourly wages are not in violation of wage controls. However, in competing with one another to hire various kinds of labor services, companies may well resort to giving workers longer lunch and coffee breaks, longer paid vacations, and more paid holidays. While recorded hourly wages may be held in check by the enforcement of wage controls, the amount of hours *actually* worked will be less. Total hours on the job are different than hours actually worked. In effect, the same number of dollars spent on wages is buying fewer hours of actual work. Again, wages per actual hour of work—measured to take account of all these ways of evading controls—would reveal that in truth wages are increasing at a rate in excess of that allowed by controls. Like prices, recorded wages may appear to be held in check by controls when in reality wages per actual hour worked are rising more rapidly. And the latter is the meaningful measure of inflation. Reported prices and wages can really disguise, even hide altogether, the true rate of inflation.

#### Questions

1. Give some examples of products for which it would be difficult to evade

price controls through product change.

2. How would the degree to which a good is subject to product change affect the observed shortage associated with price control?

## SUMMARY

**1.** The economy grows through time but exhibits fluctuations about its growth trend called business cycles. The four phases of the business cycle—recession, trough, expansion, peak—may vary considerably in magnitude and duration from one cycle to the next, and no two cycles are ever exactly alike.

**2.** The business cycle affects different industries and segments of the economy in varying degrees. Durable goods industries tend to experience larger fluctuations than nondurable goods industries. These are usually industries with a few large, dominant (monopoly-type) firms that tend to have larger fluctuations in output and employment than in product price. Industries with many small competitive firms tend to show larger fluctuations in product price than in output and employment—typically these are nondurable goods industries.

**3.** While many determinants of the business cycle reflect the internal structure of the economy, others are considered exogenous (external). The distinction is not always clear-cut, however.

**4.** Three basic types of unemployment may be identified: frictional, structural, and cyclical. There are several measures of unemployment along with considerable controversy over which is the most appropriate one. There is reason to believe that the economy's so-called natural rate of unemployment has risen since World War II.

**5.** The greater the economy's total demand for goods and services, the greater the total demand for labor needed to produce them. As a result, the level of employment is higher and the level of unemployment is lower. One measure of the cost of unemployment is the GNP gap, the dollar value of the goods and services not produced when there is idle labor. Though often hard to measure, there are also psychological and social costs associated with unemployment. Moreover, the burden of unemployment is quite unevenly distributed among different groups in our economy.

**6.** Inflation is a rise in the general level of prices of all goods and services. Inflation reduces the purchasing power of money. The effects of anticipated inflation will be accounted for in the terms of economic contracts of all kinds.

**7.** Unanticipated inflation will result in a loss of purchasing power (wealth and income) among creditors, fixed-dollar income groups, and fixed-dollar asset holders. It results in an arbitrary redistribution of income and wealth. Uncertainty about inflation breeds a fear of these consequences of unanticipated inflation, and this inhibits the economy's ability to perform at its full-employment potential. For these reasons price stability is a major goal of economic policy.

**8.** The consumer price index (CPI) is a measure of the general level of prices in the economy, and as such is often interpreted as a measure of the "cost of living." The CPI most likely overstates the rate of inflation because the market basket weights are changed infrequently, new products are not included, and there is no allowance for the changing quality of the goods included in the market basket.

**9.** Wage-price controls make it illegal to increase wages and prices beyond limits set by government. Controls are difficult and costly to enforce because they cause shortages. Frustrated buyers willing to pay a higher price for the good give suppliers an economic incentive to evade controls. In addition to selling at prices above the legal limit, evasion can take the form of changing product quality and the compensation of labor in ways that effectively reduce the quantity of work actually performed for the same wage.

## KEY TERMS AND CONCEPTS

business cycles
consumer price index (CPI)
depression
expansion
fixed-dollar assets
GNP gap
indexing
inflation
labor force
peak
potential GNP
recession
seasonal variation
trough
unanticipated inflation
unemployment
variable-dollar asset
wage-price controls

## QUESTIONS AND PROBLEMS

**1.** Can you give reasons why the average length of business cycle expansions should be longer than the average length of recessions, as indicated in Table 6–1?

**2.** How would you expect changes in the size of the armed forces to affect potential GNP? How would failure to take account of this manifest itself in Figure 6–5, part b?

**3.** Suppose you are an interviewer in an unemployment office. As a practical matter, how would you distinguish the frictionally unemployed from the cyclically unemployed from the structurally unemployed?

**4.** Since the early 1960s the growth rate of the total population has been considerably lower than it was during the 1950s and late 1940s—the years of the so-called baby boom. Assuming that the population growth rate remains constant at its present lower level, what are the implications for unemployment in the early part of the twenty-first century?

**5.** In the event of an unanticipated inflation, which of the following assets would you prefer to own: a stamp collection, savings bonds, cash, a collection of old English coins, common stock, a fast-food restaurant, a contract to deliver towels and linen to a hotel chain, a deposit in a savings and loan bank, a mortgage on your neighbor's house?

**6.** How does inflation affect fixed-dollar income groups? What does it do to their share of real GNP?

# APPENDIX The Accelerator Principle

## THE ACCELERATOR PRINCIPLE: AN INSIGHT

We have argued that one reason durable goods industries experience more severe fluctuations than nondurable goods industries is that durable goods purchases can be put off more easily than nondurable goods purchases. The so-called *accelerator principle* provides yet another insight into the causes of this greater variability in durable goods industries.

### An Example

The way the accelerator principle works is perhaps best illustrated by an example. Suppose we consider the relationship between shoe sales by the shoe industry (a nondurable or semidurable goods industry) and the sale of shoemaking machines by the shoe machinery industry (a durable goods industry). We will assume that in order to produce $1,000 worth of shoes the shoe industry needs to have roughly $2,000 worth of shoe machinery. In other words, the production of $1 worth of the nondurable good requires the aid of approximately $2 worth of the durable good. What does this say about the relationship between changes in the year-to-year level of shoe sales and changes in the year-to-year level of the sales of shoe machines?

An answer to this question is given by the data in Table A6–1. In year 1, retail shoe sales are $10 million (column 1). The shoe industry uses $20 million worth of shoe machinery (column 2) to produce this quantity of shoes. We will assume that it has this stock of shoe machinery on hand at the beginning of year 1, so that it does not need to *add* to its capital stock of shoe machines during year 1. Net investment in shoe machinery is therefore zero (column 3). Suppose, however, that $2 million worth of shoe machines wear out every year. The shoe industry must therefore buy $2 million of shoe machines from the shoe machine industry for replacement (column 4). Hence in year 1, shoe industry output and sales are $10 million (column 1), while the shoe machine industry's output and sales are $2 million (column 4).

Now suppose that in year 2 annual retail shoe sales increase by 30 percent to $13 million (column 1). The shoe industry now needs $26 million worth of shoe machines (column 2) to produce this amount of shoes. Hence the additional $3 million of shoe production means the industry must add $6 million worth of new shoe machinery (column 3) to its stock of shoe machines. This plus the annual replacement of $2 million worth of shoe machinery brings total shoe machine sales to $8 million (column 4). The upshot is that a 30 percent increase in shoe industry sales between years 1 and 2 causes a 300 percent increase in the sales of the shoe machine industry. In other words, there is an accelerator effect.

When shoe sales rise by 54 percent to $20 million in year 3 (column 1), the shoe industry needs $40 million worth of shoe machinery (column 2). Therefore net investment in shoe machinery rises to $14 million (column 3). This plus replacement expenditures

**TABLE A6-1 The Accelerator Principle:**
**Retail Shoe Sales and Shoe Machine Sales**
(Hypothetical Data in Millions of Dollars)

| | Shoe Industry | | | Shoe Machine Industry |
|---|---|---|---|---|
| | (1) | (2) | (3) | (4) |
| | Annual Retail Shoe Sales | Stock of Capital: Shoe Machines[a] | NI = Net Investment in Shoe Machines | Sale of Shoe Machines = NI + Replacement |
| Year 1 | $10 | $20 | $ 0 | $ 0 + $2 = $ 2 |
| Year 2 | 13 | 26 | 6 | 6 + 2 = 8 |
| Year 3 | 20 | 40 | 14 | 14 + 2 = 16 |
| Year 4 | 27 | 54 | 14 | 14 + 2 = 16 |
| Year 5 | 31 | 62 | 8 | 8 + 2 = 10 |
| Year 6 | 31 | 62 | 0 | 0 + 2 = 2 |

[a] Assumes that $2 worth of shoe machinery is needed to produce every $1 worth of shoes.

causes total shoe machine sales to rise to $16 million (column 4). Hence a $7 million, or 54 percent, increase in shoe sales between years 2 and 3 (column 1) causes an $8 million, or 100 percent, increase in shoe machine sales (column 4). Again we see an accelerator effect.

But now suppose the increase in shoe sales between years 3 and 4 is again $7 million, the same as it was between years 2 and 3 (column 1). The shoe industry now needs $54 million worth of shoe machines (column 2). Net investment in shoe machines is once again $14 million (column 3). This plus the annual $2 million replacement expenditure means that shoe machine sales (column 4) are once again $16 million. The startling conclusion is that shoe sales must keep growing at $7 million per year if shoe machine sales are just to stay the same!

When shoe sales increase by only $4 million between years 4 and 5 to $31 million (column 1), the shoe industry's net investment in shoe machines declines to $8 million (column 3). This plus the annual $2 million for replacement means that total shoe machine sales are now only $10 million (column 4), down from the $16 million of the previous year—this despite the fact that annual shoe sales still increased! Suppose that in

year 6 shoe sales don't increase at all (column 1). There is now no need for the shoe industry to increase its stock of shoe machines (column 2), so net investment in shoe machines falls to zero (column 3). The shoe machine industry's total sales fall to $2 million (column 4), the annual replacement requirement of the shoe industry. If shoe sales fall in subsequent years, the shoe industry might even cut back on these replacement expenditures.

The annual shoe sales (column 1) and the annual shoe machine sales (column 4) are plotted in Figure A6–1 to give a graphic illustration of the accelerator principle. In general, *the accelerator principle says that ever larger increases in the level of retail sales are needed in order for net investment in capital or durable goods to rise. For net investment to remain constant, retail sales must increase by a constant amount every year. When the expansion of retail sales begins to slow down, the level of net investment will actually fall.* Table A6–1 and Figure A6–1 clearly show that due to the accelerator principle the mere expansion and subsequent leveling off of retail shoe sales caused an expansion, a peak, and a recession in the sale of shoe machinery—a complete business cycle in the shoe machinery industry.

**FIGURE A6-1**   **The Accelerator Principle: Retail Shoe Sales and Shoe Machine Sales** (Hypothetical Data)

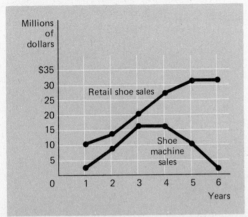

The graph of retail shoe sales is plotted from the data in column 1 of Table A6-1, and the graph for shoe machine sales is plotted from the data in column 4.

The ever larger increases in shoe sales between years 1 and 2 and between years 2 and 3 cause an even more pronounced rise in the sale of shoe machines over this time span. This is known as the accelerator effect. When the rise in shoe sales between years 3 and 4 is the same as that between years 2 and 3, shoe machine sales flatten out. When the expansion of shoe sales slows down between years 4 and 5, shoe machine sales actually decline—a downward accelerator effect. When the sale of shoes flattens out between years 5 and 6, the resulting decline in shoe machine sales is even greater. Hence the expansion and subsequent flattening out of shoe sales results in an expansion, a peak, and a recession in shoe machine sales—a complete business cycle in the shoe machine industry. This is an example of the accelerator principle in action.

## Qualifications and Extensions

Capital goods—goods used to produce other goods—make up a large part of the output of the economy's durable goods industries. (Consumer durables, such as passenger cars, also account for a sizeable portion.) While other factors also affect investment in capital goods, the accelerator principle would seem to provide a key insight into the relatively large fluctuations in the behavior of capital investment in our economy. However, two qualifications on the way the accelerator principle works should be noted. First, if the economy is in the early stages of an expansion, there may be excess capacity in nondurable goods industries, so that expansion can occur with no increase in capital goods. Second, in the later stages of an expansion, there may be no excess capacity in capital goods industries, so that nondurable goods industries cannot get more capital.

*The accelerator principle is also relevant to inventory investment, both in durable and nondurable goods.* For example, suppose that for every $1 worth of sales of canned goods, grocers want to keep $2 worth of canned goods in inventory. Table A6–1 and Figure A6–1 could then represent canned goods sales (column 1); the desired inventory of canned goods (column 2); net inventory investment in canned goods (column 3); and gross inventory investment in canned goods, which would include the replacement expenditure that is due to damaged canned goods (column 4).

## QUESTIONS AND PROBLEMS

1. Using the same sales figures in column 1 of Table A6–1, suppose the shoe industry needed roughly $3 worth of shoe machinery for each $1 of shoes produced and sold. How would this affect the behavior of shoe machine sales in column 4? What insight does this give you into the role of capital intensity (the amount of capital required to produce a dollar's worth of output) as a factor in the behavior of business cycles?

2. Would you expect the effect of the accelerator principle on investment expenditures to be the same during the expansion phase of the business cycle as during the recession phase? Why or why not?

# 7

# Measuring National Income and Product

---

AFTER READING THIS CHAPTER, YOU WILL BE ABLE TO:

1. Explain how, for purposes of national income accounting, GNP may be viewed from two sides—the expenditure side and the income side.

2. State the relationship between gross national product, net national product, national income, personal income, and disposable income.

In this chapter we will focus on national income accounting. National income accounting provides us with aggregate measures of what is happening in the economy. It is the way we measure the various flows depicted in the flow diagrams of Chapter 5.

## WHY IS NATIONAL INCOME ACCOUNTING IMPORTANT?

When you drive your car, you usually keep an eye on the speedometer to see how fast you are going. You check the fuel gauge before starting out to make sure you have enough gas to reach your destination. The temperature gauge warns you about engine overheating before serious damage is done (the radiator boils over or the radiator hose breaks). Without the information these gauges provide, you could find yourself in a dangerous situation. The same is true with respect to the performance of our economy.

When our economy plunged into the Great Depression of the 1930s, the general lack of any timely, systematic measurements of what was happening became painfully apparent. This experience spurred the government to develop today's national income accounting procedures. Armed with relatively recent statistical measurements of the economy's performance, businesses, households, and government policymakers are better informed about what has been happening in the economy and where it appears to be headed. Businesses and households are therefore in a better position to make economic plans. Government policymakers need this kind of information to assess the economy's performance in order to implement timely policies to improve that performance. Shy of this lofty ambition, policymakers need such information at least to avoid policy actions that may harm the economy's performance.

### The Two Sides of GNP

Envision a sales counter in any store or business. On one side stands the customer paying out money in exchange for the good or service that the store provides. On the other side stands the proprietor, giving the customer the good or service in exchange for the customer's money. Corresponding to every purchase there is a sale, since there are always two sides to every transaction. We know from our discussion of value added in Chapter 5 that all the money received on the seller's side of the counter ultimately is paid out in wages, rent, interest, and profit as compensation to the owners of the factors of production used to produce and distribute the product. Therefore all the money received on the seller's side of the counter is income to all the owners of the factors of production—land, labor, and capital.

We may think of all such counters in the economy across which all final goods and services flow as one big sales counter. The total of all the money flowing across the counter in exchange for all the final goods and services produced in a year is the money GNP. When we view GNP from the buyer's side of the counter, where expenditures are made and goods are taken off the counter, we are viewing GNP from the expenditure, or output, side. This viewpoint is often referred to as the *expenditure, or output, approach* to GNP. On the other hand, if we look at GNP from the seller's side of the counter, where all the income is received and ultimately distributed to the owners of productive factors, we are viewing GNP from the income, or earnings, or allocations side—often called the *income approach* to GNP. These two sides of GNP may be summarized by the following equation, which is *always* valid:

$$\left.\begin{array}{l}\text{total}\\\text{expenditures}\\\text{on final goods}\\\text{and services}\end{array}\right\} = \text{GNP} = \left\{\begin{array}{l}\text{total income}\\\text{from production}\\\text{and distribution}\\\text{of final output}\end{array}\right.$$

The left side of this equation may be thought of as representing the lower flow channel in Figure 5–2 of Chapter 5, and the right side as representing the upper flow channel.

To understand the elements that go into

national income accounting and the basic concepts used in much macroeconomic analysis, we need to look at both ways of viewing GNP in more detail. In fact, this is necessary even if you only want to make some sense out of an everyday news item about the state of the economy.

## THE EXPENDITURE SIDE OF GNP

The economy can be divided into four distinct sectors: household, business, government, and foreign. Total expenditure on GNP can be divided up according to which of these sectors makes the expenditure. Personal consumption expenditures are made by households; private domestic investment expenditures by businesses; government expenditures by state, local, and federal government; net exports reflect our trade with foreigners.

### Personal Consumption Expenditure (*C*)

**Personal consumption** expenditures by households are often simply termed *consumption,* or designated *C.* These are household expenditures on consumer durables such as cars and household appliances, on consumer nondurables such as food and clothing, and on services such as medical care, shelter, beauty treatments, haircuts, and dry cleaning. Also included are imputed household expenditures, such as the value of food that farm families produce and consume themselves.

### Gross Private Domestic Investment (*I*)

Recall the distinction we made in Chapter 1 between the common usage of the term *investment* and that used by economists. In common usage people often speak of investing money in stocks and bonds, for example.

However, these are only financial transactions representing the purchase of titles of ownership. When economists and national income accountants use the term **investment**, they are referring primarily to business firms' expenditures on new capital goods—goods that are used to produce other goods and services.

The term *private* means we are referring to expenditures by private business firms, as opposed to government agencies, whereas the term *domestic* means we are speaking of investment expenditures in the United States. The term *gross* will be explained below. **Gross private domestic investment,** often designated *I,* includes all final purchases of new tools and machines by business firms, all construction (residential as well as business), and changes in inventories. Several clarifying remarks are in order.

1. Only *new* tools and machines are included because, as we have already stressed, purchases of secondhand goods are not included in GNP.

2. Residential construction of owner-occupied dwellings is included along with factories and apartment buildings. These dwellings are income-producing assets in the sense that they produce a service, shelter, that could be rented out—just like an apartment or other commercial structure. (You might wonder why cars and furniture, which can also be rented, are included in consumption, since the line of reasoning we've been using suggests that they could be included in investment. The fact that they are included under consumption simply illustrates that there is a certain arbitrariness in national income accounting conventions.)

3. Why are changes in business inventories included in gross private domestic investment? First of all, inventories are included in investment because they are a necessary part of the productive process just like any other capital good. Inventories consist of stocks of raw materials and other inputs, goods in various stages of completion, and finished goods not yet sold. The firm has money invested in inventories just as it has

money invested in other capital goods. The basic reason for taking account of inventory changes is that GNP is supposed to measure the economy's output of goods and services during a year. But what do inventory changes have to do with this?

Suppose that the economy's production of output for the year exceeds the quantity of output actually sold during the year. The amount of output not sold must go into **inventories**, stocks of unsold goods. Inventories at the beginning of the year consist of goods produced in previous years (and therefore not included in this year's GNP). Therefore, inventories at the end of the year will be larger by the amount of output produced but not sold this year. Therefore, in order to correctly measure *this year's* total output, or GNP, we must add this increase in inventories to this year's sales of final goods and services.

Alternatively, suppose the quantity of output sold during the year exceeds the quantity of output produced by the economy. Since this excess of sales over production can only occur by selling goods out of inventories, inventories will be lower at the end of the year than at the beginning. Since inventories at the beginning of the year consist of goods produced in previous years, the sale of those goods should not be included in this year's GNP. Hence, the decrease in inventories must be subtracted from this year's total sales of final goods and services in order to correctly measure *this year's* total output, or GNP.

### Gross Versus Net Investment: Depreciation

Capital goods wear out and get "used up" during the course of producing other goods—they are subject to **capital depreciation**. Machines, tools, and equipment need to be repaired or replaced. Factories and buildings require maintenance. That part of gross private domestic investment expenditures that goes toward these replacement activities simply maintains the economy's ex-

isting stock of capital. What is left over represents a net addition to the economy's capital stock and is therefore called **net private domestic investment.** *Gross private domestic investment* equals replacement investment plus net private domestic investment.

For example, in 1984 gross private domestic investment in the United States was about $637 billion. Of this amount about $403 billion was replacement investment, or what national income accountants call capital consumption allowances. This means that there was roughly $234 billion ($637 billion minus $403 billion) worth of net addition to the capital stock in the United States in 1984.

### Investment and Capital Formation

To a large extent, the economy's ability to produce goods and services depends on its stock of capital goods. (Land and labor are its other important factors of production.) Growth in the economy's capital stock is therefore important because it contributes to growth in the economy's GNP. When gross investment is greater than replacement investment, net investment is positive and there is growth in the capital stock. When gross investment equals replacement investment, net investment is zero and there is no growth in the capital stock. If gross investment is less than replacement investment, net investment is negative and the economy's capital stock is wearing out faster than it is being replaced.

The relationship between gross investment, replacement investment, and net investment since 1929 is summarized in Figure 7–1, which plots the ratio of gross investment to replacement investment. When this ratio is greater than 1, gross investment is greater than replacement investment. This means that net investment is positive and the capital stock is growing. Figure 7–1 shows us that this has been the case for every year since the end of World War II in 1945. In only one year, 1942, did gross investment just equal replacement investment, so that their ratio equaled 1 (circled on the graph) and the economy's capital stock remained unchanged—net investment was zero. During the Great Depression of the 1930s, gross investment was less than replacement investment from 1931 through 1935 and also in 1938. The ratio is therefore less than 1 for these years, as Figure 7–1 shows. The same is true for the war years 1943, 1944, and 1945. Therefore during the Great Depression and World War II, there were years (the shaded areas in Figure 7–1) when net investment was negative and the economy's capital stock, and hence its productive capacity, was actually declining.

## Government Spending (G)

Government spending, often designated G, includes spending on final goods and services by government at all levels—federal, state, and local. Expenditures on services include wages paid to all government employees, civilian and military. We have already noted that government transfer payments are not included in GNP because they are not purchases of current production. These payments are not included in government expenditures for the same reason they are not included in GNP.

## Net Exports (X)

The total expenditures on final goods and services in our economy include those made by foreigners on our output as well as those made by our own citizens on foreign goods and services. Foreign purchases of our output are **exports**. Our purchases of foreign output are **imports**. Since GNP is supposed to be a measure of productive activity in our economy, it should only measure the output

**FIGURE 7–1** **The Ratio of Gross Private Domestic Investment to Replacement Investment in the United States Since 1929**

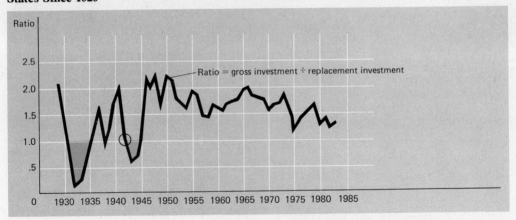

When the ratio of gross investment to replacement investment is greater than 1, net investment is positive and the economy's capital stock is growing. This has been true in every year since the end of World War II. When the ratio equals 1, net investment is zero and the capital stock remains unchanged, as was the case in 1942 (circled on the graph). When the ratio of gross investment to replacement investment is less than 1, net investment is negative. This means that the capital stock is wearing out or being used up faster than it is being replaced. This was true during the Great Depression of the 1930s and for several years during World War II, as indicated by the shaded areas.

actually produced domestically. Imports are already counted in C, I, and G. Imports must therefore be subtracted from total expenditures on final goods and services when measuring GNP. Exports are not included in C, I, and G. Since exports represent goods produced domestically they must be added in. National income accountants do this by simply adding in exports and subtracting out imports. That is, they add in the difference between exports and imports, or **net exports**, which are designated X.

$$X = \text{net exports} = (\text{exports} - \text{imports})$$

Net exports can be either positive or negative depending on whether exports are larger or smaller than imports.

## Summary of the Expenditure Side of GNP

When GNP is viewed from the expenditure side, it is equal to the sum of personal consumption expenditures C, gross private domestic investment I, government expenditures G, and net exports X. In brief, from the expenditure side:

$$\text{GNP} = C + I + G + X$$

---

**CHECKPOINT\* 7-1**
**The Commerce Department's chief economist was reported to have made the following observation about GNP growth: ". . . though the fourth quarter growth rate probably won't exceed the third quarter's, 'the composition will be better' as more growth will come from personal consumption and less from inventory accumulation." Why do you think she felt this particular composition of growth in the fourth quarter was better than that of the third quarter?**

\*Answers to all Checkpoints can be found at the back of the text.

---

## THE INCOME SIDE OF GNP

Now let's consider GNP from the seller's side of the counter. Viewed from this vantage point, GNP is distributed as payments or income to the owners of all the inputs that contribute to its production. These payments consist of wages, interest, rent, and profit. In addition, a certain amount goes to pay indirect business taxes and a portion is provided for capital consumption allowances. We will consider the last two items first.

### Indirect Business Taxes

**Indirect business taxes** consist of sales and excise taxes and business property taxes. Because sales and excise taxes are levied on the goods and services businesses produce and not on the businesses themselves, the term *indirect* is used to describe them.

Since indirect business taxes are paid to the government, they are not a payment or earned income to a factor directly used by the firm to produce a product, as is the case for wages, interest, rent, and profit. Nonetheless, indirect business taxes must be paid out of the sales price of the product. For example, suppose a business firm must receive $10 per unit of a good to cover the costs of all the factors used to produce it. If the government levies a 7 percent sales tax, the firm must charge a price of $10.70 to cover both its factor costs and the $.70 it owes the government. Since $10.70 is what must be spent to get a unit of the product (the expenditure side of GNP), the $.70 indirect business tax must be included on the income side of GNP if the two sides are to be equal. This is necessary even though the sales tax is not an item of earned income for any factor of production.

### Capital Consumption Allowances: Depreciation

We have already discussed the concept of depreciation, or capital consumption allowances—the difference between gross investment and net investment. When the economy produces its annual output of final goods and services, part of its capital stock or productive capacity is worn out, or used up. If you produce 10 hammers but wear out 2 hammers in the process, it would be misleading to say that you are 10 hammers ahead. Similarly, after deducting indirect business taxes from GNP, it would be misleading to say that *all* of the remainder is income earned by the factors of production in the form of wages, interest, rent, and profit. An allowance must first be made for the capital stock that was worn out in the process—the depreciation of machines, tools, and commercial and residential buildings. Therefore, *when GNP is viewed from the income side, in addition to deducting indirect business taxes, it is also necessary to deduct depreciation, or capital consumption allowances, before we may view the remainder as income earned in the form of wages, interest, rent, and profit.*

## Wages

Wages, or employee compensation, consist of all payments to employees for labor services of any kind. Hourly wages, salaries, bonuses, and tips come immediately to mind. Also included, however, are employer contributions to the social security system and to private pension and health insurance plans, as well as employer payments in kind—the personal use of a company car or plane, for example. These so-called supplemental benefits to wages and salaries are viewed as part of the necessary wage payments that employers must make to obtain the labor services they want.

## Interest

Consistent with the notion that earned income is the payment for the use of productive factors, interest is the payment made by businesses for the use of financial capital. It is calculated as the difference between interest payments made by the business sector and the interest payments it receives from all other sectors, plus the difference between interest payments to other countries and those received from them. Interest payments within sectors—business, consumer, or government—are not included because they have a zero net effect on the sector. Interest payments made by the government and consumer sectors to each other or to the business sector are not included because they are not regarded as payment for the use of a productive factor. Payments within the business and the consumer sectors are shown as transfer payments in the national income accounts.

## Rent

In the national income accounts rent includes the income earned by households for the use of their real property holdings such as land and buildings of all kinds. It also includes the imputed rent of owner-occupied dwellings, as noted previously. In addition it embraces income payments received by households from copyrights, patent rights, and royalties from the use of things such as a famous name or an endorsement by a famous person.

## Profit

National income accounts break profit into two categories: proprietors' income and corporate profits.

### Proprietors' Income

**Proprietors' income** is the income earned by the owners of unincorporated businesses. Doctors, lawyers, farmers, and many other small businesses are not incorporated. After these owner-operated businesses have paid wages, rent, and interest to all the factors of production they hire, what remains out of their total sales revenue is income or profit to the owners—proprietors' income.

### Corporate Profits

The profits of corporations, or incorporated businesses, are, of course, derived in the same way. Corporate profits are subject to different tax laws than proprietors' income, however. Proprietors' income is subject to income taxes just like wages and salaries are. Corporate profits are subject to a corporate profits tax. What is left of corporate profits after this tax may be paid out entirely or in part as dividends to stockholders—the owners of the corporation. The part of after-tax corporate profits that the corporation does not pay out in dividends is called undistributed corporate profits, or retained earnings. These are used by the corporation either to invest in capital or to pay off debt obligations of the firm.

## Summary of the Two Sides of GNP

Table 7-1 summarizes our discussion of the two sides of GNP. The items on the expenditure or output side are on the left, and the items on the income or allocation side are on the right. Data for the United States economy for 1983 are given to illustrate how the sum of the expenditure items on the left-hand side of the table add up to the sum of the income items on the right-hand side of the table. Each side, of course, sums up to GNP.

### CHECKPOINT 7-2

**It is often argued that corporate profits are treated unfairly by our tax laws relative to the treatment of proprietors' income because corporate profits are subject to double taxation. That is because corporations must pay a corporate profits tax and then dividends paid to stockholders are subject to the income tax. How does this double taxation most likely affect the size of retained earnings relative to the size of dividend payments?**

## RELATED NATIONAL INCOME ACCOUNTING CONCEPTS

There are four other important and related national income accounting concepts needed for a complete picture of the basics of national income accounting. These are net national product, national income, personal income, and disposable income. Each may be viewed as a link between the total sales of final goods and services, or GNP, and the amount of those total sales receipts that households receive.

**TABLE 7-1 The Expenditure Side and the Income Side of GNP: 1983** (in Billions of Dollars)

| Expenditure or Output Side of GNP | | | Income or Allocation Side of GNP | |
|---|---|---|---|---|
| Personal consumption | $2,155.9 | | $ 280.7 | Indirect business taxes |
| | | | 377.4 | Capital consumption allowances |
| Gross private domestic investment | 471.6 | GNP = $3,304.7 = | 1,984.9 | Wages (compensation of employees including supplements) |
| | | | 256.6 | Interest |
| | | | 58.3 | Rental income |
| Government spending | 685.5 | | 121.7 | Proprietors' income |
| | | | 225.2 | Corporate profits |
| Net exports | −8.3 | | −.1 | Miscellaneous adjustments |

SOURCE: U.S. Department of Commerce. Figures may not add to total GNP because of rounding.

## Net National Product (NNP): GNP Minus Depreciation

We noted above that if you wear out 2 hammers while producing 10 hammers, you are 8 hammers "better off," not 10. True, 10 hammers were produced and that quantity is a measure of total productive activity over some period of time. But in order to assess what that productive activity has actually provided, it is necessary to deduct the 2 hammers used up to get the *net* product of our efforts.

Similarly, GNP is a measure of the economy's total productive activity. But it makes no adjustment to account for the quantity of the year's output that must be used to replace the goods used up in producing this year's output. To do so we *subtract the annual depreciation of the economy's capital stock, or capital consumption allowance, from GNP to get the economy's* **net national product (NNP)**. *Net national product measures the dollar value of the economy's annual output of final goods and services after adjustment is made for the quantity of the year's output needed to replace goods used up in producing that output.*

Net national product may be obtained by deducting the capital consumption allowance of $374.4 billion from both the right-hand side and the left-hand side of Table 7–1. On the left-hand side we may view it as being deducted from gross private domestic investment to give net investment. The subtraction of capital consumption allowances from GNP to give NNP for our economy in 1983 is shown in Table 7–2.

## National Income (NI): NNP Minus Indirect Business Taxes

We have already noted that when GNP is viewed from the income side, we are basically interested in how the income earned from the sale of the economy's output is paid out to the owners of the productive factors that produced it. Net national product contains one item that does not represent pay-

**TABLE 7-2 Deriving Net National Product, National Income, Personal Income, and Disposable Personal Income from GNP: 1983** (in Billions of Dollars)

| | |
|---|---|
| Gross National Product (GNP) | $3,304.7 |
| Less: Capital consumption allowance | −377.4 |
| Equals: Net National Product (NNP) | 2,927.3 |
| Less: Indirect business taxes | −280.7 |
| Equals: National Income (NI) | 2,646.6 |
| Less: Corporate income taxes | −75.7 |
| Less: Undistributed corporate profits | −56.3 |
| Less: Social security contributions | −176.2 |
| Plus: Transfer payments | 403.5 |
| Equals: Personal Income (PI) | 2,741.9 |
| Less: Personal taxes | −406.3 |
| Equals: Disposable Income (DI) | $2,335.6 |

SOURCE: U.S. Department of Commerce.

ment to a factor of production—namely, indirect business taxes. These go to government. In order *to arrive at a figure for the total wage, interest, rent, and profit income earned in the economy during a year, it is necessary to subtract indirect business taxes from net national product to get national income.* **National income (NI)** *measures the income earned by the suppliers of all factors of production used to produce the economy's total output of final goods and services for the year.*

National income may be calculated by adding up all the items on the right side of Table 7–1 except capital consumption allowances and indirect business taxes. The subtraction of indirect business taxes from net national product to arrive at national income is shown in Table 7–2.

## Personal Income (PI): Income Received

While national income measures the income earned by factors of production, it does not represent *income actually received by households,* or what is called **personal income (PI)**. That part of national income earned but not received consists of corporate income (or profits) taxes, undistributed corporate profits, and social security contributions (collected by the government in the form of payroll taxes). On the other hand, some income received by households is not earned currently and some is not really earned at all. This income is represented by public and private transfer payments. Transfer payments consist of such things as social security, welfare, unemployment, and veterans' benefits. Also included are the interest payments on government debt and interest paid by consumers.

To move from income currently earned by households, national income, to income actually received, personal income, it is necessary to subtract from national income the three types of income not received and to add transfer payments. Hence, *personal income equals national income plus transfer payments minus corporate income taxes, undistributed corporate profits, and social security contributions.* This calculation is illustrated in Table 7–2.

## Disposable Income (DI): PI Minus Personal Taxes

**Disposable income (DI)** *equals personal income minus personal taxes.* Personal taxes consist of inheritance taxes, property taxes, and personal income taxes, which are by far the largest of the three as well as the most familiar to the typical working person. After paying personal taxes out of personal income, what is left is literally disposable in the sense that households may use it any way they wish. The largest part of disposable in-

**FIGURE 7-2  Summary of Expenditure and Income Side of GNP and Relationship Between GNP, NNP, PI, and DI**

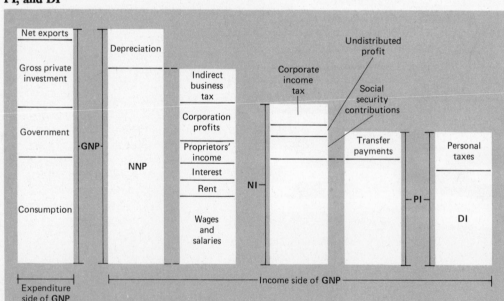

come is typically spent; this constitutes the personal consumption expenditures, which we have already discussed. The relationship between personal income and disposable income is illustrated in Table 7–2.

At this point you should examine Table 7–2 from top to bottom. It summarizes the relationship between five important accounting measures: (1) gross national product (GNP), (2) net national product (NNP), (3) national income (NI), (4) personal income (PI), and (5) disposable income (DI). Figure 7–2 summarizes our discussion of the expenditure side and the income side of GNP, as well as the relationship between GNP, NNP, NI, PI, and DI.

## CHECKPOINT 7-3
**Where do the transfer payments in Figure 7-2 come from—that is, point out their sources in Figure 7-2.**

## SUMMARY

**1.** When GNP is viewed from the expenditure, or output, side it equals the sum of personal consumption expenditures, made by households; gross private domestic investment expenditures, made by business firms; government expenditures, made by federal, state, and local governments; and net exports, the difference between foreign purchases of our goods and our purchases of foreign goods.

**2.** When GNP is viewed from the income side, it appears as payments, or income, in the form of wages, interest, rent, and profit to the owners of all the inputs that contribute to its production. In addition, a certain amount goes to pay indirect business taxes and a portion is provided for capital consumption allowances.

**3.** In addition to GNP, there are four other important and interrelated national income accounting concepts: (1) net national product, which equals gross national product mi-

nus capital consumption allowances or depreciation; (2) national income, which equals net national product minus indirect business taxes; (3) personal income, which equals national income minus income earned but not received (corporate income or profits taxes, undistributed corporate profits, and social security contributions) plus income received but not currently or necessarily earned (public and private transfer payments); and (4) disposable income, which equals personal income minus personal taxes.

## KEY TERMS AND CONCEPTS

capital depreciation
disposable income (DI)
exports
gross private domestic investment
imports
indirect business taxes
inventory
investment
national income (NI)
net exports
net national product (NNP)
net private domestic investment
personal consumption
personal income (PI)
proprietors' income

## QUESTIONS AND PROBLEMS

**1.** GNP is supposed to measure the economy's output of final goods and services. But in what way and to what extent could it also be said to be a measure of the value of the services of productive factors?

**2.** The following national income accounting data are for the United States in 1929 (in billions of dollars), the last year before the onset of the Great Depression of the 1930s.

| | |
|---|---|
| Transfer payments | $ 4.0 |
| Gross private domestic investment | 16.2 |
| Indirect business taxes | 7.0 |
| Personal taxes | 2.6 |

Net exports of goods and ser-
vices                                     1.1
Undistributed corporate profits           2.8
Capital consumption allowances            7.9
Personal consumption expendi-
tures                                    77.2
Corporate income taxes                    1.4
Interest paid by consumers                1.5
Contributions for social insur-
ance                                       .2
Government purchases of goods
and services                             8.5

Use the above data to answer the following questions about the year 1929. Show your work.

a. How much was GNP?

b. What was the amount of personal saving?

c. What was the amount of income earned but not received?

d. What was the amount of income earned by factors of production?

e. What was the amount of personal income?

f. Show two different ways of arriving at the amount of disposable personal income.

g. What was the amount of the addition to the nation's stock of capital?

h. What was national income?

i. Could dividends have been larger?

j. What was net national product?

k. What amount of income was available to households for saving?

l. By how much would you say the economy came out ahead as the result of the year's production?

m. What was the amount of income earned in the form of interest, wages, rent, and profit?

# 8

# Aggregate Demand and Supply: The Income-Expenditure View

---

**AFTER READING THIS CHAPTER, YOU WILL BE ABLE TO:**

1. State the reasons why classical economists thought a capitalistic, laissez faire economy would automatically tend to operate at a full-employment equilibrium.

2. Distinguish between the classical view and the Keynesian analysis in terms of aggregate demand and aggregate supply.

3. Explain the concepts of the consumption function and the saving function and the determinants of consumption and saving.

4. Explain the nature of investment expenditures and their determinants.

5. Explain how the equilibrium level of total income is determined according to the income-expenditure approach.

Chapter 6 introduced some of the characteristics of the economy's performance, along with two problem areas of major concern—unemployment and inflation. And in Chapter 7 we saw how we keep tabs on the economy's performance by the use of national income accounting. However, in order to better understand aggregate economic activity in general, we need to become familiar with the way aggregate demand and aggregate supply interact to determine total income, output, employment, and the economy's price level, a subject briefly introduced in Chapter 5.

Our journey begins in this chapter. First off we will examine why many economists from Adam Smith's time up through the 1930s believed that capitalistic, market-oriented economies naturally tended to operate at full employment—a view that essentially assumes the aggregate supply curve is vertical. Then we will see why and how the Great Depression of the 1930s forced a major rethinking on this issue—the Keynesian revolution. This gave rise to the income-expenditure theory, an approach that assumes the economy's price level is inflexible so that the aggregate supply curve is horizontal and the equilibrium level of total income, output, and employment is determined solely by aggregate demand. We will examine this approach here and in the next chapter. Government expenditure and taxation will be introduced into this framework in Chapter 10. Then in Chapter 11 we will allow the price level to vary with changes in total income, output, and employment, and will see more generally how aggregate demand and supply jointly determine the economy's price level and its total income, output, and employment levels.

## THE CLASSICAL VIEW OF INCOME AND EMPLOYMENT

Classical economists subscribed to the notion that capitalistic, market-oriented economies naturally tended to operate at a full-employment output level. The classical economist's faith in this point of view was based on Say's Law,[1] an appealing yet deceptive argument.

### Say's Law

Simply put, **Say's Law** *states that supply creates its own demand.* According to Say's Law, people only work to produce and supply goods and services because they want to acquire the income to buy goods and services. A level of total dollar spending insufficient to purchase the full-employment output of goods and services was considered impossible because the total income earned from the production of the economy's total full-employment output would be spent to purchase that output.

Classical economists subscribed to two fundamental assumptions about how the economy worked—*two assumptions essential to a belief in Say's Law. First, prices and wages always adjust quickly to clear markets. Second, the interest rate always adjusts to equate saving and investment.*

### *Prices and Wages Adjust to Clear Markets*

*The classical economists argued that if the economy's aggregate demand for goods and services declined, flexible prices and wages would quickly adjust downward until the total quantity of goods and services demanded was once again restored to the initial full-employment total output level.* Let's briefly examine their argument.

A decline in the economy's aggregate demand is reflected in leftward shifts in the demand curves in each of the economy's many product markets. Product prices fall in response, and laborers quickly and willingly accept lower wages in order to keep their jobs. This adjustment occurs in every product market in the economy so that each continues to produce and sell the same quantity

[1] Initially put forth by the French economist Jean Baptiste Say (1767–1832).

of output and employ the same amount of labor as before the initial decrease in demand. Therefore the economy continues to produce the full-employment total output level that it did before the downward adjustment of all prices and wages.

### Saving and the Income-Expenditure Flow

Our examination of the circular-flow diagrams of the economy in Chapter 5, and our discussion in Chapter 7 of how GNP may be viewed either from the expenditure side or the income side, both indicated that:

$$\left.\begin{array}{l}\text{total expenditure}\\ \text{on final goods and}\\ \text{services}\end{array}\right\} = \left\{\begin{array}{l}\text{total income from}\\ \text{the production and}\\ \text{sale of final output}\end{array}\right.$$

For the purpose of simplifying our discussion of this relationship, we will assume there is no government expenditure or taxation.

Consideration of the total-expenditure-equals-total-income relationship immediately suggests a possible problem for a believer in Say's Law. *While it is undeniably true that every dollar of expenditure on goods and services creates a dollar of income, it does not follow that the person receiving the income necessarily spends all of it.* What happens when households save some of their income? As long as there is a saving leakage from total dollar income, won't total dollar expenditure and total dollar output and income continue to get smaller and smaller? The answer is yes. The continuing fall in total demand that results when households do not spend all their income means wages and prices would have to fall continually to maintain full employment—hardly a realistic state of affairs!

### The Interest Rate Equates Saving and Investment

But classical economists had an answer to the problem posed by the saving leakage from the income-expenditure flow. *If that part of*

*total income that is saved is just matched by an equivalent amount of investment expenditure by businesses,* then the leakage from the income-expenditure flow that results from saving is offset by the injection of investment into that flow.

But what assures that the amount of investment expenditures businesses intend to make will be equal to the amount of saving that households intend to do? Classical economists contended that in a capitalist economy the **interest rate** would always adjust—like the price in any other market—to ensure that total intended investment in the economy would equal total intended saving. If the interest rate is viewed as the price of borrowing, businesses will demand more borrowed funds for investment at low interest rates than at high rates. Therefore, the investment curve for the economy must slope downward (like any demand curve), as shown in Figure 8–1. Saving out of income involves a sacrifice by households—the forgone consumption they could have enjoyed. Therefore, it is necessary to pay households a higher interest rate to induce them to save more. Hence, the saving curve for the economy—the supply of dollars available to be loaned out of total income—is upward sloping (like any supply curve), as shown in Figure 8–1.

The intersection of the saving and investment curves in Figure 8–1 corresponds to the equilibrium level of the interest rate, $i_e$. As in any other market, if the price (interest rate) is above this level, the supply of dollars to loan (saving) exceeds the demand for dollars to invest (investment) and price will be bid down to $i_e$. Similarly, if the price (interest rate) is below this level, demand exceeds supply, and price will be bid up to $i_e$. Because of the market adjustment of the interest rate, classical economists argued that the savings plans of households would always be equal to the investment plans of businesses.

Therefore, classical economists maintained that the economy would operate at its full-employment output level without the need

**FIGURE 8-1   Classical Economists Argued That the Interest Rate Would Make Saving and Investment Equal**

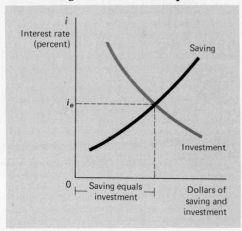

For businesses, the interest rate is the price of borrowing. Consequently, they will demand more borrowed funds for investment at low interest rates than at high rates. Thus the investment curve slopes downward.

Classical economists contended that saving out of income by households is a sacrifice in the form of forgone consumption. Therefore households can be induced to save more only by paying them a higher interest rate. Hence, the saving curve slopes upward.

The equilibrium interest rate, $i_e$, equates the quantity of dollars demanded for investment by businesses with the quantity of dollars households are willing to save. According to classical economists, this equality ensured that the economy would operate at full employment.

for continually falling wages and prices. *Say's Law assumed that the unfettered forces of free markets and laissez faire capitalism would guarantee full employment with price stability. If there were disturbances that caused investment or saving curves to shift, or shifts in demand and supply curves in any other market, adjustments in wages, prices, and the interest rate would always return the economy to a position of full-employment equilibrium.*

The classical view of the economy can be represented in terms of the *aggregate demand (AD)* and *aggregate supply (AS)* curves (introduced in Chapter 5) shown in Figure 8-2. The aggregate supply curve *AS* is vertical at the full-employment total output level $y_f$ (horizontal axis), reflecting the classical view that prices, wages, and the interest rate will always adjust quickly to any shift in aggregate demand to keep the economy operating at $y_f$. Suppose the *AD* curve is intitially $AD_1$ so that the economy's price level is $p_1$, corresponding to the intersection of $AD_1$ and *AS* at $e_1$. If aggregate demand declines as represented by a leftward shift in the *AD* curve from $AD_1$ to $AD_2$, then the economy's price level (the average of all prices, including wages) falls to $p_2$, corresponding to the intersection of $AD_2$ with *AS* at $e_2$. The equilibrium output level is still $y_f$.

**CHECKPOINT\* 8-1**
**Suppose the economy is operating at full-employment equilibrium. Assume the classical economists' point of view that wages and prices are perfectly flexible. Describe the adjustment process that would occur in product markets in response to an increase in the economy's total demand. When equilibrium is once again restored, will wages and prices be higher, lower, or unchanged? Suppose the economy is operating at full-employment equilibrium and that we take account of the role of saving and investment as envisioned by the classical economists. Suppose the investment curve in Figure 8-1 shifts leftward, but that for some reason the interest rate cannot fall below the level $i_e$. Will wages and prices rise, fall, or stay the same? Explain your answer.**

\*Answers to all Checkpoints can be found at the back of the text.

**FIGURE 8-2  Aggregate Demand and Supply in the Classical View**

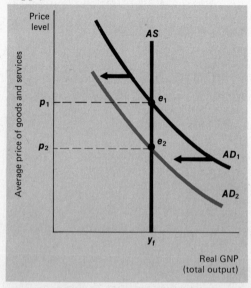

The aggregate supply curve *AS* in the classical view is vertical at the full-employment level of total output $y_f$ (vertical axis) because prices, wages, and the interest rate always adjust quickly to maintain full employment in response to any change in aggregate demand. For example, if the *AD* curve shifts leftward from $AD_1$ to $AD_2$ the economy's equilibrium price level would fall from $p_1$ to $p_2$ while total output would remain at $y_f$.

## AGGREGATE DEMAND AND EMPLOYMENT: THE INCOME-EXPENDITURE APPROACH

Classical economists had always acknowledged that capitalistic, market-oriented economies might experience occasional, temporary bouts of unemployment, possibly caused by rapid shifts in the composition of demand or by such things as wars and crop failures. But then came the 1930s. A prolonged depression—the Great Depression—gripped the capitalist, market-oriented economies of the world. The gap between classical theory and fact was now too great to ignore.

In the United States alone, the unemployment rate was never lower than 14.3 percent in the years from 1931 through 1940. Indeed, from 1932 through 1935, it hovered between 20 and 25 percent. Money GNP fell by roughly 50 percent between 1929 and 1933 while gross investment fell by over 90 percent.

### The Keynesian Revolution

A group of Cambridge University economists led by John Maynard Keynes offered an explanation that went beyond the bounds of the classical framework and sparked what has come to be called the Keynesian revolution. In 1936 Keynes published his analysis—*The General Theory of Employment, Interest, and Money* which argued that the inevitability of full-employment equilibrium was an unlikely proposition at best and simply wrong in general. Keynes argued that it is irrelevant whether complete wage and price flexibility would ensure full employment if *in fact* wages and prices are slow to adjust in the real world. During the Great Depression economists noted that this was true in a number of markets and that wages were particularly slow to adjust downward. Keynes also argued that disposable income—not the interest rate—is the main determinant of saving. Given this, Keynes questioned the ability of the interest rate to equate saving and intended investment as required by Say's Law.

### The Keynesian Analysis

In the classical model the equilibrium level of total output (constant dollar total income or real GNP) is determined on the supply side by virtue of Say's Law's assertion that the economy automatically tends to operate at full employment, as represented by the vertical *AS* curve at $y_f$ in Figure 8-2. Aggregate demand serves only to determine the price level which is assumed to adjust quickly to any shift in the *AD* curve.

The Keynesian analysis switches the emphasis from the supply side to the demand side. *Keynesian analysis focuses on how the equilibrium level of total income, output, and employment is determined in an economy that operates at less than full employment and where the price level is not flexible.* The equilibrium level of total output and employment is completely determined by aggregate demand, as shown in Figure 8–3. The aggregate supply curve *AS* is horizontal at the fixed (inflexible) price level $p_0$. If the *AD* curve is $AD_1$ then the equilibrium level of total output is $y_1$ (horizontal axis), corresponding to the intersection of $AD_1$ and *AS* at $e_1$, a level less than the full-employment

output level $y_f$. Suppose aggregate demand falls as represented by a shift from $AD_1$ to $AD_2$. Now total output declines (but not the price level, as in the classical model) from $y_1$ to $y_2$ and the associated level of employment falls as well (it takes less labor to produce less output). In sum, *the level of total income, output, and employment vary directly with aggregate demand and are completely demand determined.*

## The Income-Expenditure Approach: Determining Aggregate Demand

The upshot of the Keynesian analysis is straightforward. In an economy that operates at less than full employment and where the price level is not flexible, an explanation of the determination of total output, income, and employment requires an explanation of the determination of aggregate demand—why is the *AD* curve where it is and why does it shift? An analysis known as the income-expenditure approach provides an answer to this question. It boils down to an explanation of the behavior of the four main expenditure categories—consumption *C*, investment *I*, government *G*, and the net exports *X*—that constitute the expenditure side of GNP (discussed in the previous chapter), the left side of the relationship:

$$\left.\begin{array}{l}\text{total expenditure}\\\text{on final goods and}\\\text{services}\end{array}\right\} = \left\{\begin{array}{l}\text{total income from}\\\text{the production and}\\\text{sale of final output}\end{array}\right.$$

In the next section we will examine consumption and investment spending, two of the key components of total expenditure. Then we will see how consumption and investment combine to determine the equilibrium level of total income, output, and employment according to the income-expenditure approach, under the simplifying assumption that government spending and net exports are zero. Throughout our discussion it will be assumed that the price level is unchanging. Ultimately we will want to exam-

**FIGURE 8-3  Aggregate Demand and Supply in the Keynesian Analysis**

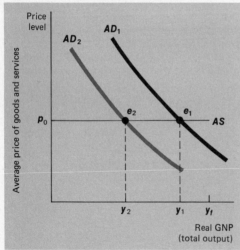

When the price level is not flexible the aggregate supply curve *AS* is horizontal at the fixed price level, indicated here as $p_0$ (vertical axis). Shifts in the aggregate demand curve, such as from $AD_1$ to $AD_2$, cause total output and employment to change. Total output, income, and employment are completely demand determined.

ine what causes the price and output levels to change at the same time, a more complicated issue that will be taken up in Chapter 11 and subsequent chapters.

---

## CHECKPOINT 8-2

**How would you describe the way saving and investment plans were matched for Robinson Crusoe in his one-man island economy? Could he have an unemployment problem? How well would Say's Law describe the way his economy worked? What is it about modern industrialized economies, as compared to Robinson Crusoe's, that leads to difficulties for Say's Law?**

---

# THE CONSUMPTION AND SAVING FUNCTIONS

*Consumption is the portion of their disposable income that households spend on goods and services. Personal saving is the remaining part, the portion of disposable income that households refrain from spending.* Therefore, whatever explains consumption behavior must also explain personal saving behavior.

## Consumption and Saving Depend on Income

Keynes contended that the single most important determinant of consumption expenditure and personal saving is the household's disposable income. Statistical studies tend to bear out that claim.

Using hypothetical data, Table 8–1 shows the total amount of consumption (column 2) that the economy's households would plan to do at different levels of disposable income (column 1). The difference between disposable income and consumption is the amount of saving (column 3). This is the amount that households refrain from spending at each level of disposable income. Note that as income increases so do both consumption and

**TABLE 8-1 The Consumption and Saving Schedules** (Hypothetical Data in Billions of Dollars)

| (1) Disposable Income (DI) | (2) Con- sumption (C) | (3) Saving (S) |
|---|---|---|
| | | S=(1)−(2) |
| 300 | 320 | −20 |
| 325 | 335 | −10 |
| 350 | 350 | 0 |
| 375 | 365 | 10 |
| 400 | 380 | 20 |
| 425 | 395 | 30 |
| 450 | 410 | 40 |
| 475 | 425 | 50 |
| 500 | 440 | 60 |

saving. All other factors that affect consumption are assumed to be given—that is, fixed and unchanging.

## The Consumption Function: Graphical Representation

The income-consumption relationship may be represented graphically by measuring consumption expenditures on the vertical axis and disposable income on the horizontal axis. In Figure 8–4, part a, both axes are measured in the same units, billions of dollars. The consumption data from column 2 of Table 8–1 and the disposable income data from column 1 are plotted in Figure 8–4, part a, to give the consumption curve C. When actual levels of the economy's consumption expenditures are plotted against the associated levels of the economy's disposable income, economists have found a relationship that looks very much like the consumption curve C shown in part a.

Note the 45° line that bisects the 90° angle formed by the horizontal and vertical axes of the diagram. Any point on the 45° line corresponds to the same dollar magnitude on either axis. This line serves as a very useful reference for interpreting the relation-

**FIGURE 8-4  The Consumption Function
and the Saving Function**

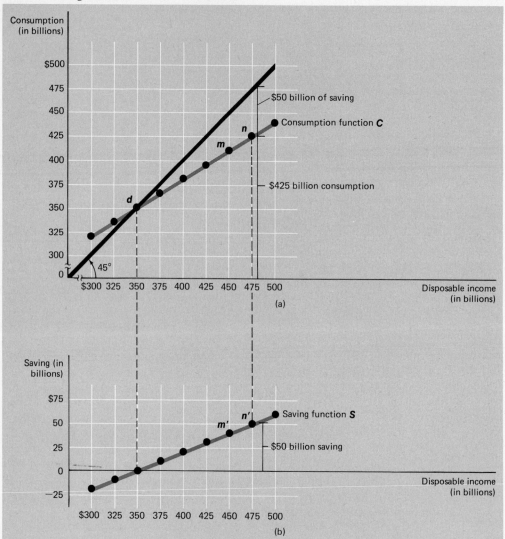

The consumption function $C$ in part a is plotted from the data in columns 1 and 2 of Table 8–1. Note that as disposable income increases, consumption also increases, but by a smaller amount. Movement along the consumption function is caused by a change in disposable income, while all other things that affect consumption are assumed to remain unchanged.

The amount of saving at any disposable income level is represented by the vertical distance between the consumption function and the 45° line in part a. In other words, what households don't consume they save.

Using the data from columns 1 and 3 in Table 8–1, saving also may be plotted against disposable income (part b) to give the saving function $S$. The saving function slopes upward, reflecting the fact that the level of planned saving rises as disposable income rises.

ship between disposable income, consumption, and saving. At any given level of disposable income, the vertical distance between the corresponding point on the consumption curve *C* and the 45° line represents the amount of saving, or the amount of that disposable income households refrain from spending. For example, at a disposable income level of $475 billion (horizontal axis) the vertical distance to the corresponding point on the consumption curve (point *n*) measures the $425 billion of consumption spending (vertical axis) that takes place at that disposable income level. The vertical distance from that point on the consumption curve up to the 45° line measures the $50 billion of saving that takes place when disposable income is $475 billion.

At point *d*, where the consumption curve intersects the 45° line, the entire $350 billion of disposable income goes into consumption expenditure—saving is zero. At disposable income levels greater than $350 billion, saving is positive and is equal to the vertical distance between the 45° line and the consumption curve.

At disposable income levels less than $350 billion, the consumption curve lies above the 45° line and the economy's households spend more than the amount of disposable income. Households are able to spend more than disposable income either by drawing on wealth accumulated in the past or by borrowing. This amounts to negative saving, or what may be called dissaving.

The relationship between the level of disposable income and the level of consumption, represented by the consumption curve *C*, is called the **consumption function**. The term *function* is used here because the level of consumption expenditure is determined by (is a function of) the level of disposable income. *The consumption function shows that as disposable income increases, consumption also increases, but by a smaller amount. Movement along the consumption function is caused by a change in disposable income, while all other things that affect consumption are assumed to remain unchanged.*

## The Saving Function: Graphical Representation

What households don't consume out of income they save. When income increases, consumption increases by a smaller amount because part of any increase in income goes into saving. And saving obviously gets larger as income increases.

Another very useful representation of the relationship between disposable income and saving is shown in part b of Figure 8–4. The axes are drawn to exactly the same scale as those in part a of Figure 8–4, except that saving is measured on the vertical axis. The saving function *S* is plotted from the data in columns 1 and 3 of Table 8–1.

The vertical distance between the saving function and the horizontal axis represents the amount of saving that the economy's households would desire to do at each income level. At any given income level the vertical distance between the saving function and the horizontal axis in part b is the same as the vertical distance between the consumption function and the 45° line in part a. This correspondence is pointed out at the $475 billion disposable income level, for example, and is also obvious at the break-even point.

*The* **saving function** *shows the relationship between the economy's level of disposable income and the level of desired or planned saving. It slopes upward, reflecting the fact that the level of planned saving rises as income rises.*

## Movements Versus Shifts in Consumption and Saving

In Chapter 4 we discussed the difference between movement along a good's demand curve and shifts in the position of its demand curve. A similar distinction must be made between movement along a consumption function or a saving function and shifts in these functions.

### Movements Along the Consumption and Saving Functions

Movement along a consumption function can only be caused by a change in disposable income, all other things affecting consumption assumed to be unchanged. Of course, for any movement along a consumption function, there is a corresponding movement along the associated saving function. For example, in Figure 8-4, part a, if disposable income rises from $450 to $475 billion, there is a movement along the consumption function from point $m$ to point $n$ and a corresponding movement along the saving function in Figure 8-4, part b, from point $m'$ to point $n'$.

### Shifts in the Consumption and Saving Functions

When any of the other things (besides disposable income) that affect consumption changes, there is a shift in the consumption and saving functions. For example, suppose the consumption function is initially in the position $C_0$, as shown in part a of Figure 8-5. The associated saving function is $S_0$, as shown in part b. If the consumption function shifts downward from $C_0$ to $C_1$, the saving function then shifts upward from $S_0$ to $S_1$. At any given disposable income level, households now consume less and save more. On the other hand, if the consumption function shifts upward from $C_0$ to $C_2$, the saving function then shifts downward from $S_0$ to $S_2$. In this case households now consume more and save less at any given disposable income level.

## Other Determinants of Consumption and Saving

What are the "other things" that can change and thereby cause shifts in the consumption and saving functions? Some are the following.

### 1. Credit conditions

The easier it is for consumers to obtain credit and the lower the interest rate they pay for it, the more likely they are to borrow from banks and other financial institutions to buy cars, household appliances, and other goods on credit. This would tend to shift the consumption function upward and the saving function downward. Tougher credit conditions and a higher interest rate have the opposite effect.

### 2. Wealth

The size and composition of the stocks of assets (bank accounts, cash, bonds, stocks, houses, etc.) owned by consumers is an important determinant of consumer spending. Disposable income is not the only source of funds consumers have. Consumption spending can also be financed by withdrawals from bank accounts or by cashing in other forms of wealth. An increase in wealth would tend to shift the consumption function upward and the saving function downward—a decrease would have the opposite effect.

### 3. Expectations about employment, prices, and income

Consumer expectations about the course of the economy play a crucial role in their willingness to spend. For example, if consumers begin to expect lower levels of employment and income, they might try to save more for possible rainy days ahead. The result would be a downward shift in the consumption function and an upward shift in the saving function. Changes in expectations about inflation also affect consumption and saving, but the direction of the shift is not as clear.

---

*CHECKPOINT 8-3*

**Suppose a news item reports that "most forecasters still look for somewhat lower interest rates and expect consumer outlays to remain strong." If the forecasters are right, how will the consumption function shift and why? How will the saving function shift?**

**FIGURE 8-5   The Consumption and Saving Functions Shift When the "Other Things" Change**

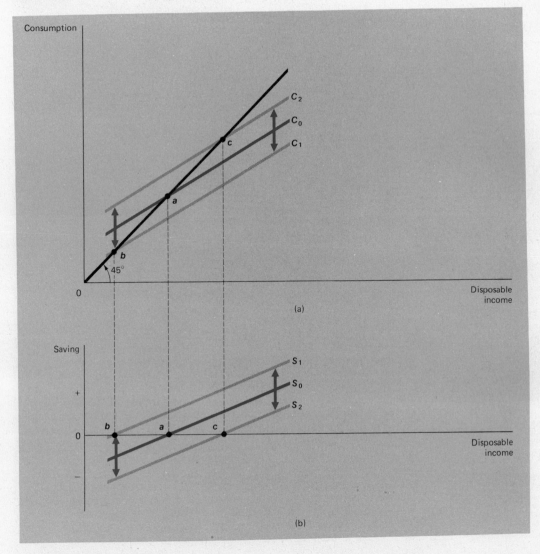

(a)

(b)

Movement along the consumption function or the saving function is due to changes in disposable income. All other things that affect consumption are assumed to be unchanged. When any of these other things change, they cause a shift in the consumption and saving functions.

Suppose the consumption function is initially $C_0$ (part a) and the associated saving function is $S_0$ (part b). If the consumption function shifts downward from $C_0$ to $C_1$, the saving function then shifts upward from $S_0$ to $S_1$. At any given income level, households now consume less and save more. Similarly, if the consumption function shifts upward from $C_0$ to $C_2$, the saving function then shifts downward from $S_0$ to $S_2$. Households consume more and save less at any given disposable income level.

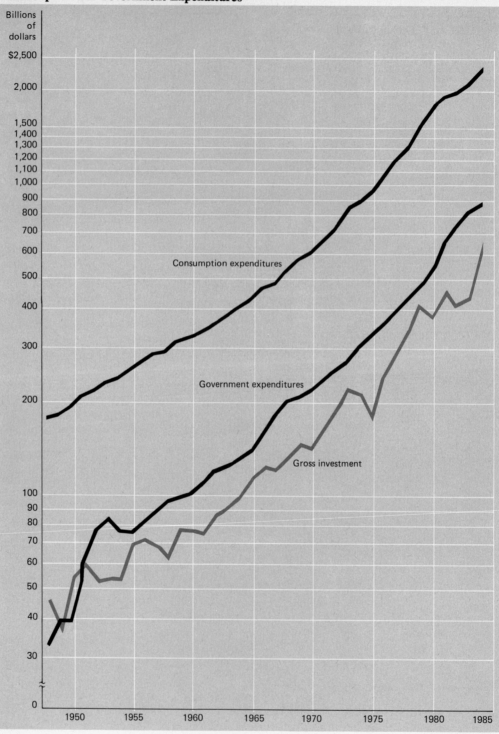

**FIGURE 8-6  Investment Varies More Than Consumption and Government Expenditures**

Billions of dollars

Consumption expenditures

Government expenditures

Gross investment

# INVESTMENT AND ITS DETERMINANTS

Of the three major categories on the expenditure side of GNP—consumption, investment, and government—investment expenditures vary the most. This is evident from the graphic representation of these three categories in Figure 8–6. As long as members of households are employed and have a steady source of income, consumption varies very little, growing rather steadily through time with the growth of the economy. Government expenditure, while not quite as steady as consumption, has certainly been less variable than investment. What are the main determinants of investment expenditure, and what accounts for its variable behavior?

## Investment and Profit

If businesses anticipate that revenue from the sale of goods and services produced with the aid of capital goods will more than cover all costs of production, so that there is a profit, they will invest in the capital goods. Otherwise they won't. A major underlying reason why investment is so variable (as illustrated in Figure 8–6) is the fact that the decision whether or not to invest in capital goods depends on business expectations about future profits.

### Forecasting Future Profit

Put yourself in the shoes of an investment decision maker. In order to forecast prospective profits in any meaningful way, you have to forecast the magnitudes of all of the ingredients that will enter into the calculation of profit: sales revenues and the level of costs (wage rates, rents, interest rates, materials prices, utilities payments, various taxes and tax rate changes). Based on these forecasts, come up with your "best" forecast of the future profits (or losses) likely to result from any investment currently undertaken.

### Changing Expectations

Quite obviously profit forecasts are dependent on the current expectations held by businesses about the future. Changes in these expectations cause changes in profit forecasts, which in turn lead to changes in the amount of investment businesses want to do. Expectations can be very volatile, buffeted by continually changing information about markets, government policies, political events, and even the weather.

## The Investment Schedule and Its Determinants

When we develop the basic theory of how the economy's level of total income and employment are determined according to the income-expenditure approach, we will need to add the consumption plans of households to the investment plans of businesses to get the economy's total intended or planned expenditure on goods and services. In order to do this we will need to relate the level of businesses' investment spending plans to income, just as consumption spending plans are related to income by the consumption function. To simplify the ensuing discussion we will assume government taxes are zero and make no distinction between DI, PI, NI, NNP, and GNP because we will ignore all those things that differentiate these measures from one another.

---

Shown here are consumption, gross investment, and government expenditures over the post–World War II period. (Note that the vertical axis is a logarithmic, or ratio, scale on which equal distances represent equal percentage changes.) Investment expenditures have been the most variable of these major components of the expenditure side of GNP during this period.

The relationship between income and planned investment is represented by the investment schedule $I$ shown in Figure 8-7, part a. The economy's total dollar income, or total output, is measured on the horizontal axis, and its gross investment expenditures are measured on the vertical axis. As drawn, the investment schedule $I$ shows that businesses in aggregate plan to spend an amount equal to $I_0$ on plant, equipment, and inventories no matter what the level of income in the economy—*all other things remaining the same.* Therefore, the investment schedule $I$ is perfectly horizontal at the level $I_0$. Our discussion of the determinants of investment, the "other things," will indicate what determines the position of the $I$ schedule and how it may be shifted by changes in these determinants. Remember that the question of what determines investment expenditure in our economy is basically one of what determines the prospects for profit. Some of the more important determinants are the following.

### 1. Variation in Total Income

It seems reasonable to believe that the higher the level of current economic activity as measured by the level of total income, the more optimistic businesses will be about prospects for future profits. This optimism may well encourage them to invest more at higher income levels. If so, the investment schedule $I$ may slope upward as shown in Figure 8-7, part b.

### 2. The Interest Rate

The funds that businesses use to make investment expenditures on capital goods either must be borrowed from outside the firm or must be generated internally in the form of the firm's business saving (also called retained earnings). If they are borrowed from outside the firm, the cost of borrowing is the interest rate that must be paid to the lender. If they are generated internally, the cost to the firm is the forgone interest the firm could have earned if it had lent the funds to someone else. In either case the interest rate is the

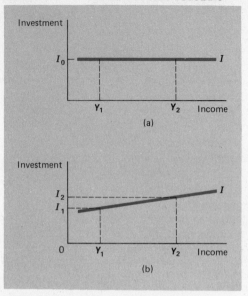

**FIGURE 8-7   The Investment Schedule**

In these diagrams the amount of investment expenditure in the economy is measured on the vertical axis and the economy's total income on the horizontal axis. The investment schedule $I$ shows the total amount of investment businesses desire to make at each level of the economy's total income, all other things remaining the same.

The investment schedule in part a is perfectly horizontal. This means that desired investment expenditure in the economy equals $I_0$ no matter what the level of total income.

The investment schedule in part b slopes upward on the assumption that businesses will be more optimistic about profit prospects the higher is the current level of economic activity as measured by total income. Therefore, desired investment will be larger at higher income levels. For example, desired investment will equal $I_1$ at income level $Y_1$, and the larger amount $I_2$ at the higher income level $Y_2$.

cost of the funds invested in capital goods. The higher the interest rate, the more this cost cuts into profit and reduces the incentive to invest in capital goods. Conversely, the lower the interest rate, the larger the profit and the greater the incentive to make investment expenditures.

Since the interest rate is among the "other things" assumed unchanged for any *movement along* the investment schedule, a change in the interest rate will cause the $I$ schedule to shift, as shown in Figure 8–8. In sum, *increases in the interest rate shift the investment schedule downward and decreases in the interest rate shift it upward.*

### 3. Technological Change and New Products

Technological change often makes existing capital equipment obsolete. Firms that fail to invest in capital goods that feature the latest technological breakthrough will find themselves at a competitive disadvantage relative to those that do. Those that acquire the latest capital first will get a competitive jump on rivals. Given these carrot-and-stick incentives, technological change often results in an upward shift in the investment schedule, such as from $I_0$ to $I_2$ in Figure 8–8.

**FIGURE 8-8  Shifts in the Investment Schedule**

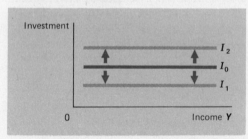

The investment schedule shows the total amount of investment businesses desire to do at each level of income, all other things that affect investment remaining the same. If one or more of these other things should change, it will cause the investment schedule to shift, either upward from $I_0$ to a position such as $I_2$, or downward to a position such as $I_1$. Among the other things that can cause such shifts are changes in the interest rate, technology, expectations about prospective profits, and the development of new products.

The development of new products opens up new markets. Lured by the resulting profit opportunities, firms will want to invest in the capital goods necessary to produce these new products. This too will cause an upward shift in the investment schedule.

### CHECKPOINT 8-4

**How would an increase in the prices of new capital goods affect the investment schedule? How do you think the investment schedule would be affected if labor unions and management in major industries throughout the country successfully negotiated new labor contracts without resorting to strikes?**

## TOTAL EXPENDITURE AND TOTAL INCOME: DETERMINING EQUILIBRIUM

Now we will see how the consumption function and the investment schedule combine to determine the economy's equilibrium level of total income, output, and employment. We will continue to make no distinction between GNP, NNP, NI, PI, and DI because we assume there is no government expenditure or taxation, that all saving is personal saving, and that capital depreciation is zero. We also continue to assume that net exports are zero and that the price level is fixed.

*The **equilibrium income level** is the one income level, among all possible income levels, at which the dollar value of the economy's total expenditure on output is just equal to the dollar value of total output that the firms in the economy produce. The equilibrium income level is also the level of total income that will be sustained once it is achieved.* Let's see how the equilibrium income level is determined.

### Total Expenditure Equals Consumption Plus Intended Investment

We have examined how the level of consumption expenditure and intended investment expenditure can be shown in a graph with the income level measured on the horizontal axis and desired consumption expenditures (Figure 8-4, part a) or intended investment expenditures (Figure 8-7) measured on the vertical axis. We may now combine these two components to form the economy's total spending or *total expenditure schedule*. We assume that the only components of total expenditure are consumption and investment.[2]

The hypothetical example of Table 8-2, which is shown graphically in Figure 8-9, shows how this is done. At each level of total income, column 1 of Table 8-2, the economy's households wish to spend an amount given by the associated level of consumption expenditures *C* shown in column 2. Column 3 of Table 8-2 shows the level of intended or planned investment expenditures *I* for the entire economy associated with each level of total income in column 1. Our example assumes that the amount of intended investment is the same ($300 billion) no matter what the level of total income. (This pattern of investment could be represented by a horizontal investment schedule like that shown in

[2] Government expenditures will be introduced in Chapter 10 and net exports will be ignored until we discuss international trade in a later chapter.

Figure 8-7, part a.) The total exenditure level, column 4 of Table 8-2, is obtained by adding the level of consumption expenditures (column 2) to the intended investment expenditures (column 3). It is represented in Figure 8-9 as the economy's *total expenditure schedule E*.

The economy's total expenditure schedule represents the amount of total spending on final goods and services that the economy's households and businesses desire to do at each possible level of total income.

## Total Income Equals Expected Total Spending

Total income is the sum of *all* payments received by the suppliers of all productive factors—land, labor, capital, and all other inputs—used in the production of the economy's total output. Therefore total income is the dollar value of this total output. The economy's firms produce this total output because they *expect* to sell it. That is, the dollar value of this total output (which equals total income) equals the level of *expected total spending* on final goods and services—the level of total *sales expected by the economy's businesses* which they therefore produce to meet.

**TABLE 8-2 Total Expenditure Equals Consumption Plus Intended Investment** (Hypothetical Data in Billions of Dollars)

| (1)<br>Total Income | (2)<br>Consumption Expenditure (*C*) | | (3)<br>Intended Investment (*I*) | | (4)<br>Total Expenditure (*E*)<br>*D* = (2) + (3) |
|---|---|---|---|---|---|
| $   200 | $   300 | + | $300 | = | $   600 |
| 400 | 400 | + | 300 | = | 700 |
| 600 | 500 | + | 300 | = | 800 |
| 800 | 600 | + | 300 | = | 900 |
| 1,000 | 700 | + | 300 | = | 1,000 |
| 1,200 | 800 | + | 300 | = | 1,100 |
| 1,400 | 900 | + | 300 | = | 1,200 |
| 1,600 | 1,000 | + | 300 | = | 1,300 |
| 1,800 | 1,100 | + | 300 | = | 1,400 |

**FIGURE 8-9** **Determining the Equilibrium Level of Total Income**

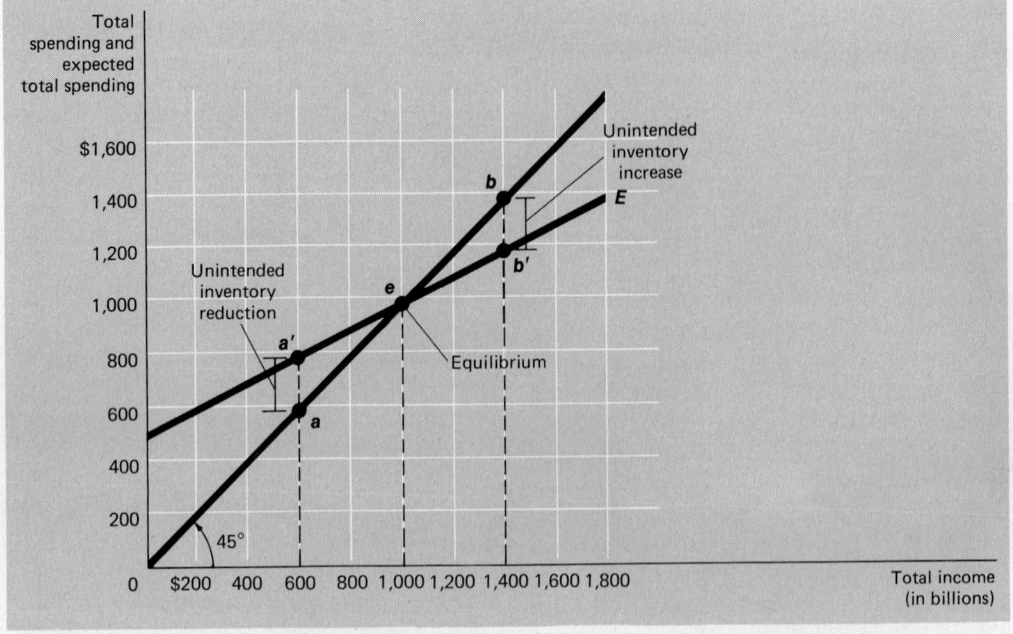

The economy's total expenditure schedule *E* combines with the 45° line to determine the equilibrium level of total income, which equals $1,000 billion, corresponding to the intersection at point *e*. This level of total income gives rise to a level of total spending that just buys up the total output the economy's businesses produce. Thus, there are no changes in inventories.

At total income levels lower than the equilibrium level, total expenditure is greater than total output. Therefore, unintended inventory reduction is necessary in order to satisfy the excess of total spending over total output. This will lead the economy's businesses to increase total output, causing total income to rise toward the equilibrium level.

At total income levels greater than the equilibrium level, total expenditure is less than total output. There are unintended inventory increases equal to the excess of total output over total spending. Therefore, the economy's businesses will decrease total output, causing total income to fall toward the equilibrium level.

The data on which Figure 8–9 is based are shown in Table 8–3.

This concept is also represented graphically in Figure 8–9. Expected total spending is measured on the vertical axis and total income on the horizontal axis. Since total income (horizontal axis) is always equal to expected total spending (vertical axis), this relationship may be represented by the already familiar 45° line. Why? Because any point on this line corresponds to a dollar magnitude

on either axis that is exactly equal to the corresponding dollar magnitude on the other axis.

For example, suppose the economy's business firms expect total spending to be $1,000 billion (vertical axis), which corresponds to point *e* on the 45° line. They will then proceed to produce $1,000 billion of total output, an amount just sufficient to satisfy expected total spending. Since this $1,000 billion is the total of all payments for the factors used to produce the total output, it is the level of total income in the economy. Measured on the horizontal axis, a total income level of $1,000 billion also corresponds to point e on the 45° line.

## Determining the Equilibrium Level of Total Income

We can now see how the economy's equilibrium level of total income is determined. This is the level of total income that will be sustained once it is achieved. To do this we combine the economy's total expenditure schedule E with the 45° line that represents the relationship between expected total spending and total income. This combination in Figure 8–9 is based on the hypothetical data of Table 8–3. First we will consider two possible nonequilibrium levels of total income. It will then be readily apparent why the equilibrium level of total income occurs where the total expenditure schedule E intersects the 45° line at point e.

### Unintended Inventory Reduction

Let us suppose that the economy's business firms *expect* total spending (vertical axis) to

be $600 billion. This corresponds to point a on the 45° line of Figure 8–9. Acting on the basis of this expectation, they produce $600 billion worth of total output. Since this represents $600 billion of payments to all the factors used to produce this total output, the economy's total income level (horizontal axis) is $600 billion, which also corresponds to point a on the 45° line. However, with a total income level of $600 billion, the *actual* level of total spending in the economy will turn out to be $800 billion, corresponding to point a' on the economy's total expenditure schedule E. But the economy only produced $600 billion worth of total output during the period. Consequently, the only way the total spending of $800 billion can be satisfied is for businesses to sell $200 billion of goods from inventories, stocks of goods produced and accumulated during *past* periods. The amount of this *unintended inventory reduction* is represented by the vertical distance between point a' on the economy's total expenditure schedule E and point a on the 45° line. It is *unintended* because the economy's business firms underestimated what the level of total spending in the economy was going to be.

The fact that the economy's business firms have to sell from inventories tells them that they underestimated total spending. If they

---

**TABLE 8-3 How the Economy's Equilibrium Total Income Level Is Determined** (Hypothetical Data in Billions of Dollars)

| (1) Expected Total Spending | (2) Total Income | (3) Total Expenditure (E) | (4) Change in Inventories | (5) Total Income Will Tend to |
|---|---|---|---|---|
| $   200 | $   200 | $   600 | $−400 | rise |
| 400 | 400 | 700 | −300 | rise |
| 600 | 600 | 800 | −200 | rise |
| 800 | 800 | 900 | −100 | rise |
| 1,000 | 1,000 | 1,000 | 0 | equilibrium |
| 1,200 | 1,200 | 1,100 | +100 | fall |
| 1,400 | 1,400 | 1,200 | +200 | fall |
| 1,600 | 1,600 | 1,300 | +300 | fall |
| 1,800 | 1,800 | 1,400 | +400 | fall |

were to continue doing this, unintended inventory reduction would also continue. Eventually, perhaps quickly, this would cause them to revise their expectations of total spending upward. The dollar value of total output produced, and hence the level of the economy's total income, would rise accordingly. This adjustment process will continue as long as there is any unintended reduction of inventories.

When and where will the adjustment stop? When unintended inventory reduction ceases—at the income level at which the level of total spending is just equal to that expected. In Figure 8–9 this occurs at a total income of $1,000 billion, corresponding to the intersection of the total expenditure schedule E with the 45° line at point e. It is therefore the equilibrium level of total income.

Starting from any level of expected total spending—and hence total income—less than $1,000 billion, total income will tend to rise until the equilibrium level is reached and there is no longer any unintended reduction of inventories. This is illustrated in Table 8–3. You should check the numbers shown there and relate them to Figure 8–9.

### Unintended Inventory Increase

Consider what happens at total income levels greater than the equilibrium level. Suppose the economy's business firms expect total spending (vertical axis) to be $1,400 billion, corresponding to point b on the 45° line in Figure 8–9. Therefore, they produce that amount of total output and the economy's total income (horizontal axis) is $1,400 billion. But at that total income level, actual total spending (vertical axis) will turn out to be only $1,200 billion, point b' on the economy's total expenditure schedule E. This means that $200 billion of the economy's total output will go unsold and therefore end up as an unintended inventory increase. This increase is represented by the vertical distance between points b and b' in Figure 8–9.

The $1,400 billion level of total income will not be sustained. Why? Business firms will not go on producing more output than they can sell, thereby increasing their unsold inventory. Instead, they will revise their expectations of total spending downward and produce less. As a result, total income will fall to the equilibrium total income level of $1,000 billion, which corresponds to the intersection of the economy's total expenditure schedule E and the 45° line at point e in Figure 8–9. We can now see that, starting from any level of total income greater than the equilibrium level, total income will tend to fall to the equilibrium level. Again this is illustrated in Table 8–3. You should check the numbers in this table and relate them to Figure 8–9.

In sum, *the economy's equilibrium level of total income gives rise to a level of total spending that just purchases the total output that the economy's businesses desire to produce. In equilibrium there is no change in inventories because total spending just matches the dollar value of total output.*

### Equilibrium Without Full Employment

Recall that we are assuming the economy's price level is fixed. Therefore if total spending and total income change, the entire change is due to a change in the number of actual physical units of output produced by the economy. And this requires a change in the amount of labor used in production. Consequently, every level of total income on the horizontal axis of Figure 8–9 corresponds to a different level of total employment.

These considerations suggest that *a major implication of the income-expenditure approach is that the level of employment associated with the equilibrium level of total income need not correspond to full employment, and typically will not.* For example, suppose that the labor force will be fully employed only when the economy produces the level of total output associated with a total income level equal to $1,400 billion. However, we have

## POLICY PERSPECTIVE

### The Great Depression—Attempts to Explain a Paradox

One of the most frightening things about the Great Depression is that no one, especially economists, seemed to have an adequate explanation that might suggest a policy for dealing with it.

In almost any city, long lines of unemployed workers could be seen seeking a free meal or some sort of assistance for their impoverished families. Somehow it all seemed a paradox. Why was it that able-bodied workers, who wanted nothing so much as a job in order to buy badly needed food and other goods, could not find work producing these products? Wouldn't the income they earned give rise to the demand that would justify the production that would give them employment? Couldn't failing businesses see the connection between the lack of customers at the front door and the long line of unemployed workers seeking jobs at the back door? How could this situation go on for so long? These riddles led to a growing fear. Had Karl Marx been right all along—would capitalism fall by its own weight? What was the matter?

### Wage and Price Flexibility

Many economists of the day, schooled in the classical tradition, argued that the problem lay in a number of markets where wages and prices were "sticky." They contended that in some product markets large monopoly-type firms were not willing to lower product prices as rapidly as was necessary in the face of declining product demand. Similarly, they argued that many unemployed workers were too reluctant to accept lower, or low enough, wages to gain employment. Hence, these economists concluded that classical wage and price flexibility was not allowed to work to bring the economy back to a full-employment equilibrium. Even though wages and prices did fall during the Great Depression, as shown in Figure P8-1, they contended that the decline was not far enough or fast enough. However the evidence in Figure P8-1 certainly provides room for debate on this issue. Some of these same economists, and others as well, also argued that government interference in banking and financial markets was keeping the interest rate from adjusting properly to equate saving and investment plans.

### Can the Interest Rate Match Saving and Investment Plans?

Perhaps the weakest link in the classical argument was the idea that interest rate adjustment would ensure the equality of saving and investment plans.

#### Many Things Affect Saving

The classical economists' argument that households are induced to save more at high interest rates than at low rates raises some questions. Even if the assertion is true, it may take large changes in interest rates to really affect the level of saving much at all, other things remaining the same. Indeed, many of the "other things" may be much more important determinants of saving plans than the interest rate is.

For example, much household saving is directed toward accumulating the funds needed to make some future purchase—a house, an automobile, a college education, a vacation, and so forth. Saving may also be aimed at providing a "nest egg" for unforeseen emergencies such as job loss, illness, or simply a general sense of secu-

**FIGURE P8-1  Wage and Price Levels in the United States During the Great Depression**

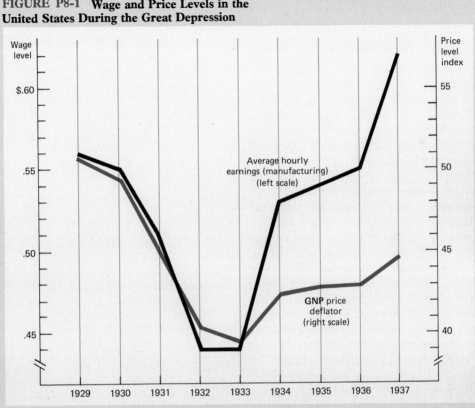

SOURCE: U.S. Department of Commerce and Bureau of Labor Statistics.

rity. Saving can also provide for retirement years. Some people may simply want to accumulate enough wealth to be able to live off the interest it can earn. The last motive has an interesting implication. The higher the interest rate, the less wealth it takes to earn a given level of income. If the interest rate is 5 percent, it takes $10,000 to earn $500 per year. At an interest rate of 10 percent, it takes half that amount, or $5,000, to earn $500 per year. Therefore, if people save in order to accumulate just enough wealth to be able to earn a certain income level from it, the higher the interest rate the less will be the amount of saving necessary to achieve their goal. Of course, this is just the opposite of the classical proposition that saving will increase when the interest rate increases.

### Investment—How Important Is the Interest Rate?

During the Great Depression capital consumption, or depreciation of the economy's capital stock, was actually larger than the amount of gross investment in each of the years from 1931 through 1935! In other words, net investment was negative. Many economists question whether interest rates lower than those that actually prevailed would have substantially increased investment expenditures in those years. A host of other factors are generally considered to be more important determinants of the level of investment.

For example, our discussion of the accelerator principle in the appendix of Chapter 6 indicated that the behavior of retail or final sales is extremely important. Since total income is just the receipts from total sales of the economy's total output of final goods and services, the accelerator principle suggests that the economy's total investment will be strongly affected by the behavior of total income. The fact that money GNP fell by roughly 50 percent between 1929 and 1933 would seem to have some bearing on the fact that gross investment fell by over 90 percent during this same period of time. No matter how low the rate of interest, dramatically falling sales would hardly seem likely to encourage businesses to invest in new plant and equipment or more inventories.

Regarding the interest rate, Keynes argued that there might well be a lower limit (above zero) to how far it could fall. Without getting into the complexity of his argument, this meant that the interest rate might not be able to fall low enough to match saving and investment plans and ensure full employment. Keynes also noted that even if the interest rate fell to zero, investment plans might still be less than saving plans, as shown in Figure

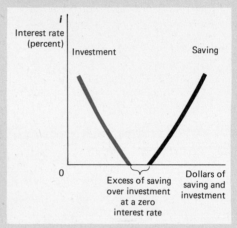

**FIGURE P8-2  Even at a Zero Interest Rate Saving May Not Equal Investment**

Here intended saving, represented by the saving curve, exceeds intended investment, represented by the investment curve, even when the interest rate is zero.

P8–2. The leakage from saving would then lead to a continuing fall in aggregate demand for goods and services.

### Questions

1. Could you envision the paradox described here occurring in Robinson Crusoe's world (one person living alone on an island)? Why or why not?

2. How might a decline in the total income level affect the saving curve $S$ in Figure P8–2?

already seen that if the economy's total expenditure schedule is $E$ (Figure 8–9), total spending is not sufficient to sustain this level of total income. Consequently, some of the labor force will be unemployed. In general, the lower the equilibrium level of total income, the higher the unemployment rate.

*CHECKPOINT 8-5*
**Give the explanation of what happens in the economy starting at any level of expected total spending and proceeding from column 1 to 2 to 3 to 4 to 5 in Table 8–3.**

## SUMMARY

**1.** Classical economists argued that a capitalistic, laissez faire economy would automatically tend to operate at a full-employment equilibrium. This contention was based on Say's Law, which states that supply creates its own demand.

**2.** The classical argument held that if wages and prices were perfectly flexible, a drop in total demand would result in a downward adjustment in wages and prices sufficient to reestablish a full-employment level of total output. In addition, the leakage from the income-expenditure flow due to saving would create no problem because the interest rate would adjust to ensure that saving plans always equaled investment plans.

**3.** The Great Depression of the 1930s led to a critical reexamination of the classical position. It became obvious that in a number of markets, prices and particularly wages were sticky, or slow to adjust downward. The notion that saving and investment plans could be equated by interest rate adjustments alone was brought into question.

**4.** The Keynesian revolution led to the development of income-expenditure theory and its basic building blocks—the consumption function, the saving function, and the investment schedule. The consumption function shows the amount households want to consume (spend) and the saving function the amount they want to save (not spend) at each disposable income level. The investment schedule shows the amount businesses want to invest at each income level.

**5.** Movements along the consumption and saving functions are caused by changes in disposable income, all other things that influence consumption and saving remaining the same. Changes in one or more of the other things will cause shifts in the consumption and saving functions. Important among these other things are credit conditions, consumer wealth, and consumer expectations about unemployment, prices, and income.

**6.** Investment expenditures are more vari-

able than the other two major components of the expenditure side of GNP, consumption and government expenditures. The expectation of profit is what determines the level of desired investment expenditure. The variability of investment expenditure results from the difficulty and complexity of forecasting prospective profits combined with the sensitivity of expectations to changes in the economic environment.

**7.** The investment schedule represents the relationships between the level of planned investment and the level of total income. Several important determinants of profit prospects that can cause shifts in the investment schedule are interest rate changes, technological change, and the development of new products.

**8.** According to the income-expenditure approach the equilibrium level of total income, output, and employment occurs where the total expenditure schedule intersects the 45° line. At equilibrium the total income earned from production of the economy's total output corresponds to a level of total spending just sufficient to purchase that total output.

**9.** At levels of total income less than the equilibrium level, total spending is greater than total output and there is unintended inventory reduction. This leads the economy's business firms to increase total output, so that total income and employment rise toward the equilibrium level. At levels of total income greater than the equilibrium level, total spending is less than total output and there are unintended increases in inventories. The economy's business firms then reduce total output, so that total income and employment tend to fall toward the equilibrium level.

## KEY TERMS AND CONCEPTS

consumption function
equilibrium income level
interest rate
saving function
Say's Law

## QUESTIONS AND PROBLEMS

**1.** According to Say's Law, supply creates demand. Why couldn't this law be stated the other way around, namely, that demand creates supply?

**2.** Suppose you were a completely self-sufficient farmer and trapper living in the wilderness. What would be the relationship between your saving and investment decisions? What would be the significance of the notion of involuntary unemployment?

**3.** Explain why wage and price flexibility are not sufficient to restore a full-employment equilibrium subsequent to a fall in total demand.

**4.** Using a diagram like Figure 8–1, illustrate what would happen if there were no positive level of the interest rate that would equate saving and investment plans. Describe what would be happening in the economy in this situation.

**5.** How do you think the following would affect the consumption and saving functions and why?

a. Employer-subsidized pension plans for employees are set up throughout the economy.

b. There is a decline in the stock market.

c. The government announces that gasoline will be rationed to consumers starting 3 months from now.

d. Households anticipate that the rate of inflation is going to rise from 5 percent per year to 15 percent per year during the next 6 months.

e. Households begin to doubt the financial soundness of the social security system, causing concern about the level of future retirement benefits that the system will be able to pay them.

**6.** What do you think would be the effect on prospective profit of each of the following and how would the investment schedule shift as a result?

a. Unions demand that employers make larger contributions to employee pension plans.

b. New sources of natural gas are discovered.

c. Congress passes a law allowing larger tax write-offs for research and development costs.

d. Congress passes a law mandating stiffer controls on industrial disposal waste.

e. War breaks out in the Middle East, threatening the destruction of oil fields in the area.

f. The president calls for price ceilings on final products and an increase in social security taxes.

**7.** Compare and contrast the way businesses decide to invest with the way households decide how much to consume, and explain why investment is more variable than consumption.

**8.** How do you think the position of the total expenditure schedule $E$ in Figure 8–9 would be affected by each of the following?

a. a decline in the expected profitability of business;

b. a rise in the interest rate;

c. an increase in the wealth of households;

d. an increase in consumer indebtedness.

**9.** Why does total income equal expected total spending? In what sense are inventories a buffer against mistakes in forecasting?

**10.** In Table 8–3, suppose the economy's level of total expenditure (column 3) is higher by $100 billion at every level of total income (column 2). What would be the new equilibrium level of total income, and how would columns 4 and 5 be changed? Can you sketch this change in Figure 8–9?

**11.** Why is it that the unintended inventory increase represented by the vertical distance between $b$ and $b'$ in Figure 8–9 is included in total income, while the unintended inventory reduction equal to the vertical distance between $a'$ and $a$ is not?

# 9

# Total Expenditure and the Multiplier in Income Determination

**AFTER READING THIS CHAPTER, YOU WILL BE ABLE TO:**

1. Distinguish between realized and intended investment and explain their relationship to saving and equilibrium.

2. Describe and explain the paradox of thrift.

3. Define and explain the marginal and average propensities to consume and to save.

4. Define the multiplier and illustrate why autonomous changes in the components of total expenditure have multiplier effects.

In this chapter we will examine more closely the Keynesian view of how the economy's equilibrium level of total income, output, and employment is determined. First, we will focus on the relationship between investment and saving in the determination of equilibrium. Then we will examine the so-called paradox of thrift. Finally we will define and explain the marginal propensity to consume and the marginal propensity to save. We will use these concepts to explain the important Keynesian concept of the multiplier, which tells us how total income will change in response to a change in total expenditure.

We will continue to make no distinction between GNP, NNP, NI, PI, and DI because for the time being, we will assume there is no government expenditure or taxation, that all saving is personal saving, and that capital depreciation is zero. We also continue to assume that net exports are zero. Throughout this chapter we will also assume that wages and prices are unchanging, an assumption that simplifies the analysis without interfering with the learning objectives in any way. The concepts developed in this chapter will prove very useful to us in the next chapter, where we introduce government expenditure and taxation into this framework.

## EQUILIBRIUM AND REALIZED VERSUS INTENDED INVESTMENT

So far, our discussion of how the equilibrium level of total income is determined has focused on the total expenditure schedule $E$ and its relationship to the 45° line. Now let's look at this relationship more closely. First, we will explicitly recognize that the total expenditure schedule $E$ is equal to the sum of consumption and the level of intended or desired investment, as was shown in Table 8–2. Then we will explicitly recognize the relationship between total income and consumption (the consumption function) and total in-

come and saving (the saving function). These relationships were shown in Figure 8–4 of Chapter 8.

Continuing with our hypothetical example, the data from Tables 8–2 and 8–3 are shown again in columns 1, 2, 4, 5, and 6 of Table 9–1. Also shown is the level of saving (column 3), which is equal to the difference between total income and consumption (column 1 minus column 2). Realized investment, which is equal to the sum of columns 4 and 6, is shown in column 7. These relationships are shown in Figure 9–1, part a, which is the same as Figure 8–9 except that the consumption function has been added. This function is the level of consumption expenditure $C$ (column 2) associated with each level of total income (column 1). We will use Figure 9–1 to help us define the concept of realized investment and its relationship to intended investment. We will then examine the relationship between these two types of investment and saving, both when the economy is at its equilibrium income level and when it is not.

## Realized Investment Always Equals Saving

In Chapter 7 gross private domestic investment was defined as including all final purchases of new tools and machines by business firms, all construction expenditures, *and all changes in inventories.*

### At Total Income Levels Below Equilibrium Level

We have seen that when the economy is at a below-equilibrium level of total income, there is an unintended inventory change. This change is an inventory reduction, which is represented by the vertical distance between the total expenditure schedule $E$ and the 45° line. For example, when total income is $600 billion (Figure 9–1, part a), there is an unintended inventory reduction of $200 billion, which is represented by the vertical distance between $a'$ and $a$. The amount of

**TABLE 9-1 Determination of the Equilibrium Level of Total Income, and the Relationship Between Intended Investment, Realized Investment, and Saving**
(Hypothetical Data in Billions of Dollars)

| (1) | (2) | (3) | (4) | (5) | (6) | (7) |
|---|---|---|---|---|---|---|
| Total Income and Output | Con- sumption Expenditure (C) | Saving (S) | Intended Investment (I) | Total Expenditure (E) or Total Spending | Unintended Inventory Change Equals Total Output Minus Total Expenditure | Realized Investment Equals Intended Investment Plus Unintended Inventory Change |
| | | $S = (1) - (2)$ | | $D = (2) + (4)$ | $(1) - (5)$ | $(4) + (6)$ |
| $ 200 | $ 300 | $-100 | $300 | $600 | $-400 | $-100 |
| 400 | 400 | 0 | 300 | 700 | -300 | 0 |
| 600 | 500 | 100 | 300 | 800 | -200 | 100 |
| 800 | 600 | 200 | 300 | 900 | -100 | 200 |
| 1,000 | 700 | 300 | 300 | 1,000 | 0 | 300 |
| 1,200 | 800 | 400 | 300 | 1,100 | 100 | 400 |
| 1,400 | 900 | 500 | 300 | 1,200 | 200 | 500 |
| 1,600 | 1,000 | 600 | 300 | 1,300 | 300 | 600 |
| 1,800 | 1,100 | 700 | 300 | 1,400 | 400 | 700 |

intended investment, or the investment that business firms *desire* to do, is $300 billion, which is represented by the vertical distance *a'* to *a"* between the total expenditure schedule E and the consumption function C. However, this $300 billion investment expenditure, when combined with the $500 billion of consumption expenditure (a sum equal to $800 billion), exceeds the $600 billion of total output produced during the period, corresponding to point *a* on the 45° line, by $200 billion. Hence, $200 billion of goods has to be sold from inventory to satisfy this excess of total spending over total production. The $200 billion decrease, or *negative change*, in inventories is an offset to the $300 billion of intended investment. It is often called a disinvestment. Actual investment, or **realized investment,** therefore amounts to only $100 billion, which is represented by the vertical

distance between point *a* on the 45° line and point *a"* on the consumption function C.

Note that this vertical distance between point *a* on the 45° line and point *a"* on the consumption function also represents the amount of saving that households do out of the $600 billion total income. Therefore, it follows that *realized investment is equal to saving.* At any total income level less than the equilibrium level of total income (which is equal to $1,000 billion in our example), intended investment is always greater than realized investment. A comparison of columns 4 and 7 of Table 9-1 for the total income levels (column 1) less than the equilibrium level bears this out. At any of these total income levels, it is also always true that realized investment equals saving (compare columns 3 and 7). You should relate these numbers to Figure 9-1.

**FIGURE 9-1** **Determinations of the Equilibrium Level of Total Income, and the Relationship Between Intended Investment, Realized Investment, and Saving**

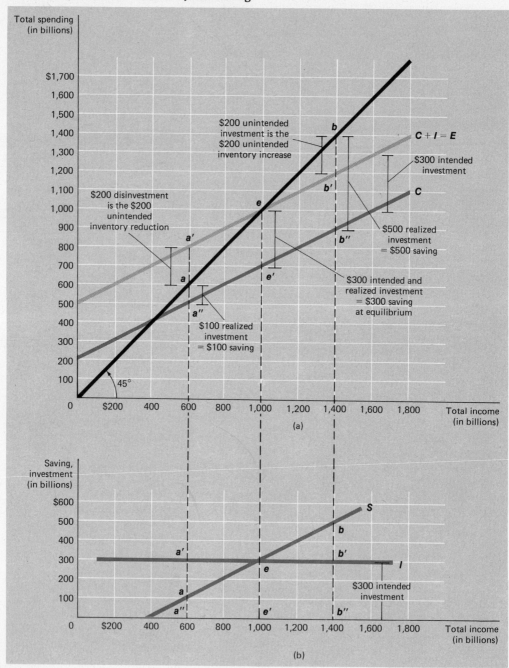

(a)

(b)

### At Total Income Levels Above Equilibrium Level

At total income levels greater than the equilibrium level, we observed that there are unintended inventory increases represented by the vertical distance between the total expenditure schedule E and the 45° line. For instance, at a total income level of $1,400 billion (Figure 9–1, part a), we see a $200 billion unintended inventory increase. This increase is equal to the vertical distance between b and b'. Once again the amount of intended investment that the economy's business firms desire to do equals $300 billion. This desired investment is represented by the vertical distance between point b' on the total expenditure schedule E and point b'' on the consumption function C. This amount of investment expenditure plus the $900 billion of consumption expenditure gives a total spending level of $1,200 billion. But this level is $200 billion lower than the $1,400 billion level of total output produced during the period (point b on the 45° line). As a result, $200 billion of unsold goods remain on shelves and in warehouses as inventory. This $200 billion increase or *positive change*

in inventories is unintended investment, an unplanned addition to the $300 billion of intended investment. Therefore, actual or *realized investment* amounts to $500 billion, which is equal to the vertical distance between point b on the 45° line and point b'' on the consumption function C.

Again this vertical distance represents the amount of saving, equal to $500 billion, that takes place when the total income level is $1,400 billion. Once more we see that *realized investment is equal to saving.* Indeed, this is true at any total income level greater than the equilibrium level. For example, in Table 9–1 compare columns 3 and 7 for each of the total income levels in column 1 greater than the $1,000 billion equilibrium level. It is also true that at any total income level greater than the equilibrium level, realized investment is always greater than intended investment, as we can see by comparing columns 4 and 7. Again, you should relate these numbers to Figure 9–1.

### Equilibrium Level of Total Income

Now consider the equilibrium level of total income, which is $1,000 billion. It is only

The diagram in part a is the same as that in Figure 8–9 except that the components that make up total expenditure E, consumption C, and intended investment I are explicitly shown along with the level of saving (which is equal to the difference between consumption C and the 45° line). At total income levels larger than the equilibrium level of $1,000 billion, realized investment exceeds intended investment by the amount of unintended inventory increase. At total income levels less than the equilibrium level, intended investment is greater than realized investment by the amount of unintended inventory reduction. Realized investment always equals saving, no matter what the level of total income. But intended investment equals saving, hence realized investment, only at the equilibrium level of total income.

The diagram in part b shows an alternative but completely equivalent way to represent the determination of the equilibrium level of total income. It combines the saving function S, corresponding to the consumption function in part a, with the investment schedule I, which shows the level of intended investment; the investment schedule I is the same as the vertical distance between the total expenditure schedule E and the consumption function C in part a. The points corresponding to a, e, b, and so forth in part a are similarly labeled in part b. The vertical distances between these points have exactly the same interpretation in part b as in part a. The equilibrium level of total income is determined by the intersection of the saving function S and the investment schedule I at point e.

here that the level of intended investment is equal to the level of realized investment, in this case $300 billion, which is represented by the vertical distance from $e$ to $e'$ in Figure 9–1, part a. This reflects the fact that there is no unintended change in inventory because the $1,000 billion level of total spending just equals the $1,000 billion of total output produced. Again observe that realized investment equals saving, just as at all other levels of total income. But only at equilibrium is it also true that intended investment equals saving.

By way of summary, we can say that:

1. Actual or realized investment always equals saving no matter what the level of total income.
2. Intended investment equals saving only at the equilibrium level of total income.
3. Realized investment and intended investment are equal only at the equilibrium level of total income. At all other levels of total income, they differ by the amount of unintended inventory change.

## Leakages-and-Injections Interpretation of Equilibrium

In Figure 8–4 of Chapter 8, we examined the correspondence between the consumption function and the saving function. The saving function $S$ in Figure 9–1, part b, corresponds to the consumption function $C$ in Figure 9–1, part a, in exactly the same manner. The saving function is based on the data from columns 1 and 3 of Table 9–1. Figure 8–7, part a, of Chapter 8 showed us that when the level of intended investment is the same at all income levels, it may be represented by a horizontal investment schedule. Hence, the $300 billion level of intended investment represented by the vertical distance between the consumption function $C$ and the total expenditure schedule $E$ in Figure 9–1, part a, also can be represented by the investment schedule $I$ in Figure 9–1, part b. This invest-

ment schedule is based on the data from columns 1 and 4 of Table 9–1.

The combination of the saving function $S$ and the investment schedule $I$ in Figure 9–1, part b, is an alternative but completely equivalent way to that shown in part a for representing how the equilibrium level of total income is determined. The points corresponding to $a$, $e$, $b$, and so forth in part a are similarly labeled in part b. The vertical distances between these points have exactly the same meaning in part b that they have in part a. However, the combination of the saving function $S$ and the investment schedule $I$ in part b suggests another interesting interpretation of the determination of the equilibrium level of total income. This is the leakages-and-injections interpretation.

### The Circular Flow

We anticipated this interpretation in Chapter 8. There we noted that the circular-flow nature of the total-spending-equals-total-income relationship suggests that saving is like a leakage from the ongoing flow, while investment is like an injection to that flow. Investment spending by businesses acts as an offset to the saving by households (their refraining from spending out of income) and can prevent a sharp drop in the ongoing level of total spending. This is so because not all of the economy's output is sold to consumers. Some of it is sold to businesses in the form of capital goods; thus, investment spending takes a portion of total output off the market.

What will be the equilibrium, or unchanging, level of the total-spending-equals-total-income circular flow? It will be that level of total income at which the associated amount of leakage due to saving is just exactly offset by the amount of injection due to intended investment—the level of total income at which intended investment equals saving. This level is represented in Figure 9–1, part b, by the intersection of the saving function $S$ and the investment schedule $I$ at point $e$, which corresponds to a total income level of $1,000 billion.

### At Total Income Levels Above Equilibrium Level

At total income levels greater than the equilibrium level, the leakage from saving will be larger than the injection from intended investment. This can be seen by comparing columns 3 and 4 of Table 9–1, and it is also represented by the fact that the saving function S lies above the investment schedule I to the right of point e. For example, at a total income level of $1,400 billion, point b″, the leakage from total income due to saving equals $500 billion, which is represented by the vertical distance from b″ to b. However, the injection due to intended investment is only $300 billion, the vertical distance from b″ to b′. This means that of the $500 billion of total output *not* purchased by consumers only $300 billion is taken off the market through intended investment spending by businesses. The rest, amounting to $200 billion and represented by the vertical distance from b′ to b, is left unsold on shelves and in warehouses as an unintended addition to inventory. This addition to inventory will lead the economy's businesses to reduce production of total output and thereby cause the level of total income to fall, as we discussed earlier in looking at Figure 9–1, part a. Total income will continue to fall until the amount of total output consumers refrain from purchasing—the amount consumers save—equals the amount businesses purchase—their intended investment spending. This equality occurs only at the equilibrium total income level of $1,000 billion, the level at which intended investment and saving both equal $300 billion, as represented by the vertical distance between point e′ and e in Figure 9–1, part b.

### At Total Income Levels Below Equilibrium Level

At total income levels less than the equilibrium level, the leakage from saving will be less than the injection from intended investment. This may be seen by comparing columns 3 and 4 of Table 9–1. It is also represented by the fact that the saving function lies below the investment schedule to the left of point e in Figure 9–1, part b. For instance, at a total income level of $600 billion, point a″, the leakage from total income due to saving is only $100 billion, represented by the vertical distance from a″ to a. But the injection from intended investment amounts to $300 billion, which is equal to the distance from a″ to a′. The difference, amounting to $200 billion, is the excess of total demand or spending over total output, which is represented by the vertical distance between a and a′. In order to satisfy this excess demand, producers must sell goods from inventories. But this reduction in inventories will lead the economy's businesses to increase the production of total output. Consequently the economy's total income will rise, as we discussed earlier in connection with part a of Figure 9–1. Total income will continue to rise, and the amount of leakage due to saving will continue to increase until it equals the amount of injection into the circular flow due to intended investment. Again, this equality occurs only at the equilibrium total income level of $1,000 billion, the level at which the saving function S intersects the investment schedule I at point e in Figure 9–1, part b.

### Equilibrium Level of Total Income

*The equilibrium level of total income, corresponding to the intersection of the saving function S and the investment schedule I, is the only level where the total of the saving plans of the economy's households just matches the total of the investment plans of the economy's businesses. At any other level there will be a discrepancy between the plans of these two groups.*

### CHECKPOINT* 9–1

**Explain why realized investment is *always* equal to saving. Explain why it is sometimes said that "this is obvious because the part of total output that is not consumed must go someplace."**

*Answers to all Checkpoints can be found at the back of the text.

---

### ECONOMIC THINKERS

---

#### John Maynard Keynes — 1883–1946

John Maynard Keynes, the great British scholar, was doubtless the most influential economist of the first half of the twentieth century. In 1936 he published *The General Theory of Employment, Interest, and Money,* a book that had about the same impact on affairs as had Adam Smith's *The Wealth of Nations.*

Up to this point Keynes had generally accepted the elements of neoclassical economics as espoused by such great economists as Alfred Marshall, the English economist who had been his teacher at Cambridge. Neoclassical economics assumed that Say's Law of markets was valid, that full employment was the natural case when the economy was in equilibrium. Prices and interest rates would be flexible, varying with demand and supply. Free competition would be the normal case. If unemployment occurred, there would be a tendency toward the restoration of full employment. There would at all times be sufficient demand to take the goods produced off the market. Any deviations from this norm would be brief (of course there might be hard times, the business cycle, etc.) but these would be abnormal and largely self-correcting.

Keynes objected to these concepts in whole or in part. He contended that the economy might well be in equilibrium and at the same time at a position of less than full employment. That is, aggregate demand for goods and services might be inadequate to support full employment. Of course there was increasing evidence that prices and wages were often rigid due to monopolistic elements in the economy, unions, price fixing, nonprice competition, and other factors. U.S. economists especially argued that this was in fact most often the case.

However, Keynes's theory did not rest merely on the existence of rigid prices and wage rates. In his view the volume of employment was determined by the level of "effective demand." Even if wages were flexible, the same problem might exist due to the possible rigidity of interest rates.

Keynes suggested increased government expenditures to supplement private expenditures for consumption and investment in the event that these expenditures were inadequate to provide full employment, which was often the case.

In the United States some American economists battling the Depression advocated Keynesian measures as part of the "New Deal" machinery. These battles were fought throughout the 1930s, but President Roosevelt's advisors were not really active Keynesians until after 1938, and Roosevelt himself was never convinced of the virtue of budget deficits. By the 1950s Keynesian economics had become well integrated into basic theory.

FOR FURTHER READING

Harrod, R. F. *The Life of John Maynard Keynes.* New York: Harcourt Brace Jovanovich, 1951.
Norton, Hugh S. *The Employment Act and the Council of Economic Advisers 1946–1976.* Columbia: University of South Carolina Press, 1977.

---

## THE PARADOX OF THRIFT: WHAT DID BEN FRANKLIN SAY?

You have probably heard the old saw, attributed to Ben Franklin: "A penny saved is a penny earned." It seems like good advice for a household. But it may not be good for the economy if all households do so. It is a case of the fallacy of composition—what is true of the part is not necessarily true of the whole.

Suppose the equilibrium level of total in-

## POLICY PERSPECTIVE

### A Common Misconception About the Saving-Investment Process— The Role of Banks

During the Great Depression more than 5,000 banks failed between 1929 and 1933 in the United States. Many economists place at least some of the blame on the policymakers responsible for regulating the banking system at that time, arguing that they had the authority and the means to keep any bank from having to close (as we will see in Chapter 13). What was not well understood then was the exact nature of the crucial role that banks play in the economy's saving-investment process. Because of this role widespread bank failures can cause severe interruptions in the saving-investment process and hence in the economy's income-expenditure flow, thereby contributing to, or even causing, a severe economic downturn.

The extent of the role of banks in maintaining the income-expenditure flow was often not fully appreciated because of a common misconception, namely, the idea that dollars from saving must somehow flow from the hands of savers into the hands of investors in order for investment expenditures to be able to occur. But in fact households may bury their unspent dollars in the backyard if they wish. In a modern economy the banking system is able to create money (we shall see how in a later chapter) and lend it to businesses that want to invest in plant, equipment, and inventories. As long as the amount of money banks lend to businesses in this way is equal to the amount households desire to save, investment plans will continue to equal saving plans and there need be no interruption in the income-expenditure flow.

The fact that dollars do not literally have to flow from the hands of savers into those of investors illustrates how much the motives and decisions of savers may be disconnected from those of investors. It also highlights an important point. If households put their savings in sugar bowls and mattresses or bury them in the backyard, investment will have to be financed by the banking system. Widespread bank failures, such as those that occurred during the 1930s, remove this source of financing and cause intended investment spending to fall, thereby reducing the economy's equilibrium level of total income, output, and employment as well.

#### Questions

1. We have noted that if households put their savings in sugar bowls and mattresses or bury them in the backyard, investment will have to be financed by the banking system. What bearing does this have on the fact that total spending is always greater than total income at levels of total income less than the equilibrium level?

2. What effect do you think widespread bank failures would have on the consumption function?

come and output in the economy is $1,400 billion. This level is determined by the intersection of the saving function $S_0$ with the investment schedule $I$ at point $e_0$ in Figure 9-2, part a. The level of saving and investment (vertical axis) is $400 billion. Now suppose the economy's households follow Ben Franklin's advice. They decide to save more at every level of total income. The result would be an upward shift in the saving function from $S_0$ to $S_1$. But look what happens! The equilibrium level of total income and

FIGURE 9-2 **The Paradox of Thrift**

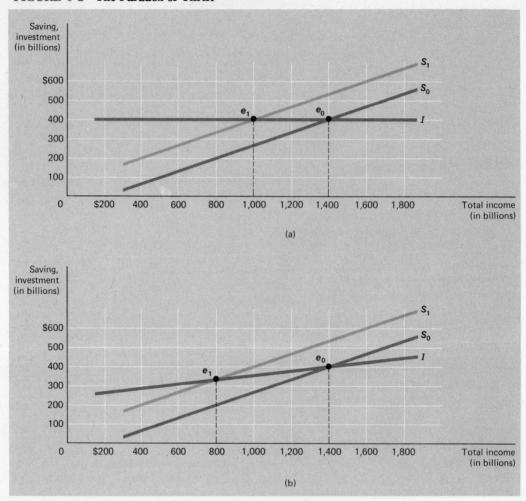

(a)

(b)

It may well be good advice for a household to try to save more, but bad for the economy if all households attempt to do so.

Suppose the economy's equilibrium level of total income is initially $1,400 billion, as determined by the intersection of the saving function $S_0$ and investment schedule $I$ at point $e_0$. If the economy's households attempt to save more, the saving function will shift up to the position $S_1$. Given the investment schedule $I$ in part a, total income and output will fall to $1,000 billion and the amount of saving will in fact remain unchanged at $400 billion. If the level of intended investment varies with the level of total income and output, as shown in part b, the attempt to save more actually causes the amount saved to fall!

output falls from $1,400 billion to $1,000 billion, as determined by the intersection of $S_1$ and $I$ at $e_1$. Furthermore, the amount of saving that actually takes place remains unchanged at $400 billion. A penny saved is not a penny earned. Quite the contrary, the *attempt* to save more results in no increase in saving and, worse yet, leads to an actual decline in the total income earned!

This **paradox of thrift** is even more pronounced if the level of intended investment varies with the level of total income, so that the investment schedule $I$ slopes upward as shown in Figure 9–2, part b. Then the same upward shift in the saving function from $S_0$ to $S_1$ results in an even greater fall in total income and output, from \$1,400 billion to \$800 billion, as determined by the intersection of $S_1$ and $I$ at $e_1$. Moreover, the amount of saving that actually takes place is now smaller! The attempt by the economy's households to save more leads to the paradoxical result that they end up saving less.

What explains the paradox of thrift? The answer is that the attempt to save more results in a larger leakage from total income. At the initial equilibrium level of total income, \$1,400 billion in our example, the leakage exceeds the amount of intended investment spending. Consequently, the level of total income falls as the economy's businesses cut back the production of total output in order to avoid unintended inventory increases. This fall in total output and income continues until the level of saving, or leakage, is once again brought into equality with the level of intended investment, or injection. At this point there is no unintended inventory accumulated and the economy is once again at equilibrium.

### CHECKPOINT 9-2

**Explain the paradox of thrift in terms of what happens if the economy's households attempt to save less. To do so, use Figure 9–2, parts a and b. Suppose a news item suggests that consumers may attempt to rebuild "their savings" that have "dwindled." What do you as an "analyst" think about this? What are the possible implications for auto workers and steelworkers?**

## MARGINAL AND AVERAGE PROPENSITIES TO CONSUME AND TO SAVE

Students often confuse the concepts of marginal and average. The distinction between

them is important to our understanding of the consumption and saving functions and their role in the theory of income and employment determination. In particular, the marginal propensity to consume and the marginal propensity to save are needed to understand the important Keynesian concept of the multiplier, as we shall see.

### Marginal Propensity to Consume and to Save

The **marginal propensity to consume (MPC)** is the fraction or proportion of any *change* in disposable income that is consumed:

$$MPC = \frac{\text{change in consumption}}{\text{change in disposable income}}$$

The term *marginal* refers to the fact that we are interested *only* in the *change* in the level of consumption brought about by a *change* in the level of disposable income. Similarly, the **marginal propensity to save (MPS)** is the fraction or proportion of any *change* in disposable income that is saved:

$$MPS = \frac{\text{change in saving}}{\text{change in disposable income}}$$

These concepts are shown in Table 9–2. As we move from one level of disposable income to the next in column 1, the *change* ($\Delta$) in the level of disposable income, $\Delta DI$, is given in column 2. The associated *change* in the level of consumption, $\Delta C$, brought about by the *change* in disposable income, $\Delta DI$, is given in column 4. The associated marginal propensity to consume, MPC, is shown in column 7. In this case, MPC (which is $\Delta C \div \Delta DI$) equals .60. Similarly, the change in the level of saving, $\Delta S$, brought about by the *change* in disposable income, $\Delta DI$, is given in column 6. The associated marginal propensity to save, MPS, is given in column 8. In this case, the MPS (which is $\Delta S \div \Delta DI$) equals .40.

Suppose, for example, that disposable income rises from \$450 billion to \$475 billion, an increase of \$25 billion (column 2). What do households do with this increase? Accord-

**TABLE 9-2 The Consumption and Saving Schedules, the Marginal Propensity to Consume, and the Marginal Propensity to Save** (Hypothetical Data in Billions of Dollars)

| (1) | (2) | (3) | (4) | (5) | (6) | (7) | (8) |
|---|---|---|---|---|---|---|---|
| Disposable Income (DI) | Change in DI (ΔDI) | Consumption (C) | Change in C (ΔC) | Saving (S) | Change in S (ΔS) | Marginal Propensity to Consume (MPC) | Marginal Propensity to Save (MPS) |
| | | | | $S = (1) - (3)$ | | $MPC = \dfrac{(4)}{(2)}$ | $MPS = \dfrac{(6)}{(2)}$ |
| 300 | | 320 | | −20 | | | |
| | 25 | | 15 | | 10 | .60 | .40 |
| 325 | | 335 | | −10 | | | |
| | 25 | | 15 | | 10 | .60 | .40 |
| 350 | | 350 | | 0 | | | |
| | 25 | | 15 | | 10 | .60 | .40 |
| 375 | | 365 | | 10 | | | |
| | 25 | | 15 | | 10 | .60 | .40 |
| 400 | | 380 | | 20 | | | |
| | 25 | | 15 | | 10 | .60 | .40 |
| 425 | | 395 | | 30 | | | |
| | 25 | | 15 | | 10 | .60 | .40 |
| 450 | | 410 | | 40 | | | |
| | 25 | | 15 | | 10 | .60 | .40 |
| 475 | | 425 | | 50 | | | |
| | 25 | | 15 | | 10 | .60 | .40 |
| 500 | | 440 | | 60 | | | |

ing to Table 9–2, they consume .60 of it, which is $15 billion (column 4), and save .40 of it, which is $10 billion (column 6). These are the only two things households can do with the increase—consume part of it and save the rest. By definition, then, the fraction of the increase in disposable income consumed, MPC, plus the fraction saved, MPS, when added together are equal to the whole increase in disposable income. Therefore, *the sum of MPC and MPS must always equal 1:*

$$MPC + MPS = 1$$

The data in Table 9–2 show us that this is true, since

$$.60 + .40 = 1$$

*The marginal propensity to consume is represented graphically by the slope of the consumption function,* as shown in Figure 9–3,

part a. (Figure 9–3 is the same as Figure 8-4.) The slope of any line is the ratio of the amount of vertical change in the line to the associated amount of horizontal change. For the consumption function, the vertical change ΔC is associated with the horizontal change ΔDI. Similarly, *the marginal propensity to save is represented graphically by the slope of the saving function* as shown in Figure 9–3, part b.

If the consumption function is a straight line, then so is the saving function. When the consumption function is a straight line, its slope (*MPC*) has the same value at every point along the line. The same is true of the slope (*MPS*) of the straight-line saving function. The consumption and saving functions of Figure 9–3 are both straight lines. If, however, the consumption function were a curve that was less steeply sloped at higher

**FIGURE 9-3  The Marginal Propensity to Consume and the Marginal Propensity to Save**

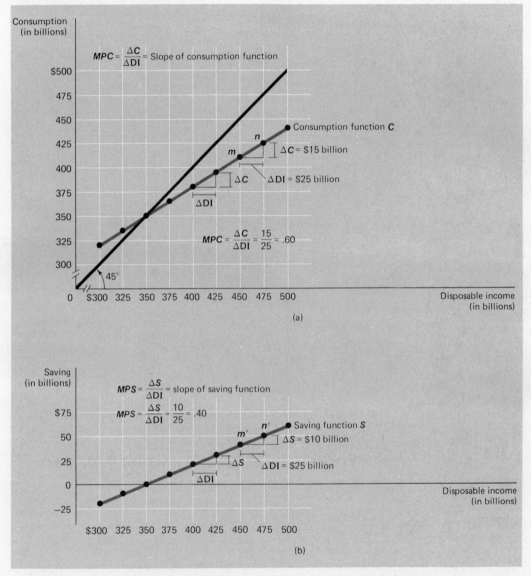

(a)

(b)

The slope of a line is the ratio of the amount of vertical change in the line to the associated amount of horizontal change.

For the consumption function, the vertical change $\Delta C$ is associated with the horizontal change $\Delta DI$, as shown in part a. Hence, the slope of the consumption function is $\Delta C \div \Delta DI$, which is the marginal propensity to consume, MPC. Similarly, the slope of the saving function is $\Delta S \div \Delta DI$, which is the marginal propensity to save, MPS, as shown in part b.

Both of these functions are straight lines. Therefore, the marginal propensity to consume is the same no matter where it is measured along the consumption function. The same is true of the marginal propensity to save measured anywhere along the saving function. In the examples shown here, which are based on the data in Table 9-2, the MPC equals .60 and the MPS equals .40.

**TABLE 9-3 The Consumption and Saving Schedules, the Average Propensity to Consume, and the Average Propensity to Save** (Hypothetical Data in Billions of Dollars)

| (1) Disposable Income (DI) | (2) Consumption (C) | (3) Saving (S) | (4) Average Propensity to Consume (APC) | (5) Average Propensity to Save (APS) |
|---|---|---|---|---|
| | | $S = (1) - (2)$ | $APC = \frac{(2)}{(1)}$ | $APS = \frac{(3)}{(1)}$ |
| 300 | 320 | −20 | 1.07 | −.07 |
| 325 | 335 | −10 | 1.03 | −.03 |
| 350 | 350 | 0 | 1.00 | .00 |
| 375 | 365 | 10 | .97 | .03 |
| 400 | 380 | 20 | .95 | .05 |
| 425 | 395 | 30 | .93 | .07 |
| 450 | 410 | 40 | .91 | .09 |
| 475 | 425 | 50 | .89 | .11 |
| 500 | 440 | 60 | .88 | .12 |

disposable income levels, then the saving function would be a curve that gets more steeply sloped at higher disposable income levels. In that case the *MPC* would be smaller at higher income levels and the *MPS* would be larger. Draw such consumption and saving functions and illustrate these characteristics.

## Average Propensity to Consume and to Save

The **average propensity to consume (APC)** is the fraction or proportion of *total* disposable income that is consumed:

$$APC = \frac{\text{consumption}}{\text{disposable income}}$$

Note that whereas the *MPC* is the ratio of the *change* in consumption to the *change* in disposable income, the *APC* is the ratio of the *level* of consumption to the *level* of disposable income. The *APC* and the *MPC* are therefore two distinctly different concepts.

Table 9–3 shows the same data in columns 1, 2, and 3 for DI, *C,* and *S* as in columns 1,

3, and 5 of Table 9–2. The average propensity to consume for each level of disposable income (column 1), and its associated level of consumption (column 2), is shown in column 4. *APC* equals *C* ÷ DI, which is the consumption data in column 2 divided by the disposable income data in column 1. Note that unlike the *MPC* (column 7 of Table 9–2), the *APC* (column 4 of Table 9–3) declines as disposable income increases.

The **average propensity to save (APS)** is the fraction or proportion of *total* disposable income that is saved:

$$APS = \frac{\text{saving}}{\text{disposable income}}$$

Again, the *APS* and the *MPS* are distinctly different concepts. While the *MPS* is the ratio of the *change* in saving to the *change* in disposable income, the *APS* is the ratio of the *level* of saving to the *level* of disposable income.

The *APS* of our example is shown in column 5 of Table 9–3. Note that while *APC* (column 4) falls as disposable income increases, the *APS* (column 5) increases. In other words, if the fraction of total disposable income consumed gets smaller at higher disposable income levels, it follows that the fraction of total disposable income saved must get larger. Since all disposable income is either consumed or saved, it also follows that

$$APC + APS = 1$$

---

### CHECKPOINT 9-3

**Show graphically how the consumption function would have to look if its *MPC* and *APC* are always equal to each other, no matter what the disposable income level. What would be true of the relationship between the *MPS* and the *APS* of the saving function in this case, and what would the saving function look like? How would the consumption function have to shift for the *APC* to increase and the *MPC* to remain unchanged? Show what would happen to the saving function in this case.**

---

### AUTONOMOUS EXPENDITURE CHANGE AND THE MULTIPLIER EFFECT

Our examination of the business cycle in Chapter 6 indicated that total income, output, and employment are always "on the move." One of the main reasons for this movement is that total expenditure frequently shifts. In the simple economy we are considering in this chapter, where government expenditure and taxation are ignored, shifts in total expenditure can be caused by shifts in either or both of its components—consumption and intended investment. Such shifts are represented by changes in the position of the total expenditure schedule that are reflected in changes in the equilibrium levels of total income, output, and employment.

Shifts in the consumption and saving functions, the investment schedule, and hence the total expenditure schedule, are due to causes *other than* changes in the level of total income. Changes in the level of total income cause *movement along* these curves. Changes in all other things—expectations, wealth, interest rates, and so forth—cause *shifts or changes in the position* of these curves. In order to keep this extremely important distinction in mind, changes in expenditure which cause the total expenditure schedule to shift are often referred to as *exogenous*, or *autonomous*, expenditure changes.

*Shifts in total expenditure, whatever the underlying cause, give rise to even larger changes in total income and output. This is referred to as the multiplier effect. Given the dollar amount of the shift in total expenditure, the resulting change in total income and output will be several times larger, or some multiple of this amount. This multiple is called the* **multiplier**. For instance, if intended investment rises by $10 billion and the resulting change in total income amounts to $30 billion, the multiplier is 3. If the rise in total income is $40 billion, the multiplier is 4. Let's see why there is a multiplier effect and what determines the size of the multiplier.

### Graphical Interpretation of the Multiplier Effect

Suppose the economy's business firms believe that sales are going to pick up in the coming year and that they are going to need more productive capacity to meet this increase. Let's suppose that investment spending increases from $200 billion to $400 billion.

The effect of this increase on total income and output is shown in Figure 9–4. In this figure the economy is initially in equilibrium at a total income level of $800 billion. This is the level at which the total expenditure schedule $E_0$ (which equals $C_0 + I_0$) and the 45° line intersect, point *a* in part a. Equivalently, it is the point at which the investment schedule $I_0$ and the saving function $S$ intersect, point *a* in part b. A $200 billion autonomous increase in investment from $I_0$ to $I_1$

**FIGURE 9-4  Shifts in Total Expenditure Have a Multiplier Effect on Total Income and Output**

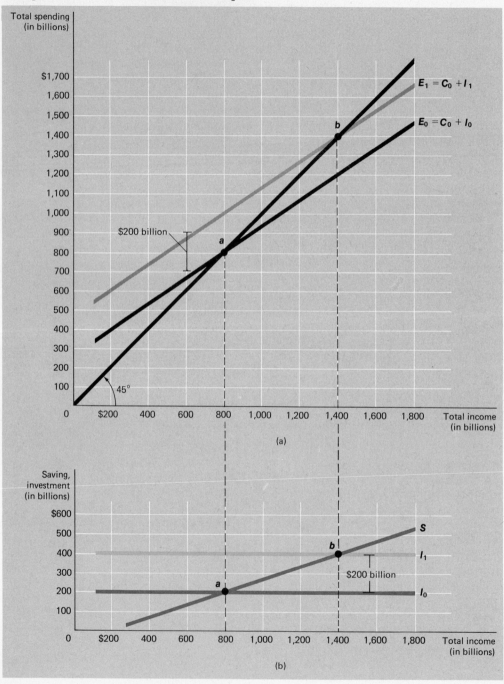

causes the total expenditure schedule in part a to shift upward from $E_0$ (which equals $C_0 + I_0$) to $E_1$ (which equals $C_0 + I_1$). Equivalently, this is represented in part b by the upward shift in the investment schedule from $I_0$ to $I_1$. Each of the diagrams shows that the equilibrium level of total income rises from $800 billion to $1,400 billion—given by the intersection of $E_1$ and the 45° line at point $b$ in part a and by the intersection of $S$ and $I_1$ at point $b$ in part b. In other words, the $200 billion increase in investment causes a $600 billion increase in total income and output. This is the multiplier effect. The value of the multiplier is 3 in this hypothetical example.

The multiplier effect also applies for any autonomous decrease in the level of investment spending. For example, suppose that the economy is now at the equilibrium total income level of $1,400 billion. Then suppose the economy's business firms' expectations about future sales turn pessimistic, and investment spending shifts downward $200 billion from $I_1$ to $I_0$. This is represented in Figure 9-4, part a, by a downward shift in the total expenditure schedule from $E_1$ (which equals $C_0 + I_1$) to $E_0$ (which equals $C_0 + I_0$). Equivalently, it is represented in part b by a $200 billion downward shift in the investment schedule from $I_1$ to $I_0$. In either diagram we can see that total income and output fall by $600 billion, from $1,400 billion to $800 billion. Once again, the multiplier effect is at work, and the value of the multiplier is 3.

## A Numerical Interpretation of the Multiplier Effect

We can also provide a numerical interpretation of the example of the multiplier effect that is illustrated in Figure 9-4. In this example, the marginal propensity to consume $MPC$, which is the slope of the consumption function, is $2/3$. Hence, the marginal propensity to save $MPS$, the slope of the saving function, is $1/3$. We will see how the $MPC$ and the $MPS$ play a crucial role in the multiplier effect and in the determination of the size of the multiplier.

To do so, let's consider the data in Table 9-4. Again, we will assume that the economy is initially in equilibrium at a total income level of $800 billion. The table shows how an autonomous increase in investment expenditure of $200 billion has a chain-reaction effect on the economy. The autonomous expenditure increase causes an increase in income. Part of this income increase is spent, causing a further increase in income, part of which is spent, and so on, round after round. At the first round firms react to the increase in total expenditure by increasing total output by $200 billion. This increased output, of course, is received as increased income

The total expenditure schedule in part a will be shifted by a shift in either or both of its components, the consumption function (hence the saving function) and the investment schedule. If the investment schedule shifts upward by $200 billion from $I_0$ to $I_1$, the total expenditure schedule will shift upward from $E_0$ (which equals $C_0 + I_0$) to $E_1$ ($C_0 + I_1$). Consequently, the equilibrium level of total income and output will rise from $800 billion to $1,400 billion, or by three times the amount of the investment spending increase. This is the multiplier effect. The multiplier equals 3 in this example.

Part b shows an equivalent representation of this shift in terms of the investment schedule and the saving function. This diagram indicates clearly why there is $600 billion increase in total income in response to the $200 billion increase in investment spending. The $600 billion increase in total income gives rise to a $200 billion increase in saving, or leakage, that is just enough to offset the initial $200 billion increase in investment, or injection.

**TABLE 9-4 Multiplier Effect of an Expenditure Increase, Round by Round** (Hypothetical Data in Billions of Dollars)

| Expenditure Round | (1) Change in Income and Output | (2) Change in Consumption | (3) Change in Saving |
|---|---|---|---|
| | | $MPC = 2/3$ | $MPS = 1/3$ |
| First round | $200.0 ⟶ | $133.4 | $ 66.6 |
| Second round | 133.4 ⟵⟶ | 89.0 | 44.4 |
| Third round | 89.0 ⟵⟶ | 59.4 | 29.6 |
| Fourth round | 59.4 ⟵⟶ | 39.6 | 19.8 |
| Fifth round | 39.6 ⟵⟶ | 26.4 | 13.2 |
| Rest of the rounds | 78.6 ⟵⟶ | 52.2 | 26.4 |
| Totals | $600.0 | $400.0 | $200.0 |

(column 1) in the form of wages, rents, interest, and profit by the households who own the factors of production used to produce the increased output. Given an *MPC* of 2/3, households will spend $133.4 billion of this income increase (column 2) and save $66.6 billion (column 3).

At the second round firms react to this $133.4 billion increase in total expenditure by increasing total output an equivalent amount. This gives rise to another increase in payments to factors of production and a further rise in total income of $133.4 billion (column 1). In turn, 2/3 of this, or $89 billion, is spent (column 2), and $44.4 billion is saved (column 3).

At the third round, the $89 billion increase in total expenditure again causes a like increase in total output, factor payments, and hence income (column 1). Then 2/3, or $59.4 billion, of this increase is spent at the fourth round, $39.6 billion is spent at the fifth round, and so forth until the additions to total income ultimately become so small they are insignificant. Adding up all the round-by-round increases in total income in column

1, the total increase in total income and output is $600 billion. This is the same result we saw in Figure 9-4.

Why does the expansion in total income end here? The reason is that the $600 billion increase in total income gives rise to a $200 billion increase in the amount of saving, or leakage (column 3), that is just enough to offset the initial $200 billion increase in investment, or injection. At this point the economy is once again in equilibrium. Total income has increased by three times the initial increase in investment because the economy's households save 1/3 of any increase in income. The multiplier is 3, just as it was in Figure 9-4.

## The Multiplier and the *MPS* and *MPC*

Our example of the multiplier effect, illustrated in Figure 9-4 and Table 9-4, suggests that the size of the multiplier depends on the size of the *MPS* or its complement, the *MPC*. (Remember that *MPS* + *MPC* = 1, always.)

Recall that the *MPS* is represented by the slope of the saving function (see Figure 9–3, part b). The *MPS*, or slope of the saving function *S*, in Figure 9–4, part b, is $\frac{1}{3}$. This means that every \$1 increase in saving (vertical movement) corresponds to a \$3 increase in total income (horizontal movement). Consequently, when the investment schedule shifts upward by \$200 billion from $I_0$ to $I_1$, saving likewise rises by \$200 billion (vertical axis) and total income rises by \$600 billion (horizontal axis). Every \$1 of increase in investment spending gives rise to a \$3 increase in total income. The multiplier is therefore 3. But this is just the reciprocal of the *MPS*— the value of the *MPS*, which is equal to $\frac{1}{3}$, turned upside down.

When we look at the numerical illustration of our example in Table 9–4, the same conclusion emerges. When the *MPS* equals $\frac{1}{3}$, every \$1 of increased investment ultimately results in \$3 of increased total income—the \$200 billion increase in investment spending ultimately results in a \$600 billion increase in total income. The multiplier is 3. If the *MPS* had been $\frac{1}{2}$, the ultimate increase would have been \$400 billion—the multiplier is 2. If the *MPS* had been $\frac{1}{4}$, the increase would have been \$800 billion—the multiplier is 4.

In sum, for the simple economy of this chapter (no net exports, no government expenditures, no taxation), *the multiplier is equal to the reciprocal of the MPS:*

$$\text{the multiplier} = \frac{1}{MPS}$$

If *MPS* equals $\frac{1}{3}$, for example, then

$$\text{the multiplier} = \frac{1}{\frac{1}{3}} = 3$$

Note that because $MPC + MPS = 1$, it is true that $MPS = 1 - MPC$, and so we can also say

$$\text{the multiplier} = \frac{1}{1 - MPC}$$

Also note that *the smaller the MPS, and therefore the larger the MPC, the larger the*

*multiplier. Conversely, the larger the MPS, and hence the smaller the MPC, the smaller the multiplier.* (Convince yourself of this by computing the multiplier first when $MPS = \frac{1}{2}$, hence $MPC = \frac{1}{2}$; and second when $MPS = \frac{1}{4}$, hence $MPC = \frac{3}{4}$.)

### Two Important Points

Finally, two important points should be made about our discussion of the multiplier effect and the multiplier. First, our example assumed that the multiplier effect was triggered by an autonomous shift in investment spending. Exactly the same results would have followed if the trigger had instead been an autonomous shift in consumption spending, as represented by a shift in the consumption and saving functions. Second, the multiplier effect and the multiplier are just as applicable to downward shifts in investment or consumption spending as they are to upward shifts.

### CHECKPOINT 9-4

**Suppose that the total expenditure and investment schedules are $E_0$ and $I_0$ in parts a and b respectively in Figure 9–4. Show what the effect would be in both parts a and b if there were a \$200 billion upward shift in the consumption function. Suppose the *MPS* is $\frac{1}{5}$. Show what the effect of a \$100 billion *downward* shift in consumption would be in a table like Table 9–4. Also, illustrate this effect graphically, using a figure like Figure 9–4, parts a and b. Suppose a news item notes that "consumers have spent so heavily in recent months that their savings have dwindled. . . ." In what sense is the word *savings* used? Suppose the news item seems to be talking about both movements along and shifts in the consumption function. Illustrate what is being said in terms of a diagram like Figure 9–4.**

## SUMMARY

**1.** Realized investment is always equal to saving. Intended investment equals saving only at the equilibrium level of total income. Therefore, intended investment and realized investment are equal at the equilibrium level of total income but differ from each other by the amount of unintended inventory change at all other levels of total income.

**2.** Intended investment may be viewed as an injection into the circular flow of spending and income, while saving may be viewed as a leakage from that flow. At the equilibrium level of total income, the injection of intended investment is equal to the leakage due to saving. Graphically, this corresponds to the point at which the investment schedule intersects the saving function. At levels of total income greater than the equilibrium level, the leakage due to saving exceeds the injection due to intended investment, and total income will tend to fall toward the equilibrium level. At less than equilibrium levels of total income the leakage due to saving is less than the injection from intended investment. This inequality causes total income to rise toward the equilibrium level.

**3.** If households try to save more, the economy's total income will fall and the level of saving will be no higher than it was initially, or it may even be lower. This is the paradox of thrift.

**4.** The marginal propensity to consume (*MPC*) is the fraction of any change in disposable income that is consumed—represented graphically by the slope of the consumption function. The marginal propensity to save (*MPS*) is the fraction of any change in disposable income that is saved—represented graphically by the slope of the saving function. The sum of the *MPS* and the *MPC* always equals 1.

**5.** The average propensity to consume (*APC*) is the fraction of disposable income that is consumed, and the average propensity to save (*APS*) is the fraction of disposable income that is saved. The sum of the *APC* and the *APS* always equals 1.

**6.** Autonomous spending changes represented by shifts in the total expenditure schedule cause changes in total income that are several times the size of the initial spending change. This multiplier effect may be triggered by changes in either or both of the components of total expenditure—the consumption function (and therefore the saving function) and the investment schedule. In the simple economy of this chapter, the multiplier equals the reciprocal of the marginal propensity to save.

## KEY TERMS AND CONCEPTS

average propensity to consume (*APC*)
average propensity to save (*APS*)
marginal propensity to consume (*MPC*)
marginal propensity to save (*MPS*)
multiplier
paradox of thrift
realized investment

## QUESTIONS AND PROBLEMS

**1.** Why does realized investment always equal saving? When realized investment and intended investment are not equal, why does the level of total income, output, and employment tend to change?

**2.** When injections exceed leakages, what happens to the economy's level of total income? What is the relationship between intended investment and realized investment in this situation? If the level of total income is falling, what must be the relationship between saving and intended investment? If the level of total income is rising, what must be the relationship between realized investment and saving?

**3.** Explain the paradox of thrift in terms of Figure 9–1, part a. Suppose the marginal propensity to consume *MPC* decreases because households want to save more out of income so they won't be so hard pressed for funds when Christmas shopping time rolls around. What do you predict this decrease in *MPC* will do to ease their budget problems come Christmas?

4. Show what happens to the consumption and saving functions as a result of the following:

    a. The *MPS* decreases.

    b. The *APC* increases.

    c. The *APC* decreases and the *MPS* increases.

    d. The *APS* and the *MPS* decrease.

    e. The *APC* and the *MPC* increase.

    f. The *APC* decreases and the *MPC* increases.

5. If the saving function shifts downward, what must happen to the investment schedule in order for the total demand schedule to remain unchanged? What will happen to the level of employment in this instance? Why will this happen?

6. What happens to the value of the multiplier if the consumption function becomes steeper? What happens to the value of the multiplier if the saving function shifts downward to a position parallel to its initial position? What is the effect on the level of total income in this case?

# 10

# Government Spending, Taxation, and Fiscal Policy

**AFTER READING THIS CHAPTER, YOU WILL BE ABLE TO:**

1. Explain how government spending and taxation affect total expenditure and the equilibrium level of GNP.

2. Explain the practical limitations of discretionary fiscal policy.

3. Describe how automatic stabilizers work to moderate the cyclical swings in our economy.

4. Outline the major views of budget policy and be able to explain the concept of the high-employment budget.

5. Explain the financing effects of budget surpluses and deficits.

6. Describe the differences between public and private debt and the nature of the possible burdens of the government debt.

**W**e are now familiar with the basic explanation of why the equilibrium level of total income may be less than the full-employment level. This chapter brings the role of government into the analysis and shows how **fiscal policy**—government's management of its spending, taxing, and debt-issuing authority—affects the equilibrium level of total income, output, and employment. One of the primary objectives of present-day fiscal policy is to smooth out the ever present fluctuations in economic activity and prod the economy closer to full-employment without inflation. While fiscal policy cannot be expected to accomplish such a task alone, it must play a key role.

In this chapter we will continue to assume that wages and prices are inflexible so that the economy's general price level is fixed. We will relax this assumption in the next chapter and allow the price level to vary with changes in total income, output, and employment, as determined by the interaction of aggregate demand and supply.

## THE GOVERNMENT BUDGET

Like any budget, *the federal* **government's budget** *is an itemized account of expenditures and revenues over some period of time.* In this case, the time period is the fiscal year beginning October 1 and ending September 30 of the following year. The expenditure, or outlay, side of the budget consists mainly of defense expenditures and transfer payments in the form of social security and welfare payments, unemployment compensation, medical payments, and interest on the government debt (see Figure 3–1, Chapter 3). Revenues to cover these outlays come largely from corporate and personal income taxes and from social insurance taxes, which are paid into the social security system by employers and employees. These are followed by excise taxes, which are taxes levied on the sale of certain products, such as alcohol and tobacco. Interest on government-managed trust funds and customs duties levied on certain internationally traded goods also provide revenue.

An examination of state and local government budgets shows the largest proportion of outlays going to education. Next come expenditures for police and fire protection, the administration of judicial and legislative operations, the development of natural resources, and the establishment and maintenance of recreation programs and facilities. The largest proportion of the remaining expenditures goes into highways and roads, hospitals, and health and welfare programs. The major sources of revenue for state and local governments are property taxes (on land and buildings, and sometimes on personal property and financial assets) and retail sales taxes. However, the fastest growing source of state and local revenues in recent years is state and local income taxes.

From World War II to 1974, state and local government tax revenues increased much more rapidly than federal tax revenues. This reflected the growing economic importance of state and local government activities. Since 1974 federal tax revenues have increased on average at a somewhat faster rate than state and local government tax revenues.

### Deficits and Surpluses

A government has a **balanced budget** if total expenditures equal total tax revenues. It has a **budget surplus** if expenditures are less than tax revenues. It has a **budget deficit** if expenditures are greater than tax revenues. The federal budget in our economy has shown a deficit in all but eight years since 1931. The last time there was a budget surplus was 1969, and the last time there were back-to-back surpluses was in 1956 and 1957. During one string of 16 years, 1931 through 1946 (the Great Depression and war years), there was a federal budget deficit virtually every year. The number of consecutive budget deficit years since 1969 surpasses this mark. In this chapter we will see why budget deficits generally tend to stimulate income, output, and employment, while surpluses have the opposite effect.

## Fiscal Policy and the Employment Act of 1946

The Great Depression of the 1930s made people fearful that the economy might plunge into another depression when peacetime conditions returned at the end of World War II. This led Congress to pass the Employment Act of 1946, which declared that "it is the continuing policy and responsibility of the Federal Government . . . to coordinate and utilize all its plans, functions, and resources . . . in a manner calculated to foster and promote free competitive enterprise and the general welfare . . . to promote maximum employment, production, and purchasing power."

This act clearly called for the federal government to use its taxing and spending authority to prevent recessions and inflationary booms. Recent developments in economic theory, due to Keynes and his followers, suggested that the consumption and investment decisions of individual households and businesses could give rise to either too little or too much aggregate demand. The collective effect of private decisions based on self-interest could result in either excessive unemployment or excessive inflation. By contrast, Keynesian theory suggested that government acting for society as a whole could manage its spending and taxing activities to prevent these unwanted developments. This is the spirit of Keynesian fiscal policy. Let's see how it works both in theory and in practice.

## PRINCIPLES OF DISCRETIONARY FISCAL POLICY

*Discretionary fiscal policy is the government's deliberate regulation of its spending and taxing activities to attempt to smooth out business fluctuations and ensure maximum employment with as little inflation as possible.* Our discussion of discretionary fiscal policy will be simplified by assuming that the only kind of taxes collected by the government are personal income taxes. This means that personal income, PI, now differs from disposable income, DI, by the amount of these taxes. We will continue to make no distinction between GNP, NNP, NI, and PI. They are all the same—what we called total income in the previous chapter. From now on we generally will use the term GNP when referring to total income. In our simplified world, then, GNP differs from DI only by the amount of personal income taxes $T$.

## Government Expenditure and Total Expenditure

Suppose initially that government spending and taxation are zero. Assume that the equilibrium level of GNP is $1,200 billion as determined by the intersection of the total expenditure schedule $C + I$ and the 45° line in Figure 10–1, part a. This intersection corresponds to the intersection of the saving function $S$ and the investment schedule $I$ in Figure 10–1, part b. If the full-employment level of GNP is $1,600 billion, the economy is plagued by a considerable amount of unemployment when GNP is only $1,200 billion.

The economy can be pushed to full employment if the government spends $200 billion on goods and services. This amount of government spending $G$ then adds another layer onto the total expenditure schedule, pushing it vertically upward by $200 billion to the position $C + I + G$ in Figure 10–1, part a. Given that the $MPC$ is assumed to equal 1/2 (hence the $MPS$ equals 1/2), the multiplier is 2. Therefore, GNP increases by $400 billion from $1,200 billion to $1,600 billion, corresponding to the intersection of the total expenditure schedule $C + I + G$ with the 45° line.

This also may be shown in terms of Figure 10–1, part b. Here the $200 billion of government spending $G$ adds another layer onto the investment schedule $I$ to give the schedule $I + G$. The intersection of $I + G$ with the saving function $S$ is the point at which the leakage from saving, equal to $600 billion, is just offset by the sum of the injections from intended investment $I$, equal to $400

**FIGURE 10-1  Effect of Government Spending on Equilibrium GNP**

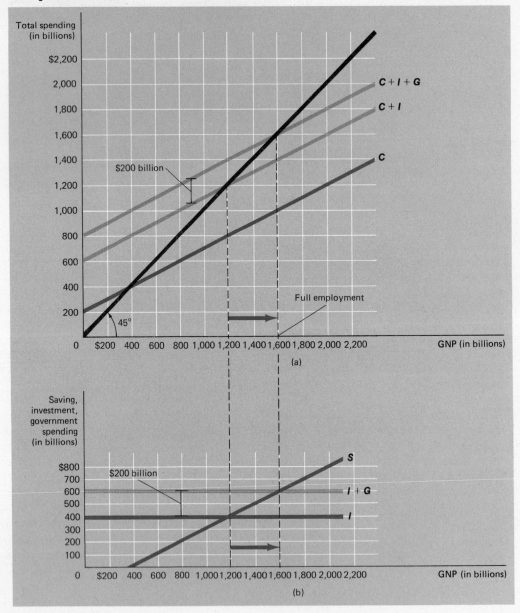

Government spending of $200 billion causes the total expenditure schedule to shift upward from $C + I$ to $C + I + G$ in part a. The equilibrium level of GNP is thereby increased from $1,200 billion, corresponding to the intersection of $C + I$ and the 45° line, to $1,600 billion, corresponding to the intersection of $C + I + G$ and the 45° line. This can be shown equivalently in terms of leakages and injections in part b. The $200 billion, and government spending, equal to $200 billion. When we bring government spending into the picture, we see that it is no longer necessary for intended investment to equal saving at equilibrium. What is important is that the leakages from income equal the injections into it, or that $S = I + G$, in this case. (Note that government expenditures do not have to be financed by taxes, although they can be, as we shall see below.)

Of course, a decline in $G$ will cause the total expenditure schedule (part a) and the $I + G$ schedule (part b) to shift downward and the equilibrium level of GNP to fall. In sum, *increases in the level of government spending will cause increases in the level of GNP, just like upward shifts in the level of intended investment and consumption. Decreases in government spending will cause decreases in GNP.*

## Taxation and Total Expenditure

Government spending is one side of fiscal policy. Taxation is the other. Suppose the government decides to finance its $200 billion expenditure by levying a lump-sum tax of $200 billion. This is a lump-sum tax in the sense that government will collect $200 billion in taxes no matter what the level of GNP. How will this affect the equilibrium level of GNP?

Figure 10-2 demonstrates what will happen. The equilibrium of Figure 10-1, part a, determined by the total expenditure schedule $C + I + G$, is shown again in this figure. Initially GNP equals DI. When the government imposes the lump-sum tax, a wedge equal to $200 billion will be driven between GNP and disposable income DI at every

level of GNP. Since part of every dollar of DI is consumed and the rest saved, it follows that the reduction in DI will be reflected partly in a reduction in consumption and partly in a reduction in saving. The degree of reduction in each category is determined by the size of the $MPC$ and the $MPS$. The $MPC$ and $MPS$ are each equal to $\frac{1}{2}$ in this case. Therefore, the $200 billion tax will cause a $100 billion reduction in consumption and a $100 billion reduction in saving at every level of GNP. The consumption function is the only component of the total expenditure schedule affected by the tax. It is shifted down by $100 billion from $C$ to $C_1$ at every level of GNP. Consequently, the total expenditure schedule is shifted downward by $100 billion from $C + I + G$ to $C_1 + I + G$, as shown in Figure 10-2, part a. The equilibrium level of GNP therefore declines from $1,600 billion, the full-employment level, to $1,400 billion. This $200 billion change is the result of the multiplier effect.

We get the same result if we take the leakages-injections point of view. The equilibrium of Figure 10-1, part b, determined by the intersection of the saving function $S$ and the $I + G$ schedule, is shown again in Figure 10-2, part b. When the $200 billion lump-sum tax is imposed, DI is reduced by this amount at every level of GNP. With an $MPS$ of $\frac{1}{2}$ this means that saving is reduced by $100 billion at every level of GNP, so that the saving function shifts downward from $S$ to $S_1$. In addition to the leakage from GNP due to saving, now there is also a $200 billion leakage due to taxes at every level of GNP. Adding this to the saving function gives us the total leakage function $S_1 + T$. The equilibrium level of GNP is now $1,400

billion of government expenditure adds another layer $G$ onto the investment schedule $I$ to give the $I + G$ schedule. The new equilibrium level of GNP at $1,600 billion corresponds to the intersection of the saving function $S$ and the $I + G$ schedule. Here the $600 billion leakage from saving is exactly offset by the injections which equal the sum of the $400 billion of intended investment $I$ and the $200 billion of government spending $G$.

**FIGURE 10-2** **Effect of Government Taxation on Equilibrium GNP**

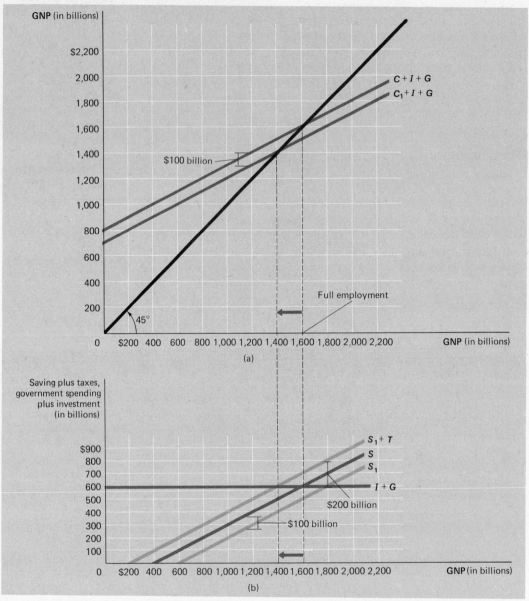

Suppose the government imposes a lump-sum tax of $200 billion. This means that DI will be $200 billion less at every level of GNP.

Assuming that the *MPC* equals $1/2$ and therefore that the *MPS* is also $1/2$, consumption will be $100 billion less at every level of GNP. The consumption function will be shifted downward by this amount. The total expenditure schedule will therefore shift downward by this amount, from $C + I + G$ to $C_1 + I + G$ in part a. The equilibrium level of GNP will fall from $1,600 billion to $1,400 billion.

billion, determined by the intersection of $S_1$ + $T$ and $I$ + $G$ in Figure 10-2, part b. Here the sum of the leakages from GNP, which is equal to saving plus taxes, is just offset by the sum of the injections, which is equal to intended investment plus government spending. At equilibrium, $S_1$ + $T$ = $I$ + $G$.

Whether we look at it from the total expenditure schedule vantage point of part a or from the leakages-injection vantage point of part b, we see that imposing a tax will cause the equilibrium level of GNP to fall. Similarly, removing the tax would cause the total expenditure schedule to rise or, equivalently, the $S$ + $T$ function to fall, so that the equilibrium level of GNP would increase. In sum, *increases in taxes will cause decreases in GNP. Decreases in taxes will cause increases in GNP.*

### The Balanced Budget Multiplier

Note that the $200 billion of government spending alone *increases* the equilibrium level of GNP from $1,200 billion to $1,600 billion (Figure 10-1). However, the $200 billion lump-sum tax collected to finance the spending *decreases* the equilibrium level of GNP from $1,600 billion to $1,400 billion (Figure 10-2). The net increase in the equilibrium level of GNP—from $1,200 billion to $1,400 billion—is therefore $200 billion. In short, a $200 billion increase in government spending, financed by a $200 billion increase in taxes, results in a $200 billion increase in GNP.

This illustrates the **balanced budget multiplier**: *a government expenditure increase balanced by an equivalent increase in taxes will result in an increase in GNP of exactly the same size. The balanced budget multiplier equals 1.* The increase in GNP is equal to 1 times the amount of the government expenditure increase, or 1 times the amount of the government tax increase. Similarly, a government expenditure decrease balanced by an equivalent decrease in taxes will result in a decrease in GNP of exactly the same size. The balanced budget multiplier equals 1 no matter what the size of *MPS* and *MPC*.

What explains the operation of the balanced budget multiplier? Consider our example again. The government expenditure increase of $200 billion is in part offset by the $200 billion increase in taxes. Why? Because with an *MPC* of $1/2$, and therefore an *MPS* of $1/2$, the tax increase causes a $100 billion decrease in consumption spending. The net result is an increase in total spending of $100 billion—the difference between the $200 billion increase in government spending and the $100 billion reduction in consumption spending. This is only the initial effect, however. The $100 billion net increase in total spending times the multiplier 2 ultimately gives a net increase in GNP of $200 billion.

In the example shown in Figures 10-1 and 10-2, GNP must equal $1,600 billion if there is to be full employment. Starting from a GNP level of $1,200 billion, the balanced budget multiplier tells us that a $200 billion increase in government spending, financed by a $200 billion increase in taxes, will only

In terms of the leakages-injections approach of part b, with an *MPS* of $1/2$ the $200 billion reduction in DI will cause saving to be $100 billion less at every level of GNP. Hence, the saving function will be shifted downward by this amount, from $S$ to $S_1$. The $200 billion tax leakage must be added to the saving leakage at every level of GNP to give the total leakage function $S_1$ + $T$. The new equilibrium level of GNP is $1,400 billion, determined by the intersection of the $I$ + $G$ schedule and the $S_1$ + $T$ function. At this level the leakage, which equals saving plus taxes, is just offset by the injections, which equal intended investment plus government spending. At this level $S_1$ + $T$ = $I$ + $G$.

increase GNP to $1,400 billion. This is what we found in Figure 10–2. Assuming that we want a balanced government budget, how much would government spending and taxes have to be increased in order to raise GNP from $1,200 billion to $1,600 billion? According to the balanced budget multiplier, both government spending and taxes would have to be raised by $400 billion.

## Discretionary Fiscal Policy in Practice

Our analysis of the effects of government expenditure and taxation on the equilibrium level of GNP indicates how discretionary fiscal policy might be used to combat recessions and overheated, inflationary booms.

Reductions in government expenditures, increases in taxes, or both may be used to reduce the level of total expenditure when economic expansions create excessive inflationary pressures. If the government budget is in deficit to begin with, a reduction in the deficit or possibly its replacement with a surplus will be required to reduce total expenditure. If the budget is balanced to begin with, the creation of a budget surplus will be required to reduce total expenditure. If a surplus exists initially, an even larger surplus will be required.

When the economy is slipping into a recession, increases in government expenditures, reductions in taxes, or both may be used to increase total expenditure. If the government budget is initially in deficit, these actions will give rise to an even larger deficit. If the budget is balanced to begin with, a deficit will result. And if a surplus exists initially, the surplus will be reduced or replaced by a deficit.

These prescriptions for the ideal exercise of discretionary fiscal policy are not so easy to carry out in practice. Let's see why.

### Politics and Priorities

Federal government expenditure and tax programs are ultimately formulated and passed by Congress. This political process is affected by many different special interest groups and lobbies, each with a list of priorities that often conflicts with the goals of discretionary fiscal policy. For example, suppose prudent fiscal policy calls for a reduction in government expenditures to reduce inflationary pressures. But nobody wants government expenditures that affect his or her region to be cut back. The other alternative is to increase taxes. But which taxes, and who shall pay them? Neither politicians nor the public ever like increasing taxes.

The politics of working out compromises between various interest groups with conflicting objectives takes time. Hence the question is whether Congress can resolve the various issues associated with an expenditure or a tax bill and pass it in time to counteract either inflationary pressures or a recession.

### Forecasting, Recognition, and Timing

The sluggishness of the democratic political process is not the only thing that can throw off the timing of fiscal actions. This problem aside, it is necessary to be able to forecast the future course of the economy fairly accurately. Otherwise, it is not possible to take appropriately timed fiscal actions to head off expected recessions or curb inflationary booms. Forecasting is still more an art than a science, despite the development of large economic (that is, statistical or econometric) models of the economy. The record of economic forecasters, both in government and out, is mixed at best.

It is not only difficult to forecast where the economy is going. Often it is almost as hard to recognize where the economy is. Frequently the economy has been in a recession for several months before economists, policymakers, and other observers have recognized and agreed that this is the case. Part of the problem is the fact that many important measurements of the economy's performance are only available sometime after the events that they measure have occurred. For instance, statistics on GNP become available every quarter year. The first measurement of GNP for the third quarter of the year (July through September) may not be available until sometime in November, for example. In general, what is the result of this recognition lag? It is that discretionary fiscal policy tends to be more of a reaction to past developments in the economy than an anticipation of those to come.

*In practice, the forecasting and recognition problems combine with political considerations and the sluggishness of democratic decision making to create serious timing problems for discretionary fiscal policy.* In addition, even when a change in government spending or taxes finally takes place, there is often a considerable time lag before its full effect on the economy is realized. Given all these considerations, it is not hard to see how a government spending increase—or a tax cut—intended to offset a recession might be badly timed. Such actions could end up taking place in the expansion phase of the business cycle, *after* the trough of the recession has passed. Rather than reducing the depth of the recession, these actions would simply add inflationary pressures to the expansion phase of the cycle that follows. Similarly, a government spending decrease—or a tax increase—intended to offset inflationary pressures during a boom in the economy could end up taking place after the boom has passed. Such actions could actually cause or worsen the next recession. To this extent, *the timing problems associated with discretionary fiscal policy can make economic fluctuations worse.*

### State and Local Governments

Discretionary fiscal policy might be more effective if it represented a coordinated effort of federal, state, and local governments. However, the Employment Act of 1946 applies only to the federal government. If anything, state and local governments tend to conduct their fiscal activities in ways that contribute to, rather than smooth out, the fluctuations of the business cycle. This hap-

pens largely because state and local governments are under more pressure to balance their budgets than is the federal government. Their ability to tax and raise money to finance expenditures rises and falls with the business cycle. Therefore, they tend to spend more heavily on postponable projects such as schools and highways during periods of general economic prosperity than during recessions.

---

### CHECKPOINT* 10-1
**Consider again the example of Figures 10-1 and 10-2, and suppose that the *MPS* is ¼ and the *MPC* is ¾. Explain how the total expenditure schedule is now affected by a $100 billion increase in government expenditures financed entirely by a $100 billion increase in lump-sum taxes. Give an explanation in terms of the leakages-injections approach. Explain why the balanced budget multiplier equals 1 no matter what the value of *MPC* and *MPS*.**

*Answers to all Checkpoints can be found at the back of the text.

---

## AUTOMATIC STABILIZERS: NONDISCRETIONARY FISCAL POLICY

Discretionary fiscal policy requires deliberate action by Congress. The decisions to change the level of government spending, taxation, or both must be made on a case-by-case basis. However, our economy also contains automatic stabilizers. **Automatic stabilizers** *are built-in features of the economy that operate continuously without human intervention to smooth out the peaks and troughs of business cycles.* They are comparable to the automatic pilot that keeps an airplane on course. Like an automatic pilot, the economy's automatic stabilizers don't necessarily eliminate the need for deliberate action. But they do reduce it. Let's look at some of the more important built-in stabilizers and how they work.

## POLICY PERSPECTIVE

### The Variety of Taxes and Their Effects on Spending

There are a variety of different taxes—income taxes, sales taxes, corporate profit taxes, property taxes, and so forth. All of them have one thing in common. They take spending power away from those taxed. However, beyond this, these taxes differ in the burden each places on different groups in the economy.

Roughly speaking, a particular tax is said to be *progressive* if it takes a larger percentage out of a high income than it takes out of a low income. The personal income tax is an example of a progressive tax. (We will define this term in more detail shortly.) A sales tax on Rolls Royces is another progressive tax because typically only people with high incomes buy them. A particular tax is said to be a **regressive tax** if it takes a smaller percentage out of a high income than it takes out of a low income. For example, a sales tax on food is considered regressive because the percentage of income spent on food by a low-income household is usually larger than that spent by a high-income household. Therefore, the amount of food sales tax paid by the low-income household, measured as a percentage of its income, is larger than the corresponding percentage for a high-income household.

A given amount of tax revenue could be collected by using progressive taxes or regressive taxes or some combination of both. However, it is not clear in general whether progressive or regressive taxes have a more depressing effect on total income and expenditures. Some economists

argue that progressive taxes on personal and business income reduce the incentive to work and depress investment spending. Therefore, they feel progressive taxes depress total spending more than regressive taxes. Other economists claim that regressive taxes depress total spending more because of their effect on consumption. They argue that low-income groups consume more of their income than high-income groups. Since regressive taxes fall heaviest on low-income groups, these economists contend that consumption spending is more depressed by regressive taxes.

Such considerations indicate that raising or lowering taxes to bring about a *given size change in GNP* is far more difficult than was suggested by our discussion of Figure 10–2. In the real world Congress has to decide which of a wide variety of taxes to change. Often there is only the vaguest idea of what the effects on GNP will be.

#### Questions

1. The levying of the lump-sum tax illustrated in Figure 10–2 amounts to collecting a fixed sum of money from every adult in the economy. Would you regard this as a progressive or a regressive tax?

2. Name some special interest groups in our economy and indicate how you think they would stand on the issue of progressive versus regressive taxes.

## Tax Structure

Up to now we have used only lump-sum taxes in our analysis, so that the amount of tax revenue is the same no matter what the level of GNP. In reality, the tax structure of

the U.S. economy is such that the amount of tax revenue rises when GNP increases and falls when GNP declines. The significance of this for economic stability is illustrated in Figure 10–3. There it is assumed that the level of government and intended investment expenditures is the same at all levels of GNP—the $I + G$ schedule is flat.

Part a of Figure 10-3 shows the lump-sum tax case with which we are already familiar. Suppose that the sum of investment and government expenditure is initially $300 billion, as represented by the $I_0 + G$ schedule. The equilibrium level of GNP is $1,200 billion, determined by the intersection of $S + T$ and $I_0 + G$. If investment spending increases by $100 billion from $I_0$ to $I_1$, the $I_0 + G$ schedule shifts up to $I_1 + G$ and the equilibrium level of GNP increases by $400 billion, from $1,200 billion to $1,600 billion. If at this point investment were to decrease by $100 billion, the $I_1 + G$ schedule would shift back down to $I_0 + G$. GNP would decrease by $400 billion, from $1,600 billion to $1,200 billion, in response to a $100 billion fluctuation in investment.

### Proportional Taxes

Now consider the effect of the same fluctuation in investment, given the same saving function $S$, when the economy's tax structure is such that tax revenues rise and fall *proportionally* with GNP. This situation is shown in part b of Figure 10-3. The tax revenue at each level of GNP is represented by the vertical distance between the saving function $S$ and the saving plus tax function $S + T$. This distance gets proportionally larger as GNP increases. *With a* **proportional tax**, *an X percent rise (or fall) in GNP always results in an X percent rise (or fall) in tax revenues.* For example, suppose the proportional tax rate is .2. If GNP increases by 10 percent, from $1,000 billion to $1,100 billion, tax revenues will increase by $20 billion from $200 billion (.2 × $1,000 billion) to $220 billion (.2 × $1,100 billion). That is, tax revenues also increase by 10 percent. Given the position of the saving function $S$, the larger (smaller) is the proportional tax rate, the steeper (less steep) will be the $S + T$ function in part b.

When the $I + G$ schedule is in the position $I_0 + G$, the equilibrium level of GNP is

$1,300 billion. When the $100 billion increase in investment shifts the schedule up to $I_1 + G$, the equilibrium level of GNP increases by $200 billion to $1,500 billion. Similarly, a $100 billion fall in investment pushing the $I + G$ schedule down from $I_1 + G$ to $I_0 + G$ would cause a $200 billion fall in GNP, from $1,500 billion to $1,300 billion. In short, the same $100 billion fluctuation in investment causes a smaller fluctuation in GNP under a proportional tax structure than under a lump-sum tax structure—a $200 billion versus a $400 billion GNP fluctuation. Why is this?

Recall that taxes, like saving, are a leakage that drains off potential spending on goods and services. With a lump-sum tax the tax leakage does not change with changes in GNP. But with a proportional tax the leakage increases as GNP increases and has an *ever greater* braking effect on further rises in GNP. Hence, a rise in injections due to increased investment or government spending or both is more quickly offset by an increase in leakages under a proportional tax structure than under a lump-sum tax structure. Similarly, a fall in the level of injections results in a more rapid decline in leakages under a proportional tax structure. Therefore, GNP does not have to decline as far to reestablish the equality between injections and leakages.

The stabilizing effect of the proportional tax structure is greater the larger is the proportional tax rate or the percent of GNP that is collected in taxes. An increase in the proportional tax rate makes the $S + T$ function in part b steeper. This means that the shift in the $I_0 + G$ schedule to $I_1 + G$, or from $I_1 + G$ to $I_0 + G$, will cause an even smaller change in GNP. Hence, the economy is more stable in that it is less sensitive to such a disturbance.

### Progressive Taxes

In reality, tax revenues in our economy tend to rise and fall more than proportionally with increases and decreases in GNP. This happens largely because personal and business

**FIGURE 10-3   The Tax Structure as an Automatic Stabilizer**

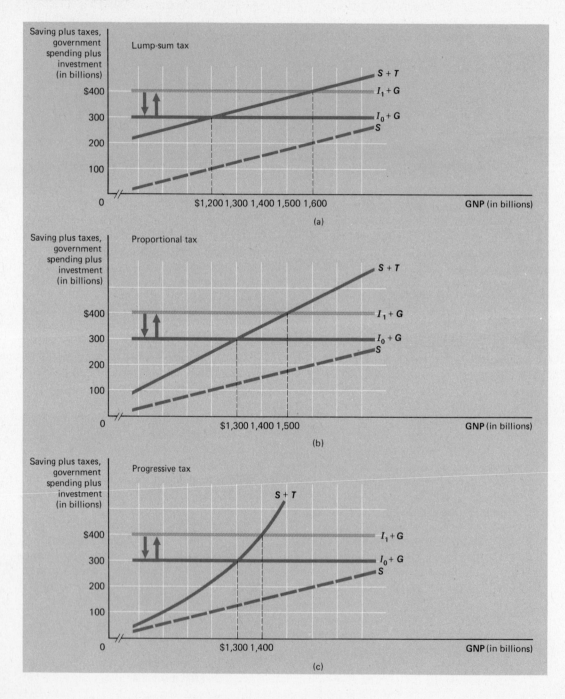

(a)

(b)

(c)

income is subject to a progressive tax. *A* **progressive tax** *on income imposes successively higher tax rates on additional dollars of income as income rises.* For example, the first $10,000 of an individual's income might be subject to a 20 percent tax rate, the second $10,000 to a 30 percent rate, the third to a 40 percent rate, and so forth. This means that the fraction of total income taxed away gets larger as total income rises. If the individual in our example makes $10,000, then 20 percent, or one-fifth, of it goes to taxes; if the individual's income is $20,000, then 25 percent (equal to the average of 20 percent and 30 percent), or one-fourth, of it goes to taxes, and so forth. By contrast, with a proportional tax rate the fraction of total income taxed away is the same no matter what the level of total income.

The effect of a progressive tax structure on the economy's stability is illustrated in Figure 10–3, part c. The saving function $S$ is the same as in parts a and b. However, the $S + T$ function now curves upward, reflecting the fact that taxes rise more than proportionally with increases in GNP and fall more than proportionally with decreases. Now the same $100 billion fluctuation in investment considered in parts a and b results in an even smaller fluctuation in GNP. When $I_0 + G$ shifts up to $I_1 + G$, there is only a $100 billion increase in GNP, from $1,300 billion to $1,400 billion. By comparison, under the proportional tax rate of part b, this shift resulted in a $200 billion increase in GNP.

With the lump-sum tax of part a, there was a $400 billion increase.

In general, *the progressive nature of the U.S. economy's tax structure acts as a built-in stabilizer by automatically increasing tax leakages more than proportionally as GNP rises and by reducing such leakages more than proportionally as GNP falls. This is generally desirable because increasing leakages during an inflationary expansion will have a dampening effect on the economy. Conversely, decreasing leakages during a recession will tend to buoy up spending.*

## Unemployment Compensation

Since the 1930s **unemployment compensation** has become an increasingly important automatic stabilizer in our economy. Recessions swell the ranks of the unemployed. Without some form of assistance, laid off workers must cut back their spending drastically. This only makes the recession worse. Paying laid off workers unemployment benefits enables them to better sustain their consumption spending and thus cushions the downturn. These unemployment benefits are paid out of unemployment trust funds that are built up with unemployment taxes during periods of economic expansion. These taxes constitute an increase in leakages during boom periods. As such, they help to curb excessive inflationary expansions. In sum, *during recessions injections into the economy from unemployment benefits tend to exceed the leak-*

---

Proportional taxes and progressive taxes act as automatic stabilizers because they increase leakages when GNP rises and decrease leakages when GNP falls.

The leakages-injections diagrams of parts a, b, and c all have the same saving function and the same $100 billion $I + G$ schedule shifts. The only difference between the diagrams is that they each assume different tax structures. When taxes are lump sum (part a), the leakage due to taxes is the same no matter what the level of GNP. A $100 billion shift in the $I + G$ schedule, from $I_0 + G$ to $I_1 + G$ or vice versa, causes a $400 billion change in GNP. By comparison, the same shifts in the $I + G$ schedule under a proportional tax structure (part b) cause a smaller change (equal to $200 billion) in GNP. The same shifts under a progressive tax structure result in a still smaller change (equal to $100 billion) in GNP.

*ages due to unemployment taxes, and the economy is stimulated on balance. During expansionary periods leakages due to unemployment taxes tend to exceed injections from unemployment benefits and the net effect is to curb inflationary pressures.*

## Other Automatic Stabilizers

Other automatic stabilizers in our economy include family assistance programs, price-support programs for agriculture, and a tendency for older workers laid off during recessions to start claiming their social security retirement benefits. Let's briefly look at each of these automatic stabilizers.

Not surprisingly, during recessions many families find themselves forced into financial straits that make them eligible for certain forms of family assistance. This aids them in sustaining their otherwise sagging purchasing power.

Farm product prices tend to fall during recessions. Government price-support programs keep them from falling below a certain level and thus prop up farm family incomes and spending.

After older workers have been laid off for a certain period of time, their prospects for reemployment often diminish rapidly. Once they have used up the amount of unemployment benefits to which they are entitled, they frequently retire and claim social security retirement benefits. These benefits thus pick up where unemployment benefits leave off for this group of workers. To this extent social security retirement benefits tend to automatically cushion recessions in the same way as unemployment compensation.

## Automatic Stabilizers Are a Double-edged Sword

The same characteristics of automatic stabilizers that make them desirable can also make them very undesirable under certain circumstances. For example, the tendency of the U.S. tax structure to increase leakages when GNP rises helps to curb inflationary pressures when the economy is near full employment. However, if the economy is coming out of the depths of a recession, the same tendency for leakages to rise acts as a drag on economic recovery.

---

### CHECKPOINT 10-2

**Suppose the government spending component of the $I + G$ schedules in Figure 10–3 is always equal to $200 billion, whatever the level of GNP. For each of the cases shown in parts a, b, and c of Figure 10–3, explain how the government budget changes as a result of the $100 billion change in investment, both when it represents an increase from $I_0$ to $I_1$ and when it represents a decrease from $I_1$ to $I_0$. That is, for each case, does the budget remain balanced, go from surplus to deficit or from deficit to surplus, or what? In light of your findings, how might you state the way the automatic stabilization effect works in terms of the government budget?**

---

## BUDGET POLICY

Government budget policy is the joint result of government spending and tax policy. Budget policymakers have to consider such questions as: When and how often should the budget be balanced? When should it be in surplus, when in deficit? How should deficits be financed—by printing money or issuing bonds? And what should be done with surpluses? These questions have always provoked controversy.

## Different Views on Budget Policy

The following represent three of the most often heard views on budget policy. Now that we are familiar with how government spending and taxation can affect the economy, we can consider the economic implications of each of them.

## POLICY PERSPECTIVE

### Discretionary Versus Nondiscretionary Expenditures

While automatic stabilizers tend to smooth out the peaks and troughs of business cycles, they do not eliminate them entirely. Research on the matter suggests that the amplitude of business cycles (the difference in GNP from trough to peak) may be reduced by anywhere from one-third to one-half as a result of the presence of automatic stabilizers. This means there is still a role for well-timed discretionary fiscal policy in eliminating that part of the business cycle not smoothed out by the automatic stabilizers.

Discretionary fiscal policy expenditures usually have a different impact on the economy than do the expenditures arising from nondiscretionary fiscal policy. Discretionary government expenditures are typically for goods and services—roads, buildings, trucks, research grants, and so forth. Nondiscretionary government spending usually takes the form of transfer payments, such as unemployment compensation, welfare benefits, and interest on the government debt. Hidden behind a given dollar figure for government expenditure is a variety of decisions about the role of government in our economy.

Viewed only in terms of the expansionary impact on the economy, however, most economists regard government spending on goods and services as more expansionary than transfer payments. For example, suppose that the multiplier equals 2 and that the economy is not operating at full employment. Government spending of $20 billion on goods and services will cause the economy to produce $40 billion of additional output—$20 billion to meet government purchases and $20 billion to meet increased consumer spending as a consequence of the multi-plier effect. Alternatively, if the government paid out the $20 billion in unemployment compensation benefits, no increase in output would be needed to satisfy government purchase orders. The government would simply hand unemployed workers $20 billion. The unemployed will spend half of this on goods and services (because a multiplier of 2 implies an *MPC* of $1/2$), or $10 billion. The operation of the multiplier effect on this $10 billion expenditure means that the economy's total output increases by $20 billion. In sum, a $20 billion government expenditure on goods and services causes the economy's total output to increase by $40 billion. But a $20 billion transfer payment causes total output to rise by only $20 billion.

#### Questions

1. In 1970 transfer payments were equal to roughly 10 percent of GNP. By the mid-1980s they had risen to about 17 percent of GNP. Over the same period of time federal government purchases of goods and services as a share of GNP fell from 10 percent to the equivalent of about 8 percent. What implications about fiscal policy might you draw from these trends over this time period?

2. If the trends reported in question 1 had been just the opposite how do you think the GNP gap would have been affected compared to the way it actually behaved?

## Classical View: Balance the Budget Annually

The classical economists generally believed that government expenditures should be matched by government tax revenues every fiscal year—that is, that the budget should be balanced annually. As a result of the Great Depression of the 1930s and the loss of faith in the classical theory of full employment, few economists subscribe to this view today. Yet, there are still politicians and others who believe that the government budget should be balanced annually. Generally, they view the government budget in the same way as the budget of a household or business firm. Households and businesses that have budget deficits often go bankrupt.

However, if the government budget is balanced every year, the income-expenditure view argues that fiscal policy will add to economic instability rather than reduce it. For example, suppose the economy is in the expansionary phase of a business cycle. As GNP rises tax revenues rise even faster because of a progressive tax structure. Given the level of government expenditures, the increase in tax revenues may well give rise to a budget surplus. In order to keep the budget balanced, the government will have to cut taxes or increase government expenditures or both. However, we have seen that increases in government expenditure, as well as reductions in taxes, push up total expenditure. This will add to the economic expansion.

On the other hand, suppose the economy is entering a recession. As GNP declines, tax revenues will fall. Given the level of government expenditure, this may result in a budget deficit. In order to keep the budget balanced, the government will have to increase taxes or reduce government spending or both. But such actions will reduce total expenditure even further and make the recession worse.

Thus, the annually balanced budget would make the expansion phase of the business cycle larger and the recession phase deeper. Business cycles would be more severe.

## Balance the Budget Cyclically

Another point of view argues that the budget should be balanced over the course of the business cycle. That is, the budget should be balanced over whatever period of time it takes for a complete business cycle, measured from either trough to trough or peak to peak. Those who favor this approach contend that balancing the budget in this way will at the same time permit the exercise of a stabilizing fiscal policy. During a recession the government would run a budget deficit by increasing spending and reducing taxes to stimulate the economy. During the expansion and boom phase of the cycle, the government would run a surplus by cutting back its spending and increasing taxes in order to curb inflationary pressures. Ideally, the size of the deficit that occurs in the recession is just matched by the size of the surplus during the boom. The budget is therefore balanced over the business cycle.

In reality, it is very difficult to do this because recessions and expansions typically differ from one another in length and magnitude. Therefore, the size of the deficit incurred while fighting the recession is not likely to be the same as the size of the surplus generated by attempts to curb an inflationary expansion.

## Functional Finance

The functional finance point of view contends that the goals of economic stabilization and full employment without inflation should come ahead of any concern about balancing the budget. This means that the budget may have to run in deficit over a period of several years in order to keep employment high or run in surplus to curb inflation. Proponents of functional finance argue that any difficulties associated with ongoing deficits or surpluses are far outweighed by the benefits of high employment without inflation.

Critics of the functional finance approach argue that it throws away the fiscal discipline imposed by a balanced budget objective.

Generally, the critics do not argue for slavish pursuit of a balanced budget. Rather, they believe that it should be a rough guideline used to keep inflationary deficit spending under control.

## The Cyclically Adjusted Budget

Each of the viewpoints on budget policy we have just mentioned has obvious drawbacks. The annually balanced budget is destabilizing. Balancing the budget over the business cycle is very difficult if not impossible. Functional finance seems to lack any standard for evaluating budget policy performance. Another budget concept—the cyclically adjusted budget—has gained popularity among economists and policymakers because it provides a way of judging to what extent fiscal policy is pushing the economy toward a high-employment level of GNP. (A high-employment level might be deemed to be a level of GNP where the unemployment rate is 6 percent, for example.)

### The Actual Budget and the Cyclically Adjusted Budget

The *actual* government budget surplus or deficit is equal to the difference between *actual* government expenditures and *actual* tax revenues. Suppose actual GNP is less than the high-employment level of GNP. Given that the tax structure is progressive, the actual tax revenues are less than the amount that would be collected at the high-employment GNP level. The actual government budget might well show a deficit, as prudent fiscal policy would say it should during a recession. Injections from government spending exceed tax leakages (there is a net injection). But is this actual budget deficit large enough to combat the recession? How can we tell?

Suppose we compare this actual level of government spending with the amount of tax revenue that would be collected *if* GNP were at the high-employment level. It might turn out that the high-employment level of tax revenue would exceed actual government spending. In other words, if the economy were at the high-employment level of GNP, there would be a budget surplus. And this means that actual fiscal policy would be a force tending to push GNP down and away from the high-employment level! Clearly, the *actual* budget deficit is not as large as it should be if fiscal policy is to be oriented toward pushing GNP up to the high-employment level.

We conclude that *compared to the actual budget deficit or surplus, a more meaningful measure of the impact of fiscal policy is the difference between the actual level of government spending and the level of tax revenue that would be collected if the economy were operating at a high-employment level of GNP. This is the* **cyclically adjusted budget**. If actual GNP is below the high-employment level of GNP and there is a cyclically adjusted budget deficit, fiscal policy may be viewed as a force favorable to the achievement of a high-employment level of GNP. On the other hand, if under these same circumstances there is a cyclically adjusted budget surplus, fiscal policy may be viewed as not sufficiently expansionary for the purpose of achieving a high-employment level of GNP. If actual GNP is above the high-employment level of GNP, the existence of a cyclically adjusted budget deficit would suggest that fiscal policy is overly expansionary and is contributing to inflationary pressures. However, if under these same circumstances there is a cyclically adjusted budget surplus, fiscal policy may be viewed as a force favorable to curbing excessive expansion.

Finally, note carefully the following point. Even if the cyclically adjusted budget (deficit or surplus) indicates that the current stance of fiscal policy is favorable to the achievement of a high-employment level of GNP, it is no guarantee that this goal will be realized. Consumption and investment spending may be either so expansionary or so contractionary that a high-employment equilibrium level of GNP cannot be reached or maintained. Put another way, even though the cyclically adjusted budget may be favorable to the achievement of a high-employment level of GNP, the *size* of the cyclically adjusted budget (deficit or surplus) may not be large enough given the existing level of consumption and investment spending.

### Recent Budget Experience

Figure 10-4 compares the difference between actual government spending and actual tax revenues (the actual budget deficit or surplus) with the difference between actual government spending and high-employment GNP tax revenues (the cyclically adjusted budget deficit or surplus) for the years since 1971. Observe that in most of these years the actual budget deficit was larger than the cyclically adjusted budget deficit. If one only looked at the actual budget deficit, the expansionary impact of fiscal policy would generally appear more pronounced than is indicated by the cyclically adjusted budget deficits. Nonetheless, the cyclically adjusted budget was in deficit in each of these years, indicating that fiscal policy was expansionary over this period. Largely due to the automatic stabilizers, it was particularly expansionary, as was desirable, during the latter stages of the severe recession that reached its trough at the end of the first quarter of 1975, and during the even more severe recession which reached its trough in the fourth quarter of 1982.

## Effects of Deficit Financing on the Economy

By definition, a budget deficit means that tax revenues are less than government expenditures. How and where does the government get the funds to finance the difference? There are two ways in which the government can obtain the needed funds: (1) it can borrow the money from the public by selling government bonds, or (2) it can print the money. It can also do some combination of both. The expansionary effect on the economy of a budget deficit varies, depending on which method is used to finance the deficit.

### Bond Financing

Like any other bond, a government bond is a contract whereby the borrower (the government) agrees to pay back the lender (the buyer of the bond) the amount lent plus some rate of interest after some specified period of time. For example, consider a $1,000 government bond that pays a 5 percent rate of interest and promises to pay back the lender after 1 year. At the end of 1 year the lender, or bond buyer, gets back $1,050 (the original $1,000 plus 5 percent of $1,000, or $50) from the government, the bond seller. As with any bond, the only way the government can sell the bond (borrow the $1,000) is by paying a high enough rate of interest to induce people to buy it (lend the $1,000).

The government must sell its bonds in the bond market, in competition with bonds sold by businesses that are trying to borrow funds to finance their investment spending. In order to induce the public to buy these government bonds instead of those issued by the business sector, the government will have to pay an interest rate high enough to make their bonds relatively more attractive. This competition between the financing needs of the government and those of the business sector will push up the rate of interest. We know from our discussion in Chapter 8 (see Figure 8-8) that this interest rate rise will cause the level of investment spending to fall, as represented by a downward shift in the investment schedule. Therefore, *when a government deficit is financed by selling government bonds, the expansionary effect of the deficit on the economy is somewhat offset by a downward shift in investment spending.*

### Printing Money

The other way in which the government can finance the deficit is to create the needed

**FIGURE 10-4   The Actual Budget and
the Cyclically Adjusted Budget Since 1971**
(in Constant 1972 Dollars, GNP Deflator)

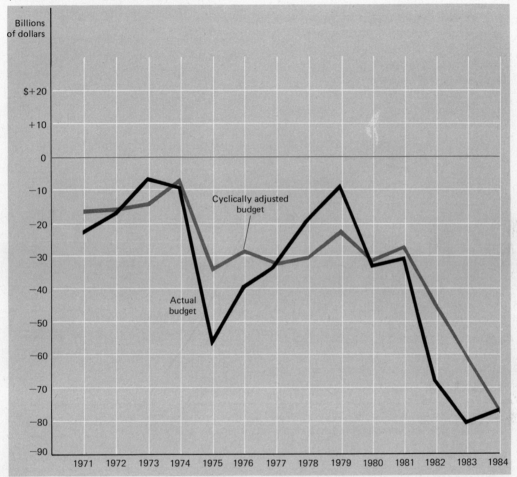

The actual budget deficit or surplus equals the difference between actual government
spending and actual tax revenues. The cyclically adjusted budget deficit or surplus equals
the difference between actual government spending and the level of tax revenues that
would be collected at the high-employment GNP level. The cyclically adjusted budget
deficit or surplus is a better indicator of how well the government is managing fiscal
policy.

For most of the periods shown here both the actual budget and the cyclically adjusted
budget have shown a deficit. But the actual budget deficit has been greater than the
cyclically adjusted budget deficit because actual GNP has been below the high-
employment level of GNP for much of this period. The fact that the cyclically adjusted
budget was in deficit throughout most of this period indicates that fiscal policy was geared
toward pushing the economy to the high-employment level of GNP.

money. We will be able to describe the way this is done in a modern economy after we have studied how the banking system works in Chapters 12 through 14. For the moment, we will simply assume that the government cranks money out with a printing press. Using this method means that there is no longer a need to issue bonds and, hence, there is no rise in the interest rate that depresses investment spending. It follows that *when the government finances a deficit by creating new money, the expansionary effect of the deficit on the economy will be greater than when the deficit is financed by borrowing (issuing bonds).*

## What to Do with a Budget Surplus

The government may collect more tax revenue than it spends (have a budget surplus) in the boom phase of an expansion. (Note, however, that budget surpluses have been rare.) The budget surplus is desirable at this phase of the business cycle because it is anti-inflationary, meaning that it dampens inflationary pressures. But the extent of this dampening effect depends on what the government does with the surplus. There are two possibilities. The government can use the surplus to retire some of the outstanding government debt by paying back bondholders. Alternatively, the government can simply hold on to the surplus as idle funds. This amounts to withdrawing the money from the economy.

Suppose the surplus is used to retire outstanding debt. Think of the surplus as the net leakage—the excess of the leakage due to taxes over the injections of government spending. Returning the surplus to the economy by retiring debt offsets this net leakage to the extent that it puts money back into the hands of the public, who then spend it. Debt retirement thereby reduces the anti-inflationary effect of the budget surplus. However, if the government simply holds the surplus as idle funds, there is no offset to reduce this net leakage. We conclude that the *anti-inflationary effect of a government budget surplus is greater when the surplus funds are held idle than when they are used to retire government debt.*[1]

**CHECKPOINT 10-3**
**Compare Figure 10-4 with Figure 6-5, part b, and describe how well fiscal policy has performed in view of the behavior of the GNP gap since 1971. What are the implications for the cyclically adjusted budget concept of the fact that the expansionary impact of a deficit depends on how it is financed? Similarly, what are the implications for this concept of the different ways of disposing of a surplus?**

## THE GOVERNMENT DEBT

The government debt is a subject of controversy and a source of concern to many people. Should we be concerned about it? Who owes what to whom? How can we tell whether the debt is too big or not? What are the burdens of the debt? Almost every citizen worries about these questions from time to time.

### What Is the Government Debt?

Since the beginning of World War II government budget deficits have far outnumbered surpluses. Financing these deficits by selling government bonds has resulted in a large increase in the stock of bonds outstanding—the size of the government debt. Figure 10-5 shows that most of this increase was concentrated in the war years, 1941–1945, and in the years since 1967.

[1] Note that retiring government debt removes government bonds from the bond market and thus reduces competition with private bonds. This tends to reduce the interest rate and thereby stimulate investment spending. This is another source of stimulus to the economy that occurs when there is debt retirement.

## POLICY PERSPECTIVE

### The Deficit Problem—Crowding Out Capital Formation

In recent years there has been increasing concern about the size of federal government budget deficits—government spending in excess of tax revenue. While deficits only amounted to roughly .3 percent of GNP in the 1960s, their size increased to equal approximately 2.5 percent of GNP during the 1970s, and it is estimated that their average size for the 1980s will turn out to be considerably higher yet.

A critical concern often expressed about federal deficits is that they absorb resources that would otherwise be available to build up the economy's capital stock. It is therefore often said that deficits "crowd out" investment, or capital formation. The argument may be illustrated in terms of the leakages-injections relationship which says that the sum of the injections, investment ($I$) plus government spending ($G$), must equal the sum of the leakages, saving ($S$) plus taxes ($T$), or $I + G = S + T$. When there is a deficit government spending $G$ is larger than tax revenue $T$, which means $S$ is larger than $I$. Part of the economy's saving $S$ must go to finance the deficit leaving the rest to finance investment $I$. If part of saving did not have to finance the deficit it would be available to finance a larger level of investment spending, or capital formation.

For example, suppose $I$ and $G$ each equals $500 billion and that $S$ equals $600 billion while $T$ equals $400 billion. Then $I + G = S + T$ is (in billions) $500 +

$500 = $600 + $400, and the government budget deficit equals $G - T = $500 - $400 = $100. Since tax revenue ($T = $400) is not sufficient to finance all of government spending ($G = $500), $100 of saving ($S = $600) must go to finance the deficit, leaving $500 of saving to finance investment ($I = $500). In other words, part of the economy's saving $S$ must be used to finance the deficit and the other part is used to finance investment $I$. What if government spending were larger, say, $G = $900 instead of $500? Then the deficit would be larger, $G - T = $900 - $400 = $500. This $500 excess of government spending over tax revenue would have to be financed out of saving, leaving only $100 of the total saving ($S = $600) to finance investment. Now $I + G = S + T$ would be $100 + $900 = $600 + $400. Investment $I$ is now only $100. The larger deficit has crowded out investment, reducing it from $500 to $100! Our example illustrates how growing deficits can cause the economy's rate of capital formation to decline due to crowding out.

#### Questions

1. In our initial example what would have to happen to investment if taxes were cut to $100?

2. In our initial example how would balancing the budget by raising taxes affect the rate of capital formation?

## Public Versus Private Debt

Most of us are accustomed to thinking in terms of private debt, the personal debt people incur when they borrow money to buy a car, a house, or a college education. The chief fear is that of not being able to pay the debt off as repayments come due. If you can't, your assets—the car, the house, the furniture—may be seized by those who have

**FIGURE 10-5   Government Debt**

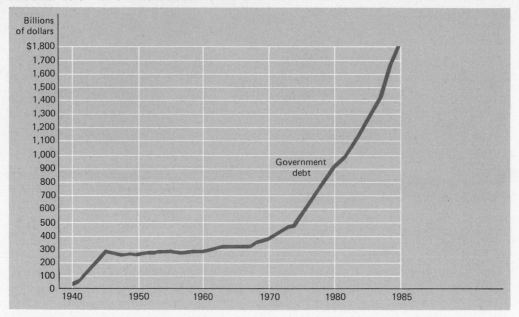

Since 1940 the government debt has grown roughly twentyfold, reflecting the fact that government deficits have far outnumbered surpluses. The increase was mostly concentrated in the World War II years and in the years since 1967.

lent you money. They may even be able to put a lien on your paycheck. This is a legal claim that allows them to take a part of every paycheck (direct from your employer) until they have been paid back the amount originally lent to you. In short, a private debt is what one party, the debtor, owes another, the creditor. Failure by the debtor to repay the creditor on time can result in severe hardship and loss for the debtor. Of course, the creditor is made poorer as well, possibly losing all that was originally loaned.

The government, or public, debt is different from a private debt in certain important respects, though it is similar in others. Consider the following hypothetical example. Suppose that the government's debt is held entirely by its own citizens, and that each citizen owns the same number of government bonds as every other citizen. Since it is the citizens' government, the government debt is the citizens' debt, or what the citizens owe themselves! Suppose the government decided to pay off the entire debt by levying and collecting a tax of the same size from each citizen. The amount of taxes that each citizen would pay the government would be just equal to the amount of money each would receive from the government for the government bonds that each holds. It is the same as if each citizen were to take X dollars out of his or her left pocket and put the X dollars back into the right pocket.

What about interest payments on a government's debt held entirely by and distributed equally among its own citizens? Again, suppose the government levies and collects a tax of the same size from every citizen to pay the interest on the debt. Each citizen would then pay an amount of taxes exactly equal to the interest payments received on the government bond he or she holds. Again, what each citizen takes out of the left pocket matches what is put back into the right pocket.

Obviously, in our hypothetical example the existence and size of the government debt is of no consequence whatsoever. The example shows how different a government, or public, debt can be from a private debt.

## The Burden of the Government Debt

Our hypothetical example serves another important purpose. It suggests that any cause for concern about the government debt lies in the fact that certain of the example's assumptions don't hold in reality. Because of this, the government debt imposes certain burdens similar to those of a private debt.

### Distribution Effects

First of all, government bonds outstanding are not distributed equally among the nation's citizens. Some people hold none and others own a great number. However, any attempt to retire some or all of the debt would have to be financed out of taxes that are paid by all citizens (except those who somehow avoid paying taxes). This large transfer payment would result in a redistribution of income. Some citizens would

would pay out more than they would get back. Others would be net gainers in this transfer. Their tax payment toward the debt retirement effort would be less than their holdings of government bonds.[2]

Interest payments on the government debt have the same distribution effects. These interest payments are transfer payments, fi-

[2] Many government bonds are held by trust funds, banks, insurance companies, and other businesses. A multitude of citizens either own or have claims on these institutions and therefore own government bonds indirectly. This makes no difference to our argument.

nanced by taxes on the general population and paid to those holding government bonds. A citizen is a net gainer if the amount received in interest payments exceeds his or her share of the tax payments used to pay interest on the debt. Otherwise the citizen is a net loser in this transfer.

In sum, the issue of public debt burden may be viewed in terms of the distribution effects of the transfer payments used to retire the debt or pay interest on it. It is a burden to those citizens who are net losers in this transfer. *For them the burden is similar to that of a private debt.*

### Relative Size of Public Debt and GNP

It is difficult to give an accurate statistical measure of the burden created by redistribution effects. Whatever they are, the economy's ability either to retire the public debt or to pay interest on it is all relative to the economy's capacity to pay taxes. A reasonable measure of this ability is the size of the GNP relative to the size of the debt and to the amount of the interest payments that must be paid on it.

Figure 10–6 indicates that since World War II, GNP has become much larger relative to the size of the government debt. In the immediate postwar years, 1945–1947, the debt was actually larger than GNP. From then until 1974, however, GNP grew until it was roughly three times as large as the gov-

Since then, and particularly in recent years, the ratio of GNP to the size of the debt has declined, suggesting that the debt burden is increasing.

What about the size of GNP relative to the amount of the interest payments on the debt? From the end of World War II up through the middle 1960s, these payments amounted to between 1.5 and 2 percent of GNP. In recent years they have increased, representing about 3.0 percent of GNP. Though this still seems a small fraction of total GNP, the increase is cause for concern if it continues.

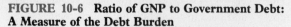

**FIGURE 10-6    Ratio of GNP to Government Debt:
A Measure of the Debt Burden**

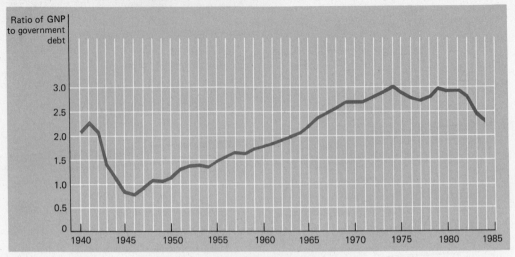

One measure of the burden of the government debt is its size relative to that of GNP, shown here as the ratio of GNP to the government debt. During World War II the debt grew much faster than GNP, and the ratio fell. Since World War II GNP has generally grown faster than the debt. In the immediate postwar years, the debt was larger than GNP—the ratio was less than 1. GNP was roughly three times larger than the debt by 1974. To the extent that GNP represents the tax capacity to pay off the debt as well as to pay interest on it, the burden of the debt on the economy has declined since World War II. In recent years the ratio has begun to fall, however, suggesting that the debt burden is increasing.

### External Versus Internal Debt

Government debt (bonds) held by U.S. citizens is what these citizens collectively owe to themselves. The redistribution effects associated with taxation and transfer payments only redistribute the economy's total output domestically. As a nation there is no loss in total output. That part of government debt held by foreigners is another matter. Interest payments on such debt, as well as the retirement of that debt, amounts to a transfer of purchasing power from a nation's citizens to foreigners. In other words, a part of the nation's output must be given up to another nation. It is like private debt in that one party loses purchasing power by virtue of the obligation to pay another.

In the United States the portion of government debt held by foreigners has in-creased in recent years. In the late 1960s foreigners held anywhere from 3 to 5 percent of the total government debt. During the 1970s this figure increased to around 12 to 14 percent, a level that has persisted into the 1980s. While this is still a small portion of the total debt, the increase is somewhat disturbing. Some say it reflects the fact that political turmoil abroad has caused foreign investors in general to seek the relatively safe haven provided by U.S. government bonds.

### Is the Debt a Burden on Future Generations?

It is sometimes argued that government debt creation imposes a burden on future generations. Is this true? Yes and no.

Debt creation does saddle future generations with the redistribution effects associ-

## POLICY PERSPECTIVE

### Deficits and the Growing Government Debt— Facing Up to a Problem

Whatever the size of a government budget deficit, financing that deficit results in the creation of an equivalent amount of new government debt. One of the major concerns about the large deficits of recent years is that they have caused an increase in the rate of growth of the government debt.

#### Debt Growing Faster than GNP

In contrast to most of the postwar period, since 1979 the rate of growth of government debt has generally exceeded the rate of growth of GNP, resulting in a decline in the ratio of GNP to government debt, as can be seen from Figure 10–6. Given the rate of interest that must be paid on government debt, total interest payments on the debt tend to become an ever larger factor in the government's budget as long as the debt grows at a faster rate than GNP. While interest payments on the debt represented 7.2 percent of the government budget in 1975, by 1985 they represented over 12 percent (see Figure 3–1, Chapter 3).

Obviously the rate of growth of government debt cannot exceed the rate of growth of GNP indefinitely. Eventually the interest payments on the debt would take up the whole government budget, crowding out all other government expenditure categories (education, national defense, social security payments, and so forth), until finally the government would simply be forced to repudiate the debt— the government would literally be bankrupt. No doubt political pressures would build up to reduce deficits and curb growth of the government debt long before this point were reached.

#### Limiting Growth of Deficits

What kind of limit on the size of government deficits is necessary if the growth rate of the government debt is not to exceed the growth rate of GNP? The answer is that the dollar size of the deficit must not exceed the growth rate of nominal GNP multiplied by the dollar size of the government debt. For example, if the debt equals $1 trillion and nominal GNP is growing at 5 percent per year, then the deficit should not exceed $50 billion. A $50 billion deficit would require the government to issue (sell) $50 billion of new government bonds, thus increasing the debt by another $50 billion (to $1.05 trillion), or at a 5 percent annual rate. Actual deficits were so large from 1975 through 1983 that the government debt grew at an average rate of about 15 percent per year while nominal GNP grew only about half as fast, at an average rate of about 8 percent per year. Eventually politicians and policymakers are going to have to reduce government deficits in order to bring the growth rate of government debt down to or below the rate of growth of nominal GNP.

#### Questions

1. How might changes in the level of interest rates affect the urgency of the need to bring down the growth rate of the government debt?

2. How does the distribution of holdings of government debt among citizens bear on the urgency to bring down the growth rate of government debt?

ated with the taxes and transfer payments needed to make ongoing interest payments on the debt. To the extent that taxpayers and bondholders are not necessarily the same people, this redistribution of income will be a burden to some members of future generations.

The creation of public debt during times when the economy is operating at full employment *may* represent a burden to future generations, but not necessarily. New government bonds may "crowd out" bonds being issued by businesses when the economy is producing at maximum capacity. To this extent business may have to cut back on capital expansion for lack of funds. The government gets the funds and uses the resources that would otherwise go to businesses for something else. Suppose the government spends the funds from its bond sales inefficiently or on something society doesn't want—fighter planes that don't fly or fancy inaugural dances. Present and future generations are *burdened* because of the forgone capital that would have allowed the economy to produce more now and tomorrow. Note, however, that the government might have raised taxes instead of selling bonds to get the funds for those foolish expenditures. *Only* when selling bonds is easier than raising taxes (due to political considerations, say) is it true that creating government debt is a cause of the burden. Even then the real cause is poor fiscal policy.

Creation of public debt can be a blessing under certain conditions. Suppose the economy is in a recession. Prudent fiscal policy would call for increased government spending and reduced taxes—in short, a deficit. And creating this deficit requires the creation of more government debt.[3] If the government didn't take these actions, the economy would have a longer and deeper recession than otherwise. Goods and services, includ-

ing capital goods, that otherwise could be produced would not be. This year's forgone production would be forever lost to society. Society would be saddled with *the burden of doing without goods it could have had*—now and in the future.

---

*CHECKPOINT 10-4*
**Suppose that half of the nation's citizens each hold an equal share of the government debt and that all citizens each pay an equal share of the taxes used to pay interest on the debt. Given this situation, how large do you think the total debt could be in relation to GNP before serious unrest might develop? What would government bankruptcy mean in this case?**

---

## SUMMARY

**1.** The government budget is an itemized account of government expenditures and revenues over the course of a year. The budget is said to be balanced, in surplus, or in deficit depending, respectively, on whether government spending equals, is less than, or is greater than government tax revenues. The Employment Act of 1946 gives the government responsibility for maintaining full employment. Achieving this goal must therefore be a major concern of budget policy.

**2.** The equilibrium GNP can be raised by increasing government expenditures or by lowering taxes or by doing both. Conversely, the equilibrium GNP can be lowered by decreasing government expenditures or by raising taxes or by doing both. According to the balanced budget multiplier, a simultaneous increase in government expenditures and taxes of a matched, or balanced, amount will result in an increase in GNP equal to the increase in government spending. The converse is true of a decrease.

**3.** During a recession a suitable discretionary fiscal policy calls for Congress deliber-

---

[3] Even if the government financed the deficit by creating more money ("printing" it), it would be necessary to create more bonds under modern central banking arrangements, the subject of Chapters 12 through 14.

ately to increase government spending and reduce taxes. An inflationary expansion would call for a decrease in government spending and an increase in taxes. In practice, discretionary fiscal policy is hampered by the difficulty of forecasting the future; timing problems due to the politics and sluggishness of democratic processes and to lags in recognizing the current state of the economy; the tendency of fiscal actions by state and local government to accentuate contractions and expansions; and the variety of taxes that Congress may change, each having a quantitative impact that is difficult to assess.

**4.** Nondiscretionary fiscal policy relies on the economy's built-in automatic stabilizers. Chief among these are a progressive tax structure and unemployment compensation programs, which cause tax revenues to vary more than proportionally with changes in GNP. These automatically tend to generate expansionary budget deficits during recessions and budget surpluses that dampen inflationary pressures during expansions. Automatic stabilizers reduce but do not eliminate the need for discretionary fiscal policy. Sometimes they pose a problem, for they can slow down the recovery from a recession and, to this extent, hinder rather than help the economy.

**5.** Annually balanced budgets tend to accentuate the business cycle. A cyclically balanced budget policy is difficult to follow because the expansion phase of a business cycle typically differs in length and magnitude from the recession phase. Consequently, functional finance is the budget policy most often followed.

**6.** Given the actual level of government spending, the cyclically adjusted budget measures what the budget deficit or surplus would be if GNP were continually at a high-employment level. The cyclically adjusted budget deficit or surplus is a more accurate measure of the impact of fiscal policy than is the actual budget deficit or surplus.

**7.** A budget deficit has a more expansionary impact on the economy if it is financed by creating new money than if it is financed by borrowing. A budget surplus has less of a contractionary impact on the economy if the surplus is used to retire debt outstanding than if it is simply left to accumulate in the government treasury.

**8.** The government debt, or the stock of government bonds outstanding, was larger than GNP in the immediate post–World War II years. Up through 1974 GNP grew faster than the debt until it was roughly three times the size of the debt. By this criterion the debt became less of a burden over time. In recent years the ratio of GNP to government debt has declined, suggesting that the debt burden is increasing.

**9.** The government debt may be a burden to the extent that the taxes and transfer payments needed to make interest payments on the debt cause a redistribution of income among citizens, to the extent that the debt is held by foreigners, and to the extent that debt creation allows the financing of unproductive or unnecessary government spending.

## KEY TERMS AND CONCEPTS

automatic stabilizers
balanced budget
balanced budget multiplier
budget deficit
budget surplus
cyclically adjusted budget
fiscal policy
government budget
progressive tax
proportional tax
regressive tax
unemployment compensation

## QUESTIONS AND PROBLEMS

**1.** Suppose that the government budget is balanced and that the economy is experiencing an inflationary boom. Assuming the economy's *MPC* is ⁴/₅, compare and contrast each of the following discretionary fiscal actions in terms of their effectiveness in dealing with this situation:

    a. increase lump-sum taxes by $10 billion;

    b. decrease government spending by $10 billion;

    c. decrease both government spending and lump-sum taxes by $10 billion;

    d. decrease government spending by $16 billion and lump-sum taxes by $20 billion.

**2.** From 1931 through 1940 the unemployment rate never fell below 14.3 percent (1937), yet the government had a budget deficit in every one of those years. If deficits are expansionary, what were the possible problems? Use a leakages-injections diagram to illustrate your answer. (Any of the diagrams from Figure 10–3, parts a, b, or c will do, but show both the government spending schedule and the investment schedule separately, as well as their sum.)

**3.** Assume a $100 billion downward shift in consumption spending. Using the diagrams in parts a and b of Figure 10–3, what would be the difference in the discretionary change in government spending required to keep the equilibrium GNP from changing, comparing the lump-sum tax case with the proportional tax case? What does this illustrate about the relationship between the role of automatic stabilizers and the need for discretionary fiscal action?

**4.** A number of economists have argued that discretionary fiscal policy is not well suited to deal with the relatively brief recessions that the United States has experienced since World War II. They contend that it is necessary to rely more on the built-in stabilizers to deal with such recessions. On the other hand, they argue that the relative importance of discretionary versus nondiscretionary fiscal policy is just the reverse in a depression like that of the 1930s. Explain why you would agree or disagree with these economists.

**5.** It has been argued by some economists that financing government deficits by borrowing may actually result in completely offsetting the expansionary effect of the deficit. What must they be assuming about the degree of difficulty of inducing the public to buy government bonds and the degree of sensitivity of investment spending to interest rate changes? These economists would refer to this as a situation of "complete crowding out," where the real issue is one of *who* will decide how resources are to be used—the government or the private market. Explain.

**6.** Relative to other views on budget policy, it has been said that "functional finance isn't so much a deliberate budget policy as a rationalization for what actually happens." Considering all the difficulties associated with discretionary fiscal policy, as well as the difficulties of pursuing the other budget policies, give an assessment of this statement.

**7.** In what sense is the public debt "what we owe ourselves"? In what sense, and why, might this not be true from the standpoint of an individual taxpayer? Why do foreign holdings of our nation's government debt put us in a position like that of an individual who is in debt?

# 11

# Aggregate Demand and Supply: Inflation and Supply-Side Economics

## AFTER READING THIS CHAPTER, YOU WILL BE ABLE TO:

1. Derive the aggregate demand curve from the total expenditure schedule, and explain why and how the aggregate demand curve shifts.

2. Explain the shape of the aggregate supply curve, and why and how the curve shifts.

3. Use the aggregate demand and supply curves to describe the difference between demand-pull and cost-push inflation and to explain stagflation.

4. Describe supply-side economics and explain its implications for fiscal policy.

**I**n a money-using, market-oriented economy such as that of the United States, total output and the general price level are jointly determined by the interaction of aggregate demand and aggregate supply. So far our analysis of the determination of total income, output, and employment has assumed that prices and wages, hence the general price level, are fixed. In sum, we have assumed that the aggregate supply curve is perfectly horizontal at the unchanging general price level, as shown in Figure 8-3 in Chapter 8. This means that any change in the dollar value of total income and output is due entirely to a change in the quantity of real output—so many bushels of wheat, pairs of shoes, tons of steel, and so forth. Now we want to allow for the real-world situations in which *both* the general price level and total output change at the same time.

In this chapter we will examine in greater detail the way in which aggregate demand and aggregate supply interact to jointly determine total income, output, employment, and the economy's price level. Our analysis will allow us to distinguish between demand-pull and cost-push inflation and the closely related problem of stagflation. It also will provide a framework for examining supply-side economics and some of the policies of the Reagan administration, often referred to as Reaganomics.

## THE AGGREGATE DEMAND CURVE

When we introduced the aggregate demand curve *(AD)* in Chapter 5 we saw that it shows the relationship between the economy's total demand for real GNP, or total output, and the economy's price level. It was argued that the *AD* curve has a negative slope because a higher price level, by reducing the purchasing power of consumer wealth, causes consumers to cut back on the quantity of goods and services they demand.

Now we can use the income-expenditure approach developed in the last three chapters to see more clearly why this is true, and also to examine the causes of shifts in the *AD* curve.

## The Price Level and Total Expenditure

In Chapter 8 we noted that an increase in consumer wealth would tend to shift the consumption function upward, while a decrease in wealth would tend to shift it downward. Much consumer wealth consists of fixed-dollar assets such as money, corporate and government bonds, and saving accounts. We pointed out in Chapter 5 that when the price level rises the real value or purchasing power of fixed-dollar assets declines, and that when the price level falls their purchasing power increases. Hence an increase in the price level reduces consumers' real wealth (the purchasing power of a given dollar amount of wealth), while a fall in the price level increases it. Therefore an increase in the price level, by reducing real wealth, will shift the consumption function downward. Conversely, a fall in the price level, by increasing real wealth, will shift the consumption function upward.

Since the consumption function is a major component of the total expenditure schedule (as shown in Figure 10-1), any shift in the consumption function will cause the total expenditure schedule to shift and thus cause the equilibrium level of real GNP to change. Therefore, *a fall in the price level, by shifting the consumption function upward, causes the aggregate expenditure schedule to shift upward and the equilibrium level of real GNP to increase. A rise in the price level has the opposite effect, causing the total expenditure schedule to shift downward and the equilibrium level of real GNP to decrease.*

## Derivation of the *AD* Curve

Figure 11-1, part a, shows the determination of the equilibrium level of real GNP by the total expenditure schedule for three different possible price levels. The total expenditure schedule $E_1$ associated with the lowest of the three price levels, $p_1$, determines an equilibrium level of real GNP equal to $2,000 billion, corresponding to the interaction of $E_1$ with the 45° line at point $e_1$. For a higher price level $p_2$ the associated total expenditure schedule is $E_2$ and equilibrium real GNP is lower, equal to $1,400 billion. And for a yet higher price level $p_3$ the associated expenditure schedule $E_3$ and equilibrium real GNP of $800 billion are even lower.

Each combination of equilibrium real GNP and its associated price level in part a determines a point on the aggregate demand curve $AD$ in part b of Figure 11–1. Points $e_1$, $e_2$, and $e_3$ on the $AD$ curve in part b correspond respectively to the points $e_1$, $e_2$, and $e_3$ in part a. The negative slope of the $AD$ curve reflects the fact that increases in the price level cause equilibrium real GNP to fall while decreases cause it to rise.

*Changes in the price level cause shifts in the total expenditure schedule that change equilibrium real GNP, and correspond to movements along the AD curve. Therefore movement along the AD curve shows the response of equilibrium real GNP to changes in the price level.*

## Shifts in the $AD$ Curve

In Chapters 9 and 10 we saw that any autonomous, or exogenous, change in consumption and investment spending, in government spending and tax rates, or in net export expenditure will cause the total expenditure schedule to shift and equilibrium real GNP to change.[1] We shall now show that such exogenous changes also cause the $AD$ curve to shift.

[1] In Chapters 9 and 10 we ignored net exports. Recognizing such expenditure simply adds one more layer to the consumption, investment, and government spending that add up to give the total expenditure schedule, as shown in Figure 10–1 for example.

We have seen that any change in the price level will cause the total expenditure schedule to shift and give rise to *movement along the AD curve*, as illustrated in Figure 11–1. But for a given price level we know that any exogenous expenditure or tax rate change will also cause the total expenditure schedule to shift and equilibrium real GNP to change. (These were the only kinds of cases considered in Chapters 9 and 10.) Since the price level is given, or unchanged, such a change in real GNP certainly can't be represented by movement along an $AD$ curve. Therefore it must be represented by a shift in the $AD$ curve.

This is illustrated in Figure 11–2. Suppose the price level is given as $p_0$ and the total expenditure schedule is $E_0$ in part a of Figure 11–2. The equilibrium real GNP is $1,000 billion and the point corresponding to $e_0$ in part a is $e_0$ on the $AD$ curve in part b. Suppose there is an exogenous expenditure increase (an increase in government spending, say) that shifts the total expenditure schedule up from $E_0$ to $E_1$ and increases equilibrium real GNP to $2,000 billion, corresponding to point $e_1$ in part a. Given the price level $p_0$, the $AD_0$ curve in part b is shifted rightward to $AD_1$ and the equilibrium point $e_1$ on $AD_1$ corresponds to point $e_1$ in part a.

The conclusions of Chapters 9 and 10 about the effects of exogenous expenditure and tax rate changes on the total expenditure schedule can now be stated in terms of their effects on the $AD$ curve.

1. *An exogenous increase in consumption, investment, government or net export expenditure will shift the AD curve rightward. An exogenous decrease in any of these expenditures will shift the AD curve leftward.*

2. *A tax rate increase will shift the AD curve leftward. A tax rate decrease will shift the AD curve rightward.*

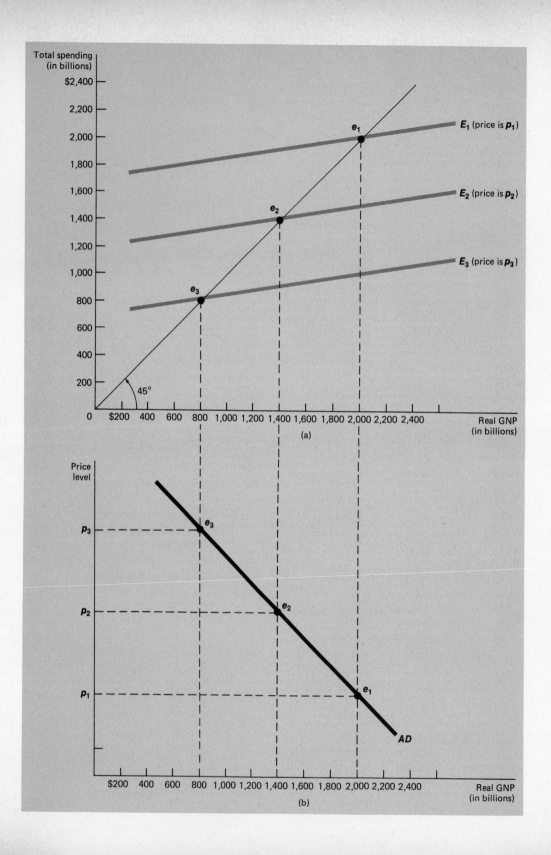

## CHECKPOINT* 11-1

**Explain why changes in the price level cause movement along the *AD* curve and why exogenous expenditure changes cause the *AD* curve to shift. What would be the effect on the *AD* curve of a $100 billion increase in government expenditures financed by a $100 billion increase in lump-sum taxes?**

*Answers to all Checkpoints can be found at the back of the text.

## THE AGGREGATE SUPPLY CURVE

When we introduced the aggregate supply curve (*AS*) in Chapter 5 we saw that it shows the amounts of total output, or real GNP, that the economy's business will supply at different price levels. Now we will examine the shape of the *AS* curve in greater detail as well as consider how and why it can shift.

### Shape of the *AS* Curve

A typical aggregate supply curve (*AS*) is shown in Figure 11-3. Three distinctly different ranges of the curve are readily apparent. It is horizontal to the left of point *a*. It increases at an increasing rate between points *a* and *c*, and then becomes vertical above point *c*.

### Horizontal Range— Only Output Changes

When the economy's firms produce any level of real GNP less than $y_a$, corresponding to point *a* on the *AS* curve, they have a great deal of unused capacity. In fact, there is so much unemployed labor and idle plant and equipment to the left of *a* on the *AS* curve that firms would produce and sell more at prevailing prices if there were only more buyers. Therefore *real GNP can be increased along the horizontal range of the AS curve without any change in the economy's price level $p_0$ because there is so much excess capacity in the economy*. Over this "Keynesian" range of the *AS* curve any change in aggregate demand changes real GNP but has no effect on the economy's price level, as illustrated earlier in Figure 8–3 (Chapter 8).

### Intermediate Range— Both Price and Output Change

The *AS* curve slopes upward over the range from *a* to *c* indicating that as the price level rises the economy's firms produce more output, or real GNP, *other things remaining the same*. When we introduced the *AS* curve in Chapter 5 we noted that the positive slope reflects short-run conditions. In particular, in the short run when the price level (the average of all prices) rises over the range from *a* to *c*, the prices of firms' products tend to rise while the prices of firms' inputs (such as the wages paid labor) are assumed to remain unchanged, or "the same." Hence firms' profits rise along the positively sloped range of the

---

**FIGURE 11-1 The Relationship Between Total Expenditure and the Aggregate Demand Curve**

Increases in the economy's price level from $p_1$ to $p_2$ to $p_3$ cause the total expenditure schedule to shift downward from $E_1$ to $E_2$ to $E_3$ and the equilibrium level of real GNP to decline from $2,000 billion to $1,400 billion to $800 billion as shown in part a. In part b we plot these price levels and their associated levels of equilibrium real GNP to get the points $e_1$, $e_2$, and $e_3$ on the aggregate demand curve AD, corresponding to the points $e_1$, $e_2$, and $e_3$ in part a. Note that changes in the price level cause *shifts* in the total expenditure schedule that correspond to movements along the AD curve.

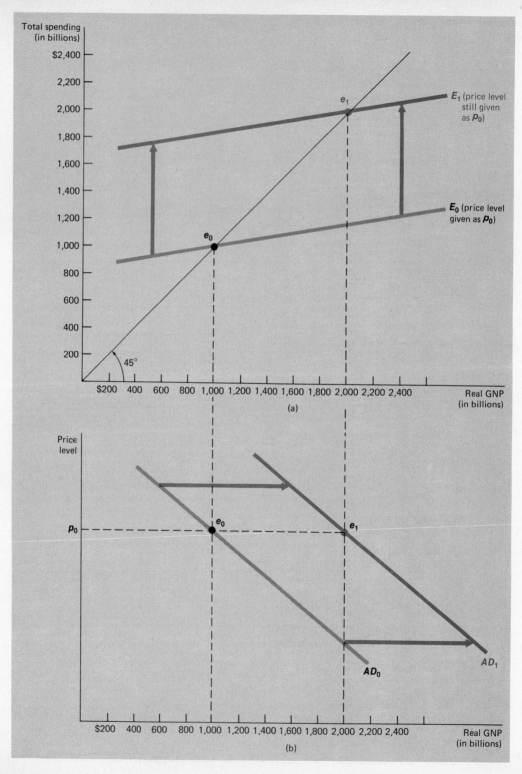

**FIGURE 11-3   The Aggregate Supply Curve**

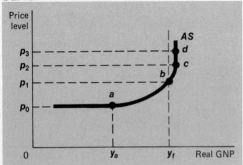

The aggregate supply curve AS is horizontal over the "Keynesian" range up to point a because there is so much unemployment and idle capacity that the economy's firms will increase output (real GNP) at the existing price level if there is demand for it. The AS curve rises over the intermediate range from a to c because as the economy's price level rises product prices rise relative to fixed input prices in the short run and firms are induced by rising profits to increase output. On the vertical or "classical" range of the AS curve above point c the economy is up against the limits of its capacity to produce output so that changes in the price level cause no change in output. This capacity constrained level of real GNP is larger than the real GNP level $y_f$ —the "full-employment" level—associated with a so-called natural rate of unemployment.

AS curve from a to c and they respond by increasing output—real GNP increases.

There are a number of reasons why the assumption that input prices remain unchanged in the short run is a fair approximation to reality. Some labor contracts between firms and workers set money wages up to 3 years in advance. Even in areas of the economy without such contracts money wages are usually increased only about once a year and remain fixed in the meantime. The prices of other inputs are often essentially fixed in the short run as well. For example, purchasing contracts between firms and supppliers are often entered into at prearranged prices that are renegotiated after completion of the contract, which may take a considerable amount of time. Similarly, plant and equipment leasing agreements as well as building rental contracts can fix the prices of such inputs for up to several years.

Another important characteristic of the AS curve over the range from a to c is that the slopes increases *at an increasing rate.* This reflects the fact that as firms expand output in the short run and operate closer to full capacity production becomes less efficient. Consequently *increasingly* larger amounts of labor and other inputs are required per additional unit of output produced. Therefore, even though wages and other input prices remain unchanged, the cost per additional unit produced increases at

**FIGURE 11-2   The Relationship Between Shifts in the Total Expenditure Schedule and Shifts in the AD Curve**

Assume a given, or unchanging, price level $p_0$. Then an exogenous increase in consumption, investment, government, or net export expenditure, or a reduction in tax rates, shifts the total expenditure schedule upward from $E_0$ to $E_1$, part a. This shift increases equilibrium real GNP from the level associated with point $e_0$ to that associated with point $e_1$. Corresponding to the shift from $E_0$ to $E_1$, part a, the aggregate demand curve shifts rightward from $AD_0$ to $AD_1$, part b. Given the price $p_0$, the points $e_0$ and $e_1$ on $AD_0$ and $AD_1$ correspond to points $e_0$ and $e_1$ in part a and the associated equilibrium levels of real GNP. An exogenous reduction in consumption, investment, government, or net export expenditure, or an increase in tax rates, shifts the total expenditure schedule downward and the aggregate demand curve leftward, given the price level $p_0$.

an increasing rate. Hence to keep profits rising, and induce firms to supply more output, increasingly higher product prices must be received by firms to cover their increasingly higher per unit production costs. For this reason the economy's price level rises at an increasing rate per additional unit of total output, or real GNP, over the range from $a$ to $c$ along the $AS$ curve. In sum:

*The AS curve rises over the intermediate range because while input prices remain unchanged in the short run, product prices (hence the economy's price level) can rise, thereby increasing profits and inducing the economy's firms to increase output. The AS curve rises at an increasing rate over the intermediate range because per unit production costs rise at an increasing rate and product prices (hence the economy's price level) must do likewise if profits are to rise and induce further increases in output.*

### The Vertical Range— Only Price Changes

When the economy's price level has risen to $p_2$, corresponding to point $c$, the $AS$ curve becomes vertical. The economy has reached the absolute limit of its productive capacity. Over this range increases in the price level, such as from $p_2$ to $p_3$, corresponding to movement from $c$ to $d$ along $AS$, will not result in any increase in real GNP—nothing more can be produced. Shifts in aggregate demand over the vertical or "classical" range of the $AS$ curve only change the price level and cause no changes in real GNP, as illustrated earlier in Figure 8–2.

Finally it should be emphasized that when the economy is up against its productive capacity limit it produces a level of real GNP greater than the economy's potential real GNP level $y_f$ associated with a so-called natural level of unemployment (discussed in Chapter 6), or what might be termed the "full-employment" level of real GNP. This is indicated in Figure 11–3 by the fact that the vertical range of the $AS$ curve lies to the right of $y_f$ which corresponds to point $b$ on the $AS$ curve at price level $p_1$.

## Shifts in the *AS* Curve

There are a number of reasons why the $AS$ curve can shift. Among the most important are changes in input prices, productivity changes, and changes in the size of the economy's labor force and its capital stock.

### Changes in Input Prices

We have emphasized that in the short run input prices are assumed to remain unchanged. They are among the other things assumed to remain the same when there is *movement along* the $AS$ curve. Recalling our discussion of market demand and supply curves in Chapter 4 immediately suggests that any change in any of those "other things," such as input prices, will cause a shift in the $AS$ curve.

One particularly important input price is the money wage rate. Given the prices firms are receiving for their products, if workers demand and get higher money wages, firms will find their profits reduced or possibly even eliminated. Consequently whatever their current output levels, firms will only be willing to continue producing at those levels if they receive higher prices. Therefore whatever the real GNP, the associated price level will have to be higher if the economy's firms are to continue to produce that level of real GNP. Thus the $AS$ curve will shift up, such as from $AS_0$ to $AS_1$ in Figure 11–4.

For example, suppose the economy's firms had been willing to produce the real GNP $y_0$ at price level $p_0$ prior to the increase in money wages, corresponding to point $a$ on $AS_0$. After the money wage increase they will be willing to produce $y_0$ only if the price level is $p_1$, corresponding to point $b$ on $AS_1$ in Figure 11–4. Equivalently, prior to the money wage increase the economy's firms were willing to produce a real GNP level $y_1$ at price level $p_1$, corresponding to point $c$ on $AS_0$. After the increase they are only willing to produce a smaller real GNP level $y_0$ at the price level $p_1$, corresponding to point $b$ on $AS_1$. In sum:

*An increase in money wages or any other*

## FIGURE 11-4 Increases in Input Prices Shift the AS Curve Upward

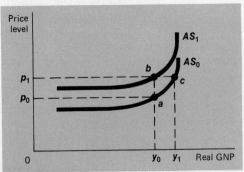

At any given level of real GNP an increase in money wages or any other input price will reduce or eliminate firms' profits. Therefore they will only continue to produce their current levels of output if they receive higher product prices. This means that whatever the level of real GNP, the economy's associated price level will have to be higher as represented by an upward shift in the AS curve, such as from $AS_0$ to $AS_1$.

*input price will cause an upward shift in the AS curve. A decrease in money wages or any other input price will shift the AS curve downward.*

### Changes in Productivity

Another important item assumed to remain the same along the AS curve is technology—the state of scientific and managerial knowledge. Improvements in technology increase labor productivity which means each worker can produce more. Given money wage rates and the prices of other inputs this means that production costs per unit of output go down. The economy's firms are therefore willing and able to produce and sell their products at lower prices. Moreover, given the size of the labor force and the quantity of the economy's other resources, the maximum amount of output the economy can produce is increased. Consequently the AS curve shifts

down and to the right, such as from $AS_0$ to $AS_2$ in Figure 11-5.

*An increase in productivity shifts the AS curve downward and to the right, reflecting the fact that the economy's firms are now willing to produce any level of real GNP at a lower price level, and that the maximum real GNP the economy can produce is increased.*

### Changes in Labor Force and Capital Stock

If the size of the economy's labor force and its stock of capital increase, there will be an increase in the maximum level of real GNP that the economy can produce. This will cause the AS curve to shift rightward, such as from $AS_0$ to $AS_1$ in Figure 11-5.

## FIGURE 11-5 Increased Productivity Shifts the AS Curve Downward and Rightward

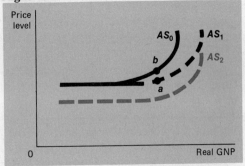

Given money wage rates and the prices of other inputs, an increase in productivity causes production costs per unit of output to go down so that the economy's firms are willing and able to sell their products at lower prices. In addition, the maximum amount of output the economy can produce is increased. Therefore a productivity increase shifts the AS curve downward and to the right, such as from $AS_0$ to $AS_2$.

Given money wage rates and input prices, an increase in the size of the economy's labor force and its capital stock shifts the AS curve rightward, such as from $AS_0$ to $AS_1$.

Note that for any level of real GNP over the intermediate ranges of $AS_0$ and $AS_1$, the corresponding point on $AS_0$ is higher than the corresponding point on $AS_1$—point $b$ is higher than point $a$, for example. This is explained by recalling that when output is increased over the intermediate range of the $AS$ curve production becomes less efficient as the economy gets closer to full capacity. With a larger labor force and capital stock these inefficiencies do not become as severe along $AS_1$ as along $AS_0$ until higher levels of real GNP are reached.

## CHECKPOINT 11-2

**Explain how a decline in the price of imported oil would affect the $AS$ curve. During the worst years of the Great Depression in the United States net investment was negative. Explain how this would affect the $AS$ curve.**

## INTERACTION OF AGGREGATE DEMAND AND SUPPLY

Our analysis of the determination of total income, output, and employment in Chapters 8, 9, and 10 assumed the $AS$ curve was horizontal. Therefore the price level remained unchanged whenever the $AD$ curve shifted, as in Figure 8–3 in Chapter 8. Now we will examine the way in which that analysis is modified when the price level can vary with output because of the existence of the upward sloping intermediate and vertical ranges along the $AS$ curve, such as shown in Figure 11–3. In addition, we will examine the distinction between demand-pull and cost-push inflation, and gain some understanding of the problem of stagflation.

### Modification of the Analysis When the Price Level Changes

Figure 11–2 showed the change in real GNP at a given price level in response to an exogenous, or autonomous, expenditure increase (in consumption, investment, government, or net export spending), or a tax rate reduction, which shifts the total expenditure schedule upward and the $AD$ curve rightward. Such a shift is repeated again in Figure 11–6, but now allowing for the price level to change along the upward sloping intermediate range of the $AS$ curve. The adjustment can be broken into two steps.

*Step 1.* The total expenditure schedule $E$ shifts upward from $E_0$ to $E_1'$ in part a of Figure 11–6, causing the $AD$ curve to shift rightward from $AD_0$ to $AD_1$, as shown in part b. *If* the economy's firms were willing to increase output *at the price level* $p_0$ in response to the increase in aggregate demand, real GNP would increase from $y_0$ to $y_1'$, corresponding to a move from point $e_0$ to point $e_1'$. The adjustment would be exactly the same as that already described in Figure 11–2. The increase in real GNP from $y_0$ to $y_1'$ would be equal to the multiplier effect discussed in Chapters 9 and 10. Now, however, because the $AS$ curve is upward sloping, the economy's firms are not willing to produce a real GNP greater than $y_0$ at the price level $p_0$. Therefore at $p_0$ there is an excess demand for total output equal to the distance between point $e_0$ and $e_1'$.

*Step 2.* The excess demand causes the economy's price level to rise. The increase in the price level will cause the total expenditure schedule to shift downward from $E_1$ in part a, which gives rise to movement up along the $AD_1$ curve, part b, as previously shown in Figure 11–1. The adjustment is complete once the total expenditure schedule has shifted down to $E_1$, part a, and the price level has risen to $p_1$ corresponding to the intersection of $AD_1$ and $AS$ at point $e_1$ in part b. Compared to the increase in real GNP that occurs when the price level remains unchanged (from $y_0$ to $y_1'$), real GNP now increases by a smaller amount (from $y_0$ to $y_1$) because some of the increase in aggregate demand is absorbed by a rise in the price level. In sum:

*When the economy is operating along the intermediate range of the $AS$ curve, an exoge-*

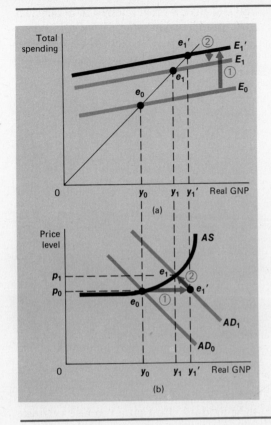

**FIGURE 11-6  Change in Real GNP and the Price Level Due to Exogenous Expenditure Change**

Initially equilibrium real GNP is $y_0$ and the equilibrium price level is $p_0$ at point $e_0$ in both part a and part b. An exogenous expenditure increase shifts the total expenditure schedule upward from $E_0$ to $E_1'$ (arrow 1, part a) and the $AD$ curve rightward from $AD_0$ to $AD_1$. If the economy's firms were willing to increase output in response to the increase in aggregate demand at price level $p_0$, real GNP would increase from $y_0$ to $y_1'$ (arrow 1, part b), an amount equal to the simple multiplier effect. However, because the $AS$ curve is upward sloping there is instead an excess aggregate demand at $p_0$. Therefore the price level rises causing the total expenditure schedule to shift downward to $E_1$ (arrow 2, part a) and movement up along the $AD_1$ curve (arrow 2, part b), restoring equilibrium at point $e_1$ (parts a and b), at real GNP level $y_1$, and price level $p_1$. The multiplier effect on real GNP (equals the increase from $y_0$ to $y_1$) is smaller when the price level rises compared with the effect ($y_0$ to $y_1'$) when the price level remains unchanged.

nous expenditure change, or an exogenous tax rate change, will have a smaller multiplier effect on real GNP than when the economy is operating along the horizontal range of the AS curve.

Finally, note that along the vertical range of the $AS$ curve the multiplier effect on real GNP equals zero. Any exogenous expenditure or tax rate change will only cause a change in the price level along the vertical range.

## Demand-Pull Inflation: Shifts in the *AD* Curve

Suppose the $AD$ curve is initially in the position $AD_0$ in Figure 11-7 so that the equilib-

rium price level and real GNP are $p_0$ and $y_0$ respectively, corresponding to point $e_0$ on the $AS$ curve. An exogenous expenditure increase, or tax rate reduction, which shifts the $AD$ curve rightward from $AD_0$ to $AD_0'$ increases equilibrium real GNP from $y_0$ to $y_0'$. However, along this horizontal, or Keynesian, range of $AS$ from point $e_0$ to $e_0'$ there is so much excess capacity and unemployment that firms are willing to increase output at existing prices in response to increased demand—the price level remains unchanged at $p_0$.

Further increases in aggregate demand, such as represented by shifts from $AD_0'$ to $AD_1$ to $AD_2$, along the intermediate range of the $AS$ curve between points $e_0'$ and $e_2$ cause

**FIGURE 11-7   Demand-Pull Inflation**

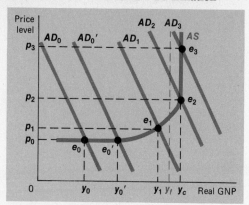

The rise in the price level caused by increased aggregate demand is called demand-pull inflation.

When aggregate demand increases from $AD_0$ to $AD_0'$ over the horizontal, or Keynesian, range of the $AS$ curve real GNP increases from $y_0$ to $y_0'$ while the price level remains unchanged at $p_0$. Increases in aggregate demand over the intermediate range, such as from $AD_0'$ to $AD_1$ to $AD_2$, pull up the price level to an ever greater extent (from $p_0$ to $p_1$ to $p_2$) relative to the increase in real GNP (from $y_0'$ to $y_1$ to $y_c$). Increases in aggregate demand, such as from $AD_2$ to $AD_3$, over the vertical or classical range of the $AS$ curve pull up the price level (from $p_2$ to $p_3$) without increasing real GNP at all.

the price level to rise. Moreover, the rise in the price level becomes ever larger relative to the increase in real GNP as the economy moves closer and closer to its full-employment real GNP level $y_f$, and then beyond to its capacity level $y_c$ where the price level rises to $p_2$, corresponding to point $e_2$. Further increases in aggregate demand, such as from $AD_2$ to $AD_3$, move the economy up along the vertical, or classical, range of the $AS$ curve and pull the price level up from $p_2$ to $p_3$ while real GNP remains unchanged at $y_c$.

The increase in the price level which is caused by increases in aggregate demand along the intermediate and vertical ranges of

the $AS$ curve is often referred to as demand-pull inflation. **Demand-pull inflation** *originates on the demand side of the economy's markets for goods and services and is caused by increases in aggregate demand.*

## Cost-Push Inflation: The Stagflation Problem

We have seen how an increase in money wages or any other input price will cause the $AS$ curve to shift upward, as shown in Figure 11–4 for example. Such upward shifts give rise to **cost-push inflation.**

### Cost-Push Inflation

Cost-push inflation may originate in the labor market where powerful unions coerce firms to pay higher wages under the threat of labor walkout or strike. The resulting rise in per unit costs of production is then likely to cause these firms to charge higher product prices. Similarly, a few large firms in key industries might use their market power to try to raise profits by charging higher prices for their products. Cost-push can also originate with an increase in the price of any vital resource needed to produce a variety of products. The sharp rise in the price of imported oil in 1973–1974 and again in 1979 drove up the cost of energy, a necessary ingredient to any production process. The resulting rise in per unit production costs pushed up the prices of almost all products, as was reflected in the dramatic rise in the general price level.

### Stagflation

During these cost-push episodes of the 1970s the unemployment rate rose at the same time that the inflation rate increased, a phenomenon often referred to as **stagflation** (from a combination of the word stagnation, meaning high unemployment, and inflation, a rising price level). We will examine stagflation more extensively in Chapter 16. However, we can begin to get some insight into the problem by examining the relationship between cost-push inflation and unemployment at this point.

Suppose the economy's aggregate supply curve is initially $AS_0$ in Figure 11-8, intersecting the aggregate demand curve $AD_0$ at $e_0$ to give a full-employment equilibrium level of real GNP $y_f$ and price level $p_f$. Now suppose the economy experiences some sort of cost-push—for example, an increase in the price of imported oil. This will push up costs of production and business firms will now charge higher prices to cover their higher costs. To induce the economy's firms to produce any given level of real GNP, the general price level will have to be higher than previously. This is represented by an upward shift in the aggregate supply curve from $AS_0$ to $AS_1$. The economy's equilibrium price level will *rise* from $p_f$ to $p_1$ while its equilibrium level of real GNP will *decline* from $y_f$ to $y_1$, corresponding to the intersection of $AS_1$ and

$AD_0$ at point $e_1$. Since the equilibrium level of real GNP is now less than the full-employment level, employment is reduced and unemployment increased. In sum, *cost-push inflation originates on the supply side of the economy. A cost-push results in a rise in both the general price level and the unemployment rate, a phenomenon known as stagflation.*

### CHECKPOINT 11-3

**Suppose the *AS* curve to the right of point $e_0$ in part b of Figure 11-6 were more steeply sloped. Given the same $AD_0$ and $AD_1$ curves, how would the total expenditure adjustment in part a now be different? Suppose a demand-pull and a cost-push inflation occurred simultaneously and in such a way that there was no change in real GNP. Construct a diagram showing how the *AS* and *AD* curves would have to shift to give rise to such an occurrence.**

### FIGURE 11-8    Cost-Push Inflation and Stagflation

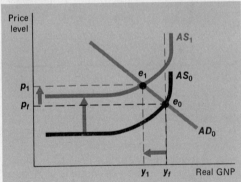

An increase in input prices shifts the *AS* curve upward from $AS_0$ to $AS_1$ along the *AD* curve $AD_0$ pushing up the price level from $p_f$ to $p_1$—a process known as cost-push inflation. The associated fall in real GNP from $y_f$ to $y_1$ raises the unemployment rate. The simultaneous increase in the price level and the unemployment rate is often referred to as stagflation.

## SUPPLY-SIDE ECONOMICS: IMPLICATIONS FOR FISCAL POLICY

Our discussion in Chapter 10 of the effects of government spending, taxation, and budget policy on the economy presented a strictly Keynesian point of view. In particular, according to the Keynesian view, taxes only affect the demand side of the economy. By causing a deficit (or surplus) in the government's budget, tax changes increase (or decrease) aggregate demand, thus increasing (or decreasing) total income, output, and employment. Moreover, we have seen that according to the Keynesian analysis, a dollar of government expenditure has a more expansionary impact on the economy than a dollar of tax cuts because the government spends the whole dollar, whereas taxpayers save part of any tax cut.

In recent years a number of economists, journalists, and politicians have been challenging the Keynesian view that tax cuts affect the economy only by affecting aggregate demand. Indeed, the views of these "supply-siders" have become an integral part of the Reagan administration's economic policy program. Basically, supply-siders argue that lower tax *rates* give rise to higher after-tax rewards or greater incentives to work, save, and invest. As people respond to these incentives the economy's capacity to produce and supply goods and services is increased. Two basic supply-side propositions follow from this.

1. The resulting increase in the economy's supply of total output, or real GNP, will put downward pressure on prices and hence help fight inflation.
2. The increase in total income and output may well give rise to an increase in tax *revenue* despite the reduction in tax *rates.* This view is just the opposite of the Keynesian view that a reduction in tax rates will always result in a reduction in tax revenue. In other words, supply-siders argue that a reduction in tax rates can reduce a government budget deficit or increase a budget surplus—just the opposite of the Keynesian view. Let's examine the supply-side reasoning underlying each of these propositions.

## Tax Rates and Incentives

Supply-side economics stresses cutting income tax *rates.* (Remember, tax rates are not the same thing as tax *revenues,* the amount of money collected from taxpayers.) In particular, supply-siders argue that marginal tax rates are what must be reduced. The **marginal tax rate** is defined as follows:

$$\text{marginal tax rate} = \frac{\text{change in tax liability}}{\text{change in income}}$$

*The marginal tax rate indicates how much of an additional dollar of one's income, the marginal or last dollar earned, must be paid in taxes.* For example, if the marginal tax rate is

.3, 30 cents of an *additional* dollar of income must be given to the government, leaving the individual with 70 cents of after-tax income.

*The marginal tax rate of a proportional income tax is constant because the same percentage of every additional dollar of income is taxed away, regardless of the amount of income earned.* If the proportional tax rate is .2, for example, then an individual earning an additional dollar will have to give 20 cents of it to the tax collector whether the individual's income is $10,000, $100,000, or $1,000,000.

*The marginal tax rate of a progressive income tax rises as income increases.* For example, suppose the progressive income tax structure is such that the first $10,000 of an individual's income is subject to a 20 percent rate, the second $10,000 to a 30 percent rate, the third to a 40 percent rate, and so forth. Then for income levels less than $10,000 the marginal tax rate on an additional dollar of income is .2, for income levels between $10,000 and $20,000 it is .3, for income levels between $20,000 and $30,000 it is .4, and so forth.

Supply-siders argue that a reduction of marginal tax will increase work effort, encourage more saving and investment, improve resource allocation, and reduce the amount of resources devoted to tax-avoidance activities. Each of these effects of reduced marginal tax rates will tend to increase the economy's aggregate supply of goods and services. Let's consider why.

### Tax Rate Effects on Work Effort

When an individual considers whether or not to work harder or longer, the relevant question is, What will be the additional after-tax income, or take-home pay, resulting from the additional effort? The larger the marginal tax rate, the smaller the after-tax reward and therefore the less the incentive to work harder or longer. This consideration is relevant not only to people contemplating the merits of additional work effort in their currently held job (more overtime, for example) but also to those contemplating promotion possibilities, career choices, new business ventures, and other forms of innovative work effort. For example, suppose the marginal tax rate on additional income above $30,000 were .95 (a marginal rate similar to the rates prevailing at this income level of the progressive tax structures of Great Britain and Sweden). Few people would want to put in the additional time and effort, acquire the additional training and education, or take on the additional responsibility and risks necessary to earn an income greater than $30,000. In sum, supply-siders argue that higher marginal tax rates encourage people to take more leisure time and work less. This can occur in many ways: a reduction in overtime; earlier retirement; more absenteeism; fewer second breadwinners in households; lower labor productivity; and greater reluctance to take more responsible (and higher paying) jobs, to pursue more demanding (and higher paying) careers, or to undertake other innovative, often risky and demanding, forms of work effort. Therefore, *supply-siders argue that reducing marginal tax rates will stimulate work effort and thereby increase the economy's aggregate supply of output.*

### Tax Rate Effects on Saving and Investment

As we have discussed before, one of the determinants of the amount of saving is the rate of return that can be earned on savings. If the rate of interest is 10 percent, an individual would receive $10 on $100 of saving after 1 year, a rate of return of 10 percent. But this is $10 of income and would be taxed just like any other form of income. Hence the higher the marginal tax rate on income, the smaller the fraction of the $10 that the individual could keep. For example, if the marginal tax rate were .3, the individual could keep only $7 after tax. The after-tax rate of return would be 7 percent. It is the after-tax rate of return that is important to the individual who is deciding how much to save. The higher the marginal tax rate, the lower the

after-tax rate of return and the smaller the incentive to save. Saving is necessary for capital formation, which increases the economy's capacity to produce goods. Therefore, *supply-siders argue that the increase in saving caused by a reduction of marginal tax rates tends to increase the economy's aggregate supply of output.*

Business willingness to invest in capital goods also depends on the after-tax rate of return on the dollars invested in capital goods. *Supply-siders argue that reduction of marginal tax rates stimulates investment spending, increasing capital formation and thereby aggregate supply.*

### Tax Rate Effects on Resource Allocation

High marginal tax rates encourage the creation and use of loopholes in the tax law, the legal ways in which payment of taxes at going marginal tax rates can be avoided. These loopholes encourage workers, savers, and investors to direct resources into activities where after-tax rates of return are relatively high only because of special tax exemptions and advantages created by the loopholes. Such tax advantages are available to those investing in real estate, for example. As a result, it is possible that the economy devotes too many resources to residential and commercial construction at the expense of other productive activities not offering tax advantages. *Supply-siders argue that reductions in marginal tax rates would reduce the "payoff" from loopholes and therefore lead to a more efficient allocation of resources, hence increasing the economy's capacity to supply goods.*

### Tax Rates and Tax Avoidance

Seeking out and taking advantage of often complicated tax loopholes typically requires the use of trained lawyers and accountants. Higher marginal tax rates make it more worthwhile for taxpayers to employ such services in order to avoid taxes. It is estimated

## POLICY PERSPECTIVE

### Tax Evasion and the Underground Economy— Another Source of Deficit Growth

Tax avoidance, the *legal* use of tax loopholes, has long been a common practice made possible by our complicated tax laws which offer a myriad of exceptions, write-offs, special deductions, and exemptions to this or that particular group in our society. However in recent years a number of industrialized countries, including the United States, have experienced a significant and growing loss of tax revenue due to tax evasion. Tax evasion is *illegal*, unlike tax avoidance, and refers to income taxes individuals and businesses should pay but do not, encompassing income earned from both legal and illegal activity. Higher tax rates encourage people to go to greater lengths to "hide" income from the tax collector, despite the risks of getting caught and having to pay stiff fines, possibly even serving a prison term. Higher tax rates increase the rewards of "cheating" and thus make it more worthwhile to take these risks.

One way people engage in tax evasion is to participate in the so-called "underground economy." It is difficult, for example, for wage earners employed by businesses, government, and other organizations to hide income from the tax authorities because of automatic tax withholding from paychecks. Higher tax rates encourage people to engage in activities where the income earned is easier to hide. Such activities include the bartering of goods and services, and "cash only" transactions. For example, a moonlighting auto mechanic might fix a farmer's tractor in exchange for a few pounds of bacon and a bushel of corn, or simply be paid off in cash. In such instances, there are no checks that can be traced from bank records, or payroll records that can be audited by tax authorities. The underground economy refers to all such barter and cash-only exchanges of goods and services wherein the income earned from such activity goes unreported and thereby untaxed.

How much tax revenue is not collected by the federal government as a consequence of tax evasion? A recent Internal Revenue Service report estimates that $90.5 billion of federal income tax was lost in the United States in 1981 due to unreported incomes, an amount approximately equal to 33 percent of total federal corporate and personal income taxes actually collected in 1981; $81.5 billion was due to unreported legal income and another $9.0 billion due to unreported income earned in illegal activities.[1] These figures refer to lost federal income tax revenue. In addition tax evasion has also resulted in lost tax revenue to state and local governments—a probably significant, though unknown amount. A major policy concern is that tax evasion contributes significantly to the size of government deficits.

### Questions

1. In Sweden, which has very high marginal tax rates, it is reported that the average worker is absent from his or her job one day a week due to "illness." Can you offer an

[1] Internal Revenue Service, Income Tax Compliance Research, Department of the Treasury, Office of the Assistant Commissioner (Planning, Finance, and Research), Research Divsion, 1983. Also see Carl P. Simon and Ann D. Witte, *Beating the System* (Boston: Auburn House Publishing Co., 1982).

explanation for this amazingly high rate of absenteeism in a country known for its generally high health standards?

2. If loopholes in our present tax laws were greatly reduced or eliminated, what effect do you think this would have on tax evasion activity?

that billions of dollars' worth of highly skilled and educated labor is employed annually in this fashion—labor that otherwise could be employed in producing goods and services more useful from society's viewpoint. Therefore, *supply-siders argue that a reduction of marginal tax rates would increase the economy's capacity to supply goods and services by reducing the use of resources for tax-avoidance activities.*

## Inflation and Tax Rate Reduction

*Supply-siders argue that the increase in the economy's supply of total output resulting from reductions in marginal tax rates will put downward pressure on prices and hence help fight inflation,* the first of the two supply-side propositions noted before. This proposition can be illustrated in terms of the economy's aggregate supply curve.

Suppose the economy initially has an equilibrium level of real GNP $y_0$ and price level $p_0$, determined by the intersection of $AD_0$ and $AS_0$ at point $a$ in Figure 11–9.

### Effect of Tax Rate Reduction on the Aggregate Supply Curve

Suppose there is a reduction in marginal tax rates. For the moment let's focus only on the effect on the aggregate supply curve. Since marginal tax rates are now lower, workers, other resource suppliers, and firms will get to keep a larger fraction of the dollars they earn from the sale of the goods and services they produce. Suppliers can supply the same quantity of goods as before, but they can now sell the goods at a lower price and still receive the same after-tax income. Hence the reduction of marginal tax rates shifts the aggregate supply curve $AS_0$ down to the position $AS_1$.

Notice also, however, that the aggregate supply curve is shifted rightward as well. This reflects the increase in the economy's capacity to supply goods caused by the re-

**FIGURE 11-9  Demand-Side and Supply-Side Effects of Reduction in Marginal Tax Rates**

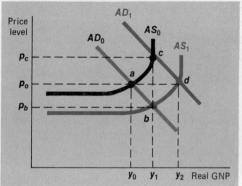

A reduction in marginal tax rates causes the economy's aggregate demand curve to shift rightward, according to the Keynesian, or demand-side, view, and the aggregate supply curve to shift downward and to the right, according to the supply-side view.

When the $AD$ curve shifts rightward from $AD_0$ to $AD_1$, real GNP increases from $y_0$ to $y_1$, and the price level rises from $p_0$ to $p_c$ if supply-side shifts are ignored. Allowing for the supply-side effects of the tax rate reduction, the $AS$ curve also shifts, such as from $AS_0$ to $AS_1$. In the example shown here, the result of both shifts is that real GNP increases from $y_0$ to $y_2$ while the price level remains unchanged at $p_0$. Hence supply-siders argue that tax rate reductions increase real GNP more and the general price level less than is suggested by a strictly Keynesian, or demand-side point of view.

## POLICY PERSPECTIVE

### Where Are We on the Laffer Curve?

Skepticism about the supply-siders' argument that lowering marginal tax rates will lead to increase tax revenues is fairly widespread. Many economists and policy-makers agree that the proposition may be true in the long run, after sufficient economic growth. As to the short run, however, many critics argue that the decrease in tax rates would not have a sufficient impact on the economy's supply side to expand income enough to actually increase tax revenues. Furthermore, many economists seriously question whether we are on the upper portion of the Laffer curve. Empirical studies of this question for the United States suggest that we are not.[1] A similar study for Sweden, which has much higher tax rates than the United States, concludes that Sweden is on the upper portion of its Laffer curve.[2]

To settle this issue for the United States requires much more empirical evidence than is currently available. We really don't know at what level of tax rates the economy's tax revenue would begin to decline.

[1] Bruce Bender, "An Analysis of the Laffer Curve," *Economic Inquiry*, July 1984, pp. 414–420. Also see Don Fullerton, "On the Possibility of an Inverse Relationship Between Tax Rates and Government Revenues," *Journal of Public Economics*, October 1982, pp. 3–22.

[2] Charles E. Stuart, "Swedish Tax Rates, Labor Supply, and Tax Revenues," *Journal of Political Economy*, October 1981, pp. 1020–1038.

duction in marginal tax rates, an increase due to increased work effort, increased capital formation, more efficient resource allocation—all the effects of marginal tax rate reductions just discussed. The economy's full-capacity output level, corresponding to the vertical segment of the aggregate supply curve, has increased—the vertical segment of $AS_1$ lies to the right of that for $AS_0$.

As a consequence of the shift in the $AS$ curve from $AS_0$ to $AS_1$, the economy's equilibrium level of real GNP increases from $y_0$ to $y_1$ while its equilibrium price level falls from $p_0$ to $p_b$, corresponding to the intersection of $AD_0$ and $AS_1$ at point $b$. We see now why supply-siders argue that reducing marginal tax rates puts downward pressure on prices and helps fight inflation.

### Supply-Side and Demand-Side Views Combined

Let's now combine the demand-side effects of a reduction in marginal tax rates, as illustrated in Figure 11–2, with the supply-side effects. On the demand side, a reduction in marginal tax rates will cause the aggregate demand curve in Figure 11–9 to shift rightward—from $AD_0$ to $AD_1$, say. Now if we ignore any supply-side effects of the tax rate reduction, as is customary in the Keynesian view, we simply move up along the aggregate supply curve $AS_0$ from point $a$ to point $c$. Real GNP increases from $y_0$ to $y_1$ and the price level rises from $p_0$ to $p_c$.

However, suppose we also take into account the shift in the aggregate supply curve from $AS_0$ to $AS_1$, the supply-side view of the effects of the reduction in marginal tax rates. Then the equilibrium level of real GNP is increased to $y_2$ while the price level remains unchanged at $p_0$, corresponding to the intersection of $AD_1$ and $AS_1$ at point $d$.

In conclusion, our example suggests that *when supply-side effects are taken into account, marginal tax rate reductions are likely to be less inflationary and lead to larger increases in output than is suggested by a strictly demand-side, or Keynesian, point of view.*

**FIGURE 11-10   The Laffer Curve**

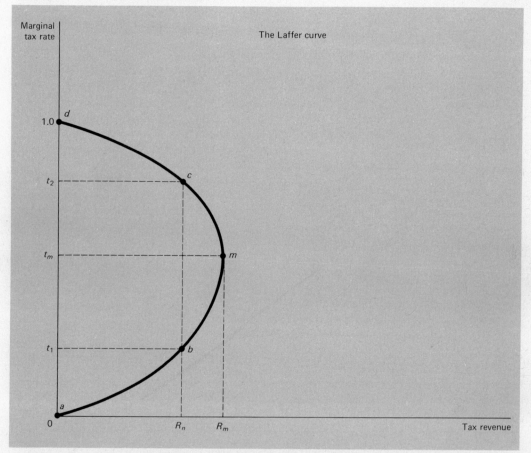

The Laffer curve suggests that tax revenue (horizontal axis) rises as the marginal tax rate is increased up to some rate $t_m$, corresponding to point $m$ on the curve, where the maximum possible tax revenue is $R_m$. Tax rates higher than $t_m$ discourage productive efforts so much that total income falls, causing tax revenue to decline. The curve implies that if the marginal tax rate is above $t_m$, rate reduction will give rise to increased tax revenue. It also implies that for every marginal tax rate above $t_m$ there exists a lower rate that would generate the same tax revenue.

## Tax Rate Reduction and Tax Revenues—The Laffer Curve

While a reduction in marginal tax rates may cause an expansion in the economy's capacity to produce goods and services, won't it also lead to larger budget deficits due to a decline in tax revenues? Some supply-siders, such as Arthur Laffer, say no. This brings us to the second supply-side proposition: *supply-siders argue that the increase in total income and output (real GNP) resulting from a reduction in marginal tax rates may well give rise to an increase in tax revenue despite the reduction in tax rates.* This proposition may be character-

## POLICY PERSPECTIVE

### Indexing Income Taxes—Putting the Brakes on Rising Tax Rates

One of the first major policy initiatives of the early years of the Reagan administration—the first piece of "Reaganomics" legislation—was the Economic Recovery Tax Act passed by Congress in 1981. In addition to cutting marginal tax rates by 23 percent over a 3-year period, the Act provided that income tax brackets would be indexed to inflation beginning in January 1985. Prior to that time our income tax structure suffered from *bracket creep*—a process whereby inflation automatically increased taxes paid to the federal government, even though Congress didn't legislate higher tax rates.

Personal income and business income in the U.S. economy are subject to a progressive tax. Recall that a progressive tax on income imposes successively higher tax rates on additional dollars of income as income rises. As a hypothetical example, suppose income tax rates are such that the first $10,000 of an individual's income is subject to a 20 percent tax rate, the second $10,000 to a 30 percent rate, the third to a 40 percent rate, and so forth. This means that as one's total income rises, the fraction of that total income that is taxed away gets larger. If the individual makes $10,000, 20 percent, or one-fifth, of it goes to taxes; if $20,000, then 25 percent (the average of 20 percent and 30 percent), or one-fourth, of it goes to taxes, and so forth.

#### Inflation and the Progressive Tax Structure

The problem with our progressive tax structure prior to January 1985 was that it was calculated on the basis of fixed-dollar amounts that didn't allow for changes in the purchasing power of the dollar resulting from inflation. Consequently, even if your dollar income rose at the same rate as the general price level, the quantity of goods you could purchase with the income you had left after paying taxes declined. This was so because as your dollar income increased, it was subjected to progressively higher rates of taxation.

Consider an example using the hypothetical progressive tax rates mentioned above. Suppose you are making $10,000 per year, which means you are taxed at a 20 percent rate. Your after-tax income is therefore $8,000. Now suppose that there is a 10 percent rate of inflation but that your dollar income also increases 10 percent, from $10,000 to $11,000, or by $1,000. The purchasing power of your before-tax income thus remains unchanged—it is an income of constant purchasing power. While the first $10,000 of your income is taxed at a 20 percent rate, the additional $1,000 is taxed at a 30 percent rate. Hence your after-tax income is now $8,700 ($11,000 minus the sum of .20 × $10,000 and .30 × $1,000, or $11,000 minus $2,300). Over the year your after-tax dollar income has increased from $8,000 to $8,700, or by 8.75 percent. Though your before-tax dollar income increased at the same rate as the general price level (10 percent), your after-tax dollar income increased at a lower rate. The purchasing power of your before-tax income is constant, but you can only purchase goods with what you have left after taxes. And since your after-tax dollar income has not kept up with the increase in the general price level, you now have less purchasing power—you are worse off. Inflation combined with a progressive income tax structure automatically taxes away purchasing power.

### How Indexing Income Taxes Works

It was often pointed out that this loss of purchasing power amounted to an unlegislated, unvoted, unsigned tax hike, literally "taxation without representation." The basis for this claim was that inflation automatically pushed people into progressively higher tax brackets. These brackets were not adjusted for the fact that the purchasing power of the dollar was reduced by inflation, however. Indexing income taxes adjusts these tax brackets upward at the same rate as the rate of inflation. Indexing therefore prevents the automatic taxing away of purchasing power.

Consider our hypothetical example once more, and assume that the tax brackets are indexed to the rate of inflation. Once again, the first tax bracket is the first $10,000 of income (taxed at a 20 percent rate), the second tax bracket applies to income earned beyond $10,000 up to $20,000 (taxed at a 30 percent rate), the third applies to income beyond $20,000 up to $30,000 (taxed at a 40 percent rate), and so forth. If the rate of inflation over the coming year is 10 percent, each tax bracket will be adjusted upward 10 percent. The first tax bracket now will be the first $11,000 of income, the second bracket will be from $11,000 up to $22,000, the third from $22,000 up to $33,000, and so forth. Now when your dollar income increases 10 percent (the same as the rate of inflation), from $10,000 up to $11,000, this increase doesn't move you into the next tax bracket as before. Therefore, your after-tax dollar income increases from $8,000 to $8,800, also an increase of 10 percent. Since your after-tax income has increased the same percentage amount as the general price level, you still have the same purchasing power.

#### Questions

1. If the income tax structure were not indexed, why might the economy be more susceptible to recession?

2. Some argue that indexing the income tax structure removes an automatic protection against inflationary booms. How could this be so?

ized in terms of the popularly known **Laffer curve** shown in Figure 11–10.

The Laffer curve shows the relationship between the marginal tax rate (vertical axis) and the amount of tax revenue the government receives (horizontal axis). It is easy to establish the two points where the Laffer curve meets the vertical axis. Clearly if the marginal tax rate is zero, the government will receive no tax revenue, which corresponds to point $a$ at the origin of the graph. At the other extreme, if the marginal tax rate is 1, so that every dollar of income is confiscated by the government, people will have no incentive to work and again tax revenue will be zero, corresponding to point $d$. If the marginal tax rate is $t_1$ (roughly .2, say), government tax revenue would equal $R_n$, corresponding to point $b$ on the Laffer curve. If the rate is increased to $t_m$, tax revenue rises to $R_m$, corresponding to point $m$ on the curve. Notice, however, that any further increase in the rate will actually cause the level of tax revenue to decline. At $t_2$, for instance, tax revenue falls back to the level $R_n$, corresponding to point $c$. Why? Above some marginal tax rate, such as $t_m$, the after-tax rewards for working and capital formation become so low that these productive activities are reduced. The resulting decline in total income is so great that tax revenues decline despite the increased marginal tax rate. For example, suppose that the economy has a proportional tax structure and the marginal

## POLICY PERSPECTIVE

### The Reagan Deficits—The Result of Supply-Side Economics or What?

A major economic policy issue confronting the Reagan administration has been the alarming size of federal government budget deficits (see Figure 10–4)—the excess of federal government expenditures over receipts. The ballooning of federal deficits during the Reagan years appears to have been associated with a combination of adverse budgetary developments rather than with a single cause, such as supply-side economic policies, as some critics would have it. An examination of government expenditures and receipts since 1969 is revealing.

#### Growth of Federal Expenditures

Federal expenditures as a share of GNP are shown in Figure P11–1. They are broken down into two major categories: the purchase of goods and services, and transfer payments (including transfer to persons, state and local governments, net interest on the federal debt, and subsidies to government enterprises). Until 1979, the share of federal expenditures in GNP changed very little, except for a temporary spurt in 1975. The surge in transfer payments was almost offset by the decline in the purchase of goods and services. However, since 1979 both components of federal expenditures have risen relative to GNP.

While national defense purchases of goods and services declined from 1968 to 1979, they rose from 4.6 percent of GNP in 1979 to 6.0 percent in 1983. This rise accounted for all of the increase in the share of government purchases in GNP, but for only 36 percent of the increase in the share of total government expenditures in GNP.

#### Federal Receipts as a Share of GNP

The share of federal receipts in GNP is shown in Figure P11–2, broken down by major components: personal tax receipts, social security contributions, and corporate income taxes. The share of social security taxes in GNP continued its upward climb from 1979 to 1983, rising from 6.6 percent to 7.1 percent. This increase largely offset the decline in the share of personal taxes from 9.5 percent to 8.9 percent over the same period. Corporate taxes declined from 3.1 percent to 1.8 percent of GNP from 1979 to 1983, a decline that largely reflected a similar decrease in corporate profits over this period.

**FIGURE P11-1  Federal Government Expenditures as a Share of GNP** (Recessions Are Shaded Areas; Data Is Seasonally Adjusted)

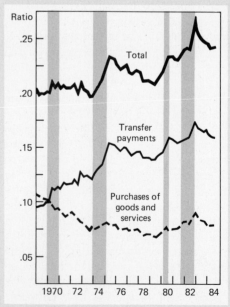

SOURCE: National Income and Product Accounts.

**FIGURE P11-2** **Federal Government Receipts as a Share of GNP**
(Recessions Are Shaded Areas; Data Is Seasonally Adjusted)

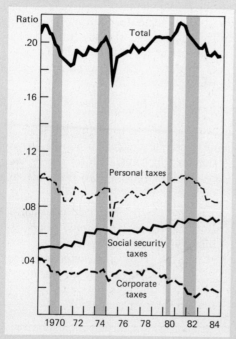

SOURCE: National Income and Product Accounts.

### Causes of Deficits During the First Reagan Term

The surge in the size of government deficits during the first term of the Reagan administration reflected the rise in total government expenditures as a share of GNP, from about 21 percent in 1979 to approximately 25 percent by 1984, coupled with a decline in total receipts as a share of GNP from around 21 percent to about 19 percent. The expenditure rise was primarily due to the continued rapid growth of transfer programs such as social security programs, Medicare, unemployment benefits, and interest on the national debt. In the meantime, receipts grew more slowly than GNP, largely reflecting a de-

cline in corporate income and corporate income tax receipts. Explanations that attribute deficit growth to the defense buildup that began in 1979 or to tax cuts seem to be inadequate.

### The Defense Argument

Growth in the share of defense spending in GNP from 1979 through 1983 accounted for only 1.4 percentage points of a 4.8 percentage point rise in the deficit as a percent of GNP (from 0.7 percent to 5.5 percent). Transfer payments in particular, as well as other government expenditures, account for a considerably larger part of the rise.

### The Tax-Cut Argument

As a consequence of the 1981 tax cuts, tax rates and taxes obviously were lower than levels they would otherwise have attained. However, despite the tax cuts of the Economic Recovery Tax Act of 1981, actual tax rates tended to rise from 1980 to 1984! This was due to the fact that the 1981 cuts in personal marginal tax rates were largely offset by inflation-induced **"bracket creep"** and social security tax hikes. The 1981 tax cuts (phased in over 3 years) were evidently a poor substitute for income tax indexing which began in January 1985.

The Tax Act of 1981 also provided business tax cuts, primarily by reducing effective tax rates on income from new investments through accelerated depreciation (the Accelerated Cost Recovery System). However overall it had only a minor impact on average tax rates or on the real tax burden on business income from 1980 to 1983. New indirect business taxes have largely offset lower tax rates on corporate income and accelerated depreciation. By far the largest share of the observed decline in corporate income taxes as a share of GNP has been related to the business cycle.

### The Role of the Business Cycle

Budget developments during the first term of the Reagan administration were largely a reflection of the business cycle. The shaded areas in Figures P11–1 and P11–2 represent recessions. Note that government expenditures, and especially transfer payments, typically rise and receipts generally fall relative to GNP during recessions (for the reasons discussed in Chapter 10). This pattern has been observed in each postwar recession, with the exception of 1953–1954 when the pattern was broken by a sharp decline in national defense spending. The greater severity of the 1981–1982 recession (relative to other postwar recessions) accentuated the cyclical swing in the deficit during the first term of the Reagan administration.

### Deficit Prospects for the Rest of the 1980s

Current Reagan administration and Congressional Budget Office deficit pro-jections indicate deficits are likely to remain large throughout the rest of the 1980s, though they may decline somewhat as a share of GNP. Projections of the so-called structural deficit, that part of the deficit not attributable to the business cycle, suggest that the structural deficit may worsen and then show little improvement through the remainder of the decade.

### Questions

1. Some claim that it was the behavior of transfer payments during the 1970s that laid the foundation for the ballooning deficits of the 1980s. Comment on this point of view using the evidence in Figure P11–1.

2. Both Keynesians and supply-siders might argue that raising taxes to reduce the deficit could actually end up making it larger. Explain the likely, but different, reasoning underlying their contention.

tax rate is increased from .5 to .6. If total income declines from $2,500 billion to $2,000 billion, tax revenues decline from $1,250 billion to $1,200 billion.

### Increasing Tax Revenue by Tax Reduction

Some supply-siders contend that current marginal tax rates in the United States are high enough that we are at a point such as $c$ on the Laffer curve. They argue that by lowering the marginal tax rate and moving down the curve, tax revenue would increase. For instance, moving from point $c$ down to point $m$ would increase tax revenue from $R_n$ to $R_m$ in Figure 11–10. Moreover, if the supply-siders are right, a lower marginal tax rate would yield the same level of tax revenue currently realized. For example, in Figure 11–10 the rate $t_1$ will yield the same tax revenue, $R_n$, as the rate $t_2$.

### CHECKPOINT 11-4

How would a strictly demand-side, or Keynesian, point of view regarding the effects of an increase in marginal tax rates be modified when supply-side effects are taken into account? How do you think closing all tax loopholes would affect the position of the Laffer curve in Figure 11–10?

### SUMMARY

1. An increase in the economy's price level causes the total expenditure schedule to shift downward and the equilibrium level of real

GNP to decrease, while a decrease in the price level shifts the total expenditure schedule upward and increases equilibrium real GNP. The aggregate demand curve (*AD*) plots this relationship between the price level and the equilibrium level of real GNP. Movement along the *AD* curve thus shows the response of equilibrium real GNP to changes in the price level.

**2.** An exogenous increase in expenditure or a tax reduction will shift the *AD* curve rightward. An exogenous decrease in expenditure or a tax rate increase will shift the *AD* curve leftward.

**3.** The aggregate supply curve (*AS*) shows the amounts of total output, or real GNP, that the economy's businesses will supply at different price levels. Over the horizontal range of the *AS* curve there is so much excess capacity that real GNP can be increased without any change in the price level. The *AS* curve rises over the intermediate range because input prices remain unchanged in the short run while product prices (hence the economy's price level) can increase thereby raising profits and inducing the economy's firms to increase output. Over the vertical range of the *AS* curve the economy has reached its production capacity limit and increases in the price level will not induce any increase in real GNP.

**4.** Changes in input prices, in productivity, in the size of the labor force, or in the capital stock will cause the *AS* curve to shift.

**5.** The *AD* and the *AS* curves jointly determine the equilibrium price level and the equilibrium level of real GNP. An exogenous expenditure change, or an exogenous tax rate change, will have a smaller multiplier effect on real GNP along the intermediate range of the *AS* curve than along the horizontal range. The multiplier effect is zero along the vertical range.

**6.** Given the position of the *AS* curve, rightward shifts in the *AD* curve along the intermediate and vertical ranges of the *AS* curve

give rise to demand-pull inflation. Upward shifts in the *AS* curve give rise to cost-push inflation. Given the position of the *AD* curve, an upward shift in the *AS* curve increases both the general price level and the unemployment rate, a phenomenon known as stagflation.

**7.** Supply-side economics takes issue with the demand-side, or Keynesian, view that tax cuts only affect aggregate demand. Supply-siders argue that lower marginal tax rates increase the economy's capacity to supply output by providing higher after-tax rewards, which encourage work effort and other productive activities.

**8.** Two basic propositions follow from the supply-side view of the effects of lower marginal tax rates: (1) the resulting increase in total output, or real GNP, will help to fight inflation; and (2) total income may increase to such an extent that tax revenue rises despite the reduction in tax rates, a proposition that is characterized by the Laffer curve.

**9.** Indexing the income tax structure in order to prevent automatic inflation-induced increases in tax rates was legislated during the first term of the Reagan administration and implemented beginning in January 1985.

**10.** The ballooning of federal government budget deficits during the first term of the Reagan administration was largely a reflection of the business cycle, not so much of the tax cuts initiated in 1981 or the increases in defense spending. The major cause of the increase in total government expenditures since the late 1960s has been the growth of transfer payments. Current predictions indicate that deficits are likely to remain large through the remainder of the 1980s.

## KEY TERMS AND CONCEPTS

bracket creep
cost-push inflation
demand-pull inflation
Laffer curve

marginal tax rate
stagflation

## QUESTIONS AND PROBLEMS

1. Explain the derivation of the *AD* curve from the total expenditure schedule. Explain how each of the following would affect the *AD* curve: an exogenous increase in consumption expenditure; an exogenous reduction in tax rates; a decrease in the price level; an exogenous increase in government spending; an exogenous decrease in net export spending; an exogenous increase in investment spending.

2. Explain the concept of the *AS* curve and its shape. Explain how and why it is affected by changes in technology.

3. Explain how and why the multiplier effect varies over the three different ranges of the *AS* curve.

4. Suppose labor unions begin to demand higher wages in order to keep up with a rising cost of living (a rising general price level) caused by rightward shifts in the *AD* curve. Using the *AD* and *AS* curves explain how this could give rise to stagflation.

5. Suppose marginal tax rates on income are reduced. Rank the following as either "much" or "little" in terms of the effect the reduction would have on work effort: self-employed house painter, mail carriers, building contractor, police officer, senator, shoe-shine person, barber, mayor, automobile company executive, librarian, realtor, owner of machine-tool shop.

6. Suppose that the economy's total income equals $2,000 billion and that income is subject to a proportional tax rate of .5. If the proportional tax rate is reduced to .4, how much would total income have to rise in order for total tax revenue to increase?

# THREE

## Money, Banking, and Monetary Policy

# 12

# The Nature and Functions of Money and Banking

**AFTER READING THIS CHAPTER, YOU WILL BE ABLE TO:**

1. Explain the nature and functions of money.

2. Describe the differences between commodity money, fiat money, bank money or checkable deposits, and near money.

3. State the nature of the relationship between the supply of money, prices, and the value of money.

4. Explain how banks evolved from a mere safekeeping function to a fractional reserve banking operation, creating money through their lending activities.

5. Describe the purposes, organization, and functions of the Federal Reserve System.

6. Describe the role of depository institutions as creators of money and as financial intermediaries.

**I**t has been said that money is "the oil that lubricates the wheels of trade." When the economy's monetary system is functioning well, this seems an apt analogy. However, history shows that money and the closely related activity of banking are often the source of economic instability, inflation, and unemployment. Indeed, monetary problems have frequently plagued our economy throughout its history.

This chapter focuses on the basic nature and functions of money and banking. In addition, we will see how and why the Federal Reserve System was developed to provide the basic structure for money and banking in our economy. Chapter 13 will study in detail the way our banking system affects the size of the economy's money supply. Chapter 14 will focus on how the money supply affects the level of aggregate demand for goods and services and on the role that money plays in determining the economy's equilibrium level of total output and employment.

## THE NATURE OF MONEY

What does money do? What are the different kinds of money? What determines the value of money?

### What Money Does

Essentially, money does three things. It functions as a medium of exchange, a unit of account, and a store of value.

### *Money as a Medium of Exchange*

Without money people would have to carry on trade by *barter*—the swapping of goods for goods. In Chapter 3 we saw that for trade to take place in a barter economy there must be a *coincidence of wants* between individuals. If I have good X to trade and I want to get good Y, I must find someone who not only wants to get good X but also coincidentally

has good Y to give in exchange. The difficulties involved in finding a coincidence of wants tend to discourage and inhibit specialization and trade in a barter economy (recall the discussion in Chapter 3). Because of this, the gains from specialization and trade cannot be fully realized and therefore the total output of the economy is less than it otherwise might be. However, if money is used to carry on trade, I can sell good X to whomever wants it and accept money in exchange. Whether the purchaser has the good Y that I want is now irrelevant. I can use the money to buy good Y from whomever has it, regardless of whether or not they want good X. Trade is now easier because **money** *is something that is generally acceptable to everyone as payment for anything.*

*The existence of money eliminates the need for a coincidence of wants. Therefore when goods are bought and sold using money as the medium of exchange, the economy is able to be more productive. Its production possibilities frontier is shifted outward.*

### *Money as a Unit of Account*

In a barter economy, comparing the relative values of different goods and services is much more complicated than in a money-using economy. For example, to get an idea of the cost of an orange in a barter economy would require a knowledge of the rate at which oranges exchange for apples, shoes, tea, bread, haircuts, and so forth. A shopping trip would entail numerous cross comparisons of the exchange rates between widely different goods and services. "Let's see, if 3 oranges will buy 8 apples and 5 apples will buy 2 pears, that must mean . . . ah . . . 15 oranges will buy 16 pears." There is no need for such complex calculations if everything is valued in terms of the same unit of account, money. Then in the above example the price of an orange is $.16, of an apple $.06, and of a pear $.15.

*Money provides a common unit of account for expressing the market values of widely dif-*

*ferent goods and services. The existence of this common unit of account greatly reduces the time and effort needed to make intelligent economic decisions. As a result, more time and effort are available for use in other productive activities. This is another reason why money shifts the economy's production possibilities frontier outward.*

### Money as a Store of Value

You can hold wealth in many forms: houses, yachts, stocks, bonds, jewelry, and so on. But *no form of wealth is as readily convertible into other goods and services as money is. This ready convertibility, or* **liquidity***, makes money an attractive store of value, or source of purchasing power.*

If you had to sell your new wristwatch within the next 5 minutes to get money to make purchases, you would probably only get a fraction of what you paid for it. If you had paid $50 for it, you might only be able to get $20—a loss of $30. If instead you had $50, you could easily make $50 worth of purchases within 5 minutes. In general, you can rank assets on a scale from the most liquid to the least liquid according to the amount of loss, including **transaction costs** (such as brokerage fees, advertising costs, and time and effort searching for a buyer), that would result if they had to be converted into money *within a short period of time.* Money of course heads the list. A car, a house, a painting, or a piece of land might be at or near the bottom.

### Kinds of Money

Throughout history money has taken many forms. Many of the oldest kinds of money are still used today, while new kinds continue to be developed. In order of their historical evolution, the principal kinds of money are commodity money, coins, paper money, and demand deposits. All these different kinds of money share one common characteristic that is the essence of "moneyness." Namely, *money is something that is generally acceptable to everyone as payment for anything.*

### Commodity Money

The earliest forms of money were commodities that often had other uses besides serving as money. Hides, furs, jewelry, precious stones and metals, and livestock are but a few examples. Even today these items often serve as money in some economically underdeveloped regions of the world. When the German deutsche mark became worthless as a result of the German hyperinflation in the early 1920s, Germans used cognac and cigarettes as money.

Some commodities are better suited for use as money than others. The ideal commodity money does not suffer from handling and time—it wears well. Eggs and other perishables won't do. It should be valuable enough that small amounts, easily carried, are sufficient to buy a week's groceries. Anything requiring a wheelbarrow instead of a pocketbook is out. The ideal commodity money is easily divisible for making change and small purchases. Diamonds, the most durable commodity, are too difficult to split. Finally, the market rate of exchange of the commodity money with other goods should be relatively stable.

Historically the precious metals, gold and silver, have been the most continuously used forms of commodity money. Small amounts are quite valuable, so that as a commodity money they are easy to carry. Both are attractive metals and interact little with other substances, though silver does tarnish and gold is soft.

### Coins

Coins were a natural outgrowth of the use of precious metals as commodity money. Using gold dust in bulk form meant that every merchant needed a scale to carry on business. Every transaction, however small, required careful and time-consuming weighing. The first coins were made by kings or rulers who weighed out an amount of precious metal and made a coin out of it. The coin had the amount of precious metal it contained stamped on it (its "face value") along with the ruler's seal as a guarantee of the weight. This made trading easier as long as the ruler was honest and the citizens didn't tinker with the coins to "clip" or remove precious metal from them. Monarchs and those they ruled being human (despite the monarchs' frequent claim to the contrary), the debasement of the coin of the realm was common.

Another problem with coins is that they often disappear from circulation whenever the market value of the precious metal they contain exceeds the amount of the face value stamped on them. Suppose a 25-cent piece contains $.30 worth of silver. Eventually circulation will bring the 25-cent pieces into the hands of someone who will melt them down for the $.30 worth of silver rather than use each coin for purchasing $.25 worth of goods, the face value stamped on the coin.

To avoid this problem governments now issue **token coins**—*coins that contain an amount of metal that is worth much less than the face value of the coin.* Such coins are **fiat money**—*money that the government declares by law to be legal tender for the settlement of debts.* This means that if you owe somebody $.25 and you offer them a quarter coin to pay off the debt, they must accept it. If they don't, they no longer have a legal claim on you. This illustrates an important characteristic of fiat money. *Fiat money is money that is not backed by or convertible into gold or any other precious metal. It is acceptable because the government declares it to be acceptable, not because of the value of the materials contained in it. It is acceptable not as a commodity itself but rather because people know that it can be used to buy goods and services.*

### Paper Money

*Paper money,* the bills in your wallet, is also money in today's economy. It too illustrates that money is acceptable because it will buy goods. The value of the bills themselves as a commodity is next to nothing. Indeed, the materials needed to make a $1 bill, or a $10,000 bill, cost but a tiny fraction of a cent. Today all paper money in the United States is issued by the Federal Reserve System (which we shall look at shortly) in the form of Federal Reserve notes. At one time the Treasury issued paper money, but no longer.

### Demand Deposits

If you place currency (coins and paper money) in a **demand deposit** at a commercial bank, the bank is legally obligated to give that money back to you the moment you ask for it—that is, on demand. Demand deposits are also called checking accounts because you can write checks against them.

A check is nothing more than a slip of paper, a standardized form, on which you write the bank an order to withdraw funds from your checking account and pay them either to someone else or to yourself. The check is a convenience that makes it unnecessary for you to go to your bank and withdraw currency from your demand deposit every time you need money to make a purchase or pay a bill. The receiving party (an individual, business, or other institution) has only to sign, or endorse, the check to receive the funds from your bank out of your demand deposit. Often the party receiving the check will simply endorse and deposit it in his or her own checking account, frequently in a different bank. The banks conveniently handle the transfer of funds from your checking account to that of the receiving party.

*Demand deposits function as money by virtue of the check-writing privilege.* Compared to currency they have several advantages. Lost or stolen currency is almost impossible to recover. Lost or stolen checks are much more difficult for another party to use, so that a demand deposit is relatively secure from such mishaps. Checks may be sent through the mail much more readily and safely than currency. Checks therefore make trade possible between parties separated by great distances. They also provide a convenient record of completed transactions. Given these advantages, it is not surprising that in terms of dollar value checks account for by far the largest amount of transactions in our economy. One disadvantage of demand deposits is that by law commercial banks are not allowed to pay interest on them.

*Today almost all economists regard demand deposits as money because they can be converted into currency on demand and because checks are such a widely used medium of exchange.*

### Other Demand-Deposit-Type Accounts

During the 1970s our financial system began to develop other types of deposits, which carry check-writing privileges similar to those of the traditional commercial bank demand deposit, but have the advantage that they earn interest as well. These demand-deposit-type accounts became even more extensive when Congress passed the Depository Institutions Deregulation and Monetary Control Act of 1980.

1. *NOW Accounts.* These accounts are interest-earning savings accounts at any depository institution (commercial bank, mutual savings bank, savings and loan association, or credit union). The holder of a NOW account can have funds transferred to a designated party simply by sending the depository institution a checklike form, a **negotiable order of withdrawal (NOW).** A NOW is written exactly as one would write a check. NOW accounts do not make commercial bank demand deposits obsolete, however, since only individuals and certain nonprofit organizations are allowed to hold NOW accounts. Businesses must still use demand deposits to have check-writing privileges.

2. *Automatic Transfer Service.* Commercial and mutual savings banks are authorized to offer **automatic transfer services (ATSs)** from a savings account to a checking account or to some similar type of checkable account. With ATS a depositor can keep funds in an interest-earning savings account and the bank will automatically transfer them to his or her non-interest-earning checking account only when checks are written against the account. ATS effectively makes savings accounts into demand-deposit-type checking accounts.

3. *Share Drafts.* Federally insured credit unions are authorized to offer **share draft** accounts, which work just like NOW accounts. Share draft accounts are effectively demand-deposit-type checking accounts.

The new demand-deposit-type accounts can perform the medium-of-exchange function of money because in effect checks can be written against them. This has given rise to a "modern" narrow definition of money, termed **M1:**

M1 = currency + checkable deposits

"Checkable deposits" include demand deposits at commercial banks, NOW and ATS balances, share drafts held at credit unions, and demand deposits at thrift institutions.[1]

### Near Money

Currency, demand deposits, and other checkable deposits are regarded as money because they seem to perform all three functions of money (as a medium of exchange, a unit of account, and a store of value) better than any other asset. But there are several other kinds of assets that fulfill the unit of account and store of value functions at least as well. In addition, they can be converted rather easily into currency or checkable deposits. These assets are often called **near money**—they are like money except that they are not usually regarded as a medium of exchange.

1. *Time Deposits.* **Time deposits** earn a

---

[1] For a more detailed definition see any recent *Federal Reserve Bulletin.*

fixed rate of interest and must be held for a stipulated amount of time. Withdrawal before the stipulated maturity date is penalized, often by a loss of or a reduction in the interest rate earned. Some depository institutions, such as commercial banks and savings and loan associations, offer time deposits called **certificates of deposit (CDs).** CDs differ from other kinds of savings deposits in that they require that the depositor deposit a specified amount of money (such as $1,000 or $5,000) for a certain length of time (such as for 6 months or a year). In return, the depositor is guaranteed a specified rate of interest on the deposit for that length of time. Withdrawal before that length of time has expired incurs a penalty—typically in the form of a lower rate of interest received on the deposit. In addition to the penalty, it takes time and effort (a trip to the bank) to convert CDs into checkable deposits or currency whenever the medium of exchange function is needed. But the higher the interest rate on CDs, the more worthwhile it is to hold funds in that form—the return makes up for the inconvenience and penalty of shifting to currency and checkable deposits when necessary.

2. *Savings Deposits.* Various kinds of savings deposits in commercial banks, mutual savings banks, savings and loan associations, and credit unions fit the description of near money. However, as we discussed above, the Deregulation Act of 1980 and the development of NOWs, ATSs, and share drafts have blurred the distinction between checkable deposits and savings deposits. Nonetheless, since it costs depository institutions something to administer these various checklike mechanisms, savings accounts that do not carry such medium-of-exchange-type conveniences can be expected to pay somewhat higher interest rates.

3. *Money Market Fund Shares.* **Money market fund shares** pay shareholders a rate of interest that is competitive with the highest rates of return available on large denomination ($10,000 and up) short-term government and corporate bonds and on other financial instruments typically too large for the average depositor to buy alone. Money market mutual funds are able to do this by pooling the relatively small deposits of the shareholders and investing them in the large-denomination financial instruments. After deducting a small management fee, the money market mutual fund passes on most of the return earned on these instruments to its shareholders.

Most money market mutual funds require shareholders to make minimum initial investments, roughly ranging from $500 to $10,000, and to maintain a minimum balance of at least $250. Most funds calculate and pay interest on shares daily, and shares can be redeemed at any time either by wire transfer or by writing a check against the shares. The check-writing privilege makes money market shares nearly as liquid, or moneylike, as demand deposits in commercial banks— nearly, because the funds usually put a minimum size restriction on checks (usually they must be at least $250) and because shares are not insured, whereas commercial bank demand deposits are (up to $100,000).

4. *Short-Term Government Bonds.* Some argue that short-term government bonds, such as **Treasury bills**, that mature 1, 3, or 6 months after the day they are issued are also near money. These are less liquid than savings deposits because their prices fluctuate with changes in the interest rate between the day they are issued and the day they mature. Therefore, unlike a savings deposit, one cannot be sure of the amount of purchasing power that can be realized from the sale of a short-term government bond at any time except the maturity date. In addition, a brokerage fee must be paid when buying or selling a bond. Moreover, it is not possible to buy fractions of a bond, and this "lumpiness" makes them less attractive to individuals than they are to large corporations, banks, and

other financial institutions (pension funds, trust funds, and insurance companies).

**5.** *Negotiable Certificates of Deposit.* For similar reasons, the large **negotiable certificates of deposit** (CDs with a minimum denomination of $100,000) issued by commercial banks are also attractive to large investors. Unlike the CDs described earlier (often called nonnegotiable CDs), negotiable CDs may be bought and sold at any time just like a bond. Hence, their price also fluctuates on a day-to-day basis just like that of a bond.

### Broader Definitions of Money

Because of the near-money nature of money market fund shares and the different kinds of savings deposits and certificates of deposit, broader definitions of money that include these items have gained increased attention in recent years. The basic argument for including these near-money assets in the broader definitions is that the near moneys are almost as liquid as currency, demand deposits, and savings deposits that carry NOW or ATS privileges. Most savings deposits without these privileges are less liquid than currency and demand deposits only because of the transactions costs (a trip to the bank, a postage stamp, or a phone call) incurred when they are transferred into currency and demand deposits. As already noted, the narrowest definition of money, M1, equals the sum of currency and checkable deposits. The broader definitions of money are essentially as follows. **M2** *is defined as M1 plus money market mutual fund shares plus savings and small time deposits that do not carry checklike privileges.* **M3** *is defined as M2 plus large negotiable CDs.* Table 12–1 provides an idea of the sizes of M1, M2, and M3, along with the relative importance of the various components that make up each of these definitions of money.

### Credit Cards and Trade Credit

A near money is often just as good a store of value as currency and demand deposits. But a near money is not a medium of exchange, though it can be readily converted to one. Credit cards and trade credit have very much the opposite properties of near money. They cannot serve as a store of value, but they are a medium of exchange.

If a business will sell you goods and services without requiring your immediate payment in the form of cash or a check, we say the business has extended you credit. If you carry a recognized credit card, many businesses will sell goods and services to you on the spot in exchange for nothing more than your signature on a credit slip bearing your credit card number. This allows you to defer payment by cash or check for some period of time. The credit card essentially serves as a short-term medium of exchange, a substitute for a check or cash. It is short term because the business ultimately expects to receive either currency or a check.

Businesses often extend credit to other businesses that are regular customers—a wholesaler supplying a retailer, for example. Such credit is called **trade credit**. It allows one business to buy goods from another without making immediate full payment by check or with currency. Trade credit is usually extended on the basis of past dealings that have convinced the seller that the buyer is financially sound and reliable—that the buyer will ultimately "pay up" with currency or a check. Like the credit card, trade credit serves as a short-term medium of exchange even though it is not a store of value.

*Credit cards and trade credit reduce the need for currency and checkable deposits as mediums of exchange. They cannot replace currency and checkable deposits, however, because such credit is not a store of value.*

### What Determines the Value of Money or What Backs Money?

Money in our economy today is neither backed by nor convertible into gold or any other precious metal. Coins contain an

**TABLE 12-1 Measures of Money in the United States:**
**M1, M2, M3** (Seasonally Adjusted,
Billions of Dollars, 1984)

| | | Percentage of | | |
|---|---|---|---|---|
| | | M1 | M2 | M3 |
| Currency | $ 155.0 | 28.4 | 6.8 | 5.4 |
| Plus: Demand deposits (at commercial banks)[a] | 247.1 | 45.3 | 10.8 | 8.6 |
| Plus: NOWs, ATSs, other demand-type deposits Equals: | 143.5 | 26.3 | 6.3 | 5.0 |
| M1 – – – – – – – – – – – – – – – – – – | 545.6 | 100.0 | | |
| Plus: Money market fund shares and savings and small time deposits[b] Equals: | 1,740.9 | | 76.1 | 60.9 |
| M2 – – – – – – – – – – – – – – – – – | 2,286.5 | | 100.0 | |
| Plus: Large negotiable CDs[c] Equals: | 569.8 | | | 19.9 |
| M3 – – – – – – – – – – – – – – – – – | 2,856.3 | | | 100.0 |

SOURCE: *Federal Reserve Statistical Release* H.6 (508), October 11, 1984.
[a]Includes $5.2 billion of U.S. traveler's checks of nonbank issuers.
[b]Includes certain specialized overnight assets.
[c]Includes other specialized assets.

amount of metal that is worth much less than their face value. Paper money is just that— pieces of paper. Both coins and paper money are money because the government declares it so—they are fiat money. Checkable deposits are just bookkeeping entries. Indeed, the government has not even declared checkable deposits to be money, which only shows that general acceptability in exchange is more important than a government declaration. If coins, currency, and checkable deposits are not backed by gold or any other precious metal, and if they have no value in and of themselves, then what determines their purchasing power or real value? The value of money is determined by supply and demand, just like the value of anything else. Let's see why.

### Money Demand and Supply

Money's value derives from its scarcity relative to its usefulness in providing a unique service. The unique service lies in the fact that money can be readily exchanged for goods and services. The economy's demand for money derives from its demand for this service. Therefore, the economy's demand for money is largely determined by the total dollar volume of its current transactions as well as its desire to hold money for possible future transactions.

What determines the supply of money? In the next chapter we will see how our economy's depository institutions as a whole can create money in the form of checkable deposits. We will also see how the government,

**POLICY PERSPECTIVE**

### Money and Prices—Two Cases of Hyperinflation

There are interesting historical illustrations of the relationship between the amount of money supplied to the economy, the price level, and the value of a unit of money.

During the Revolutionary War in our country, it was very difficult for the government to raise sufficient revenue through taxation to finance military operations. Consequently, both the states and the Continental Congress resorted to printing money to pay for supplies, weapons, and troops. As a result, the supply of paper money in the economy increased by an enormous amount between 1774 and 1781. This increase in the supply of paper money greatly exceeded the growth in the economy's capacity to produce goods and services. Hence, the growth in the money supply was much larger than the growth in the quantity of transactions involving the purchase and sale of goods and services. As a result, the prices at which these transactions took place rose rapidly, and the purchasing power of a unit of paper currency fell accordingly. State laws passed in an effort to control the rapid rise in the price level and the deteriorating value of the dollar were fruitless because they attacked the symptom, the hyperinflation, rather than the cause of the problem, the tremendous increase in the money supply. Public jawboning, private threats, ostracism, boycotts, fines—all proved useless against the flood of paper money.

A more recent example of hyperinflation occurred in Germany between 1921 and 1923. The German government increased the supply of currency to such an extent that the wholesale price index rose to a level in November 1923 that was 30 billion times higher than it was in January 1921! By this point the deutsche mark's value as money had been destroyed. An item purchased for a mark in 1921 cost 30 billion marks in 1923. Cases of hyperinflation like this one are relatively rare. But many governments, particularly in underdeveloped countries, regularly print fiat money to finance their expenditures. Inflation rates on the order of 50 to 200 percent per year are not uncommon in these countries.

through the Federal Reserve System, can promote or limit this kind of money creation. Therefore, not only is the government in a position to control the supply of fiat money (coins and paper money), it also is able to regulate the supply of money more broadly defined.

### Money Demand and Supply Determine Money's Value

The value of a unit of money (such as a dollar) is its purchasing power, or the amount of goods and services that it will buy. The higher the economy's price level, the smaller the quantity of goods and services that a unit of money will buy. Conversely, the lower the price level, the larger the quantity of goods and services a unit of money will buy.

If you are going to the grocery store to buy four loaves of bread and the price of bread is $.50 per loaf, then you will need $2 of money to exchange for the bread. However, if the price of a loaf of bread is $1 per loaf, you will need $4 of money. There is obviously a relationship between the total quantity of such transactions in the economy, the prices at which they take place, and the economy's demand (need) for money. Over-

**FIGURE 12-1  Money and Consumer Prices in the United States Since 1905**

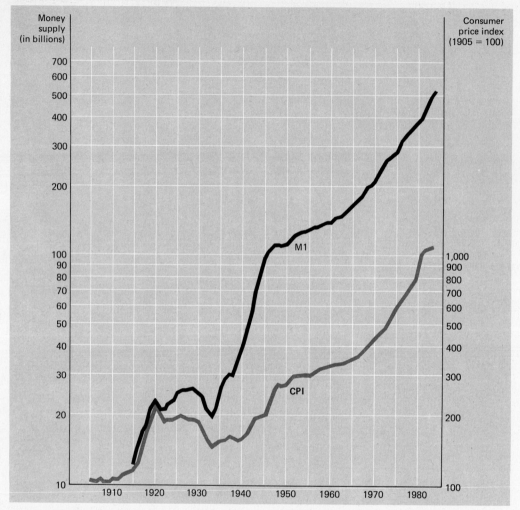

The general level of consumer prices and the money supply tend to move together. This is illustrated by the behavior of the Consumer Price Index (CPI) and the money supply, defined as M1. The data are plotted on a ratio scale so that equal vertical distances represent equal percentage changes.

simplifying somewhat, the following tends to be true. Given the economy's total quantity of transactions (such as the number of bread loaves purchased) and its demand for money needed to execute these transactions, the greater the supply of money, the higher the price level at which these transactions will take place. Conversely, the smaller the supply of money, the lower the price level at which these transactions will tend to take place. Thus, the supply of money and the demand for it play an important role in determining the price level in the economy. Therefore, it follows that the supply and demand for money play an important role in determining the purchasing power, or value, of a unit of money.

In sum, *given the demand for money, the larger the supply of money, the higher the price level will tend to be and, hence, the less the purchasing power, or value, of a unit of money. Conversely, the smaller the supply of money, the lower the price level will tend to be and hence the greater the purchasing power, or value, of a unit of money.*

The tendency for the general level of prices and the money supply to move together is illustrated in Figure 12–1. In this figure, money, defined as M1, is plotted along with the Consumer Price Index (CPI) for the years since 1905. The data are plotted on a ratio scale so that equal vertical distances represent equal percentage changes.

---

### CHECKPOINT* 12-1

**What would you rather use for money, $10 worth of aluminum or $10 worth of steel? Why? Rank the following in terms of their liquidity: a savings deposit, a $100,000 negotiable CD, a $10 bill, a 90-day Treasury bill, a stamp collection, a $1,000 bill, a demand deposit, a Master Charge credit card, a lot in a suburb. Rank each of the above items as a store of value, given that there is a 10 percent rate of inflation. Explain this quote: "Money is acceptable because it is acceptable." Using the information in Figure 12–1, evaluate how a dollar bill has served as a store of value over the period since 1905.**

* Answers to all Checkpoints can be found at the back of the text.

---

## THE DEVELOPMENT OF BANKING

An examination of the nature and development of early banking practices will enable

us to better understand how modern banks function. It will also reveal why it was felt necessary to create the Federal Reserve System in order to put commercial banking on a sounder footing. In addition, we will gain further insight into the nature of money and how it functions.

### Primary Functions of Banks

Modern banks have three primary functions: (1) they provide safekeeping services for all kinds of assets, not just money; (2) they make loans; and (3) as a group they create money. Originally the provision of safekeeping services was their only function. The functions of lending and money creation developed later, although today these functions represent by far the most important role of banks in our economy.

### Safekeeping— The Oldest Banking Function

Goldsmiths were the forerunners of early banks. They had to have strong safes in order to protect and keep gold. Aware of this, people would often bring their own gold to the goldsmith for deposit in the safe. Usually the goldsmith received a fee for this safekeeping service. The depositor received a receipt designating the amount of gold deposited and attesting to the depositor's right to withdraw the gold on demand upon presentation of the receipt. When gold depositors needed their gold to purchase goods and services, they simply presented their receipts to the goldsmith, who then gave them back their gold. Perhaps the closest counterpart of the goldsmith's safe in a modern bank is the safe-deposit box you rent from the bank for an annual fee.

### Lending—The First Commercial Banks

We might think of early commercial banking as evolving from the original safekeeping activities of goldsmiths. Suppose such a bank

**TABLE 12-2  Balance Sheet of an Early Commercial Bank**

| Assets | | | Liabilities | |
|---|---|---|---|---|
| Ounces of gold | 1,000 | | Ounces of gold receipts | 1,000 |
| Ounces of total assets | 1,000 | = | Ounces of total liabilities | 1,000 |

opens and accepts 1,000 ounces of gold from depositors. The depositors in turn receive receipts—their legal claim to the gold. The bank's balance sheet is shown in Table 12-2. Like any balance sheet, the left-hand side shows the assets of the bank, or what it has in its possession. In this case, the bank's assets consist of the 1,000 ounces of gold. The right-hand side shows the bank's liabilities— the claims on the bank's assets, or who owns them. In this case the liabilities consist of the depositor's receipts, which are their proof of legal ownership, or claim to the gold. Like all balance sheets, total assets must equal total liabilities—assets amounting to 1,000 ounces of gold are balanced by liabilities or receipts laying claim to 1,000 ounces of gold.

On a typical day the quantity of receipts turned in at the bank's deposit window by depositors wishing to withdraw their gold amounts to only a small fraction of the total 1,000 ounces of gold. Moreover, these withdrawals are often approximately offset by new deposits of gold with the bank. As a consequence, our early banker observes that there is usually a sizeable amount of gold standing idle in the safe. It occurs to the banker that in addition to the fees earned for providing safekeeping services, there is another possible moneymaking activity. Why not lend out some of this idle gold to people who are willing to pay the banker interest to borrow it? As long as the banker keeps enough gold in the safe to meet withdrawal demands of depositors, the depositors never even need to know that some of their gold is being lent to other people. Even if they do

know, they won't care as long as they can always get their gold back on demand.[2]

Suppose the banker observes that depositors never withdraw more than 15 percent of the gold in the safe on any one day. The banker therefore decides it is safe to loan out about 80 percent, or 800 ounces, of the gold. This leaves 20 percent, or 200 ounces, in the safe as a reserve to satisfy depositors' withdrawal demands, somewhat more than the banker's experience suggests is necessary. The banker receives an IOU from each party that borrows gold. This note, a contract signed by the borrower, states the amount of gold owed to the bank, the date it must be paid back, and the interest rate that the borrower must pay the banker for the loan. The bank's balance sheet now appears as shown in Table 12-3. Comparing this balance sheet with that in Table 12-2, we see that for assets the bank now has 200 ounces of gold plus a number of pieces of paper, the IOUs, stating that various borrowers owe the bank 800 ounces of gold. For liabilities the bank still has obligations to give depositors 1,000 ounces of gold on demand, represented by paper gold receipts in the hands of depositors.

The bank will have no difficulties as long as the depositor's demands for withdrawal do not exceed 200 ounces of gold in any one day. Should this happen, the bank would be

---

[2] One ounce of gold is indistinguishable from any other. Depositors are therefore only concerned about being able to get back the number of ounces of gold deposited, not the exact same particles of gold they deposited.

**TABLE 12-3 Early Commercial Bank's Balance Sheet After Loaning Out 800 Ounces of Gold**

| Assets | | | Liabilities | |
|---|---|---|---|---|
| Ounces of gold (reserves) | 200 | | Ounces of gold receipts | 1,000 |
| Ounces of gold in IOUs | 800 | | | |
| Ounces of total assets | 1,000 | = | Ounces of total liabilities | 1,000 |

unable to honor its commitment to give depositors their gold on demand.

### Money Creation and the Early Commercial Banks

Now that we have looked at the principle behind the way in which early banks evolved to combine safekeeping and lending functions, it is not difficult to see how they became creators of money as well.

It takes time and effort for depositors to go to the bank to withdraw gold every time they need it to make purchases of goods and services. In the community in which our early bank operates, suppose that the merchants know their customers fairly well and that the bank has a sound reputation. Merchants are therefore willing to sell goods in exchange for customers' gold receipts. The customer simply signs the paper gold receipt and specifies that its ownership has been transferred to the merchant. The merchant can either take the receipt to the bank to claim gold or use it to make purchases from someone else, transferring its ownership once again in the same manner. The receipt itself is now used as money. It is acceptable in trade because people know it can be redeemed for gold on demand at the bank. It is used as money because it eliminates the need for frequent trips to the bank. And receipts are also easier to carry.

*Expanding the Bank's Lending Activities.* Once the gold receipts are being used as

money, the banker sees a way to expand the bank's lending activity. At present the banker has to keep only a fraction of the gold as reserves—the rest is loaned out. Specifically, 200 ounces is kept in the safe and 800 ounces leaves the bank on loan. But if gold receipts are now acceptable as money, why not just give borrowers paper gold receipts rather than actual gold in exchange for their IOUs? The borrower can use the receipts just as readily as the gold to make purchases. The banker previously felt that it was necessary to keep only 200 ounces of actual gold on hand (asset side of Table 12-3) when there were gold receipts outstanding amounting to claims on 1,000 ounces (liability side of Table 12-3). If this was workable, wouldn't 1,000 ounces of gold in the safe be adequate if there were gold receipts outstanding amounting to claims on 5,000 ounces? There would still be gold receipt claims on 5 ounces for every 1 ounce of actual gold, just as before.

*As a consequence of the fact that gold receipts are acceptable as money,* the banker can now keep all 1,000 ounces of deposited gold in the safe and print up and loan out gold receipts amounting to claims on 4,000 ounces of gold. Now the banker can earn interest on 5 times as many IOUs, generated by the lending of 4,000 ounces of gold as represented by the gold receipts given to borrowers (previously the banker earned interest on IOUs for 800 ounces of gold). These receipts will have the same claim on the gold in the safe as the receipts received by the original

**TABLE 12-4  Early Commercial Bank's Balance Sheet After Loaning Out Gold Receipts for 4,000 Ounces of Gold**

| Assets | | | Liabilities | |
|---|---|---|---|---|
| Ounces of gold (reserves) | 1,000 | | Ounces of gold receipts | 5,000 |
| Ounces of gold in IOUs | 4,000 | | | |
| Ounces of total assets | 5,000 | = | Ounces of total liabilities | 5,000 |

gold depositors. Our early commercial bank's balance sheet now looks as shown in Table 12–4. All 5,000 ounces' worth of gold receipts are now circulating in the economy as money. Note, however, that there are only 1,000 ounces of actual gold.

As in the case depicted by Table 12–3, it is also true here that if all holders of these gold receipts brought them into the bank at one time and demanded gold, they could not be satisfied. The bank would not be able to honor its commitments to give out gold on demand. However, as long as no more than 20 percent of the gold receipts are presented for payment at one time, there is no problem.

### Bank Notes and Fractional Reserve Banking

It is now easy to see how banks got into the business of issuing paper money in the form of **bank notes**. The gold receipts of our hypothetical early commercial bank are but a short step removed from the status of these notes. To take this short step all the bank has to do is give a gold depositor bank notes instead of a receipt with the depositor's name on it.

Suppose the bank decides to print up a bank note that says "one dollar" across the front of it and, in smaller letters below this, "this note is redeemable for one ounce of gold on demand." Now the note could just as well have been called "one John," "one Sue," "one Kleebop," or "one Mark." The dollar was chosen as the basic unit of account in the

United States by the Coinage Act of 1792.[3] As far as the money-using public was concerned, the important thing was that the bank note could be converted into gold at the bank on demand. Our hypothetical early commercial bank's balance sheet now appears as shown in Table 12–5. Compare this with Table 12–4.

During much of the nineteenth century, each bank in the United States could issue its own uniquely engraved bank note or currency. Through their lending activity such banks typically ended up issuing an amount of bank notes considerably larger than the amount of gold they had to back up the notes. That is, the bank notes had only fractional backing, thus giving rise to the term **fractional reserve banking**. There was usually nothing wrong with this if a bank used good judgment and didn't issue "too many" bank notes. But the main difficulty with a system that combined fractional reserve banking with a convertible currency (convertible into gold) was that even a well-managed bank could get caught short. Banks frequently found themselves confronted with demands to exchange gold for their bank notes that exceeded the amount of gold in their safes. When this happened a bank would be forced to close its doors. People left

---

[3] The name derives from the old German word *thal*, meaning "valley." Its early origin stems from coins used in the valley of Saint Joachim in Bohemia as early as 1519. These coins were called *Joachimsthaler* and then *thaler*, which in English became "dollar."

**TABLE 12-5 Early Commercial Bank's Balance Sheet After One-Dollar Bank Notes Replace Gold Receipts**
(Hypothetically, $1 = 1 Ounce of Gold)

| Assets | | | Liabilities | |
|---|---|---|---|---|
| Gold reserves (1,000 ounces) | $1,000 | | Bank notes | $5,000 |
| IOUs | 4,000 | | | |
| Total assets | $5,000 | = | Total liabilities | $5,000 |

holding that bank's currency were really holding only worthless pieces of paper.

Fractional reserve banking of this kind typified the so-called wildcat period of banking in the United States from 1836 to 1864. A large number of note-issuing private and state banks came into existence during this time. The term *wildcat bank* was used to describe many of these banks because they often issued bank notes far in excess of the amount of gold they had on hand. And they would locate in remote regions (where the wildcats were) to discourage people from trying to turn the bank notes in for gold. By 1863, there were roughly 1,600 different kinds of bank notes in circulation in the United States. To correct the excesses of the wildcat period, Congress passed the National Bank Acts of 1863 and 1864. These acts provided for a national currency and created national banks that were allowed to issue bank notes.

## Bank Panics and Economic Instability

The National Bank Acts did not put an end to the nation's monetary and banking problems. Just as the banks had created bank notes when they made loans, they could also create demand deposits. When they granted a loan and received an IOU, they simply credited the amount of the loan to a demand deposit in the borrower's name. Banks now came to use national currency as reserves, either keeping them in their own safe or possibly on deposit at another bank. Again the reserves typically amounted to only a fraction of the amount of their demand deposit liabilities. As an example, the asset side of the balance sheet in Table 12–5 would now have $1,000 of national currency as reserves and, as before, the $4,000 of IOUs. The liability side would have $5,000 of demand deposits.

### The Nature of Bank Panics

The problem, as before, was that if too many depositors attempted to withdraw currency from their demand deposits, the bank might not have enough reserves to satisfy their demands. Because of this, bank panics and financial crises were still frequent. Even a rumor that a bank had made some bad loans (an IOU that some borrower wasn't meeting interest payments on or couldn't pay off) could cause people holding deposits at the bank to panic. There would then be a "run on the bank" as depositors rushed to withdraw currency from their accounts—"to get their money out." Even if the rumor were false, the bank might be forced to close because the sudden increase in demand for deposit withdrawals could exceed the amount of currency in its safe. Paradox: the rumor of possible bankruptcy could cause bankruptcy.

In general, bank failures caused by runs on banks could be triggered by an adverse turn of events anywhere in the economy. Once banks started to fail, a chain reaction could set in, causing a recession throughout the economy. One of the most common causes of these financial crises was the growth of the economy itself as the United States developed into an industrial power in the last third of the nineteenth century. Let's see why.

### Limits to Money Supply Expansion

Commercial banks themselves could not increase the total amount of the national currency available in the economy. They could of course provide credit (make loans) to feed economic expansion. The increase in deposits created by this loan expansion meant that the amount of demand deposits would get ever larger relative to the amount of currency available for bank reserves. Compounding the problem was the fact that more currency was also needed to serve as a medium of exchange in an expanding economy. The result was that bank reserves would become an ever smaller fraction of deposit liabilities, and banks would become more susceptible to a sudden surge of deposit withdrawals. The bank caught short might scramble to withdraw currency from its deposit at another bank, setting off a chain of bank failures and a general financial crisis. Consumers and businesses who dealt with these banks would suffer financial losses. This would cause a general decline in consumption and investment expenditures—that is, a decline in aggregate demand. GNP would fall, unemployment would rise, and the economy would be plunged into recession.

It was clear that the nation's monetary system, its money-creating mechanism, was not responsive enough to the economy's ever growing need for money—the money supply mechanism was not "elastic" enough. The money supply could not readily "stretch out" to meet the increasing demand for money caused by economic expansion. This was so often the case in nineteenth-century America that recessions were typically referred to as financial crises or panics. After the financial crisis of 1907, Congress set up a National Monetary Commission to study the problem. The commission's recommendations resulted in the Federal Reserve Act of 1913.

**CHECKPOINT 12-2**
**Why might a bank note be said to be like an IOU? When currency is convertible into gold, how does the amount of gold in the economy put a limit on the amount of money in the economy? Describe how you think people's opinions about the soundness of banks at any particular time would affect the upper limit to the amount of the economy's money, defined as currency plus demand deposits. If bankers were to become cautious about the business outlook, how do you think this would affect the amount of IOUs on their balance sheets, and why and how would this affect the amount of money in the economy? How do you think this would affect total demand for goods and services?**

## THE FEDERAL RESERVE SYSTEM: ORGANIZATION AND FUNCTIONS

The basic recommendation of the National Monetary Commission was that control over the economy's money supply and the nation's commercial banks should be centralized. This control was to be vested in a central bank, an arm of the federal government, that would deliberately manage the money supply to foster economic stability with maximum output and employment and as little inflation as possible. (Indeed, several other nations already had central banks.) The Federal Reserve Act of 1913 gave life to this concept by forming the Federal Reserve System.

The Depository Institutions Deregulation and Monetary Control Act of 1980 (or simply the Monetary Control Act of 1980) extended certain of the Federal Reserve System's controls to all depository institutions—mutual savings banks, savings and loan associations, and credit unions, as well as commercial banks. Federal Reserve System controls over member commercial banks are still more extensive than over the other depository institutions. But the act subjects all to the same regulations regarding the reserves they are required to hold against checkable deposits—demand deposits, NOWs, ATSs, and share drafts.

## Organization of the Federal Reserve System

Rather than having one central bank as in most countries, the United States has 12, each representing and serving one of the 12 districts into which the country is divided by the Federal Reserve System.[4] All are under the control of a central policymaking body called the Board of Governors of the Federal Reserve System, often referred to as the Federal Reserve Board, located in Washington, D.C. The Board of Governors has the responsibility and authority for the administration of the Federal Reserve System and the nation's monetary policy.

Each Federal Reserve bank is responsible for carrying out board policy as directed by the Board of Governors. Each does so by virtue of its authority over the member commercial banks and other depository institutions in its region. The Board of Governors is assisted in its policymaking by the Federal Open Market Committee (FOMC) and, to a lesser degree, by the advice of the Federal Advisory Council. This broad organizational outline of the Federal Reserve System is shown in Figure 12–2.

### The Board of Governors

There are seven governors on the board, each appointed by the president and subject to confirmation by the Senate. Each governor serves for a term of 14 years, and the terms

[4] The Federal Reserve banks are in Boston, New York, Philadelphia, Cleveland, Richmond, Atlanta, Chicago, Saint Louis, Minneapolis, Kansas City, Dallas, and San Francisco.

**FIGURE 12-2  Organization of the Federal Reserve System**

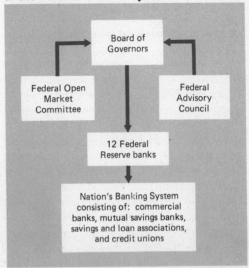

The Board of Governors, assisted by the Federal Open Market Committee and advised by the Federal Advisory Council, is responsible for the formulation of the nation's monetary policy and the regulation of the nation's money supply and banking system. The 12 Federal Reserve banks are responsible for implementing the board's policies in their respective regions of the country.

are staggered so that one governor is appointed every 2 years. This gives the board stability and a certain degree of independence from political pressures. Otherwise, the political party in power might be able to pressure the board to pursue partisan objectives rather than goals that are consistent with the best interests of the economy as a whole. The president appoints one governor to serve as chairman of the board for a 4-year term.

The board, assisted by the Federal Open Market Committee (FOMC), is charged with controlling and regulating the nation's money supply and banking system to promote economic stability and maximum output and employment with minimum inflation. To accomplish this (1) it can conduct open market operations; (2) it can set reserve requirements for all depository institutions—commercial banks, mutual savings banks, savings and loan associations, and credit unions; and (3) it can set the level of the discount rate. The board also has the power to impose selective controls on stock market purchases, on interest rates paid by commercial banks on time deposits (the Monetary Control Act of 1980 will gradually phase out interest rate controls), and on certain kinds of consumer credit. We will discuss the three main tools of monetary policy along with other powers in greater detail in the next two chapters.

*The Federal Open Market Committee (FOMC).* The FOMC is composed of the seven Federal Reserve Board governors plus five presidents of Federal Reserve banks. The president of the New York Federal Reserve bank is a permanent member of the committee, like the governors, whereas the other four positions are rotated on a regular basis among the other 11 Federal Reserve bank presidents. The FOMC meets once a month in Washington, D.C. to evaluate the economy's current condition and where it appears to be headed. In light of this evaluation, the FOMC decides what monetary policy should be during the coming month in order to best promote the achievement and maintenance of maximum output and employment with a minimum of inflation. In short, the FOMC is responsible for the formulation of monetary policy.

*The Federal Advisory Council.* The Federal Advisory Council is made up of 12 commercial bankers, one selected from each Federal Reserve district by the district's Federal Reserve bank. Though the council meets periodically with the board, it is only an advisory body to the board and has no policymaking powers.

## The Federal Reserve Banks

There are 12 regional Federal Reserve banks rather than one central bank because it was originally felt that this arrangement would make the Federal Reserve System more sensitive to particular regional needs.

Each Federal Reserve bank is technically "owned" by the member commercial banks in its respective district. However, ownership of Federal Reserve bank stock is in the nature of an obligation of membership in the Federal Reserve System. It does not carry with it the rights of control and financial interest ordinarily attached to stock ownership in corporations that are operated for profit. Moreover, the policies followed by the Federal Reserve banks are dictated by the governmentally appointed and controlled Board of Governors, not by the member commercial banks. The objective of the board is not to make profit for the Federal Reserve banks but rather to foster prosperity for the economy as a whole. The policymaking body, consisting of the board, the other members of the FOMC, and the 12 Federal Reserve banks, is often referred to as "the Fed."

The Federal Reserve banks do not deal with the public directly. They operate as banker to depository institutions. Just as depository institutions hold the deposits of households and businesses, the Federal Reserve banks hold deposits of depository institutions. Just as depository institutions make loans to the public, Federal Reserve banks make loans to depository institutions. In addition, the Federal Reserve banks are given the authority under the Federal Reserve Act to issue currency in the form of Federal Reserve notes. Commercial banks are no longer allowed to issue currency, or bank notes, as they were in the nineteenth century.

## The Member Commercial Banks

There are approximately 15,000 commercial banks in the United States, of which roughly 5,500 are members of the Federal Reserve System. However, in terms of the dollar value of deposits, member banks account for about 70 percent of total deposits at commercial banks.

Commercial banks may be divided into two classes—**state banks** and **national banks**. About one-third of all commercial banks are national banks and the rest state banks. National banks are chartered by the federal government, state banks by state governments. All national banks are *required* by law to be members of the Federal Reserve System. State banks may become members of the Federal Reserve System if they wish, and if they meet certain requirements.

The number of state bank members declined from 1,915 in 1950 to roughly 1,000 by 1980, so that the number of member banks as a percentage of all commercial banks fell from about 86 percent to roughly 40 percent over this period. The main reason for the decline was that nonmember commercial banks were subject only to state reserve requirements, which were more lenient than those imposed by the Federal Reserve System. In particular, the percentage reserve requirements were lower, so that nonmember banks did not have to hold as high a percentage of their assets in non-interest-bearing earning reserves. Apparently for many state banks the loss of income due to the higher reserve requirements was considered too high a price to pay for the benefits of Federal Reserve membership. Benefits included free check-clearing services, free shipment of coin and currency, use of Federal Reserve wire facilities for funds transfers, and the ability to borrow from the Federal Reserve.

### The Monetary Control Act of 1980: Major Change in the Federal Reserve System

The decline in commercial bank membership, coupled with the rapid growth in checklike deposits (NOWs, ATSs, share drafts) at other types of depository institutions (mutual savings banks, savings and loans, credit unions) outside the control of the Federal Reserve System, gave rise to in-creasing concern that the Fed was losing its ability to control and regulate the nation's money supply and banking system. This concern, among others, led Congress to pass the Depository Institutions Deregulation and Monetary Control Act of 1980.

*The act gives the Fed the power to set reserve requirements that apply uniformly to all transactions accounts at all depository institutions—commercial banks, mutual savings banks, savings and loans, and credit unions. For this purpose, transactions accounts are defined to include demand deposits, NOW accounts, ATSs, accounts subject to telephone transfer, and share drafts. The act also provides that all depository institutions that hold transactions accounts or nonpersonal time deposits are entitled to the same discount and borrowing privileges at the Fed as member commercial banks.* In addition, the act makes all depository institutions eligible for other Federal Reserve services as well—currency and coin shipment services, check-clearing and collection services, wire-transfer services, and securities-safekeeping services. The Fed will charge a price for these services to cover costs. The act calls for a gradual phase-in of the new reserve requirements during the 1980s.

The act all but eliminates any distinction between member and nonmember commercial banks, and it certainly blurs the distinction between commercial banks and other types of depository institutions. However, the checking accounts (demand deposits) at commercial banks are still somewhat more universal in that NOW accounts cannot be used by businesses, as noted before. Since the economy's business sector is a substantial user of checking accounts, commercial banks still have an edge over other depository institutions as providers of checking services.

### How the Fed Affects the Money Supply

We have seen how a commercial bank or any depository institution can make a loan by accepting the debt instrument, or IOU, of an individual or business and crediting a demand deposit or any checkable deposit in the borrower's name for the amount of the loan. The asset side of the bank's balance sheet is increased by the dollar amount of the IOU, and the liability side is increased by the same amount in the form of a checkable deposit held in the name of the borrower. The borrower or depositor may then write checks against this deposit, and the bank is obliged to honor these checks. Hence, **commercial banks** *or any* **depository institution** *can create money by extending credit in the form of loans to businesses and households.* We will investigate this process in more detail in the next chapter.

The amount of money supplied to the economy through deposit creation is limited only by the amount of reserves that depository institutions have. And the Fed can control the amount of reserves through its open market operations, its setting of legal reserve requirements, and its willingness to lend reserves to depository institutions. Regarding the latter, a depository institution is entitled to borrow funds for short periods from its regional Federal Reserve bank. In principle this is an important privilege. Recall that in the nineteenth century banks were frequently forced to close because of a lack of reserves to satisfy depositors' withdrawal demands. The borrowing privilege of the Federal Reserve System was intended to make it possible for a bank with otherwise sound assets to borrow whatever reserves were needed to meet a sudden surge of deposit withdrawals. In practice, many economists feel that this borrowing privilege has not always been granted when it should have been, citing especially experiences during the Great Depression.

In sum, *it is the control over depository institution reserves that gives the Fed the ability to influence the size of the economy's money supply and thereby affect the level of total demand for goods and services in the economy. It is through this mechanism that the Board of Governors must try to implement monetary policy.* We will examine this process in more detail in the next three chapters.

## Depository Institutions as Financial Intermediaries

A **financial intermediary** *is a business that acts as a middleman (intermediary) by taking the funds of lenders and making them available to borrowers. A financial intermediary tries to cover its costs and make a profit on the difference between the interest it charges borrowers and the interest it must pay to attract the funds of lenders.* When a financial intermediary accepts a lender's funds, it issues an obligation against itself, a liability, to pay the lender back. When the intermediary in turn lends these funds to a borrower, it takes on an asset in the form of the borrower's IOU, or obligation, to pay the funds back.

The liabilities that a commercial bank issues are in the form of demand, savings, and time deposits. Savings deposits might be in the form of passbook saving accounts, tailored to small depositors. Time deposits might be in the form of large negotiable certificates of deposit (CDs) that are usually issued in denominations of $100,000. CDs are much like short-term bonds and are tailored to the needs of large businesses and other institutions seeking to earn interest on the large amounts of funds they have at their disposal from time to time. In addition to creating checkable deposits through their lending activities, commercial banks also receive funds deposited in demand, savings, and time deposits, which they can then lend out.

Savings and loan associations, mutual savings banks, and credit unions issue liabilities against themselves that are much like the savings and time deposits of commercial banks. In recent years they have also been issuing checkable accounts (NOWs, ATSs, and share drafts), as we have already noted. Savings and loan associations and mutual savings banks make loans mostly to people buying homes and other real estate, thereby acquiring mortgages as assets. Credit unions acquire assets in the form of claims against people to whom they make consumer loans. Though they are not depository institutions, insurance companies are also financial intermediaries. Insurance companies issue liabilities in the form of insurance policies. The premiums they collect from policyholders are used to acquire assets such as mortgages, various kinds of bonds, and corporate securities.

### The Role of Financial Intermediaries

What special services and advantages do financial intermediaries provide for our economy? Basically, there are three.

1. *Financial intermediaries have expertise as credit analysts. They have the ability and experience to evaluate and compare the risk and return, or credit worthiness, of different kinds of loan opportunities.* Imagine trying to prudently loan out your money by doing this in your spare time, after performing a day's work as a carpenter or doctor or whatever. Credit analysts do this full time for a living, just as carpenters and doctors work full time. Credit analysis is just another area of specialization in a modern, industrialized economy.

2. *Financial intermediaries take the many different-sized amounts of funds that households, businesses, and other institutions want to lend and package them into the typically different-sized amounts that individual borrowers want to borrow.* For example, many small depositors at a commercial bank can indirectly make a $50,000 loan to a business.

3. *Financial intermediaries provide an opportunity for small lenders with small amounts of money to participate in risk-reducing diversification.* By depositing a small amount of money in a financial intermediary, a depositor in effect takes a proportional share of every loan the intermediary makes. Simply stated, the depositor has not put all of his or her eggs in one basket. The likelihood of loss is therefore reduced.

## Additional Functions of the Federal Reserve System

The Fed's most important and most difficult task is to attempt to manage the economy's money supply in a manner that avoids inflation while at the same time promoting the achievement and maintenance of a high-employment level of GNP. However, in addition to this and its other functions already mentioned, there are several rather routine but nonetheless important functions that are indispensable to the smooth operation of our monetary system.

1. *The Federal Reserve banks serve as clearinghouses for the collection of checks.* Recall that a check is simply a standardized form on which you write your bank an order to withdraw funds from your checking account and pay them to another party. If the other party deposits the check in his or her checking account, and that account happens to be in the same bank as yours, your bank can simply draw down (debit) your account by the amount of the check and increase (credit) the account of the other party by this amount. However, the other party is more likely to have an account at a different bank, perhaps in another part of the country. In that case the Federal Reserve banks will collect the funds from your account and deposit them in the account of the party to whom you wrote the check. We will examine the mechanics of this process in more detail in the next chapter.

2. *The Federal Reserve banks serve as the bankers for the federal government.* The checking accounts of the U.S. Treasury are for the most part kept at Federal Reserve banks. Federal government bond sales and redemptions, as well as tax collections, are also handled by these banks. In short, the Federal Reserve banks are the government's fiscal agents.

3. *The Federal Reserve banks provide the economy's paper money.* When people need more cash, they typically withdraw it from their deposits at depository institutions. The

## POLICY PERSPECTIVE

### The Bank Panic Problem Returns Again

During the Great Depression of the 1930s some 10,000 banks failed (from 1929 through 1933). Between the Depression and 1980, only one major bank failure occurred—at Franklin National Bank in 1974. But after uninsured depositors lost money in the failure of Penn Square Bank in July 1982, the inability of banks to stop deposit withdrawals by nervous depositors has once again emerged as a key problem in the U.S. financial system, as illustrated in Figure P12–1. The most dramatic example was provided in 1984 when major institutional depositors around the world made their run on huge Continental Illinois Bank and Trust Company in Chicago, accelerating a decline that finally brought a federal takeover. A lesson of Continental's failure was that the Federal Deposit Insurance Corporation (FDIC) couldn't stop a giant run by institutional depositiors even after it issued an unprecedented guarantee protecting them.

#### The Problem of Big Depositors' Runs

It seems unlikely that runs or other liquidity strains will lead to widespread bank failures, as they did in the Great Depression. For one thing federal insurance of deposits of up to $100,000 each provides a safety net that didn't exist back then, and the Federal Reserve can intercede as lender of last resort to support any depository institution. Moreover, the runs have so far been limited to banks that have generally depended too heavily on large institutional deposits of over $100,000 which are often removed by money managers at the first hint of trouble.

However politicians and regulators are hard-pressed to come up with any real solutions to runs by big institutional depositors. Such depositors typically place $5 million to $200 million at individual banks, choosing the bank by its reputation since the $100,000 deposit insurance limit provided by the FDIC is of little use to them. Because they are using other people's money, the institutional depositors holding most of the uninsured deposits feel they can't do business with a bank that gets into trouble. Once the reputation of a bank is sullied by ballooning losses or rumors, these big depositors tend to move in a herd to safer alternatives for their cash. Witnessing the fate of Continental, healthy banks are reassessing the wisdom of relying on big uninsured foreign and domestic deposits as a stable source of funds. Many of the largest banks, such as Bank of America, are seeking out "retail" deposits from individuals which are thought to be more stable than institutional deposits.

#### Criticizing the FDIC— Big Bank Favoritism

The FDIC has received a lot of criticism for the double standard it seems to apply to troubled banks depending on their size. In the case of giant Continental the FDIC rescued all depositors, not just those holding $100,000 or less. When smaller banks have failed (Continental was the largest ever) the depositors holding deposits in excess of $100,000 have had to take their losses. Not surprisingly, smaller banks have complained of losing bigger deposits to the largest banks as depositors sense from the Continental experience that deposits over $100,000 are more likely to be protected in the bigger banks.

**FIGURE P12-1   Value of Deposits of Banks Suspending Operations**

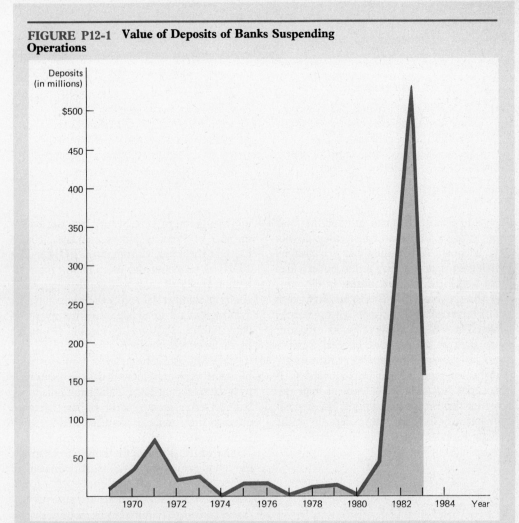

Value of deposits of banks that closed temporarily or permanently on account of financial difficulties. This does not include failed banks whose deposit liabilities were assumed by other banks.

SOURCE: Federal Deposit Insurance Corporation.

One criticism of the government's provision of deposit insurance has been that it may encourage banks to engage in riskier lending practices because bankers know that small depositors' money is protected by the FDIC in the event of failure. If the FDIC is now prepared to protect all depositors at the largest banks, as it did in the case of Continental, many critics argue that these institutions will be encouraged to engage in even riskier lending activities. And since the FDIC is a government agency, it is the taxpayer who may end up footing the bill for any really large bank failures.

### Questions

1. The FDIC actually only has reserves equivalent to about 1 percent of the total amount of bank deposits it insures. How does this fact, coupled with the experiences associated with recent large bank failures, affect the argument that the existence of deposit insurance is the "ounce of prevention" that forestalls the need for a "pound of cure"?

2. Some would say that the way the FDIC has dealt with recent large bank failures may in itself be a source of instability in our banking system. Explain why this might be true.

---

depository institutions can provide this cash from their vaults. However, if they do not have adequate funds, they can get cash by drawing on their accounts at the Federal Reserve banks, the bankers' banks, in the same way that people write checks to draw cash out of their checking accounts at commercial banks. The Federal Reserve banks can print more cash, in the form of Federal Reserve notes, to supply the depository institutions' demand for cash if need be. Conversely, if depositors deposit a lot of cash in their deposits at depository institutions, the depository institutions can in turn deposit at the Federal Reserve banks what they don't want to keep in their vaults.

## Promoting Sound Banking and Protecting Depositors

A long history of bank failures and truly tragic stories of depositors "losing their money" has led to the establishment of a number of ways for government to supervise banks. Every state has banking commissions that regulate state-chartered banks. At the federal level, the Federal Reserve banks continually examine the operations and practices of member banks and enforce correction of irregularities where necessary. The U.S. Comptroller of the Currency has supervisory authority over all national banks, a power granted under the National Bank Acts of 1863 and 1864.

One of the most significant pieces of banking legislation in U.S. history was the Banking Act of 1933, which created the Federal Deposit Insurance Corporation (FDIC). The FDIC is probably the most important protection provided to depositors. It insures deposits at commercial banks and savings banks against loss up to $100,000 in the event of bank failure. This greatly forestalls runs on banks by panicking depositors—the rumor of trouble that itself often causes the most trouble. The very existence of deposit insurance puts depositors at ease. If the bank fails, they still get their money back. It has the same effect as the "ounce of prevention" that forestalls the need for "the pound of cure."

The FDIC also has the power to examine the loans made by insured banks because, of course, deposits are no safer than the loans into which depositor's funds are put. All national banks are required to be insured by the FDIC. State banks may be covered if they choose. In fact, almost every bank carries federal deposit insurance, paying insurance premiums to the FDIC that are proportional to the total amount of their deposits.

Similar deposit insurance is provided for savings and loan associations by the Federal Savings and Loan Association, and for credit unions (federally chartered) by the National Credit Union Administration.

## Where Do We Go from Here?

In the next chapter, we will examine in more detail the nature of the modern bank and how it works. We will also study how the whole banking system functions to create money and how this process is influenced by the Fed. In Chapter 14, we will examine how the money supply affects the level of aggregate demand for goods and services, and the role that money plays in determining the economy's equilibrium level of total output and employment.

---

### CHECKPOINT 12-3
**How does the Federal Reserve System give elasticity to the money supply? Why do you suppose the Fed is sometimes referred to as the "lender of last resort"? Some say deposit insurance is more effective in dealing with the problem of bank panics than is the depository institutions' privilege of borrowing from the Federal Reserve banks. Why?**

---

### SUMMARY

**1.** Money is anything that functions as a medium of exchange, a store of value, and a unit of account. Money is the most liquid of all assets.

**2.** The basic kinds of money are commodity money, currency (fiat money consisting of coin and paper money), demand deposits (checking accounts), and other checkable deposits. A near money can function as a unit of account and store of value like money, but not as a medium of exchange—though it is readily convertible into money.

**3.** Money in our economy is neither backed by nor convertible into gold. It has value because of the goods and services it will buy due to its acceptability in trade. The purchasing power of money depends on the price level. And this in turn depends on the government's management of the money supply.

**4.** Banks evolved from the safekeeping service provided by goldsmiths to become lend-

ers as well. After gold receipts began circulating as money, banks were able to create money (bank notes) through the expansion of their lending activities. This eventually gave rise to present-day fractional reserve banking, with demand deposits and other checkable deposits serving as money by virtue of the check-writing privilege.

**5.** The Federal Reserve System was established to provide the economy with a more elastic money supply so that the bank panics and financial crises that plagued nineteenth-century America might be avoided. The Federal Reserve System consists of the Board of Governors of the Federal Reserve System and the 12 regional Federal Reserve banks.

**6.** The Board of Governors of the Federal Reserve System has responsibility for the supervision of the economy's banking system and the management of the economy's monetary policy. The board's policy orders are carried out by the 12 Federal Reserve banks. They serve as central banks, dealing directly with, and serving as bankers to, the economy's depository institutions. The Federal Reserve banks are owned by the member commercial banks but are controlled and directed by the board.

**7.** The economy's depository institutions function as financial intermediaries, accepting deposits and making loans. Depository institutions can create money by creating checkable deposits through their lending activities. Because of the Fed's control over the reserves of depository institutions, the Fed has the ability to influence the size of the economy's money supply and hence the level of total demand for goods and services in the economy.

**8.** The Federal Reserve System also serves as a clearinghouse for the collection of checks and as the banker for the federal government, provides the economy's paper money, and supervises and regulates the banking practices of member banks. The Federal Reserve System's supervisory activity is supplemented and augmented by a number of other government agencies. These include state banking commissions, the U.S. Comptroller of the Currency, and the Federal Deposit Insurance Corporation, which provides deposit insurance.

## KEY TERMS AND CONCEPTS

automatic transfer service (ATS)
bank note
certificate of deposit (CD)
commercial bank
demand deposit
depository institution
fiat money
financial intermediary
fractional reserve banking
liquidity
M1
M2
M3
money
money market fund share
national bank
near money
negotiable certificates of deposit
negotiable order of withdrawal (NOW)
share draft
state bank
time deposit
token coins
trade credit
transactions costs
Treasury bill

## QUESTIONS AND PROBLEMS

**1.** What are the differences between inflation and deflation in terms of their effects on the three basic functions of money?

**2.** Compare and rank the different definitions of money—M1, M2, and M3—in terms of their relative merits (1) as mediums of exchange and (2) as stores of value. What difference would it make for your answer to (2) if (a) there was an inflation, (b) there was a deflation, or (c) there was neither inflation nor deflation?

**3.** Our money is no longer backed by nor convertible into gold or any other precious metal. Why is it still valuable?

**4.** The following item appeared in the *Wall Street Journal*, June 12, 1978.

> The Treasury revoked 1974 rules that prohibited exporting, melting or otherwise treating or processing pennies. The ban was imposed in April 1974 because high copper prices made it profitable to melt the coins for their metal content or to export them. Because of stabilized prices, the prohibitions aren't necessary any longer, the agency said.

Explain this news item, taking care to distinguish between commodity money and fiat money.

**5.** Why might fractional reserve banking be described as the "swapping of one debt obligation for another?"

The U.S. economy was largely agricultural in the nineteenth century. In the spring, banks would make many loans to farmers, who needed money to plant crops. It was anticipated that once the crops were harvested and sold, the farmers would be able to pay off their loans to the banks in the late summer and early autumn. Describe the likely chain of events resulting from a drought. Suppose you were the banker in a farm community, and in the middle of the summer farmers came to you requesting loans so that they could construct irrigation ditches in their fields. What would you do? Why? What role might rumor play in all of this, depending on the *likely* outcome of your decision on these loan requests?

**7.** Why and how might central banking (the existence of the Federal Reserve System) have greatly reduced bank panics in the nineteenth century? Why might deposit insurance also have helped?

**8.** Describe how the basic functions of the Federal Reserve System are supposed to contribute to economic stability.

**9.** Why and how is financial intermediation important to our economy?

# 13

# Banks, Money Creation, and the Role of the Federal Reserve System

**AFTER READING THIS CHAPTER, YOU WILL BE ABLE TO:**

1. Explain the nature of the balance sheet of a bank.

2. Describe the conflict between the bank's desire to make profits and its need for liquidity and security.

3. Characterize the differences and similarities between the operation of an individual bank in a system of many banks and the operation of the banking system considered as a whole.

4. Describe how deposit expansion and money creation takes place in our banking system.

5. Explain and describe the three main tools used by the Federal Reserve System to affect the economy's money supply.

6. Define the major determinants of the demand for money.

7. Explain how money demand and money supply interact to determine the equilibrium level of the interest rate in the money market.

**H**ow do the Fed's (Federal Reserve System) actions affect our banking system, the money supply, and the level of economic activity in general? To answer this question we must first look more closely at the way banks operate. We will then examine the process by which our banking system as a whole is able to expand and contract the total amount of demand deposits and other checkable deposits, a principal component of the money supply. We will also examine the tools and methods that the Fed uses to control this process and thereby pursue its monetary policy objectives. Finally, we will consider the major determinants of the demand for money and see how money demand and supply interact to determine the equilibrium level of the interest rate in the money market.

## THE BANKS

The previous chapter described the origins and basic nature of banks and the way they function. We saw that a bank is a business seeking to make a profit, just like any other kind of business. We also saw that banks create money in the process of extending credit through their loan-making activity, their principal source of earnings.

Our discussion was aided by the use of a highly simplified version of a bank's balance sheet. In order to better understand how modern banks operate, we need to look at the bank balance sheet in more detail. We also need to consider the distinction between actual, excess, and required reserves in order to understand the deposit expansion (or contraction) process by which our banking system increases (or decreases) the economy's money supply. The bank's need for liquidity on the one hand and its desire to make a profit on the other bear closely on how this deposit expansion (or contraction) process works. With this in mind, we will also consider how banks juggle the often conflicting goals of liquidity and profitability.

Our discussion could be conducted in terms of any one of the different types of depository institutions that issue checkable deposits (commercial banks, mutual savings banks, savings and loan associations, or credit unions). However, we will focus on commercial banks because their demand deposits are the least restrictive in terms of who can hold them and in terms of the size of checks that may be written against them. The basic principles of deposit expansion and money creation illustrated by the commercial banks, as well as the problem of balancing liquidity against profitability, apply in similar fashion to any type of depository institution that offers checkable deposits.

## The Balance Sheet: Assets and Liabilities

Our discussion of how a bank gets started and the way in which it manages its assets and liabilities will be conducted in terms of the bank's balance sheet.

### Starting a Bank

Suppose a group of people decide to start a commercial bank, calling it Citizens' Bank. Say they put $100,000 of their own money into the business and receive in exchange shares of capital stock—paper certificates indicating their ownership of the bank. The owners' $100,000 of capital stock is the equity, or net worth, of the bank. Part of the $100,000, say $85,000, is used to buy a building and other equipment needed to operate a bank. Assume that the remaining $15,000 is needed to buy stock in the district Federal Reserve bank to establish Citizens' Bank's membership in the Federal Reserve System. At this point Citizens' Bank's balance sheet is as shown in Table 13–1. The left, or asset, side of the balance sheet shows what the bank owns. The right, or liability and equity, side of the balance sheet shows the claims against the bank. The bank's total assets equal its total liabilities and equity, of course, because everything the bank possesses is claimed by someone.

**TABLE 13-1 Balance Sheet of Citizens' Bank**

| Assets | | Liabilities and Equity | |
|---|---|---|---|
| Stock in Federal Reserve bank | $ 15,000 | | |
| Building and equipment | 85,000 | Equity (stock certificates of Citizens' Bank) | $100,000 |
| Total assets | $100,000  = | Total liabilities and equity | $100,000 |

### The Bank Opens Its Doors

The bank is now ready for business. When its doors open suppose that customers deposit $1,000,000 in currency. The bank now adds $1,000,000 in demand deposits to the liability and equity side of its balance sheet and $1,000,000 cash to the asset side. Its balance sheet now appears as shown in Table 13-2. Those who have claims on the bank, represented on the liability and equity side of the balance sheet, are divided into two groups—the owners of the bank and the non-owners. The claims of the owners represent the bank's equity, or net *worth,* amounting to $100,000 (the value of the stock certificates issued by Citizens' Bank). The claims of the nonowners are represented by the $1,000,000 of demand deposits. The nonowners' claims constitute the bank's liabilities. Hence, **equity** (*or* **net worth**) *equals the difference between total assets and total liabilities.*

### Required Reserves, Actual Reserves, and Excess Reserves

Suppose the legal **required reserves** imposed by the Fed on banks is 20 percent. This means that a bank is required by law to hold an amount of reserves equal to 20 percent of the total amount of its demand deposits. *The ratio of required reserves to the total amount of demand deposits is the* **required reserve ratio**. *The law defines* **reserves** *as the cash held in the bank's vault and the deposits of the bank at its district Federal Reserve bank.* Since Citizens' Bank has $1,000,000 of demand deposits, it must hold at least $200,000 (20 percent of $1,000,000) in the form of reserves. Suppose it deposits $200,000 of its $1,000,000 of cash in its account at the Federal Reserve bank. Citizens' Bank's balance sheet now appears as shown in Table 13-3. While its legally required reserves amount to $200,000, its total reserves actually amount to $1,000,000—$200,000 on deposit at its district Federal Reserve bank and $800,000 in the form of cash in its vault. Citizens' Bank's total reserves now exceed its required reserves by $800,000. This amount is called its **excess reserves**.

In sum, *total (or actual) reserves are equal to required reserves plus excess reserves.* Required reserves are the reserves that a bank is legally required to hold against demand deposits. Required reserves are equal to the amount of demand deposits multiplied by the

**TABLE 13-2 Balance Sheet of Citizens' Bank**

| Assets | | Liabilities and Equity | |
|---|---|---|---|
| Cash | $1,000,000 | Demand deposits | $1,000,000 |
| Stock in Federal Reserve bank | 15,000 | | |
| Building and equipment | 85,000 | Equity (stock certificates of Citizens' Bank) | 100,000 |
| Total assets | $1,100,000  = | Total liabilities and equity | $1,100,000 |

**TABLE 13-3 Balance Sheet of Citizens' Bank**

| Assets | | Liabilities and Equity | |
|---|---|---|---|
| Reserves | $1,000,000 | Demand deposits | $1,000,000 |
| On deposit at Federal Reserve bank | 200,000 | | |
| Cash | 800,000 | | |
| Stock in Federal Reserve bank | 15,000 | | |
| Building and equipment | 85,000 | Equity (stock certificates of Citizens' Bank) | 100,000 |
| Total assets | $1,100,000 = | Total liabilities and equity | $1,100,000 |

required reserve ratio. Excess reserves are the reserves held above and beyond the amount needed for required reserves. Excess reserves are equal to total reserves minus required reserves.

### Loaning Out Excess Reserves

At this point Citizens' Bank has excess reserves of $800,000. A bank's largest potential source of earnings is the interest it can earn by making loans and buying and holding various kinds of bonds and securities. Citizens' Bank therefore will want to put these excess reserves to work rather than hold "idle" cash, which earns no interest at all.

Suppose it loans out $300,000 to consumers who want to buy cars, household appliances, and perhaps bonds and stocks. Suppose $200,000 is loaned to businesses that need money to stock inventories of goods and raw materials and to buy equipment. The bank holds IOUs from these consumers and businesses in the form of notes (typically the IOUs of consumers and small businesses) and commercial paper (the IOUs of large corporations). Suppose the bank also purchases $100,000 worth of U.S. government securities and $100,000 of other securities, such as corporate bonds and state and local government bonds. As a precautionary measure, Citizens' Bank elects to keep $100,000 of its cash as excess reserves—to meet sudden withdrawal demands by depositors or to

**TABLE 13-4 Balance Sheet of Citizens' Bank After Loaning Out Excess Reserves**

| Assets | | Liabilities and Equity | |
|---|---|---|---|
| Reserves | $ 300,000 | Demand deposits | $1,000,000 |
| On deposit at Federal Reserve bank | 200,000 | | |
| Cash | 100,000 | | |
| Consumer loans | 300,000 | | |
| Business loans | 200,000 | | |
| Government securities | 100,000 | | |
| Other securities | 100,000 | | |
| Stock in Federal Reserve bank | 15,000 | | |
| Building and equipment | 85,000 | Equity (stock certificates of Citizens' Bank) | 100,000 |
| Total assets | $1,100,000 = | Total liabilities and equity | $1,100,000 |

be able to provide credit to a regular loan customer on short notice. Citizens' Bank's balance sheet now appears as shown in Table 13–4.

### Real-World Bank Balance Sheet

The stages of development of our hypothetical Citizens' Bank, illustrated in Tables 13–1 through 13–4, are like those of a real-world commercial bank. The Citizens' Bank balance sheet shown in Table 13–4 is now very similar to the balance sheet of a typical commercial bank in our economy.

Consider, for example, the consolidated balance sheet of all the U.S. commercial banks shown in Table 13–5. This consolidated balance sheet is obtained by adding together the assets and liabilities of all the individual commercial banks in the economy. The distribution of assets and liabilities in Table 13–5 is fairly representative of that of a typical commercial bank. We can see that the asset side of the balance sheet of our hypothetical Citizens' Bank in Table 13–4 is similar to the asset side of this consolidated balance sheet.

A comparison of the liability and equity sides of these two balance sheets reveals two important items that we didn't introduce in our Citizens' Bank example—namely, time and savings deposits (discussed in the previous chapter). The Fed imposes a legal reserve requirement on time and savings deposits just like that imposed on demand deposits. The total amount of time and savings deposits at commercial banks is larger than the amount of demand deposits in Table 13–5.

## Liquidity and Security Versus Profit: Bank Portfolio Management

As a financial intermediary, a commercial bank primarily engages in making short-term loans to businesses and households, as well as purchasing and holding bonds and other securities. *The bank's income-earning assets—its loans, bonds, and securities—together with its excess reserves constitute the bank's portfolio.* A bank manages its portfolio by adjusting the relative proportions of the different income-earning assets it holds in such a way as to satisfy two often conflicting objectives: (1) the maintenance of liquidity and security and (2) the realization of profit.

### Maintenance of Liquidity and Security

In the previous chapter, we saw how banks could fail if they didn't have adequate reserves to meet depositors' demands to withdraw their funds. It is clear from Table 13–5 that modern commercial banks hold an amount of reserves equal to only a fraction of

**TABLE 13-5 Consolidated Balance Sheet of All U.S. Commercial Banks, December 1983**
(in Billions of Dollars)

| Assets | | Liabilities and Equity | |
|---|---|---|---|
| Reserves: cash assets including reserves with Federal Reserve banks | $ 205.0 | Demand deposits | $ 383.2 |
| | | Savings deposits | 461.3 |
| Loans | 1,149.3 | Time deposits | 680.4 |
| U.S. government securities | 186.9 | Other liabilities | 433.6 |
| Other securities | 250.6 | | |
| Other assets: bank premises and other property | 321.3 | Capital accounts: includes equity | 154.6 |
| Total assets | $2,113.1 = | Total liabilities and equity | $2,113.1 |

SOURCE: *Federal Reserve Statistical Release* H.8 (510), January 12, 1984.

their deposit liabilities. Moreover, the largest part of a bank's reserves typically are held to satisfy the legal reserve requirement, and the bank can't really use these to satisfy depositors' withdrawals. (We shall see shortly that the main purpose of required reserves is to give the Fed control over the banking system's money creation process.) Hence, in practice a bank will have to use its excess reserves to meet any sudden surge of deposit withdrawals. And if these excess reserves are not adequate, it will then have to liquidate some of its income-earning assets—that is, convert them into funds that can be used to meet deposit withdrawals.

A bank therefore needs to restrict itself to holding income-earning assets that are relatively liquid and secure. As we saw in the previous chapter, *the more liquid an asset is, the easier it is to convert into money without loss. The security of an asset refers to the degree of likelihood that the contracted obligations of the asset will be met.* For example, a bond is a contract stipulating that the borrower, the bond issuer, will pay the lender, or bondholder, a certain amount of interest on specified dates and return the amount of money borrowed (the principal) on the maturity date of the bond. U.S. Treasury bonds are the most secure asset a bank can hold. Loans made to consumers and households are less secure and, of course, the degree of security will vary from one consumer or business to the next.

It is important to recognize that liquidity and security, though related, are not the same thing. For example, a U.S. Treasury bill that matures in 90 days is for all intents and purposes just as secure as a U.S. Treasury bond that matures in 5 years. Yet the market value or price of the 5-year Treasury bond will tend to fluctuate more on a day-to-day basis than that of the 90-day Treasury bill. The Treasury bill is, therefore, considered more liquid. (A simple, but not complete, explanation is that a Treasury bill is typically closer to its maturity date—the date when its price is guaranteed.) This is true in general of shorter-term bonds as compared to longer-term bonds.

In the case of loans to consumers and businesses, represented by financial paper and notes (IOUs of businesses and consumers), and in the case of bonds issued by corporations and local governments, the shorter the term to maturity, the greater the degree of security generally associated with such assets. This is so because there is more certainty about the likely financial situation of the borrowers in the short run than in the long run. In general, a bank restricts its holdings of earning assets to shorter-term loans, bonds, and securities because of the relatively higher degree of liquidity and security associated with these assets. This restriction is dictated by the large amount of deposit liabilities subject to withdrawal on demand.

### Balancing Profit Against Liquidity and Security

A commercial bank is like any other business in that it wants to maximize the profits realized by its owners, the stockholders. First and foremost, however, the bank is obliged to meet deposit withdrawals on demand. Whenever it is unable to do this, the bank is out of business.

Obviously, if a bank held nothing in its portfolio but vault cash, it would maximize liquidity and security. It would never have any problem satisfying demands for deposit withdrawal. But without any earning assets in its portfolio the bank wouldn't be very profitable either. At the other extreme, if a bank holds no excess reserves and tries to hold only those earning assets that yield the highest return, it may earn large profits. But the bank will run a high risk that it will not be able to meet a sudden surge of deposit withdrawals. Clearly, *there is a conflict between the maintenance of liquidity and security on the one hand and the realization of profit on the other. The main task of bank portfolio management is to strike a balance between these conflicting objectives.*

Borrowers whose ability to repay loans is questionable typically must pay higher interest rates to obtain loans. Similarly, the lower the probability that the contractual obligations of a bond or security will be met, the higher is the interest it must yield to get a lender to buy it. In short, the less security an earning asset offers, the greater the return that can usually be realized from holding it. The higher return is compensation for the higher probability that the asset holder, or lender, may suffer a sizeable loss if the asset does not meet its contractual obligations (the borrower fails to make interest payments or pay the loan, or principal, back or both). Obviously, there is a temptation to acquire earning assets that offer less security but higher returns in order to increase bank profits, hoping of course to avoid the possible losses.

It is also tempting for a bank to hold longer-term bonds because their market value fluctuates more than that of short-term bonds. Consequently, if the portfolio manager can purchase a long-term bond when its market value is low and sell it when its value rises, sizeable profits can be realized. Of course, if the bank needs money to meet a sudden surge of deposit withdrawals on a given day, it might be forced to sell some of its long-term bonds for considerably less than it paid for them. In short, the greater profits that can possibly be realized on long-term bonds must be weighed against the fact that they are less liquid than short-term bonds.

The balance between the need for liquidity and security and the desire for profit is reflected in the consolidated balance sheet for all U.S. commercial banks, Table 13–5:

1. The banks' *reserves* are of course their most liquid and secure assets. However, reserves (vault cash and deposits at Federal Reserve banks) earn no interest.[1]

2. Among the income-earning assets,

holdings of *U.S. government securities* consist mostly of short-term U.S. Treasury bills, which are highly liquid and just as secure as vault cash or deposits at the Federal Reserve banks. These are sometimes referred to as secondary reserves.

3. *Loans to businesses and consumers* represent by far the largest portion of the income-earning assets. Their degree of security is considerably less than that of reserves and U.S. Treasury bills, but they yield much higher rates of return and are the main source of commercial bank earnings. The loans are predominantly short term, some for periods less than a month but few for a period longer than 5 to 10 years. The loans are represented by notes (typically the IOUs of consumers and small businesses) and commercial paper (the IOUs of large corporations) of varying degrees of liquidity.

4. *Other securities* consist mostly of longer-term federal, state, and local government bonds. Most of these generally yield a higher rate of return than U.S. Treasury bills but a lower return than loans to businesses and consumers. This difference is largely a reflection of the fact that their degree of security is greater than that of such loans.

The relative proportions of these four categories of assets in commercial bank portfolios reflect each individual bank's choice of balance between liquidity, security, and profitability. However, these proportions also reflect certain legal limitations on the kinds of assets commercial banks are allowed to hold in their portfolios. For example, they are generally not allowed to hold common stocks.

---

[1] One exception pertains to a *supplemental reserve requirement,* which can be imposed on every depository institution by an affirmative vote of five members of the Board of Governors. The supplementary reserves, not to exceed 4 percent of transactions accounts, earn interest at a rate determined by the Fed. The supplemental reserve requirement provision was created by the Monetary Control Act of 1980.

---

### CHECKPOINT* 13-1
**From 1933 through 1940 commercial banks kept a considerably larger portion of their assets in the form of excess reserves than is the case today. Why do you suppose they did this?**

* Answers to all Checkpoints can be found at the back of the text.

**TABLE 13-6a  Balance Sheet of Citizens' Bank**

| Assets | | Liabilities and Equity | |
|---|---|---|---|
| Reserves | $1,000,000 | Demand deposits | $1,000,000 |
| Required reserves | 200,000 | | |
| Excess reserves | 800,000 | | |
| Stock in Federal Reserve bank | 15,000 | | |
| Building and equipment | 85,000 | Equity | 100,000 |
| Total assets | $1,100,000    = | Total liabilities and equity | $1,100,000 |

## DEPOSIT EXPANSION AND THE BANKING SYSTEM

In the previous chapter we saw how a commercial bank can make a loan by accepting the IOU of an individual or business and crediting a demand deposit in the borrower's name for the amount of the loan. The asset side of the bank's balance sheet is increased by the amount of the IOU, and the liability side is increased by the same amount in the form of a demand deposit held in the name of the borrower. The borrower may then write checks against this demand deposit and the bank is obliged to honor these checks. We will now examine how the banking system as a whole, consisting of many such banks, creates money through this process. Again we will focus on commercial banks. It should be emphasized, however, that the process of money creation described applies to all depository institutions that issue checkable deposits and that the banking system as a whole includes all of these institutions.

First we will consider the position of an individual bank in a system of many banks.

We will then examine the process of money creation when there are a large number of commercial banks in the economy.

### The Individual Bank in a System of Many Banks

Consider once again the Citizens' Bank when it is in the position shown by its balance sheet in Table 13-3, reproduced here as Table 13-6a. It has $1,000,000 in demand deposit liabilities and holds $1,000,000 of reserves. Again assuming that the legal reserve requirement is 20 percent, the required reserves amount to $200,000. Therefore, the bank has $800,000 of excess reserves and is in a position to make loans by creating demand deposits.

What amount of loans and, hence, demand deposits will the Citizens' Bank create? It cannot create more than $800,000 worth. At this stage Citizens' Bank's balance sheet appears as in Table 13-6b. The bank cannot lend out more than $800,000 because borrowers will most likely immediately spend

**TABLE 13-6b  Balance Sheet of Citizens' Bank After Making Loans of $800,000 But Before Checks Are Written Against Bank**

| Assets | | Liabilities and Equity | |
|---|---|---|---|
| Reserves | $1,000,000 | Demand deposits | $1,800,000 |
| IOUs: loans to businesses, to consumers | 800,000 | | |
| Stock in Federal Reserve bank | 15,000 | | |
| Building and equipment | 85,000 | Equity | 100,000 |
| Total assets | $1,900,000    = | Total liabilities and equity | $1,900,000 |

these funds by writing checks against the $800,000 of demand deposits that the bank has credited to them. Since Citizens' Bank is just one among thousands of banks in the banking system, it is highly likely that these checks will be made payable to parties who deposit their money in these other banks. Therefore, when all of these checks are presented to the Citizens' Bank for collection of payment, Citizens' Bank will have to pay out its $800,000 of excess reserves to satisfy the checks, which are orders to withdraw the $800,000 of deposits on demand. Assume that this happens. Citizens' Bank's balance sheet will now appear as in Table 13-7.

Note that the bank is now "fully loaned up." It has just the amount of reserves on hand to meet the legal reserve requirement—$200,000 of reserves held against $1,000,000 of demand deposits. There are no excess reserves. While the Citizens' Bank now has the same amount of demand deposits it had in the beginning, it has created $800,000 more money in the economy. That money is now deposited in other banks. Although unlikely, it could have happened that all of the checks written against the $800,000 of demand deposits created by Citizens' Bank in Table 13-6b were paid to parties who redeposited them at Citizens' Bank. The deposits of those who wrote the checks would then be reduced by $800,000, while the deposits of those who received the checks would be increased by $800,000. The total amount of demand deposit liabilities at Citizens' Bank would remain unchanged at $1,000,000. Also unlikely, but possible, the $800,000 of demand deposits created in Table 13-6b might be withdrawn by the borrowers in the form of currency, so that the final position of the bank would be as shown in Table 13-7.

In general, *a single bank in a banking system composed of many banks cannot lend more than the amount of its excess reserves. This is so because borrowers will most likely write checks against the deposits that will cause the bank to lose these excess reserves, along with the deposits, to other banks.* This means that a single bank cannot permanently increase the amount of its demand deposit liabilities (by making loans) beyond the amount it had to begin with.

## A Banking System of Many Banks

We will now see that a banking system made up of many banks can make loans and create demand deposits equal to several times the amount of total excess reserves in the system.

Why is this so? Recall that a single bank in a banking system of many banks cannot permanently increase the amount of its demand deposits because the demand deposits it creates by lending are transferred by check-writing borrowers to other banks. As a result, the demand deposits of other banks are increased. Therefore, the amount of demand deposits in the *whole* banking system is increased. Reserves and deposits cannot be lost to other banks outside the banking system because there are no banks outside the system. Let's now explore in more detail lending and deposit creation in a banking system consisting of many banks. We will see why

---

**TABLE 13-7 Balance Sheet of Citizens' Bank After Checks For $800,000 Are Written Against Bank**

| Assets | | Liabilities and Equity | |
|---|---|---|---|
| Reserves | $   200,000 | Demand deposits | $1,000,000 |
| IOUs: loans to businesses and    consumers | 800,000 | | |
| Stock in Federal Reserve bank | 15,000 | | |
| Building and equipment | 85,000 | Equity | 100,000 |
| Total assets | $1,100,000    = | Total liabilities and equity | $1,100,000 |

the amount of money created is some multiple of the total amount of excess reserves.

## Money Creation in a Banking System of Many Banks

Suppose somebody deposits $1,000 of currency in a demand deposit at Bank A. Assume that the legally required reserve ratio is 10 percent, or .10, and that the bank was fully loaned up prior to the time of the $1,000 deposit. Bank A now has $1,000 more demand deposits as liabilities and $1,000 more reserves as assets, of which $100 are required reserves and $900 are excess reserves. (In the discussion to follow, we will ignore all items on the bank's balance sheet but those that change as a result of deposit expansion.) Bank A's balance sheet changes as follows:

**BANK A**
(Bank A receives $1,000 in demand deposits.)

| Assets | | Liabilities | |
|---|---|---|---|
| Reserves | + $1,000 | Demand deposits | + $1,000 |
| Required reserves | + 100 | | |
| Excess reserves | + 900 | | |
| Assets+ | $1,000 | Liabilities+ | $1,000 |

Bank A, as an individual bank, can now lend out $900 by creating $900 of new demand deposits, an amount equal to its excess reserves. At this point Bank A's balance sheet changes like this:

**BANK A**
(Bank A makes $900 of loans, increasing demand deposits by $900.)

| Assets | | Liabilities | |
|---|---|---|---|
| Reserves | $1,000 | Demand deposits | $1,000 |
| Loans | + 900 | Demand deposits | + 900 |
| Assets | + $1,900 | Liabilities+ | $1,900 |

Presumably, the party borrowing the $900, in whose name Bank A creates the $900 demand deposit, will soon spend that $900 by writing a check against the deposit for that amount. That is, the borrower will use the money to pay for some good or service. Suppose the recipient of that check deposits the check in another bank, Bank B. Since the check is drawn against Bank A, $900 of reserves will be transferred from Bank A to Bank B. After all this, the change in Bank A's balance sheet is the following:

**BANK A**
(Bank A loses $900 of reserves and deposits after check is written against it.)

| Assets | | Liabilities | |
|---|---|---|---|
| Reserves ($1,000 − $900) | + $ 100 | Demand deposits ($1,900 − $900) | + $1,000 |
| Loans | + 900 | | |
| Assets | + $1,000 | Liabilities+ | $1,000 |

Bank A is now fully loaned up. It has $1,000 of demand deposits and holds $100 of reserves, just the amount required by law, given that the required reserve ratio is .10. It has no excess reserves.

When the $900 check drawn on Bank A is deposited in Bank B, and $900 of reserves are transferred from Bank A to Bank B, the following changes are made in Bank B's balance sheet:

**BANK B**
(Bank B receives $900 deposit from Bank A, and $900 of reserves are transferred to Bank B.)

| Assets | | Liabilities | |
|---|---|---|---|
| Reserves | + $900 | Demand deposits | + $900 |
| Required reserves | + 90 | | |
| Excess reserves | + 810 | | |
| Assets | + $900 | Liabilities | + $900 |

Bank B's demand deposits and reserves are each increased by $900. With a required reserve ratio of .10, the increase in the amount of its legally required reserves amounts to $90, while the increase in its excess reserves amounts to $810.

Suppose that Bank B now creates demand deposits by lending out $810, an amount equal to its excess reserves. Bank B's balance sheet will now change as follows:

### BANK B
(Bank B makes $810 of loans, increasing demand deposits by $810.)

| Assets | | Liabilities | |
|---|---|---|---|
| Reserves | $ 900 | Demand deposits | $ 900 |
| Loans | + 810 | Demand deposits | + 810 |
| Assets | + $1,710 | Liabilities | + $1,710 |

Now suppose the borrower writes a check for $810 against this newly created demand deposit. If the recipient of the check deposits it in another bank, Bank C, $810 of reserves will then be transferred from Bank B to Bank C. The change in Bank B's balance sheet appears as follows:

### BANK B
(Bank B loses $810 of reserves and deposits after check is written against it.)

| Assets | | Liabilities | |
|---|---|---|---|
| Reserves ($900 − $810) | + $ 90 | Demand deposits ($1,710 − $810) | + $900 |
| Loans | + 810 | | |
| Assets | + $900 | Liabilities | + $900 |

Now Bank B has $900 of demand deposits and $90 of reserves. The reserves are equal to 10 percent of the amount of demand deposits, just the amount it is legally required to hold. Bank B is fully loaned up—it has no excess reserves.

*The Pattern of Lending and Deposit Creation.* There is a pattern to this process of lending and deposit creation. Bank A's excess reserves allow it to make loans and create new demand deposits equal to the amount of its excess reserves, which are then transferred by check-writing borrowers to Bank B. Bank B acquires all of Bank A's excess reserves in this process. Bank B is required to hold a fraction (equal to the legally required reserve ratio) of these new reserves against its newly acquired demand deposits. The remainder are excess reserves that allow B to make loans and create new demand deposits, which are in turn transferred by check-writing borrowers to Bank C, and so on. After borrowers write checks transferring Bank C's newly created demand deposits, along with its excess reserves, to Bank D, the change in Bank C's balance sheet will be as follows:

### BANK C

| Assets | | Liabilities | |
|---|---|---|---|
| Reserves | + $ 81 | Demand deposits | + $810 |
| Loans | + 729 | | |
| Assets | + $810 | Liabilities | + $810 |

And repeating the same pattern another step further, the change in Bank D's balance sheet would appear as follows:

### BANK D

| Assets | | Liabilities | |
|---|---|---|---|
| Reserves | + $ 73 | Demand deposits | + $729 |
| Loans | + 656 | | |
| Assets | + $729 | Liabilities | + $729 |

And similarly, for Bank E the change is:

### BANK E

| Assets | | Liabilities | |
|---|---|---|---|
| Reserves | + $ 66 | Demand deposits | + $656 |
| Loans | + 590 | | |
| Assets | + $656 | Liabilities | + $656 |

The complete process of demand deposit expansion throughout the banking system is summarized in Table 13-8. Starting with the initial demand deposit of $1,000 at Bank A (column 1), follow the arrows and notice that the successive increases in demand deposits at Banks B, C, D, and so on become smaller and smaller. This reflects the fact that when a bank receives demand deposits and reserves from another bank, only a portion of these reserves, the excess reserves (column 2), can be passed on to yet another bank through lending and the creation of new demand deposits. The other portion must be kept as required reserves (column 3). If we want to know the total amount of new demand deposits that this process creates—the total

amount of money creation—we must add up all the deposit increases throughout the banking system, as shown in column 1.

*The Process of Deposit Creation Completed.* When the entire process of deposit expansion is complete, all banks in the banking system are fully loaned up—there are no excess reserves anywhere in the banking system. The initial $1,000 increase in reserves is totally tied up as required reserves (column 3). Including the initial increase in demand deposits of $1,000 at Bank A, the total increase in demand deposits and, therefore, money for the whole banking system amounts to $10,000. That is, the total increase in demand deposits (column 1) is 10 times the ini-

**TABLE 13-8 Expansion of the Money Supply by Lending and Deposit Creation by the Banking System** (Legally Required Reserve Ratio Is .10)

| Bank | (1) New Reserves and Demand Deposits | (2) Excess Reserves Equal to the Amount Bank Can Lend, Equal to New Money Created | (3) Required Reserves |
|---|---|---|---|
| | | (1) − (3) | (1) × required reserve ratio of .10 |
| A | $ 1,000 | $ 900 | $ 100 |
| B | 900 | 810 | 90 |
| C | 810 | 729 | 81 |
| D | 729 | 656 | 73 |
| E | 656 | 590 | 66 |
| F | 590 | 531 | 59 |
| G | 531 | 478 | 53 |
| H | 478 | 430 | 48 |
| All remaining banks | 4,306 | 3,876 | 430 |
| Total | $10,000 | $9,000 | $1,000 |

## POLICY PERSPECTIVE

### Bank Failure and Deposit Contraction—How Serious Is the Threat?

Historically banking crises have often been identified as major contributors to economic downturns. During the Great Depression the domino effect of bank failures (see Figure P13-1)—one bank failure triggering another and so on—proved costly not only to the depositors, shareholders, and loan customers of the banks directly affected, but ultimately contributed to the length and depth of the Depression itself.

However there are major differences between today's banking system and that of the Great Depression era, the main one being the existence of federal deposit insurance. Deposit insurance alleviates the fear of small depositors that they will not be able to convert their deposits into currency, and thus eliminates a potentially major source of reserve drainage from the banking system as a whole, which was the underlying cause of the domino effect.

**FIGURE P13-1  Number of Banks Suspending Operations During the Great Depression, 1929–1933**

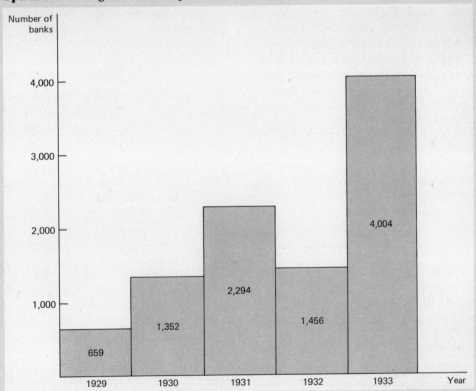

This graph shows the number of banks that closed temporarily or permanently because of financial difficulties. It does not include failed banks whose deposit liabilities were assumed by other banks.

SOURCE: Federal Deposit Insurance Corporation.

A net currency outflow from a fractional reserve banking system such as ours is equivalent to a reserve drain that sets off a multiple contraction of deposits and credit at all banks as each tries to raise cash to finance the deposit loss. When banks have to liquidate assets at below-market prices, they may incur sufficiently large losses to be driven into bankruptcy. However currency drains have not occurred in any banking crisis since 1933, the year federal deposit insurance was established.

Such a currency drain didn't even occur in Chicago in 1984 with the failure of the huge Continental Illinois National Bank, the seventh largest commercial bank in the United States. The deposit runs that did occur at Continental Bank were by large, effectively uninsured depositors. But they didn't withdraw their deposits in the form of currency, which is not a useful medium of exchange for large corporations. Rather they transferred their deposits into other, presumably safer, banks. Therefore, while the deposits were lost to Continental, they were not lost to the banking system as a whole. Hence the multiple deposit contraction associated with a currency drain, and the resulting domino effect, never occurred.

Some large depositors may feel safer removing their funds from the banking system altogether and investing them in United States Government Treasury securities, a nearly risk-free asset. But again, the funds are not lost to the banking system. Ownership of the deposit account is transferred to the seller of the Treasury securities, another depositor in the banking system.

Today bank failures are much less likely to set off a chain reaction of other bank failures and ever larger deposit losses because there is typically no loss of currency and thus no reserve drain from the banking system as a whole. Deposit insurance has largely immunized healthy banks from unhealthy banks. And individual large bank failures are perhaps no longer any more or less serious to the economy than the failure of any large company.

### Questions

1. Why is it that currency withdrawals can result in a multiple deposit contraction throughout the banking system?

2. Why is it that deposit withdrawals from a troubled bank are less likely to result in a domino effect in today's banking system than they were in the banking system of the early 1930s?

---

tial $1,000 increase in reserves at Bank A. This multiple of 10 is the reciprocal of the required reserve ratio of .10. Similarly, viewed in terms of the initial increase in excess reserves of $900 at Bank A, the total amount of new money created by the expansion process is $9,000 (column 2). Again, the multiple is 10.

In sum, *a single bank in a banking system cannot permanently increase the amount of its demand deposits by lending out its excess reserves. But when each individual bank in the system lends out its excess reserves, the banking system considered as a whole can. That is, the total expansion in demand deposits throughout the entire banking system is equal to a multiple of any increase in reserves. The multiple is equal to the reciprocal of the required reserve ratio.*

### Deposit Contraction: Destruction of Money by the Banking System

The deposit expansion or money creation process is also reversible. Suppose the banking system is fully loaded up and a depositor at Bank A decides to withdraw $1,000 of currency. In essence this leads to a reversal of the process summarized in Table 13–8— think of the direction of the arrows as now being reversed.

Initially Bank A loses $1,000 of reserves in the form of cash (column 1). Since it has $1,000 less demand deposits, it no longer needs to hold the $100 in required reserves (column 3) against these deposits. But since Bank A was fully loaned up to begin with, it is now short $900 of the amount of required reserves it must hold against its remaining deposits. Consequently, Bank A will have to get rid of $900 of other assets in its portfolio (column 2) to replenish its reserves. Suppose it does this by selling $900 of government bonds to someone who holds demand deposits in Bank B. This party writes a check against Bank B for $900 (column 1) payable to Bank A. Bank A deposits this $900 check in its deposit at its district Federal Reserve bank. Since deposits at the Fed count as reserves, Bank A now has just the amount of reserves needed to satisfy its legal reserve requirement.

However, when Bank A's account at the Fed is marked up, or credited, $900, Bank B's account at the Fed is drawn down, or debited, $900. While Bank B no longer needs to hold $90 of required reserves (column 3) because it has lost $900 of demand deposits (column 1), it is now short $810 of the amount of required reserves it must hold against its remaining deposits. Therefore, Bank B sells $810 of government bonds to someone who holds demand deposits in Bank C. This party writes a check against Bank C for $810 (column 1) payable to Bank B. Bank C then loses deposits and finds itself short of required reserves, and the whole contraction process is repeated over and over with respect to Banks D, E, F, and so forth. In the end, the total reduction in demand deposits for the whole banking system amounts to $10,000 (column 1). Hence, the initial decrease in demand deposits and, therefore, reserves of $1,000 results in a total reduction in the amount of demand deposits that is 10

times greater. Note again that this multiple is the reciprocal of the required reserve ratio $^1/_{10}$, or .10.

In sum, *the process of multiple contraction of demand deposits is just the reverse of the process of multiple expansion of deposits.*

## Determining the Deposit Multiplier

We have seen that any initial increase in reserves can result in an increase in the total amount of demand deposits, or new money, that is equal to a multiple of the amount of increase in reserves. This was true for the banking system consisting of many banks, provided they were fully loaned up. The multiple equals the reciprocal of the required reserve ratio $r$, or $^1/_r$. This reciprocal is often called the **deposit multiplier**:

$$\text{deposit multiplier} = \frac{1}{r}$$

If the required reserve ratio is 20 percent, or .20, the deposit multiplier $^1/_r$ equals $^1/_{.20}$, or 5. If the required reserve ratio were 10 percent, or .10, then the deposit multiplier would equal $^1/_{.10}$, or 10. In this case, for example, the maximum increase in the dollar amount of new demand deposits resulting from a $10 increase in reserves would be $100. We can express this through the following equation:

$$\$10 \times \frac{1}{r} = \$10 \times 10 = \$100$$

In general, if $E$ is the change in reserves and $D$ is the maximum increase in demand deposits, then

$$D = E \times \frac{1}{r}$$

Of course, the deposit multiplier is applicable to a decrease in reserves as well as to an increase. That is, if reserves are removed from the banking system when it is fully loaned up, there will be a contraction in the amount of demand deposits in the system that is equal to the amount of reserves removed multiplied by the deposit multiplier $1/_r$. For example, in our discussion of multiple deposit contraction, the legally required reserve ratio was .10. The deposit multiplier was therefore 10. Assuming that the banking system was fully loaned up, we saw that an initial $1,000 reduction in reserves resulted in a total loss of demand deposits amounting to $10,000 for the whole banking system ($1,000 × 10).

## Other Determinants of the Size of the Deposit Multiplier

By now you have probably been struck by the similarity between the deposit multiplier and the income or expenditure multiplier discussed in Chapter 9. Indeed, the deposit expansion process of Table 13–8 looks very similar to the income expansion process of Table 9–4. Just as the deposit expansion multiplier is equal to the reciprocal of the required reserve ratio, the expenditure multiplier is equal to the reciprocal of the marginal propensity to save. Just as the expenditure multiplier reflects the fact that expenditure by one party is income for another, the deposit multiplier reflects the fact that reserves and deposits lost by one bank are reserves and deposits gained by another. The size of the expenditure multiplier is determined by the amount of leakage into saving at each round of expenditure, as determined by the size of the *MPS*. Similarly, the size of the deposit multiplier is determined by the amount of leakage of reserves into required reserves at each round of the deposit expansion process.

The similarity between the two multipliers ends here, however. This is so because the expenditure multiplier deals with a flow, income, while the deposit multiplier deals with a stock, the money supply. Moreover, money and income are completely different concepts. Nonetheless, the leakage concept is very useful to our understanding of the other determinants of the size of the deposit multiplier.

### Leakages into Excess Reserves

Up to this point in our discussion of the deposit multiplier, we have assumed that leakage into required reserves is the *only* type of leakage from the deposit expansion process. In other words, we have assumed that banks are always fully loaned up. In reality, this is not always the case.

For example, as part of their portfolio management policy banks may want to keep a certain amount of excess reserves on hand for liquidity purposes. This constitutes another source of leakage from the deposit expansion process in addition to the leakage into required reserves. This means that a greater portion of the reserves one bank receives from another is set aside at each round of deposit expansion—part to satisfy legal reserve requirements and part to be held as excess reserves to satisfy the liquidity objectives of a bank's self-imposed portfolio management policy. In short, a smaller amount of reserves is now passed on from one bank to the next and, therefore, the full amount of deposit expansion will be less. This makes the deposit multiplier smaller. For example, if the legal reserve requirement is 10 percent and in addition banks set aside as excess reserves another 10 percent of any reserves received, the deposit multiplier is equal to 1 ÷ .20 (the sum of .10 and .10), or 5.

Similarly, the deposit multiplier for the deposit contraction process will be smaller if banks choose to keep excess reserves on hand for liquidity purposes. Why? Each bank will be able to meet deposit withdrawals out of excess reserves before it needs to start selling off assets, which would lead to further deposit withdrawals at other banks, in the manner we have already described.

### Leakages Due to Cash Withdrawal

Another source of leakage from the deposit expansion process is cash withdrawal. In our discussion it was assumed that when a check was written against a deposit at one bank, the recipient deposited the entire amount in another bank. In reality, the recipient may deposit only part of the amount of the check and hold the rest in cash. Since cash in banks constitutes reserves, this means that a smaller amount of reserves ends up being transferred from one bank to the next, and the full amount of the deposit expansion process is reduced accordingly. For example, suppose that in addition to the 10 percent leakage into excess reserves, there is another 10 percent leakage due to cash withdrawals by the public at each step of the deposit expansion process. The deposit expansion multiplier will now be equal to 1 ÷ .30 (the sum of .10, .10, and .10), or 3.3.

### Variation in Willingness to Lend and Borrow

Finally, the willingness of banks to lend and the eagerness of businesses and consumers to borrow tends to vary with economic conditions. At one extreme, if there is no lending and borrowing, there will be no deposit expansion at all. At the other extreme, when banks are fully loaded up there is the maximum possible amount of deposit expansion. The amount of deposit expansion usually lies somewhere between these two extremes, depending on the banks' willingness to lend and the demand for loans by borrowers. Generally, banks are more cautious and eager borrowers less numerous when the economy is in the contraction phase of a business cycle. Obviously, therefore, the amount of excess reserves banks hold will tend to vary over the course of the business cycle. Consequently, so will the size of the deposit multiplier.

In sum, *the theoretical deposit multiplier calculated as the reciprocal of the required reserve ratio assumes that banks are fully loaded up. It tells us the maximum amount of deposit expansion or contraction that can take place in response to a change in excess reserves. In reality, banks are not always fully loaded up and there are also leakages due to cash withdrawal by the public. Consequently, the size of the ac-*

*tual deposit multiplier is typically variable as well as smaller than the theoretical deposit multiplier.*

---

### CHECKPOINT 13-2

**Change the required reserve ratio in Table 13–8 to .25 and show how the deposit expansion process will look as a result. How might the actions of one bank or one depositor put a stop to this expansion process? Suppose bankers' willingness to lend increases. Describe how and why this will affect the economy's money supply. With a required reserve ratio of .25, what will be the maximum possible effect on the economy's money supply if you decide to withdraw $100 in cash from your bank? Under what conditions will your withdrawal have the least possible effect on the money supply? (Define the money supply as demand deposits plus currency held *outside* of banks.)**

---

## THE ROLE OF THE FEDERAL RESERVE SYSTEM

The Board of Governors of the Federal Reserve System, the Fed, is responsible for the conduct of *monetary policy* in our economy. *Monetary policy is deliberate action taken to affect the size of the economy's money supply for the purpose of promoting economic stability and maximum output and employment with a minimum of inflation.*

The Fed is able to affect the size of the economy's money supply by controlling the quantity of reserves in the banking system. If the Fed increases the quantity of reserves, money creation takes place through the process of deposit expansion. If the Fed decreases the quantity of reserves, the amount of money in the economy is reduced through the process of deposit contraction. In this section we will examine the tools the Fed actually uses to conduct monetary policy. We will also look at the so-called federal funds market and its relationship to the way in which the Fed conducts monetary policy. Finally, we will examine the "minor" tools of monetary policy.

## The Three Major Tools of Monetary Policy

There are three major tools that the Fed can use to conduct monetary policy: (1) open market operations, (2) setting reserve requirements for commercial banks and other depository institutions, and (3) setting the level of the discount rate—the interest rate it charges commercial banks and other depository institutions when it lends them reserves. We will consider each of these tools in turn.

Again we will illustrate our discussion in terms of commercial banks. However, again we emphasize that the discussion also applies to all depository institutions that issue checkable deposits and that the banking system includes all such institutions.

### Open Market Operations

The Fed can directly affect the amount of bank reserves by buying or selling government securities, such as U.S. Treasury bills, in the open market where these securities are traded. Such transactions are called **open market operations**. Open market operations are the Fed's most important tool for carrying out monetary policy. *When the Fed conducts open market purchases, it buys government bonds and puts reserves into the banking system, causing an expansion of demand deposits and other checkable deposits and hence an increase in the economy's money supply. When the Fed conducts open market sales, it sells government bonds and takes reserves out of the banking system, causing a contraction of demand deposits and other checkable deposits and hence a decrease in the economy's money supply.* Let's consider how each of these operations works in more detail.

1. *Open Market Purchases.* Suppose the Fed buys $100,000 of Treasury bills in the open market and the seller is a commercial bank. (We will focus only on those items in the Fed's and the commercial bank's balance sheet that are affected by this transaction.) The Fed pays the commercial bank by increasing (crediting) the commercial bank's reserve account at its district Federal Reserve bank by the amount of the purchase, or $100,000. Hence, the Fed has $100,000 more assets in the form of Treasury bills and $100,000 more liabilities in the form of commercial bank reserve deposits at the Fed. The changes in the Federal Reserve bank's balance sheet look like this:

**FEDERAL RESERVE BANK**

| Assets | | Liabilities | |
|---|---|---|---|
| Treasury bills | + $100,000 | Commercial bank reserve deposits | + $100,000 |

The commercial bank now has lost $100,000 of assets in the form of Treasury bills sold to the Fed, but it has gained $100,000 of assets in the form of reserves—deposits at the Fed. The changes in the commercial bank's balance sheet therefore look like this:

**COMMERCIAL BANK**

| Assets | |
|---|---|
| Reserves: deposits at the Fed | + $100,000 |
| Treasury bills | − $100,000 |

Note that while the total amount of the commercial bank's assets have not changed, the commercial bank now has more reserves. If the commercial bank previously was fully loaned up, it now has $100,000 of excess reserves. It is now in a position to make new loans by creating demand deposits if it wishes. We have seen how this can lead to deposit expansion, or money creation, throughout the banking system.

Suppose that the Fed buys $100,000 of Treasury bills in the open market, but the seller is one individual or a business other than a bank. The Fed simply makes out a check for $100,000 drawn against a Federal Reserve bank and payable to the seller of the Treasury bills. Suppose the seller deposits the check in a commercial bank. The commercial bank then presents the check to its district Federal Reserve bank for collection, and the commercial bank's reserve account at the Federal Reserve bank is increased (credited) by $100,000. The changes in the Federal Reserve bank's balance sheet are as follows:

### FEDERAL RESERVE BANK

| Assets | Liabilities | |
| --- | --- | --- |
| Treasury + $100,000<br>bills | Com-<br>mercial<br>bank<br>reserve<br>deposits | + $100,000 |

Again, the Fed has $100,000 more assets in the form of Treasury bills and $100,000 more liabilities in the form of commercial bank reserve deposits.

The commercial bank now has $100,000 more liabilities in the form of demand deposits and $100,000 more assets in the form of reserves represented by deposits at its Federal Reserve bank. These changes in the commercial bank's balance sheet look like this:

### COMMERCIAL BANK

| Assets | Liabilities | |
| --- | --- | --- |
| Reserves: + $100,000<br>de-<br>posits<br>at the<br>Fed | Demand<br>de-<br>posits | + $100,000 |

Again, we see that commercial bank reserves are increased by the amount of the open market purchase. Assuming that the commercial bank was initially loaned up, it now has excess reserves because it is only required to hold a fraction of its new reserves against its newly acquired $100,000 of demand deposits. Deposit expansion and money creation can take place just as before.

In sum, *commercial bank reserves are increased by the amount of Federal Reserve open market purchases no matter whether the seller of the securities is a bank or a nonbank.*

2. *Open Market Sales.* Suppose the Fed sells $100,000 of Treasury bills in the open market and the buyer is a commercial bank. The Fed takes payment from the commercial bank by reducing the commercial bank's reserve deposit with its Federal Reserve bank by $100,000. In other words, the Fed's liability to the commercial bank is reduced by $100,000, while its assets are reduced to the extent of the $100,000 of Treasury bills it sells. The changes in the Federal Reserve bank's balance sheet look like this:

### FEDERAL RESERVE BANK

| Assets | Liabilities | |
| --- | --- | --- |
| Treasury − $100,000<br>bills | Com-<br>mercial<br>bank<br>reserve<br>deposits | − $100,000 |

The commercial bank has gained $100,000 of assets in Treasury bills purchased from the Fed. But it also has had to give up $100,000 of its reserve deposits at its Federal Reserve bank to pay for them. The changes in the commercial bank's balance sheet look like this:

### COMMERCIAL BANK

| Assets | |
| --- | --- |
| Reserves:<br>deposits<br>at the Fed | − $100,000 |
| Treasury<br>bills | + $100,000 |

While the total amount of the commercial bank's assets has not been changed by these transactions, the commercial bank now has less reserves. This can set in motion the deposit contraction process, or reduction in the money supply, we have already discussed.

What if the buyer of the $100,000 of Treasury bills sold by the Fed is an individual or business other than a bank? Suppose payment is made to the Fed with a check drawn against the buyer's deposit at a commercial bank. When the Fed receives the check, it decreases (or debits) the commercial bank's reserve deposits at its Federal Reserve bank by $100,000. Once again, payment to the Fed is represented by a reduction of a Federal Reserve bank's liability to a commercial bank. The change in the Federal Reserve bank's balance sheet looks like this:

### FEDERAL RESERVE BANK

| Assets | Liabilities | |
|---|---|---|
| Treasury − $100,000 bills | Commercial bank reserve deposits | − $100,000 |

The commercial bank's demand deposit liabilities are reduced by $100,000 because of the check written by its depositor, the buyer of the Treasury bills. The commercial bank's assets are likewise reduced $100,000 by the reduction in its reserve deposits at the Federal Reserve bank that takes place when its depositor's check clears. The commercial bank's balance sheet is changed as follows:

### COMMERCIAL BANK

| Assets | Liabilities | |
|---|---|---|
| Reserves: − $100,000 deposits at the Fed | Demand deposits | − $100,000 |

Again, we see that $100,000 of commercial bank reserves are removed from the banking system by the Fed's open market sale of $100,000 of Treasury bills.

In sum, *bank reserves are decreased by the amount of Federal Reserve open market sales, regardless of whether the buyer is a bank or a nonbank.*

### Legal Reserve Requirements

A news item reports that the Fed "may have to dig deeper into its bag of credit-tightening tricks to stem the sharp rise in the nation's money supply." It suggests that the Fed may resort to an increase in legal reserve requirements because "stiffer reserve requirements normally will temper the banking system's lending ability." Let's see why this is so.

The Fed has the authority to set the required reserve ratios within limits established by Congress. Recall that the required reserve ratio establishes the minimum amount of reserves that banks must hold against demand deposit liabilities. These reserves may take the form of vault cash or deposits at a Federal Reserve bank or both. How does the Fed affect the economy's money supply by changing bank reserve requirements?

Suppose that all banks in the banking system are fully loaned up and that the required reserve ratio is .10. None of the banks has any excess reserves. The balance sheet of a typical commercial bank would look like this (only its reserves and demand deposits are shown):

### TYPICAL COMMERCIAL BANK

| Assets | Liabilities | |
|---|---|---|
| Reserves  $100,000 | Demand deposits | $1,000,000 |

The bank has $100,000 of reserves, which is just equal to 10 percent of its demand deposit liabilities of $1,000,000.

*Increase in the Legal Reserve Requirement.* Suppose that the Fed wants to tighten up the economy's money supply, or bring about a "credit tightening," as it is put in the news item. This means that the Fed wants to force the banks in the banking system to reduce their lending activity or their holdings of other earning assets. This will cause a deposit contraction throughout the banking system and hence a reduction in the money supply.

To bring this about, suppose the Fed increases the legal reserve requirement from 10 percent to 12 percent. Our typical bank is now required to hold $120,000 of reserves against its $1,000,000 of demand deposits (.12 × $1,000,000). Since it only has $100,000 of reserves, it is $20,000 short. In order to make up this deficiency, the bank must reduce its loans or sell off $20,000 of its other earning assets (or do some combination of both totaling $20,000). This will set in motion the deposit contraction process, or the reduction in the money supply, we have discussed before.

*Decrease in the Legal Reserve Requirement.* On the other hand, if the Fed wants to ease up on credit, or increase the money supply, it can reduce the reserve requirement. Suppose, for example, that it reduces the required reserve ratio from .10 to .08 (from a 10 percent reserve requirement to an 8 percent reserve requirement). Our typical bank is now required to hold only $80,000 of reserves against its $1,000,000 of demand deposits. Therefore, it has $20,000 of excess reserves. If it loans this out, deposit expansion, or money creation, can take place throughout the banking system in the manner we have already discussed.

In sum, *an increase in the required reserve ratio will force a deposit contraction, or money supply reduction, if banks are fully loaned up. This contraction will be less pronounced to the extent that banks have excess reserves. A decrease in the required reserve ratio increases the amount of excess reserves, encouraging banks to increase lending and deposit expansion, thereby increasing the money supply.*

In practice the Fed does not change reserve requirements very often. This is so largely because reserve requirement changes of even a half of a point (from 15 percent to 15.5 percent, for example) can require quite an abrupt adjustment throughout the banking system.

### Setting the Discount Rate

In the previous chapter we noted that just as depository institutions make loans to the public, Federal Reserve banks make loans to depository institutions. *The interest rate that the Fed charges banks who borrow reserves from the Federal Reserve banks is called the* **discount rate**. As a figure of speech, it is often said that a bank borrows at the **discount window** when it borrows reserves from its Federal Reserve bank.

The Federal Reserve bank lends the bank reserves by increasing (crediting) the bank's reserve deposit with the Federal Reserve bank by the amount of the loan. When banks borrow from the Fed, these additional reserves enable them to make more loans and create more deposits. Therefore, borrowing at the discount window allows more deposit expansion and money creation to take place throughout the banking system than would otherwise be possible.

Banks naturally find it attractive to borrow from the discount window whenever the interest rates they can earn from making loans to businesses and consumers or by purchasing securities are greater than the discount rate. And the greater the difference, the greater the inducements for banks to borrow. On the other hand, when the discount rate is higher than these interest rates, banks are discouraged from borrowing at the discount window. It follows that *another possible way for the Fed to affect the amount of reserves in the banking system is by its setting of the discount rate. If the Fed raises the discount rate, bank borrowing is reduced and the amount of reserves in the banking system falls. This tends to cause deposit contraction and a reduction in the size of the money supply. If the Fed lowers the discount rate, bank borrowing rises, causing an increase in reserves and deposit expan-*

*sion and hence an increase in the money supply.*

## Minor Tools of Monetary Policy

In addition to the three major tools of monetary policy we have discussed, the Fed also has the power to regulate lending for stock market purchases and to regulate certain kinds of credit during emergencies, such as wartime.

### Stock Market Credit and Margin Requirements

The Fed has the authority to set margin requirements on stock market purchases. The **margin requirement** is the minimum percentage of a stock purchase that must be paid for with the purchaser's own funds. For example, if the margin requirement is 70 percent, a minimum of 70 percent of the price of the stock must be paid for with the purchaser's own money, while the remainder may be financed with borrowed funds. Congress originally gave the Fed the power to set the margin requirement so that the Fed would be able to control the amount of stock speculation financed with borrowed funds. When the Fed (specifically, the Board of Governors) feels that stock market speculation is increasing, it can put a damper on such activity by increasing the margin requirement. This is intended to prevent the development of conditions that might lead to a rapid fall in stock prices.

### Credit Regulation During Wartime

During wartime Congress often has given the Fed the authority to regulate the availability of credit for financing various kinds of consumer and business spending that threatens to direct resources and productive activity away from the war effort. The Fed does this by establishing stringent minimum downpayment requirements and fairly short repayment periods for the financing of such purchases.

---

### CHECKPOINT 13-3
It has been argued by a number of economists that the discount window and the setting of the discount rate is no longer a very useful tool for monetary policy. They claim, in fact, that it really reduces the Fed's control over the money supply. Why do you think this might be true? On the other hand, some economists argue that the existence of the discount window provides the banking system some protection against an unnecessarily restrictive monetary policy. How do you think the argument supporting this point of view might go?

---

## MONEY DEMAND AND SUPPLY AND THE INTEREST RATE

The demand for money interacts with the supply of money to determine the rate of interest in what is often referred to as the *money market*. We have seen how the Federal Reserve System regulates the supply of money. Now let's examine the determinants of the demand for money. We will then put these pieces—demand and supply—together and examine the nature of equilibrium in the money market.

### Transactions and Precautionary Demands for Money

Part of the demand for money stems from the service it provides as a medium of exchange. In short, money is needed to transact the purchase and sale of goods and services. This need is referred to as the **transactions demand** for money. What determines the size of this demand? The amount of transactions taking place in the economy, of course. One rough measure of the amount of such transactions is the level of total income, as represented by the level of money GNP for example. *When total income rises, the transac-*

*tions demand for money increases, and when total income declines, the transactions demand decreases.*

Money is also needed for precautionary purposes. Hence, there is a **precautionary demand** for money. Unforeseen events or emergencies often require immediate expenditures. Money is the most liquid asset and, therefore, ideally suited to meet such contingencies. For this reason most of us carry a little more currency with us than is needed to cover anticipated transactions for such things as lunch and bus fare. Some people even keep sizeable amounts of currency in safes and safe-deposit boxes just in case some of their other assets cannot be readily liquidated. It is probably generally true that the precautionary demand for money in the economy varies with the level of total income, as does the transactions demand.

## Money Demand and the Interest Rate

The level of total income is an important determinant of money demand primarily because of its relationship to the transactions and precautionary motives for holding money. The interest rate is also regarded as an important influence on the demand for money.

### The Interest Rate: An Opportunity Cost

It has been said that "money is barren." Money in the form of currency is barren because it does not earn interest. Money in the form of demand deposits and other checkable accounts is barren to the extent that there are regulations limiting the maximum interest rate that depository institutions are allowed to pay on such accounts. Those who hold them must forgo the opportunity to earn the higher rates of return available on other assets, such as stocks and bonds. Therefore the opportunity cost of holding money (whether for transactions, precautionary, or any other

purposes) is the forgone interest that could be earned on other assets.

In a simplified world where the only two assets are barren money and interest-earning bonds the interest rate may be thought of as the price of holding money. As with any good or service, people will demand less money when its price is high than when it is low, all other things remaining the same. That is, the higher the interest rate, the lower the quantity of money demanded; and the lower the interest rate, the greater the quantity demanded. This inverse relationship between the demand for money and the interest rate is illustrated by the demand curve for money $L$ shown in Figure 13–1. (The letter $L$ is used to designate the demand curve for money simply as a reminder that money is the most liquid asset—the demand for money is the demand for liquidity.)

### The Interest Rate and Bonds

The interest rate is an important determinant of the demand for money because people also desire to hold money for speculative purposes (in addition to the desire to hold money for transactions and precautionary purposes). However, before considering the speculative demand for money, it is necessary to understand why interest rates and bond prices always move in opposite directions.

A bond is a promissory certificate issued by borrowers (typically businesses and governments) in exchange for funds provided to them by lenders. The bond represents the borrower's promise to pay back to the lender (the bondholder) the amount of money borrowed (the principal) at the end of a certain number of years (the maturity date). The bond also promises that the borrower will make payments (coupon payments) of a set number of dollars to the lender at regular intervals (annually, for example). The coupon payments represent the rate of return, or the interest rate, that induces the lender to loan money to the borrower.

Consider a bond that promises to make

**FIGURE 13-1   The Demand for Money Is Inversely Related to the Interest Rate**

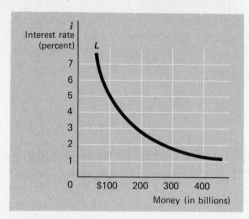

The demand curve for money slopes downward from left to right for two reasons.

First, the interest rate represents the opportunity cost of holding money. Therefore, a smaller quantity of money is demanded at a high than at a low interest rate.

Second, the nature of the speculative demand for money suggests that people will desire to hold more money and fewer bonds when the interest rate is below what is considered its normal level. This is so because bond prices are then above their normal levels, and it is thought likely that they will once again decline to those levels, resulting in losses to bondholders. On the other hand, if the interest rate is above its normal level, bond prices are below their normal levels. People will desire to hold less money and more bonds because it will be thought likely that bond prices will rise to their normal levels and bondholders will realize gains. In sum, the speculative demand for money also suggests that a smaller quantity of money is demanded at a high than at a low interest rate.

coupon payments of $10 per year, year in and year out, forever. (Such bonds, called consols, are issued by the British government, for example.) If you purchased (invested in) such a bond for $100, you would

earn a 10 percent rate of interest—the $10 coupon payment divided by the $100 purchase price, expressed as a percentage. If you paid $200 for the bond, you would earn a 5 percent rate of interest—$10 divided by $200, expressed as a percentage. Obviously, the higher the price you pay for the bond, the lower the interest rate you receive. Conversely, the lower the price paid, the higher the interest rate. Calculation of the interest rate earned on a bond with a set maturity date is more complicated, but the link between the interest rate realized on the bond and the price of the bond is the same. *The price of a bond and its interest rate always move in opposite directions.*

### The Speculative Demand for Money

Suppose people believe that there is some average, or "normal," level for the interest rate, a level determined by their observation of the interest rate in the past. Because bond prices and the interest rate are linked, this means there is also some normal level of bond prices.

If the interest rate is currently above what people consider to be its normal level, bond prices will be below their normal level. People will tend to believe that the interest rate is likely to fall and, therefore, that bond prices will rise. People will therefore prefer to hold more bonds and less money because of the gains they will realize if the likely rise in bond prices occurs. On the other hand, if the interest rate is currently below its normal level, bond prices will be above their normal level. People will tend to believe that the interest rate is likely to rise and that bond prices are likely to fall. They will want to hold more money and fewer bonds because of the losses on bonds that would result if the likely fall in bond prices occurs. Thus, the **speculative demand** for money provides another reason why less money is demanded at a high than at a low interest rate.

*The demand curve for money in Figure 13–1 slopes downward left to right not only because of the opportunity cost of holding money, represented by the interest rate, but also because of the speculative demand for money arising from the fact that interest rates and bond prices fluctuate.*

## Changes in the Demand for Money

A change in the quantity of money demanded is represented by movement along the money demand curve of Figure 13-1. This movement occurs when the interest rate changes, all other things remaining the same. A change in the demand for money is represented by a shift in the position of the money demand curve. Such a change occurs when one or more of the other things changes. (Recall the distinction made in Chapter 4 between a change in quantity demanded and a change in demand.)

Among the other things that can change, the economy's total money income (or money GNP) is a particularly important determinant of the transactions demand for money. It also influences the demand for money for precautionary purposes. (Recall the distinction between money GNP and real GNP made in Chapter 5. Hereafter, the term total income is always taken to mean total money income or money GNP.) If total income increases, both the transactions and the precautionary demand for money rise. A decline in total income has the opposite effect. Therefore, a rise in total income will increase the demand for money and cause the demand curve for money to shift rightward, such as from $L_0$ to $L_1$ in Figure 13-2. A decline in total income would cause a leftward shift, such as from $L_1$ to $L_0$.

## The Money Supply

Through its control over bank reserves and the setting of reserve requirements, we have seen how the Fed affects the deposit expansion or contraction process and the creation or destruction of money. In short, we have seen how the Fed controls the economy's money supply.

At any given time, the supply or stock of

**FIGURE 13-2    Changes in the Demand for Money: Shifts in the Money Demand Curve**

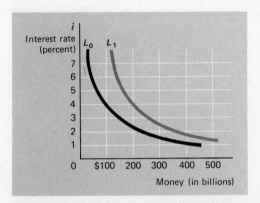

Changes in the demand for money are represented by shifts in the money demand curve, such as from $L_0$ to $L_1$. Shifts are caused by changes in one or more of the other things assumed constant when we move along a demand curve. Among these other things, the economy's total income is particularly important because when total income rises, it increases the transactions demand and the precautionary demand for money; when total income declines, it has the opposite effect. Therefore, an increase in total income shifts the demand curve for money rightward, such as from $L_0$ to $L_1$. A decline in total income would shift it leftward, such as from $L_1$ to $L_0$.

Changes in the quantity of money demanded are represented by movement along a fixed money demand curve. Such movement occurs when the interest rate changes, all other things remaining the same.

money available to satisfy the demand for money is fixed. The fixed supply of money may be represented by a vertical supply curve such as $M_0$ in Figure 13-3. (The vertical supply curve means that the money supply is unresponsive to the interest rate.) $M_0$ represents a stock of money equal to $200 billion. If the Fed were to increase the money supply by $100 billion, the money

**FIGURE 13-3  The Money Supply Curve**

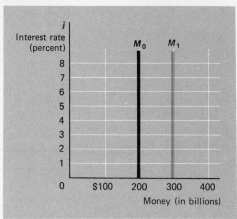

The fixed supply or stock of money available to satisfy demand may be represented by a vertical supply curve. (The fact that the supply curve is vertical means that the money supply is unresponsive to the interest rate.)

For example, $M_0$ represents a stock of money equal to $200 billion. If the Fed were to increase the money supply by $100 billion, the money supply curve would be shifted rightward from $M_0$ to $M_1$. A decrease in the money supply would be represented by a leftward shift in the money supply curve, such as from $M_1$ to $M_0$.

supply curve would be shifted rightward from $M_0$ to $M_1$, as shown in Figure 13-3. A decrease in the money supply would be represented by a leftward shift in the money supply curve.

## The Money Market: The Interaction of Supply and Demand

Now we are ready to bring money demand and money supply together to form the money market. At the outset we should remind ourselves that the supply of money and the demand for money are measured as stocks, not flows.

## Equilibrium and Disequilibrium

Suppose that money demand and supply are represented by the demand curve $L$ and supply curve $M$ shown in Figure 13-4. The supply or stock of money made available by the Federal Reserve System amounts to $300 billion. Given the demand curve $L$, the quantity of money demanded will equal $300 billion only if the interest rate equals 6 percent, corresponding to the intersection of $L$ and $M$ at point $e$. Hence, 6 percent is the equilibrium level of the interest rate. If the interest rate were higher or lower than this, the money market would be in disequilibrium, and market forces would move the interest rate back to the 6 percent equilibrium level.

*Interest Rate Below the Equilibrium Level.* For example, if the interest rate were 4 percent, the quantity of money demanded would equal $500 billion, represented by point $d$ on the demand curve. At this interest rate, there would be an excess demand for money of $200 billion (equal to the $500 billion demanded minus the $300 billion supplied). This excess demand is represented by the distance between $c$ and $d$ in Figure 13-4. In their attempts to obtain more money people try to convert other assets, such as bonds, into money by selling them. While each individual thinks he or she will be able to get more money in this way, obviously society as a whole cannot increase the amount of money it has. A seller of securities gains the money balances that the buyer of the securities loses, and so the total money supply is unaltered. The total amount of money available is fixed at $300 billion, and every bit of this is always held by somebody.

Consequently, as people try to sell bonds for money, they only succeed in pushing bond prices down. This means that the interest rate will rise. When the interest rate rises, the quantity of money demanded declines (as represented by the movement up along the demand curve away from point $d$), and the amount by which money demand exceeds money supply gets smaller. When will this

**FIGURE 13-4  The Money Market: Equilibrium and Disequilibrium**

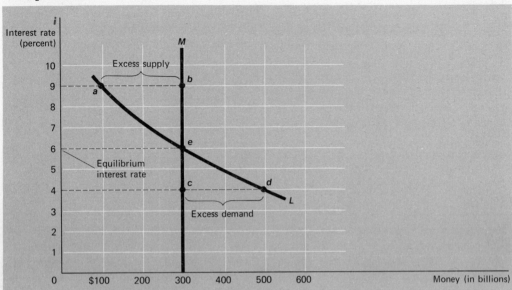

Money market equilibrium occurs at that interest rate at which the money demand curve *L* intersects the money supply curve *M* at point *e*, corresponding to a 6 percent interest rate in this case.

At interest rates below the equilibrium level, there is an excess demand for money. For example, at a 4 percent interest rate the excess demand for money amounts to $200 billion, which is represented by the distance between *c* and *d*. In their attempts to get more money people will try to sell bonds, pushing bond prices down and the interest rate up until it reaches the 6 percent equilibrium level.

At interest rates above the equilibrium level, there is an excess supply of money. For example, at a 9 percent interest rate the excess supply of money amounts to $200 billion, which is represented by the distance between *a* and *b*. In their attempts to reduce their holdings of money people will try to buy bonds, pushing bond prices up and the interest rate down until it reaches 6 percent, the equilibrium level.

process stop? When bond prices have fallen far enough to raise the interest rate level to 6 percent. At this point people will demand, or be satisfied to hold, just that quantity of money that is supplied (as represented by the intersection at point *e* of the money demand curve *L* and the money supply curve *M*).

*Interest Rate Above the Equilibrium Level.* Alternatively, what if the interest rate is above the equilibrium level of 6 percent? Suppose it is 9 percent. At this level, the quantity of money demanded equals $100 billion (represented by point *a* in Figure 13-4). There is an excess supply of money amounting to $200 billion (equal to the $300 billion supplied minus the $100 billion demanded), represented by the distance between points *a* and *b*. Of course, every bit of the $300 billion of money supplied would be held by people. But at an interest rate of 9 percent, this is more than people desire to hold. Consequently, people will try to convert their excess money holdings into other assets, such as bonds. The attempts to buy bonds will cause bond prices to rise and the interest rate to fall. As the interest rate falls, the quantity of money demanded increases (represented by the movement down along the demand curve away from point *a*), and the excess supply of money gets smaller. Finally, when bond prices have risen far enough to lower the interest rate level to 6 percent, the money market will be in equilibrium. At a 6 percent interest rate, the $300 billion money supply is just the amount people desire to hold.

## Summary: Money Demand and Supply and the Interest Rate

In sum, *there are three basic sources of money demand: the transactions demand, the precautionary demand, and the speculative demand. These three combined make up the demand for money as represented by the demand curve for money. The money supply is determined by the Federal Reserve System. The demand for money and the supply of money jointly determine the equilibrium rate of interest in the money market.*

### CHECKPOINT 13-4
**Which of the following would have the greatest effect on the interest rate: (1) an increase in money demand accompanied by an increase in money supply, (2) an increase in money demand alone, and (3) an increase in money demand accompanied by a decrease in money supply? Illustrate each of these cases—(1), (2), and (3)—graphically. How do you think the demand curve for money would be affected if people were to revise upward their notions of the normal level of the interest rate? How do you think the demand curve for money would be affected if people became more uncertain about their jobs, say, as the result of the onset of a recession? Why?**

## SUMMARY

**1.** The composition of the typical bank's portfolio of earning assets reflects a compromise between two often conflicting objectives: (a) the maintenance of liquidity and security and (b) the realization of profit.

**2.** A commercial bank generally restricts its holdings of earning assets to short-term loans, bonds, and securities because of their relatively high degree of liquidity and security. This restriction is dictated by the large amount of commercial bank deposit liabilities that are subject to withdrawal on demand.

**3.** In general, the amount of demand deposits, or money, that a single commercial bank can create through lending cannot exceed the amount of its excess reserves. This is so because borrowers will most likely write checks against these newly created deposits that the check recipients will deposit in other banks.

**4.** By contrast, when each individual bank in the banking system lends out its excess reserves, the banking system as a whole can create an amount of demand deposits, or money, that is a multiple of the total amount of excess reserves in the system. While individual banks in the banking system can lose reserves and deposits to other banks in the system, the system as a whole cannot.

**5.** The multiple for the banking system as a whole is the reciprocal of the required reserve ratio. This multiple is called the deposit multiplier. It also applies to deposit contraction, which is just the reverse of the deposit expansion process.

**6.** The three major tools used by the Fed to conduct monetary policy are (a) open market operations, (b) the setting of reverse requirements for commercial banks and other depository institutions, and (c) the setting of the level of the discount rate.

**7.** Open market operations refer to the Fed's buying and selling of government securities in the open market. When the Fed buys government securities, it puts reserves into the banking system, causing an expansion of demand deposits and other checkable deposits and hence an increase in the economy's money supply. When the Fed sells government bonds, it takes reserves out of the banking system, causing a contraction of demand deposits and other checkable deposits and hence a decrease in the economy's money supply.

**8.** An increase in the required reserve ratio will force a deposit contraction, or money supply reduction. The extent of reduction will depend on the amount of excess reserves in the banking system. A decrease in the required reserve ratio increases the amount of excess reserves, encouraging banks to increase lending and deposit expansion, thereby increasing the money supply.

**9.** When the Fed raises the discount rate, bank borrowing is discouraged. The amount of reserves in the banking system falls, and this tends to cause deposit contraction and a reduction in the size of money supply. If the Fed lowers the discount rate, bank borrowing tends to rise, resulting in an increase in reserves and deposit expansion and an increase in the money supply.

**10.** Minor tools that the Fed can use to affect lending in the economy include (a) the setting of margin requirements on the purchase of stocks, (b) the use of Regulation Q to set interest rate ceilings on time deposits at commercial banks, and (c) the authority granted the Fed by Congress during wartime to regulate the lending for various kinds of consumer and business spending.

**11.** There are three basic components of the demand for money: the transactions demand, the precautionary demand, and the speculative demand. The transactions and precautionary demands for money vary directly with the level of total income. The speculative demand for money varies inversely (negatively) with the level of the interest rate.

**12.** Both because of the speculative demand for money and the fact that the interest rate is the opportunity cost of holding money, the money demand curve slopes downward. Because of the transactions and precautionary demands for money, the money demand curve is shifted rightward by an increase in total money income and leftward by a decrease.

**13.** The money supply curve is vertical, representing the assumption that the Federal Reserve System controls the money supply. The money supply and demand curves jointly determine the equilibrium interest rate in the money market. An increase in the money supply lowers the equilibrium interest rate, a decrease raises it.

## KEY TERMS AND CONCEPTS

deposit multiplier
discount rate
discount window
equity
excess reserves
margin requirement
net worth
open market operations
precautionary demand
required reserve ratio
required reserves
reserves
speculative demand
transactions demand

## QUESTIONS AND PROBLEMS

**1.** Consider the consolidated bank balance sheet of Table 13–5 and suppose that the required reserve ratio for time, savings, and demand deposits is 10 percent (.10). Does the banking system have excess reserves, and if so, how much? What is the amount of new loans and demand deposits that could be created? Alternatively, what is the amount of government securities that could be purchased?

2. Consider the balance sheet of the following individual bank, Bank X, in a banking system of many banks:

| BANK X | | |
|---|---|---|
| Assets | Liabilities and Equity | |
| Reserves $ 220,000 | Demand deposits | $ 950,000 |
| Loans, securities, and other assets  780,000 | Equity | 50,000 |
| Total assets $1,000,000 = | Total liabilities and equity | $1,000,000 |

Assume the required reserve ratio is 20 percent (.20).

a. How much excess reserves does Bank X have?

b. Suppose Bank X creates an amount of demand deposits through lending that equals the amount of its excess reserves multiplied by the deposit multiplier. What will be the amount of the new loans it has created? What will Bank X's balance sheet look like before any checks have been written against the new deposits?

c. Given your answer to part b, suppose now that borrowers write checks against the newly created demand deposits and that the recipients of these checks deposit them in other banks. What will happen to the level of reserves in Bank X? What now will be the level of excess reserves in Bank X?

d. Given your answers to part c, describe what Bank X must do to get its house in order. Once it has done so, how will its balance sheet look?

e. What does this example tell us about the difference between an individual bank and the banking system as a whole?

f. Starting again with the answer to part a, if you were running Bank X, describe what you would do at this point. How would Bank X's balance sheet now look after your management strategy had been carried out?

3. It is sometimes said that there is a "trade-off" between bank profits on the one hand and liquidity and security on the other. Describe what is meant by this and why it is so. How does the trade-off affect the size of the deposit multiplier?

4. Suppose Bank A's balance sheet looks as follows and that the required reserve ratio is 15 percent (.15):

| BANK A | | |
|---|---|---|
| Assets | Liabilities and Equity | |
| Reserves $ 200,000 | Demand deposits | $ 900,000 |
| Loans, securities, and other assets  800,000 | Equity | 100,000 |
| Total assets $1,000,000 = | Total liabilities and equity | $1,000,000 |

a. What would be the maximum amount of cash that depositors could withdraw before Bank A would be forced to do something about the amount of loans, securities, and other assets it holds?

b. Suppose Bank A decides to make loans by creating demand deposits. Assume that Bank A and all other banks in the banking system expect that 5 percent of any loans they make will be withdrawn immediately in the form of cash. What will be the maximum amount of deposit expansion, or money creation, that will take place throughout the banking system as a whole?

c. Show the deposit expansion process of part b in a table like Table 13–8.

**5.** What is the effect on the size of the actual deposit multiplier of increases and decreases in the public's desire to hold currency? If the public's desire to hold currency rises during recessions and falls during the expansionary phase of the business cycle, over the course of the business cycle how does this affect the Fed's ability to change the money supply per dollar of any open market purchase or sale?

**6.** Of the three major tools of monetary policy, which one do you think is probably the least effective for controlling the amount of reserves in the banking system? Why?

**7.** It has been said that the Fed can be much more effective when it wants to contract the money supply than when it wants to expand the supply. Why might this be so? Explain in terms of each of the three major tools of monetary policy.

**8.** What role do Federal Reserve bank liabilities to commercial banks play in the way that open market operations affect the economy's money supply?

**9.** How can it be that when there is an excess supply of money, people hold more than they want, yet when equilibrium is restored, they are content to hold the same amount? Where did the excess go? If there is an excess demand for money, what must be true of people's desired holdings of bonds?

**10.** How would the money demand curve change if people's demand for money became more sensitive to changes in the interest rate? Show how this would affect the money demand curve *L* passing through point *e* in Figure 13–4. Would a money supply increase now have a larger or smaller effect on the equilibrium level of the interest rate? If the money demand curve shifts rightward by an amount equal to $200 billion from point *e*, would the rise in the interest rate be greater or less than would have been the case before the demand for money became more sensitive to changes in the interest rate?

# 14

# The Role of Money in Income Determination

**AFTER READING THIS CHAPTER, YOU WILL BE ABLE TO:**

1. Explain why the interest rate is a determinant of the level of investment spending.

2. Describe and explain the Keynesian view of how money affects aggregate demand.

3. Describe and explain the equation of exchange and the monetarist view of how money affects economic activity.

4. Compare and contrast the monetarist and Keynesian views on the stability of velocity in the equation of exchange.

5. Describe the evidence on the behavior of velocity in the United States.

In the last chapter we examined how the Fed is able to change the level of bank reserves and thereby cause the economy's money supply to expand or contract. But how and why do changes in the economy's money supply affect the general level of economic activity? In this chapter we will focus on this question.

We should note at the outset that economists are not in complete agreement on just how and to what extent money affects the economy. In this chapter we will focus first on the Keynesian view by introducing money into the Keynesian analysis of income determination we developed in Chapters 8 and 9. Then we will examine the monetarist point of view and compare it with the Keynesian interpretation.

## ROLE OF THE MONEY MARKET IN INCOME DETERMINATION: KEYNESIAN VIEW

We will now combine our understanding of the workings of the money market, developed in the previous chapter, with the Keynesian analysis of income determination that we developed in Chapters 8 and 9. We will then be able to examine the role of money in the determination of total income, output, employment, and the price level from the Keynesian viewpoint.

Our first step in putting the pieces together is to show the relationship between the money market, the interest rate, and the level of investment expenditures in the economy. We will then be able to examine the relationship between the money market and the economy's aggregate demand for goods and services and, hence, the relationship between the money supply provided by the Fed and total income, output, employment and the price level.

### Money, Interest, and Investment

What is the relationship between the money market and investment expenditures? To an-swer this we first recall the relationship between the interest rate and investment expenditures discussed in Chapter 8. We will then see how the interest rate serves to link the money market and the level of investment expenditures.

### *Investment and the Interest Rate*

In Chapter 8 we argued that the interest rate is the cost to a firm of funds invested in capital goods. If such funds are borrowed from outside the firm, the cost of borrowing is the interest rate that must be paid to lenders. If the funds are generated internally, the cost is the forgone interest the firm could have earned by lending the funds to someone else.

*Interest Rate Versus Expected Rate of Return.* When a firm considers whether or not to purchase or invest in a capital good, it must compare its expected rate of return on the capital good with the interest rate. If the firm is going to use its own funds, the two relevant choices are either to lend the funds to some other party or to invest them in the capital good. If the expected rate of return is higher than the interest rate, the firm can earn more by investing internally generated funds in the capital good than by lending them out. The firm will earn the difference between the expected rate of return on the capital good and the interest rate. Similarly, if the firm borrows outside funds to invest in the capital good, it will earn exactly the same difference—the difference between the expected rate of return on the capital good and the interest rate that must be paid on the borrowed funds. However, if the expected rate of return on the capital good is less than the interest rate, it will not pay to invest in the capital good.

*Expected Rate of Return on a Capital Good.* What is the expected rate of return? *The expected rate of return is the amount of money a firm expects to earn per year on funds invested in a capital good expressed as a percent of the funds invested.*

What determines the expected rate of return on a capital good? Profit, or the anticipation of profit—as noted in Chapter 8. For example, suppose that the annual revenue anticipated from the sale of goods and services produced with the aid of a capital good amounts to $500. Suppose that the anticipated annual costs of production, *excluding* the interest rate cost of the funds invested in the capital good, equals $400. The difference, in this case $100, is the amount of money the firm expects to earn per year on the funds invested in the capital good. If the price of the capital good is $1,000, the expected rate of return on the $1,000 investment in the capital good is 10 percent—$100 ÷ $1,000, expressed as a percentage.

If the interest rate is 9 percent, the firm could borrow the $1,000 at a cost of $90 per year. Alternatively, $1,000 of internal funds could earn $90 per year if lent out at 9 percent. Either way the firm will come out ahead $10 per year if it invests in the capital good. The capital good is therefore a profitable investment, and the firm should buy it. If on the other hand the interest rate is 11 percent, the same calculations show that the firm will lose $10 per year if it invests $1,000 in the capital good. The good will not be a profitable investment, and the firm should not buy it. In sum, *a firm will invest in a capital good if its expected rate of return is higher than the interest rate. It will not invest if the expected rate of return is less than the interest rate.*

*Inverse Relationship Between Interest Rate and Investment Spending.* At any given time a typical firm has a number of investment projects it could undertake—build a new plant, buy a new fleet of trucks, build a new loading dock, and so on. The firm forms an expectation of what the rate of return would be for each of these projects. The lower the interest rate, the larger is the number of these projects having expected rates of return higher than the interest rate. Hence, the lower the interest rate, the greater the amount of investment expenditure by the firm. Of course, the higher the interest rate, the smaller the number of projects with ex-

pected rates of return above the interest rate—therefore, the smaller the amount of investment expenditure by the firm.

If we consider all the firms in the economy, the total amount of investment spending will increase as the interest rate decreases. This inverse, or negative, relationship between the interest rate and investment is illustrated by the downward-sloping investment demand curve $I_d$ in Figure 14-1. *The investment demand curve shows the total dollar amount of investment projects, or capital goods formation, that the economy's firms will demand or desire to do at each interest rate.* The investment demand curve is just another way of representing the relationship between the interest rate and investment spending that we discussed in Chapter 8 (Figure 8-8).

### The Money Market and the Level of Investment

Now we can see how the money market and the level of investment spending in the economy are related. The connecting link between them is the interest rate. This is illustrated in Figure 14-2, where the money market is shown in part a and the investment demand curve is shown in part b.

Suppose initially that the money supply provided by the Federal Reserve System amounts to roughly $215 billion, represented by the money supply curve $M_0$ in part a. Given the money demand curve $L$, the equilibrium interest rate in the money market is 7 percent, determined by the intersection of $M_0$ and $L$ at point $a$. The number of investment projects with expected rates of return greater than 7 percent is such that there will be $300 billion of investment spending when the interest rate is at that level, corresponding to point $a'$ on the investment demand curve $I_d$ in part b.

Suppose the Fed increases the money supply (by open market purchases, by lowering reserve requirements, by lowering the discount rate, or some combination of these) from $215 billion to $300 billion. This in-

**FIGURE 14-1 The Investment Demand Curve: Investment Spending Varies Inversely with the Interest Rate**

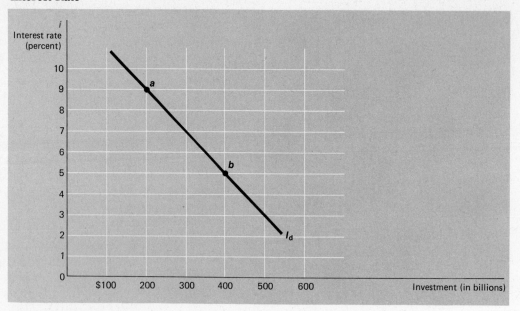

The investment demand curve $I_d$ is downward sloping, reflecting the inverse, or negative, relationship between the level of the interest rate and the amount of investment expenditure in the economy. For instance, if the interest rate were 9 percent, there would be $200 billion of investment spending, corresponding to point *a* on the investment demand curve $I_d$. At a lower interest rate, such as 5 percent, the amount of investment spending would be larger, equal to $400 billion, corresponding to point *b*.

The reason for the inverse relationship between the interest rate and investment is that the lower the interest rate, the larger the number of investment projects that have an expected rate of return greater than the interest rate. The economy's firms will invest in all those projects that are profitable, as represented by the fact that their expected rates of return are higher than the interest rate.

crease is represented by the rightward shift in the money supply curve from $M_0$ to $M_1$ in part a. At the original 7 percent interest rate, there is now an excess supply of money. As people attempt to convert this excess into other assets such as bonds, bond prices rise and the interest rate falls to 6 percent. This is the new equilibrium interest rate represented by the intersection of $M_1$ and $L$ at point *b*. The drop in the interest rate from 7 to 6 percent increases the amount of investment spending in the economy by $50 billion to $350 billion, corresponding to point *b'* on the investment demand curve $I_d$. This happens because investment projects with expected rates of return between 6 and 7 percent now become profitable. Therefore, they are undertaken in addition to all those having expected rates of return greater than 7 percent.

In sum, *the Fed can influence the amount of investment spending in the economy through its control over the money supply.* Increases in the money supply lower the interest rate and cause investment spending to increase. De-

**FIGURE 14-2**  **The Money Market and Investment Spending Are Linked by the Interest Rate**

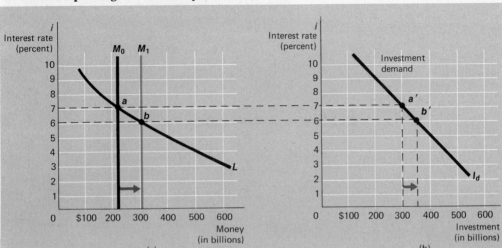

The intersection of the money demand and money supply curves in part a determines the equilibrium level of the interest rate. Given the investment demand curve $I_d$, this interest rate determines the amount of investment spending in part b.

Suppose the money supply provided by the Federal Reserve System amounts to $215 billion, represented by the money supply curve $M_0$ in part a. The equilibrium interest rate is then 7 percent, determined by the intersection of the money demand curve $L$ and the money supply curve $M_0$ at point a. The 7 percent interest rate will give rise to $300 billion of investment spending, corresponding to point a' on the investment demand curve $I_d$ in part b.

Suppose the Fed increases the money supply from $215 billion to $300 billion, represented by the rightward shift in the money supply curve from $M_0$ to $M_1$ in part a. The interest rate will then fall to a new equilibrium level of 6 percent, determined by the intersection of the money demand curve $L$ and the money supply curve $M_1$ at point b. This drop in the interest rate will cause an increase in investment spending to $350 billion, corresponding to point b' on the investment demand curve $I_d$ in part b.

creases in the money supply raise the interest rate and cause investment spending to decrease.

## Money, Real GNP, and the Price Level

We know from our discussion in Chapters 8 and 9 that investment spending is an important part of total spending in the economy. We saw that it plays a crucial role in determining the level of the total expenditure

schedule, which in turn determines the equilibrium level of real GNP, as in part a of Figure 11-2. We are now in a position to introduce the money market into that analysis.

### The Interconnecting Links Between the Money Market, Investment, and Real GNP

Consider the upper half of Figure 14-3. Suppose initially that the money supply curve $M_0$ (representing a money supply of $300

**FIGURE 14-3 Money Supply Change:
Partial Versus General Equilibrium Analysis**

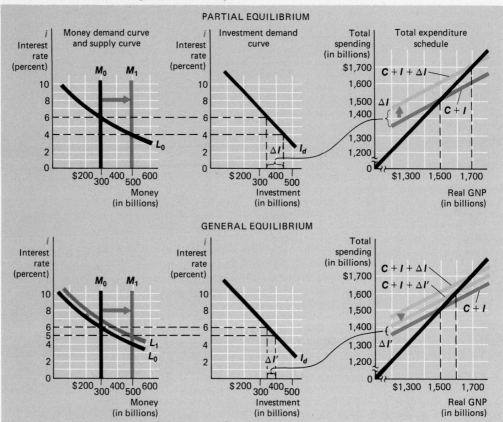

The top half of the figure shows the partial equilibrium analysis of the effects of a $200 billion increase in the money supply. The interest rate falls from 6 percent to 4 percent, causing a rise in investment Δ*I* of $100 billion, which in turn causes the total expenditure schedule to shift upward from *C* + *I* to *C* + *I* + Δ*I*. This upward shift in turn causes real GNP to rise from $1,500 billion to $1,700 billion. This analysis is partial because it doesn't allow for the effect of the rise in real GNP on money demand and hence on the interest rate.

The bottom half of the figure shows the general equilibrium analysis of the effects of the same $200 billion money supply increase. Now the interest rate falls a smaller amount, from 6 percent to 5 percent, because of allowance for the fact that the rise in real GNP causes the money demand curve to shift rightward from *L*₀ to *L*₁. Because of this, the rise in investment Δ*I*′ of $50 billion is smaller. Hence, the total expenditure schedule shifts upward a smaller amount, from *C* + *I* to *C* + *I* + Δ*I*′, and therefore the rise in real GNP is less, from $1,500 billion to $1,600 billion.

billion) and money demand curve $L_0$ (corresponding to a total income of $1,500 billion) determine a 6 percent interest rate. Given the position of the investment demand curve, this interest rate in turn gives rise to a level of investment of $350 billion. This amount of investment spending determines the position of the total expenditure schedule $C + I$, which in turn determines the equilibrium level of real GNP of $1,500 billion. This level of real GNP determines the position of the money demand curve $L_0$ (because the transactions and precautionary demand for money are influenced by the level of real GNP), which together with $M_0$ determines the 6 percent interest rate.

*Partial Equilibrium Analysis.* Now suppose the Fed increases the money supply by $200 billion (from $300 billion to $500 billion), represented by the rightward shift in the money supply curve from $M_0$ to $M_1$, the upper half of Figure 14–3. At the initial interest rate of 6 percent, there would now be an excess supply of money. This excess causes the interest rate to fall from 6 percent to 4 percent, determined by the intersection of $M_1$ and $L_0$. The decline in the interest rate from 6 percent to 4 percent means that there would be an increase in the number of investment projects having expected rates of return greater than the interest rate. The resulting increase in investment spending $\Delta I$ (change in $I$) would amount to $100 billion (a rise from $350 billion to $450 billion). This increase would cause the total expenditure schedule to rise from $C + I$ to $C + I + \Delta I$ and real GNP to increase from $1,500 billion to $1,700 billion.

This is only a partial equilibrium analysis, however. *In **partial equilibrium analysis** we focus on a change in one market and its consequences for that market, and possibly a few others. All other markets are assumed to be unchanged. In **general equilibrium analysis** we consider the adjustments that a change in one market may cause in each and every other market.*

Our analysis of the consequences of a money supply change in the upper half of Figure 14–3 is a partial equilibrium analysis because it does not take into account the effect the rise in real GNP will have on the money demand curve and hence on the interest rate. A general equilibrium analysis of the consequences of the $200 billion increase in the money supply from $M_0$ to $M_1$ must take account of this effect.

*General Equilibrium Analysis.* The general equilibrium analysis is shown in the lower half of Figure 14–3. As the interest rate falls and increased investment causes a rise in real GNP, the rise in real GNP causes the money demand curve to shift rightward at the same time. This shift in the money demand curve keeps the interest rate from falling as far as it does when the shift is ignored, as in the partial equilibrium analysis in the upper half of Figure 14–3. Consequently the rise in investment $\Delta I'$ is now less, amounting to only $50 billion. The resulting upward shift in the total expenditure schedule is now smaller—from $C + I$ to $C + I + \Delta I'$. The rise in real GNP is therefore smaller—from $1,500 billion to $1,600 billion. The position of the money demand curve at $L_1$ corresponds to (is determined by) the $1,600 billion real GNP level. In the general equilibrium analysis, the level of the interest rate falls to 5 percent, a higher level than the 4 percent of the partial equilibrium analysis.

In conclusion, our analysis indicates that *an increase in the money supply causes a decrease in the interest rate and an increase in the level of real GNP. A decrease in the money supply will have the opposite effect, causing an increase in the interest rate and a decrease in the level of real GNP.*

*Easy Money Versus Tight Money.* When the Federal Reserve increases the money supply, it is often said to be following an easy-money policy, or to be "easing credit." This manner of speaking reflects the fact that the fall in the interest rate makes it cheaper

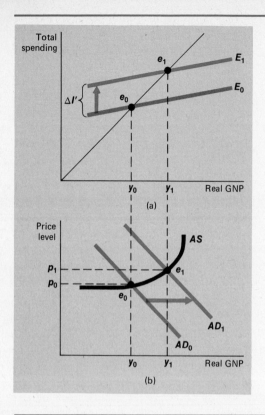

**FIGURE 14-4   Changes in the Money Supply Affect Real GNP and the Price Level**

An increase in the money supply increases investment spending by $\Delta I'$ thereby shifting the total expenditure schedule upward from $E_0$ to $E_1$, part a, and the aggregate demand curve rightward from $AD_0$ to $AD_1$, part b.

Real GNP increases from $y_0$ to $y_1$ and the price level rises from $p_0$ to $p_1$, part b, as the economy moves from its initial equilibrium position, corresponding to point $e_0$ in parts a and b, to its new equilibrium, corresponding to point $e_1$. The amount of change in the price level relative to that in real GNP depends on the state of the economy, as reflected in the slope of the $AS$ curve over the range where the shift in the $AD$ curve occurs.

to borrow, or to get credit. An easy-money policy stimulates the economy because it leads to a rise in real GNP. On the other hand, a tight-money policy, or a policy of "credit tightening," refers to the opposite situation—a reduction in the money supply leading to a rise in the interest rate and a decline in real GNP.

### The Link Between Money and the AD Curve

In Chapter 11, Figure 11-6, we saw how a shift in the total expenditure schedule due to an exogenous expenditure change will cause the aggregate demand curve *(AD)* to shift. Similarly, the shift in the total expenditure schedule caused by the money supply change shown in Figure 14-3 will also cause the *AD* curve to shift. This is illustrated in Figure

14-4. The increase in the money supply causes the increase in investment spending $\Delta I'$ which in turn shifts the total expenditure schedule upward from $E_0$ to $E_1$ in part a of Figure 14-4. This corresponds to the upward shift in the total expenditure schedule by the amount $\Delta I'$ in the general equilibrium in Figure 14-3. Corresponding to the upward shift in the total expenditure schedule, the *AD* curve in part b shifts rightward from $AD_0$ to $AD_1$. In sum:

*According to the Keynesian view, an increase in the money supply lowers the interest rate, thereby causing an increase in investment spending which shifts the total expenditure schedule upward and the AD curve rightward. A decrease in the money supply raises the interest rate which decreases investment spending, thereby shifting the total expenditure schedule downward and the AD curve leftward.*

### The Link Between Money and the Price Level

Thus far we have shown that an increase in the money supply shifts the $AD$ curve rightward so that there is an increase in the quantity of total output (real GNP) demanded *at any given price level*. But what actually happens to the price level? We are now on familiar ground which we already explored in Chapter 11. There we saw that to determine the price level it was necessary to bring the aggregate supply curve *(AS)* into the picture.

When we take account of the interaction of the $AS$ curve with the $AD$ curve in part b of Figure 14-4 we see that the price level was initially $p_0$, determined by the intersection of $AD_0$ and $AS$ at point $e_0$. The increase in the money supply that shifts the $AD$ curve rightward from $AD_0$ to $AD_1$ causes the price level to rise to $p_1$, corresponding to the intersection of $AD_1$ and $AS$ at point $e_1$.

Recall our discussion of general equilibrium, the lower half of Figure 14-3. There the money demand curve was shifted rightward from $L_0$ to $L_1$ by the increase in real GNP. Recall however from the previous chapter (Figure 13-2) that a change in total income, or money GNP, causes the money demand curve to shift. Money GNP can be thought of as equal to the product of the price level and total output (in a simple widget economy the price per widget times number of widgets), where real GNP is a measure of total output. Therefore a shift in the money demand curve caused by a change in money GNP can be due to a change in either real GNP or the price level, or both. Since the rightward shift in the $AD$ curve in part b of Figure 14-4 causes both real GNP and the price level to increase, we see now that in the general equilibrium determined by the intersection of $AD_1$ and $AS$ the rightward shift in the money demand curve in the lower half of Figure 14-3 is due to an increase in *both* real GNP and the price level—the increase in money GNP, or total income.

In general, the response of the price level to an increase in the money supply is determined by the slope of the $AS$ curve along the range over which the $AD$ curve shifts. If the $AD$ curve shifts along the horizontal range of the $AS$ curve, where the economy has a great deal of excess capacity and unemployment, there will be no increase in the price level. If the shift is over the immediate range, as in part b of Figure 14-4, where the economy is operating ever closer to its capacity limit, then both real GNP and the price level increase. Rightward shifts of the $AD$ curve along the vertical range of the $AS$ curve only increase the price level because the economy is up against the limit of its productive capacity.

### Summary of the Keynesian View on How Money Affects the Economy

*According to the Keynesian view, a change in the money supply changes the interest rate, thereby causing a change in investment spending, which in turn shifts the total expenditure schedule and hence the AD curve. The resulting change in real GNP and the price level depends on the amount of excess capacity and unemployment in the economy, as reflected in the slope of the AS curve along the range over which the AD curve shifts.*

### CHECKPOINT* 14-1

**Suppose the investment demand curve in Figure 14-2, part b, is pivoted clockwise about point $a'$ so that it is now steeper. Given the increase in the money supply from $M_0$ to $M_1$ shown in Figure 14-2, part a, will the resulting increase in investment spending in part b now be larger or smaller than before? Suppose the money demand curve $L$ in part a is pivoted clockwise about point $a$ so that it is steeper. Given the money supply increase from $M_0$ to $M_1$, will the resulting increase in investment spending (given the original investment demand curve $I_d$ shown in part b) now be larger or smaller than before? In the lower half of Figure 14-3, if money demand were more**

## POLICY PERSPECTIVE

### Ideological Differences Between Keynesians and Monetarists

Before beginning our discussion of monetarism, it should be recognized that monetarists and modern-day Keynesians (sometimes called neo-Keynesians) typically have differing political views and opinions on the proper role and size of government in our economy. Monetarists tend to favor a more laissez faire or free-market economy, with government intervening mainly to restrain monopoly and other forms of anticompetitive market practices. They believe that the market system generally does a good job of efficiently allocating resources to answer the basic economic questions of what to produce, how to produce it, and for whom. Those who adhere more to the Keynesian point of view tend to be less satisfied with the results provided by the market mechanism in a number of areas of the economy. They believe that the government can and should play a more effective and active role in correcting the shortcomings of the market mechanism. Monetarists, on the other hand, tend to view government as generally inefficient, bureaucratically cumbersome, and prone to making large mistakes when dealing with problems. Moreover, they generally fear the political implications of increasing government's control over the economy's decision-making process. They argue that increased government control poses a threat to personal freedoms and puts a damper on individual initiative.

In view of these ideological differences,

it should not be surprising that monetarists are leery of fiscal policy as a stabilization tool. We have already discussed (in Chapter 10) the timing problems associated with discretionary fiscal policy. Quite aside from this, however, monetarists fear that fiscal policy gives rise to too much direct government intervention in the economy. On the other hand, Keynesians feel government intervention is needed to solve other kinds of social and economic problems. So, why shouldn't the government also use its spending and taxation authority to attack the problems of economic instability, unemployment, and inflation? Besides, Keynesians see the Great Depression of the 1930s as evidence that the self-regulating forces of the marketplace are not sufficient to ensure that the economy will continuously operate near its full-employment capacity. They also argue that monetary policy alone was incapable of coping with such a depression. In contrast, monetarists see regulation of the money supply as a much more powerful tool for affecting the economy. They argue that the Great Depression was so severe largely because the Fed did a particularly bad job of managing monetary policy. Moreover, monetarists feel comfortable using monetary policy to regulate economic activity. It doesn't require the same direct and potentially extensive government intervention in the economy as fiscal policy.

---

sensitive to a change in total income (that is, if the change in the transactions and precautionary demand for money is greater per dollar of change in total income), would the increase in total income resulting from

the increase in the money supply from $M_0$ to $M_1$ be larger or smaller than before?

* Answers to all Checkpoints can be found at the back of the text.

## MONETARIST VIEW ON THE ROLE OF MONEY

The Keynesian view of how money affects economic activity went largely unchallenged up until the 1960s when a school of thought known as **monetarism** began to assert itself. The monetarists, largely led by Milton Friedman (winner of the 1976 Nobel Prize in Economics), argue that money plays a much more important role in determining the level of economic activity than is granted to it by the Keynesian view. We will now examine the monetarist view and also consider some of the main differences between it and the Keynesian view. We will begin by examining the equation of exchange, a notion that goes back to the classical economists.

### Monetarism and the Equation of Exchange

The dollar value of the purchases of final goods and services produced by the economy during a year is the economy's money GNP—the GNP expressed in terms of the prices at which the goods are actually purchased. (Recall the distinction between real GNP and money GNP made in Chapter 5.) Each purchase typically requires the buyer to give money in exchange for the good or service provided by the seller. The economy's money supply, its total stock of money, is used to transact all these exchanges during the course of a year.

Money GNP, a flow, is usually several times larger than the economy's money stock. This means that the money stock must be used several times during the year to carry out all the transactions represented by the money GNP. In effect, the money stock must go around the circular flow of money exchanged for goods (discussed in Chapter 5) several times during the course of a year. This idea is given expression by the **equation of exchange**, which is written

$$M \times V = p \times Q$$

In this equation $p \times Q$, price times quantity, is money GNP. For example, if the economy produces nothing but widgets, $p$ would be the price per widget and $Q$ the quantity of widgets produced per year. More realistically, for an economy that produces many kinds of goods, $Q$ may be thought of as real GNP and $p$ as an index of current prices (the prices at which goods are currently bought and sold). $M$ is the economy's money supply. $V$ is the number of times the money stock must "turn over" during a year in order to transact all the purchases of final goods and services that add up to money GNP. In other words, $V$ is the number of times a typical dollar of the money stock must go around the circular flow of money exchanged for final goods and services during a year. For this reason $V$ is called the velocity of circulation of money, or simply the **velocity** of money.

For example, if the economy's money supply $M$ is $300 billion and its money GNP is $1,500 billion, the equation of exchange would be

$$\begin{array}{ccc} M & V & GNP \\ \$300 \times & 5 & = \$1,500 \end{array}$$

The velocity of money $V$ is therefore 5. This means that the money stock must turn over five times per year. A dollar of the money stock typically would be used five times per year in the purchase of final goods and services.

### The Equation of Exchange as Definition

The equation of exchange as it stands is true simply by definition. If you know the size of the money supply and the level of the money GNP, you can calculate the value of $V$. By definition $V$ has to take on whatever value is necessary to maintain the equality between the two sides of the equation $M \times V = p \times Q$. However, suppose you took annual money GNP data and money stock data for a series of years in an economy and calculated the value of velocity for each of those years. If the calculated values of velocity didn't change much from year to year and from the earlier to the later years, your curiosity should be aroused. You should be even more curious if the same calculations for different economies revealed the same kind of regularity for $V$.

Regularity in any phenomenon is the watchword of science. When Galileo dropped objects of unequal weight from the same height on the Leaning Tower of Pisa, he discovered that they always reached the ground at the same time. No matter how different the weights, he always found this to be true. He thus discovered the law of falling bodies. Had he found no regularity in the relationship between the time taken for objects of different weights to reach the ground, his experiments would have been of little interest. It is regularity that leads to the formulation of theories—and often to controversy. Galileo's experiments and his formulation of the law of falling bodies went against the then prevailing opinion that heavier bodies fall faster than light ones. This opinion was so strong that he was forced to resign from his position as professor of mathematics at the University of Pisa.

The story of Galileo gives us some perspective on the depth of feeling that often characterizes the clash between monetarist and Keynesian viewpoints about the role of money. Here, too, regularity is a large part of the issue. *Monetarists argue that velocity $V$ in the equation of exchange is fairly stable or regular.* Those leaning toward the Keynesian point of view dispute this contention. You might well ask why not settle the argument by an appeal to facts—the calculations of velocity already mentioned. As in Galileo's time, facts aren't always convincing. Moreover, the facts about velocity are not as clear-cut as those about falling bodies, as we shall see later.

### The Equation of Exchange as Theory: The Quantity Theory of Money

What does it mean to say that velocity $V$ is stable? It means that $V$ is more than just a symbol that takes on whatever value is necessary to ensure equality between the left- and right-hand sides of the equation of exchange. The classical economists contended that $V$ was reasonably stable because it reflected the institutional characteristics of the economy. These characteristics include the frequency with which people are paid, the organization of banking, and the level of development of the transportation and communications systems. They argued that these determinants of the economy's payments mechanism were slow to change and that therefore $V$ was stable. This view of the equation of exchange became known as the **quantity theory of money**.

With the assumption that $V$ is stable, the equation of exchange passes from the realm of definition to that of theory because it enables us to predict the consequences of an event, namely a change in the money supply. (You might want to review the discussion of the characteristics of a theory in Chapter 1.) If the money supply is increased by a certain percent, then money GNP will increase by a like percent. In the previous example where $M$ equals $300 billion, $V$ equals 5, and the money GNP equals $1,500 billion, suppose the money supply $M$ is increased from $300 billion to $400 billion—a 33 percent increase. If $V$ is stable at a value of 5, money GNP will increase 33 percent, from $1,500 billion to $2,000 billion.

### Monetarist View of the Money Transmission Mechanism

Monetarism may be viewed as a sophisticated version of the quantity theory of money. Monetarists contend that the effects of money supply changes on the economy are transmitted through a host of channels, not just via the interest rate route, which is so strongly emphasized in the Keynesian point of view. In particular, monetarists argue that an increase in the economy's money supply initially increases the money holdings of consumers and businesses. That is, there is an excess supply of money. The excess money holdings are then spent on goods and ser-

---

## ECONOMIC THINKERS

---

### Milton Friedman — 1912–

Milton Friedman, who has spent most of his career at the University of Chicago, was awarded the Nobel Prize for Economics in 1976.

Friedman is perhaps best known for his "monetarist" views, which put emphasis on the importance of the money supply in the economy, and for his view that the role of government should be severely limited. Fiscal (Keynesian) policy is, in his view, less effective than monetary policy for affecting economic activity.

Friedman maintains that the general prosperity since World War II has not been due to "fine tuning" by the Council of Economic Advisers and others, or to various countercyclical devices, but to the fact that the great economic errors of the interwar period were largely avoided, especially severe reductions in the supply of money. Friedman holds that neither monetary nor fiscal policy will eliminate minor business fluctuations. Consequently, an automatic policy designed to increase the money supply by some given figure each year would be far superior to actions of the Fed or to policies devised by the Council. This automatic policy would work much more effectively if accompanied by meaningful efforts to reduce price rigidity stemming from monopolistic elements in the economy. Furthermore, he believes, a modest but steady increase in the money supply is the best way to try to maintain aggregate demand at the level of full employment.

Friedman's other claim to fame is his frequent questioning of most governmental policies designed to stimulate or regulate economic activity. Friedman would largely confine the government to the role of rule maker and umpire. Friedman sees these "rules" as having to do largely with property rights, contracts, and the provision of the money supply. The role of umpire is played by the police, the courts, and the monetary authorities.

FOR FURTHER READING
Among Friedman's major works are *Price Theory: A Provisional Text* (1962); *A Monetary History of the United States* (coauthored with Anna J. Schwartz, 1963); *The Optimum Quantity of Money and Other Essays* (1969); *A Theory of the Consumption Function* (1957); *Essays in Positive Economics* (1953); *Freedom and Capitalism* (1962); and *Free to Choose* (1980).

---

vices, directly pushing up aggregate demand and money GNP (equal $p \times Q$). Conversely, a decrease in the economy's money supply creates an excess demand for money. In an attempt to increase their money holdings, consumers and businesses cut back on their spending. This causes aggregate demand for goods and services to fall and money GNP to decrease.

In sum, *monetarists tend to believe that the cause-effect transmission from changes in the money supply to changes in money GNP are reasonably direct and tight. That is, in terms of the equation of exchange, monetarists believe that V, the velocity of money, is quite stable. Hence, they argue that changes in the money supply have a fairly direct effect on money GNP.*

An extreme version of monetarism would assume that velocity is an unchanging constant—as in the hypothetical example above where velocity was assumed always to equal 5. If this crude version of monetarism were true, monetary policy would indeed be a powerful and reliable tool for affecting the level of money GNP, or total income. The

Federal Reserve would know that it could change money GNP by any percentage amount it desired simply by changing the economy's money supply by that percentage amount. However, not even the most ardent monetarists subscribe to the view that velocity is constant.

## Monetarist Versus Keynesian Views of the Equation of Exchange

The Keynesian view of the equation of exchange holds that $V$, the velocity of money, is much less stable than the monetarists contend. Moreover, the Keynesian view argues that velocity $V$ may in fact move in the opposite direction from changes in the money supply $M$. Hence, attempts to affect the level of money GNP by changing the money supply are largely thwarted by offsetting changes in velocity.

To illustrate the differences between the monetarist and Keynesian views of velocity it is helpful to interpret the equation of exchange in terms of the Keynesian transmission mechanism. As already pointed out, monetarists argue that money supply changes affect the economy through other channels in addition to the interest rate channel. The monetarist view which we now present pertains only to the interest rate channel.

The Keynesian view that velocity is not very stable is consistent with a particular view of the Keynesian transmission mechanism, namely, that money demand is quite sensitive to changes in the interest rate while investment demand is not. The monetarist view that velocity is stable is consistent with a view that investment demand is quite sensitive to changes in the interest rate while money demand is not. The implications of these views are illustrated in Figure 14-5. (Note that this figure is similar to Figure 14-3.)

### *Effects of a Money Supply Change on Money GNP*

In the ensuing discussion we assume for simplicity that the price level is fixed. Therefore money GNP and real GNP are the same and we call them total income.

The top half of Figure 14-5 corresponds more closely to the Keynesian view of the interest rate sensitivity of investment demand and money demand than does the bottom half, or monetarist view. For instance, the money demand curve $L_1$ is less steeply sloped than the money demand curve $L_2$. Hence, money demand as represented by $L_1$ is more sensitive to a change in the interest rate (the Keynesian view) than is money demand as represented by $L_2$ (the monetarist view). For example, a drop in the interest rate from 8 percent to 7 percent would result in a $100 billion increase in money demand along $L_1$. But the interest rate would have to drop from 8 percent to 6 percent for there to be a $100 billion increase in money demand along $L_2$. The investment demand curve $I_1$ is more steeply sloped than the investment demand curve $I_2$. Investment demand as represented by $I_2$ is, therefore, more sensitive to a change in the interest rate (the monetarist view) than is investment demand as represented by $I_1$ (the Keynesian view). For example, a drop in the interest rate from 8 percent to 7 percent would result in an increase in investment of $50 billion along $I_1$. Along $I_2$ such a drop in the interest rate would result in an increase in investment of $100 billion.

Suppose the Fed increases the money supply by $100 billion, represented by the rightward shift in the money supply curve from $M_0$ to $M_1$. Let's compare the difference in the effects on total expenditure and total income that result from the difference between $L_1$ and $L_2$ and between $I_1$ and $I_2$. (We will ignore the effects of the total income change on the money demand curve because it only complicates our analysis without affecting our comparison of the different points of view.) In the upper half of Figure 14-5 (the Keynesian view), the money supply increase causes the interest rate to fall from 8 percent (the intersection of $M_0$ and $L_1$) to 7 percent (the intersection of $M_1$ and $L_1$). In the lower half of Figure 14-5 (the monetarist view), the same money supply increase results in a larger drop in the interest rate, from 8 per-

**FIGURE 14-5   Differing Views on the Impact of a Change in the Money Supply**

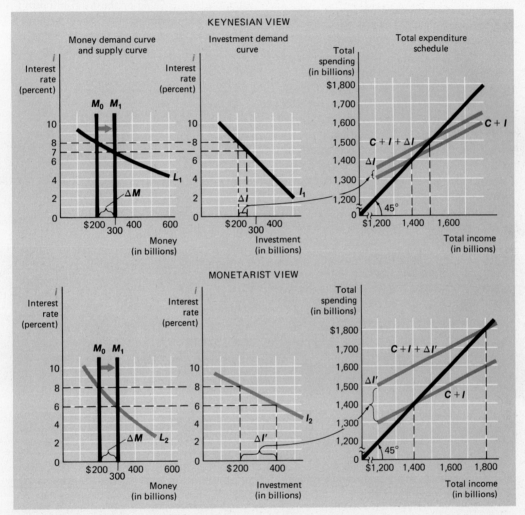

An increase in the money supply causes less of a change in total income according to the Keynesian view (top half of figure) than it does according to the monetarist view (bottom half of figure). This difference is due to the fact that money demand is more sensitive to interest rate changes in the Keynesian view than in the monetarist view, while investment demand is less sensitive to interest rate changes in the Keynesian view than in the monetarist view. Comparing the money demand curves, this means that $L_1$ is less steeply sloped than $L_2$, while for the investment demand curves $I_1$ is more steeply sloped than $I_2$. Consequently, in the monetarist view the increase $\Delta M$ in the money supply from $M_0$ to $M_1$ results in a larger reduction in the interest rate, a larger increase in investment, and hence a larger increase in the total expenditure schedule and total income than occurs in the Keynesian view.

cent to 6 percent, because the money demand curve $L_2$ is steeper than $L_1$.

The larger drop in the interest rate, combined with the fact that $I_2$ is not as steep as $I_1$, results in a larger increase in investment spending in the lower half of Figure 14-5 than in the upper half. The increase in investment spending $\Delta I$, in the upper half of the figure, amounts to $50 billion. This increase in investment shifts the total expenditure schedule upward by $50 billion from $C + I$ to $C + I + \Delta I$, resulting in a $100 billion increase in total income from $1,400 billion to $1,500 billion in the upper half of Figure 14-5. In the lower half of the figure, the $200 billion increase in investment shifts the total expenditure schedule upwards by $200 billion from $C + I$ to $C + I + \Delta I'$, causing a $400 billion increase in total income from $1,400 billion to $1,800 billion. Clearly, a $100 billion increase in the money supply would cause one to predict a greater effect on total expenditure and income if one takes the monetarist rather than the Keynesian point of view.

### Changes in Velocity

What do the two points of view expressed in Figure 14-5 imply about the stability of velocity? At the initial equilibrium position in both the upper and lower halves of Figure 14-5, the money supply is $200 billion and total income (or money GNP) is $1,400 billion. In both cases the equation of exchange is

$$\$200 \times V = \$1,400$$

In the initial equilibrium position velocity $V$ therefore equals 7. After the $100 billion increase in the money supply, the equation of exchange at the new equilibrium in the upper half of Figure 14-5 (the Keynesian view) is now

$$\$300 \times V = \$1,500$$

Therefore velocity must now equal 5. In the Keynesian view velocity has fallen from 7 to 5.

At the new equilibrium in the lower half of Figure 14-5 (the monetarist view), the equation of exchange is now

$$\$300 \times V = \$1,800$$

Velocity must now equal 6. In the monetarist view velocity has fallen from 7 to 6. Therefore, velocity changes by less in the monetarist view (from 7 to 6) than in the Keynesian view (from 7 to 5).

In sum, we can now see why *Keynesians argue that the effects of a money supply increase can be largely offset by a movement in velocity in the opposite direction, and why monetarists believe such offsetting effects are relatively weak.*

### Velocity in the Real World

What do real-world data show about the relationship between the money supply and money GNP? How does velocity actually behave?

---

**FIGURE 14-6    The Money Supply and Money GNP**

There is a striking parallel in the movements of the money supply and money GNP. Monetarists cite this as evidence to support their claim that the money supply is an important causal determinant of money GNP. Keynesians claim that this parallel movement is equally supportive of the view that causation runs in the opposite direction—from money GNP to the money supply. They argue that total expenditure $C + I + G$ can shift upward for reasons unrelated to money. As total expenditure shifts upward, consumers and business increase their demand for loans from banks in order to carry out their plans for increased spending. As a result, banks increase loans through the deposit expansion process that gives rise to an increase in the money supply.

---

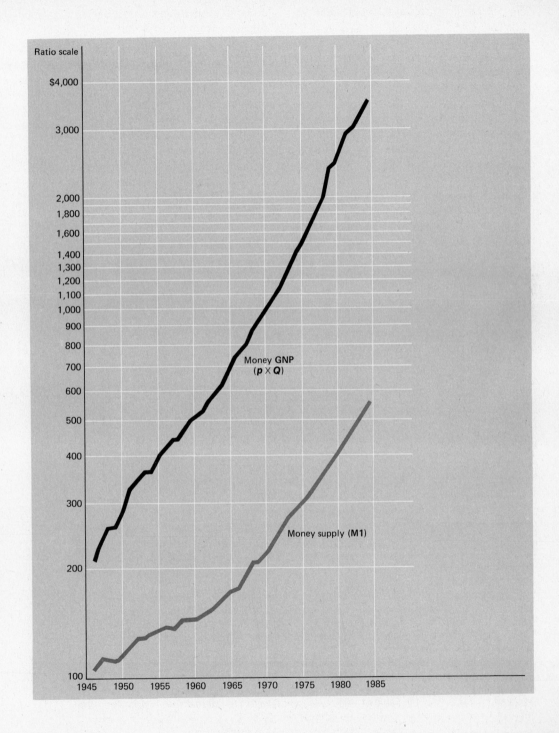

## The Money Supply and Money GNP

Figure 14-6 illustrates the behavior of the money supply (M1, defined as currency plus demand deposits plus other checkable deposits) and money GNP in the United States for the years since 1946. Monetarists contend that the almost parallel movement shown by the money supply and money GNP reflects a causal relationship running from the money supply to money GNP. However, Keynesians reply that the observed relationship is equally supportive of their point of view. They argue that the causality can also run in the other direction—from money GNP to the money supply. They point out that the economy's total expenditure schedule $C + I + G$ can shift upward for a host of reasons that have nothing to do with money supply changes. Technological change, changes in profit expectations, and the development of new products can cause investment $I$ to rise. Changes in consumer tastes, an increase in consumer optimism, population growth, and so forth can cause the consumption function $C$ to shift upward. Government expenditures $G$ may increase for reasons of national defense or to build more highways, schools, and so forth. Keynesians argue that these autonomous increases in total spending in the economy lead to an increase in the demand for loans from banks as businesses and consumers borrow to finance their spending. Banks *respond* by lending out excess reserves and thereby create money through the deposit expansion process we studied in the previous chapter. Growth in the money supply is, therefore, caused by the increase in the total expenditure on goods and services rather than the other way around.

The ongoing debate between monetarists and Keynesians finds both sides enlisting the data of Figure 14-6 as support for their point of view.

## The Evidence on Velocity

Velocity can be calculated from the money supply and money GNP data given in Figure 14-6. We can do this simply by recognizing that the equation of exchange $M \times V = p \times Q$ may also be expressed as

$$V = \frac{p \times Q}{M}$$

Dividing money GNP ($p \times Q$) by money supply data ($M$) gives us velocity in the United States since 1930, plotted in Figure 14-7, part b. This figure shows us that velocity gradually declined over the 1930–1946

---

**FIGURE 14-7   The Behavior of Velocity and the Interest Rate**

Velocity, plotted in part b, is calculated by dividing money GNP by the money supply (M1). It shows a long-run declining trend from 1930 to 1946 and a long-run rising trend since 1946. The short-run stability of velocity is more easily judged from the year-to-year percentage changes in velocity plotted in part c.

Monetarists believe that the evidence in parts b and c covering the period since the early 1950s shows that velocity is reasonably stable. The more variable behavior of velocity from 1930 through 1951 seems less supportive of this view. It is argued that the long-run rising trend in velocity since 1946 is due to the increased use of credit cards and availability of short-term credit.

Keynesians take special note of the way that the interest rate in part a moves in a parallel manner to velocity in part b. This is consistent with their view that money demand is sensitive to the interest rate. Our discussion of velocity in connection with Figure 14-5 showed how this view implies that velocity is sensitive to the interest rate, rising when the interest rate rises and falling when the interest rate falls.

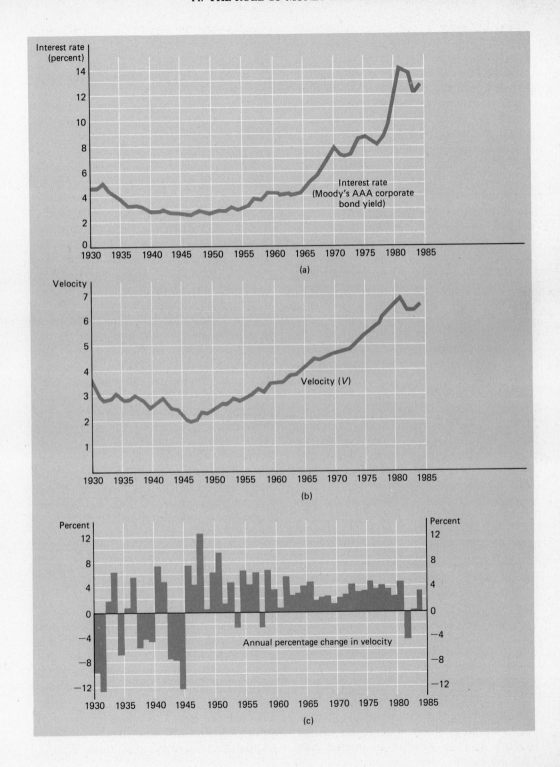

(a)

(b)

(c)

period. But since World War II velocity has climbed steadily upward from a value of about 2 to around 6. In addition to these long-run trends, velocity has varied on a year-to-year basis. This variation is illustrated in Figure 14–7, part c, which shows the year-to-year percentage change in the velocity data plotted in part b.

Monetarists believe that the growth in velocity has been reasonably slow and predictable. They suggest that the long-run upward trend in velocity since World War II reflects the increased use of credit cards and the increased availability of short-term credit for consumer purchases. Both of these developments make it possible for individuals or businesses to transact any given amount of purchases of final goods and services with a smaller balance of money on hand. Hence, the economy's money supply turns over more often, or goes around the circular income-expenditure flow more times, during the course of a year—velocity increases.

Keynesians acknowledge the impact of these same developments on velocity. But they also note that the long-run rise in velocity has been accompanied by a long-run rise in the interest rate, shown in part a of Figure 14–7. We have already discussed the fact that Keynesians believe both that money demand is quite sensitive and investment demand relatively insensitive to interest rate changes. And we saw how this implied that velocity is more unstable in the Keynesian view as compared to the monetarist view in which money demand is less sensitive and investment demand more sensitive to interest rate changes—our discussion of Figure 14–5. In particular, while the interest rate went from 8 percent to 7 percent, velocity changed from 7 to 5 in the Keynesian view (top half of Figure 14–5). By comparison, in the monetarist view (bottom half of Figure 14–5), while the interest rate went from 8 percent to 6 percent, velocity only changed from 7 to 6, despite the fact that change in the interest rate was larger. Hence, Keynesians believe velocity is quite sensitive to interest rate changes. And Keynesians claim the long-run rise in the interest rate (Figure 14–7, part a) that accompanies the long-run rise in velocity (Figure 14–7, part b) is consistent with their point of view. As further support for this view, Keynesians also note that the gradual decline in the interest rate that occurred from 1930 through 1946 accompanied the decline in velocity over this period.

Since the early 1950s velocity has never increased by more than about 6.5 percent from one year to the next, and it has never decreased by more than about 2.5 percent (Figure 14–7, part c). Monetarists argue that this amount of short-run variability of velocity over this period is consistent with their view that velocity is quite stable. However, Keynesians are quick to point out the relatively greater instability of velocity that is evident during the more turbulent years from 1930 through 1951. For example, consider the 12.8 percent drop in velocity that occurred from 1931 to 1932 in the depths of the Great Depression. At the same time, money GNP fell 23.4 percent. In terms of the equation of exchange $M \times V = p \times Q$ this means that more than half of the drop in money GNP ($p \times Q$) reflects the drop in $V$. Keynesians see this as evidence for their contention that increases in the money supply $M$ aimed at getting the economy out of the Great Depression would have had to overcome the sizeable offsetting effect of a declining $V$.

## A Constant Money Growth Rate

Monetarists believe there is a fairly stable relationship between the money supply and money GNP—in other words, a fairly stable $V$. But they do not advocate attempts to offset recessions and curb excessive economic expansions by alternately expanding and contracting the money supply. They generally argue that such a discretionary monetary policy is more likely to aggravate economic fluctuations than to minimize them. Why?

### Time Lags in Monetary Policy

Monetarists contend that changes in the money supply affect the level of economic activity over a long and variable period of time. Yes, a change in the money supply will definitely affect the level of money GNP. But there is a time lag between the point when the money supply change occurs and the point when its effect on money GNP is fully realized. Moreover, monetarists claim that the length of this time lag is quite variable and difficult to predict. Research by the foremost monetarist, Milton Friedman, suggests that the length of this time lag may vary anywhere from roughly a half year to two and a half years. As a result, monetarists argue that it is almost impossible for policymakers to schedule expansions or contractions in the money supply so that they will have their impact on the economy at the desired time. An expansion of the money supply, intended to offset a recession, may have its greatest impact a year or more down the road, after the economy has recovered and is already expanding. Hence, the money supply increase may end up adding fuel to a potentially inflationary situation rather than offsetting a recession. Similarly, a contraction of the money supply, intended to curb an overheated economy, may end up having its greatest impact after the economy has already begun to slow down. As a result, the money supply contraction may actually contribute to an ensuing recession.

Most monetarists contend that the historical record since the founding of the Federal Reserve System in 1913 suggests that discretionary monetary policy has in fact tended to destabilize rather than stabilize the economy. Therefore, monetarists claim that monetary policy mismanagement must bear some of the blame for economic instability.

### Implications for Monetary Policy

What is the upshot of the monetarist contentions? Some prominent monetarists, such as Milton Friedman, argue that the most appropriate monetary policy is to avoid discretionary decisions to expand or contract the rate of growth of the money supply. Instead, they recommend *a constant money growth rate rule,* whereby the Fed concentrates on expanding the money supply at a constant rate, year-in and year-out. Monetarists argue that this will automatically tend to smooth out the business cycle. When the economy's rate of growth (the growth rate of money GNP) falls below the constant money supply growth rate, during a recession, the continually increasing money supply will automatically provide a stimulus to get the economy going again. When the economy's growth rate rises above this rate, during a boom, the slower growing money supply will automatically put a curb on the excessive economic expansion.

Keynesians generally regard the constant money growth rule as unnecessarily cautious. They feel that there are definitely times when discretionary changes in the rate of growth of the money supply are obviously called for. This issue continues to be hotly debated by the two camps.

---

**CHECKPOINT 14-2**

**What is the main distinction between the equation of exchange viewed as a definition and as a theory? Consider again the money supply increase discussed in Figure 14–5. Keynesians have argued that the money demand curve becomes flatter at lower interest rate levels. At some very low interest rate, they argue, the curve may become perfectly flat. If the money supply is increased enough to push the interest rate down to this level, Keynesians argue that further increases in the money supply will be completely offset by decreases in velocity $V$. Can you explain why in terms of a diagram like Figure 14–5?**

---

---

## POLICY PERSPECTIVE

### Monetarist Experiment?—How the Fed Under Volcker Slowed Inflation

The monetarist idea that the Fed should concentrate more on controlling the growth rate of the money supply and less on stabilizing interest rates at targeted levels gained more serious attention as inflation worsened during the late 1960s and early 1970s. In 1975 Congress passed a joint resolution requiring the Fed to state its money supply growth rate targets a year in advance.

Monetarists say the Fed responded by using a variety of money measures (M1, M2, M3, and so on), emphasizing whichever one was most consistent at any given time with its continued desire to concentrate on controlling interest rates. Moreover, whenever the Fed missed its money growth target for a particular quarter during the latter half of the 1970s it simply started anew to try to achieve it in the next quarter, rather than trying to correct for the overly rapid or sluggish money growth of the previous quarter.

#### The Switch to Controlling Money Growth

In October 1979, amid panic over the rapidly rising inflation rate (see Figure P14–1), the Fed, led by its new chairman Paul Volcker, announced that henceforth it would concentrate much more on hitting its money growth targets and much less on controlling interest rates. Mr. Volcker and other Fed officials said from the outset that they wouldn't be pure monetarists, but would take other factors such as interest rates into account when deciding how tightly to control money growth. Nonetheless, from October 1979 to October 1982 the Fed made its most determined effort to follow monetarist

prescriptions, sharply cutting back money supply growth (see Figure P14–1).

The Reagan administration provided broad support for the Fed's goal of reducing inflation with slow money growth. But the administration also pushed through major tax cuts that would, it was argued, enable the economy to grow rapidly at the same time inflation was declining. This supply-side line of reasoning argued that the economic incentives created by the tax cuts would stimulate production so much that, even in a booming economy, price increases would be slowed by huge new supplies of goods and services as well as by the tight monetary policy.

#### What Happened

The tax cuts were phased in over a 2-year period beginning in October 1981 while the Fed slowed money growth with a vengeance during the latter half of 1981 (see Figure P14–1). Inflation declined rapidly and unemployment soared to over 10 percent by late 1982 as the economy plunged into a deep recession (Figures P14–1 and P14–2). Some economists warned of a possible depression. The supply-side contention that inflation would be cured painlessly without the throes of a recession wasn't accurate. Most economists said the main reason was that the Fed's slowing of the money growth rate simply overwhelmed the stimulus of the tax cut.

By July of 1982 the Fed, alarmed by the severity of the recession and under increasing pressure from Congress, wanted to give the economy more breathing room. Finally, at the Federal Open Market Committee (FOMC) meeting in Octo-

FIGURE P14-1   **Money Growth Rate and Inflation**

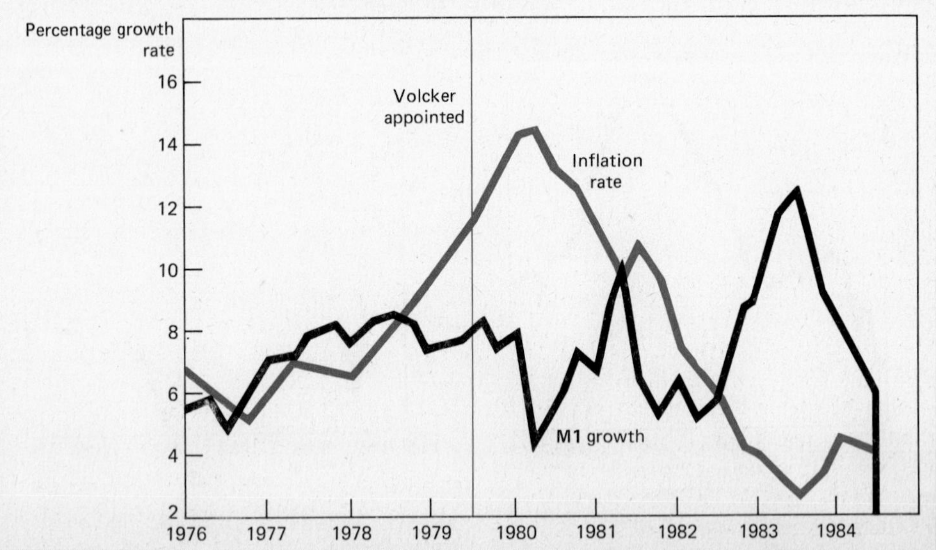

Percentage growth of the money supply (M1) and consumer prices, by quarter, from a year earlier.

Before 1979, the trend of money supply increases and inflation was steadily upward. Under Chairman Volcker, the Fed adopted the monetarist goal of slowing money growth, and inflation fell. But M1 growth became more erratic, not smoother as the monetarists wanted.

SOURCE: Morgan, Stanley & Co.

ber 1982, the FOMC accepted Chairman Volcker's argument that it was time to suspend the policy of focusing so heavily on controlling money supply growth, and adopt a broader, more flexible approach. The Fed eased credit and suspended pursuit of its money growth rate targets for the second half of 1982. Since then it has based its actions on a variety of factors, including interest rates, the behavior of prices, and economic growth.

### An Assessment of the "Monetarist" Experiment

The Fed's policy during the 1979–1982 period helped bring about a drastic reduction in inflation, with the rate of consumer price increases tumbling from 13.3 percent in 1979 to 3.9 percent in 1982. At the same time, however, money growth was extremely erratic (see Figure P14-1), not slow and steady as monetarists advocated.

Monetarists contend that the volatility of money growth means that monetarism was never really followed as prescribed. Anna Schwartz, who collaborated with Milton Friedman in research on the relation between money supply movements and the economy, believes the Fed espoused monetarist principles as a smokescreen for raising interest rates (Figure P14-3). Even a Fed governor has conceded that setting money growth rate targets helped shield the Fed against criti-

**FIGURE P14-2** **The Unemployment Rate Surged**

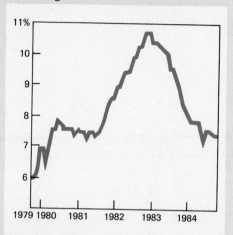

Unemployment as a percent of the civilian labor force.

**FIGURE P14-3** **Interest Rates Jumped**

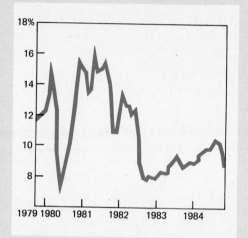

Monthly average rates on 3-month treasury bills.

cism that would be associated with a policy of setting interest rates high enough to curb inflation. Schwartz contends that the high interest rate policy's side effects (high unemployment and a deep recession) have been unfairly attributed to monetarism whose prescription for slow but *steady* money growth was never really followed.[1]

### What Has Monetarism Accomplished?

The cause of monetarism has not always been served well even by its truest believers. In late 1983 Milton Friedman predicted a recesssion for the first half of 1984 and a resurgence of inflation by the second half. The sharp slowdown in M1 growth in late 1983 (see Figure P14-1) was the basis for the recession forecast. And he said inflation would surge because of the rapid growth of the money supply

[1] "Money's Role," *Wall Street Journal,* Dec. 10, 1984, p. 16.

from mid-1982 to mid-1983. He was wrong. The economy experienced a strong expansion in the first half, and there was no major resurgence of inflation in the second half.

Monetarism's clout has declined since 1979 when the Fed first seemed to embrace it. Overall however, many economists contend that in future years inflation rates are likely to be lower than they would have been before monetarism focused so much attention on the importance of controlling money supply growth.

### Questions

1. Monetarists argue for a slow steady growth in the money supply because they claim no one understands the economy well enough to adjust the rate of money growth appropriately for any given time. Given this assertion, it could be said that it was inconsistent for Milton Friedman to predict the course of the economy in

1984 on the basis of the behavior of money growth in 1982. Why?

2. What evidence do you see in Figure P14–3 that the Fed relaxed its focus on controlling money supply growth and "broadened" its focus to include other factors?

## SUMMARY

**1.** Businesses will invest in those capital goods having an expected rate of return greater than the interest rate. The lower the interest rate, the larger the amount of investment spending that is profitable by this criterion. Hence, the investment demand curve slopes downward because more investment spending will take place at low than at high interest rates.

**2.** According to the Keynesian view the money market is linked to the level of investment spending by the interest rate. The level of investment spending determines the level of the total expenditure schedule and hence the level of real GNP. The level of real GNP in turn determines the position of the money demand curve in the money market.

**3.** An increase in the money supply lowers the interest rate. According to the Keynesian view this increases investment spending, which pushes up the total expenditure schedule, raising the level of real GNP. The rise in real GNP pushes the money demand curve rightward, causing the interest rate to rise, though not enough to offset the full effects of the initial decrease in the interest rate. A partial equilibrium analysis would ignore the effect on the money demand curve of the rise in real GNP.

**4.** According to the Keynesian view increasing the money supply lowers the interest rate and raises the real GNP level—this is often referred to as an easy-money policy. Decreasing the money supply raises the interest rate and lowers the real GNP level—this is often called a tight-money policy.

**5.** An increase in the money supply causes the aggregate demand curve *(AD)* to shift rightward, while a decrease in the money supply causes it to shift leftward. The *AD* curve and the aggregate supply curve determine the price level.

**6.** Keynesians tend to favor government intervention in the economy because they see shortcomings in the way the market system answers the economic questions of what to produce, how, and for whom. They are also doubtful that markets have the self-regulating ability to ensure economic stability and full employment without the aid of an active fiscal policy. Monetarists tend to see government intervention as an unnecessary and harmful interference with the market system, a threat to individual freedom, and a dampener on individual initiative.

**7.** The equation of exchange, $M \times V = p \times Q$, is a definitional relationship between the economy's money stock $M$ and the economy's total money income, or money GNP, which is equal to the price level $p$ times the quantity of real output $Q$. $V$ is the velocity of circulation of money. When $V$ is regarded as stable—a reflection of institutional characteristics of the economy—the equation of exchange becomes the expression for the quantity theory of money.

**8.** Monetarism may be regarded as a sophisticated version of the quantity theory of money. Monetarists argue that the cause-effect transmission from changes in the money supply to changes in money GNP are reasonably direct and tight. They argue that the effects of a money supply change are transmitted through a host of channels, not just the interest rate channel so strongly emphasized by the Keynesian view. While monetarists regard velocity as stable, Keynesians believe the velocity of money is unstable, consistent with their view that money demand is sensitive and investment demand relatively insensitive to interest rate changes.

**9.** Keynesians favor discretionary monetary policy. Monetarists argue that such a policy is likely to aggravate the business cycle rather than diminish it. Therefore, some prominent monetarists argue for a constant money growth rate rule.

**10.** The Fed under Chairman Volcker switched to a policy that focused more on controlling money supply growth and less on stabilizing interest rates during the 1979–1982 period. While this helped bring the inflation rate down, the economy experienced a severe recession with high unemployment. Monetarists claim the Fed really didn't follow monetarist prescriptions because while money growth slowed it was very erratic, not steady as monetarists advocate. Monetarism's main contribution has been to focus more attention on the importance of controlling money growth to control inflation.

## KEY TERMS AND CONCEPTS

equation of exchange
expected rate of return
general equilibrium analysis
monetarism
partial equilibrium analysis
quantity theory of money
velocity

## QUESTIONS AND PROBLEMS

**1.** Using a partial equilibrium analysis, start with the initial equilibrium position in the top half of Figure 14–3 (money supply $M_0$ equal to $300 billion) and trace through the likely effects of each of the following (indicate the direction of changes where it is not possible to measure the precise magnitudes of changes):

   a. The Fed increases the discount rate.

   b. The Fed reduces the required reserve ratio.

   c. The Fed makes an open market sale of bonds.

   d. The Fed reduces the money supply by $75 billion.

**2.** How would your answers to question 1 be affected if full adjustment in all markets is taken into account—that is, how would the answers in each case be different if a general equilibrium analysis were carried out instead of a partial equilibrium analysis?

**3.** In Figure 14–3, how would the slopes of the money demand curve $L_0$ and the investment demand curve $I_d$ have to be different for the $200 billion increase in the money supply to have a larger impact on real GNP? What implications do the slopes of the money demand and investment demand curves have for the effectiveness of monetary policy?

**4.** Link up the analysis in the top half of Figure 14–3 with the analysis in Figure 14–4, and describe how monetary policy affects the level of real GNP and the price level $p$. Do the same thing using the bottom half of Figure 14–4 and explain how the effect on real GNP and the price level would be different.

**5.** Suppose the Fed is prone to making mistakes in its exercise of discretionary monetary policy. According to which view, Keynesian or monetarist, would the resulting fluctuations in money GNP be the greatest? Why? What bearing does this have on the Keynesian view versus the monetarist view about discretionary monetary policy?

**6.** Assume the Fed decides to implement monetary policy by always keeping the interest rate at the same target level. For instance, if the interest rate falls below the target level, the Fed conducts open market sales to push it back up, while if the interest rate rises above the target level, the Fed conducts open market purchases to push it back down. Suppose there are autonomous changes in spending, reflected in shifts in the total expenditure schedule. Do you think the Fed's constant interest rate policy would tend to stabilize or destabilize the economy? Why?

7. What problems does discretionary monetary policy share with discretionary fiscal policy? (Recall the discussion of discretionary fiscal policy in Chapter 10.) In what ways would the exercise of discretionary monetary policy differ from the exercise of discretionary fiscal policy?

# FOUR

## Inflation, Unemployment, Economic Stability, and Growth

# 15

# Monetary and Fiscal Policy and Budget Deficits

**AFTER READING THIS CHAPTER YOU WILL BE ABLE TO:**

1. Explain the differences between Keynesian and monetarist views on the extent to which fiscal policy actions affect real GNP and the price level.

2. Explain the different effects on the economy of pure fiscal policy actions as distinguished from those accomplished by money supply changes.

3. Give reasons and explain why it is often difficult to coordinate monetary and fiscal policy.

4. Describe how monetary policy and government deficits can combine to give the economy an inflationary bias.

5. Describe the difference between the money interest rate and the real interest rate, and explain how this difference complicates the conduct of monetary and fiscal policy.

The basic question to be addressed in this and the next chapter is: To what extent can monetary and fiscal policy smooth out economic fluctuations (the so-called business cycle) and prod the economy closer to full employment without excessive inflation? In this chapter we will first focus on why Keynesians and monetarists hold differing opinions on the effectiveness of fiscal policy. Then we will examine why fiscal actions that cause government budget deficits have monetary implications that make it difficult to distinguish purely fiscal from purely monetary effects. We will then see how budget deficits can give rise to conflicts between monetary and fiscal policy.

## FISCAL POLICY: KEYNESIAN VERSUS MONETARIST VIEWS

Aside from the ideological differences we discussed in the last chapter, why do Keynesians have more faith than monetarists in the ability of fiscal policy to smooth out the business cycle, foster full employment, and curb inflation? How can fiscal policies which cause deficits have monetary effects? Are fiscal and monetary policies well coordinated or do they frequently work at cross-purposes with each other? Let's now consider each of these questions in turn.

### Pure Fiscal Policy and Crowding Out

The basic differences between the Keynesian and monetarist views on the effectiveness of fiscal policy are perhaps most clearly illustrated in terms of pure fiscal policy. *Pure fiscal policy* consists of changes in government expenditure, taxation, or both that do not change the money supply.

Monetarists argue that pure fiscal policy causes very little change in total income and employment. For example, the monetarist view holds that an increase in government expenditure leads to the **crowding out** of private sector expenditure, particularly investment spending. Hence, any expansionary effect on aggregate demand caused by an increase in government spending is largely offset by an accompanying decline in investment spending. In contrast, Keynesians argue that crowding out is not that significant.

### Why There Is Crowding Out

What is the explanation for the crowding-out effect and the difference in opinion between Keynesians and monetarists regarding its size? The answer hinges on the effect of a rise in total income on money demand, the interest rate, and investment spending.

Recall the increases in the economy's total income cause the money demand curve to shift rightward, as illustrated in Figure 13–2, Chapter 13. Our discussion of general equilibrium (Figure 14–3 in Chapter 14) showed us how this rightward shift in the money demand curve would tend to dampen an expansion in total expenditure and real GNP, and therefore the amount of rightward shift in the $AD$ curve in Figure 14–4.

Consider now Figure 15–1 where the differences in slope between the investment demand curves, $I_1$ and $I_2$, and the money demand curves, $L_1$ and $L_2$, reflect the differences between the Keynesian and monetarist views discussed earlier in Figure 14–5. For a *given* increase in total income, there will be a certain amount of rightward shift in the money demand curve as shown in Figure 15–1. $L_1$ shifts to $L_1'$ (Keynesian view), and $L_2$ shifts to $L_2'$ (monetarist view). The amount of this shift, equal to the distance beween $a$ and $b$, is of course the same in both cases because both shifts are caused by the same given increase in total income. Note, however, that in the monetarist view the resulting rise in the interest rate is larger (from 5 to 7 percent) than in the Keynesian view (from 5 to 6 percent). The larger rise in the interest rate, combined with the fact that $I_2$

**FIGURE 15-1   Keynesian View Versus Monetarist View
of the Effects of an Increase in Total Income on
Investment**

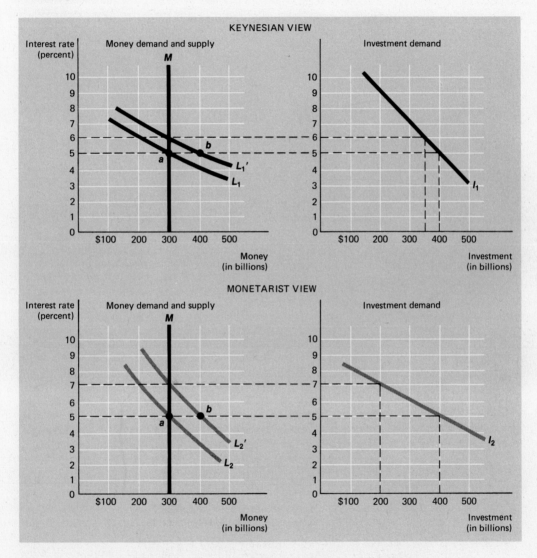

A given increase in total income will shift the money demand curve rightward, from $L_1$ to $L_1'$ in the Keynesian view and from $L_2$ to $L_2'$ in the monetarist view. At the initial equilibrium interest rate of 5 percent, the amount of this rightward shift equals the distance from *a* to *b*. The money demand curve is more steeply sloped in the monetarist than in the Keynesian view. Therefore, the interest rate rises further in the monetarist view (from 5 to 7 percent) than in the Keynesian view (from 5 to 6 percent). Combined with the fact that the investment demand curve $I_2$ is less steeply sloped than $I_1$, this means that investment spending is reduced more in the monetarist than in the Keynesian view.

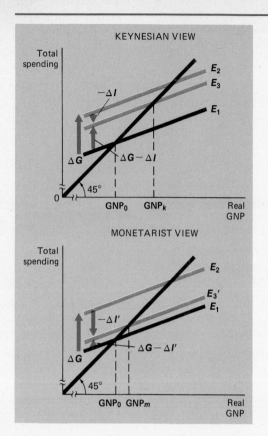

**FIGURE 15-2 The Crowding-Out Effect of Fiscal Policy**

An increase in government expenditure $\Delta G$ pushes the total expenditure schedule from $E_1$ up to $E_2$ if we momentarily ignore the effects of the rise in real GNP on money demand, the interest rate, and investment. Taking account of such effects (as illustrated in Figure 15–1), the rise in real GNP increases the demand for money, which pushes up the interest rate and causes a reduction, or crowding out, of investment spending.

This crowding out of investment spending is larger according to the monetarist view (bottom half of Figure 15–1) than according to the Keynesian view (top half of Figure 15–1). Consequently, there is a greater offsetting change in investment in the monetarist view, equal to $-\Delta I'$, than in the Keynesian view, equal to $-\Delta I$. As a result, the total expenditure schedule only rises from $E_1$ to $E_3'$ increasing GNP from $GNP_0$ to $GNP_m$, in the monetarist view. By comparison the exact same increase in government spending, $\Delta G$, increases the total expenditure schedule from $E_1$ to $E_3$ and GNP from $GNP_0$ to $GNP_k$ in the Keynesian view.

has a flatter slope than $I_1$, results in a larger reduction in investment spending, or more crowding out, in the monetarist view than in the Keynesian.

### The Crowding-Out Effect

The effect of crowding out on the total expenditure schedule and hence on real GNP is shown in Figure 15-2. Here the economy's total expenditure schedule is $E_1$, which means that the equilibrium level of real GNP is $GNP_0$, as shown in both the upper and lower half of the figure. Now suppose government spending increases by the amount $\Delta G$. If we momentarily ignore the effects of

the resulting rise in real GNP on money demand, the economy's total expenditure schedule is shifted up to $E_2$ (upper and lower half of Figure 15-2). However, if we allow for the effects of the real GNP rise on money demand, the interest rate, and the level of investment spending, as shown in Figure 15-1, the total expenditure schedule cannot rise to the position $E_2$ in Figure 15-2. Why? Because the effect of the rise in government spending will be offset in part by the reduction, or crowding out, of investment spending that results from the rise in the interest rate. According to the Keynesian view (upper half of Figure 15-2), the crowding out of investment will equal $-\Delta I$, so that the total expenditure schedule is shifted up to $E_3$—or by an amount equal to $\Delta G - \Delta I$. Equilib-

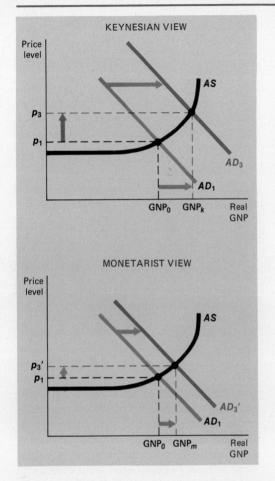

**FIGURE 15-3  Crowding-Out Effect on Aggregate Demand**

An exogenous government expenditure increase, or an exogenous tax reduction, causes less crowding out of investment spending and therefore gives rise to a larger rightward shift of the *AD* curve according to the Keynesian view than according to the monetarist view. Consequently the Keynesian view holds that such fiscal policy actions cause larger increases in real GNP and the price level than is the case according to the monetarist view.

rium real GNP rises from $GNP_0$ to $GNP_k$. According to the monetarist view (lower half of Figure 15-2), the crowding out of investment will be larger, equal to $-\Delta I'$. The total expenditure schedule is shifted up by a smaller amount, equal to $\Delta G - \Delta I'$, to $E_3'$, and real GNP rises only from $GNP_0$ to $GNP_m$.

Figure 15-3 shows how crowding out affects the *AD* curve and hence both the price level and real GNP. Recall that a shift in the total expenditure schedule due to an exogenous expenditure change shifts the *AD* curve, as shown previously in Figure 11-6, Chapter 11. Corresponding to the shift in the total expenditure schedule from $E_1$ to $E_3$ according to the Keynesian view, Figure 15-2, the *AD* curve shifts from $AD_1$ and $AD_3$ along the *AS* curve in Figure 15-3 and the price level rises from $p_1$ to $p_3$ as real GNP increases from $GNP_0$ to $GNP_k$. Corresponding to the shift in the total expenditure schedule from $E_1$ to $E_3'$ according to the monetarist view, Figure 15-2, the *AD* curve shifts from $AD_1$ to $AD_3'$ along the *AS* curve in Figure 15-3 and the price level rises from $p_1$ to $p_3'$ as real GNP increases from $GNP_0$ to $GNP_m$. Clearly the increase in the price level and real GNP is smaller according to the monetarist view.

### Crowding Out and Taxation

Our illustration of the crowding-out effect has assumed that the fiscal action taken was an increase in government spending. But a tax reduction also shifts the total expenditure schedule upward and the *AD* curve rightward, as we saw in Chapters 10 and 11, and results in the same type of crowding-out effect. Similarly, an increase in government expenditures matched by an increase in taxes (a balanced budget increase) shifts the total expenditure schedule upward (discussed in Chapter 10) and the *AD* curve rightward, giving rise to the crowding-out effect.

In sum, *monetarists believe fiscal policy actions have very little effect on real GNP, the price level, and employment because of the offsetting crowding-out effect. The Keynesian view holds that fiscal policy has a sizeable effect because the offsetting crowding-out effect is not that significant.*

### Fiscal and Monetary Effects Combined: Financing Budget Deficits

Fiscal policy has monetary effects whenever a fiscal action is accompanied by a change in the money supply. This may happen whenever a change in government expenditure, taxation, or both gives rise to a government budget deficit or surplus.

### Financing Budget Deficits Without a Money Supply Change

Recall our discussion of the financing of government budget deficits in Chapter 10. There we noted that whenever government expenditure exceeds tax revenues the government must finance the difference by issuing government bonds. If the public (businesses, individuals, and private institutions) buys the bonds, they typically write checks against their demand deposits or other checkable deposits. These checks are made payable to the U.S. Treasury for the amount of government bonds purchased. The government then spends this money, putting it right back into the hands of the public. There is no change in the supply of money in the economy when the government deficit is financed in this fashion. Hence, the only question is how much the expansionary effect of the government expenditure increase, tax reduction, or both is offset by the crowding-out effect—the same issue we discussed in connection with Figures 15–2 and 15–3.

### Financing Budget Deficits with a Money Supply Change: Monetizing the Government Debt

In Chapter 10 we observed that if the government chooses not to finance its deficit by selling bonds to the public, it can "print the money" it needs. Now that we've seen how the Federal Reserve System can create money (Chapters 12 and 13), we can see exactly how this is done.

*A Hypothetical Example.* The Federal Reserve is the arm of the government that "prints the money." The following hypothetical example illustrates how this can occur. Rather than sell the deficit-financing government bonds to the public, suppose the U.S. Treasury simply sells them directly to the Fed. How can the Fed pay for the bonds? Since the Fed is the government's banker, suppose it simply credits or adds to the U.S. Treasury's account at the Fed (the government's checking account) the amount of funds necessary to cover the purchase of the bonds. Then the government writes checks against this account when it purchases goods and services in the economy. The check recipients, who provide the goods and services, deposit the checks in their banks and the economy's money supply is increased by this amount. In sum, one arm of the government, the Federal Reserve, creates money for another arm of the government, the U.S. Treasury. The Treasury spends this money, thereby increasing the entire economy's money supply.

## The Politics of Coordinating Fiscal and Monetary Policy

In principle, the goals of monetary and fiscal policy are the same—to smooth out economic fluctuations, to promote full employment, and to curb inflation. Ideally, therefore, those who advocate the use of discretionary, or "activist," policies would argue that policymakers should coordinate monetary and fiscal actions to achieve these ends. For example, during a recession appropriate fiscal policy should give rise to a deficit, while appropriate monetary policy should increase the rate of expansion of the money supply. On the other hand, if the economy is operating close to full employment and inflationary pressures are increasing, prudent fiscal policy should generate a budget surplus, and monetary policy should reduce the rate of expansion of the money supply. In practice, monetary and fiscal policies are not so easily coordinated.

### Fiscal Policy and the Political Process

A major reason coordination is difficult is that the size and timing of government expenditure and tax programs are influenced by other considerations in addition to those of economic stabilization. Expenditure and tax programs are a product of the political processes of Congress and reflect the objectives and priorities of many different special interest groups and regions of the country. There is often little regard for the fiscal policy implications of expenditure and tax programs conceived under these conditions.

A typical member of Congress finds it difficult, if not politically unrewarding, to consider actions taken on behalf of constituents in terms of their impact on the overall government budget. For example, a representative or senator who votes for

closing down Army bases in his or her district because the Army no longer needs them risks defeat at the polls. It may be true that the base closings will help trim the federal government's budget and relieve inflationary pressures in the economy. But local voters will be more concerned about the adverse impact of the base closings on the local economy.

In principle, the executive branch of the federal government is in a better position to have a broader perspective on fiscal policy. Moreover, the president is typically held accountable by voters for the overall state of the economy. Nonetheless, the president still must deal with Congress in order to have fiscal policy actions approved. A concerned president, seeking to avoid a recession by initiating a tax cut or a spending program, may be stymied by congressional politics. Or the president, seeking to curb inflation and an overheated economy, may have to resort to the exercise of presidential veto power over expansionary expenditure and tax programs passed by Congress. Even then, if the president vetoes a spending program or tax cut considered inflationary, Congress can override such a veto by passing the legislation again by a two-thirds majority of both houses.

The question is not whether or not to have fiscal policy. Whenever decisions are made about government spending and taxation, for whatever reasons, the resulting government expenditure and tax actions unavoidably affect total income, output, employment, and the level of prices. All such actions amount to a fiscal policy, even when they are taken primarily in pursuit of other objectives unrelated to maintaining economic stability, reasonably full employment, and a rein on inflation. *A basic difficulty with fiscal policy as a stabilization tool is that there are so many other objectives that often take precedence in the determination of government spending and tax policy. It is largely for this reason that fiscal policy often conflicts with monetary policy.*

### The Process of Monetary Policy

Unlike fiscal policy, monetary policy is made by a relatively small group of people: the Federal Open Market Committee (FOMC), consisting of the seven governors of the Federal Reserve Board plus five Federal Reserve bank presidents. The FOMC meets once a month in a closed-door session to hammer out monetary policy. The minutes of these secret meetings are not available to the public until 2 months after each meeting. Furthermore, the public does not have direct ballot box control or influence over FOMC members as it does over members of Congress. Indeed, the general public hardly knows what the Federal Reserve System is, let alone that monetary policy is made by the members of the FOMC. Hence, compared to members of Congress, FOMC members are sheltered from, and largely

unaccountable to, public pressures. Because of these institutional differences, FOMC members are relatively more free to pursue economic stabilization objectives than are members of Congress.

In sum, compared to fiscal policy, the process of making and carrying out monetary policy is more organized. It is also easier for monetary policy to focus more continuously on the pursuit of economic stabilization goals since, compared to fiscal policy, it is relatively less hampered by other considerations and the more direct political pressures that often dominate Congress. Nonetheless, between presidential jawboning and congressional oversight, the Fed may not be as independent as it sometimes appears.

### Questions

1. Even if it were possible to coordinate monetary and fiscal policy *initiatives,* what other problems might cause the *results* of such efforts to be uncoordinated?

2. What do you think a monetarist would say about the idea of coordinating monetary and fiscal policy?

---

*"Printing Money" in the Real World.* It may have struck you that this process is very similar to what happens when the Federal Reserve makes an open market purchase of government bonds. The major difference is that in our example the Fed buys the bonds directly from the U.S. Treasury rather than from the public. In fact, the direct sale of bonds by the U.S. Treasury to the Fed is illegal. However, in essence this is what happens when the Treasury sells government bonds to the public while at the same time the Fed makes an open market purchase of an equivalent amount of government bonds

from the public. In effect, the Fed (one arm of the government) is buying up the government debt issued by the Treasury (another arm of the government) to finance the government deficit. It's a "wash." In essence the government deficit is financed by the government's creation of money. When the Fed finances government deficit spending in this way, it is said to be *monetizing the government debt*—turning newly issued government bonds directly into newly created money. That is, the Fed is "printing money." The Fed may purchase an amount of bonds equal only to a portion of the bonds sold by the

Treasury to finance the budget deficit. In that case, only that portion of the deficit spending is financed by "printing money."

When deficit spending is financed by monetizing the government debt, the money supply is increased. And we know that such an increase will cause a rightward shift in the economy's *AD* curve and a rise in real GNP and the price level (Figure 14–4). This shift is an addition to the rightward shift in the *AD* curve and the rise in the price level that results from the increase in government spending, reduction in taxes, or both (Figure 15–3). In sum, *deficit spending financed by the creation of money—monetizing the government debt—is more expansionary than deficit spending financed only by selling bonds to the public—that is, without the creation of money.*

### Keynesian View Versus Monetarist View on Deficit Financing

Monetarists argue that deficit spending has a pronounced expansionary effect on the economy only to the extent that it is financed by the creation of money. This position is dictated by the monetarist view that money supply increases are very expansionary (bottom half of Figure 14–5), while government expenditure increases, tax reductions, or both are largely offset by crowding out (bottom halves of Figure 15–2 and Figure 15–3). The Keynesian view doesn't see money supply increases as nearly so expansionary (top half of Figure 14–5) or the crowding-out effect as nearly so large (top halves of Figures 15–2 and Figure 15–3). Consequently, the Keynesian view holds that deficit spending is expansionary largely because of the direct effects of government expenditure, tax reduction, or both on the economy's aggregate demand curve for goods and services. Keynesians would agree that deficit spending is more expansionary if it is financed by money creation than by the sale of bonds to the public without money creation. However, they don't think the method of financing makes nearly as much difference as the monetarists do.

## MONETARY POLICY AND GOVERNMENT DEFICITS

In the preceding Policy Perspective we discussed some of the difficulties of coordinating monetary and fiscal policy. We will now focus more specifically on the role that the interest rate plays in the conflict between government deficit financing and the objectives of monetary policy.

Autonomous increases in consumption and investment spending and increases in government spending, reductions in taxes, or both, cause the total expenditure schedule to shift upward and the *AD* curve rightward. However, the resulting rise in total income, or money GNP, will lead to an increase in the demand for money. This in turn will cause the interest rate to rise. The result is a cutback in investment spending that tends to dampen the rise in aggregate demand, with the extent of the cutback depending on the interest rate sensitivity of investment demand and money demand. (Recall the Keynesian view versus the monetarist view on this issue.) The only way to avoid this interest rate rise is for the Federal Reserve to increase the money supply. Of course, if the economy is already operating at or close to full employment, such a monetary expansion will result in a rise in the price level as the *AD* curve shifts rightward along the upward-sloping aggregate supply *(AS)* curve.

## Interest Rate Stability and Deficit Spending

Over the years critics of the Federal Reserve have frequently claimed that it is overly concerned with maintaining interest rate stability. As a result, such critics allege, the Fed often expands the money supply to keep the interest rate from rising when the rise itself is caused by an inflationary increase in aggregate demand. It would be wiser for the Fed to refrain from increasing the money supply and, thus, allow the interest rate rise to check the expansion of aggregate demand, thereby dampening inflationary pressures. Instead, when the Fed expands the money supply in such a situation, it adds further fuel to the inflationary increase in aggregate demand.

Critics go on to argue that these inflationary implications of the Fed's preoccupation with interest rate stability are of even more concern in the presence of government deficit spending. Why?

### Interest Rate and Aggregate Demand

Recall our discussion of government deficit spending. There we observed that a government deficit must be financed by issuing new government bonds. Recall that when these bonds are sold to the public, there is no change in the economy's money supply as long as the Federal Reserve doesn't engage in open market purchases (monetize the debt). The money that the public gives to the U.S. Treasury in exchange for the new bonds is returned to the economy when the government spends it. This government spending shifts the *AD* curve rightward, increasing

real GNP and the price level, and thus the demand for money. *The interest rate rises* and cuts back investment spending (the crowding-out effect), which tends to dampen the rightward shift in the *AD* curve.

However, if the Fed does not want the interest rate to rise, it must engage in open market purchases. That is, as soon as the interest rate begins to rise, the Fed will carry out open market purchases to keep it down. But this amounts to financing the government deficit by printing money, or monetizing the government debt. The money supply is increased. Government deficit spending financed in this way causes the economy's *AD* curve to shift rightward, both because of the spending increase and because of the increase in the money supply. Clearly, if the Fed does not want the interest rate to rise, the curb on the rise in aggregate demand due to the crowding-out effect is absent and inflationary pressures are greater.

### An Inflationary Bias

This is the reason that critics of the Fed contend that a preoccupation with interest rate stability gives monetary policy an inflationary bias that is accentuated by government deficit spending. They claim that this bias has been of particular concern since the middle 1960s. There has been only one government budget surplus (1969) since then. More alarming, however, has been the behavior of the cyclically adjusted budget, which economists generally regard as a more accurate measure of the expansionary impact of fiscal policy (see Chapter 10). Critics of the Fed note that the government ran a cyclically adjusted budget *surplus* throughout the last half of the 1950s and the first half of the 1960s—fiscal policy was contractionary. Since the beginning of 1966, except for 1969, the government has run a cyclically adjusted budget *deficit*—fiscal policy has been predominantly expansionary (see Chapter 10, Figure 10–4). To the extent that the Fed has been preoccupied with interest rate stabilization, critics argue that monetary policy and fiscal policy jointly contributed to the inflationary pressures that plagued the economy throughout the 1970s and up until the 1981–1982 recession which occurred shortly after the Fed began putting more emphasis on controlling money growth and less on stabilizing the interest rate. (See the Policy Perspective at the end of Chapter 14, pp. 338–341.)

## Inflation and the Interest Rate: Real Versus Money Interest Rate

There is another important consideration that bears on the issue of interest rate stability and monetary policy: the relationship between inflation and the interest rate. Whenever there is inflation, it is necessary to recognize the existence of two distinct measures of the interest rate: the real interest rate and the money interest rate.

### The Real Interest Rate

The **real interest rate** *is the interest rate calculated in terms of its purchasing power over goods and services.* Suppose I agree to lend you $100 for 1 year at an interest rate of 10 percent. At the end of 1 year you will pay me back the $100 plus $10, or $110. If there is *no change in the general price level* in the meantime, I give up $100 of purchasing power over goods today in exchange for $110 of purchasing power over goods a year from now. In 1 year I will get back 10 percent more purchasing power than I originally gave up. Hence, in this example the real interest rate equals 10 percent. The real interest rate is the rate that we would actually see in the market when the general price level is stable—that is, when there is no inflation (or deflation).

### The Money Interest Rate

The **money interest rate** *(sometimes called the nominal or market rate) is the interest rate calculated in terms of units of money, not purchasing power over goods.* Only when the general price level is expected to be stable is it true that the money interest rate equals the real interest rate. This is so because under these circumstances the purchasing power of a unit of money remains unchanged. When-

ever there is anticipated inflation (or deflation), the money interest rate and the real interest rate will differ from each other by the amount of the anticipated inflation (or deflation). This is so because when there is a change in the general price level, the purchasing power of a unit of money changes.

### Anticipated Rate of Inflation

*The anticipated rate of inflation is the difference between real and money interest rates.* To illustrate the difference between the real interest rate and the money interest rate, consider our $100 loan example again. To be willing to lend you $100, I again insist on getting back 10 percent more purchasing power in 1 year than I originally gave up. But now suppose both you and I *expect* a 5 percent rate of inflation. This means we both expect the purchasing power of a unit of money, a dollar, to decline by 5 percent over the next year. Therefore, I must charge you an additional 5 percent just to compensate myself for the anticipated loss in purchasing power on each unit of money, or dollar, that I lend you. Hence, I lend you $100 at a money rate of interest of 15 percent. The 15 percent money rate of interest equals the 10 percent real rate of interest plus the anticipated rate of inflation of 5 percent. This additional 5 percent may be thought of as an inflation premium that is added on to the real rate of interest. You will be willing to pay the 15 percent money rate of interest to borrow the $100 from me. Why? Because you will recognize that you are going to pay me back dollars that have lost 5 percent of their purchasing power due to inflation.

In short, the 15 percent money rate of interest means that I lend you $100 of money now, and in 1 year you repay me $115 of money. The 10 percent real rate of interest means that I lend you $100 of purchasing power *now*, and in 1 year you repay me the equivalent amount of purchasing power *plus* another 10 percent of purchasing power.

In summary:

money interest rate = real interest rate + anticipated rate of inflation

If the anticipated rate of inflation is zero, then the money interest rate and the real interest rate are the same. The money interest rate is the one we actually observe in the market for loans and bonds. The real interest rate is unobservable unless the anticipated rate of inflation is zero. In everyday life, the "interest rate" that people talk about is the money interest rate.

Now let's consider the implications of the distinction between the money and the real interest rate for the interest rate stabilization issue.

## Interest Rate Stability and Anticipated Inflation

Critics who claim that the Fed is too preoccupied with interest rate stability are referring to the money interest rate, since it is the rate observed in the market. The alleged inflationary bias of such a policy seems even more likely when this fact is recognized.

For example, assume the economy is operating close to full employment, somewhere along the steeply sloped range of the *AS* curve. Now suppose there is an increase in aggregate demand (possibly due to an increase in government deficit spending, an increase in autonomous investment and consumption spending, or both). The resulting rise in real GNP and the price level causes money demand to increase, which in turn leads to a rise in the money interest rate. Now the Fed reacts by increasing the money supply in order to bring the money interest rate back down (say, by making an open market purchase). But this causes a further rightward shift in the *AD* curve, which causes another increase in GNP and the price level. The increases in the price level cause people to begin to anticipate inflation. The onset of anticipated inflation causes the money interest rate to increase more as lenders now add on a larger inflation premium to the real interest rate. But this leads the Fed to again increase the money supply. The increase in the money supply causes another increase in aggregate demand, a further rise in real GNP

and the price level, another increase in the anticipated rate of inflation and hence in the money interest rate, and so on for another round.

*By trying to stabilize the level of the money interest rate, the Fed actually triggers self-defeating increases in the anticipated rate of inflation, which cause the money interest rate to rise even more as inflation gets worse!* At some point in this process Fed critics contend that the Fed becomes alarmed at the accelerating inflation and slams the brakes on the growth of the money supply, triggering a recession and an increase in unemployment. Now the Fed feels compelled to fight the recession above all else. Once again it expands the money supply. The process repeats itself, accompanied by periodic recessions and expansions with fluctuations in the inflation rate and unemployment. The Fed's alternation between fighting inflation and unemployment has been tagged the "stop-go policy" by Fed critics.

## Implications for Fiscal and Monetary Policy

A pattern of conflict among policy goals seems to be a major contributing factor to the inflation-unemployment process. The Fed would like to stabilize interest rates, but this goal conflicts with its desire to curb inflation. And its desire to curb inflation conflicts with its desire to avoid recession and unemployment. When the fiscal policy stance is one of almost continual budget deficits, particularly cyclically adjusted budget deficits, the inflationary bias of a monetary policy oriented toward interest rate stabilization is accentuated by the inflationary bias of fiscal policy.

Many critics of fiscal and monetary policy make the following recommendations. (1) The Federal Reserve should worry less about interest rate stabilization. These critics contend that this would help reduce the Fed's contribution to the inflationary bias jointly shared by fiscal and monetary policy. They

## POLICY PERSPECTIVE

### Why Have Real Interest Rates Been So High?

The persistently high level of real interest rates since 1980 has been a major concern of policymakers, the business community, and any person who borrows money. Since only nominal or money rates of interest are directly observable, it is necessary to subtract an estimate of the anticipated inflation rate from a nominal interest rate to obtain a measure of the real interest rate (recall that the nominal interest rate = the real interest rate + the anticipated rate of inflation). This is how the real interest rate was obtained from the nominal interest rate shown in Figure P15–1. Figure P15–1 indicates how high real interest rates have been by historical standards because the level of the real rate during the mid-1970s is representative of the level for the entire post-World War II period. What has caused the high level of real rates?

#### Monetary and Budget Deficit Explanations

It would appear that the initial increase from 1980 to 1981 was caused by the Fed's severe tightening of monetary policy which occurred at that time (see the Policy Perspective at the end of Chapter 14, pp. 338–341). Many observers blame the large federal budget deficits for the continuing high level of real interest rates since 1981. However studies attempting to assess the magnitude of the effect of deficits on real interest rates have provided mixed results. Though some studies have found significant effects, a number of studies using different methods have found the effects to be quite small. As the economic recovery proceeded from the 1981–1982 recession, neither the tight-money nor the budget deficit explanation

of high real interest rates seemed consistent with the strength of investment during the recovery.

#### Tax Policy and the Investment Boom

Another possible explanation attributes the high level of real interest rates to the increased business capital depreciation allowances for tax purposes enacted in 1981. This change in the tax law raised the real aftertax rate of return on new business investment. The higher rate of return on new investment makes it worthwhile for businesses short of cash to borrow at higher interest rates to finance good investment opportunities. Similarly, businesses with good cash flow find it profitable to invest in plant and equipment (real assets) rather than in financial assets or investments abroad. The tax law change explanation therefore argues that the real rate of interest in financial markets has been pulled up by the substantial increase in the prospective aftertax rate of return on business investment. Both investment and the real rate of interest in financial markets would probably have been lower if aftertax returns to investment had been lower according to the tax law change argument.

#### So Why Have Real Rates Been High?

It is not easy to assess the relative magnitudes of the effects on real interest rates of monetary restriction, large budget deficits, and high aftertax rates of return on new business investment. However a reasonably persuasive argument can be made that the effect of a higher aftertax rate of return on new business investment has dominated over the 1981-1984 period as a

**FIGURE P15-1  Nominal and Real Interest Rates**

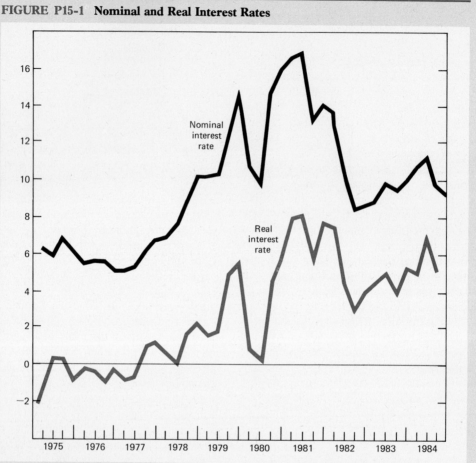

Nominal and real interest rate on 3-month Treasury bills. [Technical note: nominal interest rate measured as nominal yield to maturity; real interest rate measured as nominal yield less anticipated rate of inflation (measured as change in GNP implicit price deflator) over period to maturity.]

SOURCE: National Bureau of Economic Research/American Statistical Association, *Economic Outlook Survey*.

whole, and certainly over the recovery years of 1983 and 1984. The principal evidence supporting the argument is the coexistence of the strength of business investment and the high real rate of interest. Had tight-money or budget deficit effects been dominant, then high interest rates due to these effects would have overwhelmed the new incentives to invest and caused business investment to be relatively weak instead of relatively strong.

**Questions**

1. What would the evidence seem to suggest about the strength of the

crowding-out effect on investment caused by budget deficits in recent years?

2. How would you assess the extent of

coordination between monetary and fiscal policy over the 1981–1984 period?

claim that if the Fed focused less on interest rate stabilization, it could more effectively restrain demand-pull inflation. This in turn would go far to eliminate the Fed's periodic need to tighten the money supply in an attempt to curb an acceleration of inflation, efforts that often bring on recession and unemployment. (2) Congress must act more responsibly to curb excessive deficit spending, particularly during those times when the economy is experiencing inflationary expansion. At such times, a reduction or elimination of the cyclically adjusted budget deficit would in turn make it easier for the Fed to control inflation without causing a recession.

From October 1979 to October 1982 the Fed was less concerned about interest rate stabilization. (See the Policy Perspective in Chapter 14, pp. 338–341.) Since then the Fed's objectives have been less clear. However, large government deficits have persisted into the 1980s. During the 1979–1982 period the Fed's increasing concern with inflation led it to pursue a tight-money policy, resulting in high interest rates. In the opinion of many observers, this contributed significantly to the recessions of 1980 and 1981–1982. Though the inflation rate was finally reduced to under 10 percent in 1981 and then to under 5 percent in 1982, 1983, and 1984, the Fed was increasingly criticized for causing both high interest rates and high unemployment rates. It seems the Fed can't win as long as Congress allows deficit spending to continue unchecked.

### CHECKPOINT 15-2

**If the general price level declined over a long period of time (as it did in the United States during the latter part of the nineteenth century) so that people came to expect deflation, would the money interest rate be above or below the real interest rate? Why? Starting with the early 1960s, compare the behavior of the money interest rate shown in Figure 14-7, part a, with the annual percentage rate of change of the price level shown in Figure 6-5, part a. How might you explain the relationship between these two measures?**

### SUMMARY

**1.** Keynesians argue that fiscal policy is a more powerful economic stabilization tool than monetary policy. Disagreeing, monetarists claim that pure fiscal policy actions have little effect on total income and employment because of offsetting crowding-out effects on private spending, particularly investment. Keynesians, on the other hand, do not believe the crowding-out effect is that significant. Monetarists argue that deficit spending stimulates the economy only to the extent it is financed by money creation.

**2.** It is often difficult to coordinate fiscal and monetary policy in order to achieve economic stability and reasonably full employment with a minimum amount of inflation. A major reason is that many other considerations and political pressures affect government expenditure and tax programs, and these often take priority over economic stabilization objectives. By contrast, the monetary policymaking process is more organized, relatively more sheltered from political pressure, and, therefore, more easily and continuously focused on economic stabilization goals.

**3.** A monetary policy that is preoccupied with interest rate stability tends to have an inflationary bias, particularly in the presence of government deficit spending. This bias is accentuated by the onset of anticipated inflation, which causes the money interest rate to be greater than the real interest rate. Critics of such a policy argue that the inflation-unemployment problem would be lessened if monetary policymakers worried less about interest rate stability and fiscal policymakers avoided high-employment budget deficits during periods of inflationary economic expansion.

**4.** The high levels of real interest rates since 1980 are unprecedented in the post-World War II years. It has been variously argued that the causes are tight monetary policy, continuously large budget deficits, and increased business capital depreciation allowances which have raised the aftertax rate of return on new business investment. The latter explanation seems most plausible in view of the coexistence of strong business investment and high real rates of interest over the 1981–1984 period.

## KEY TERMS AND CONCEPTS

crowding out
money interest rate
real interest rate

## QUESTIONS AND PROBLEMS

**1.** How are Federal Reserve open market purchases similar to the financing of government deficits through money creation? How are they different?

**2.** It is often said that the extent of the crowding-out effect that results from a pure fiscal policy action is different when the economy is in a recession than when it is operating close to full-employment capacity. Explain why this might be so. Suppose a deficit is financed entirely by money creation. Can there still be a crowding out? Explain.

**3.** Suppose the economy is in a deep depression like the Great Depression of the 1930s. Suppose also that the money demand curve becomes very flat at a low level of the interest rate, and suppose that the equilibrium interest rate is at this low level. Would a pure fiscal policy action, such as a balanced budget government expenditure and tax increase, have a crowding-out effect? Under these conditions, would it make any difference whether the government resorts to a pure fiscal policy action as opposed to deficit spending financed by money creation?

**4.** Consider the interest rate that your local bank is currently paying on savings or time deposits. Using the currently reported rate of inflation, calculate what you think is the real rate of interest earned on such deposits. Remember that the money interest rate you earn is taxable income. Taking this into account, what do you think of the real rate of interest you earn on such deposits?

**5.** A number of economists claim that the Federal Reserve can push the money interest rate down in the short run. That is, they say that open market purchases have the initial effect of pushing it down but that these same purchases "sow the seeds" leading to a later rise in the interest rate. Explain how and why this might be so.

# 16

# The Inflation-Unemployment Trade-off: Supply-Side, Accelerationist, and New Classical Views

---

**AFTER READING THIS CHAPTER, YOU WILL BE ABLE TO:**

1. Explain the concept of the Phillips curve.

2. Explain why cost-push inflation or stagflation can cause the inflation rate and the unemployment rate to increase at the same time, contrary to the Phillips curve.

3. Explain the accelerationist view of the inflation-unemployment trade-off.

4. Explain the new classical view and its implications for monetary and fiscal policy.

5. Describe how the changing nature of the labor force can affect the aggregate supply curve and worsen the inflation-unemployment trade-off.

**I**t is conventional to associate a rising rate of inflation with a declining unemployment rate during the expansion phase of the business cycle. The behavior of inflation and unemployment during the 1960s certainly seemed to exhibit such a relationship. Until recent years it was also conventional to expect a declining rate of inflation along with a rising unemployment rate during recessions. However during the 1970s and until the recession of 1981–1982, inflation declined little, if at all, during periods of rising unemployment. These experiences have baffled the public and sent perplexed economists scrambling for explanations.

In this chapter we will look at the recent behavior of inflation and unemployment in the United States. We will begin by asking whether there is an inflation-unemployment trade-off, as suggested by a concept known as the Phillips curve. While there has been much controversy over the possible existence of such a curve, that debate has given rise to some interesting new explanations of inflation and unemployment that go beyond the Keynesian and monetarist analyses considered in previous chapters. We will examine these new developments in economic thinking as well as their implications for monetary and fiscal policy. We will also look at the changing nature of the unemployment problem and its implications for inflation.

## IS THERE AN INFLATION-UNEMPLOYMENT TRADE-OFF?

Ever since the late 1950s, economists, policymakers, and politicians have speculated and argued about the existence of a trade-off between inflation and unemployment. Many have claimed that it is possible to reduce unemployment if we are willing to tolerate higher rates of inflation. Conversely it is often claimed that inflation can be reduced only by incurring higher rates of unemployment. The implication is that there exists a trade-off—we can have less unemployment for more inflation, or less inflation for more unemployment.

The graphical representation of this trade-off is known as the **Phillips curve**, after the British economist A. W. Phillips, who in 1958 put forward empirical evidence of such a trade-off for the British economy over the period 1862–1957. Economists have subsequently devoted considerable effort to investigating the possible existence of Phillips curve trade-offs in industrialized countries for the postwar period. The experience with inflation and unemployment during the 1960s, 1970s, and the early 1980s suggests that such a trade-off is not so simple or straightforward. Indeed, the experience of recent years has raised serious questions about whether such a trade-off even exists.

### The Phillips Curve

Recall our discussion of the upward-sloping range of the aggregate supply curve in Figures 11–3 and 11–7 in Chapter 11. There we saw that increases in aggregate demand cause output and employment to increase, unemployment to fall, and the economy to move closer to full employment and beyond to full utilization of its productive capacity. However, over this range of the *AS* curve increases in aggregate demand result in ever larger increases in the general price level and ever smaller increases in employment and the quantity of output, or real GNP. Similarly, the ever larger increases in the general price level are accompanied by ever smaller reductions in the unemployment rate. This description characterizes the onset of demand-pull inflation as the economy approaches full employment. It suggests that we can only have a lower unemployment rate if we are willing to have a higher rate of inflation. This is the essence of the logic underlying the Phillips curve concept.

### *Graphical Representation of the Phillips Curve: A Menu of Choices*

A hypothetical Phillips curve is shown in Figure 16–1. The annual percentage rate of increase in the price level, the rate of inflation, is measured on the vertical axis, and the

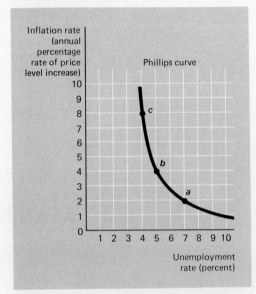

The Phillips curve is downward sloping left to right, suggesting that there is a trade-off between inflation (vertical axis) and unemployment (horizontal axis). The curve implies that the economy typically will experience both inflation and unemployment at the same time and that price stability and full employment are not compatible goals of fiscal and monetary policy. Most economists agree that increases in aggregate demand will lead to higher rates of inflation and lower unemployment rates, a movement up along the curve. However, today most would question whether this process is reversible—namely, whether the economy could move back down the *same* curve if there is a decrease in aggregate demand.

unemployment rate is measured on the horizontal axis. The curve slopes downward left to right, a reflection of the fact that a lower unemployment rate can only be achieved by having a higher rate of inflation, and vice versa.

The Phillips curve represents a menu of choices for monetary and fiscal policy. For example, the hypothetical Phillips curve of Figure 16-1 suggests that if policymakers want to keep the rate of inflation at 2 percent or less, they must be willing to settle for an unemployment rate of 7 percent or more, as represented by point *a* on the Phillips curve. On the other hand, if policymakers are willing to tolerate a 4 percent inflation rate, the unemployment rate can be reduced to 5 percent, point *b* on the Phillips curve. The trade-off between inflation and unemployment, represented by the slope of the curve between points *a* and *b*, is a reduction of 2 percentage points in the unemployment rate in exchange for a 2 percentage point increase in the inflation rate. However, the trade-off worsens between points *b* and *c*. If policymakers want to reduce the unemployment rate from 5 percent to 4 percent, they must be willing to settle for an increase in the inflation rate from 4 percent to 8 percent.

The lower right-hand portion of the Phillips curve suggests that to achieve a zero rate of inflation would require an unacceptably high rate of unemployment. Conversely, the upper left-hand portion suggests that a reduction of the unemployment rate below 4 percent would give rise to prohibitively high rates of inflation. The Phillips curve reminds us that economics is a study of choices, and that every choice has an associated cost. For example, choosing point *b* instead of point *a* means choosing a 5 percent instead of a 7 percent unemployment rate, a reduction in unemployment that is considered desirable. However, the cost of this choice is an additional 2 percentage points of inflation, from a rate of 2 percent at point *a* to 4 percent at point *b*—a move that is undesirable but necessary in order to achieve the lower unemployment rate.

It should be emphasized that the Phillips curve shown in Figure 16-1 is strictly a hypothetical example. The curve could lie to the left or right of the position shown. It might conceivably intersect the horizontal axis at a 10 percent unemployment rate. This would suggest that if we were willing to settle for a 10 percent unemployment rate, we could have a zero rate of inflation.

## Implications of the Phillips Curve: The Reversibility Issue

One important implication of the Phillips curve is that the economy typically will experience both inflation and unemployment at the same time. In other words, price stability and full employment are not compatible goals of fiscal and monetary policy. Another implication is that the economy can move up along the Phillips curve, reducing the unemployment rate and increasing the rate of inflation. However, the Phillips curve also implies that this process is reversible—that the economy can move back down the curve, as from point *c* to point *b* to point *a*, reducing the rate of inflation and increasing the unemployment rate. This implication is far more questionable and controversial than the others. Why?

It appears to most observers of the U.S. economy that the rate of inflation rises more readily than it falls. Almost all economists would agree that an increase in aggregate demand is likely to lead to an increase in the rate of inflation and a reduction in the unemployment rate, a movement up the Phillips curve. But few would argue that the economy is likely to follow the same path back down the Phillips curve in response to a decrease in aggregate demand. What does the evidence show?

## The Evidence: Is There a Stable Phillips Curve?

Figure 16–2 plots the rate of inflation (vertical axis) and the associated unemployment rate (horizontal axis) for the U.S. economy in each year since 1953. The data strongly suggest that there is not a stable Phillips curve relationship.

This figure shows us that periods during which the inflation rate rose and the unemployment rate fell were followed by periods in which the inflation rate fell by less than the previous rise as the unemployment rate increased. Clearly movements up along any alleged Phillips curve are not followed by reverse movements back down the same Phillips curve. Moreover, even more striking are

**FIGURE 16-2 The Relationship Between Inflation and Unemployment**

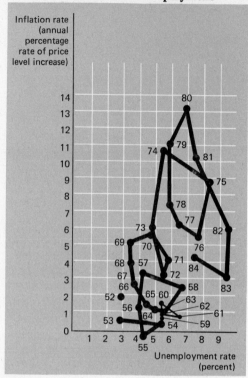

The relationship between the inflation rate (vertical axis) and the unemployment rate (horizontal axis) in the U.S. economy suggests that the Phillips curve is not stable. Periods of increasing rates of inflation accompanied by reductions in the unemployment rate were followed by periods in which the inflation rate fell by less than the previous rise as the unemployment rate increased. Even more striking are the instances in which both the inflation rate and the unemployment rate rose (1956 to 1957, 1962 to 1963, 1969 to 1970, 1973 to 1974, and 1979 to 1980). Such movements are completely contrary to the alleged shape of the Phillips curve.

the instances in which both the inflation rate and the unemployment rate rose (1956 to 1957, 1962 to 1963, 1969 to 1970, 1973 to 1974, and 1979 to 1980). These movements are completely contrary to the alleged shape of the Phillips curve. The data in Figure 16–2 suggest that the economy has experienced an upward spiraling inflation rate associated with a cyclical unemployment rate. Also, on average, the unemployment rate seems to have increased during the 1970s and early 1980s. Much of the rest of this chapter is concerned with possible explanations for the phenomena shown in Figure 16–2.

## Supply-Side Shocks and Stagflation

The concept of the Phillips curve really derives from the notion that increases in aggregate demand tend to increase inflation and reduce unemployment, while decreases in aggregate demand tend to reduce inflation and increase unemployment. However, during the 1970s the U.S. economy suffered a number of severe shocks on the supply side—large increases in the price of imported oil and other fuels, as well as intermittent worldwide food and raw materials shortages. These shocks have led economists to focus more attention on the role of aggregate supply and its interaction with aggregate demand as an explanatory factor underlying the behavior of inflation and unemployment.

Recall our discussion in Chapter 11 of cost-push inflation and the way it might be represented in terms of the aggregate supply curve, as illustrated in Figure 11–8. (You may want to reread that discussion at this point.) There we noted that a cost-push inflation could occur in a number of ways. It might come about because powerful unions force firms to pay higher wages by threatening to strike. These firms then pass on the resulting rise in per unit costs, at least in part, in the form of higher product prices. Cost-push inflation may also result because a few large firms in key industries exercise their market power to raise profits by increasing the prices they charge for their products. Another source of cost-push inflation, which was common during the 1970s, is increases in the prices of vital resources, such as energy and strategic raw materials. Again, such increases cause increases in per unit production costs that push up the prices of

almost all goods and services, as reflected by a rise in the general price level. In Figure 11–8 we saw how cost-push inflation is represented by an upward shift of the aggregate supply curve. For example, the aggregate supply curve $AS_0$ in Figure 11–8, part a, shifted upward to $AS_1$.

Given a cost-push, the economy can experience an increase in both the rate of inflation and the unemployment rate at the same time—the phenomenon termed stagflation, discussed previously in Chapter 11 and illustrated in Figure 11–8. Note that this is contrary to the conventional Phillips curve trade-off. Note also, however, that it does provide a possible explanation for the simultaneous increases in the rate of inflation and the unemployment rate incurred from 1956 to 1957, from 1962 to 1963, from 1969 to 1970, and certainly for the periods 1973 to 1974, and from 1979 to 1980, as shown in Figure 16–2. The 1973 to 1974 and 1979 to 1980 episodes in particular were clearly the consequence of supply shocks, resulting in each instance from dramatic increases in the price of imported oil.

### CHECKPOINT* 16-1

**Suppose the Phillips curve in Figure 16-1 shifts in such a way that unemployment can be reduced with a smaller increase in the rate of inflation. Sketch how the new Phillips curve might look. Suppose the Phillips curve in Figure 16-1 shifts so that the economy can have a zero percent rate of inflation when it has a 9 percent unemployment rate, and yet require larger increases in the inflation rate for each percentage point of reduction in the unemployment rate. Sketch how such a Phillips curve might look. If the Phillips curve represents a menu of choices, is the policymaker's selection of a point on the curve a normative or a positive issue? Why?**

*Answers to all Checkpoints can be found at the back of the text.

**FIGURE 16-3** **The Accelerationist View**

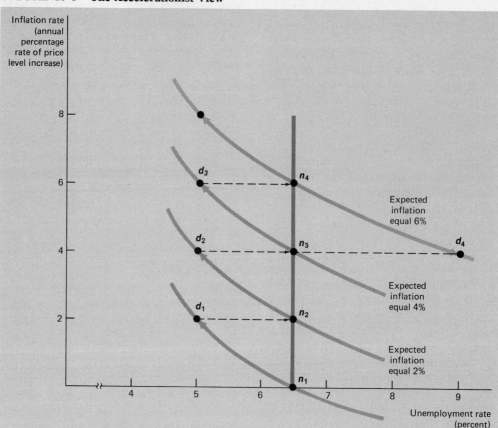

The accelerationist view holds that in the long run the economy tends to operate at its natural rate of unemployment, here hypothetically assumed to be 6.5 percent. An increase in aggregate demand increases profit and hence output and employment in the short run, thereby temporarily reducing the unemployment rate below the natural rate while increasing the inflation rate ($n_1$ to $d_1$). However workers, recognizing the decline in their real wages, then demand higher money wages which reduce profits causing production to fall and unemployment to return to its natural rate ($d_1$ to $n_2$). Repetition of this process causes the inflation rate to accelerate and the short-run Phillips curve to shift upward as workers' expected rate of inflation rises in recognition of the increases in the actual inflation rate. Hence there is no stable long-run Phillips curve trade-off between the inflation rate and the unemployment rate.

## ACCELERATIONIST AND NEW CLASSICAL VIEWS

While the simultaneous increase in the inflation and unemployment rates of 1973–1974 and 1979–1980 were caused by supply-side shocks, the factors underlying the inflation-unemployment rate pattern for other years shown in Figure 16–2 are less clear. Only the years 1963–1969 and 1976–1979 bear a resemblance to the hypothetical Phillips curve of Figure 16–1, and even these years suggest that the Phillips curve has shifted over time. Moreover these years were characterized by the expansion of aggregate demand in the economy. An example of the lack of reversibility back down a stable Phillips curve is illustrated by the recession of 1969–1970. This recession was largely due to a tightening of monetary policy in an attempt to curb what was then regarded as an alarmingly high inflation rate (about 5.3 percent). The consequence was a contraction of aggregate demand. Unfortunately this resulted in little change in inflation but a rather large increase in the unemployment rate, from 3.5 percent up to 4.9 percent. In general, what does the pattern of data points in Figure 16–2 suggest? If there is a Phillips curve it appears to be shifting upward and to the right.

Attempts to explain the data of Figure 16–2 have contributed to the development of the accelerationist view of the inflation-unemployment trade-off. This view essentially holds that the Phillips curve shifts upward as workers increase their expected rate of inflation. Milton Friedman, in his Nobel prize address, has added to this view the notion that increasing variability of the inflation rate increases the average level of the unemployment rate. Finally, probably the most controversial and dramatic development in macroeconomic thinking in recent years has been the emergence of the new classical view which is based on the theory of rational expectations. The new classical view concludes that *systematic* monetary and fiscal policy is essentially unable to affect unemployment and the level of total output in the economy! We will consider each of these views in turn.

## The Accelerationist View and the Natural Rate

The **accelerationist view** contends that in the long run a downward-sloping Phillips curve (such as that in Figure 16–1) does not exist. Instead it is argued that in the long run the economy tends to operate at its **natural rate of unemployment,** described earlier in Chapter 6. Basically *the accelerationist view holds that expansionary monetary and fiscal policies aimed at reducing the unemployment rate below the natural rate will result in an ever increasing, or accelerating, rate of inflation.* Let's see why.

## Adjustment to the Natural Rate: The Short-Run Trade-Off

Assume, for example, that the natural rate of unemployment is 6.5 percent, corresponding to point $n_1$ in Figure 16–3. However suppose policymakers and politicians think that a 6.5 percent unemployment rate is too high—that disgruntled voters will turn on them if something isn't done to reduce it. Consequently expansionary monetary and fiscal policies are initiated thereby increasing aggregate demand which in turn pulls up the price level. *Given the level of money wages,* firms will realize increased profits and therefore expand output and hire more labor. As a result, in the short run the economy moves from point $n_1$ to point $d_1$ in Figure 16–3. The unemployment rate has been reduced to 5 percent but the inflation rate has risen from zero percent to 2 percent. Thus there is a Phillips curve type trade-off, at least in the short run, according to the accelerationist view.

However the position $d_1$ cannot be maintained in the longer run. Why? Because while the general price level of final goods and services has risen, the money wages of workers have remained unchanged.[1]

This means that a worker's *real wage,* which equals the money wage divided by the general price level, has fallen. A worker gets paid the same number of dollars but these dollars buy less. Correctly perceiving themselves as worse off, the labor force demands and receives a higher money wage in order to

[1] When total demand increases, businesses are the first to become aware of it. They notice that goods are moving off shelves faster, that inventories are becoming more rapidly depleted, and that there is an increase in their backlogs of unfilled orders. Only *after* firms have increased prices do workers in general begin to become aware of the price increases—for example, during the course of shopping around for various goods and services.

"catch up" with the rise in the general price level. However when the money wage has risen to restore the real wage level that initially existed at $n_1$, firms' profits will be reduced back to their initial level. Firms therefore reduce output back to its initial level. Hence the unemployment rate returns again to the natural rate level of 6.5 percent. Now however the inflation rate is 2 percent, so that the economy is at point $n_2$ in Figure 16-3.

Note that at the initial point $n_1$ the inflation rate was zero percent and so workers had come to *expect* a zero percent rate of inflation. Only *after* the economy has made the short-run move to point $d_1$ do workers become aware that their expectation of a zero rate of inflation is no longer valid, that the inflation rate is in fact 2 percent. Along with the catch-up increase in their money wage which moves the economy to point $n_2$ workers revise their *expected* rate of inflation upwards to 2 percent. Hence according to the accelerationist view there is a short-run Phillips curve passing through points $n_1$ and $d_1$ that is stable as long as workers expect a zero rate of inflation. When they revise their expected inflation rate upwards to 2 percent, the short-run Phillips curve shifts upwards until it passes through point $n_2$.

### Policy Implications: No Long-Run Trade-off

The whole process may be repeated. Frustrated by the return of the unemployment rate to the 6.5 percent level, suppose policymakers once again use expansionary monetary and fiscal policies to stimulate aggregate demand.

Starting from point $n_2$ with the inflation rate already at 2 percent, prices accelerate ahead of money wages once again, profits rise and firms again expand output and employment. The economy moves from point $n_2$ to point $d_2$ up along the short-run Phillips curve corresponding to a 2 percent expected rate of inflation. Again there is a short-run reduction of the unemployment rate to 5 per-

cent, but the inflation rate now rises to 4 percent. Workers realize their real wage has fallen and that their expectation of a 2 percent rate of inflation is too low since the actual inflation rate is now 4 percent. Hence they ask for and receive a money wage increase that restores their real wage to its previous level. Profits fall again to their original level and therefore the unemployment rate returns to the natural rate of 6.5 percent, corresponding to point $n_3$. The short-run Phillips curve has shifted upward to a position, at point $n_3$, corresponding to an expected inflation rate of 4 percent. Unfortunately, the long-run consequence of policymakers' efforts to reduce the unemployment rate below the natural rate is an undesirable acceleration of the inflation rate from 2 percent to 4 percent *without* any reduction of the unemployment rate at all!

The process could be repeated again and again with the economy moving from $n_3$ to $d_3$ to $n_4$ and so forth, the inflation rate rising to ever higher levels. The downward-sloping short-run Phillips curves through points $n_1d_1$, $n_2d_2$, $n_3d_3$, and so on, correspond to successively higher expected inflation rates. Policymaker efforts to move along a short-run Phillips curve such as $n_1d_1$ cause it to shift upward to a less desirable position such as $n_2d_2$. And repeated efforts result in yet higher and even less desirable positions. In short, a stable Phillips curve representing an unchanging inflation-unemployment trade-off simply doesn't exist according to the accelerationist view. For example, in the *long run* an inflation rate of 2 percent cannot be continuously maintained *together with* a 5 percent unemployment rate, as represented by point $d_1$. If policymakers wanted to keep the unemployment rate at 5 percent they would have to expand aggregate demand continuously. But such a policy would unavoidably cause the inflation rate to increase from 2 percent (point $d_1$) to 4 percent (point $d_2$) to 6 percent (point $d_3$), and so on.

In the long run there can be an unchanging inflation rate only if the economy's unemployment rate is equal to the natural rate of unemployment. That is, the inflation rate can remain unchanged only if the economy is at a point on the vertical line through points $n_1$, $n_2$, $n_3$, and $n_4$.

In sum, *according to the accelerationist view there is no stable long-run Phillips curve trade-off between the inflation rate and the unemployment rate. Persistent attempts by policymakers to stimulate aggregate demand to reduce the unemployment rate below the natural rate will cause an ever increasing rate of inflation.*

What happens if restrictive monetary and fiscal policies are implemented in an attempt to reduce the inflation rate? Suppose the economy is at point $n_4$ in Figure 16–3 where the actual inflation rate is 6 percent and the short-run Phillips curve through $n_4$ corresponds to an expected inflation rate of 6 percent. Suppose the Fed shows money growth so that the growth rate of aggregate demand declines and firms now find that the growth rate of prices of their products slows down from a 6 percent to a 4 percent rate. Since workers still expect a 6 percent inflation rate they continue to push up their money wages at a 6 percent rate. Therefore firms experience declining profits and cut back output and employment. The unemployment rate increases to 9 percent as the economy moves back down the Phillips curve to point $d_4$. When workers finally realize that their expected inflation rate is higher than the actual rate of 4 percent, they revise their expected inflation rate to 4 percent and become willing to settle for a 4 percent rate of increase in their money wage. Firms' profits rise and they expand output and employment until the unemployment rate returns to the natural rate corresponding to point $n_3$. The Phillips curve has shifted down to the position $n_3d_3$.

### The Inflation Rate and the Natural Rate: Friedman's View

The vertical line through $n_1$, $n_2$, $n_3$, and $n_4$ in Figure 16–3 represents the long-run relationship between the inflation rate and the natural rate of unemployment. The fact that the line is vertical represents the *assumption* that the natural rate of unemployment is unchanged regardless of the level of the inflation rate. Taking issue with this assumption, Milton Friedman (Nobel prize winner in economics, 1976) has put forward the view that the natural rate of unemployment is *not* constant. Rather, he argues that it tends to be larger the higher the level of the inflation rate. Instead of the vertical line of Figure 16–3, Friedman suggests that the line representing the long-run relationship between the inflation rate and the natural rate of unemployment is positively sloped as represented, say, by the line through $u_1$, $u_2$, $u_3$, and $u_4$ in Figure 16–4. A simplified explanation of why this should be so follows.

*Friedman's Analysis: The Role of Inflation Variability.* Friedman argues that increasing *variability* of the inflation rate causes a reduction in the efficiency with which market prices guide economic activity. Recall from our discussion in Chapter 2 how market prices serve as a signaling mechanism that determines how the economy's different kinds of labor and other resources are *allocated* to those uses for which they are best suited. Recall also from Chapter 2 that whenever there is a misallocation of labor and other resources the economy will not be able to operate on its production possibilities frontier—that is, there will be economic inefficiency and the economy will produce less than its maximum possible total output level. Friedman's argument in essence is that increased variability of the inflation rate is reflected in greater variability of all market prices. This adds "noise" to the market price signaling mechanism which reduces its allocative efficiency and thereby the economy's "on-average" or natural rate of output level, thus increasing the natural rate of unemployment. Therefore the greater the degree of inflation variability the higher is the natural rate of unemployment. Friedman observes that historically inflation variability tends to be larger the higher the level of the inflation rate. Hence, it follows, *Friedman concludes,*

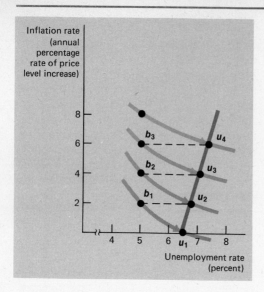

Inflation rate (annual percentage rate of price level increase)

Unemployment rate (percent)

**FIGURE 16-4   Accelerationist View When Natural Rate Rises With Inflation Rate**

According to Milton Friedman's view of the natural rate, increased variability of the inflation rate reduces the efficiency with which market prices guide economic activity, thereby reducing the economy's natural rate of output and hence increasing its natural rate of unemployment. Since greater inflation rate *variability* appears to be associated with higher *levels* of the inflation rate, the natural rate of unemployment tends to rise with the level of the inflation rate, as indicated by the points $u_1$, $u_2$, $u_3$, $u_4$. Combining this view of the natural rate with the accelerationist view of the short-run Phillips curve, the implication is that persistent policy attempts to reduce unemployment below the natural rate will cause ever increasing inflation along with a rising natural rate of unemployment ($u_1$ to $b_1$ to $u_2$ to $b_2$ and so forth).

that the natural rate of unemployment tends to be larger the higher the level of the inflation rate.

We can modify the accelerationist view to account for Friedman's view of the natural rate as shown in Figure 16-4. The line through $u_1$, $u_2$, $u_3$, and $u_4$ representing the long-run relationship between the inflation rate and the natural rate of unemployment is now positively sloped—the natural rate is larger the higher the inflation rate. For example (using hypothetical data), when the inflation rate is zero percent the natural rate of unemployment is 6.5 percent (point $u_1$), for a 2 percent inflation rate the natural rate is 6.8 percent (point $u_2$), and for a 4 percent inflation rate it is 7.1 percent (point $u_3$). Instead of the adjustment path (Figure 16-3) $n_1$ to $d_1$ to $n_2$ to $d_2$, and so forth, the adjustment path (Figure 16-4) is now $u_1$ to $b_1$ to $u_2$ to $b_2$, and so on.

In sum, *combining the accelerationist view with Friedman's view of the natural rate it*

*follows that persistent attempts by policymakers to stimulate aggregate demand to reduce the unemployment rate below the natural rate will cause an ever increasing rate of inflation as well as an increasing natural rate of unemployment.*

*The Evidence.* The data points in Figure 16-2 do suggest that the variability of the inflation rate has increased over time. That is, the magnitude of the up and down movements in the inflation rate (measured on the vertical axis) appears to have increased during the 1970s and early 1980s. Also, it appears that the level of the inflation rate has on-average increased along with the rise in inflation variability, as Friedman has observed. And along with these increases the average level of the unemployment rate seems to have increased as well, consistent with Friedman's view that there exists a long-run relationship wherein the natural rate of unemployment tends to increase with the level of the inflation rate.

How well does the accelerationist view combined with Friedman's view of the natural rate conform to the evidence in the data? A suggestive interpretation comparing the facts of Figure 16–2 with the theory as represented in Figure 16–4 is shown in Figure 16–5. Examining Figure 16–5 one should remember that, like beauty, the degree of apparent conformity between fact and theory is all in the eye of the beholder.

## The New Classical View

According to the accelerationist view policymakers can keep the unemployment rate below the natural rate, though the benefits to society of a higher level of employment can be achieved only at the cost of an ever increasing rate of inflation. By contrast, *the new classical view argues that policymaker attempts to reduce the unemployment rate below the natural rate cannot succeed, and, worse yet, they still impose the costs of an ever increasing inflation rate on society.* In brief, while the accelerationist view offers the prospect of a trade-off between the benefit of lower unemployment and the cost of ever increasing inflation, the new classical view argues there will be only the cost and no benefit. The linchpin of the new classical view is the theory of rational expectations.

### Rational Expectations

*The* **theory of rational expectations** *holds that people form their expectations about the future course of economic activity (wages, prices, employment, and so forth) on the basis of their knowledge, experience, and understanding of how the economy works, including the effects of monetary and fiscal policy. Furthermore they make use of all relevant, available economic data and information when they form their expectations.* The theory of rational expectations implies that people do not persist in making the same mistakes (that is, systematic mistakes) over and over when

predicting future events. Rather, they become aware of their systematic errors and alter their behavior to eliminate them. In short, the theory of rational expectations asserts that people go about forming their expectations in a reasonable, or rational, way.

### The Policy Ineffectiveness Argument

Consider now how the theory of rational expectations would change the accelerationist scenario described in Figure 16–3. Recall that there an increase in aggregate demand, caused by an increase in the money supply, say, led to an increase in the price level. Given the *unchanged* level of many wages in the short run, profits rose, stimulating output and employment and thereby reducing the unemployment rate below the natural rate ($n_1$ to $d_1$). In the long run workers realized that the price level had risen, hence that their real wages had fallen, and demanded and received money wage increases that restored real wages to their initial level. Thus profits fell to their initial level and unemployment rose back to the natural rate ($d_1$ to $n_2$). The process could be repeated over and over again.

Note that in this scenario it was the fact that workers' *expectation* of the inflation rate was lower than the actual inflation rate during each expansion phase ($n_1$ to $d_1$, $n_2$ to $d_2$, and so forth) which made the short-run unemployment rate reduction possible. Workers incorrectly perceived that their real wage was higher because while they were immediately aware of the increase in their money wage, they were not immediately aware of the *actual* rate of increase in the price level. For example, along the short-run Phillips curve $n_1$ to $d_1$ (Figure 16–3) workers expected a zero rate of inflation, but in fact the price level rose at a 2 percent rate. Along the short-run Phillips curve from $n_2$ to $d_2$ they expected a 2 percent rate of inflation, but the price level actually rose at a 4 percent rate.

According to rational expectations theory workers will not keep making this same (systematic) mistake over and over. They will know the way the system works and form

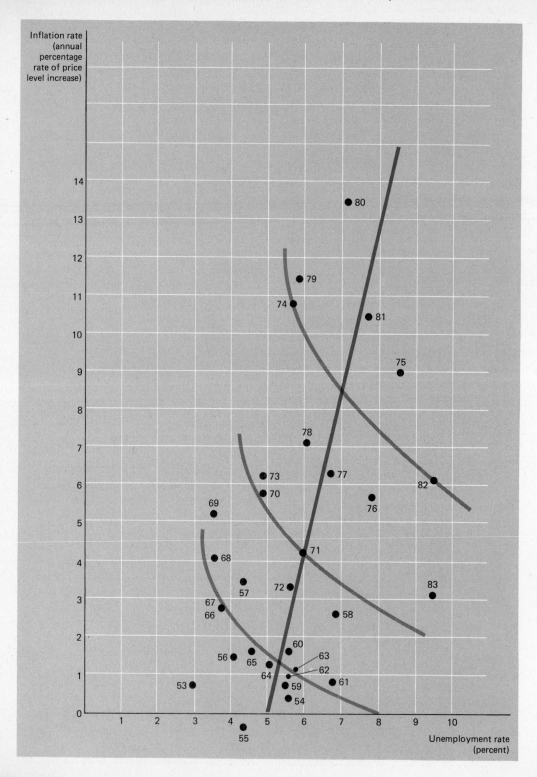

their expectations on the basis of that knowledge. In particular, they will know that the inflation rate increases whenever the monetary authority expands the money supply in an attempt to reduce the unemployment rate below the natural rate. They will immediately expect the higher inflation rate and immediately realize that they must push up their money wage simply to maintain the level of their real wage. Hence firms' profits will not increase in response to the increase in aggregate demand because the increase in the price level will be offset immediately by increases in money wages. Consequently there will be no reduction in the unemployment rate below the natural rate. Monetary policy attempts to lower the unemployment rate will only succeed in causing an ever increasing rate of inflation. The economy will move directly from $n_1$ to $n_2$ to $n_3$, and so on, in Figure 16–3. There is not even a short-run Phillips curve trade-off. Hence, *according to the new classical view, systematic policymaker attempts to affect real variables in the economy, such as total output (real GNP) and the unemployment rate, will be ineffective. Thus the new classical view implies that systematic monetary and fiscal policy efforts to smooth out the business cycle will be ineffective.*

Note that the new classical view emphasizes that it is *systematic* policy efforts that have no effect on real variables. Systematic policy actions are those that are predictable because, according to rational expectations theory, people understand both how the economy works (from experience) and how government policymakers react to the economy's performance—for example, by slowing money supply growth during business cycle expansions and increasing it during recessions. The only kind of policy actions that will affect real variables are those that are unpredictable. They come as "surprises"— they are random events. But as the new classical view points out, monetary and fiscal actions that are random must be totally unrelated to the economy's performance except by chance. Such actions can hardly be said to constitute a meaningful policy.

### Reasons Why Policy Is Still Effective

The new classical view's conclusion that systematic monetary and fiscal policy will not affect the economy's real variables is certainly contrary to what most economists and policymakers believe. Even the most ardent supporters of the new classical view would likely agree that there are considerations that suggest why systematic monetary and fiscal policy actions are still able to affect the economy's real variables.

*Learning and Lags.* The theory of rational expectations (the backbone of the new classical view) assumes that people form expectations on the basis of what they have learned about the economy through experience and information gathering. If we envision a world where there is no change in technology, institutions, laws, customs, and tastes, then it would seem that one could become fairly well informed about how the economy works. In the real world all of these things are subject to ongoing change in varying degrees. Therefore learning about "how the system works" is more difficult. Learning about change is subject to time lags, and new knowledge is already in the process of becoming obsolete.

---

**FIGURE 16–5  Combined Accelerationist-Friedman Natural Rate Views: Theory Versus Facts**

Combining the data of Figure 16–2 with the theory represented in Figure 16–4 suggests that there may be a "rough" correspondence between theory and fact. There is obviously considerable room for interpretation and disagreement on this issue however.

---

## POLICY PERSPECTIVE

### Viewpoints on the Costs of Reducing Inflation*

The cost of reducing the rate of inflation through restrictive monetary and fiscal policy can be measured in terms of the amount of output not produced (the GNP gap described in Chapter 6) due to the increased unemployment caused by such disinflation policies. The double-digit inflation of the 1970s unleashed a debate over the size of these costs while events of the early 1980s provided some evidence. Two principal viewpoints emerged on this issue: One may be termed the "mainstream" and the other the "credibility" view, the latter representing to varying degrees adherents of the new classical view, or those who are at least sympathetic to the theory of rational expectations.

#### The Mainstream View

The mainstream view puts the highest estimate on the cost of disinflation, arguing that the downward rigidity, or inertia, of U.S. prices and money wages would require a severe recession to reduce inflation significantly. According to many economists, a principal cause of the inertia observed in U.S. data is the unique North American institution of the 3-year union wage contract with expiration dates staggered across different industries. Indeed, cross-country evidence from most European countries and Japan suggests that the form of labor contracts is an important factor underlying inflation inertia in the United States. A suggested remedy is an alternative institutional arrangement, such

*Based on R.J., Gordon, " 'Credibility' vs. 'Mainstream': Two Views of the Inflation Process," in W.D. Nordhaus, ed., *Inflation: Prospects and Remedies, Alternatives for the 1980s,* no. 10 (Washington: Center for National Policy), October 1983, pp. 25–34.

as the system of 1-year contracts with simultaneous expiration dates prevalent in Japan.

#### The Credibility View

The credibility view asserts that the degree of responsiveness of inflation to restrictive monetary and fiscal policies is influenced by people's expectations about the future behavior of policymakers, clearly a view with a rational expectations orientation. If a recession is typically expected to lead to a policy stimulus, then firms will typically expect a short recession. Rather than cut prices to sell excessive product inventories, they are more likely to await recovery in the expectation that shortly their inventories may be sold without the lost profits implied by price cuts. The credibility view holds that if firms and workers *believe* that policymakers are prepared to fight inflation with sustained restrictive policies, no matter how severe the resulting recession, firms will be quicker to lower prices to sell off excessive inventories and workers more willing to forgo wage increases out of fear for their jobs. Therefore the credibility view argues that to the extent policymakers establish credibility in their intentions to fight inflation, the output loss caused by restrictive monetary and fiscal policy will be considerably less than that predicted by the mainstream view.

#### What Does the Evidence Say?

Empirical research suggests that inflation inertia was less important in earlier eras in U.S. history, and in some other countries during the postwar era, such as in Japan for example. The apparent shift toward greater inertia in the United States

**FIGURE P16-1   Reduction in Inflation Rate and Increase in Unemployment Rate, 1979–1984**

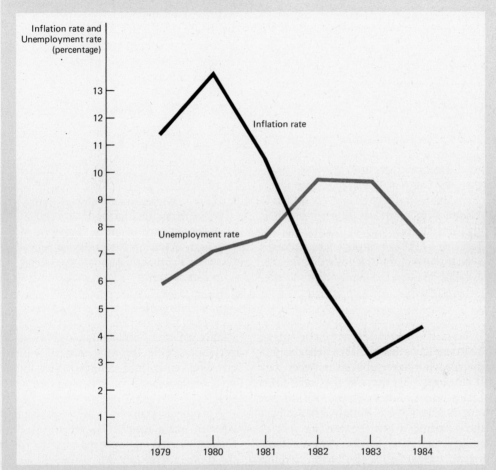

about 1950 could be explained equally well by either the mainstream or the credibility view. The mainstream view points to the development of the 3-year wage contract. The credibility view points to the national policy shift to commitment to fight recessions (the Employment Act of 1946), and the belief by firms and workers that the government really will act promptly to stimulate the economy

when confronted by a recessionary downturn in demand.

But there were other nations in the postwar era that made a new commitment to maintain full employment, and some of them exhibit less inflation inertia than the United States. Such cases suggest that the form of the labor contract may play an important role in inflation inertia in the postwar United States. Three-year staggered contracts contribute to inertia because union wage negotiations tend to look backward to the rate of wage gain realized in other industries in last year's negotiations, rather than forward to the likely stance of monetary and fisal policy.

### Experience From the 1981–1982 Recession

The benefit of hindsight makes it clear that the Fed's commitment to fight inflation with a tight monetary policy contributed significantly to the 1981–1982 recession, by many measures the most severe since the Great Depression. As shown in Figure P16–1, the resulting reduction in the inflation rate was significant, but the fact that in 1982 unemployment reached a record postwar high suggests that the cost was enormous, a fact which tends to support the mainstream view. Advocates of the credibility view may argue that the public's 15 years of experience with rising inflation rates understandably led to a belated recognition that at last the Fed was seriously committed to fighting inflation, even at the expense of serious damage to incomes and jobs.

### Questions

1. It may well be said that the evidence from the 1981–1982 recession is consistent with both the mainstream view and the credibility view. Why?

2. Why might automatic cost-of-living adjustments tied to the inflation rate make the issue of union contract length irrelevant to the debate between the mainstream and credibility points of view?

Policymakers and politicians come and go so that predicting policymaker behavior and knowing policymaker objectives (what they will do versus what they say they will do) is not easy. Just as history shows that no two business cycles are ever exactly alike, policymaker response to such cycles (the mix of monetary and fiscal action, its magnitude, duration, and timing) is also bound to differ from one cycle to the next. To this extent there is always a certain amount of unpredictability and surprise in any "systematic" policy action. Returning to Figure 16–3, for example, workers must be able to perfectly predict the amount of monetary expansion and its effect on the price level. Having done so, they must then increase their money wages in unison with the price level if firms are not to experience any increase in profits which would cause them to increase employment and output.

*Fixity of Contracts.* The new classical view's policy ineffectiveness argument implicitly assumes prices and money wages are perfectly flexible. But in fact buyers and sellers often enter into contracts that fix the price of a good or service for some period of time.

A familiar example is a union contract wherein union members agree to work for some stipulated money wage over the life of the contract, typically 2 to 3 years in length. Suppose the economy is initially at point $n_1$ in Figure 16–3 and that at least some members of the total labor force have entered into such a union contract. Suppose further that the monetary authority announces that it is going to expand the money supply—there is no surprise. Despite the fact that all workers now know and expect what is about to happen, those under union contract cannot increase their money wage (it is fixed by the contract) in anticipation of the increase in the price level. When the price level increase occurs, those firms employing the union labor will realize increased profits causing them to increase employment and output. Unemployment will be reduced below the natural rate, at least until the union contract expires and union workers are able to negotiate a higher money wage. In the meantime, because of the money wage fixed by contract, systematic (predictable) monetary policy is able to affect real variables in the economy, such as output and unemployment.

---

### CHECKPOINT 16-2

**Perhaps you would disagree with the locations of the short-run Phillips curves shown in Figure 16-5; study the data points in that figure again and sketch in short-run Phillips curves in a way that you think is more consistent with the accelerationist view. Explain why it is, or is not, reasonable to believe that short-run Phillips curves are shaped such as those in Figure 16-4 for example.**

---

## INFLATION AND THE CHANGING NATURE OF UNEMPLOYMENT

What level of the unemployment rate corresponds to "full employment"? This is the level that is regarded as the acceptable, or the normal or natural, unemployment rate. Recall our discussion of this question in Chapter 6. (You may want to reread that discussion.) There we observed that many economists believe that since the mid-1960s there has been a definite rise in the *level* of the unemployment rate that corresponds to the natural unemployment rate. What are the implications of this rise for efforts by policymakers to deal with the problems of inflation and unemployment? To answer these questions, let's first consider the changing nature of the unemployment rate, and then the way this change is reflected in the aggregate supply curve.

## The Changing Nature of Unemployment

The Department of Labor actually publishes six different measures of the unemployment rate. The level of unemployment can appear considerably different depending on which measure we look at. However, the news media, the public, politicians, and policymakers all tend to focus on only one of these. It is considered the official unemployment rate.

The official unemployment rate goes back to the 1930s. Then it was designed to measure unemployment among adult male heads of household. At that time, adult male heads of household did in fact constitute nearly the entire labor force. Over the years, however, the composition of the labor force has changed drastically, so that now the official unemployment rate covers a much more diverse group of people. Today work by male heads of household still accounts for about two-thirds of all hours worked because these men are primarily full-time workers. But now they constitute no more than 40 percent of the labor force. The other 60 percent of the labor force is made up of the following types of workers:

1. Slightly more than 50 percent of the country's population of adult females now work or are seeking work. The great majority of these are not "heads of household," but "dependents" holding part-time jobs.

2. People who are officially "retired," but available for part-time work up to the point at which their earnings would reduce payments from their social security benefits.

3. Young single adults who maximize their incomes by alternating between periods of full-time employment and periods of official "unemployment," when they draw tax-free "unemployment" compensation.

4. Unemployables registered for "employment" in order to be eligible for welfare checks and food stamps.

5. A sizeable number of full-time students who are available for part-time work only.

In sum, the composition of the labor force has changed over time so that male heads of household represent a smaller portion, while all others (the five categories listed above) represent a larger portion. Many economists argue that a large number of the people in the "all other" portion are in circumstances that do not compel them to find work with the same urgency as the typical adult male head of household. Others in the all other portion are simply not as employable, either because of a lack of marketable job skills or because of disabilities of one form or another. Hence, many economists claim that the growing importance of the all other portion of the labor force means that the level of the official unemployment rate corresponding to the notion of "full employment" has risen.

Remember from Chapter 6 that another factor that may contribute to this rise in the natural unemployment rate is the more rapid rate of growth of the labor force relative to the rate of growth of the total population. This situation reflects an influx of young workers born in the postwar "baby boom" combined with a sharp drop in the birthrate since the early 1960s. Yet another possible factor in the rise of the natural unemployment rate is the increased flow of nonpaycheck money in the form of more liberal unemployment compensation and welfare benefits. It is argued that this makes it easier for people to remain unemployed longer while looking for a job, and may lead some to list themselves as unemployed even though they are not trying very hard to find work.

## Aggregate Supply and Inflation: Policy Implications

The changing nature of unemployment has implications for the aggregate supply curve and the relationship between inflation and unemployment. These implications are illustrated in the hypothetical example of Figure 16–6. The aggregate supply curve corresponding to the situation *before* the changes in the nature of unemployment just described is $AS_1$, and $AS_2$ is the aggregate supply curve *after* these changes.

**FIGURE 16–6  The Changing Nature of the Labor Force Affects the Aggregate Supply Curve**

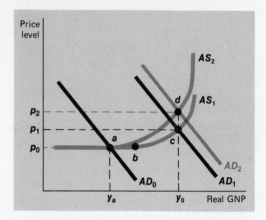

The changing nature of the labor force has caused price level increases to be larger when the economy approaches full employment.

Such change causes the aggregate supply curve to change shape from $AS_1$ to $AS_2$. As a result, if monetary or fiscal policy attempts to reduce unemployment by increasing real GNP from $y_a$ to $y_0$, for example, the $AD$ curve must be shifted rightward from $AD_0$ to $AD_2$ along $AS_2$, a larger amount than the shift to $AD_1$ required along $AS_1$. Consequently the increase in the price level from $p_0$ to $p_2$ along $AS_2$ is greater than that from $p_0$ to $p_1$ along $AS_1$. Thus the changing nature of the labor force tends to worsen the short-run inflation-unemployment trade-off along the Phillips curves in Figures 16–3 and 16–4.

Assume that these changes make no difference in the economy's ability to produce any real GNP up to $y_a$, corresponding to point $a$ on the aggregate supply curves. However, beyond point $a$ $AS_2$ lies above $AS_1$. This reflects the fact that along $AS_2$ beyond point $a$, as compared to $AS_1$, it is harder for the economy's producers to obtain and efficiently use the additional labor needed to increase output because the "all other" portion of the labor force described above is much larger for $AS_2$ than for $AS_1$. (Remember that money wages and other input prices are fixed for any movement along an $AS$ curve—$AS_2$ doesn't rise more rapidly than $AS_1$ because of any change in money wages or input prices.) Hence for increases in real GNP beyond $y_a$ *per unit production costs rise more rapidly along $AS_2$* because of production inefficiencies associated with using labor that is less well trained and less committed to continuous employment. This, in turn, causes a more rapid rise in the prices firms charge for their products. Therefore, for any given increase in real GNP beyond point $a$, the economy's price level rises more along $AS_2$ than along $AS_1$.

### Implications for Fiscal and Monetary Policy

Consider the implications of this for fiscal and monetary policy. Assume the economy's $AD$ curve is initially at $AD_0$ in Figure 16–6, so that real GNP is $y_a$ and the price level is $p_0$. Suppose policymakers want to reduce unemployment by stimulating aggregate demand enough to increase real GNP to $y_0$ where the associated unemployment rate is 6 percent. This is done by either increasing the money supply or government expenditures, reducing taxes, or some combination of these.

If the aggregate supply curve is $AS_1$ the price level doesn't begin to rise until the economy reaches point $b$ on the aggregate supply curve. The policymakers' goal is achieved once the $AD$ curve has been shifted to $AD_1$ where it intersects $AS_1$ at point $c$ on $AS_1$. The economy's price level rises from $p_0$ to $p_1$. By comparison, suppose instead the economy's $AS$ curve is $AS_2$, reflecting the changes in the nature of the labor force described above. Now in order for policymakers to achieve their goal the $AD$ curve must be shifted further to the right to the position $AD_2$. The economy's price level rises more, from $p_0$ to $p_2$, corresponding to point $d$ on $AS_2$.

### Summary of Implications of the Changing Nature of Unemployment

In sum, as a result of the changing nature of the labor force, the economy has to incur a larger rise in the price level in order to reduce the unemployment rate. Policymakers' attempts to reduce the official unemployment rate to levels considered natural or "acceptable" in the past now seem to generate higher rates of inflation. This is why policymakers and economists over the past 2 decades have tended to move the "full-employment" benchmark for the official unemployment rate upward from around 4 percent to 6 to 6.5 percent. It is argued that this helps avoid excessively expansionary fiscal and monetary policy. Taking account of the effect on the aggregate supply curve of the changing nature of the labor force only worsens the short-run inflation-unemployment trade-off along the Phillips curves shown in Figures 16–3 and 16–4.

### CHECKPOINT 16–3
**Look at the data in Figure 16–2 again. Do you see any pattern in these data that might, at least in part, be attributable to the changing nature of the labor force?**

### SUMMARY

**1.** Economists have speculated that there is a trade-off between inflation and unemployment. The trade-off may be represented by the Phillips curve, which indicates that lowering the unemployment rate means accepting more inflation, and that reducing inflation means accepting more unemployment. However, evidence suggests that movements up the Phillips curve (increasing inflation and reducing unemployment) cannot be followed by movements back down the same curve (reducing inflation while increasing unemployment). Data show that the economy has experienced an upward-spiraling inflation rate associated with a cyclical unemployment rate.

**2.** Increases in the price of inputs to production that are initiated on the supply side of the economy raise production costs and give rise to cost-push inflation. This is represented by an upward shift of the aggregate supply curve. Given the position of the *AD* curve, the price level rises, output declines, and the rate of unemployment increases. Such a process underlies stagflation wherein the economy experiences an increase in both the inflation and unemployment rates at the same time.

**3.** The accelerationist view of the possibility of an inflation-unemployment trade-off holds that in the long run a downward sloping Phillips curve does not exist. In the short run the accelerationist view argues that there is a trade-off. However, in the long run policymaker actions that move the economy up along short-run Phillips curve will cause the curve to shift upward as workers increase their expectation of the rate of inflation to match the actual rise in the inflation rate. Therefore expansionary monetary and fiscal policies intended to reduce the unemployment rate below the natural rate will cause an ever increasing, or accelerating, rate of inflation. Milton Friedman has argued that the natural rate itself is not fixed, but rather tends to increase with the level of the inflation rate.

**4.** The new classical view is based on the theory of rational expectations which holds that people form their expectations about the future course of economic activity on the basis of all relevant economic knowledge, experience, and data, and in such a way that they do not make repeated, or systematic, mistakes. Because of rational expectations, the new classical view holds that there is not even a short-run trade-off between inflation and unemployment, and that policymakers' attempts to reduce the unemployment rate below the natural rate will *only* cause an ever increasing rate of inflation.

**5.** In general, the new classical view argues that monetary and fiscal policy are ineffective influences on real variables in the economy, such as output and the unemployment rate. However critics of this view point out that lags in learning about a changing economy and "how the system" works, coupled with the fact that policymakers are never perfectly predictable or systematic, make it highly unlikely that firms and workers can anticipate policy actions so well as to render them ineffective.

**6.** Since World War II the composition of the labor force has changed, so that male heads of household represent a declining portion. Many economists argue that this has caused the aggregate supply curve to rise more sharply as real GNP is increased. Consequently, policymakers' attempts to reduce the official unemployment rate to levels considered "acceptable" in the past now cause sharper rises in the general price level, or more inflation. Therefore, a number of economists and policymakers advise that the "full-employment" benchmark of the official unemployment rate should be moved upward in order to avoid excessively inflationary fiscal and monetary policy. The changing nature of the labor force worsens the short-run inflation-unemployment trade-off along the Phillips curve.

## KEY TERMS AND CONCEPTS

accelerationist view
natural rate of unemployment
new classical view
Phillips curve
rational expectations theory

## QUESTIONS AND PROBLEMS

**1.** Which years in Figure 16–2 most strongly suggest the possible existence of a Phillips curve? What is the reversibility issue, and how do the data in Figure 16–2 bear on this issue?

**2.** Classify each of the following changes according to whether you think they affect the economy's aggregate demand curve, the economy's aggregate supply curve, or both. Explain your answer in each case.

a. an increase in personal income taxes;

b. an increase in employers' legally required contribution to employee social security taxes;

c. a worldwide strike by dockworkers;

d. an increase in employee absenteeism;

e. the outbreak of war;

f. a major discovery of oil within the continental United States;

g. a stock market crash;

h. an announced upward revision of the White House's forecast of GNP growth in the coming year.

**3.** Explain in what ways the credibility view described in the Policy Perspective, Viewpoints on the Costs of Reducing Inflation, is a compromise between the mainstream view and the new classical policy in effectiveness argument.

**4.** According to the new classical view an anticipated (expected) increase in the money supply will affect *nominal* GNP. Why is it that the adjustment of expectations that offsets any real effects of such an increase does not offset the nominal effects also?

**5.** You read about the classical view of income and employment in Chapter 8. How is the new classical view similar to the (old) classical view? How are they different?

**6.** How do you think each of the following would affect the shape of the aggregate supply curve and why?

a. increasing unemployment benefits and relaxing the requirements for eligibility;

b. setting up job-market clearinghouses that provide extensive information about job openings across the country;

c. increasing the age at which people become eligible for retirement benefits.

# 17

# Guidelines, Controls, Indexing, and Jobs

**AFTER READING THIS CHAPTER, YOU WILL BE ABLE TO:**

1. Describe how wage and price guidelines work and list the pros and cons of incentive programs to induce voluntary compliance with guidelines.

2. Describe how wage and price controls work and how they affect the economy.

3. Outline the most recent experience of the United States with wage and price controls.

4. Explain how indexing may be applied to the U.S. tax structure and to fixed-dollar assets in order to protect purchasing power.

5. Summarize the different views on how indexing affects economic stability.

6. Outline policies, other than conventional fiscal and monetary policy, for dealing with unemployment.

Policymakers, politicians, and economists have not always been satisfied with attempts to deal with the problems of inflation and unemployment by using the conventional tools of fiscal and monetary policy. Since the late 1960s in particular, increased rates of inflation coupled with high unemployment rates have led to the formulation of other policy measures aimed at dealing with these problems.

Some of these measures have been tried in the past. For example, price controls were imposed during World War II and during 1951 and 1952, Korean War years. Varying degrees of price controls were also imposed by the Nixon administration from 1971 to 1974. Wage-price guidelines were used by the Kennedy and Johnson administrations from 1962 to 1966, as well as by the Carter administration in the late 1970s. Various forms of public works projects and government-sponsored manpower training programs aimed at reducing unemployment trace their origins to the depression-era New Deal legislation of the 1930s. A number of other measures have been proposed and given serious consideration by both Congress and the executive branch of government in recent years. One of these, which we will consider in this chapter, is indexing, a procedure that ties wages, income tax rates, and fixed-dollar assets to the rate of inflation in order to keep their real value (purchasing power) constant.

In this chapter we will consider the pros and cons of several of these measures, both the old and the new, the tried and the untried. Controversy surrounds all of them with respect to their effectiveness and the way they affect different groups in the economy. First we will examine policy measures for dealing with inflation. Then we will turn to policy measures aimed at the problem of unemployment.

## POLICIES FOR DEALING WITH INFLATION

Whenever policymakers are either unwilling or unable to conduct monetary and fiscal policy in such a way as to avoid inflation, there is inevitably a hue and cry to do "something" about inflation. Even when inflation is caused by an excessively expansive fiscal and monetary policy, it is always tempting to tackle the symptom—rising prices—rather than the cause. The logic is simple. If prices are rising, grab them and hold them down. *A* **wage-price guidelines** *policy attempts to curb inflation by getting business and labor to refrain voluntarily from increasing wages and prices at rates in excess of some guideline rate specified by the government. If voluntary compliance isn't forthcoming or is deemed unworkable, government may make compliance mandatory by imposing so-called* **wage-price controls**.

We will now examine guidelines and controls policies. In particular, we want to consider how they are carried out, their workability, and their effectiveness. Along the way we will also look at some of their implications for resource allocation and some of the ways they affect different groups in the economy.

### Wage-Price Guidelines

Wage-price guidelines are effective only to the extent that business and labor voluntarily comply with them. When the Carter administration initiated such a program in late 1978, it requested that annual increases in wages and private fringe benefits (health and pension benefits) not exceed 7 percent. Business firms were asked to limit price increases to one-half of one percentage point below their average annual rate of price increase during 1976 and 1977. Labor was reluctant to comply with the wage guideline because at the time the rate of inflation of the general price level exceeded 7 percent. Labor feared that compliance would mean a loss in the purchasing power of their wages. Many businesses were reluctant to comply because they feared that the prices of inputs and the wages of labor would rise faster than the allowable increases in the prices of their products under the guidelines. In short, they feared that compliance would squeeze profits and possibly even cause losses. The dilemma facing individual workers, unions, and business firms in voluntary compliance is like that of individuals in a crowd standing at a football game. No one can see any better when everyone is standing than when everyone is sitting down. But those who voluntarily sit down are relatively worse off if others remain standing. Hence, no one is willing to sit down.

Since one of the basic problems with a wage-price guidelines policy is that of ensuring voluntary compliance, a number of policies have been proposed or used to provide economic incentives for compliance. Two that have been considered, but as yet not tried, are wage insurance and the so-called tax-based income policy (TIP). Another method is to use moral suasion, or jawboning, backed by thinly veiled threats that the government may take more drastic measures if compliance is not forthcoming.

### Wage Insurance

Let's say that the wage guideline is 7 percent—that is, government requests that labor not seek wage increases greater than 7 percent per year. But suppose labor is reluctant to comply with the guideline for fear that consumer prices may rise at a rate greater than 7 percent, thus reducing the purchasing power of a wage that rises only 7 percent. One way to alleviate labor's fear is for the government to offer wage insurance. **Wage insurance** *guarantees that the government will repay labor for the purchasing power that they lose if they comply with the guideline but consumer prices, measured by the consumer price index (CPI), rise faster than the guideline rate for wages.* The repayment would be calculated on the basis of the difference between the annual percentage rate of growth in the CPI and the guideline rate for wages. For example, suppose a worker making $10,000 per year agreed to accept a 7 percent raise (the guideline rate) and the CPI then rose 8 percent over the year. The government's wage insurance program would pay the worker $100, which is 1 percent of

$10,000. If the CPI rose 10 percent, the worker would get $300, or 3 percent of $10,000.

By providing wage insurance the government hopes to be able to get labor to comply voluntarily with a wage guideline. However, critics contend that those workers who think they can bargain for wage increases greater than the increase in the CPI would still not comply. But suppose all wage and salary workers do comply and an overly expansive fiscal and monetary policy causes the CPI to increase at a rate greater than the guideline rate. Critics argue that a wage insurance policy would not only become incredibly expensive, but self-defeating as well. For example, suppose wages and salaries totaled $1 trillion per year. Wage insurance payments would amount to $10 billion for every percentage point of inflation above the guideline rate. Moreover, the wage insurance payments would amount to the government giving everybody the money they had voluntarily refrained from taking in the form of wage increases in the first place. As a result, critics contend that inflation would continue just as if there had never been compliance with the wage guideline.

Critics also point to technical problems that make the workability of a wage insurance program doubtful. For example, should fringe benefits be included in the wage guideline? Suppose they are not included. Unions can take the wage increases they forgo under the guideline in the form of increased fringe benefits instead. They would bargain with employers for higher-cost retirement and health compensation benefits. On the other hand, suppose fringe benefits are included in the wage guideline. How do you place a value on them? For example, the cost of increased pension benefits to be received in the future depends on assumptions about how long the worker lives after retirement and how long his or her dependent spouse lives. Different assumptions give different answers. The paperwork and labor hours required to set up and enforce answers to these questions can grow rapidly for both the government and private employers.

## Tax-Based Income Policy (TIP)

There are two basic versions of the **tax-based income policy (TIP)**. Both attempt to provide an economic incentive for compliance with a wage guideline. But one uses the carrot while the other uses the stick.

*The Carrot Version.   What we may call the carrot version of TIP rewards with tax credits (reductions in income taxes) those workers who keep their wage increases below the guideline rate.* For example, suppose the guideline rate for wage increases is 7 percent. A worker earning $10,000 per year who settles for a wage increase of 6 percent, or $600, would get a tax credit of $100 (the difference between 7 percent of $10,000 and 6 percent of $10,000). That is, the worker's income tax bill would be reduced by $100. If the worker had settled for a 7 percent wage increase, the guideline rate, there would be no $100 tax credit. But, of course, the worker would have $100 additional income. However, this extra income would be subject to the income tax. If the tax rate were 20 percent, the worker could keep only $80 of the additional income. This is $20 less than what the worker would have by settling for a 6 percent wage increase and having $100 less taxes to pay. Clearly, the carrot version of TIP gives labor an incentive to settle for wage increases below the guideline rate. However, critics are quick to point out that while this version of TIP would encourage compliance with the guideline, labor's purchasing power would not be reduced. Indeed, it would be slightly greater, and it is argued that this would only add to inflationary pressures—the basic problem guidelines seek to control.

*The Stick Version.   What we may call the stick version of TIP is aimed at forcing employers to comply with a wage guideline. The stick version punishes with tax penalties employers who grant wage increases in excess of the guideline rate.* The tax penalties are supposed to stiffen management's resistance to union demands for wage increases larger than the guideline rate.

However, what happens if unions respond by becoming more militant in their wage demands? Is it not possible that more or longer labor strikes will result? If so, then firms may find the higher costs (in terms of lost sales) of more or longer shutdowns greater than the tax penalties incurred by granting wage increases that exceed the guideline rate. In that case, firms would be better off by giving in to the excessive wage increases. Of course, one way to deal with this possible shortcoming would be to make the tax penalties high enough so that the higher costs of more or longer strikes would still be less than the tax penalties. Critics argue that there then would be more or longer shutdowns due to strikes. As a result firms would end up producing less output, giving rise to shortages. Since shortages cause prices to rise, the rate of inflation would increase rather than slow down—just the opposite result of that intended by a wage guideline policy.

According to critics, there is also another reason why the stick version of TIP may cause inflation to increase rather than to decrease. Suppose firms experiencing increased demand for their output want to respond to the increased profit opportunities by expanding production. They may have to increase wages more than the guideline rate in order to hire the additional labor needed to produce more output. Because of the tax penalty they will incur, the size of the prospective profits will be decreased. And this will diminish the incentive for the firms to expand output. Hence, output will increase less in response to the increased demand than it would if there were no tax penalties, and, consequently, prices will increase more. In this situation, the existence of tax penalties curbs wage increases but accentuates product price increases. The more rapidly increasing product prices will in turn cause labor to press even harder for larger increases in wages in order to keep up with the rising cost of living.

## Jawboning and Arm-Twisting

One approach frequently used to gain compliance with wage-price guidelines is "jawboning"—government appeals to business and labor's sense of patriotic responsibility. This may take the form of presidential statements to the effect that "every American should do his or her part to help fight inflation." Or if a particular corporation increases its product price by an excessive amount, or if there is a particularly excessive wage settlement in some industry, the president may publicly express "disappointment" and "concern" that more restraint was not used. Corporate executives and union leaders may be contacted directly or even called to the White House for a discussion of the matter. The president may request a price "rollback" or very publicly "keep an eye" on the final stages of a particular labor contract negotiation.

When jawboning doesn't work, the government may resort to "arm-twisting." The government simply announces that it is prepared to take actions directly affecting those who don't comply with the guidelines. For example, companies either seeking or holding government contracts (companies selling products to the government under contract) may be required to certify that they are complying with the guidelines. The president may direct government agencies to purchase only from those companies observing the guidelines. The government may also campaign to encourage consumer boycotts of companies that don't comply with the guidelines. Those industries that are sheltered from foreign competition by tariffs (a tax added on to the price of an imported good) and other types of import restrictions may be threatened with removal of those restrictions if they don't comply with the guidelines. Without such restrictions, firms in those industries would be under greater pressure from foreign competition to hold down wage-price increases.

## Wage-Price Controls

Experience with wage-price guidelines and voluntary compliance suggests that such a policy has little, if any, effect on inflation. A principal problem is that compliance by business executives and union leaders requires that they voluntarily behave in a manner contrary to their primary responsibilities. Business executives are hired and paid to run companies as efficiently and profitably as possible. Executives who comply with price guidelines at the expense of company profits may well have to answer to angry stockholders and boards of directors. Similarly, union leaders are chosen by the rank-and-file union members to get them the best possible wage settlement. Union leaders who honor the wage guideline instead of rank-and-file goals may be replaced. Another problem is that those firms and unions that do comply voluntarily with wage-price guidelines run the risk of losing economic ground relative to those that don't—the problem of the standing crowd at the football game.

Wage-price controls make compliance with government-specified guidelines mandatory. The limits on the rate of wage-price increases are no longer mere guidelines, but standards—like posted speed limits on highways. To exceed them is to break the law. However the temptation to do so can be great, for the reasons discussed in the Policy Perspective (Wage-Price Controls—A Difficult Way to Curb Inflation) at the end of Chapter 6. Like speed limits, wage-price controls require enforcement. And enforcement can be costly and difficult because evasion can take many forms.

### Cost of Enforcing Controls

The larger the army of enforcement agents, the more likely it is that the various forms of evasion of wage-price controls will be detected and kept in check. However, the policing activity itself can become very costly.

This point is perhaps best illustrated by an example. Suppose 1 percent of the economy's labor force was lured away from whatever they were doing and employed by the government as enforcement agents for wage-price controls. Each of them can now be assigned to police full time the economic activities of each member of the other 99 percent of the labor force. Employers' attempts to evade price controls by changing product quality, or to evade wage controls by compensating workers with longer coffee breaks and so forth, would be detected more often and prevented, though probably not completely. "Under-the-counter" deals or "middle-of-the-night" trades between consumers and retailers at prices exceeding control limits would also be detected more often and prevented, though again probably not completely.

Note, however, that with 1 percent of the labor force now employed full time as enforcement agents, the goods and services that 1 percent previously produced are no longer available. Only 99 percent of the economy's former output of goods and services can be produced now. The other 1 percent has been replaced with the output of wage-price control enforcement services. The cost, the opportunity cost, of evasion-preventing enforcement is the 1 percent of the GNP that could otherwise have been produced. Moreover, with 99 percent as many goods and services available—that is, with supply reduced—there will be additional upward pressure on prices. The enforcement agents would have their hands full, not only with those they were policing but in limiting their own demand for goods as well. For don't forget, to hire 1 percent of the labor force away from their previous jobs usually requires that they be paid wages that are at least equal to what they previously made. And enforcement agents would spend their wages just like everyone else. The irony is that in an attempt to keep people from having to pay higher prices for goods, we have seen to it that they don't get 1 percent of the goods and services they used to get. Is this cost of enforcement worth it? That is a question society has to confront when considering the use of controls.

A number of critics of wage-price controls claim there is another cost of controls that is also very important, although difficult to measure. They worry that enforcement activities pose a threat to individual freedoms and the democratic processes on which our form of government is based. They fear that wage-price controls constitute too much government interference with the rights of individuals to enter into private contracts (agreements to buy and sell) at mutually agreed-upon terms.

## Effects of Wage-Price Controls on the Economy

Controls affect the way markets allocate the economy's resources. In addition, controls affect different groups in the economy to different degrees, and this raises questions of equity. Moreover, the mere prospect of controls can generate undesirable effects on expectations.

### Effect of Controls on Resource Allocation

In a market-oriented economy, prices provide the signals that determine what to produce, how to produce it, and for whom. Critics argue that wage-price controls (and guidelines as well) interfere with this crucial function, and that as a result, they give rise to the misallocation of resources (land, labor, and capital). In a dynamic economy there are a multitude of different markets in which supply and demand are continually shifting due to changes in technology, consumer tastes, and a host of other factors. If wages and prices are not free to change to reflect these shifts in supply and demand, there are no effective signals to redirect the use of resources in response to these changes. For example, suppose the demand for a particular good increases. If price controls prevent the price of the good from rising, there will be no signal indicating to suppliers society's desire that more resources be devoted to the production of this good. As a result there will be a shortage of the good, such as that shown in Figure 17–1.

In a changing economy with extensive wage-price controls that are effectively enforced, shortages and bottlenecks will occur in many markets as time passes. Buyers will

**FIGURE 17-1    Price Controls Cause Shortages**

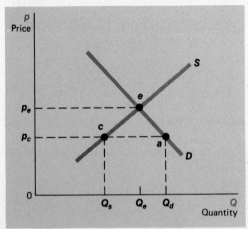

The intersection of the demand curve $D$ and supply curve $S$ at point $e$ determines the equilibrium price $p_e$ and quantity $Q_e$ in a freely functioning market. If price controls forbid suppliers to sell their product at a price higher than $p_c$ they will supply quantity $Q_s$ to the market, corresponding to point $c$ on $S$. But buyers will demand the larger quantity $Q_d$, corresponding to point $a$ on $D$. Therefore there will be a persistent shortage equal to $Q_d$ minus $Q_s$.

not be able to buy all they want at the controlled price. With controls, markets simply cannot function to equate supply and demand. For example, in a typical market, such as that shown in Figure 17-1, there is a shortage at the controlled price $p_c$ equal to the quantity demanded $Q_d$ minus the quantity supplied $Q_s$. Since all buyers can't be satisfied, who will decide which buyers get the quantity $Q_s$ of the product and which don't?

One way is simply to sell to those first in line—first come, first served. In many markets, however, sellers will take care of their friends first. The trouble with either of these possibilities is that some buyers get all they want while the rest get none. To many this

seems a most unfair and undesirable aspect of a wage-price controls program. One way around the problem is for the government to issue ration coupons to all who want the good. The total amount of these coupons will be just enough to lay claim to the total quantity of the good supplied, which in Figure 17-1 is $Q_s$. Since each buyer who wants the good at price $p_c$ will be given some of the coupons, all will be assured of getting some of the good. Obviously, some buyers will not be able to get all they would have liked, but this seems more equitable than a situation in which some get none at all. Such a ration coupon system was used during World War II.

No matter how the shortages that result from wage-price controls are handled, economists generally agree on one point. The extent of resource misallocation and the severity of shortages will become more pronounced the longer wage-price controls are imposed.

### Controls and Equity

Controls invariably affect different groups in the economy to different degrees. Critics of controls claim that this isn't equitable. The largest business firms and unionized labor tend to be watched more closely for control violations than smaller firms and nonunionized labor. This is partly due to the fact that larger firms and unionized labor are more visible and, hence, easier to watch. Furthermore, it is often argued that large business firms and unions account for such a large share of the economy's output, and represent such a large concentration of economic power, that they serve as a bellwether for wages and prices in the rest of the economy. Some argue, therefore, that it is necessary to make them the focal point of wage-price control efforts.

Labor unions often complain that wage controls tend to be more heavily policed than price controls. Since labor must negotiate wages with management, it is to some extent unavoidable that some of the responsibility for wage controls must be borne by management. This irks labor because it seems to them that an "army" of "patriotic" business executives will help enforce wage controls, but that no comparable army will help enforce price controls.

Many critics argue that perhaps the greatest inequity of all is that interest rates, dividends, rents, profits, and other forms of income are not usually controlled to the same extent that wages are. Since higher-income groups tend to derive a larger share of their income from these sources than do lower-income groups, the inequity favors higher-income groups.

### Effect of Controls on Expectations

A news item reports that a study by a congressional committee concluded that "Capitol Hill discussion of mandatory controls would cause business and labor to rush to raise prices and wages prior to the controls period." Because wage-price controls have to be legislated by Congress, such a program is unavoidably preceded by a good deal of public debate. It's a little like a football team yelling its next play from the huddle. The other team is then able to anticipate and prepare for what is about to happen. Business and labor may react to the congressional debate by initiating price and wage increases they otherwise might not have made until later—better take what they can get while they can. The effect of the debate is to trigger more inflation, the very thing a wage-price control program is intended to prevent.

Some contend that the way to avoid this problem is for Congress to give the president standing authority to impose wage-price controls. It is argued that the president could then simply switch on the controls at any time, thereby reducing business and labor's chance to "jump the gun." Critics of this idea feel uncomfortable about giving the president such unlimited authority. Besides, they claim, when inflation heats up, business and labor would be on the lookout for possible presidential action. As a result, they

might mistakenly jump the gun several times, increasing wages and prices even though the president takes no action. Such mistaken anticipation would only add more fuel to inflation.

Despite the jumping-the-gun problem, it is often argued that once wage-price controls are imposed they will tend to dampen inflationary expectations. In the last chapter we saw how inflationary expectations, once established, can create severe problems for fiscal and monetary policy. A number of economists contend that imposing well-enforced wage and price controls for a short period of time can check the rise in wages and prices, thereby causing a downward revision of inflationary expectations and a deceleration of inflation. Others are afraid that controls would have to be imposed for too long a period for this to occur, and that the result would be a serious misallocation of resources.

## Controls and Fiscal and Monetary Policy

Wage-price controls have appealed on occasion to policymakers who think that controls can be used to combat inflation without using restrictive fiscal and monetary policy. Their argument is that controls can be used to curb inflation, thereby freeing fiscal and monetary policy to push the economy toward full employment without fear of the usual inflationary consequences. Indeed, this was the reasoning underlying the controls program imposed by the Nixon administration during the early 1970s.

### Arguments Against Controls as a Substitute for Restrictive Fiscal and Monetary Policy

However, many economists claim that the idea that controls can curb inflation in the face of an expansionary fiscal and monetary policy is simply wishful thinking. In particular, they argue that if the money supply con-

## POLICY PERSPECTIVE

### Our Most Recent Experience with Wage-Price Controls

Most of the U.S. economy's experience with wage-price controls occurred during World War II and then again during the Nixon administration.

When the Nixon administration took office in January 1969, the economy was experiencing its highest rate of inflation since the end of the Korean War in 1953 (see Figure 6–5, part a). The administration attempted to curb inflation by exercising fiscal and monetary restraint. As a result, the government had an actual budget surplus in 1969 for the first time since 1960 and a cyclically adjusted budget surplus for the first time since 1965. But despite the restrictive stance of fiscal policy, the rate of inflation ended up even higher in 1969 than it had been in 1968. Policymakers became even more concerned in 1970, when a slight recession and a rise in the unemployment rate (from 3.5 percent in 1969 to 4.9 percent in 1970) were still accompanied by a high rate of inflation (see Figure 16–2, the years 1968, 1969, and 1970). It seemed that the years of almost continually increasing rates of inflation since 1963 (Figure 16–2) had given rise to firmly entrenched inflationary expectations. By 1971 the outlines of the stagflation problem were becoming apparent.

On the one hand, the Nixon administration wanted to reduce the unemployment rate. On the other hand, the administration feared that a more expansionary fiscal and monetary policy would cause even higher rates of inflation. To get around this policy dilemma, the administration decided to impose wage-price controls to check inflation. The administration hoped this program would permit a more expansionary fiscal and monetary policy to reduce unemployment without at the same time making inflation worse.

### Phases I and II of the Nixon Plan

Congress gave President Nixon the authority to impose wage-price controls when it passed the Economic Stabilization Act of 1970. The administration did not use this authority until August 1971. Then it imposed a controls program that went through several phases before the president's authority to use controls expired in April 1974. Phase I lasted about 3 months (August 15, 1971, to November 19, 1971) and imposed a freeze on all wages and prices throughout the economy. Phase II lasted about 14 months (November 19, 1971, to January 11, 1973) and represented a relaxation of the controls of Phase I. Under Phase II wage increases were not supposed to exceed 5.5 percent per year while prices could be raised to cover increased costs—which meant businesses were not allowed to increase profit margins. While the rate of inflation remained reasonably stable during Phases I and II, the rate of inflation had begun to fall in 1970, considerably before the Phase I freeze (see Figure 16–2). Hence, it is not clear how effective Phases I and II controls actually were. It could be that the drop in the rate of inflation from 1970 to 1972 was really a reflection of the widening gap between potential and actual GNP (the GNP gap) that took place during these years (see Figure 6–5, part b).

### Phases III and IV

A further loosening of controls began with the imposition of Phase III, which lasted about 7 months (January 11, 1973, to August 13, 1973). During this period the economy's aggregate demand for goods and services began to expand sharply and the GNP gap was closed (Figure 6–5, part b). The rate of inflation rose quite sharply (Figure 16–2, the years 1972 and 1973). Because Phase III controls appeared to be losing badly to inflation, Nixon reimposed a complete freeze from August 13 to September 12, 1973—Phase III$\frac{1}{2}$. Phase III$\frac{1}{2}$ briefly checked the rise in the inflation rate, but shortages became such a problem that the cure seemed worse than the inflation. Hence, Phase III$\frac{1}{2}$ gave way to Phase IV, during which decontrol was extended to more and more sectors of the economy until Congress allowed the authority to impose controls to expire in April 1974.

The experience with Phases III and IV did much to confirm the idea that loosely enforced controls are almost useless in the face of a strong expansion of aggregate demand. (The energy crisis that occurred during Phase IV also added to the inflation problem.) And when a freeze, Phase III$\frac{1}{2}$, was imposed during this period, it seemed to bear out the contention that strict controls create severe resource misallocation and shortages. There have been many studies of the effectiveness of the Nixon wage-price controls program. By and large, their conclusions have been very much the same as those of a congressional study of the 1971–1974 mandatory control period. Namely, that the long-run inflation rate wouldn't have been substantially different in the absence of price controls.

### Questions

1. Why is it difficult to tell how effective the wage-price controls were in curbing the inflation rate?

2. It might be said that the Nixon administration's reason for imposing controls was flawed because of incompatible objectives. Why?

tinues to expand at a faster rate than the economy's output of goods and services, there will continue to be upward pressure on prices. A monetary expansion to finance large government deficits as the Federal Reserve monetizes the government debt (as described in Chapter 15) will make it very difficult for wage-price controls to check inflation. If differences in enforcement mean that some prices are more restrained by controls than others, the less restrained prices may very well rise faster than they otherwise would. This happens because shortages will tend to develop where controls are effective, and when consumers with more money in their hands can't get all they want in some markets, they will tend to spend more on goods they can get in other markets. In short, uncontrolled prices will be bid up even more with the funds made available by the increasing money supply. Unless, that is, the controls somehow keep people from spending the additional money, so that the velocity of money $V$ in the equation of exchange ($M \times V = p \times Q$) is reduced. And saving the money in financial institutions such as banks doesn't count, since that money is loaned out and spent. Essentially, it is argued, controls only work if they make people stuff the additional money in mattresses or bury it in the ground.

In sum, these critics contend that in the face of expansionary fiscal and monetary policy, the prices of controlled products may be held down, but those of uncontrolled, or loosely controlled, products will be driven even higher than otherwise. As a result, the average level of all prices, and the overall rate of inflation, will be affected very little by controls. Critics ask how this can possibly justify the numerous shortages and misallocations of resources that controls cause.

### Arguments for Controls as a Substitute for Restrictive Fiscal and Monetary Policy

However, there is another school of thought that argues that fiscal and monetary policy cannot be counted on to curb inflation because of the existence of large corporations and unions. Some economists claim large unions and corporations aggressively push up wages and prices simply because they can exercise so much market power.

Whenever unions and corporations use their market power in this way, the aggregate supply curve shifts upward. This causes the economy's total output to decline and unemployment to rise, as discussed in Chapter 11. Fiscal and monetary policy could allow such recessionary developments to persist until sagging demand deters the large unions and corporations from trying to push up wages and prices still further. However, it is argued that policymakers, fearful of the rise in unemployment, quickly react with expansionary policies that pump up demand. The result is that the big unions and corporations push up wages and prices, and policymakers quickly move to accommodate these increases in order to avoid recessionary developments. Unions and corporations act, and policymakers react, over and over again. The result is inflation, with the unions and corporations calling the tune. Proponents of this version of the inflationary process argue that unless policymakers are willing to take a firmer stance against inflation and worry less about unemployment, wage-price controls are the only policy that will break this vicious cycle.

### CHECKPOINT* 17-1

**Some critics of wage-price controls argue that such regulations control wages and prices "artificially," and that as a result when controls are removed, there is a "price explosion." What do you think these critics mean, and how might you explain their position in terms of Figure 17-1? A study by a** congressional committee concluded that Capitol Hill discussion of mandatory controls would lead to a rush to raise wages and prices prior to the control period, and that the resulting jump in prices would force the Fed to tighten the money supply so that "recession will arrive that much sooner and be that much deeper." Can you explain the study's conclusion in terms of the aggregate supply and demand framework?

\* Answers to all Checkpoints can be found at the back of the text.

## INDEXING—PROTECTING PURCHASING POWER FROM INFLATION

Wage-price guidelines and controls are aimed at curbing inflation. By contrast, **indexing** *is a policy aimed at protecting people against the loss of the dollar's purchasing power that is caused by inflation. Indexing keeps constant the purchasing power of wages, taxes, and fixed-dollar, or nominal, assets by adjusting their dollar-denominated values for the change in the general price level.* (Recall our discussion in Chapter 6.) For example, suppose an employer has agreed to index employees' wages, which currently are $5 per hour. If there is a 10 percent rate of inflation over the coming year, the employer automatically increases the wage to $5.50. Thus, while goods cost 10 percent more, an employee's dollar-denominated wage has also increased 10 percent. The employee is being paid the same amount of purchasing power, or the same real wage, per hour.

We have previously examined how our income tax is indexed to inflation (recall the Policy Perspective, Indexing Income Taxes—Putting the Brakes on Rising Tax Rates, Chapter 11). As of yet however, capital gains taxes and government bonds are not indexed to inflation. Let's examine how indexing might be used to adjust capital gains taxes and government bonds for the effects of inflation, and also consider how indexing can be used in the private sector.

## Indexing Capital Gains Taxes

**Capital gains taxes** *are taxes levied on any gain one realizes from selling an asset at a price greater than the original purchase price.* Many have criticized capital gains taxes because they do not make any distinction between gains that merely reflect an increase in the general level of prices and those that represent an increase in the asset owner's purchasing power, or a real capital gain.

### *Taxing Paper Gains Instead of Real Gains*

Let's assume capital gains are taxed at a rate of 25 percent. Suppose you bought a piece of land for $10,000 10 years ago. Assume that in the meantime inflation has taken place, so that the general level of prices has risen 100 percent, or doubled. Now suppose that you sell your land today for $20,000. Despite the fact that you get twice as many dollars for the land as you originally paid for it, you are still just getting back the same amount of purchasing power. Why? Because the dollar you receive today buys only half of what it did 10 years ago. However, the capital gains tax does not recognize that fact. You will be taxed 25 percent of the dollar, or paper, gain. That is, you will have to pay the government 25 percent of the difference between the $20,000 sale price and the $10,000 purchase price, or $2,500 (.25 × $10,000). The result is that after tax you keep $17,500. In effect you get back 75 percent more dollars than you originally paid, but since the general level of prices has increased 100 percent you are getting back less purchasing power. In terms of purchasing power, or so-called real terms, you have actually taken a loss. You are only getting back 87.5 percent of the purchasing power ($17,500 ÷ $20,000) originally paid for the land. In real terms you have been taxed 12.5 percent for selling an asset on which there was no real capital gain.

This simple example illustrates how the capital gains tax collects taxes where there has been no real capital gain at all. Worse yet, suppose the price of an asset rises but at a rate less than the rate of inflation. If the owner sells it, less purchasing power will be received than was paid for it. Adding insult to injury, the capital gains tax will then take some more away! In fact (with a capital gains tax rate of 25 percent), it is necessary for the price of an asset to rise *more* than 25 percent *more* than the rise in the general level of prices for the seller of the asset to realize any real gain after tax at all.

For example, suppose today you sell for $23,333 the land that you paid $10,000 for 10 years ago. Again, suppose the general price level has risen 100 percent in the meantime. The price of your land has gone up 33.3 percent more than the rise in the general price level (from $10,000 to $23,333 is a rise of 133.3 percent). The paper gain of $13,333 ($23,333 − $10,000) would be taxed at the 25 percent rate, and you would pay $3,333 in taxes (.25 × $13,333). This effectively taxes away your entire real gain! You are left with $20,000, exactly the amount of purchasing power you paid for the land 10 years ago.

Critics conclude that the capital gains tax combined with inflation imposes such severe penalties on the sale of assets that it discourages investment. Why? The prospective return on investment in new assets (machines, buildings, and land) must be quite high to induce people to sell existing assets and incur the capital gains tax. Hence, critics contend that the flow of financial capital out of old assets and into new ones is impeded.

### *Indexing—Taxing Only the Real Gains*

Many critics point out that capital gains tax laws were originally written when there was little or no inflation. Little thought was given to the way these laws might affect real after-tax gains and losses in an inflationary environment. Tax reformers now argue that capital gains taxes should be indexed to the rate of inflation so that the tax only applies to the real gain, and not the so-called paper gain.

The way to do this would be to adjust the original purchase price of the asset upward by the amount of the inflation that has taken place since the asset was originally purchased.

Consider again our initial example in which you paid $10,000 for land 10 years ago and sell it for $20,000 today, while the general level of prices has risen 100 percent. With an indexed capital gains tax you would owe no tax at all. Why? Because when we adjust the original purchase price for inflation, it becomes $20,000 in terms of the purchasing power of today's dollars. Hence, there is no real capital gain to tax because the inflation-adjusted purchase price is the same as the sale price.

Consider again the case where the price of the asset rises 33 percent more than the rise in the general price level. That is, you sell for $23,333 the land that you paid $10,000 for 10 years ago. Again, suppose that the general price level has risen 100 percent in the meantime. If the capital gains tax is indexed, the original purchase price will be calculated as $20,000. In terms of today's dollars (which buy half as much as a dollar did 10 years ago), this is exactly the amount of purchasing power that was originally paid for the land. The capital gains tax rate of 25 percent then would be applied to the real gain of $3,333 ($23,333 − $20,000), so that you would pay the government $833.25 (.25 × $3,333) in capital gains taxes. Recall that in this case, when the capital gains tax was not indexed, the entire real gain was taxed away.

Tax reformers contend that indexing the capital gains tax, like indexing the income tax, would deprive the government of another source of "unvoted and unlegislated" tax revenue. It is also alleged that indexing would remove the damper on investment imposed by a nonindexed capital gains tax. A study conducted at the National Bureau of Economic Research by Martin Feldstein and Joel Slemrod measured the total excess taxation in 1973 of corporate shares of stock caused by inflation. They found that the total capital gains taxes paid on dollar (as opposed to real) capital gains by individuals amounted to $1.1 billion. With indexing, the tax liability on the real capital gains would have been only $661 million. Hence, inflation raised tax liabilities by almost $500 million, roughly doubling the overall effective tax rate on corporate stock capital gains. Although the Economic Recovery Tax Act of 1981 reduced the tax rates on capital gains, it did not index the capital gains tax rates to inflation.

## Indexing Government Bonds

Recall our discussion of anticipated versus unanticipated inflation in Chapter 6. (You may find it helpful to reread that section at this point.) We saw that whenever there is an unanticipated inflation, there is a redistribution of wealth from lenders to borrowers—borrowers gain at lenders' expense. American citizens have loaned enormous sums to the U.S. government over the years, testified to by the fact that the government debt amounts to more than a trillion dollars. To the extent that there is unanticipated inflation, the government gains at citizens' expense. Because bonds are fixed-dollar assets, the government repays citizens the same number of dollars originally borrowed. However, the dollars repaid have less purchasing power due to inflation.

Let's suppose a citizen loans the government $100 for 1 year by buying a government bond that pays a 5 percent rate of interest. Furthermore, suppose that the citizen buys the bond anticipating that there will be no inflation during the year. Hence, the citizen loans the government $100 of purchasing power because of the prospect of getting back 5 percent more purchasing power in 1 year, or $105. The citizen assumes that each dollar will have exactly the same purchasing power as that originally loaned. However, suppose that over the course of the year there is a 10 percent rise in the general price level, a 10 percent rate of inflation that was completely unanticipated by the citizen. Now when the government pays the citizen $105 at the end of the year, the $105 has only about 95 percent of the purchasing power of the $100 that the citizen originally loaned the

## POLICY PERSPECTIVE

### Indexing and the Fight Against Inflation

Most economists agree that indexing can eliminate many of the arbitrary windfall gains and losses caused by unanticipated inflation. It can protect people's savings in fixed-dollar assets, such as bonds and savings accounts, from losing their real value. It is often argued that middle- and lower-income groups have few alternatives to holding their savings in the form of fixed-dollar assets. Therefore, indexing would reduce the uncertainty they face when making long-run saving plans to buy a house or car, to educate their children, or to provide for old age.

### Indexing Not a Cure

While many agree that indexing can reduce the pain of inflation, far fewer believe that it is a cure for inflation. The reason is that indexing deals with the symptoms of inflation, not its basic causes—such as overly expansive fiscal and monetary policy and aggregate supply shocks. However, some economists contend that indexing would remove government's incentive to follow such expansionary fiscal and monetary policies. They argue, for example, that if the tax structure were indexed, the government wouldn't be able to collect more tax revenues by using inflation to push people into higher tax brackets. Similarly, the government wouldn't be able to pay off government debt with inflation-depreciated dollars. Supposedly this would make legislators more cautious about generating large bond-financed deficits. Yet other economists contend just the opposite. They argue that if policymakers felt people were protected from inflation by indexing, there would be even less concern about the inflationary consequences of continuous deficit spending.

### Income Tax Indexing and Stability

Opponents of income tax indexing claim it is destabilizing. They argue that the automatic reduction in purchasing power that occurs when inflation pushes people into higher tax brackets acts to dampen inflationary booms. Proponents of indexing acknowledge this point, but claim that there is another aspect of the stability question that argues even more strongly for indexing. Without indexing the after-tax purchasing power of a before-tax income of constant purchasing power declines (as discussed in the Policy Perspective, Indexing Income Taxes—Putting the Brakes on Rising Tax Rates, Chapter 11). Suppose wage and salary earners' before-tax incomes rise at the same rate as the general level of prices. Without indexing, they find themselves worse off because the purchasing power of their after-tax income has declined. To "catch up" they must push for increases in their before-tax wages and salaries that are greater than the rate of inflation. But this will tend to push the rate of inflation even higher as employers pass these wage and salary increases along to the consumer in the form of higher prices. The rate of inflation will accelerate. Even though before-tax wages and salaries may keep pace with inflation, the purchasing power of after-tax wages and salaries will continue to lose ground. The cycle goes faster and faster, like a dog trying to catch its own tail. Proponents claim that income tax indexing is necessary to eliminate this source of accelerating cost-push inflation.

government. The citizen gets back 5 percent more dollars than originally loaned, but each dollar now buys 10 percent less. The 10 percent rate of inflation has more than offset the 5 percent rate of interest. Because the citizen did not anticipate the inflation, the government has gained the purchasing power and the citizen has lost it.

Many feel that when citizens lend to their own government, they should not be subject to the risk of loss due to unanticipated inflation. Since the government controls fiscal and monetary policy, it is in a position to generate an unanticipated inflation and thereby reduce in real terms (purchasing power) the amount of the debt it has to pay back. It is highly doubtful that government creates inflation for this reason. However, fiscal and monetary policymakers are not immune from making mistakes that can cause inflation. And as we saw in the last two chapters, the complexities that beset fiscal and monetary policy management in today's world can, and have, led to this result. Therefore, many argue that government bonds should be indexed to the rate of inflation to ensure that their real value remains constant.

To see how the indexing of government bonds would work, let's consider our bond example again. Suppose the $100 government bond were indexed to the rate of inflation. Again, suppose there is a 10 percent rate of inflation. At the end of the year, when the bond matures, the bondholder would automatically get back $110, the amount of purchasing power the bondholder loaned to the government initially. In addition, the bondholder receives the 5 percent interest rate on the purchasing power loaned. That is, the bondholder receives an additional $5.50, or 5 percent of $110. Hence, the citizen gets

back the amount of purchasing power after 1 year that was originally anticipated when the bond was purchased.

## Other Applications of Indexing

Besides its application to taxes and bonds, there are several other ways that indexing can be used in both the government and the private sector of the economy.

Corporate bonds, mortgage loans, and savings deposits are fixed-dollar assets just like government bonds. Unanticipated inflation also causes losses for those lenders who put money into these assets. Lenders and borrowers could agree to index such assets in exactly the same way described for government bonds. The indexing of these assets has not yet occurred to any significant extent in the United States, possibly because inflation has not yet been severe enough. One exception is the development of the variable-rate home mortgage, where the homeowner's interest payments on the mortgage are indexed to the rate of inflation.

Wages in the United States have been indexed to varying degrees in some areas of the economy. These areas include the wages of certain government workers, as well as those of workers in unions that have wage escalator clauses in their contracts. **Escalator clauses** *or COLAs (cost-of-living allowances) effectively index wages to inflation by stipulating that wages must be adjusted upward periodically to keep pace with the rising cost of living, as measured by the consumer price index, for example.*

Congress has legislated the indexing of social security payments and federal retirement benefits. On the other hand, the indexing of retirement pension benefits in the private sector of the economy has not been extensive. If the inflation problem persists, however, the practice of indexing private pension benefits will probably become more widespread.

===

### CHECKPOINT 17-2

**Between 1968 and 1981 Congress cut taxes on five different occasions. Some say that in part this was done to offset the effects of inflation on taxes, that it was a discretionary form of income tax indexing. From a politician's viewpoint, can you think of two reasons why discretionary tax adjustment might be preferable to the automatic adjustment provided by an indexed income tax? Some people object to indexing government bonds because they claim it might have an adverse effect on the private sector's ability to borrow. Why might this be so? Recently, a high ranking government official said he didn't think much of indexing because it meant "you've given up the fight against inflation." What do you think of this point of view?**

===

## DEALING WITH UNEMPLOYMENT

What options are there for dealing with unemployment besides the conventional tools of fiscal and monetary policy? One problem with expansionary fiscal and monetary policy is that it tends to push up demand in all areas of the economy. This increased demand can cause prices to rise in industries already operating at full capacity and wages to rise where the required kinds of labor are already fully employed or in short supply. The result is more inflation, but little reduction in unemployment. Meanwhile stubborn pockets of unemployment may still persist in certain areas of the economy. Trying to get at those pockets by expanding aggregate demand is a little like trying to paint a picture with an 8-inch-wide house painter's brush. You hit a lot of areas that you don't want to touch.

In an effort to get around this problem, a number of policies have been proposed that focus on unemployment in more specific ways. A few of these have actually been tried while some have only been considered. Their effectiveness is a subject of ongoing debate. Let's consider a few of them—namely, manpower programs, public works projects, and job tax credits.

### Manpower Programs

**Manpower programs,** *also known as job-training programs, are aimed at developing the job skills of the young and unemployed in order to increase their employability.* These programs also attempt to upgrade the job skills of older unemployed workers whose previous jobs have been eliminated by technological change and shifts in product demand. For example, the need for coal miners has been greatly reduced by both the mechanization of coal mining and the increased use of other kinds of fuel since the 1930s. As a result, miners who can no longer find employment require new skills for use in industries where workers are needed.

### CETA and Other Programs

Several programs were undertaken to upgrade the job skills of low-income groups during the 1960s and early 1970s. Many of these individual programs were brought together under the Comprehensive Employment and Training Act (CETA) in 1973. CETA established a community manpower system to give people training and transitional public-service employment with the aim of enhancing their employability in the private sector. The federal government's role in CETA was to provide support and technical assistance to local programs. The Older American Community Service Employment Act of 1973 has subsidized jobs for older workers. Other federal activities have included apprenticeship programs, the Job Corps, and the Work Incentive Program (WIN). The federal government has also helped support apprenticeship programs run by employers, often jointly with labor unions, to train workers on the job in a skilled trade. The Job Corps has undertaken the training of disadvantaged youth, largely at residential centers, and has conducted nontraditional training for women. The Work Incentive Program has provided manpower, placement, and other services to help people receiving Aid to Families with Dependent Children get and keep jobs.

### Program Effectiveness

Have these programs been very effective at improving employability and helping to reduce the unemployment rate?

Some say that the Job Corps's experience with efforts to train disadvantaged youths, the "hard-core" unemployed among the young, suggests that progress is possible. However, high costs and drop-out rates are a problem. Moreover, Job Corps training, like any job-training program, has little value if there is no job to enter once training is completed. Particularly discouraging is the high unemployment rate among black teenagers. It has climbed with little interruption for over a quarter of a century until now roughly 35 percent are unemployed, as compared to 16.5 percent in 1954. Analysts who monitor this problem offer various explanations. Notably, they say government job programs don't focus enough on inner-city neighborhoods where black teenagers predominate. Also, new jobs are emerging farther from inner-city areas. Many claim that the minimum wage eliminated many jobs that would otherwise be available to unskilled workers. Another factor cited is inadequate educational facilities.

Public-service jobs funded by CETA were intended to reduce hard-core unemployment and provide temporary, entry-level jobs into the economic mainstream for people without much training or work experience. But critics note that local projects have often called for workers with sophisticated skills. They also cite some large cities where funds intended for jobs for poor blacks, Hispanics, and welfare mothers have been used to rehire municipal workers laid off in budget cutbacks. Critics also point out that federal public-service money, rather than creating new jobs, has often been diverted into supporting activities that state and local governments might have provided from their own budgets.

The CETA program spent some $60 billion during its 9 year existence but managed only to get 30 percent of its participants into private-sector jobs. All in all, the CETA program was mostly a jobs-subsidy program, offering money to state and local governments to create "make-work" jobs. Only 18 cents of every CETA dollar was spent on training people for jobs in the private sector.

### The Job Training Partnership Act— Private Sector Involvement

The Job Training Partnership Act (JTPA) of 1982 went into effect in 1983, replacing CETA with training programs focused almost entirely on the private sector. Under JTPA at least 70 cents of each training dollar must be used for direct training costs, as compared to CETA's 18 cents. JTPA uses federal funds to provide seed money for state and local governments to set up, with the help of industry, local training centers that give training tailored to the available jobs in those communities. The program has created nearly 600 Private Industry Councils, involving 11,000 business volunteers, who advise the training centers about which job skills are most in demand in their areas. So far the program has been much more successful than CETA in getting participants jobs in the private sector.

## Public Works Projects

Since the days of the Great Depression, public works projects have been seen as a way to use government expenditures to put the unemployed back to work while meeting important community needs. However, it is not always easy to devise projects that are truly worthwhile on their own merits and not just excuses to spend money to "make work." During the Great Depression, the Works Progress Administration (WPA) put many unemployed people to work on a variety of projects, such as developing park areas, building roads, constructing dams and public buildings, and so forth. While many of these projects were considered worthwhile, others were of a "make-work" nature—leaf raking, construction projects using men and shovels where motorized equipment would have been more efficient, and so on. Today many proponents of public works projects contend that unemployed young people could be employed on such projects as slum clearance and urban rehabilitation. It is argued that these activities would create jobs in inner cities where unemployment among youth, particularly blacks, is highest.

Ideally, it is desirable to locate public works projects in those areas of the country where unemployment rates are highest. This has proved difficult in practice, however. Federal statistics are often not precise enough to identify areas with the highest unemployment. The national jobless rate is based on a monthly survey of 50,000 households, but the sample doesn't produce precise rates for particular geographic areas. Building trades unions, for example, complain that the government seems to have difficulty pinpointing places where their numbers are particularly hard-hit by unemployment. Some states that work up their own figures often seem to underestimate dramatically the number of the long-term, chronically unemployed.

The idea of timing public works projects so that they are initiated and carried out during the recession phases of business cycles has turned out to be largely unworkable. We have already noted in Chapter 10 how the timing of discretionary spending aimed at offsetting recessions is hindered by the uncertainties of forecasting and recognition and the sluggishness of the democratic decision-making process. As a result, slow-starting projects may aggravate inflation later by tightening up labor markets in an improving economy.

## Employment Tax Credit

The basic idea behind an employment tax credit is to reduce the cost of labor to business firms so that they will hire more labor. *The* **employment tax credit** *allows firms to exclude a certain amount of their income from taxation, an amount equal to some specified percent of the wages they pay labor.* This credit effectively reduces the cost of employing labor, thus encouraging firms to hire more workers than they would otherwise.

Some economists view the employment tax credit as a less inflationary way of stimulating the economy and increasing employment than reductions in personal and corporate income taxes. They contend that cuts in personal and corporate income taxes put extra dollars in the hands of consumers and businesses without initially expanding the supply of goods that will be demanded with these dollars. By contrast, it is argued that an employment tax credit puts extra dollars in circulation through bigger payrolls, while at the same time expanding production through the hiring of additional workers. Proponents also claim that by lowering production costs such a credit encourages businesses to hold down prices.

Some economists think that an employment tax credit is a cheaper, more effective, more permanent way of putting the hard-core unemployed to work than federal spending on public works or public-service jobs. We have noted that public-service jobs, such as those that were funded by CETA, are intended to provide temporary, entry-level jobs into the economic mainstream for the hard-core unemployed and others without much training or work experience. Those who prefer the employment tax credit approach argue that it puts these people into the economic mainstream immediately and gives them on-the-job training that is difficult to duplicate in public-service jobs. However, some economists contend that subsidizing wages via the employment tax credit inhibits investment in labor-saving machinery, which is needed to increase productivity. On the other hand, others argue that less emphasis on capital and more on labor is appropriate for a society trying to conserve energy and other natural resources and prevent pollution.

## SUMMARY

**1.** A wage-price guidelines policy attempts to curb inflation by getting business and labor to refrain voluntarily from increasing wages and prices at rates in excess of some guideline rate specified by government.

**2.** Two measures designed to provide incentives for compliance with wage-price guidelines are wage insurance and the tax-based income policy (TIP). Wage insurance guarantees that the government will repay labor for the purchasing power that they lose if they comply with the guideline and consumer prices rise faster than the guideline rate for wages. The carrot version of TIP rewards with tax credits (reductions in income taxes) those workers who keep their wage increases below the guideline rate for wage increases. The stick version of TIP punishes with tax penalties employers who grant wage increases that exceed the guideline rate.

**3.** High administration officials usually resort to jawboning and arm-twisting in their attempts to gain voluntary compliance with guidelines.

**4.** Wage-price controls affect resource allocation because wages and prices are not free to move to reflect shifts in supply and demand in different markets. Controls also raise questions of equity because enforcement efforts tend to focus more heavily on some groups than others and to control wages and prices more than interest rates,

dividends, rents, profits, and other forms of income.

**5.** The mere expectation that controls are about to be imposed may lead to an acceleration of wage-price increases. Whether or not the existence of wage-price controls dampens inflationary expectations remains a question of debate.

**6.** Experience suggests that controls have not proven very effective in the face of expansionary fiscal and monetary policy.

**7.** Indexing keeps constant the purchasing power of wages, taxes, and fixed-dollar assets by adjusting their dollar-denominated values for the change in the general price level.

**8.** Indexing the capital gains tax would mean that those selling an asset would be taxed only on their real gain, not on dollar gains attributable to inflation. Indexing government bonds, mortgage loans, savings deposits, and other fixed-dollar assets would eliminate many of the arbitrary gains and losses caused by unanticipated inflation.

**9.** Some economists argue that indexing income taxes and government bonds would reduce inflation because it would make it harder for government to finance deficit spending. Others disagree, claiming that if policymakers felt people were protected from inflation by indexing, there would be even less concern about curbing an overly expansive fiscal and monetary policy.

**10.** Opponents of income tax indexing also argue that it removes the automatic reduction in purchasing power that otherwise acts to dampen inflationary booms. Proponents claim that income tax indexing eliminates accelerating cost-push inflation caused by wage and salary earners' attempts to maintain the purchasing power of their after-tax income.

**11.** Conventional fiscal and monetary policy has difficulty reducing stubborn pockets of unemployment without generating inflationary price increases in those parts of the economy already operating at capacity. Policies more specifically focused on dealing with hard-core unemployment problems seem to be necessary.

**12.** Manpower programs provide job training for the young and hard-core unemployed to increase their employability. Public works projects are often aimed at providing employment while also constructing needed public facilities, such as schools, roads, and parks. An employment tax credit is designed to reduce the cost of labor and encourage employment by giving firms tax credits equal to some specified percent of the wages paid to labor.

## KEY TERMS AND CONCEPTS

capital gains taxes
employment tax credit
escalator clause
indexing
manpower programs
tax-based income policy (TIP)
wage insurance
wage-price controls
wage-price guidelines

## QUESTIONS AND PROBLEMS

**1.** Suppose the government institutes a wage-price guidelines policy. If you are running a business, what would determine your willingness to comply with the guidelines?

**2.** Explain why some economists argue that whether the carrot version of TIP will lead to more, or less, inflation depends on how the government decides to replace the tax revenue lost when workers earn tax credits. How would a combined carrot-and-stick version of TIP affect your analysis of this issue? What advantages might a combined carrot-and-stick version of TIP have over wage insurance?

**3.** It has been said that because controls affect resource allocation, inflation actually takes place even though prices are not allowed to rise. Explain the logic underlying this view.

**4.** "Controls can affect expectations in a variety of ways, some tending to curb and others to aggravate inflation." Elaborate on this statement.

**5.** It has been argued that if all wages and salaries as well as all fixed-dollar assets were indexed, the slightest bit of excessive fiscal or monetary expansion would create an inflation that would feed on itself, getting worse and worse, eventually turning into hyperinflation. Explain why you agree or disagree with this point of view.

**6.** While job-training programs and employment tax credits are both aimed at reducing unemployment, they each have implications for inflation as well. What are the inflationary implications of each? Which do you think might be more inflationary and why?

# 18

# Economic Growth

**AFTER READING THIS CHAPTER, YOU WILL BE ABLE TO:**

1. Define the concept of economic growth.

2. Describe the ways in which economic growth and its major components are measured.

3. Explain the classical view of economic growth.

4. Summarize the sources of economic growth.

5. Describe the problems underlying the slowdown of economic growth in the United States during the 1970s, and the apparent recovery from those difficulties in the 1980s.

6. Explain the controversy over the benefits and costs of economic growth and the concern about possible limits to economic growth.

**O**ur discussion in preceding chapters has dealt mostly with the analysis of income and employment determination in the short run. We have focused on the problem of how to smooth out economic fluctuations and at the same time keep the economy operating close to full employment without generating excessive inflation. The framework of income and employment analysis that we have used throughout implicitly assumes that there is a given, unchanging quantity of resources and a given state of technology. That assumption is what makes it a short-run analysis. In the short run, there is a given amount of labor, capital, and land to employ, a given state of technological know-how, and a given population to clothe, house, and feed.

Economic growth takes place because in the long run the quantity of available resources, the state of technology, and the size of the population all change. It is necessary to study economic growth in order to understand how and why the economy's capacity to produce goods and services changes in the long run. Economic growth (or the absence of it) also has important implications for how well we can handle many of the problems that confront our economy in the short run. Emphasizing the importance of the short run, Keynes once remarked that "in the long run we are all dead." Nonetheless, the long-run phenomenon of economic growth has important consequences for how well we live in the short run.

Our first concern in this chapter will be the definition and measurement of economic growth. Then we will examine the major past and present explanations of why there is economic growth. Finally, we will consider the apparent slowdown in U.S. economic growth, the issue of the benefits and costs of economic growth, and the increasing concern about the possible limits to economic growth.

## DEFINING AND MEASURING ECONOMIC GROWTH

We can define economic growth in several different, but related, ways. Moreover, how we define economic growth largely determines how we measure it. Definition and measurement are closely related issues.

## Defining Economic Growth

Defined quite generally, **economic growth** *is the expansion of an economy's capacity to produce goods and services that takes place over prolonged periods of time, year in and year out, from decade to decade, from one generation to the next, or even over the course of centuries.*

### The Expanding Production Possibilities Frontier

Recall our discussion of the economy's production possibilities frontier in Chapter 2. Suppose the economy produces two kinds of goods—consumer goods and capital goods. The production possibilities frontier *AA* in Figure 18–1 shows the different maximum possible combinations of quantities of capital and consumer goods that the economy can produce if it fully employs all its available resources of labor, capital, and land, given the existing state of technological know-how. If there is an increase in the quantity or quality of any of these resources or if there is improvement in the state of technological know-how, the economy's production possibility frontier will shift outward to a position such as *BB*. As a result, the economy can produce more of both kinds of goods. This gives us an insight into the nature and causes of economic growth. Economic growth may be viewed as the continual shifting outward of the production possibilities frontier caused by growth in the quantity or quality, or both, of the economy's available resources, by ongoing improvement in the state of technological know-how, or by some combination of both.

### Staying on the Frontier

When the economy's production possibilities frontier shifts outward, the economy's *capacity* to produce increases. But the economy will not realize the full benefits of this capac-

FIGURE 18-1 **Economic Growth Shifts the Production Possibilities Frontier Outward**

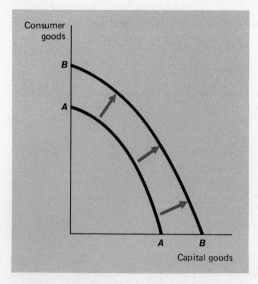

Economic growth may be represented by an outward shift of the production possibilities frontier, such as from *AA* to *BB*. The shift is caused by growth in the quantity or quality, or both, of the economy's available resources, by ongoing improvement in the state of technological know-how, or by a combination of both. To realize the full benefits of economic growth, the economy must maintain full employment and avoid inefficient allocation of its resources.

ity increase unless it is always on its production possibilities frontier. In Chapter 2 we saw that there are two reasons why the economy may operate inside its production possibilities frontier.

First, the economy will not operate on its production possibilities frontier if any of its resources are unemployed. Whenever part of the labor force is unemployed or whenever there is unused plant capacity, the economy operates inside its production possibilities frontier. In order to remain on the frontier, the economy's aggregate demand for goods and services must grow at a rate sufficient to

utilize fully the increased productive capacity provided by economic growth.

Second, the economy will not operate on its production possibilities frontier if any of its resources are underemployed—that is, if there is not efficient resource allocation. Efficient resource allocation requires that resources be employed in those activities for which they are best suited. Only then will the economy be able to realize the maximum possible output with its available resources. (Recall the example in Chapter 2 of the effect on the economy's output of wheat and oranges that results from trying to grow wheat in Florida and oranges in Minnesota.)

In sum, if the economy is to stay on its expanding production possibilities frontier and realize the gains from economic growth, it must avoid both unemployment and underemployment. While it is not possible to eliminate unemployment completely, fiscal and monetary policy must see to it that aggregate demand expands fast enough to utilize the increased productive capacity provided by economic growth. And, in order to minimize underemployment, markets must operate efficiently to allocate resources to those productive activities in which the value of their contribution to total output will be greatest.

### The Interdependence of Demand and Economic Growth

The rate of increase of aggregate demand for goods and services and the rate of economic growth are interrelated. If aggregate demand doesn't expand fast enough to keep the economy operating on its production possibilities frontier, the resulting unemployment will mean that a certain amount of capital goods that could be produced will not be. Capital goods not produced today will not be available to produce other goods tomorrow. Consequently, the outward expansion of the economy's production possibilities frontier will not be as great. There will be less economic growth than otherwise would have been possible had aggregate demand expanded fast enough to keep the economy continually operating on its production possibilities frontier.

For example, during the Great Depression aggregate demand declined so much that the nation's firms actually allowed their capital stock to wear out faster than they replaced it—net investment was negative, as was shown in Figure 7–1 in Chapter 7. This meant that the economy's capital stock actually declined. One of the major costs of the Great Depression was the enormous quantity of capital goods that the economy never produced. This lack of capital goods production resulted in a severe decline in the rate of expansion of the economy's productive capacity, and hence in its rate of economic growth.

## Measuring Economic Growth

If economic growth is represented by an outward expansion of the economy's production possibilities frontier, then *one measure of economic growth is the rate of growth of the economy's full-employment level of total output.* This is the level of total output the economy can produce when it is on its production possibilities frontier. The money value of full-employment total output can change because of a change in prices. Since we are only interested in measurements of growth that represent an increase in the output of actual goods and services, economic growth rates must be calculated using constant-dollar, or real, measures of full-employment total output. An example of such a measure is potential, or full-employment, real GNP measured in constant 1972 dollars, as was shown in Figure 6–5, part b.

### Full-Employment Real GNP

The rate of growth of full-employment real GNP is a measure of the growth in the economy's overall capacity to produce goods and services. But it tells us little about how the economy's standard of living is changing over time. One measure of the economy's standard of living is output per capita, the economy's full-employment total output level divided by the size of its population.

We can express this as

full-employment real GNP per capita

$$= \frac{\text{full-employment real GNP}}{\text{population}}$$

It is obvious from this expression that growth in full-employment real GNP does not necessarily mean an increase in the standard of living as measured by full-employment real GNP per capita. If full-employment real GNP (the numerator) grows faster than population (the denominator), full-employment real GNP per capita will grow and the economy's standard of living will increase. However, if full-employment real GNP grows at a slower rate than population, full-employment real GNP per capita declines and the standard of living goes down. Remember, however, that full-employment real GNP per capita is an average and, thus, a very rough measure of living standards. Few economists consider it an ideal measure of the economy's standard of living. For example, it doesn't tell us anything about the actual distribution of income in the economy. (At this point you should reread the discussions in Chapter 5 of what GNP does not measure.) Nonetheless, *the rate of growth of output per capita is a measure of economic growth that provides a rough indication of change in the standard of living.*

### Output per Labor Hour

Another important measure closely linked to economic growth is output per labor hour (often referred to as output per man hour). Output per labor hour is the conventional way of measuring **productivity.** It gives us some indication of how efficiently each labor hour combines with the capital stock and the existing state of technology to produce output. Output per labor hour is an appealing measure of productivity because it is a combined reflection of the quality of labor (education, technical skill, motivation), the quantity and quality of capital that labor uses, and the degree of sophistication of the state of technology. *The greater the rate of growth of output per labor hour, the larger the rate of* *growth of productivity, and this obviously contributes to the rate of economic growth.*

## Components of Full-Employment Total Output

The economy's full-employment total output $Q$ may be viewed as having four components. The size of the economy's population $N$ (the number of people) is the first component. The second is the fraction of the population that makes up the labor force. This fraction is equal to the number of laborers $L$ divided by the size of the population $N$. Note that the number of laborers $L$ may be computed as the population $N$ multiplied by the fraction of the population in the labor force:

$$L = N \times \frac{L}{N}$$

The third component is the average number of hours $H$ that each laborer actually works. The total number of labor hours actually worked by the entire labor force therefore equals $L$ multiplied by $H$. Note that the total number of labor hours $L \times H$ may be expressed as

$$L \times H = N \times \frac{L}{N} \times H$$

The fourth component is productivity, or output per labor hour, which is equal to full-employment total output $Q$ divided by the total number of labor hours $L \times H$:

$$\frac{Q}{L \times H}$$

The economy's full-employment total output $Q$ is equal to the total number of labor hours $L \times H$ multiplied by output per labor hour $Q/(L \times H)$:

$$Q = L \times H \times \frac{Q}{L \times H}$$

Since

$$L \times H = N \times \frac{L}{N} \times H$$

the economy's full-employment total output $Q$ may also be expressed as

$$Q = N \times \frac{L}{N} \times H \times \frac{Q}{L \times H} \qquad (1)$$

Equation 1 shows that the economy's full-employment total output $Q$ may be viewed as being equal to the product of the four components: the size of the population $N$ multiplied by the fraction of the population in the labor force $L/N$ multiplied by the average number of hours each laborer actually works $H$ multiplied by output per labor hour $Q/(L \times H)$. Clearly the growth of the economy's full-employment total output $Q$ will depend on the way each of these four components in Equation 1 changes over time. (Note that the $N$, $L$, and $H$ in the numerator of Equation 1 may be cancelled out by the $N$, $L$, and $H$ in the denominator of Equation 1 to give $Q = Q$, which is true by definition.)

The total output of the U.S. economy, as measured by real GNP (in constant 1972 dollars), is shown in part a of Figure 18-2. Since 1948 real GNP has increased roughly threefold. Let's examine the role that each of the four components has played in this growth.

## Role of the Components of Total Output in Economic Growth

1. *Population—P.* Population growth contributes to economic growth from both the demand side and the supply side. A growing population means a growing demand for all kinds of goods and services. On the supply side, an increasing population provides the ever larger pool of labor needed to produce the larger quantity of output required to satisfy growing demand.

Throughout its history the United States has experienced steady population growth due to a high birthrate, a declining death rate, and at times (especially during the nineteenth century) substantial immigration. The U.S. population increased from approximately 5 million persons in 1800 to approximately 76 million in 1900. By 1984 it had increased to about 237 million. In recent years the birthrate has declined somewhat,

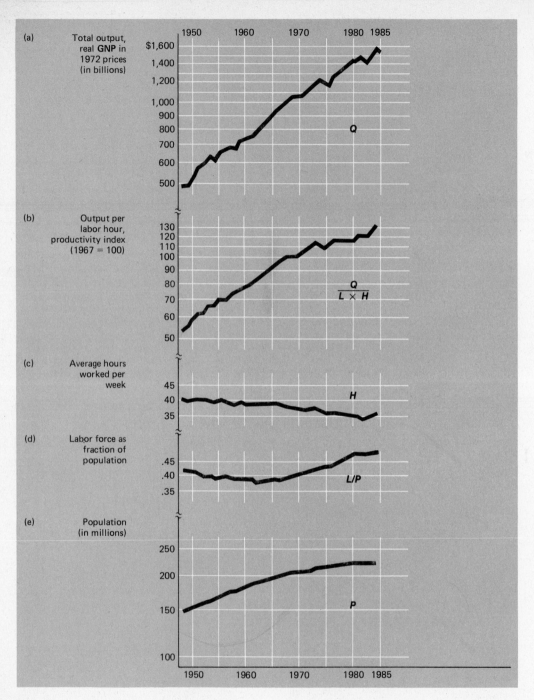

reflecting a trend toward smaller families. (This trend may be due in part to the increasing participation of women in the labor force.) Population experts project the population will grow to somewhere between 245 million and 290 million by the year 2000, the range largely reflecting the difference between assuming a low or a high birthrate. The growth in the postwar U.S. population since 1948 is illustrated in part e of Figure

18–2. Clearly, population growth has been a contributing factor to the growth in real GNP shown in part a.

2. *Labor force, as a fraction of the population—L/P.* While the population provides the source of the labor pool, it is the proportion or fraction of the population that actually joins the labor force, *L/P,* that determines the size of the labor pool. The larger the fraction, the larger the labor force provided by a given size population and hence the greater the productive capacity of the economy.

The behavior of this fraction in the postwar U.S. economy is shown in part d of Figure 18–2. Expressing the fraction *L/P* as a percentage, the percentage of the population in the labor force fell from roughly 41 percent in 1948 to somewhat less than 38 percent in 1962. Since that time it has increased steadily, reaching about 47 percent by the early 1980s where it seems to have leveled off. In other words, the labor force has been growing faster than the population. As we observed in Chapter 6, in part this has been due to a maturing post–World War II "baby boom" that swelled the working-age population during the 1960s and 1970s. Another contributing factor has been the increase in the proportion of working-age women that

have joined the labor force during these years.

3. *Hours, average hours worked per laborer—H.* In 1890 the length of the average workweek was roughly 60 hours. During the early part of the twentieth century, it declined steadily to about 43 hours in 1930. Since then the decline has continued at a more gradual pace (interrupted by an increase during World War II). From 1948 to around 1966 the average workweek only declined by about 1 hour, from about 40 hours per week down to about 39 hours, as illustrated in part c of Figure 18–2. Since then it appears to have declined to about 35 hours.

Obviously, a decline in the length of the average workweek tends to reduce the rate of economic growth. However, the reduction in hours worked reminds us that economic growth is certainly not the be-all and end-all of the "good life." Most economists argue that the steady decline in the average workweek reflects a preference for more leisure, one of the fruits made possible by the higher standard of living provided by economic growth. Indeed, while the length of the average workweek today is about 40 percent shorter than it was in 1890, real GNP per capita has increased roughly 500 percent over this time period.

---

**FIGURE 18-2  The Components of Economic Growth in the American Economy Since 1948**

The growth of total output $Q$, measured by real GNP (part a), is the product of change in four components: population, $P$; the fraction of the population in the labor force, $L/P$; the average hours worked per laborer, $H$; and productivity, or output per labor hour, $Q/(L \times H)$.

Productivity growth (part b) has been the single most important contributor to real GNP growth since 1948. Next in order of importance has been population growth (part e). The decline in the proportion of the population in the labor force (part d) from 1948 to 1962 tended to work against real GNP growth, while the increase in that proportion since 1962 has been favorable to real GNP growth. The decline in average hours worked per week (part c) tended to hold back real GNP growth. The decline in productivity growth (part b) in recent years has worked against real GNP growth (part a).

Note that the vertical axis in each diagram is a logarithmic, or ratio, scale, on which equal distances represent equal percentage changes. For example, in part a the distance from 600 to 900 is the same as the distance from 800 to 1,200 since each represents an increase of 50 percent.

4. *Output per labor hour—$Q/(L \times H)$.* Growth in productivity, or output per labor hour, is the principal component in economic growth. In all countries that have experienced sustained increases in their standard of living, productivity growth has been the wellspring. Productivity growth results from increases in the educational and skill levels of the labor force, growth in the quantity and quality of capital, and the steady advancement of the state of technological know-how. Output per labor hour has more than doubled in the U.S. economy since 1948, as shown in Figure 18–2, part b. However, the slowdown in the rate of increase in output per labor hour in recent years is a bad omen for economic growth.

Comparing parts b, c, d, and e of Figure 18–2, we can see that productivity growth (part b) has been the single most important contributor to the growth in real GNP (part a) since 1948, except during recent years. Next in order of importance has been population growth (part e). The decline in the proportion of the population in the labor force (part d) from 1948 to 1962 tended to work against economic growth, while the increase in that proportion since 1962 has been favorable to economic growth. The decline in average hours worked per week (part c) has tended to hold back growth in real GNP. But it should be stressed that if the shorter workweek represents a choice of more leisure in exchange for less growth in the output of goods, it signifies an increase in well-being.

### The Significance of Growth Rates—The "Rule of 72"

What difference does it make whether an economy grows at 3 percent, or 4 percent, or 5 percent? A great deal! A rule-of-thumb calculation known as the "rule of 72" readily shows why. For any growth rate in real GNP, the rule of 72 says that the number of years it will take for real GNP to double in size is roughly equal to 72 divided by the growth rate. For example, if the economy's real GNP grows at a rate of 2 percent, it will take approximately 36 years ($72 \div 2$) for real GNP to double. If it grows at a 3 percent rate, it will take 24 years to double ($72 \div 3$). A 6 percent growth rate would mean real GNP would double in only 12 years ($72 \div 6$)!

Consider the implications of different growth rates for our economy. Economists tend to agree that in the 1960s the economy could grow 4 percent each year without setting off demand-pull inflation. However, because of the slowdown in productivity growth during the 1970s and early 1980s, this figure may be more like 3, or even 2, percent. According to the rule of 72, at a 4 percent growth rate real GNP would double in roughly 18 years ($72 \div 4$). Starting from the year 1984, this doubling would occur in the year 2002. However, if the "safe growth" rate needed to avoid excessive inflation is 3 percent, real GNP would not double until approximately the year 2008, which is 24 years from 1984. If the safe growth rate is 2 percent, real GNP would not double until the year 2020.

Suppose we start with the actual level of real GNP in 1980 and project these two different growth paths into the future, as shown in Figure 18–3. Clearly, the farther into the future we go on these two different paths, the greater the difference in the possible levels of real GNP. In 1982 the difference amounts to roughly $40 billion. By 1990 real GNP on the 4 percent growth path is about $2,160 billion, while on the 3 percent growth path it is about $1,950 billion, a difference of $210 billion. By the year 2000 the difference amounts to about $635 billion!

### CHECKPOINT* 18–1

**From 1950 to 1981 productivity in the U.S. economy roughly doubled (Figure 18–2, part b). What does the rule of 72 tell us about the rate of growth of productivity during this time period? Suppose it is projected that productivity growth in the United States may average no more than 1.5 percent per year in coming years. What does this imply about the projected**

**FIGURE 18-3** **The Difference Between a Real GNP Growth Rate of 4 Percent and a Rate of 3 Percent**

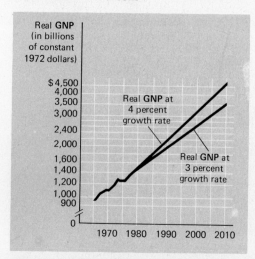

Starting from the actual level of real GNP in 1980, the difference between growing at a 3 percent and at a 4 percent rate becomes more pronounced as we proceed into the future. In 1982 the difference amounts to roughly $40 billion. But by the year 2000 it amounts to about $635 billion. (Note that the vertical axis is a logarithmic, or ratio, scale, on which equal distances represent equal percentage changes.)

**behavior of the other three components of economic growth, given a "safe growth" rate of 3 percent per year? Compare parts a and e of Figure 18-2 and give a rough estimate of how much real GNP per capita has increased since 1948 in the United States.**

\* Answers to all Checkpoints can be found at the back of the text.

# EXPLAINING ECONOMIC GROWTH

It has been difficult for economists to come up with a single, comprehensive theory that explains economic growth. How does a country that has experienced a low and unchanging standard of living for centuries transform itself into one that realizes a sustained, decade-by-decade increase in productivity and real GNP per capita? Part of the difficulty economists have with this question is that a good deal of the answer no doubt requires an explanation of the political, cultural, and sociological processes that underlie such a transformation. The classical economists, such as David Ricardo and Thomas Malthus, painted a rather gloomy picture of the prospects for economic growth. Subsequent generations of economists have had the benefit of observing economic growth on a scale that the classical economists had not anticipated. Present-day explanations of economic growth place a great deal of emphasis on such things as capital formation, technological change, and saving.

## The Classical View of Economic Growth

During the late eighteenth and early nineteenth centuries the Industrial Revolution in England was just getting under way. Much of the rest of Western Europe remained untouched by this development. Observing the world around them, it is little wonder that classical economists, such as Malthus and Ricardo, argued that a nation's economic growth would inevitably lead to stagnation and a subsistence standard of living. In its simplest form, their argument rested on two basic premises. The first was the law of diminishing returns. The second was the proposition that the population would expand to the point where the economy's limited resources would only provide a subsistence living.

### Production and the Law of Diminishing Returns

The law of diminishing returns is a proposition about the way total output changes when the quantity of one input to a production process is increased while the quantities

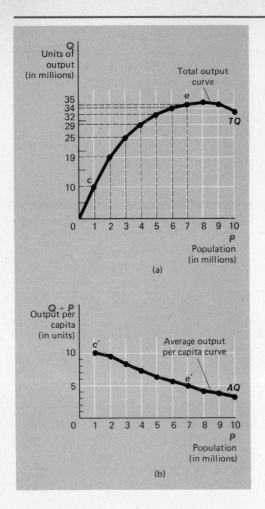

(a)

(b)

**FIGURE 18-4  Total Output, Average Output per Capita, and the Law of Diminishing Returns**

Given an unchanging state of technology, when a larger and larger population $P$ works with a fixed quantity of land and other resources, total output $Q$ (vertical axis, part a) increases by successively smaller amounts, a reflection of the law of diminishing returns. Thus the $TQ$ curve (part a), which represents the relationship between population size and total output, rises less and less steeply as population size increases. The average output per capita (vertical axis, part b) for each population size is calculated by dividing total output $Q$ by population $P$. Again reflecting the law of diminishing returns, the average output per capita curve $AQ$ declines as population increases.

of all other inputs are held constant. Classical economists applied this law to economic growth. *Given the state of technological know-how, classical economists argued that as a larger and larger population works with a fixed amount of land and other resources, the increase in total output becomes less and less.* In other words, there are diminishing returns in the form of successively smaller additions to total output. As a consequence the average output per capita declines as the population grows.

The law of diminishing returns is illustrated in Figure 18–4 for a hypothetical country. In part a, population $P$ is measured on the horizontal axis and total output $Q$ on the vertical axis. The total output curve $TQ$ shows the relationship between the size of the country's population and the quantity of total output that population can produce, assuming a fixed quantity of resources and a given state of technological know-how. With a population of 1 million the economy is able to produce a total output of 10 million units. If the population increases by 1 million, to a total of 2 million, the level of total output rises by 9 million units to a total of 19 million units. A population increase to 3 million results in an increase in total output from 19 million to 25 million units, or a rise of 6 million units, and so forth. Note that each successive 1 million person increase in the population results in a smaller increase in total output. The successively smaller increases in total output associated with each 1 million person increase in population reflect the law of diminishing returns. Once the population reaches 8 million, further increases in population actually cause total output to fall. That is, the $TQ$ curve bends over and begins to decline beyond a population of 8 million.

The consequences of diminishing returns for average output per capita are shown in Figure 18–4, part b. Average output per capita (vertical axis) is calculated for each population level $P$ (horizontal axis) by dividing the total output $Q$ (from part a) by $P$. For example, when the population size is 1 million and total output equals 10 million units, corresponding to point $c$ on $TQ$ (part a), average output per capita is 10 units, corresponding to point $c'$ (part b). The average output per capita is calculated and plotted in a similar fashion for each population size to give the average output per capita curve $AQ$. Notice that because of the law of diminishing returns, average output per capita decreases as the population size increases, as indicated by the declining $AQ$ curve. For instance, when population is 7 million and total output equals 35 million, point $e$ on $TQ$ (part a), average output per capita is 5 units, point $e'$ on $AQ$ (part b).

### The Subsistence Living Level

Another crucial ingredient of the classical theory of economic growth was the notion of a subsistence living level. *The* **subsistence living level** *may be viewed as the minimum standard of living necessary to keep the population from declining.* At the subsistence level the number of births would just equal the number of deaths. If the standard of living fell below the subsistence level, economic hardship would cause the death rate to rise above the birthrate and the population would decline. If the standard of living rose above the subsistence level, the death rate would

fall below the birthrate and the population would increase.

The subsistence living level for our hypothetical economy is illustrated in Figure 18–5. The axes in parts a and b are exactly the same as those in parts a and b of Figure 18–4. Given any population size (horizontal axis), the subsistence total output curve $SQ$ in part a indicates the minimum total output (vertical axis) necessary to maintain that population—that is, to keep it from declining. For example, the subsistence total output level necessary to sustain a population of 1 million is 5 million units of output, corresponding to point $d$ on $SQ$. Similarly, the $SQ$ curve indicates that it would take 10 million units of output to sustain a population of 2 million, 15 million units to sustain a population of 3 million, and so forth.

The subsistence living level may also be expressed in per capita terms. The average per capita subsistence level for any size population may be obtained by dividing the corresponding subsistence total output level by the population size. For example, for a population of 1 million requiring a subsistence total output of 5 million units (corresponding to point $d$ on $SQ$), the average per capita subsistence level is 5 units of output per person. Alternatively, observe from the $SQ$ curve that every additional population of 1 million requires another 5 million units of total output to maintain a subsistence level of living. Hence, whatever the population size, the average per capita subsistence living level in our hypothetical economy is 5 units of output per person, represented by the horizontal line $L$ in part b.

### Population Growth and Diminishing Returns

The classical view of economic growth combined the law of diminishing returns with the notion of the subsistence living level. Figure 18–6 illustrates the classical view by combining the $TQ$ and $AQ$ curves of Figure 18–4 with the $SQ$ and $L$ curves of Figure 18–5.

Suppose the population is initially 1 mil-

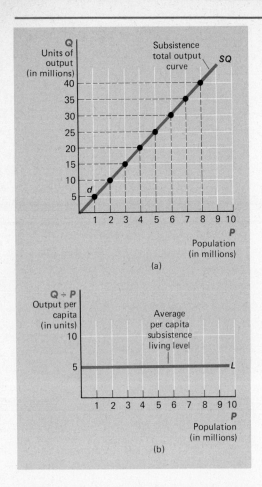

**FIGURE 18-5   The Subsistence Living Level**

The subsistence total output curve in part a shows the subsistence level of total output (vertical axis) associated with any given size population (horizontal axis) in a hypothetical economy. The subsistence level of total output for any given size population is that which provides a standard of living just sufficient to keep the total population from declining (the number of births just equals the number of deaths). The average per capita subsistence living level is equal to the subsistence level of total output for any given size population divided by the population. For the hypothetical economy shown here, the average per capita subsistence living level is 5 units of output per person, represented by the horizontal line *L* in part b.

lion. Given the fixed quantity of resources and the state of technological know-how, the economy will be able to produce a total output of 10 million units, corresponding to point *c* on total output curve *TQ* (part a). However, the subsistence total output level needed for a population of 1 million is only 5 million units, point *d* on the subsistence total output curve *SQ* (part a). In terms of total output, the economy's standard of living exceeds the subsistence level by 5 million units, represented by the vertical distance between points *c* and *d* in part a. In per capita terms, the average output per capita of 10 units (point *c'* in part b) exceeds the per capita

subsistence living level of 5 units (point *d'* in part b) by 5 units. Consequently, the death rate will be lower than the birthrate and the population will increase. Suppose the population increases to 2 million. The economy will produce a larger total output of 19 million units (point *f* in part a), which again exceeds the subsistence total output level of 10 million units (point *g* in part a), this time by 9 million units. In per capita terms, the average output per capita of 9.5 units (point *f'* in part b) again exceeds the per capita subsistence living level of 5 units (point *g'* in part b). Hence, the population will continue to increase.

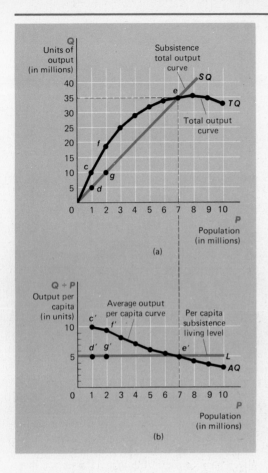

(a)

(b)

**FIGURE 18-6**   **The Classical View of Economic Growth**

At any population size less than 7 million the total output curve *TQ* lies above the subsistence total output curve *SQ* in part a. Because the quantity of total output produced (vertical axis) exceeds the subsistence total output level, the classical view argued that the birthrate would be higher than the death rate. Hence, both the population (horizontal axis) and total output would grow. At any population size greater than 7 million the total output curve *TQ* lies below the subsistence total output curve *SQ*. Since the total output produced is less than the subsistence total output level, the death rate would exceed the birthrate. Hence, both the population and total output would decline. Long-run equilibrium occurs at the intersection of *TQ* and *SQ*, point *e*, where the total output level produced is just sufficient to support a population of 7 million at a subsistence living level.

The argument may also be represented in per capita terms, part b. Consider any population size less than 7 million. Average output per capita, given by the *AQ* curve, is greater than the per capita subsistence living level of 5 units of output per person, given by the horizontal line *L*. Hence population rises, causing average output per capita to fall toward the per capita subsistence living level. Now consider any population level greater than 7 million. Average output per capita is less than the per capita subsistence level—the *AQ* curve lies below *L*. Hence, population declines and average output per capita rises toward the per capita subsistence level. The long-run equilibrium occurs at a population size of 7 million, where average output per capita just equals the per capita subsistence level, corresponding to the intersection of *AQ* and *L* at *e'*.

---

## ECONOMIC THINKERS

### THOMAS R. MALTHUS — 1766–1835

Thomas Malthus, a clergyman by training, was in many ways the epitome of the gentleman English scholar. Taking his A.B. degree from Jesus College, Cambridge, in 1788, he was appointed vicar at Albury near the family home and lived a quiet scholarly life. The economic views of Malthus fall into two broad categories: one, devoted to population problems, for which he is best known; and, two, his work on the inadequacy of aggregate demand, in which he was a forerunner of the great economist J. M. Keynes. His views on population were embodied in his famous work, *An Essay on the Principle of Population As It Affects the Future Improvement of Society* (1798), and his broader views were put forth in his book, *Principles of Political Economy,* published in 1820.

Malthus did not quarrel with the mildly cheerful view of Adam Smith relative to the future of humankind, but as he saw the future, it was a far cry from the optimistic picture drawn by his contemporaries Godwin, Condorcet, and their followers. Malthus forecast that the future was likely to be grim. He began with two postulates:

1. Food is necessary to people's existence.
2. The passion between the sexes is necessary and is likely to continue.

Following these basic postulates, he argued that "the power of the population is infinitely greater than the power of the earth to produce subsistence for man." That is, population would outstrip the ability of people to produce adequate food.

Since the science of keeping vital statistics was in its infancy and data relating to agricultural output were for all practical purposes nonexistent, the quantification of the theory was at best a theoretical approximation. This fact in no way inhibited Malthus, although later he did some empirical research to answer critical comment. His research may be summed up as follows:

| Year | 1 | 25 | 50 | 75 | 100 | 125 | 150 | 175 | 200 | 225 |
|---|---|---|---|---|---|---|---|---|---|---|
| Population | 1 | 2 | 4 | 8 | 16 | 32 | 64 | 128 | 256 | 512 |
| Subsistence | 1 | 2 | 3 | 4 | 5 | 6 | 7 | 8 | 9 | 10 |

That is, population, if unchecked, would increase 512 times after 225 years, the food supply only 10 times.

If the means are available, population will naturally increase. There are, however, two kinds of checks on population. These checks are either "preventive," reducing birthrates, or "positive," affecting the mortality rate. Among the lower classes the positive check is more common, since they suffer high rates of infant mortality and more often die from poor nutrition and general ill health resulting from lack of resources. On the other hand, those in the upper classes are more influenced by the preventive check since they tend to marry later and have fewer children, wishing to preserve their living standards. The poor have little to lose, so there is no reason to defer marriage.

As a further consequence, such policies as public relief (the "poor laws") defeat their own purpose, resulting only in an upsurge of population. Generally, Malthus favored the preventive check over the positive. All this was, to be sure, unfortunate, for "to prevent the recurrence of misery is alas, beyond the power of man." For a man of the cloth to take such a dim view of the arrangements of Providence may seem to pose a bit of a problem, and Malthus tried to answer this seeming contradiction in the last two chapters of his *Essay,* which attempt to mesh the principle of population with a view of a providentially ordered universe.

FOR FURTHER READING
Bonar, James. *Malthus and His Work.* New York: Macmillan, 1924.

According to the classical view, population and output will continue to grow as long as the economy's standard of living exceeds the subsistence living level. That is, population and total output grow as long as the total output curve *TQ* lies above the subsistence total output curve *SQ* (part a). Putting it in per capita terms, they will continue to grow as long as the average output per capita curve *AQ* lies above the per capita subsistence living level curve *L* (part b). Once the population reaches 7 million, total output produced will be 35 million units (part a), which is just equal to the subsistence level of total output needed to sustain a population of 7 million. This level corresponds to the intersection of the *SQ* and *TQ* curves at point *e* in part a. In per capita terms, at a population of 7 million average output produced per capita is 5 units, which is just equal to the per capita subsistence living level, corresponding to the intersection of *AQ* and *L* at point *e'* (part b). At this point population and output will cease to grow. Economic growth stops. The economy has reached a static, or unchanging, equilibrium position.

What a dismal equilibrium it is, characterized by stagnation and a subsistence standard of living. If the population were to rise above 7 million, total output produced would be less than the subsistence total output level required to sustain the larger population (to the right of point *e* in part a, the *TQ* curve lies below the *SQ* curve). Average output per capita would be less than the per capita subsistence living level (to the right of point *e'* in part b, the *AQ* curve lies below *L*). Consequently, famine and disease would cause the death rate to rise above the birthrate and the population would tend to fall back to the 7 million level. On the other hand, if the population were to fall below the 7 million level, total output would exceed the subsistence total output required to sustain the smaller population (the *TQ* curve lies above the *SQ* curve to the left of point *e* in part a). Living standards would rise since the average output per capita would be above the per capita subsistence living level (the *AQ* curve lies above

*L* to the left of point *e'* in part b). Unfortunately, according to the classical view, this would cause the birthrate to exceed the death rate. The population would tend to increase to 7 million again, and the standard of living would once again decline to the subsistence level.

### The "Dismal Science"

If economic growth tended to lead society to such a dismal long-run equilibrium position, the prospects for ever improving economic well-being would seem dim indeed. It is this implication of the classical view of economic growth that earned economics its designation as the "dismal science." The classical view is still relevant today in the so-called underdeveloped countries of the world. The near subsistence living standards and the high rates of population growth that plague those countries do suggest a rush toward the dismal long-run classical equilibrium. But the classical view bears little resemblance to the spectacular rise in living standards and the sustained economic growth experienced by the present-day industrialized, or developed, countries.

### Sources of Growth and Rising Living Standards

How can the long-run classical equilibrium and a subsistence living level be avoided? One way is for the total output curve, hence the average output per capita curve, to shift upward fast enough to stay ahead of population growth. Obviously, it would also help if population growth didn't increase every time output per capita rose above the subsistence living level.

Economic growth with rising living standards is depicted in Figure 18–7. Suppose the population is initially $P_1$. Total output corresponding to point *b* on total output curve *TQ* exceeds the subsistence total output level corresponding to point *a* on the subsistence output curve *SQ* (part a). Hence, average output per capita corresponding to

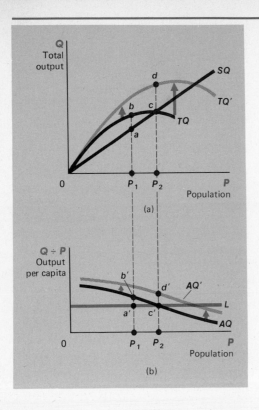

**FIGURE 18-7    Economic Growth with Rising Living Standards**

When the total output curve $TQ$ and hence the average output per capita curve $AQ$ shift upward rapidly enough, economic growth will be accompanied by rising average output per capita.

Suppose the total output and average output per capita curves are in the positions $TQ$ and $AQ$, respectively, and population is $P_1$. The standard of living exceeds the subsistence living level. Therefore, economic growth will tend toward the classical long-run equilibrium with population $P_2$ existing at a subsistence living level, corresponding to points $c$ and $c'$. However, if in the meantime $TQ$ and $AQ$ shift up to $TQ'$ and $AQ'$, average output per capita will rise, as represented by the fact that the vertical distance between $c'$ and $d'$ is greater than that between $a'$ and $b'$.

Upward shifts in $AQ$ and $TQ$ are caused by capital deepening, technological change and innovation, and an increase in the quality of the labor force caused by investment in human capital.

point $b'$ on the average output per capita curve $AQ$ exceeds the per capita subsistence level $L$ by an amount represented by the vertical distance between $b'$ and $a'$ (part b). Assume this above-subsistence standard of living causes the population to rise to $P_2$ in the manner suggested by the classical view. However, in the meantime suppose the total output curve shifts up to $TQ'$ and hence that the $AQ$ curve shifts up to the position $AQ'$. Now, even though the population grows to $P_2$, the standard of living is not driven down to the subsistence level corresponding to points $c$ and $c'$. Instead, total output rises to point $d$ on $TQ'$ and average output per capita rises to point $d'$ on $AQ'$. The standard of living has actually increased, as represented by the fact that the vertical distance between $c'$ and $d'$ is greater than that between $a'$ and $b'$.

What would cause economic growth to take place in this fashion, rather than along the lines suggested by the classical view? In particular, what causes the increase in productivity that allows any given size population to produce more, as represented by the upward shift in $TQ$ and $AQ$? And what factors might inhibit the tendency for population growth to be so responsive to increases in the standard of living? While there is no hard and fast blueprint, most economists now agree that any list of the key elements in economic growth should include capital deepening, technological change and innovation, education or investment in human capital, rising aspirations for a better standard of living, and saving and investment.

### Capital Deepening

**Capital deepening** *is an increase in the stock of capital (machines, tools, buildings, high-*

*ways, dams, and so forth) relative to the quantities of all other resources, including labor.* Capital deepening makes it possible for any given size population to produce a larger total output, so that average output per capita is increased. This, of course, is reflected in upward shifts of the *TQ* and *AQ* curves, such as those shown in Figure 18-7. Given the size of the population, the state of technology, and the quantities of all other resources, there are diminishing returns to capital deepening just as there are to increases in the population. Increases in the quantities of the *same kinds* of machines, tools, buildings, highways, and dams beyond a certain point (that is, more of the same capital goods labor is already using) obviously will not yield further increases in total and per capita output. Why? Because there will not be enough population and quantities of other resources with which to combine them in productive activities. The emphasis on "same kinds" of capital brings us to the role of technological change and innovation.

### Technological Change and Innovation

Invention and scientific discovery lead to technological change and innovation in production techniques. Even the most casual observer of economic life is struck by the changes that take place over time in the kinds of capital and procedures used to produce goods and services. When existing capital wears out, it is often replaced with *new kinds* of capital incorporating the new technology. Perfectly usable capital is often simply made obsolete by the development of new kinds of capital. As a result, even if the economy did not increase the quantity of resources devoted yearly to the replacement of worn-out or obsolescent capital, the productive capacity of the economy would grow. Hence, for any given size, population, and quantity of all other resources, total output would be larger. Again, this would be reflected in the upward shift of the *TQ* and *AQ* curves, such as that shown in Figure 18-7.

Some kinds of technological change are the result of changes in the form of a capital good, so-called **embodied technical change**. This is the kind of technological change that most often comes to mind. The diesel locomotive replaced the steam locomotive. Jet airliners have largely replaced the propeller variety. The electronic pocket calculator has made the slide rule obsolete. The list goes on and on.

Other kinds of technological change take the form of new procedures or techniques for producing goods and services, so-called **disembodied technical change**. Examples are the use of contour plowing to prevent soil erosion on farms, the development of new management techniques in business, and the pasteurization of milk. Such technological changes are not embodied in the form of a capital good. Of course, many types of embodied technical change make disembodied technical changes possible and vice versa. The electronic computer has made many new kinds of managerial procedures possible. And these procedures in turn make it possible to use new kinds of capital goods, or embodied technical changes. For example, computers enable airlines to use sophisticated procedures for scheduling and controlling the flow of passengers between airports more efficiently. This efficiency makes it practical to use certain kinds of jet aircraft.

### Education and Investment in Human Capital

Just as investment in capital goods increases productive capacity, so too does investment in human beings in the form of education, job training, and general experience. It is no accident that literacy rates and average years of schooling per capita tend to be higher in developed countries than in underdeveloped countries. Improvements in the quality of the labor force shift the *TQ* and *AQ* curves upward, as in Figure 18-7, in the same way that embodied and disembodied technical changes do.

Improvements in sanitation, disease prevention, nutrition, and the general health of the population are also forms of investment in human capital. A healthier population is more capable of learning and generally gives rise to a more productive labor force less prone to absenteeism and accidents. In addition, increases in the average life span make it possible to develop a more experienced labor force and to provide the larger pool of able managers and leaders needed to fill administrative positions.

### Rising Aspirations and Population Growth

If a society is to realize both economic growth and a rising standard of living, population growth must somehow be kept from literally "eating up" every increase in output per capita above the subsistence living level, as in the classical view. Countries that have experienced an industrial revolution and the progression from underdeveloped to developed status have somehow managed to escape from the drag of excessive population growth. One explanation is that once an economy realizes a rise in the standard of living above the subsistence level, the actual experience instills a taste for the "good life," or at least a better life. More and better food, clothing, and housing breeds a keen awareness that living *can be* more comfortable. People aspire to a better standard of living and become more aware of the relationship between curbing family size, and hence population growth, and the ability to realize these aspirations.

The effect of a rise in the aspiration level, measured in terms of average output per capita, on population size is shown in Figure 18–8. Suppose the aspiration level rises to *AL*. That is, people desire a standard of living, measured in terms of average output per capita, that exceeds the subsistence level by an amount equal to the vertical distance between *AL* and *L*. The population will not get larger than $P_a$, corresponding to the intersection of *AL* with the average output per capita curve *AQ* at point *a*. The long-run equilibrium average output per capita at point *a* is

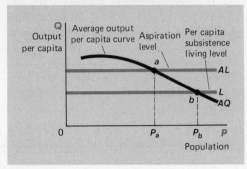

**FIGURE 18-8   The Effect of a Rising Aspiration Level on Population**

Suppose the aspiration level, measured in terms of average output per capita, is *AL*. The population will not get larger than $P_a$, corresponding to the intersection of *AL* with the average output per capita curve *AQ* at point *a*. The long-run equilibrium average output per capita at point *a* is higher than that corresponding to the classical view at point *b*, where a larger population $P_b$ exists at a subsistence living level.

higher than that corresponding to the classical view at point *b*, where the larger population $P_b$ exists at a subsistence living level. Now when capital deepening, technological change, and investment in human capital cause the *AQ* curve to shift upward, economic growth will cause population and output per capita to tend toward equilibrium positions corresponding to the intersection of the rising *AQ* curve with *AL*.

Another explanation of the decline in the population growth rate that tends to accompany economic development is that this decline is in part due to a change in the role of children. Such a change is brought about by the nature of economic development. The populations of underdeveloped countries are largely involved in agricultural activities, eking out a meager living with primitive tools. It is argued that under such circumstances children are viewed as "another pair of hands," useful for the work they can perform starting at a relatively early age. In addition, they are insurance that there will be somebody to look after aging parents. As economic development progresses, an ever larger portion of the population becomes employed in the economy's expanding industrial sector. Families earning livelihoods in factories, stores, and trades servicing a more urbanized population no longer view children as contributors to the family's economic well-being. Rather a child is primarily a dependent to be fed, clothed, and housed until he or she enters the labor force as a self-sufficient young adult. In short, in an industrial and urban setting, children are more of an economic burden on the family. The incentive to have large families that exists in a rural, agricultural setting is greatly reduced. It is therefore argued that as an increasing portion of the population moves into the industrial sector the birthrate, and hence population growth, tends to decline.

### The Role of Saving and Investment

In previous chapters we saw how saving, the refraining from consumption, makes it possible for investment to take place. Investment expenditures create new capital goods, which replace capital stock that is worn out or obsolescent, as well as increase the size of the economy's capital stock. Saving and investment are thus crucial to the capital formation and technological change that make possible economic growth and increasing output per capita.

Consider Figure 18–7 once again. The upward shift of $TQ$ to $TQ'$, and hence of $AQ$ to $AQ'$, requires saving and investment. When the population is $P_1$ and the total output curve is $TQ$, there is an excess of output above that required for subsistence. This excess is represented by the vertical distance between points $a$ and $b$ (part a). In order for capital formation to shift $TQ$ up to $TQ'$, the population must refrain from consuming all the excess output that the economy is able to produce. That is, some of it must be saved. What is not consumed is available for invest-

ment or the formation of the capital goods that increase the economy's productive capacity, as represented by the upward shift of the total output curve from $TQ$ to $TQ'$.

### Other Factors in Economic Growth

A distinguishing characteristic of developing economies is a growing *specialization of labor* accompanied by *increases in the scale of production*. In the early stages of economic development, a worker is typically engaged in many different tasks. For example, at the beginning of the Industrial Revolution in England (in the latter half of the eighteenth century), production was typically organized along the lines of the so-called cottage industry. A family occupying a cottage on a modest parcel of land would raise a small number of farm animals, tend a few crops, and engage in crafts such as spinning, weaving, and tanning. The family supplied much of its own food and made a good deal of its own clothing. An individual worker typically performed many different tasks. With the advent of the Industrial Revolution and the advancement of production technology, greater specialization and increases in the scale of production took place, thereby reducing per unit (of output) costs of production. Lower-priced, mass-produced goods led to the expansion of markets, an integral part of the economic growth process.

Another important ingredient of economic growth is the *development of extensive capital markets*, that is, markets where savers lend funds to borrowers who make the investment expenditures that give rise to capital formation. The growth of banking and other financial institutions that pool the savings of a large number of small savers and lend them out to investors plays a crucial role in the development of capital markets. Some economists even suggest that the state of development of a country's financial institutions provides the single most revealing indication of a country's state of economic development.

Economic growth requires a *favorable cul-*

*tural, social, and political environment.* Legal institutions are needed to provide law and order and to enforce contracts between parties to economic transactions. Cultural attitudes toward work and material advancement are an important determinant of the incentives for economic growth. A social structure that allows reasonably fluid upward and downward mobility based on performance and merit is more conducive to economic growth than a rigid social structure that puts a premium on the station of one's birth. Finally, economic growth rarely takes place in societies racked by political instability.

---

### CHECKPOINT 18-2
**Do you think the law of diminishing returns is applicable to technological change and investment in human capital? Why or why not? What are the implications of your answer for economic growth?**

---

## ISSUES IN ECONOMIC GROWTH

What are the aspects of economic growth that are currently of most concern to industrialized countries such as the United States? Policymakers were troubled by the slowing down in U.S. productivity growth that occurred during the 1970s and early 1980s. Since about 1982 productivity growth seems to have picked up. Will the revival continue? Quite aside from this issue, there has been considerable debate over whether the costs of continued economic growth in industrialized countries such as the United States are worth the benefits. Finally, there is the question of the limits to economic growth. Will we literally run out of resources? Will there be a doomsday?

### Recent Problems with Economic Growth in the United States

What were the causes of the slackening of productivity growth in the United States during the 1970s and early 1980s? (See Figure 18–2, part b.) Economists have offered several explanations. Among the most important are inflation, changes in the composition of the labor force, inadequate investment spending, reductions in research and development expenditures, and the increased government regulation of business.

### *Inflation*

The acceleration of inflation during the 1970s, made worse by the oil price shocks of 1973 and 1979, is widely credited with a major role in the productivity slowdown. Inflation eroded profits, reduced investment incentives, and impaired the efficiency of the market pricing system as an allocator of resources. The huge increase in energy prices increased the cost of using labor-saving machinery and fostered the use of more labor-intensive, lower productivity technologies.

### *Changes in the Labor Force*

From the mid-1960s up through the 1970s, youths born during the postwar "baby boom" represented a growing portion of the labor force. Their entry into the job market is at least part of the reason for the rise in the fraction of the population composing the labor force, as shown in Figure 18–2, part d (the other major cause is the increased labor force participation of women). Many of these young entrants to the labor force initially lacked training and experience. It took several years for them to become highly productive. The Council of Economic Advisers has estimated that during the 1970s industry's reliance on these inexperienced workers to fill jobs had the effect of shaving off a third of a point a year from the productivity index (Figure 18–2, part b). It is anticipated that as the "baby boom" population matures during the 1980s, it will cease to be a drag on productivity growth.

Labor force growth has slowed about 30 percent during the 1980s. The 16-to-24 age group has declined about 1.5 percent a year, in contrast to a 2.6 percent annual growth rate in the 1970s. On average, the work force of the 1980s is older and more experienced than that of the 1970s, and this should contribute to productivity gains.

### Inadequate Investment Spending

From 1948 to 1973 investment spending on new plant and equipment added 3 percent per year to the capital stock supporting each labor hour of work. From 1973 to 1982 this capital to labor hour ratio increased only about 1.75 percent annually. Some economists attribute this slow rate of increase to tax policies that tended to discourage investment spending. Others claim it was business fear that recession, inflation, or both would drastically reduce profit on new investment. In either case, the Council of Economic Advisers concluded that the effect was to slow the formation of cost-cutting, labor-saving capital. The end result, according to the council, was a reduction in the growth of productivity by half a percentage point each year.

### Reduced Research and Development Expenditures

Research and development (R and D) expenditures sow the seeds of technological change. It has been suggested that a decline in the intensity of research and development in the United States was a factor contributing to the productivity slowdown. Measured as a percent of GNP, R and D spending reached a peak of 3 percent in 1964. By 1977 the R and D expenditure share of GNP had dropped to an estimated 2.2 percent. Federal spending on R and D programs dropped with the end of the Vietnam War and the cutting back of the space program. The financial squeeze on private universities has also hindered research activities. It is difficult to calculate the adverse effect of reduced R and D spending on productivity growth, since it would have to be measured in terms of inventions not made and technological advances not realized.

### Regulation and Pollution Control

Some economists believe that excessive government regulation hinders productivity growth. Companies had to comply with an increasing number of antipollution regulations and health and safety rules during the 1970s, which led to increased spending and time devoted to these areas. Funds had to be diverted from buying productive machinery and developing more efficient operating methods. Industrial accidents have undoubtedly been prevented and environmental damage reduced. But the Council of Economic Advisers has estimated that compliance with such regulations may have cut annual nonfarm productivity growth by four-tenths of a percentage point.

## Negative Factors Reversed During the 1980s

Most of the factors that had a negative impact on productivity growth in the 1970s appear to have been reversed during the 1980s. Perhaps of greatest importance has been the deceleration in the general inflation rate and the decline in energy prices since 1981. The post-World War II baby boomers, who swelled the ranks of inexperienced youthful workers in the late 1960s and the 1970s, are now passing into their prime working years. Investment spending has increased significantly since the passage of the 1981 and 1982 tax acts. An Urban Institute study estimated that the marginal corporate tax rate on income from new investment has dropped from the 32.8 percent average of 1973 through 1981 to 15.8 percent. Since its low in 1977, R and D spending has risen and is contributing to an increased flow of cost-reducing inventions and innovations.

The costs to business of complying with antipollution and health-and-safety regulations have begun to level out as a percentage of GNP after major increases in 1970s. The move toward economic deregulation, which began under President Carter, has continued during the Reagan administration. It has

## POLICY PERSPECTIVE

### How Serious Are the Limits to Growth?

Predictions of an end to economic growth are certainly not new. Indeed, the dismal classical view, nearly 200 years old, seems very relevant in many of today's underdeveloped countries, a fact sometimes easily forgotten by those living in the industrialized or developed countries of the world. But in recent years the hard facts of pollution, energy shortages, urban sprawl, and traffic congestion have served as increasingly insistent reminders that there may well be limits to economic growth.

#### Resource Limitations

As we have already seen, the classical view of economic growth envisioned an inevitable tendency for countries to reach a point where both population and total output would cease to grow—a dismal long-run equilibrium of stagnation and misery. Due to the law of diminishing returns, output per capita would decline continuously until a subsistence standard of living was reached. However, capital deepening, technological change, investment in human capital, a rising aspiration level, and a favorable cultural, social, and political environment have all conspired to put off such a doomsday in the world's developed countries. But there are those who emphasize "put off." Put off for how long? It is undeniable that the earth's resources are limited. Therefore, these analysts argue that it is certainly not possible to beat the law of diminishing returns indefinitely. As the earth's resources are used up and population increases, the law of diminishing returns inevitably points to a declining per capita output.

#### Doomsday Predictions

Among the doomsday predictions, a group known as the Club of Rome (an international business association composed of business people, academicians, and scientists) has constructed an elaborate computerized model of world economic growth.[1] The Club of Rome model assumes that population and production grow at certain historically realistic percentage rates and that there are definite limits to world resources and technological capabilities. Given these assumptions, a computer is used to generate predictions of the future trends of industrial output per capita, the quantity of the world's resources, food per capita, population, and pollution. The predictions reach the alarming conclusion that the limits to growth will be reached somewhere in the years 2050 to 2100. The Club of Rome says that this conclusion follows largely from the depletion of the earth's nonrenewable resources—coal, petroleum, iron ore, aluminum, and so forth. Once the limit is reached, it is predicted that there will be an uncontrollable decline in population and productive capacity. If resource depletion does not trigger the collapse, then the precipitating factors will be famine, pollution, and disease.

What can be done to avert this doomsday prediction? Many of those who take the Club of Rome's predictions seriously argue that efforts should be made to establish zero population growth and zero economic growth. That is, establish a no-growth equilibrium. The Club of Rome suggests that by using appropriate technology, it may be possible to cut pollution, hold population growth in check, and reduce the amount of resources used per unit of output. In addition, investment in capital should be limited to the replace-

[1] Dennis L. Meadows and others, *The Limits to Growth* (Washington, D.C.: Potomac Associates, 1972).

ment of worn-out or obsolescent capital. Moreover, resources should be shifted away from the production of industrial products and toward the provision of more food and services.

### Perspective on Growth and Doomsday

Many find such doomsday predictions quite unconvincing. They observe that modern-day doomsday predictions sound very similar to the classical view of economic growth. The economic growth of the countries of Western Europe, the United States, Canada, Japan, the U.S.S.R., New Zealand, and Australia is completely at odds with the classical view. This is so largely because the classical view did not foresee the tremendous advance of technology that has taken place over the last century or more. Critics of the "doomsdayers" argue that current doomsday predictions again vastly underestimate the potentials of science, innovation, and technological change.

This criticism may be well taken. One wonders what the classical economists of the early 1800s would have thought if one of their number had predicted that in the twentieth century people would fly to the moon, jet aircraft carrying 450 passengers would cross continents in the time it takes a stagecoach to go 25 uncomfortable miles, in a split second an electronic computer would do calculations that would take a thousand clerks years, electronic communication would allow people to watch and hear a live event on the other side of the world, or most of the populous areas of the world could be obliterated in a few seconds by nuclear explosions. The list goes on and on. Imagine how farfetched such a list would seem to someone living in 1900, let alone the classical economists of the early 1800s. This puts a perspective on the pitfalls of making predictions about economic growth in the twenty-first century.

### Questions

1. Of all the resources at our disposal, which seems the most abundant?

2. Would the steps suggested to avert the doomsday predictions seem to imply more, or less, government intervention in the economy?

---

lowered prices in portions of the utility, transportation, communications, and finance sectors and increased competitive incentives for higher productivity.

## Costs and Benefits of Growth

The benefits of economic growth have always seemed quite obvious. The basic economic problem is to satisfy humanity's unlimited wants in the face of ever present scarcity. Economic growth eases this problem by reducing scarcity. Without growth the only way one person can be made better off is by taking something away from another. With economic growth there can be more for everyone—the lot of all can be improved. However, it has become increasingly apparent in the more industrialized countries, where economic growth has been most spectacular, that there are also costs to economic growth. Among these are pollution and a possible decline in the quality of life.

### *Pollution and the Environment*

When the economy produces "goods," it also produces by-products that are "bads"—smoke, garbage, junkyards, stench, noise, traffic jams, urban and suburban congestion, polluted water, ugly landscapes, and other things that detract from the general quality of life. In fact *all* output, both goods and bads, *eventually* returns to the environment in the form of waste. The more we experience economic growth, the more obvious this fact becomes. Many people are justifiably

## POLICY PERSPECTIVE

### How We Keep Running Out of Energy—The Role of the Market

At various times in the history of the United States it has appeared that we were about to run out of energy sources, important ingredients for economic growth. The alarm about an energy crisis during the 1970s and early 1980s was not the first. In the past, the dire predictions of exhausted energy reserves have always proved wrong. Why? Usually because those predictions failed to take account of the effects of rising energy prices, which encouraged people to seek out cheaper forms of energy and to develop more energy-efficient technology.

For example, prior to the Industrial Revolution in the late 1700s wood was the main source of fuel. People used so much wood it was feared that the forest would soon be exhausted, resulting in energy shortages and widespread hardship. But as the forests around towns and cities were used up, the price of wood rose and coal was gradually substituted for wood. The growing demand for coal led to the development of more efficient (less costly) mining methods, and coal soon replaced wood as the primary source of energy.

During the early 1800s in the United States, lamps burning sperm-whale oil were commonly used to light houses. Population growth and an expanding economy increased the demand for whale oil so much that people became concerned about the possible extinction of whales—and the United States had its first "oil" crisis. The price of whale oil rose about 600 percent over a period of about 35 years. This price rise led domestic and commercial users of whale oil to seek substitute fuels such as lard oil, distilled vegetable oil, and coal gas. Eventually, by the early 1850s, kerosene made from coal oil became the dominant fuel for lighting. The whale oil crisis had passed. The discovery of petroleum in the late 1850s provided an even cheaper way to make kerosene, and petroleum replaced coal oil as the major source of kerosene.

The important point to note about the wood and whale-oil "crises" is that the forces of demand and supply operated to encourage energy conservation as well as the development of alternative energy sources. For example, as the price of whale oil rose, consumers were motivated to conserve on its use (don't leave whale oil lamps burning when they're not needed for reading or sewing, and get by with less light in hallways and porches). At the same time, consumer demand for substitute fuels increased, causing their prices to rise. The rising prices of substitute fuels made them more profitable to produce, which encouraged enterprising firms and individuals to increase the supply of these fuels. Consumer demand turned from a fuel that was becoming scarce to fuels that were becoming more plentiful. All this occurred in the absence of a national energy policy or any other form of government intervention—a stark contrast to the way we have dealt with our own energy problems in recent years.

#### Questions

1. How does the market mechanism work to expand the potential for economic growth?

2. How would you explain the large increase in the number of compact cars on the road over the past 15 years?

concerned about the undesirable effects of growth on the environment and the balance of the world's ecological system. There is concern about disappearing species of wildlife and about the rising incidence of cancer related to synthetic products. There is concern about the destruction of the earth's ozone layer by the use of aerosol spray cans. Scientists also allege that the large-scale burning of fossil fuels has increased the carbon dioxide content of our atmosphere to such an extent that the earth's average temperature has increased a few degrees. The list of such worrisome by-products of economic growth goes on and on.

Critics of economic growth argue that some curbs on growth are necessary if these increasingly undesirable aspects of industrialization are to be controlled. Others caution that we must be careful not to confuse the control of growth with the control of pollution. They argue that the additional productive capacity made possible by growth could at least in part be devoted to pollution control efforts and the correction of past environmental damage. They point out that pollution control and a clean environment cost something, just like any other good, and that economic growth and increased productive capacity make it easier for society to incur that cost. (Recall our discussion of the production possibilities frontier and the production of scrubbers in Chapter 2.)

### The Quality of Life— Progress Versus Contentment

Economic growth implies change. Change is often what is most desired and needed by an impoverished population in an underdeveloped country. But many question whether continual change is as obviously beneficial in advanced industrialized economies such as the United States. Technological change, if anything, seems to have accelerated in the last half century. As a result, skills and training acquired in youth become obsolete more rapidly. There is more pressure to "keep current," to "retool," and to "update" one's skills. Fail to do so and you may be demoted or even out of a job. Such pressure creates anxiety and a sense of insecurity.

We have noted that an above-subsistence aspiration level may be necessary to avoid the tendency toward the long-run equilibrium of stagnation envisioned by the classical view. But some growth critics worry that aspiration levels in growth-oriented, industrialized countries are geared toward a "keep up with the Joneses" mentality. Goods may be valued more for the status they confer on the owner than the creature comforts they provide. ("I'd better get a new car this year or I may not look like I belong in this neighborhood.") Consequently, people work harder, produce more, enjoy it less, and complain about smog, traffic congestion, and the rat race. What there is of contentment, or peace of mind, may come largely from the sense that you're "making it," or better yet, that you've "arrived."

Since the beginning of the Industrial Revolution, many critics have argued that industrialization forces labor into dehumanizing jobs, requiring the performance of monotonous, mind-numbing tasks. Mass production, assembly-line jobs may provide bread for the table but little food for the soul. However, it has been said that those who make this criticism are not familiar with living conditions in countries where there is no industrialization.

### SUMMARY

**1.** Economic growth is the expansion of an economy's capacity to produce goods and services that takes place over prolonged periods of time. It may be viewed as a continual shifting outward of the economy's production possibilities frontier caused by growth in the quantity and quality of the economy's available resources (land, labor, and capital) and by ongoing improvement in the state of technological know-how.

**2.** The full benefits of growth will be realized only if there is an adequate expansion of aggregate demand and an allocation of resources to those productive activities where the value of their contribution to total output is greatest.

**3.** The rate of growth of full-employment real GNP provides a measure of the growth in the economy's overall capacity to produce goods and services. The rate of growth of output per capita provides a rough measure of growth in the economy's standard of living. The rate of growth of output per labor hour provides a measure of the growth in the economy's productivity—the efficiency with which each labor hour combines with the capital stock and the existing state of technology to produce output.

**4.** Growth in the economy's full-employment total output may be viewed as the product of change in each of the following four components: (1) population, (2) the fraction of the population that participates in the labor force, (3) the average hours worked per laborer, and (4) output per labor hour. The cumulative effects of seemingly small differences in growth rates become ever larger as time passes.

**5.** The classical economists' view of economic growth held that a nation's economic growth naturally tended toward stagnation and a subsistence standard of living. Citing the law of diminishing returns, they argued that as a larger and larger population works with a fixed amount of land and other resources the increase in total output becomes less and less, given the state of technological know-how. Consequently, average output per capita declines as population grows. Both output and population growth cease once output per capita has fallen to the subsistence level.

**6.** The drag on economic growth imposed by the law of diminishing returns and population growth can be overcome by capital deepening, technological change and innovation, and education and other forms of investment in human capital. The drag on rising living standards imposed by excessive population growth can be overcome by rising aspiration levels that tend to curb family size and hence population growth.

**7.** Saving and investment play an important role in economic growth because they are crucial to the process of capital formation and technological change that gives rise to sustained economic growth and increasing output per capita. Other important sources of economic growth are the increased specialization of labor, increases in the scale of production, the development of extensive capital markets, and the existence of a favorable cultural, social, and political environment.

**8.** During the 1970s and early 1980s there was an apparent slowdown in the growth of productivity in the United States. This slowdown has been attributed to a number of factors such as inflation, the influx of young, inexperienced workers into the labor force, inadequate investment spending, a slowdown in the growth of research and development expenditures, and increased government regulation of business in the form of pollution control and health and safety standards. It has also been argued that the rise in energy costs during the 1970s and the resulting increase in the cost of using labor-saving machinery has led companies to use more labor-intensive, less productive production techniques.

**9.** The factors that had a negative impact on productivity growth in the 1970s seem to have been reversed in the 1980s. Inflation has slowed, energy prices have declined, the baby boomers are now experienced workers, investment spending has expanded, R and D expenditures are up, and the costs of complying with antipollution and health-and-safety regulations are not rising as rapidly.

**10.** Economic growth is beneficial in that it reduces the burden of scarcity by increasing output. However, in recent years industrialized countries have become increasingly aware of some of the undesirable by-products of growth—pollution, congestion, uncertain effects on the ecological system, and the sense of anxiety, insecurity, and lack of contentment that may afflict citizens in a growth-oriented society.

**11.** Doomsday predictors argue that the limits of economic growth are likely to be reached sometime in the latter half of the next century, largely as a result of depletion of the earth's nonrenewable resources. Critics of these predictions contend that such a forecast is most likely wrong because it grossly underestimates the advance of science, technology, and innovation, which has always been a major source of economic growth.

## KEY TERMS AND CONCEPTS

capital deepening
disembodied technical change
economic growth
embodied technical change
productivity
subsistence living level

## QUESTIONS AND PROBLEMS

**1.** The rate of growth of real GNP is frequently used as a measure of economic growth. If we view economic growth as an outward expansion of the production possibilities frontier, what shortcomings does this suggest are associated with the use of real GNP to measure economic growth?

**2.** It is technologically possible to produce the *same* quantity of total output with different combinations of quantities of capital and labor. More capital may be used and less labor, or more labor and less capital. For example, a rise in the price of capital relative to the price (wage) of labor will typically cause firms to use more of the now relatively cheaper labor and less capital. Conversely, an increase in the price of labor relative to the price of capital would typically cause firms to use more of the now relatively cheaper capital and less labor. What are the implications of these possibilities for the use of output per labor hour as a measure of productivity? What bearing do these possibilities have on the apparent slowdown of U.S. productivity growth during the 1970s, given that energy prices increased dramatically during these years?

**3.** Population growth can be both a blessing and a curse for economic growth. Explain.

**4.** It is sometimes argued that in the short run, low productivity growth can create jobs because more workers will be required to satisfy rising demand. But it is then said that in the long run, low productivity growth means a slower growth of total output, which "hurts employment." Explain why you agree or disagree with this argument. What does a comparison of parts a, b, c, and d of Figure 18–2 suggest about the validity of this argument?

**5.** Can you explain why it might be possible for rising aspirations to cause the growth in total output to be *negative* and the growth in average per capita output to be *positive*, while at the same time there is technological progress? What are the implications of such a situation for population growth?

**6.** The classical view of economic growth envisioned a long-run equilibrium in which output per capita was just equal to the subsistence living level. However, if we consider the role played by saving and investment, is it really possible for long-run equilibrium to occur at such a position? Why or why not?

**7.** Despite the apparent slowdown in U.S. productivity growth during the 1970s, it appears that the growth of output per capita did not experience a similar slowdown. How would you explain this? (Hint: Examine Figure 18–2.) What does this suggest about the relative merits of each of these measures of economic growth?

# FIVE

## International Economics and World Trade

# 19

# International Trade and the National Economy

**AFTER READING THIS CHAPTER, YOU WILL BE ABLE TO:**

1. Describe present-day world trade flows and the pattern of U.S. trade.

2. Explain how trade affects total income, output, and employment.

3. Explain why nations can have a larger total output if they each specialize according to comparative advantage and trade.

4. Describe the nature of the barriers to trade nations often erect to protect domestic industry from foreign competition.

5. Describe briefly the trends in trade policy since the 1930s.

**V**irtually every nation finds it advantageous to trade with other nations. To varying degrees, all are linked to one another by trade flows and financial networks that circle the globe. This and the next chapter will describe and analyze the nature of world trade.

In this chapter we will examine some of the following questions: How significant is international trade in the world economy? How does international trade affect a country's total income, output, and employment? What are the underlying reasons why nations trade with one another? Finally, international trade is not viewed favorably by everybody. The desire for protection from the rigors of foreign competition has frequently led nations to erect barriers to international trade. We will critically examine some of the more common arguments for such barriers.

## THE IMPORTANCE OF INTERNATIONAL TRADE

International trade plays a significant role in the determination of living standards throughout the world. Though the United States is a relatively self-sufficient nation compared to most, its purchases of foreign cars, cameras, television sets, and oil are ever present reminders of American dependence on foreign trade. Let's first look briefly at some of the quantitative dimensions of international trade. Then we will consider how foreign trade affects an economy's total income, output, and employment.

### The Size of World Trade Flows

Table 19-1 provides an overall view of the magnitude of world trade, measured in dol-

**TABLE 19-1 World Trade Exports, 1984**

| | Value (in Billions of Dollars) | | Percentage of Total Exports |
|---|---|---|---|
| Developed Countries | $1,288.9 | | 64.3 |
| United States | | $218.0 | 10.9 |
| Canada | | 89.6 | 4.5 |
| Japan | | 168.8 | 8.4 |
| France | | 100.1 | 5.0 |
| West Germany | | 170.1 | 8.5 |
| Italy | | 72.7 | 3.6 |
| United Kingdom | | 92.7 | 4.6 |
| Other developed countries[a] | | 197.0 | 9.8 |
| Developing Countries | 470.6 | | 23.5 |
| OPEC[b] | | 185.2 | 9.2 |
| Other | | 285.3 | 14.2 |
| Communist Countries | 244.6 | | 12.2 |
| USSR | | 93.5 | 4.7 |
| Eastern Europe | | 100.0 | 5.0 |
| China | | 26.6 | 1.3 |
| Total | $2,004.1 | | 100.0 |

SOURCE: International Monetary Fund, Organization for Economic Cooperation and Development, and Council of Economic Advisers.

[a] Includes other OECD countries, South Africa, and non-OECD Europe (OECD: Organization for Economic Cooperation and Development).
[b] Organization of Petroleum Exporting Countries.

**FIGURE 19-1   Exports as Percentage of GNP, Selected Countries, 1983**

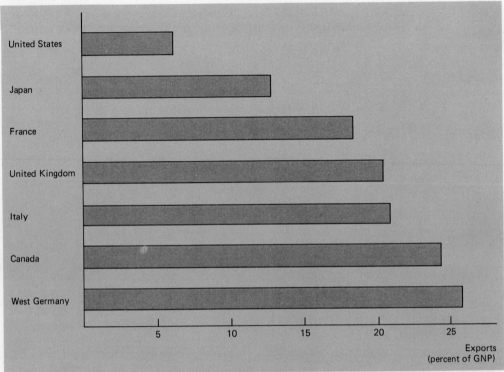

The exports of the United States to other countries represents a relatively small share of its GNP compared to other countries.

SOURCE: Council of Economic Advisors.

lars. The table shows the total dollar value of exports of goods by the nations of the world—that is, the dollar value of goods produced by each nation and then sold abroad. Some perspective on the total value of world exports is provided by comparing this figure with the GNP of the United States. This comparison indicates that the $2,004.1 billion of total world exports was the equivalent of about 55 percent of the U.S. GNP of $3,661.3 billion in 1984. It is also interesting to note that while the U.S. economy is not as dependent on international trade as many other countries, it does make a very large

contribution to total world exports. The U.S. economy provided 10.9 percent of total world exports in 1984. Indeed, the United States was actually the largest contributor to total world exports.

The nations of the world differ greatly in regard to their dependence on foreign trade. This is illustrated in Figure 19-1, which shows the value of exports of selected countries as a percentage of their respective GNP in 1983. For example, exports from the United States amounted to only 6.1 percent of its GNP in 1983, while exports for West Germany amounted to 25.8 percent of that

**TABLE 19-2 U.S. Merchandise Exports and Imports by Area, 1983**

| Exports to | Value (in Billions of Dollars) | Percentage of Total | Imports from | Value (in Billions of Dollars) | Percentage of Total |
|---|---|---|---|---|---|
| Developed Countries | $126.9 | 63.3 | Developed Countries | $154.9 | 59.3 |
| Canada | 43.8 | 21.9 | Canada | 54.4 | 20.8 |
| Japan | 21.7 | 10.8 | Japan | 41.3 | 15.8 |
| Western Europe | 54.9 | 27.4 | Western Europe | 53.9 | 20.6 |
| Australia, New Zealand, and South Africa | 6.6 | 3.4 | Australia, New Zealand, and South Africa | 5.3 | 2.0 |
| Developing Countries | 70.3 | 35.1 | Developing Countries | 105.1 | 40.2 |
| OPEC[a] | 15.1 | 7.5 | OPEC | 25.2 | 9.6 |
| Other | 55.2 | 27.6 | Other | 79.9 | 30.6 |
| Eastern Europe | 2.9 | 1.5 | Eastern Europe | 1.4 | .5 |
| Total | $200.3 | 100.0 | Total | $261.3 | 100.0 |

SOURCE: Department of Commerce, Bureau of Economic Analysis.

NOTE: Data are on an international transactions basis and exclude military shipments. Data will not add up to totals because of rounding.

[a] Organization of Petroleum Exporting Countries.

country's GNP. The differences among countries in this respect largely reflect differences in size, the extent of development of their internal markets, and the quantity and diversity of their supply of resources. The United States is so fortunate in each of these respects that its economy is relatively self-sufficient. Clearly the United States is less dependent on trade (as measured by the size of total exports relative to GNP) than the other countries in Figure 19–1. Again, however, the sheer size of the U.S. economy is reflected by the fact that the total value of its exports exceeds that of any other country.

### The Pattern of U.S. Trade

The pattern of U.S. trade with the rest of the world is illustrated by the export and import data in Table 19–2. There it can be seen that the total dollar value of U.S. imports ($261.3 billion), the goods purchased abroad, was considerably larger than the total dollar value of U.S. exports ($200.3 billion) in 1983. The dollar value of U.S. exports to Western Europe was roughly 2 percent larger than the dollar value of imports from Western Europe. The dollar value of U.S. exports to Canada were about 80 percent of the dollar value of imports from that country. The dollar value of exports to Australia, New Zealand, and South Africa was about 25 percent greater than the dollar value of imports from those countries. However, the value of U.S. imports from Japan was about 100 percent larger than the value of U.S. exports to that country. And the U.S. economy's dependence on foreign oil is reflected in the fact that its imports from OPEC (the Organization of Petroleum Exporting Countries) were 66 percent larger than the value of exports to those countries. Overall, the dollar value of U.S. imports from both the developed and the developing countries of the world was over 25 percent greater than its exports to those countries.

The composition of U.S. exports and imports by type of good is illustrated in Figure 19-2. Imports of machinery and transport equipment represented the largest share (33.4 percent) of purchases from abroad in 1983. Second in importance among U.S. imports were other manufactured goods. U.S. dependence on foreign oil is reflected in its imports of mineral fuels and related materials. Combined, these three categories represented 81.7 percent of total imports of goods. On the export side, these categories accounted for 63.2 percent of total exports of goods. It is notable that capital and manufactured goods represent a sizeable portion of U.S. imports. This testifies to the ability of other industrialized countries to compete head-on in U.S. markets with domestic manufacturers. The United States is also dependent on imports for such things as bananas, coffee, tin, nickel, tea, and diamonds. American agriculture benefits from exports of cotton, tobacco, wheat, and other foodstuffs.
one another, such as shipping services, banking services, and so forth. For example, in 1983 the United States purchased (imported) $50.3 billion of services from other nations and sold (exported) $54.9 billion of services to other nations.

## Trade Affects Total Income, Output, and Employment

Until now, our analysis of the determination of total income, output, and employment has assumed that the economy is isolated from international trade—that it is a **closed economy.** In reality, as we have just seen, ours is an **open economy**—one that trades with other nations. World trade affects the economy's aggregate demand for goods and services and, hence, the levels of total income, output, and employment. Let's see how exports and imports can be incorporated into the analysis of income determination that we initially developed in Chapters 8, 9, and 10.

### Exports, Imports, and Net Exports

Total expenditures on final goods and services in our economy include those arising from **exports**, the purchases of domestic output by foreigners. Hence, exports increase domestic production, incomes, and employment. They may be viewed as an injection into the economy's income stream, just like investment and government spending. **Imports,** on the other hand, represent expenditures by a country's citizens on output produced abroad. Such expenditures are a leakage from our economy's total income, just like saving. That is, imports also may be viewed as income *not* spent on domestically produced goods and services. As such, unlike exports, imports decrease domestic production, incomes, and employment. Therefore, the net effect of trade on a country's total income, output, and employment depends on whether the injections from exports are greater or less than the leakages due to imports. Recalling from Chapter 7 that net exports $X$ equals exports minus imports, we may say that the net effect depends on whether net exports $X$ is positive or negative. Exactly how does this difference affect the total income level?

### Determinants of Exports and Imports

To answer this question, we must first consider what determines the volume of a country's exports and imports. Certainly, differences between countries in terms of resource endowments, levels of industrial development, consumption patterns, and size are significant determinants. The extent and nature of barriers to trade are also important. We will examine the role of these considerations later in this chapter. In the next chapter we will see that exchange rates and differences in rates of inflation between nations also play an important role.

However, given all these factors, the volume of a country's exports will depend mainly on income levels in other countries. For example, if Western European countries are in the expansion phase of a business

**FIGURE 19-2** **Percent Distribution of Domestic Exports and General Imports for the United States, by Broad Commodity Groups, 1983**

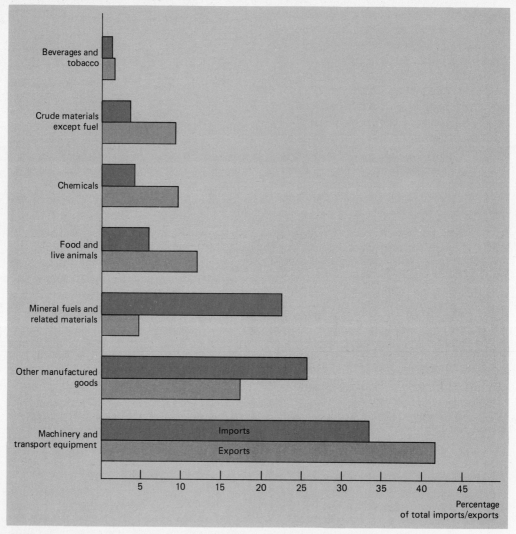

U.S. imports consist mainly of manufactured goods, mineral fuels, and related materials. Over half of total U.S. exports consist of manufactured goods.

SOURCE: U.S. Bureau of the Census, *Highlights of U.S. Export and Import Trade,* Report FT 990, monthly.

cycle, the volume of U.S. exports to them will generally rise. Conversely, a recession in these countries will tend to lower their demand for U.S. exports. On the other hand, the volume of a country's exports typically will depend very little, if at all, on its own total income level. What about the volume of a country's imports? Like consumption spending, a country's imports generally vary directly with its total income level. As a country's total income rises, its purchases of foreign products tend to increase right along with purchases of domestically produced goods.

### Trade and the Equilibrium Level of GNP

We can now examine exactly how trade affects the economy's total income level, or its level of GNP. We will use the leakages-injection approach that we developed in Chapters 9 and 10. Initially, suppose that there are no exports or imports, that the economy is a closed economy. Suppose that the sum of saving $S$ and taxes $T$, the total leakages, varies with the level of GNP as shown by the upward-sloping $S + T$ function in Figure 19–3, part a. The sum of investment spending $I$ and government spending $G$, the total injections, is represented by the $I + G$ schedule. The equilibrium level of GNP is $1,500 billion, corresponding to point $f$, at which the $I + G$ schedule and $S + T$ function intersect. At this level of GNP, the injections from government and investment spending are just equal to the leakages due to saving and taxes. In this case, $I + G = S + T = $400$ billion.

Now consider what happens when there are exports and imports—that is, when the economy is an open economy. At every possible level of GNP, the leakages due to imports must be added to those due to saving and taxes. Total leakages at each GNP level are therefore represented by the $S + T + Imports$ function shown in Figure 19–3, part a. The vertical distance between the $S + T$

function and the $S + T + Imports$ function represents the volume of imports at each level of GNP. Note that this vertical distance is greater at higher levels of GNP. This reflects the fact that the volume of imports varies directly with GNP, so that the leakage from imports is greater at higher levels of GNP.

Now consider exports. At every possible level of GNP the injections due to exports must be added to those due to investment and government spending. Total injections at each GNP level are represented by the $I + G + Exports$ schedule in Figure 19–3, part a. The vertical distance between the $I + G$ schedule and the $I + G + Exports$ schedule represents the volume of exports at each level of GNP. This vertical distance is the same at every level of GNP, a reflection of the fact that spending by foreigners on domestic output, or exports, is independent of the level of GNP. In part a, exports equal $120 billion.

*Net Exports Negative.* The equilibrium level of GNP is now $1,400 billion, corresponding to the intersection of the $S + T + Imports$ function and the $I + G + Exports$ schedule at point $e$. At this level of GNP, the sum of the injections due to investment, government, and export spending is just equal to the sum of the leakages from saving, taxes, and imports. In this case, $I + G + Exports = S + T + Imports = $520$ billion. Note that the volume of exports, represented by the vertical distance between points $d$ and $e$, is less than the volume of imports, represented by the vertical distance between points $c$ and $e$. The difference, which is equal to the vertical distance between points $c$ and $d$, equals net exports $X$ (exports minus imports). In this case net exports are negative, minus $40 billion. The leakages due to imports are greater than the injections due to exports. Hence, when net exports are negative in an open economy, the equilibrium level of GNP ($1,400 billion) is lower than the closed economy equilibrium level of GNP ($1,500 billion).

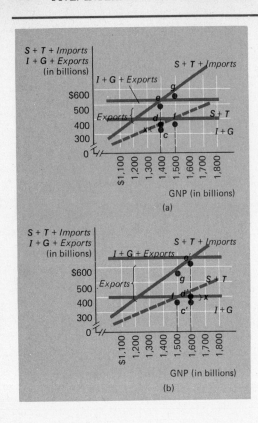

(a)

(b)

## FIGURE 19-3 Trade Affects the Equilibrium Level of GNP

Exports, the purchase of domestic output by foreigners, are an injection into the economy's income stream just like investment and government spending. Imports, purchases by a country's citizens of output produced abroad, are a leakage from the economy's income stream just like saving and taxes. In an open economy equilibrium occurs at that level of GNP where the sum of the injections due to investment $I$, government $G$, and export spending is just equal to the sum of the leakages from savings $S$, taxes $T$, and imports.

If the economy is a closed economy (it neither exports nor imports), the equilibrium level of GNP would be $1,500 billion, corresponding to the intersection of the $I + G$ schedule and the $S + T$ function at point $f$, as shown in parts a and b. In equilibrium, $I + G = S + T = $400 billion.

If the economy is an open economy (it exports and imports) with exports of $120 billion (part a), the equilibrium level of GNP is $1,400 billion, corresponding to the intersection of the $I + G + Exports$ schedule with the $S + T + Imports$ function at point $e$. In equilibrium $I + G + Exports = S + T + Imports = $520 billion. The equilibrium level of imports, which is equal to $160 billion (the vertical distance between $c$ and $e$), is larger than the $120 billion of exports (the vertical distance between $d$ and $e$). Net exports $X$, therefore, are negative, or minus $40 billion (the vertical distance between $c$ and $d$).

If exports were $260 billion, the equilibrium level of GNP would be $1,600 billion, corresponding to the intersection of the $I + G + Exports$ schedule and the $S + T + Imports$ function at point $e'$ in part b. In equilibrium, $I + G + Exports = S + T + Imports = $660 billion. The equilibrium level of imports, which is equal to $220 billion (the vertical distance between $d'$ and $e'$) is less than the $260 billion of exports (the vertical distance between $c'$ and $e'$). Net exports $X$ are positive, or $40 billion (the vertical distance between $c'$ and $d'$).

Positive net exports have an expansionary effect, and negative net exports have a contractionary effect on GNP.

*Net Exports Positive.* Alternatively, suppose the volume of exports were larger, or $1,600 billion, as shown in Figure 19–3, part b. Now the $I + G + Exports$ schedule intersects the $S + T + Imports$ function at point $e'$. The equilibrium level of GNP corresponding to this point is $1,600 billion. In this case, $I + G + Exports = S + T + Imports = $660 billion. The volume of exports ($260 billion), represented by the vertical distance between points $c'$ and $e'$, now exceeds the volume of imports ($220 billion), represented by the vertical distance between points $d'$ and $e'$. Net exports $X$ are therefore positive, represented by the vertical distance between $c'$ and $d'$ ($40 billion). The injections due to exports exceed the leakages due to imports. When net exports are positive in an open economy, the equilibrium level of GNP ($1,600 billion) is greater than the closed economy equilibrium level of GNP ($1,500 billion).

*Net Exports Zero.* Finally, suppose that the level of exports were such that the $I + G + Exports$ schedule intersected the $S + T + Imports$ function at point $g$ in parts a and b of Figure 19–3. Then exports would equal imports, as represented by the vertical distance between points $f$ and $g$. Net exports would be zero. The equilibrium level of GNP would be $1,500 billion, the same as the equilibrium level for the closed economy.

### Summary of the Effects of Trade

In sum, when the net exports of an open economy are negative, the equilibrium level of GNP is lower than the equilibrium level that would prevail if the economy were closed. Conversely, when net exports are positive, the equilibrium level of GNP is greater than the closed economy level. When net exports are zero, the open economy and the closed economy level of GNP are the same. Hence, *the effects of trade on an economy's total income, output, and employment are expansionary when net exports are positive and contractionary when net exports are negative.*

## CHECKPOINT* 19–1

**Suppose that the economy's citizens decide to reduce the volume of goods and services they buy from abroad, no matter what the level of GNP. Show how this would affect the equilibrium level of GNP in Figure 19–3, part a. At the $1,400 billion equilibrium level of GNP in Figure 19–3, part a, the leakages from imports exceed the injections from exports. How then can this be the equilibrium level of GNP? How is the effect of net exports (positive or negative) on the economy similar to the effect of a government budget deficit or surplus?**

*Answers to all Checkpoints can be found at the back of the text.

## THE BASIS FOR TRADE: SPECIALIZATION AND COMPARATIVE ADVANTAGE

We have now looked at some of the overall quantitative dimensions of world trade, as well as the basic pattern of U.S. trade. And we have also examined the way in which trade affects the determination of total income, output, and employment. We now come to the question of why nations trade with one another. What is the basis of trade? In general, trade occurs because nations have different resource endowments and technological capabilities. Because of these differences, each nation can gain by specializing in those products that it produces relatively efficiently and by trading for those it produces inefficiently or cannot produce at all. In short, international trade allows nations to increase the productivity of their resources through specialization and, thereby, to realize a higher standard of living than is possible in the absence of trade.

This general description of why nations trade sounds reasonable enough. However, to understand why it is correct requires an examination of the role of specialization and

**FIGURE 19-4    Production Possibilities Frontiers for Venezuela and the United States**
(Hypothetical Data)

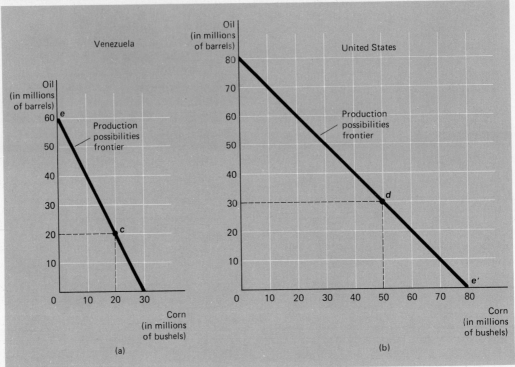

Each nation can produce both corn and oil. The production possibilities frontiers are straight lines because costs are constant—that is, the same amount of production of one good must be given up in order to produce an additional unit of the other, no matter which point on the frontier is considered.

The slope of Venezuela's production possibilities frontier (part a) indicates that 1 bushel of corn has an opportunity cost of 2 barrels of oil, or put the other way around, 1 barrel of oil has an opportunity cost of $\frac{1}{2}$ bushel of corn. The slope of the U.S. production possibilities frontier (part b) indicates that the opportunity cost of 1 bushel of corn is 1 barrel of oil, or the opportunity cost of 1 barrel of oil is 1 bushel of corn. Since the opportunity cost of corn is lower for the United States than for Venezuela, the United States has a comparative advantage in producing corn. On the other hand, since the opportunity cost of oil is lower for Venezuela than for the United States, Venezuela has a comparative advantage in producing oil.

the important principle of comparative advantage. In essence, it is the principle of comparative advantage that makes it worthwhile for nations to specialize and trade.

In order to illustrate this principle and see why it leads to specialization and trade, let's consider the following *hypothetical* example.

Suppose there are only two countries in the world economy, the United States and Venezuela. And suppose that each can produce both corn and oil, but with differing degrees of efficiency. The production possibilities frontier for each country is shown in Figure 19-4, parts a and b. (Recall from Chapter 2

### DAVID RICARDO — 1772-1823

David Ricardo was born in London, the son of a merchant-stockbroker. At 14 (after a very brief commercial education in Holland), he entered his father's business, but for family reasons left the firm at 19 and went out on his own with borrowed funds. He was an immediate success, and in a decade he had amassed a fortune of some £2 million (an immense amount by the standards of the day). He retired from trade and in 1814 purchased a country estate and a seat in Parliament. Sensitive about his lack of education, Ricardo hesitated to put his views on paper, but began to do so in 1815. Despite stylistic shortcomings, Ricardo made major advances in the science of economics,

and his contribution might well have been greater had he not died only 8 years later.

One of Ricardo's most significant contributions was his theory of rent, which he approached by putting forth the theory of diminishing returns. He observed that successive applications of inputs to a productive process resulted in lower additional returns to output. That is, in agriculture, for example, more intensive use of manpower, fertilizer, and other inputs yielded larger output, but the increases were successively smaller than those at earlier stages of production. Thus, a point might be reached where output would reach an absolute level and, in fact, decline as more inputs were applied. For a fixed resource such as land, it would be necessary over time to cultivate lands that were increasingly less productive in order to satisfy the pressing needs of increased population. As the demand for increased output rose, rent would rise (or increase) on that land of higher quality.

Ricardo was also the first to set forth the theory of comparative advantage in international trade in formal terms. According to this law, he argued, England would be better off if it imported food and exported manufactured goods. As a result, he was a supporter of the repeal of the tariff on grain as a method of lowering prices and thereby stimulating trade.

FOR FURTHER READING
St. Clair, Oswald. *A Key to Ricardo.* New York: Kelley & Millman, 1957.
Sraffa, Piero. *The Works and Correspondence of David Ricardo,* Vols. 1–9. London: Cambridge University Press, 1951–1955.

---

that each point on a production possibilities frontier represents a maximum output combination for an economy whose available resources are fully employed.) Barrels of oil are measured on the vertical axis and bushels of corn on the horizontal.

Notice that each frontier is a straight line instead of a curve, as was the production possibilities frontier discussed in Chapter 2. The frontiers here are straight lines because we are assuming that costs are constant. Along a straight-line frontier, a nation must give up the same amount of production of one good in order to produce an additional unit of the

other, no matter which point on the frontier is considered. In other words, we are assuming that the law of increasing costs (see Chapter 2), which causes the frontier to be curved, does not apply here. The assumption of constant costs makes our discussion simpler but still allows us to illustrate the principle of comparative advantage.

## Comparative Advantage: Differences in Opportunity Costs

As we can see, the production possibilities frontiers of the two nations differ. Observe that at any point on Venezuela's production possibilities frontier (part a), it is necessary to sacrifice 2 barrels of oil in order to have 1 more bushel of corn. For Venezuela, 1 bushel of corn, therefore, has an opportunity cost of 2 barrels of oil. Put the other way around, 1 barrel of oil has an opportunity cost of $\frac{1}{2}$ bushel of corn. For the United States (part b), 1 barrel of oil must be given up to have 1 more bushel of corn. Hence, for the United States, the opportunity cost of 1 bushel of corn is 1 barrel of oil, or the opportunity cost of 1 barrel of oil is 1 bushel of corn. We can see from this that the opportunity cost of corn is higher for Venezuela than for the United States. While it costs Venezuela 2 barrels of oil for each bushel of corn, it costs the United States only 1. Conversely, the opportunity cost of oil is higher for the United States than for Venezuela. It costs the United States 1 bushel of corn for each barrel of oil, while it costs Venezuela only $\frac{1}{2}$ bushel of corn for each barrel of oil.

In short, we can say that Venezuela has a *comparative advantage* (compared to the United States) in producing oil, and that the United States has a *comparative advantage* (compared to Venezuela) in growing corn. The difference in opportunity costs between the two nations reflects differences in their resource endowments, climates, and technological know-how.

## Inefficiency of Self-sufficiency— Efficiency of Specialization

As long as there is no trade between Venezuela and the United States, each is isolated and must be self-sufficient. Each country is limited to choices along its own production possibilities frontier. Suppose Venezuela chooses to produce the output combination represented by point *c* on its production possibilities frontier (Figure 19–4, part a), a combination consisting of 20 million barrels of oil and 20 million bushels of corn. Suppose also that the output combination the United States chooses to produce is represented by point *d* on its production possibili-

ties frontier (Figure 19–4, part b), 30 million barrels of oil and 50 million bushels of corn.[1] Total "world" output is therefore 50 million barrels of oil (the sum of 20 million barrels in Venezuela and 30 million barrels in the United States) and 70 million bushels of corn (the sum of 20 million bushels in Venezuela and 50 million bushels in the United States).

Figure 19–4 shows us that the world economy is not producing efficiently when each nation is isolated and self-sufficient, even though each nation is on its production possibilities frontier. Why do we say this? Suppose each nation specialized in the production of that product in which it has a comparative advantage. Venezuela would produce only oil, corresponding to point *e* (part a), and the United States would produce only corn, point *e'* (part b). Total world output would then consist of 60 million barrels of oil (Venezuela) and 80 million bushels of corn (United States). By specializing according to comparative advantage, total world output is greater by 10 million barrels of oil and 10 million bushels of corn as compared to what it is when each nation produces some of both products at points *c* and *d*. This example illustrates the principle of comparative advantage. *The principle of* **comparative advantage** *states that total world output is greatest when each good is produced by that nation having the lower opportunity cost of producing the good—that is, by that nation having the comparative advantage in the production of the good.*

When Venezuela produces 1 bushel of corn, the opportunity cost is 2 barrels of oil. It is clearly an inefficient use of the world's resources for Venezuela to produce corn when the United States can produce it at an opportunity cost of only 1 barrel of oil per bushel of corn. Similarly, it is an inefficient use of world resources for the United States to produce oil at an opportunity cost of 1 bushel of corn per barrel of oil when Venezuela can produce a barrel of oil at an oppor-

---

[1] Presumably each country's choice of output combination is made through its pricing system, as described in Chapter 2.

tunity cost of only ½ of a bushel of corn. If Venezuela produces corn, the world must give up more oil than is necessary to have corn. And if the United States produces oil, the world gives up more corn than is necessary to have oil. *The allocation of world resources is most efficient when each nation specializes according to comparative advantage.*

Since total world output of both goods is greatest when each nation specializes according to comparative advantage, clearly there can be more of both goods for both nations if each specializes and engages in trade instead of remaining isolated and self-sufficient. Let's see what particular conditions will motivate the United States and Venezuela to specialize and trade.

## Terms of Trade

Consider again the output combinations chosen by Venezuela and the United States when each is self-sufficient, represented by points *c* and *d* respectively in Figure 19–4. Note that Venezuela must forgo the production of 40 million barrels of oil in order to produce the 20 million bushels of corn associated with point *c*, since each bushel costs 2 barrels. The United States must forgo producing 30 million bushels of corn in order to produce 30 million barrels of oil—each barrel costs 1 bushel. If Venezuela could get corn by giving up *less* than 2 barrels of oil for each bushel, and if the United States could get oil by giving up *less* than 1 bushel of corn for each barrel, each would be eager to do so.

Is this possible? Yes, because of the difference in opportunity costs between the two nations. Let us now suppose that Venezuela offers to pay the United States 1½ barrels of oil for each bushel of corn it is willing to sell. For Venezuela this is cheaper than the 2 barrels per bushel that corn costs if Venezuela remains self-sufficient. For the United States, such a trade would mean that oil could be obtained at a cost of ⅔ of a bushel of corn for each barrel of oil. This is certainly cheaper than the 1 bushel of corn per barrel of oil it costs the United States if it tries to

be self-sufficient. Therefore, the United States agrees to the terms of Venezuela's offer. The **terms of trade**, the ratio of exchange between oil and corn at which both nations agree to trade, would therefore be 1½ barrels of oil per bushel of corn or, equivalently, ⅔ bushel of corn per barrel of oil.

## Specialization and Trade

Having established the terms of trade, Venezuela now specializes according to its comparative advantage in producing oil. It produces 60 million barrels of oil, which is the maximum it can produce on its production possibilities frontier. The United States now specializes according to its comparative advantage in growing corn, producing 80 million bushels, the maximum it can produce on its frontier. Though each nation specializes in production of one good, each nation's citizens want to consume both goods. This is possible, of course, because the nations can exchange goods at the agreed-upon terms of trade. This is shown in Figure 19–5, in which each nation's production possibilities frontier (exactly the same as in Figure 19–4) is shown along with its **trading possibilities frontier**. The trading possibilities frontier shows the choices that are open to a nation if it specializes in the product in which it has a comparative advantage and trades (exports) its specialty for the other product in which it has a comparative disadvantage.

When Venezuela produces 60 million barrels of oil, point *e* in part a, it can trade (export) this oil to the United States. Given the agreed-upon terms of trade of 1½ barrels per bushel, Venezuela can trade with the United States to get (import) 1 bushel of corn for every 1½ barrels of oil it exports to the United States. Starting from point *e*, such trade is represented by movement down the trading possibilities frontier as Venezuela gives up 1½ barrels for every bushel it gets. This is obviously better than the ratio of exchange along the production possibilities frontier that requires Venezuela to give up 2

**FIGURE 19-5** **Trading Possibilities Frontiers and the Gains from Trade** (Hypothetical Data)

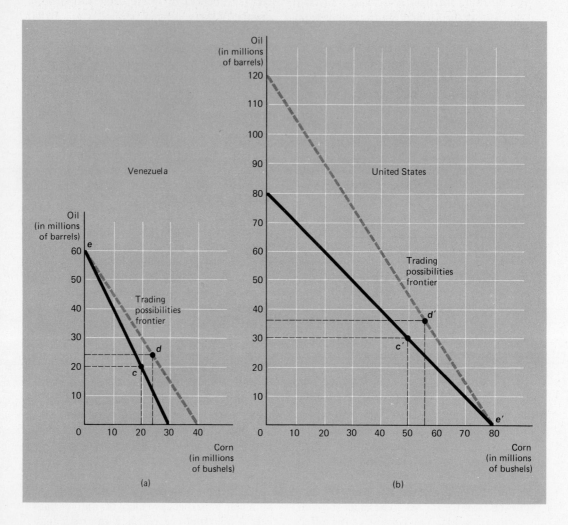

(a)

(b)

Each nation can have more of both goods if each specializes according to its comparative advantage and trades with the other.

When each nation is isolated and self-sufficient, each is forced to choose an output combination on its production possibilities frontier. For example, Venezuela may choose to produce 20 million bushels of corn and 20 million barrels of oil (point c), and the United States may choose to produce 50 million bushels of corn and 30 million barrels of oil (point c′). Alternatively, if each nation specializes according to its comparative advantage, Venezuela would produce 60 million barrels of oil (point e), and the United States 80 million bushels of corn (point e′). Then each nation could export some of its specialty in exchange for some of the other nation's specialty at terms of trade represented by the slope of the trading possibilities frontier. Such trade would move Venezuela down its trading possibilities frontier from point e to a point such as d, 24 million bushels and 24 million barrels. The United States moves up its trading possibilities frontier from point e′ to barrels for each bushel it gets. Similarly, the United States produces 80 million bushels of corn, corresponding to point $e'$ in part a. It can then move up the trading possibilities frontier by exporting 1 bushel of corn in trade for every $1\frac{1}{2}$ barrels of oil it imports from Venezuela. Again, this beats the ratio of exchange along the production possibilities frontier that requires the United States to give up 1 bushel for every barrel it gets.

In sum, the terms-of-trade ratio of exchange along the trading possibilities frontier is better than the self-sufficiency ratio of exchange along each nation's production possibilities frontier. Hence, Venezuela can get *more* than 1 bushel of corn for 2 barrels of oil if it specializes in oil and trades for corn from the United States. On this two-way street, the United States can get *more* than 1 barrel of oil for every bushel of corn if it specializes in corn and trades for oil from Venezuela.

## The Gains from Trade

Earlier we noted that if each nation specialized according to comparative advantage, total world output would be larger than if each produced some of both goods. Now we can see how trade makes this possible by allowing the citizens of each nation to consume more of both goods despite the fact that each nation produces only one of them.

Starting from point $e$, (Figure 19–5, part a), Venezuela specializes in the production of oil (60 million barrels), which it trades to the United States for corn. Starting at point $e'$ (part b), the United States specializes in the production of corn (80 million bushels), which it trades to Venezuela for oil. Given the mutually agreed-upon terms of trade of $1\frac{1}{2}$ barrels per bushel, suppose Venezuela exports 36 million barrels of its oil to the United States in exchange for imports of 24

million bushels of corn. This gives Venezuela a combination of 24 million barrels of oil and 24 million bushels of corn, represented by point $d$ on its trading possibilities frontier. Compared with the self-sufficient combination of 20 million barrels and 20 million bushels, represented by point $c$ on its production possibilities frontier, Venezuela is now able to have more of *both* goods. The 4 million more barrels of oil and 4 million more bushels of corn represent the gains from trade to Venezuela. Similarly, the United States exports 24 million bushels of its corn to Venezuela in exchange for imports of 36 million barrels of oil from Venezuela. The United States thus has a combination of 36 million barrels of oil and 56 million bushels of corn, point $d'$ on its trading possibilities frontier. This is clearly superior to the self-sufficient combination of 30 million barrels of oil and 50 million bushels, point $c'$ on its production possibilities frontier. The gains from trade for the United States amount to 6 million more barrels of oil and 6 million more bushels of corn.

We noted earlier that if each nation specialized according to comparative advantage, total world output would be larger than if each produced the output combinations represented by points $c$ and $c'$ in Figure 19–5. Specifically, we noted that specialization would increase total world output by 10 million barrels of oil and 10 million bushels of corn. Given the terms of trade ($1\frac{1}{2}$ barrels to 1 bushel), we now see how trade distributes this additional output—4 million barrels and 4 million bushels to Venezuela, and 6 million barrels and 6 million bushels to the United States. *Because of specialization and trade, there is an efficient allocation of world resources in production. Each good is produced by the nation that can produce the good at the lower cost. Consequently, each nation is able to have more of both goods.*

a point such as $d'$, 56 million bushels and 36 million barrels. Each nation is able to have more of both goods. The gains from trade for Venezuela amount to 4 million bushels and 4 million barrels (point $d$ compared to point $c$), and for the United States they amount to 6 million bushels and 6 million barrels (point $d'$ compared to point $c'$).

Finally, it should be noted that the United States is more productive than Venezuela in an absolute sense. The production possibilities frontiers in Figure 19-5 (or 19-4) show that the United States can produce any combination of corn and oil that Venezuela can *plus* more of both goods. This highlights the fundamental point that the incentive to specialize and trade stems from the fact that Venezuela and the United States have different opportunity costs in the production of corn and oil. For Venezuela the opportunity cost of producing corn is greater than that for the United States, while for the United States the opportunity cost of producing oil is greater than that for Venezuela. If the opportunity costs for Venezuela and the United States were the same, there would be no incentive to trade. However, because nations all differ in resource endowments, climate, size, and technological capabilities, it is little wonder that there is so much specialization and trade in the world.

## Some Qualifications

So far in our discussion, we have simply assumed a particular ratio of exchange as the terms of trade. But what in fact determines the terms of trade? We have also assumed constant costs throughout our discussion, so that the production possibilities frontier is a straight line. It is more realistic to assume increasing costs—that the production possibilities frontier is curved, bowed outward from the origin. How does this affect the analysis? Let's consider each issue in turn.

### Determining the Terms of Trade

We have been assuming that the terms-of-trade ratio of exchange between Venezuela and the United States is 1½ barrels of oil per bushel of corn. However, in our hypothetical example both Venezuela and the United States would find trade beneficial at terms of trade lying anywhere between 2 barrels per bushel, the ratio of exchange along Venezuela's production possibilities frontier, and 1 barrel per bushel, the ratio of exchange along

the U.S. production possibilities frontier. Any terms-of-trade ratio of exchange lying in this range allows each nation to obtain a good at a lower cost through trade than it costs to produce the good domestically.

The terms-of-trade exchange ratio within this range at which trade will actually take place depends on world supply-and-demand conditions for the two goods. If world demand for oil is strong relative to oil supply and the demand for corn is weak relative to corn supply, the price of oil will be high and the price of corn low. The terms of trade will be closer to the 1 barrel per bushel limit, which is more favorable to Venezuela than to the United States. If world demand-and-supply conditions are the opposite, the price of oil will be low and that of corn high. Then the terms of trade will be closer to 2 barrels per bushel, which is more favorable to the United States. In any event, the terms of trade are determined competitively by consumers and producers in the two countries (not by their governments).

### Increasing Costs

Suppose each nation's production possibilities frontier is curved so that it bows out from the origin. That is, each nation is faced with increasing costs as it expands production of the good in which it has a comparative advantage. Suppose Venezuela is initially at the point on its production possibilities frontier at which the cost ratio is 2 barrels of oil for 1 bushel of corn, and the United States is initially at a point on its frontier where the cost ratio is 1 barrel for 1 bushel.

Now suppose they begin to specialize and trade. As Venezuela expands its production of oil, the cost of producing it increases. That is, it will have to give up more than 1 bushel of corn to produce 2 barrels of oil. Similarly, as the United States expands production of corn, increasing cost will require it to give up more than 1 barrel of oil to produce 1 bushel of corn. Hence, the cost ratio for Venezuela goes from 2 barrels for 1 bushel to 1⅞ barrels for 1 bushel to 1¾ barrels for 1 bushel and so forth as it expands the production of oil. The cost ratio for the United States goes from 1 barrel for 1 bushel to 1⅛ barrel for 1 bushel to 1¼ barrel for 1 bushel and so forth as it expands the production of corn. The cost ratios of the two nations are now getting closer to each other.

At some point, after each nation has expanded the production of its specialty far enough, the cost ratios may become equal. At that point the basis for trade—a difference in opportunity costs between the two nations—will have been eliminated. Furthermore, at that point it is likely that each nation still produces both goods. Venezuela may still produce some corn along with its oil, and the United States some oil along with its corn. *Hence, when there are increasing costs, specialization will not be as complete, nor the volume of trade as large, as is the case when costs are constant.*

## The Argument for Free Trade

We now have seen how specialization and trade lead to an efficient allocation of world resources. They make it possible for each nation to have more of all goods than is possible in the absence of specialization and trade. While we have illustrated these points using only two nations and two goods, advanced treatments of the subject show that these conclusions hold for a multination, multiproduct world as well. Hence, it may seem odd that there are so many instances in which there is outright opposition to trade with foreign nations. The rest of this chapter will focus on the barriers to trade that nations often erect as a matter of policy. We will examine critically the most often heard arguments in favor of restricting trade. But before considering these matters, we should state the argument for free trade from a somewhat different, yet compelling perspective.

When each nation specializes in production according to its comparative advantage and trades with other nations, each nation is able to move out beyond its individual production possibilities frontier. The effect of specialization and trade is therefore the same as if each nation had gained more technological knowledge, more resources, or both. That is, the effect is the same as if each nation experienced an outward shift in its production possibilities frontier (such as we discussed in Chapter 2). It is possible for each nation to have more of all goods, thereby lessening the problem of scarcity.

---

*CHECKPOINT 19-2*
**Suppose there are two pioneers in the wilderness. Each sets up a homestead and each chops wood and grows wheat. Construct an illustration showing why it would benefit both to trade with the other. Can you think of examples that illustrate the role of the principle of comparative advantage in explaining trade between various regions of the United States?**

---

## BARRIERS TO TRADE AND ARGUMENTS FOR PROTECTION

The argument for free trade based on the principle of comparative advantage is one of the most solid cornerstones of economic analysis. No other issue seems to command such unanimous agreement among economists as the case for free trade. However, for a variety of reasons different groups in any economy are always prevailing on government to erect barriers to trade—that is, they want protection from the competition of foreign trade. We will first examine some of the commonest barriers and then consider the merits of some of the commonest arguments for protection.

### Barriers to Trade

Tariffs and quotas are the main weapons in the arsenal of protectionism. More recently, so-called antidumping legislation has also been used as a barrier to foreign imports.

## Tariffs

A **tariff (or duty)** *is a tax on imports, most often calculated as a percent of the price charged for the good by the foreign supplier.* For example, if the price of a ton of imported steel were $100, a 10 percent tariff would require the domestic purchaser to pay an additional $10 per ton. This effectively raises the price of imported steel to $110 per ton. A tariff may obviously be used as a source of revenue for the government. However, a more common purpose of tariffs is protection against foreign competition. By raising the prices of imported goods relative to the prices of domestically produced goods, tariffs encourage domestic consumers to buy domestic rather than foreign products.

For example, suppose Japanese steel companies can produce steel at a lower cost than American producers, with the result that the price of imported Japanese steel is $100 per ton while the price of domestically produced steel is $102 per ton. Domestic buyers will import the lower-priced Japanese steel. Sales of domestic steel producers will suffer. Consequently, suppose domestic producers, both company officials and steelworkers' unions, prevail on Congress to place a 10 percent tariff on imported steel. This raises the price of imported steel to $110 per ton, a price $8 higher than a ton of domestic steel. Domestic steel users now switch from importing Japanese steel to buying the cheaper domestic steel. Steel imports decline while sales and employment in the domestic steel industry rise. Recognize, however, that while domestic steel producers are better off, the rest of the nation's citizens will have to pay higher prices for all products containing steel.

Of course, tariffs need not completely eliminate imports. *As long as tariffs are not larger than the difference in production costs between domestic and foreign producers, tariffs will not completely eliminate imports.* In our example, suppose Japanese steel producers would just be able to cover costs as long as they receive a minimum of $92.73 per ton. Suppose American producers cannot afford to sell steel at a price less than $102 per ton.

With a 10 percent tariff, Japanese producers would just be able to remain competitive with U.S. producers. Japanese steel unloaded on U.S. docks at a price of $92.73 would be taxed 10 percent by the tariff, or $9.27 (.1 × $92.73), thus costing American importers $102 per ton ($92.73 paid to Japanese producers plus $9.27 in tariff revenue paid to the government). However, if the tariff were greater than 10 percent, imports of Japanese steel would cease because Japanese producers would suffer losses if they sold their steel at less than $92.73. And this price plus a tariff *greater* than 10 percent would increase the price of imported Japanese steel to domestic buyers above the price of domestic steel of $102, making Japanese steel noncompetitive.

Finally, it should be noted that the use of a tariff as a source of tax revenue runs counter to the use of a tariff for protection. A tariff generates tax revenues only to the extent that there are purchases of imported goods on which tariffs can be collected. In general, to the extent tariffs successfully serve protectionist objectives by cutting back imports, the tax revenues from tariffs are also reduced. A tariff so high as to effectively block out all imports, giving complete protection from foreign competition, would generate no tax revenue at all.

## Import Quotas

**Import quotas** *limit imports by specifying the maximum amount of a foreign-produced good that will be permitted into the country over a specified period of time (per year, for example).* Import quotas are a very effective tool of protection, unlike a tariff whose effect on the volume of imports can be hard to predict. After legislating a certain level of tariffs on a particular good, a class of goods, or even an across-the-board tariff on all goods, protectionists may find that imports are not limited to anywhere near the extent they had hoped for. Import quotas remove such uncertainty. Those favoring protection simply specify in the import quota legislation the exact quantity of a particular good that may be imported over a specified period of time.

An import quota on Japanese steel, for example, might limit imports of such steel to 1 million tons per year.

### Antidumping Laws

Domestic producers of particular products often argue that they are unfairly victimized by competing foreign imports that are "dumped" in domestic markets. The meaning of the term **dumping** is precisely captured by a complaint once registered by U.S. coal producers. They claimed that the prices paid for imported coke were not only lower than those paid for domestic coke, they were also lower than the foreign suppliers' cost of production.

**Antidumping laws** usually set a minimum price on an imported good. If the import enters the country at a price below that minimum, the law triggers a government investigation of possible dumping. Should it conclude that dumping is taking place, the imported good is not allowed to be sold at a price below the minimum, or "trigger," price. Actually, the United States has only one statute that deals with dumping. Prices are not set out in the statute. But in 1979, the Carter administration introduced a trigger-price system covering steel imports to determine more quickly if a dumping investigation is warranted.

*Difficulty of Detection.* When domestic producers of any product cry "dumping," there is always reason to suspect they are simply campaigning for protectionist measures to shelter them from foreign competition. It may well be that foreign producers are not charging prices below their costs of production, but are simply more efficient than domestic producers. That is, foreign producers can charge prices that cover their costs but yet are still below the costs of domestic producers. In that case domestic consumers reap the benefit of lower prices for imported products that cost more when produced at home. Domestic producers' claims of dumping simply amount to "crying wolf" in that case. Furthermore, it is hard to establish whether or not foreign producers are selling their goods at prices below their costs. It is difficult if not impossible for an outsider to determine just what foreign producers' costs are. And just such information is necessary to determine whether dumping exists.

*Export Subsidies and Dumping.* Nonetheless, there are circumstances under which dumping can occur and indeed does amount to "unfair" competition with domestic producers. In many nations it is not uncommon for the government to provide an **export subsidy**, or payment, to export industries to cover part of their costs of production. For example, suppose a government pays steel producers $10 for every ton of steel they export. If it costs the steel producers $90 to produce a ton of steel, the $10 subsidy from the government effectively reduces their cost to $80 per ton. Without the subsidy the steel producers could not sell steel abroad for less than $90 a ton. With the subsidy they can sell exported steel for as little as $80 a ton. Domestic steel producers in the nations importing this subsidized steel may be more efficient than the foreign producers. Let's say they can produce steel at a cost of $85 per ton. However, they will not be able to compete with the subsidized imported steel priced at $80 per ton. Domestic producers in a nation importing the subsidized steel have a legitimate complaint that imported steel is being dumped in their market.

Note that though foreign trade may increase as a result of export subsidies, it is not the kind of trade that gives rise to the world gains from trade due to specialization according to comparative advantage. In our example, the subsidized steel imports are in fact more costly to produce than the unsubsidized domestic steel. That is, the nation in which the subsidized steel is produced in fact has a comparative disadvantage in steel production relative to the nation importing the subsidized steel.

## Protecting Employment and Jobs

One of the most common protectionist arguments is that importing foreign goods amounts to "exporting jobs." It is claimed that buying foreign goods instead of domestic goods creates jobs for foreign labor that would otherwise go to domestic labor. It is charged that domestic unemployment will increase as a result. The merits of this argument depend on whether it is made with reference to the short run or the long run.

### The Short Run: Adjustment Problems

There is indeed truth to this argument in the short run. Recall again our hypothetical example of trade between Venezuela and the United States. When each was isolated and self-sufficient, each had an oil industry and a farming industry growing corn. However, when the two nations began to trade, Venezuela's farmers could no longer compete with the corn imported from the United States. All resources previously devoted to farming, including labor, had to be shifted into Venezuela's specialty industry, oil production. Similarly, in the United States oil producers could no longer compete with imported Venezuelan oil. Labor and other resources in the oil industry had to shift into the United States's specialty, corn production.

The gains from trade *after* these shifts have occurred are clear. However, the transitional period of readjustment and reallocation of resources within each country could be painful and costly to many citizens. Workers experienced and trained in farming in Venezuela and in oil production in the United States would no longer have a market for their skills. With their old jobs eliminated, many would need retraining to gain employment in their country's expanding specialty industry. Many would have to uproot their families and move to new locations, leaving old friends and severing familiar community ties. While both nations would realize the material gains from trade in the long run, it is understandable that those threatened with loss of job and an uncomfortable and personally costly transition might well support protectionist measures.

Public policy in a number of nations recognizes that changing trade patterns typically impose transition costs on affected industries and workers. In the United States adjustment assistance is provided to workers and firms that suffer from increased imports resulting from government actions, such as tariffs and quotas, that lower trade barriers. Workers are eligible for lengthened periods of unemployment compensation, retraining programs, and allowances to cover costs of moving to other jobs.

The reasoning behind a policy of transitional adjustment assistance is this: The removal of trade barriers leads to increased trade. Since the whole nation realizes gains from increased trade, some of these gains can be used to compensate those citizens who suffer losses during the period of adjustment. *Quite aside from any issue of "fairness," it may not be politically feasible to lower trade barriers unless those injured by such a move are compensated. As long as not all of the gains from trade are needed to compensate (or possibly bribe) the injured parties, the gains left over after compensation payments still make it worthwhile to lower barriers to trade.*

### The Long Run

Is there any reason why workers whose jobs have been eliminated by import competition should remain permanently unemployed? No, not as long as the economy is operating near capacity. Workers displaced by import competition will have a more difficult time making a transition to other jobs if the economy is in a recession and unemployment is high. Adjustment assistance cannot overcome a lack of alternative jobs. However, in the long run, if the economy is operating near full employment, workers displaced by foreign competition will become employed in other areas of the economy. Hence, if the argument prevails that protection from foreign competition is needed to protect domestic jobs and avoid unemployment, in the long run the nation will end up forgoing the gains from trade. *Unemployment that results from increased foreign competition should only be transitional. Any long-run unemployment problem should be blamed on fiscal and monetary policy and other domestic policies for dealing with unemployment, not on a policy of free trade.*

## Protection from Cheap Foreign Labor

Another popular argument for protection is that we must protect domestic industries from competition from cheap foreign labor. This argument appeals to the labor vote in particular because they view cheap foreign labor as a threat to their standard of living as well as to their jobs. The argument does not stand up, however. Let's see why.

Suppose two countries have exactly the *same size* labor force, but one's production possibilities frontier looks like that in part a of Figure 19–4, and the other's looks like that in part b. The labor force of part b is absolutely more productive because it can produce more of both goods. Hence, compared to the country of part a, the country of part b can pay its laborers more in both industries. Or, put the other way around, labor in the country of part a is cheaper than that of the country in part b.

But absolute differences in productivity are not the basis of trade—differences in opportunity costs are. Hence, despite the fact that labor in part b is more expensive than labor in part a, it pays for both countries to trade, as shown in Figure 19–5. Moreover, note that despite the fact that labor is cheaper in part a, it would cost the country in part b more to import corn from part a than to produce it itself. And despite the fact that labor is more expensive in part b, it still costs less for the country in part a to import corn from the country in part b than to produce it itself. Yes, it is true that the country in part b imports oil from part a *and* that labor is cheaper in part a than part b. But cheaper labor in part a is not the reason why part b imports oil from part a. It does so because the opportunity cost of producing oil in part a (2 barrels for each bushel sacrificed) is lower than

it is in part b (only 1 barrel for each bushel sacrificed).

To clinch the point, suppose the cheap labor argument prevails and insurmountable tariff barriers are erected between the two countries so that trade ceases. In each country some labor that previously worked in the industry in which the country specialized according to comparative advantage would now have to work in the less efficient industry. Real wages (the quantity of goods that can be purchased with a given money wage) would *fall* in both countries because each now has *less* output. In terms of Figure 19–5, each country is now on its production possibilities frontier at points such as c and c′, rather than on their trading possibilities frontiers at points such as d and d′. Living standards in both countries are reduced.

## Protection for Particular Industries

Industries faced with competition from foreign imports naturally have a special interest in erecting barriers to such competition. A news item reports of warnings by American steelmakers "that cut-rate imports of foreign steel 'dumped' on U.S. shores mean fewer jobs and, in the long run, a weaker American steel industry." We should be suspicious of such statements, of course. Any industry seeking protection either can't operate efficiently enough to meet the market test of foreign competition or simply wants a larger share of the domestic market and a chance to milk it by charging higher prices. In either case consumers will have to pay higher prices for the industry's products if protectionist measures are enacted into law.

The protected industry and associated special interest groups stand to gain a lot from such legislation. Hence, they organize lobbies and campaigns to pressure Congress for tariffs, quotas, and other protective barriers. The rest of the nation's citizens are often not aware of the losses that trade restrictions imply for them. The forces that might oppose such legislation are often nonexistent, disinterested, or too disorganized to offset the industry and special interest groups who favor it. The problem is that protection provides relatively large gains to a few, while freer trade helps everybody a little.

But are there circumstances that might warrant protection for a special industry because it is in the best interest of everybody? Yes, some convincing arguments have been made for protecting industries important to national defense. There is also the so-called infant-industry argument.

### The National Defense Argument

Certain industries are indispensable to any war effort—steel, transportation equipment, aircraft, mining of strategic materials, textiles, and so forth. Even though a nation may not have a comparative advantage in the production of any of these products, it may be difficult or impossible to import them when war disrupts world trade. In that case, protective tariffs and quotas may be justified to enable these industries to survive on domestic soil during peacetime. Defense considerations override the usual economic arguments. The difficulty is that many industries seek special protection in peacetime by arguing that they would be indispensable during wartime. Whether in fact they would be or not, the argument provides another vehicle for gaining protection from foreign competition. Indeed, American steelmakers could make a compelling case for protection on these grounds.

### The Infant-Industry Argument

It is sometimes argued that certain industries would develop into strong competitors in world markets if only they had a chance to get started. Unfortunately, so goes the argument, without protection from the competition of their already established counterparts in other countries, these infant industries never survive to the point where they can go head-to-head with foreign competition.

There may be some merit to this argument. However, the problem lies in correctly identifying those so-called infant industries that are destined, with the aid of temporary protective measures, to mature into productive enterprises in which the nation will definitely have a comparative advantage in a world of free trade. For example, how is it to be decided when maturity has arrived and protection can be removed? Will it eventually become the case that protective measures have simply spawned a mature special interest that is more efficient at maintaining continued protection for itself than it is at producing goods? In the meantime the nation loses in two ways. First, it forgoes the gains from trade available with the purchase of more efficiently produced foreign goods. Second, domestic resources tied up in the protected industry are not available for employment in more efficient industries elsewhere in the economy.

## The Diversification-for-Stability Argument

An economy can be highly specialized in a few products and depend to a large extent on its exports of these products for its ability to import the diversity of other goods it needs. Many developing nations fit this description. Brazil depends heavily on its coffee bean exports, New Zealand on exports of dairy products, and Saudi Arabia on its exported oil. Such nations often suffer from the risks inherent in having too many of their eggs in one basket. If world demand for their particular specialty fluctuates widely, real GNP and employment can be very unstable.

It is often argued that such nations could reduce this instability by diversifying their economies—that is, by encouraging the development of a variety of industries producing largely unrelated products. To do this, it is argued, many of these industries would have to be protected from foreign competition by tariffs, import quotas, and other barriers. Otherwise, they would not be able to compete because of their relative inefficiency compared to their foreign counterparts. The main issue here is that there presumably is a

## POLICY PERSPECTIVE

### Protection and Trade Policy—The Two-Way Street

International trade is a two-way street. It requires that nations import as well as export. However, the history of trade policy among nations clearly indicates that their eagerness to export is not matched by a similar zeal for imports. While domestic producers welcome exports as a way of expanding their markets, they often view imports as a competitive threat to be stopped if at all possible. While policymakers frequently welcome exports as a way of increasing total income and employment, they may often be concerned about the fact that imports have the opposite effect (recall our analysis of Figure 19–3). Add to these considerations the often emotional, alarmist-type arguments for protection we have previously examined, and the basis for a nation's bias in favor of exports and against imports is readily apparent.

Unfortunately, if every nation indulges this bias in the long run, international trade must cease. Why? Because every nation's exports must be another nation's imports. For example, if the United States doesn't buy goods from other nations (imports), then other nations can't earn dollars to buy goods from the United States (exports). Thus, if a nation raises tariffs, quotas, and other barriers to imports, that nation's export industries will eventually decline. Labor and other resources will have to be reallocated from the nation's shrinking export industries to its expanding industries that produce domestic goods protected by increased trade barriers. Hence, barriers to imports shift resources away from those industries in which the nation is so efficient as to have a comparative advantage. The gains from trade are lost and the nation's standard of living is diminished. If every nation cuts

imports, then every nation's exports must eventually decline as well. Everyone loses the gains from trade.

#### Tariffs of Retaliation

The process of shrinking world trade just described could begin with one nation's attempts to cut back its imports. Others might then retaliate by erecting their own barriers to imports. This has been an all too common occurrence in the history of world trade. Just as the Great Depression was beginning, Congress passed the Smoot-Hawley Tariff Act of 1930, which imposed some of the highest tariffs in U.S. history, as can be seen from Figure P19–1. If U.S. exports had remained the same, the reduction in imports caused by these tariffs would have increased net exports. This would have had an expansionary impact on total income and employment in the United States (recall our discussion of Figure 19–3). Of course, the levels of income and employment in other nations were adversely affected since a reduction in American imports meant a reduction in their exports. Hence, other nations raised trade barriers in retaliation, and U.S. exports also declined. Overall, the resulting contraction of world trade aggravated the decline in income and employment in many nations, making the Great Depression even worse.

#### Reducing Trade Barriers

Since the disastrous Smoot-Hawley Tariff Act of 1930, the United States has reduced tariffs dramatically, as can be seen from Figure P19–1. Compared with other nations, the United States today is one of the world leaders in the movement toward freer world trade. Congressional enactment of the Reciprocal Trade Agree-

**FIGURE P19-1  U.S. Tariff Rates Since 1820**

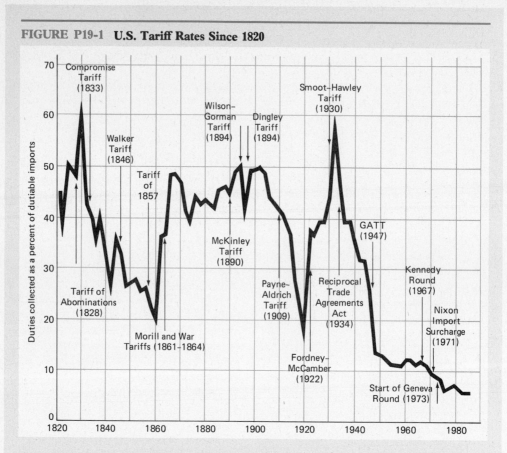

U.S. tariffs have fallen steadily since the Reciprocal Trade Agreements Act of 1934. In the postwar years they have been set at only a small fraction of the levels that prevailed throughout much of our history.

ments Act in 1934 was a major step in initiating tariff reductions in the United States. In 1947 the General Agreement on Tariffs and Trade (GATT) greatly enhanced the atmosphere for tariff reduction among nations. In the years since World War II, GATT has provided an ongoing forum for the multilateral negotiation of tariff reductions. Initially 23 nations were parties to GATT, but that number has expanded to the point where more than 90 nations are now members of GATT.

### Developments in the 1980s

The recessionary conditions that plagued the world economy during the 1981–1983 period created pressures in many countries to use trade barriers to ease domestic unemployment problems. Despite its formal commitment to GATT, even the United States took such measure as restricting imports of Japanese cars, imposing quotas on imported sugar, and restricting imports of steel from the

Common Market countries (Belgium, Britain, Denmark, France, Greece, Ireland, Italy, the Netherlands, and West Germany). The proportion of total manufacturing subject to nontariff restrictions in major industrialized countries rose to about 30 percent in 1983, up from 20 percent just 3 years earlier.

Despite substantial tariff reduction among industrialized countries since World War II, tariffs remain high in some sectors (such as textiles, footwear, steel, wood products, and shipbuilding) and among developing countries. International trade is subject to even more severe restrictions in nonmanufacturing sectors, especially in agriculture and services. An improving world economy would help provide a better political climate for the reduction of these trade barriers and the development of freer trade. An encouraging sign in the United States was the passage of the Trade and Tariff Act of 1984, a bill that generally supports freer trade.

### Questions

1. When a nation raises tariffs or imposes other restrictions on imports in an attempt to reduce domestic unemployment, it is said to be engaging in a "beggar-thy-neighbor" policy—literally, to make beggars of other nations. Explain why.

2. Why would a recovery of the world economy make it easier for governments to resist domestic pressure for protectionist measures?

trade-off between the gains from trade due to specialization according to comparative advantage on the one hand, and economic stability on the other. Some nations, like some people, prefer to have a higher *average* income level even though it means greater year-to-year income variability, rather than a lower average income with less year-to-year variability. The diversification-for-stability-through-protection argument obviously leans toward the lower average income, lower variability point of view.

### CHECKPOINT 19-3

**In a news item coke-oven makers contend that the availability of "cheap foreign coke" is causing steelmakers to postpone "much-needed construction of new coke capacity to replace old and inefficient ovens." What do you think of the coke-oven makers' argument, and where do you think they would stand on the issue of whether or not an antidumping complaint should be filed against foreign coke producers?**

### SUMMARY

**1.** The volume of world trade is roughly equivalent to 55 percent of the GNP of the United States. For many countries exports represent a sizeable portion of their GNPs—for some, as much as a half or more. Though U.S. exports and imports rarely exceed 10 percent of its GNP, the absolute dollar volume of its annual exports and imports typically exceeds that of any other nation. More than half of all U.S. exports and imports consist of capital goods and other manufactured goods. In recent years imports of oil have accounted for about 20 percent of its total imports.

**2.** Exports may be viewed as an injection into the economy's income stream, just like investment and government spending. Imports are a leakage from the economy's income stream. The effects of trade on a nation's GNP are expansionary when net exports (exports minus imports) are positive, and contractionary when net exports are negative.

**3.** The basis for international trade lies in the fact that nations differ in their resource endowments and technological capabilities.

**4.** Differing resource endowments and technological capabilities typically make the opportunity cost of producing any given good different between nations. Because of this, nations that specialize according to comparative advantage and engage in trade can have a larger total output than is possible if they remain self-sufficient and isolated.

**5.** The terms of trade determine how the larger world output made possible by specialization and trade is distributed among nations. And the terms of trade between any two traded goods depend on world supply-and-demand conditions for the two goods. Increasing costs diminish the extent of specialization and trade relative to what it would be if costs were constant.

**6.** The argument for free trade is based on the fact that when nations specialize according to comparative advantage and trade, there is a more efficient allocation of resources. The resulting increase in world output lessens the problem of scarcity and makes possible a higher standard of living.

**7.** Nations often erect barriers to trade in the form of tariffs, import quotas, and antidumping laws. These measures effectively reduce the quantity of imports and allow domestic producers to sell more at higher prices. To the extent such barriers block trade, there is a less efficient allocation of world resources and a reduced level of total world output.

**8.** Most of the arguments for protection are flawed. However, short-run adjustment problems resulting from a reduction of trade barriers can cause real hardship for those in affected industries, possibly justifying short-run adjustment assistance. In the long run the economy must operate near capacity so that the full gains from trade may be realized. Protection may be justified where national defense considerations are concerned.

**9.** U.S. tariff rates have been declining ever since the Reciprocal Trade Agreements Act of 1934. In the postwar period world trade has been spurred by the General Agreement on Tariffs and Trade (1947).

## KEY TERMS AND CONCEPTS

antidumping law
closed economy
comparative advantage
dumping
exports
export subsidy
import quotas
imports
open economy
tariff (or duty)
terms of trade
trading possibilities frontier

## QUESTIONS AND PROBLEMS

**1.** Suppose that the level of a nation's exports fluctuates from year to year. Using a diagram like Figure 19–3, can you explain why the resulting fluctuations in the nation's GNP might be smaller if it imports goods than if it doesn't import? How might the composition of imports—whether the nation imports mostly consumption goods or mostly capital goods—affect your answer?

**2.** Why is it that a doctor hires a secretary even though the doctor may be a better typist than the secretary?

**3.** Suppose there are two nations, and that one is able to produce two goods, X and Y, and the other is able to produce only good X. Is there likely to be trade between these two nations? Why or why not? If you think they would trade, what do you think would be the terms of trade?

**4.** Is it conceivable that trade between Venezuela and the United States in Figure 19–5 could lead each nation to have more of one good and less of the other—that is, say, as compared to the combinations $c$ and $c'$ that they have when there is no trade? If so, why is each still better off with trade than without it?

5. Suppose one nation (such as Australia) has a lot of land relative to the size of its population and another nation (such as Japan) has a large population relative to the amount of its land. Suppose also that these two nations have similar levels of technological know-how. What do you think might be the pattern of trade between these two nations? If, on the other hand, the nation with the higher land-to-labor ratio also had a much higher level of technological know-

how, how might this change your answer? Why?

6. It is sometimes argued that tariffs can force foreign exporters to provide their goods to us at a lower price. Can you explain why this is true?

7. One argument for protection runs as follows: "If I buy a car from Japan, Japan has the money and I have the car. But if I buy a car in the United States, the United States has the money and I have the car." Explain why you do or do not think this is a valid argument for putting a stiff tariff on imported cars.

# 20

# Balance of Payments, Exchange Rates, and the International Financial System

---

**AFTER READING THIS CHAPTER, YOU WILL BE ABLE TO:**

1. Explain the balance of payments concept and describe the major components of the balance of payments account.

2. Describe a balance of payments deficit and a balance of payments surplus.

3. Explain how flexible exchange rates eliminate balance of payments deficits and surpluses.

4. Describe how balance of payments adjustments are made under a system of fixed exchange rates.

5. Give the major arguments in the debate over a flexible versus a fixed exchange rate.

6. Explain how a gold standard works.

7. Describe the Bretton Woods system and why it has been replaced by a mixed system of flexible exchange rates and managed floats.

In the previous chapter we focused on the real aspects of international trade. That is, we looked at the way in which nations can have a larger quantity of goods, or more real output, by specializing according to comparative advantage and trading with one another. But international trade also has a monetary aspect because goods are exchanged for money and each nation has its own unique money. For example, when Americans buy goods from Great Britain, they must pay for them with British money, or pounds. Similarly, British citizens must pay for U.S. goods with dollars. In short, every movement of goods and services between nations requires a financial transaction. The flow of goods and services in one direction requires a flow of money in the other.

In this chapter we will examine how the international financial system may be organized to handle the financial transactions that accompany international trade. This requires that we become familiar with such concepts as the balance of payments, exchange rates and their determinants, and "official intervention operations." We also will examine why gold has often played an important role in international trade in the past, and how and why the present system of international financial arrangements evolved.

## EXCHANGE AND THE BALANCE OF PAYMENTS

When Americans import goods and services from other nations, they must pay for these imports with foreign currencies, often called foreign exchange. For example, German marks must be paid for goods produced in Germany, French francs for goods produced in France, Japanese yen for goods from Japan, and British pounds for goods from Great Britain. Similarly, when Americans export goods to other nations, American suppliers want to be paid with dollars. Whatever the country, domestic producers selling goods abroad want to receive payment in domestic currency because that is what they must use to pay wages and all other factors employed in production. American workers don't want to be paid in French francs, nor do French workers want to be paid in dollars.

The fundamental point is this. If a nation wants to buy goods and services (imports) from other nations, it must somehow obtain the foreign currencies needed to make payment for these imports. Broadly speaking, the only way it can do this is to export some of its own goods and services to other nations and thereby earn the foreign currencies that it needs to pay for its imports. That is, to make payments for imports, a nation must use the payments received from exports—exports must finance imports. Hence, a nation's payments to other nations must be equal to, or balanced by, the payments received from other nations. It is in this sense that there is a balance of payments.

While basically correct, this is a very simplified description of how nations obtain foreign currency. The nature of the balance of payments and the way it is calculated are also considerably more involved in reality. We need to look at currency exchange and the balance of payments in more detail.

### Currency Exchange

Suppose an American firm wishes to buy a German machine. The German manufacturer ultimately will want to receive German marks from the sale of the machine. The American firm can go to its bank, buy the amount of marks needed to pay for the machine, and send them to the German manufacturer. (The bank typically will charge the American firm a small fee for obtaining and providing the marks in exchange for dollars.) Alternatively, the American firm may pay the German manufacturer in dollars. The German manufacturer will then take the dollars to its own bank, where it will exchange them for marks. Either way, dollars are exchanged for marks.

The **exchange rate** *is the price of foreign currency. It is the amount of one currency that* *must be paid to obtain 1 unit of another currency.* Suppose, in our example, that the exchange rate between U.S. dollars and German marks is $.50 for 1 mark. Equivalently, it may be said that 2 marks can be exchanged for $1. Suppose the price of the German machine is 100,000 marks. This means that the American firm will have to give its bank $50,000 to obtain the 100,000 marks needed to pay the German manufacturer. Alternatively, the American firm may give the German manufacturer $50,000. In that case, the German manufacturer will take the $50,000 to its own bank and exchange it for 100,000 marks. Either way the American firm pays $50,000 for the machine and the German manufacturer ultimately receives 100,000 marks.

Our example illustrates that *trade between nations requires the exchange of one nation's currency for that of another.* The American purchase of a German machine gives rise to a supply of dollars and a demand for marks. Similarly, a German purchase of an American product would give rise to a supply of marks and a demand for dollars. Hence, *international trade gives rise to the international supply and demand for national currencies, or a* **foreign exchange market**. *The exchange rates between different currencies are determined in the foreign exchange market.* We will investigate how foreign exchange rates are determined and what these rates mean for the balance of payments later in this chapter. First, however, we must become more familiar with the balance of payments concept.

## Balance of Payments

*The term* **balance of payments** *means just what it says: a nation's total payments to other nations must be equal to, or balanced by, the total payments received from other nations.* When Americans supply dollars in foreign exchange markets, they are demanding foreign currencies in order to make payments to other nations. The currencies Americans receive in exchange for their dollars are supplied by foreigners who demand dollars in order to make payments to the United States. Every dollar sold must be bought, and every dollar bought must be sold. Hence, U.S. payments to other nations must be matched exactly by payments from other nations to the United States.

We have already seen how nations keep national income accounts in order to measure domestic economic activity (Chapter 7). Similarly, nations also keep balance of payments accounts in order to keep track of their economic transactions with other nations. *A nation's* **balance of payments account** *records all the payments that it makes to other nations, as well as all the payments that it receives from other nations during the course of a year.* The total volume of payments made to other nations is exactly equal to the total volume of payments received from other nations.

The balance of payments account breaks down the nation's payments to other nations into the following categories: the amount spent on foreign goods; the amount spent on foreign services; the amount loaned to foreign businesses, households, and governments; and the amount invested abroad. Similarly, the account breaks down the payments received from other nations to show the amount of foreign purchases of the nation's goods; the amount of foreign purchases of the nation's services; the amount of foreign lending to the nation's businesses, households, and government; and the amount of foreign investment in the nation. While the total volume of a nation's payments to other nations must always equal the total volume of payments received from other nations, individual categories in the balance of payments accounts need not and typically do not balance. For example, in any given year Americans may export a larger dollar volume of goods than they import or buy more services from foreigners than are sold to foreigners.

The balance of payments account for the United States is shown in Table 20–1. International transactions that give rise to pay-

**TABLE 20-1 U.S. Balance of Payments, 1983**

| Debits (−) | | Credits | | | |
|---|---|---|---|---|---|
| **U.S. Payments to Other Nations (in Billions of Dollars)** | | **U.S. Receipts from Other Nations (in Billions of Dollars)** | | **Balance (in Billions of Dollars)** | |
| Current Account | | Current Account | | | |
| (1) Merchandise imports | −$261.3 | Merchandise exports | $200.3 | Balance of trade | −$61.0 |
| (2) Income on foreign investment in United States | −53.5 | Receipts of income on U.S. assets abroad | 77.0 | | |
| (3) Services | −50.3 | Services | 54.9 | | |
| (4) Unilateral transfers | −8.7 | | | | |
| (5) Imports of goods and services | −$373.8 | Exports of goods and services | $332.2 | Balance on current account | −$41.6 |
| Capital Account | | Capital Account | | | |
| (6) Change in U.S. assets abroad | −43.3 | Change in foreign assets in U.S. | 76.5 | Balance on private capital account | $33.2 |
| (7) Change in U.S. govt. assets | −6.2 | Change in foreign official assets | 5.3 | Balance on govt. capital account | −$0.9 |
| (8) Imports of capital | −$49.5 | Exports of capital | $ 81.8 | Balance on capital account | $32.3 |
| (9) | | | | Errors and omissions | $9.3 |
| (10) | | Row 5 plus row 8 plus row 9 = | | Balance | $ 0.0 |

SOURCE: *Survey of Current Business*, July 1984.

ments to other nations are recorded as debit items (designated by a minus sign) in the balance of payments account. Such transactions supply dollars to the foreign exchange market and create a demand for foreign currency because Americans must sell dollars to obtain foreign currency. The import of a good is an example of a debit item. (Recall our example of an American business importing a German machine, which gave rise to a supply of dollars and a demand for marks.) Transactions that give rise to payments to the United States from other nations are recorded as credit items in the balance of payments account. Such transactions supply foreign currency to the foreign exchange market and

create a demand for dollars because foreigners must sell their currency to obtain dollars. The export of a good is an example of a credit item.

The credit and debit items in the balance of payments account are broadly divided into a current account and a capital account.

### The Current Account

The balance of payments on current account includes all payments received during the current period for the export of goods and services and all payments made during the current period for the import of goods and services.

*Imports and Exports of Goods—Visibles.* The largest portion of the current account is represented by merchandise imports and exports in row 1 of Table 20-1. These are the imports and exports of goods—the so-called visible items such as steel, wheat, tv sets, cars, and all the other objects that can be seen and felt. In 1983 the United States imported $261.3 billion of such merchandise and exported $200.3 billion. The difference between merchandise exports and merchandise imports is called the **balance of trade**. *When merchandise exports exceed imports, the nation has a balance of trade surplus. When imports exceed exports, the nation has a balance of trade deficit.*

In 1983 the United States had a balance of trade deficit of $61 billion ($200.3 billion of exports minus $261.3 billion of imports). As noted before, there is no particular reason why individual categories of a nation's balance of payments should in fact balance. However, when a nation has an overall balance of trade deficit, it is often said to have an unfavorable balance of trade. The balance is unfavorable in the sense that the nation is earning less from its merchandise exports than it is spending on its merchandise imports—exports of goods do not entirely finance imports of goods. However, it is not clear that it is unfavorable for a nation to get more goods from other nations than it gives in return. Besides, other categories in a nation's balance of payments will necessarily offset a balance of trade deficit because overall the balance of payments must balance. Similar observations may be made about a so-called favorable balance of trade, a balance of trade surplus.

*Imports and Exports of Services—Invisibles.* The import and export of services, or so-called invisibles, is another sizeable component of the current account. For example, Americans pay for tickets to fly on foreign airlines and pay foreign shippers to carry cargo. They also buy meals and pay for hotel rooms when traveling abroad and pay premiums for insurance provided by foreign insur-

ance companies. All of these transactions are examples of imports of services. Like the payments for imported goods, payments for imported services give rise to a supply of dollars in the foreign exchange market and a demand for foreign currencies because foreigners want to be paid in their own currencies. Similarly, Americans also export services to foreigners. Like the export of goods, the export of services gives rise to a supply of foreign currencies in the foreign exchange market and a demand for dollars.

Like services, income from foreign investment in the United States is another invisible item on the current account. Such income consists of the payment of interest and dividends on American bonds (both government and private) and stocks held by foreigners, as well as the income earned by foreign-owned businesses on American soil. It can be thought of as payment for the import of the services of the financial capital provided by foreigners to American government and industry. Such payments give rise to a supply of dollars and a demand for foreign currencies in the foreign exchange market. Similarly, receipts of income on U.S. assets abroad represent payments received by Americans (government, firms, and households) for the services of capital exported to other nations. These payments to Americans give rise to a supply of foreign currencies and a demand for dollars in the foreign exchange market.

Table 20-1, row 3, indicates that the United States purchased fewer services from other nations than it sold to them in 1983. Row 2 shows that payments to other nations for the services of foreign capital were about two-thirds as large as the payments received by Americans for providing capital to other nations.

*Unilateral Transfers.* Unilateral transfers represent payments made to another nation for which nothing is received in exchange. Private unilateral transfers are gifts given by Americans to foreigners. Government unilateral transfers consist of foreign aid. It is a convention of balance of payments accounting that such gifts are recorded as credit items under merchandise exports, just as if goods had been sold abroad. A balancing entry is made under unilateral transfers.

*Balance on Current Account.*   Row 5 shows that the total of the debit items on current account ($373.8 billion) was greater than the total of the credit items ($332.2 billion) in 1983. In other words, the total payments made by the United States to other nations on current account was greater than the total payments made by other nations to the United States. On current account the United States supplied more dollars to the foreign exchange market than other nations demanded. Or equivalently, the United States demanded more foreign currency (to pay other nations) than other nations supplied (to get dollars to pay the United States). In short, on current account, payments received from other nations were less than sufficient to finance U.S. payments to other nations. The deficit on current account amounted to $41.6 billion dollars in 1983.

## The Capital Account

There is no reason why there has to be a balance of payments on current account any more than there is a reason why merchandise imports should exactly equal merchandise exports. The current account is itself just a part of the balance of payments. Overall, however, the balance of payments must balance. Since the balance of payments is divided into the current account and the capital account, it follows that *if there is a deficit on current account, there must be a compensating surplus on capital account. Likewise, if there is a surplus on current account, there must be a compensating deficit on capital account.*

For example, if there is an excess of payments over receipts on current account (a deficit), then there must be a matching excess of receipts over payments on capital account (a surplus). That is, if more foreign currency is spent (in payments to other nations) than is

earned (in payments from other nations) on current account, the difference must come from an excess of foreign currency earned over foreign currency spent on capital account. Alternatively, an excess of receipts over payments on current account (a surplus) must be matched by an excess of payments over receipts on capital account (a deficit). In that case, less foreign currency is spent than is earned on current account, and the surplus matches the deficit on capital account, where more foreign currency is spent than is earned.

Since the balance of payments is divided into the current account and the capital account, the capital account includes all international transactions not included in the current account. Specifically, the capital account includes all purchases and sales of assets, or what is termed *capital.*

*Private Imports and Exports of Capital.* When American businesses and households invest and lend abroad (to foreign businesses, households, and governments), they receive IOUs from foreigners in the form of stocks, bonds, and other debt claims and titles of ownership. Such investments and loans are entered as debit items in the capital account. They represent an increase in American ownership of foreign assets. For example, in 1983 American households and businesses invested and loaned $43.3 billion dollars abroad (Table 20–1, row 6). Why are such transactions recorded as a debit item, just like a merchandise import? There are two basic reasons. First, these transactions represent a payment to other nations. Second, they give rise to a supply of dollars in the foreign exchange market and a demand for the foreign currencies Americans need in order to pay for foreign stocks and bonds. Moreover, you can think of Americans importing stock certificates and bonds, just like they import merchandise. Both types of payment represent the acquisition of a claim of ownership or property right from a foreign nation.

Similarly, foreign businesses and households also invest and make loans in the

United States (to American businesses, households, and governments) for which they receive American stocks and bonds. These represent an increase in foreign ownership of American assets and are entered as credit items in the capital account. Such transactions give rise to a supply of foreign currencies in the foreign exchange market and a demand for dollars needed by foreigners to make payment for their investments and loans in the United States. In exchange the United States may be thought of as exporting stock certificates and bonds—that is, exporting property rights and ownership claims. Such transactions amounted to $76.5 billion in 1983 (Table 20–1, row 6).

In 1983 the United States had a surplus on its private capital account equal to $76.5 billion minus $43.3 billion, or $33.2 billion (Table 20–1, row 6). This surplus on private capital account added to the deficit on current account (row 5) amounted to −$8.4 billion. How was this deficit financed (or paid for) so that the balance of payments balanced? For the answer, we need to consider the government capital account.

*Government Imports and Exports of Capital.* Governments also make capital account transactions. These consist mostly of loans to or from other governments; changes in government holdings of official international reserve assets such as foreign currencies, gold, and reserves with the International Monetary Fund called Special Drawing Rights or SDRs (which we will discuss later); and changes in liquid claims on official reserve assets.

Loans to other governments are debit items on the government's capital account because they represent payments to other nations for the import of their IOUs, just like lending on the private capital account. Such lending gives rise to a supply of dollars and a demand for foreign currency in the foreign exchange market. Similarly, foreign governments make loans to the U.S. government. These are recorded as credit items on the government's capital account because they

represent payments received from other nations in exchange for the export of the U.S. government's IOUs (such as U.S. government bonds and Treasury bills). Such transactions create a supply of foreign currency and a demand for dollars in the foreign exchange market.

*The government capital account transactions in official reserve assets and liquid claims on official reserve assets play an accommodating role in the balance of payments. They adjust to satisfy the requirement that overall the balance of payments must balance.* Therefore, they adjust because the total amount of foreign currency needed to make all payments to other nations *must* necessarily equal the total amount of foreign currency earned from all payments received from other nations.

For example, suppose there is a deficit on current account, a deficit on private capital account, and loans to foreign governments exceed loans received from them. The volume of foreign currency earned from other nations will be less than the volume of foreign currency paid to them. The difference will have to be made up either by using government holdings of official reserve assets or by giving other nations liquid claims on the government's holdings of official reserve assets. Payments out of holdings of reserve assets will, of course, reduce government holdings. Such payments are entered as a credit item on the government's capital account because they represent the export of official reserves (foreign currency, gold, or SDRs). Similarly, making payments by giving other nations liquid claims on holdings of official reserves is also a credit item. This item represents the export of an IOU, the liquid claim. The nation receiving the liquid claim may "cash it in" at any time (hence the term *liquid*) by demanding payment in official reserve assets.

*Overall Balance.* As already noted, in 1983 the U.S. surplus on current account (Table 20–1, row 5) plus the deficit on private capital account (row 6) totaled $8.4 billion. This deficit had to be matched by a surplus on the government capital account to give an overall balance of payments. However, we see from row 7 of Table 20–1 that the surplus on government capital account amounted to only $0.9 billion. Hence, the overall surplus on capital account (the sum of the private and government accounts, row 6 plus row 7) is $32.3 billion (row 8), which is less than the amount needed to match the $41.6 billion deficit on current account (row 5). The difference is due to errors and omissions amounting to $9.3 billion (row 9). These are errors in data collection and the government's inability to keep track of virtually all U.S. transactions with other nations. Taking these into account, the balance of payments balances (row 10), as it must.

### Balance of Payments Deficits and Surpluses

In the news we often hear or read about this or that nation's balance of payments deficit or surplus. But if the balance of payments must balance, why the talk about deficits and surpluses? Sometimes commentators are referring to the balance of trade, row 1 of Table 20–1. (To avoid confusion, they should say so explicitly.) In general, however, such references are made with respect to the balance of payments *excluding* government capital account transactions in official reserve assets (foreign currency, gold, and SDRs) and liquid claims against these reserves.

Given this interpretation, a **balance of payments deficit** means that the government is reducing its holdings of official reserve assets or that the liquid claims of foreign governments against these reserves are increasing, or both. The deficit equals the excess of the nation's payments to other nations over the payments received from other nations, exclusive of government capital account transactions in official reserves and liquid claims. A **balance of payments surplus** means the government is increasing its holdings of official reserves or its holdings of liquid claims on the official reserve assets held by foreign governments, or both. The surplus equals the excess of the payments received from other nations over the payments made to them, again exclusive of government capital account transactions in official reserves and liquid claims.

---

*CHECKPOINT\* 20-1*
**Explain how you would classify the following international transactions on the balance of payments account and why each is a credit or a debit item: as an American citizen you get a haircut in France; you give a birthday present to a cousin in Canada; you buy a Volkswagen and finance payments on it with a loan made to you by an American bank (instead, suppose you finance it with a loan made to you by Volkswagen); and the government buys French francs and finances the purchase with a liquid claim.**

\*Answers to all Checkpoints can be found at the back of the text.

---

## EXCHANGE RATES AND BALANCE OF PAYMENTS ADJUSTMENTS

The size of balance of payments deficits and surpluses, as well as the adjustment process for their elimination, depends on the role that exchange rates are allowed to play in international transactions. At one extreme, exchange rates between national currencies can be freely determined by the forces of supply and demand in the foreign exchange market. At the other extreme, exchange rates can be rigidly fixed by government intervention in the foreign exchange market. We will now examine each of these extremes.

### Flexible Exchange Rates

*When exchange rates between national currencies are freely determined by supply and de-*

*mand in the foreign exchange market, they are said to be* **flexible (or floating) exchange rates**. They are free to change in response to shifts in supply and demand.

### Currency Depreciation and Appreciation

When the exchange rate between dollars and a foreign currency increases, the foreign currency gets more expensive in terms of dollars—it takes more dollars or cents to buy a unit of foreign currency. Since this is the same thing as saying that a dollar will buy less foreign currency, we say that the value of the dollar has *depreciated* relative to the foreign currency. **Currency depreciation** *means that now more units of a nation's currency will be required to buy a unit of foreign currency.*

Conversely, if the exchange rate between dollars and a foreign currency decreases, it takes fewer dollars or cents to buy a unit of foreign currency. Since a dollar will now buy more foreign currency, the value of the dollar is said to have *appreciated* relative to the foreign currency. **Currency appreciation** *means that now fewer units of a nation's currency are required to buy a unit of a foreign currency.*

Note that *an appreciation in the value of one nation's currency is necessarily a depreciation in another's.* For example, suppose the rate of exchange between dollars and French francs is initially $1 per franc. Suppose the value of the dollar appreciates relative to the franc. For instance, say the rate of exchange decreases to $.50 per franc. It now takes half as many dollars to buy a franc. For French citizens this means the rate of exchange has risen from 1 franc per dollar to 2 francs per dollar. In other words, the value of the franc has depreciated relative to the dollar. It now takes twice as many francs to buy a dollar.

### Exchange Rates and the Price of Foreign Goods

Exchange rates allow citizens in one country to translate the prices of foreign goods and services into units of their own currency. Suppose $1 exchanges for 4 French francs on the foreign exchange market. If the price of a French-made car is 20,000 francs, its price in dollars is $5,000, or 20,000 multiplied by .25. Similarly, if the price of a ton of American wheat is $30, its price in francs is 120 francs, or 30 multiplied by 4.

*Changes in exchange rates alter the prices of foreign goods to domestic buyers and the prices of domestic goods to foreign buyers.* Suppose in the above example that the dollar depreciates, so that $1 will now only exchange for 3 francs on the foreign exchange market. Now the French-made car selling for 20,000 francs will be more expensive for an American. It will cost $6,666 (.33 × 20,000). On the other hand, a ton of American wheat selling for $30 will be less expensive to a French citizen because the depreciation of the dollar means an appreciation of the franc. The ton of wheat will now cost a French buyer 90 francs (3 × 30).

### Free-Market Determination of the Exchange Rate

In Chapter 4 we saw how supply and demand work in a freely operating market (one in which the government does not intervene) to determine the price of a good. The exchange rate is just the price of one currency stated in terms of another. And the determination of the equilibrium level of a flexible, or floating, exchange rate is determined by supply and demand just like the price of wheat or shoeshines.

For example, suppose the United States and France are the only two trading countries in the world. And suppose that the exchange rate between dollars and French francs is determined by supply and demand in the foreign exchange market as shown in Figure 20–1. (Our example uses hypothetical data.) The vertical axis measures the exchange rate, the price of a franc in terms of dollars. The horizontal axis measures the quantity of francs. The equilibrium level of the exchange rate is $.25 per franc, which

**FIGURE 20-1   Determination of the Equilibrium Level of a Flexible Exchange Rate**

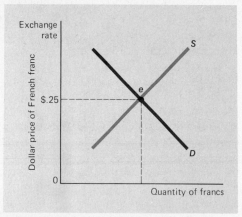

Underlying the demand curve *D* for French francs is the desire of Americans to exchange dollars for francs needed to buy French goods and services and to acquire French assets. Similarly, behind the supply curve *S* for francs is the desire of French citizens to exchange francs for dollars needed to buy American goods and services and to acquire American assets.

The equilibrium level of the exchange rate is $.25 per franc, determined by the intersection of the demand curve *D* and supply curve *S* at point *e*. If the exchange rate is less than $.25 per franc, the demand for francs in the foreign exchange market will exceed the supply and the rate will be bid up. If the exchange rate is greater than $.25 per franc, the supply of francs in the foreign exchange market will exceed the demand and the rate will be bid down.

corresponds to the intersection of the supply curve *S* and the demand curve *D* at point *e*.

The demand curve *D* shows the quantity of francs demanded by Americans at each possible level of the exchange rate. It comes from the desire on the part of Americans to exchange dollars for francs. The francs are needed to buy French goods and services and to pay interest and dividends on French loans and investments in the United States. They are also needed to make American

military expenditures in France, to make unilateral transfers such as gifts and foreign aid grants, and to pay for the American acquisition (by government, businesses, and private citizens) of French assets. In short, the demand curve *D* represents the American demand for francs needed to make payments to France—all the transactions with France that enter as debit items on the U.S. balance of payments account.

The supply curve *S* shows the quantity of francs supplied by French citizens at each possible level of the exchange rate. Underlying it is the desire of the French to exchange francs for dollars needed to pay for American goods and services and for the French acquisition of American assets. These payments are represented by all the credit items on the U.S. balance of payments account.

The supply and demand curves have the usual slopes. If the exchange rate were below the equilibrium level, the quantity of francs demanded would exceed the quantity supplied, and the exchange rate (the price of a franc) would be bid up. If the exchange rate were above the equilibrium level, the quantity of francs supplied would exceed the quantity demanded, and the rate would be bid down. At the equilibrium exchange rate, there is no tendency for the rate to change because the quantity of francs demanded is just equal to the quantity supplied.

## Flexible Exchange Rates and the Balance of Payments

The argument for flexible exchange rates is that they automatically adjust to eliminate balance of payments surpluses and deficits. Let's see how this happens.

The equilibrium in the foreign exchange market of Figure 20–1 (represented by the intersection of *D* and *S* at point *e*) is reproduced in Figure 20–2. In equilibrium there is no balance of payments deficit or surplus as we have defined these concepts. That is, there are no government capital account transactions in official reserves and liquid claims between the two nations. Moreover, the total of all other U.S. payments to France

**FIGURE 20-2  Adjustment of a Flexible Exchange Rate to Eliminate a Balance of Payments Deficit**

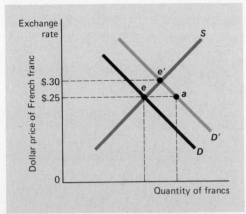

An increase in American imports of French goods will cause the demand curve for francs to shift from $D$ to $D'$ because Americans now need more francs to make payments to France. At the initial exchange rate of $.25 per franc, the United States will have a balance of payments deficit. With a flexible exchange rate the excess demand for francs, equal to the distance between points $e$ and $a$, will cause the rate to be bid up. The rise in the exchange rate will make French goods more expensive to Americans and American goods cheaper for French citizens. Therefore, American imports of French goods will decline and French imports of American goods will rise. This adjustment will continue until the exchange rate has risen to the new equilibrium level of $.30 per franc (corresponding to the intersection of $S$ and $D'$ at point $e'$). At this point, the U.S. balance of payments deficit will be eliminated.

is exactly equal to the total of all payments received by the United States from France.

Now suppose Americans step up their imports of French goods (say because more Americans develop a taste for French wines and other French goods). Total payments to France will now exceed total payments received from France. American demand for francs needed to make these payments will increase, as represented by the rightward shift in the demand curve for francs from $D$ to $D'$ in Figure 20–2. At the initial exchange rate of $.25 per franc, there will now be a shortage of francs. Equivalently, we can say there will be an excess demand for francs equal to the distance between points $e$ and $a$. The United States will now have a balance of payments deficit.

How will a flexible exchange rate eliminate this deficit? The excess demand for francs will cause the exchange rate, the dollar price of francs, to be bid up. But this will alter the prices of *all* French goods to Americans and the prices of all American goods to French citizens in the way we discussed earlier. Since Americans will now have to pay more for francs, the prices of French goods will now be higher when translated into dollars. Therefore, as the exchange rate is bid up, French goods will become more expensive for American buyers, and American imports will tend to decline. This decline is represented by a move from point $a$ toward point $e'$ along $D'$ in Figure 20–2.

But a rise in the dollar price of francs is the same thing as a fall in the franc price of dollars. (The dollar depreciates relative to the franc, and the franc appreciates relative to the dollar.) French citizens will now find that they don't have to pay as much for dollars. The prices of American goods will therefore be lower when translated into francs. Since American goods are now less expensive for French citizens, French imports will tend to increase. This increase is represented by a move from point $e$ toward point $e'$ along $S$ in Figure 20–2.

Hence, as the exchange rate rises to the new equilibrium position corresponding to $e'$, an exchange rate of $.30 per franc, American imports from France decline while American exports to France increase. The result will be to eliminate the balance of payments deficit in the United States. In sum, *when exchange rates are flexible, or freely determined by supply and demand, balance of payments deficits and surpluses will be quickly eliminated. Indeed, it is often argued that foreign exchange markets adjust so quickly that there would be no deficits or surpluses if governments didn't interfere.* (Later in this chapter we will see how governments interfere with the mechanism.)

## Factors Affecting Flexible Exchange Rates

We have just seen how a change in one nation's demand for the products of another can affect the exchange rate. Other factors can also cause shifts in supply and demand in foreign exchange markets and, hence, changes in flexible, or floating, exchange rates. Two of the more important factors in supply and demand are differences in rates of inflation between nations and changes in the level of interest rates in one nation relative to the interest rates in others.

### Differences in Rates of Inflation

Assume again that the equilibrium exchange rate between dollars and francs is $.25 per franc, determined by the intersection of *D* and *S* at point *e* in Figure 20–3. Now suppose the general price level in the United States (the prices of all American products) rises relative to the general price level in France (due to an expansionary American fiscal and monetary policy, say). As a result, French goods become less expensive relative to American goods, *given the exchange rate of $.25 per franc.* Hence, Americans increase their demand for imports from France, thereby causing their demand for francs to increase, as indicated by the rightward shift in the demand curve for francs from *D* to *D'*. At the same time, the rise in the American price level causes French citizens to reduce their demand for American goods. This results in a reduction of their supply of francs (their demand for dollars), indicated by a leftward shift of the supply curve of francs from *S* to *S'*.

At the initial exchange rate of $.25 per franc, there is now an excess demand for francs equal to the distance between points *a* and *b*. This excess demand will cause the ex-

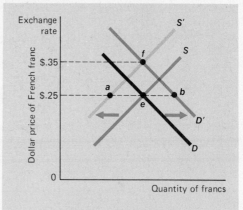

**FIGURE 20-3   Differential Changes in the Price Levels of Two Nations Cause the Exchange Rate to Change**

The rise in the general price level of American goods relative to French goods causes a depreciation of the dollar relative to the franc in the foreign exchange market.

When the general price level in the United States rises relative to the general price level in France, French goods become less expensive relative to American goods. Hence, at the initial exchange rate of $.25 per franc American demand for French imports increases and French citizens reduce their demand for American goods. The demand curve for francs therefore shifts rightward from *D* to *D'* and the supply curve for francs shifts leftward from *S* to *S'*. The resulting excess demand for francs (equal to the distance between points *a* and *b*) causes the exchange rate to be bid up to $.35 per franc. This depreciation of the dollar relative to the franc cuts back the American demand for French imports and increases French demand for American goods in exactly the manner described in connection with Figure 20–2.

change rate to be bid up from $.25 per franc to $.35 per franc, corresponding to the intersection of *S'* and *D'* at point *f*, Figure 20–3. The American demand for French imports will be cut back and the French demand for American goods will increase in exactly the manner already described in connection with Figure 20–2. In short, the rise in the general price level of American goods relative to French goods causes a depreciation of the dollar relative to the franc in the foreign exchange market.

Our hypothetical example illustrates a general observation about exchange rate movements in the real world. *Given a sufficient length of time, the exchange rate between the nations' currencies will tend to adjust to reflect changes in their price levels, all other things remaining the same.* Of course, all other things typically do not remain the same. Hence, it is usually difficult to observe real-world adjustments that are as clear-cut as our hypothetical example.

The process of exchange rate adjustment due to differential changes in national price levels operates continuously when two nations experience different rates of inflation. *If two nations are each experiencing the same rate of inflation, the relation between their general price levels remains the same. The exchange rate between their currencies will therefore remain unchanged, all other things remaining the same. However, if a nation's rate of inflation is greater than that of a trading partner, the nation with the higher inflation rate will experience an increase in its exchange rate—a depreciation of its currency—all other things remaining the same.* For instance, in our example of the United States and France, suppose the American price level continued to rise relative to that of France. Then the rate of exchange between the dollar and the franc would continue to rise. The dollar would continue to depreciate relative to the franc.

### Changes in Interest Rates

In our discussion of the capital account of the balance of payments, we observed that money is loaned and borrowed across national borders. Some of these funds are moved around the globe almost continually in search of those highly liquid financial assets (such as short-term government bonds and commercial paper) that pay the highest interest rates. When the interest rates prevailing in one country change relative to those prevailing in another, funds tend to flow toward that country where interest rates are now highest, all other things remaining the same.

For example, suppose the interest rate on U.S. Treasury bills is 7 percent, the same as that on comparable short-term French government bonds. If the interest rate on Treasury bills suddenly drops to 6.5 percent (due to Federal Reserve open market purchases, say), short-term French government bonds paying 7 percent interest will look relatively more attractive to American investors. They will therefore increase their demand for francs in order to buy more French bonds. The demand curve for francs will shift rightward, just as in Figure 20–3. Similarly, French investors will reduce the supply of francs since Treasury bills will also be relatively less attractive to them. Hence, the supply curve for francs will shift leftward, again as in Figure 20–3. The result will be a rise in the exchange rate of dollars for francs, a depreciation of the dollar relative to the franc.

*Since funds can be quickly transferred between countries, changes in the relative levels of interest rates between countries are a primary cause of day-to-day changes in flexible, or floating, exchange rates.*

### CHECKPOINT 20-2

**When one currency depreciates, why does another necessarily appreciate? In what sense is the supply curve in Figure 20–1 a demand curve for dollars, and the demand curve a supply curve of dollars? What would happen to the exchange rate of dollars for pounds if American authorities started to pursue a more expansionary monetary policy, all other things remaining the same? Why? What do you think would happen to the exchange rate of dollars for pounds if British authorities started to pursue a more restrictive fiscal policy, all other things remaining the same? Why?**

**FIGURE 20-4   Fixed Exchange Rates: Balance of Payments Deficits and Surpluses**

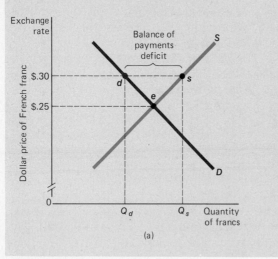

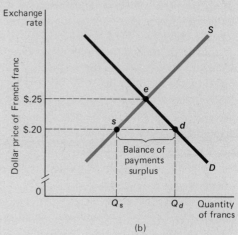

(a)                                                                      (b)

The equilibrium level of the exchange rate between dollars and francs would be $.25 per franc (the intersection at point $e$ of the supply and demand curves for francs) if the forces of supply and demand were allowed to operate freely.

However, suppose the French government wants to fix, or peg, the exchange rate above the equilibrium level at $.30 per franc, as shown in part a. Then it will have a balance of payments deficit equal to the excess supply of francs, represented by the distance between points $d$ and $s$. In order to maintain the exchange rate at $.30 per franc, the French government will have to buy up the excess supply of francs using dollars out of its holdings of official reserves.

Alternatively, suppose the French government wants to fix the exchange rate below the equilibrium level at $.20 per franc, as shown in part b. Then it will have a balance of payments surplus equal to the excess demand for francs, represented by the distance between points $s$ and $d$. In order to maintain the exchange rate at $.20 per franc, the French government will have to supply the foreign exchange market with a quantity of francs equal to the excess demand.

## Fixed Exchange Rates and the Balance of Payments

Governments have often chosen to fix, or "peg," exchange rates, which is just the opposite of allowing the forces of supply and demand to freely determine rates in the foreign exchange market. *In order to fix the exchange rate at a level above or below the equilibrium level determined by supply and demand, governments must continually intervene in the foreign exchange market.* Let's see why this is so, and how governments must intervene.

### Fixing the Rate Above Equilibrium

Consider the supply and demand for francs in Figure 20–4, part a. If the exchange rate were flexible, or floating, it would be equal to the equilibrium rate of $.25 per franc, as determined by the intersection of the demand curve $D$ and supply curve $S$ at point $e$. However, suppose the French government wants to fix, or peg, the exchange rate at $.30 per franc. At this price the quantity of francs demanded by Americans in order to make payments to France equals $Q_d$, corresponding to point $d$ on $D$. The quantity of francs supplied by French citizens in order to get dollars to make payments to the United States equals $Q_s$, corresponding to point $s$ on $S$. The quantity of francs supplied exceeds the quantity demanded—payments by France to the United States are greater than payments by the United States to France. Therefore, France has a balance of payments deficit represented by the distance between points $d$ and $s$ (also equal to $Q_s$ minus $Q_d$).

But what will keep market forces from bidding the exchange rate down to the equilibrium level at point $e$? The French government must buy up the excess supply of francs (equal to the distance between $d$ and $s$) at a price of $.30 per franc using dollars out of its holdings of official reserve assets (foreign currencies, gold, and SDRs). The French government will be able to continue fixing the exchange rate above the equilibrium level only as long as it has reserves of dollars. Once the reserves run out, the exchange will fall to the equilibrium level of $.25 per franc. When the price of a currency (the exchange rate) is pegged above the equilibrium level that would prevail in a free market, the currency is often said to be overvalued. In this case the franc is overvalued relative to the dollar.

### Fixing the Rate Below Equilibrium

Now consider the opposite case, in which the exchange rate is fixed below the equilibrium level—the franc is undervalued relative to the dollar. For example, suppose the French government wants to peg the exchange rate at $.20 per franc, as illustrated in Figure 20–4, part b. In this case the quantity of francs demanded by Americans $Q_d$ (corresponding to point $d$ on $D$) exceeds the quantity supplied by French citizens $Q_s$ (corresponding to point $s$ on $S$). Payments by France to the United States are now less than payments by the United States to France. France now has a balance of payments surplus equal to the distance between points $s$ and $d$.

How will the French government keep the

excess demand for francs from bidding up the exchange rate to the equilibrium level at point $e$? It will have to supply the foreign exchange market with a quantity of francs equal to the excess demand (the distance between points $s$ and $d$). In exchange for these francs the French government will acquire dollars, which will increase its holdings of official reserves.

## Policy Implications of Fixed Exchange Rates

*It is generally easier for a government to keep its currency undervalued (the exchange rate is pegged below the equilibrium level) than to keep it overvalued (the exchange rate is pegged above the equilibrium level).* As we have seen, a government must draw down its reserves of foreign currencies in order to keep its currency overvalued. Obviously, it can't do this indefinitely, or it will run out of such reserves. It may be able to borrow more from other nations, but again not indefinitely. By contrast, in order to keep its currency undervalued, a government only has to supply its own currency to the foreign exchange market. And, as discussed in previous chapters, a government has unlimited capacity to do this.

### Overvalued Versus Undervalued Currencies

Clearly, it is easier to keep currencies undervalued than to keep them overvalued. What are the policy implications of this fact? Suppose all nations are trading under a system of flexible exchange rates, so that there are no balance of payments deficits or surpluses. Now suppose they all agree to fix exchange rates at currently prevailing levels. As time passes supply and demand curves in foreign exchange markets inevitably shift due to changing trade patterns and differing economic developments within each nation. Since exchange rates are fixed, some nations end up with overvalued currencies and balance of payments deficits while others have undervalued currencies and balance of payments surpluses.

Nations with overvalued currencies and payments deficits must do something to correct their situation or they will run out of official reserves. By contrast, those with undervalued currencies and payments surpluses are not under this pressure—they need only keep supplying their own currency to the foreign exchange market. Hence, to eliminate its payments deficits and preserve its reserve holdings, a nation with an overvalued currency is often forced to allow its currency to depreciate. In a world of fixed exchange rates, this is called a **currency devaluation**—the exchange rate is now fixed at a lower level. Of course, the problem could also be cured if nations with undervalued currencies allowed their currencies to appreciate, called a **currency revaluation** in a world of fixed exchange rates. Obviously, if one currency is overvalued, another must be undervalued. But the pressure on the nation with the overvalued currency to devalue is simply greater than that on the nation with the undervalued currency to revalue.

## Bias Toward Contractionary Fiscal and Monetary Policy

Unfortunately, devaluing a nation's overvalued currency is not a politically popular thing for the government in office to do. It is often seen as a sign of a weakening economy and a loss of international stature. Similarly, a nation with an undervalued currency faces political obstacles to revaluation because sales abroad by its export industries benefit when its currency is underpriced in the foreign exchange market.

But the nation with the overvalued currency and the balance of payments deficit must do something to avoid running out of official reserves. One possibility is to pursue a contractionary fiscal and monetary policy, thereby curbing total demand. As we saw in the previous chapter, this also will tend to reduce the nation's demand for imports. And a reduction in imports will help to reduce its

balance of payments deficit. Unfortunately, however, curbing total demand will also increase the nation's unemployment rate and reduce its total output. Its domestic policy goals will have to be sacrificed to its international policy goal of reducing its payments deficit.

Of course, another possibility for the nation with an undervalued currency and payments surplus is to pursue an expansionary fiscal and monetary policy. Such a nation's total demand would rise, causing an increase in its imports from the nations with overvalued currencies and payments deficits. Unfortunately, this might cause unacceptable inflationary pressures in the expanding nation. Such a nation is likely to be very reluctant to sacrifice its own domestic price stability for the sake of reducing another nation's balance of payments deficit, especially since this will reduce its own payments surplus as well. Consequently, the burden usually falls on the nation with the overvalued currency (the one running out of official reserves) to pursue contractionary fiscal and monetary policy in order to reduce its payments deficit. Hence, *many critics of a fixed exchange rate system contend that it is biased toward enforcing contractionary fiscal and monetary policies on nations with overvalued currencies and chronic balance of payments deficits. As a result, they claim, worldwide unemployment rates are higher and worldwide output levels lower under such a system.*

Finally, what if a nation with an overvalued currency and a payments deficit is neither willing to devalue nor to curb total demand with restrictive fiscal and monetary policy? Such a nation may simply erect tariffs and other trade barriers to curb its imports. In that event everybody loses, as we saw in the previous chapter.

## Flexible Versus Fixed Exchange Rates

Which is to be preferred, a system of flexible exchange rates or a system of fixed exchange rates?

## Fiscal and Monetary Policy Considerations

Under a system of fixed exchange rates nations will run balance of payments deficits and surpluses because exchange rates cannot automatically adjust to equalize supply and demand in the foreign exchange markets. As we have just seen, nations with chronic balance of payments deficits may have to sacrifice high employment in order to reduce their payments deficits. Hence, critics argue that fixed exchange rates interfere with a nation's freedom to use fiscal and monetary policy to pursue domestic policy goals. These same critics often advocate flexible exchange rates because they automatically eliminate balance of payments problems, thus freeing fiscal and monetary policy to focus strictly on domestic objectives. However, some advocates of fixed exchange rates argue just the opposite. They claim that the fear of running large balance of payments deficits serves as a check on governments that might otherwise pursue excessively expansionary fiscal and monetary policies that cause inflation.

## Stability and Uncertainty

Critics contend that flexible exchange rates inhibit international trade because of the uncertainty about their future levels. For example, suppose an American woolens wholesaler puts in an order to purchase wool blankets from an English woolen mill. Suppose the current exchange rate is $2 per English pound, and that a wool blanket costs 20 pounds, or $40. At this price the American woolens wholesaler feels that the English blankets will be very competitive with American-made blankets that sell for $45. However, suppose that the blankets are delivered to the American wholesaler 3 months after the order is placed, and that in the meantime the exchange rate has increased to $2.50 per pound. The English woolen mill contracted to sell the blankets for 10 pounds apiece. But in dollars it will now cost the American woolens wholesaler $50 per blanket ($2.50 × 20), a price that will no longer be competitive with comparable American-

made wool blankets selling for $45. Clearly, fluctuations in flexible exchange rates can make international business transactions risky.

Advocates of flexible exchange rates argue that it is possible to hedge against the risks of changing exchange rates by entering into futures contracts. For instance, at the time the American woolens wholesaler placed the order for the wool blankets, a futures contract could have been obtained that guaranteed delivery of pounds to the wholesaler at a rate of $2 per pound 3 months hence. Whatever happens to the exchange rate between dollars and pounds in the meantime, the wholesaler will be assured of getting pounds at $2 per pound when it comes time to pay for the blankets. Who will enter into the futures contract agreeing to supply pounds to the wholesaler at this rate of exchange? Someone needing dollars 3 months hence who wants to be sure they can be obtained with pounds at a rate of $2 per pound. That someone might be an English firm that has ordered goods from an American firm to be delivered and paid for in 3 months.

While acknowledging the protection that hedging can offer, some critics still claim that flexible exchange rates can fluctuate wildly due to speculation—for example, the purchase of pounds at $2 per pound on the gamble that the rate will rise say to $2.25 per pound, yielding the speculator a profit of $.25 per pound. To the contrary, advocates of flexible exchange rates respond that speculative activity will tend to stabilize exchange rate fluctuations. They claim that speculators must buy currencies when they are low priced and sell them when they are high priced if they are to make money. Hence, it is argued that speculators will tend to push the price of an undervalued currency up and the price of an overvalued currency down, thus serving to limit exchange rate fluctuations.

It is often argued that fixed exchange rates invite destabilizing speculation even more than flexible exchange rates. Suppose a currency is overvalued, such as the franc in Figure 20–4, part a. And suppose word spreads that the French government is running out of the dollar reserves needed to fix the price of francs above the equilibrium level and finance its payments deficit. Anticipating a devaluation of the franc, holders of francs will rush to the foreign exchange market to get rid of their francs before the price of francs drops. This will shift the supply curve of francs rightward, making the excess supply even larger. With a larger payments deficit and reserves now declining faster, actual devaluation may be unavoidable.

### CHECKPOINT 20-3

**Describe what a government must do in order to fix an exchange rate. Why are balance of payments deficits and surpluses inevitable under fixed exchange rates? If a nation's currency was overvalued and it decided to tighten its monetary policy, what would happen to its official reserve holdings? Why?**

## THE INTERNATIONAL FINANCIAL SYSTEM: POLICIES AND PROBLEMS

The international financial system consists of the framework of arrangements under which nations finance international trade. These arrangements influence whether exchange rates will be fixed, flexible (or floating), or some combination of fixed and flexible, often called the *managed float*. The arrangements also influence the way balance of payments adjustments take place and the way nations finance balance of payments deficits. We will now examine the principal ways in which the international financial system has been organized during the twentieth century. First we will briefly consider the gold standard, which prevailed during the late nineteenth and early twentieth centuries. We will then examine the Bretton Woods system, which governed international transactions from 1944 to 1971, and finally the mixed system that prevails today.

### The Gold Standard

For about 50 years prior to World War II, the international financial system was predominantly on a gold standard. The United States was on a gold standard from 1879 to 1934 (except for two years, 1917–1918, during World War I).

#### Gold and a Fixed Exchange Rate

Under a **gold standard** gold serves as each nation's money. Each nation defines its monetary unit in terms of so many ounces of gold. The use of this common unit of value automatically fixes the rate of exchange between different currencies. For example, suppose the United States defines a dollar as equal to $1/30$ of an ounce of gold. This means the U.S. Treasury would pay $1 for every $1/30$ ounce of gold to anyone who wants to sell gold to it or give $1/30$ of an ounce of gold for every dollar of its currency to anyone who wants to buy gold. U.S. currency (coins and paper money) would be redeemable in gold. Suppose Great Britain defines its monetary unit, the pound sovereign, as equal to $5/30$ of an ounce of gold. The British Treasury would redeem its currency at the rate of $5/30$ of an ounce of gold for every pound sovereign (called a pound for short). What would be the international rate of exchange between dollars and pounds?

Obviously it would be fixed at $5 per pound. People who wanted pounds to buy British goods would never pay more than $5 per pound. Why? Simply because they could always go to the U.S. Treasury and get $5/30$ of an ounce of gold for $5, then ship the gold to Great Britain, where they could exchange it at the British Treasury for a British pound. (For simplicity, we will ignore shipping costs.) Similarly, it would not be possible to buy a pound for less than $5. Why? Because no one would sell a pound for less than this when they could exchange it at the British Treasury for $5/30$ of an ounce of gold and then ship the gold to the United States, where it could be exchanged at the U.S. Treasury for $5.

## The Gold Flow Adjustment Mechanism

Now that we see why the exchange rate was rigidly fixed under a gold standard, let's see how balance of payments adjustments took place under such a system.

Clearly, if the United States imported more from Great Britain than it exported, the United States would have to pay the difference by shipping gold to Great Britain. What would eliminate the U.S. balance of payment deficit and Great Britain's balance of payments surplus to ensure that the United States wouldn't eventually lose all its gold to Great Britain?

When the United States ran a payments deficit, the nation's money supply, its gold stock, would decrease while that of its trading partner, Great Britain, would increase. Every time an American bought British goods, dollars (U.S. currency) would be turned in to the U.S. Treasury in exchange for gold. The gold would then be shipped to Great Britain and exchanged at the British Treasury for the pounds needed to pay British exporters. Similarly, every time a British citizen bought American goods, pounds (British currency) would be turned in to the British Treasury in exchange for gold. The gold would then be shipped to the United States and exchanged at the U.S. Treasury for the dollars needed to pay American exporters. If Americans bought more from the British than the British bought from Americans, more gold would be flowing out of the United States than was flowing into it. The reverse would be true of Great Britain— more gold would be flowing in than out. Hence, Great Britain's money supply would increase while that of the United States would decrease.

Now recall the effect of money supply changes on an economy, as discussed in previous chapters. If Great Britain's money supply was increasing, this change in the money supply would increase its total demand and income. Its price level would tend to rise and its interest rates to fall. As prices of its goods rose, they would become more expensive for Americans and lead to a reduction of American imports from Britain. Similarly, the fall in British interest rates would make British securities less attractive, so that American purchases (imports) of such securities would decline. At the same time, the rise in Britain's total demand and income would tend to stimulate its imports—its purchases of American goods and services. All of these factors would amount to a reduction in American payments to Britain and an increase in British payments to the United States. All these factors would work together to reduce the U.S. balance of payments deficit and decrease Great Britain's payments surplus.

Consider what would be happening in the United States at the same time. The U.S. money supply would be decreasing, reducing its total demand and income. This would put downward pressure on its price level. The reduction in its money supply would also tend to push U.S. interest rates up. To the extent U.S. prices fell, British citizens would find American goods cheaper and would therefore buy more of them. Similarly, higher interest rates would lead British citizens to step up their purchases of American securities. Finally, the reduction in total demand and income would tend to reduce American imports of British goods. Again, all these factors would contribute to an increase in Britain's payments to the United States and a reduction in American payments to Britain.

In short, the U.S. balance of payments deficit and the British payments surplus would automatically set in motion forces that would reduce America's payments deficit and Britain's payments surplus. And, as long as an American payments deficit and a British payments surplus exist, these forces would continue to operate until both the deficit and the surplus were eliminated. At that point, the flow of gold to the United States from Britain would exactly equal the flow of gold from the United States to Britain. Balance of payments equilibrium would be restored.

To summarize, *under a gold standard nations with balance of payments deficits would lose gold to nations with balance of payments surpluses. The increase in the money supplies of the surplus nations would tend to push up their price levels, reduce their interest rates, and increase their imports from deficit nations. The decrease in the money supplies of the deficit nations would tend to reduce their price levels, increase their interest rates, and reduce their imports from surplus nations. This process would continue until balance of payments equilibrium in all nations was restored.*

### Shortcomings of the Gold Standard

The major difficulty with a gold standard is that balance of payments adjustments operate through interest rate, output, employment, and price level adjustments in each nation. Deficit nations may have to suffer recession and high rates of unemployment, while surplus nations experience unanticipated inflation with all the gains and losses that this bestows arbitrarily on different citizens. In short, domestic goals, such as the maintenance of high employment and output, as well as price stability, are completely at the mercy of the balance of payments adjustment process. Most economists feel that this amounts to letting the tail wag the dog.

Moreover, gold discoveries, which can happen at any time, can cause haphazard increases in money supplies and inflation. Conversely, a lack of gold discoveries can result in money supply growth lagging behind worldwide economic growth. Consequently, tightening money supply conditions may trigger recessions and put a damper on economic growth.

### Demise of the Gold Standard

The Great Depression of the 1930s was the undoing of the gold standard. Many nations, faced with high unemployment, resorted to protectionist measures, imposing import tariffs and quotas and exchange controls (regulations that make it difficult to exchange domestic for foreign currency). Through such measures each hoped to stimulate sagging output and employment at home by maintaining exports and reducing imports. Clearly, this was no more possible than for each participant in a footrace to run faster than everyone else. In percentage terms, world trade fell even more than world output.

As the worldwide depression deepened, nation after nation had cause to fear that if its economy began to recover while those of its trading partners remained depressed, its imports would increase while its exports remained low. Under a gold standard such a nation would lose gold, and the resulting contraction of its money supply would drag its economy back into depression. This consideration, combined with the desire to stimulate exports, led nations to devalue their currencies in terms of gold throughout the 1930s. The resolve to keep the rates of exchange between national monetary units and ounces of gold permanently fixed (and hence permanently fix rates of exchange between currencies)—the essence of an orthodox gold standard—had been broken. This state of affairs persisted until the end of World War II.

### The Bretton Woods System

In 1944 the industrial nations of the world sent representatives to Bretton Woods, New Hampshire, to establish a new international financial system for international trade. They set up a system of fixed exchange rates with the dollar serving as the key currency. That is, the United States agreed to buy and sell gold at $35 per ounce, while the other nations agreed to buy and sell dollars so as to fix their exchange rates at agreed-upon levels. Hence, all currencies were indirectly tied to gold. For example, someone holding marks could exchange them for dollars at a fixed exchange rate and then exchange the dollars for gold in the United States.

The agreements seemed a logical way to set up the new system for two reasons. First, the United States had the most gold reserves.

Second, the war-ravaged economies of Europe viewed the dollar as soundly backed by the productive capacity of the American economy. The **Bretton Woods system** (sometimes called the *gold exchange system*) clearly reflected a widespread belief that international trade would function better under a fixed exchange rate system than under one of flexible rates. It also reflected an age-old belief that money should be backed by a precious metal such as gold.

### Establishment of the
### International Monetary Fund (IMF)

Recall from our earlier discussion of fixed exchange rates that if a nation's currency is fixed above the free-market equilibrium level, it will lose holdings of official reserves. When these are gone, it simply has to devalue its currency. The International Monetary Fund (IMF) was established to deal with this problem, as well as to supervise and manage the new system in general. Member nations were required to contribute funds to the IMF. Then to bolster its ability to keep exchange rates fixed, the IMF was given the authority to lend these funds to member nations running out of reserves. For example, if the British government used up its dollar reserves purchasing pounds to fix the dollar price of pounds above the free-market equilibrium level, the IMF would lend Britain dollars to continue its support operations. The situation should be temporary, and Britain eventually should earn enough dollars in world trade to repay the IMF. A nation would be allowed to devalue relative to the dollar only if its currency were chronically overvalued, so that it continually ran a balance of payments deficit.

### Problems with the
### Bretton Woods System

We have already examined some of the major problems that plague a fixed exchange rate system. All of these troubled the Bretton Woods system until its demise in 1971. Nations often had to compromise their domestic policy goals out of concern for balance of payments considerations. The burden of adjustment usually fell on the nations with overvalued currencies and balance of payments deficits. They often had to pursue more restrictive fiscal and monetary policies to curb total demand and income in order to reduce their imports. Deficit nations also had to devalue their currencies more often than surplus nations revalued. Deficit nations were the ones borrowing from the IMF and "allegedly" the source of difficulty. In addition, as it became more apparent that a currency would have to be devalued, the day of reckoning was hastened by those selling the currency to beat the fall in the exchange rate. Was a world of such sudden readjustments really more conducive to international trade than a world of flexible exchange rates? Was the uncertainty surrounding such abrupt adjustments really less than the uncertainty that would exist under flexible exchange rates? These questions were often raised.

### The End of the Bretton Woods System

As the postwar period unfolded into the 1960s, the fixed levels of exchange rates established after World War II became increasingly out of line with the levels that would give balance of payments equilibrium in most countries. Fixed exchange rate levels established when the Japanese and European economies were still suffering from the ravages of war became increasingly unrealistic as these nations recovered and became more competitive with the United States. As a result, during the 1960s the dollar became increasingly overvalued and the United States ran chronic and growing balance of payments deficits. At the same time countries such as Germany and Japan ran chronic balance of payments surpluses as their currencies were increasingly undervalued. They found themselves continually accepting dollar claims (IOUs) from the United States. In the meantime the United States lost more than half of its gold stock. More and more foreigners became nervous about holding overvalued dollars and forced the United States to honor its commitment to exchange gold for dollars at $35 per ounce.

What could be done? The dollar, the key currency of the system, was overvalued. The United States was not willing to sacrifice domestic policy goals, such as high employment, to reduce its payments deficit. Countries with undervalued currencies often found it difficult to revalue (increase the dollar price of their currencies) because their politically powerful export industries would lose sales as their goods became more expensive to foreign customers. Finally, in 1971 the United States government announced that it would no longer buy and sell gold. The link between gold and the dollar was broken and the era of the Bretton Woods system was over.

## Flexible Exchange Rates and Managed Floats

Despite initial attempts by the industrial nations to restore fixed exchange rates in late 1971, the international financial system has become a mixture of flexible exchange rates and managed floats. Some nations have allowed their exchange rates to float freely. Many others operate a **managed float,** a system whereby exchange rates are largely allowed to float but are subject to occasional government intervention. For example, a nation with an overvalued currency may from time to time use its holdings of foreign reserves to buy its own currency, thus easing its rate of depreciation. Such a managed exchange rate policy is sometimes termed a *dirty float.* In the spirit of Bretton Woods, some countries still attempt to peg their exchange rate more or less to the dollar.

### The Declining Role of Gold

What has happened to the role of gold in the international financial system? In 1968, before the link between gold and the dollar was broken, the IMF created a paper substitute called **Special Drawing Rights (SDRs).** SDRs serve as an official reserve in addition to gold and currency holdings. SDRs are really special accounts at the IMF that can be swapped among member nations in exchange for currencies. Since this is exactly what nations used to do with gold, the SDRs are popularly dubbed "paper gold." Unlike gold, however, the IMF can create SDRs whenever it feels more official reserves are needed to meet the financial needs of expanding world trade. In this sense the creation of SDRs to expand official reserves in the world economy is much like a central bank's creation of member bank reserves in a national economy. Since the elimination of the fixed rate of exchange between the dollar and gold in 1971, gold has become more like any other metal bought and sold in world markets. In recent years both the U.S. Treasury and the IMF have attempted to de-emphasize the importance of gold as money by selling some of their gold holdings.

### Adjustment in the New Environment

The 1970s were turbulent years for the world economy. Oil prices quadrupled from 1973 to 1974 and abruptly rose again with the revolution in Iran in 1979. During 1974 and 1975 industrial nations experienced the severest recession since the Great Depression of the 1930s. Inflation emerged as a major problem for a number of nations such as the United States. And differences in domestic inflation rates between major industrial powers changed over the decade of the 1970s. All these factors required continual readjustment of exchange rates. Many economists feel that the more rigid exchange rate structure of the Bretton Woods system would never have survived these stresses and that the mixture of managed floats and flexible exchange rates has probably served the world economy better.

## CHECKPOINT 20-4
**Some economists argue that the Bretton Woods system imposed a certain amount of fiscal and monetary discipline on governments that was missing in the world economy of the 1970s and early 1980s. What do they mean?**

## POLICY PERSPECTIVE

### How Can the Dollar Be So Strong When the Trade Deficit Is So Large?

Since 1981 the United States has experienced a sharp decline in both its current account balance and its balance of trade, or equivalently, a large increase in its current account deficit and its balance of trade deficit, as shown in Figure P20–1. Both the trade and current account deficits exceeded $100 billion by 1985.

Over this same period of time the dollar appreciated steadily against a weighted average of other major currencies until by 1985 its value in terms of these currencies, or the nominal exchange rate, had increased roughly 65 percent, as shown in

Figure P20–2. Even after adjusting for the lower rate of inflation in the United States, the dollar's real value in terms of the average of these other currencies, the real exchange rate, had increased about 60 percent (see Figure P20–1). In short, relative to 1980, by 1985 the dollar bought 60 percent more in foreign markets than it did at home.

#### The Puzzle

Traditionally, an imbalance between exports and imports that produced large

**FIGURE P20-1    Balances on Trade and Current Account**

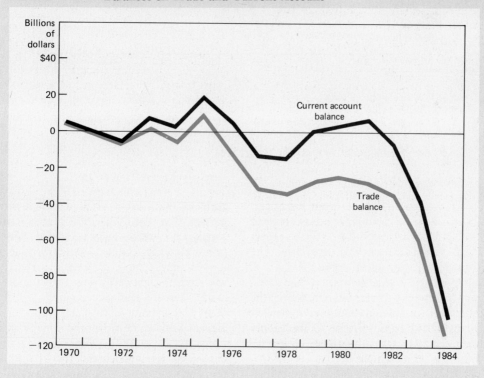

SOURCE: U.S. Department of Commerce.

**FIGURE P20-2   Nominal and Real Exchange Rates and Expected Real Interest Differential**

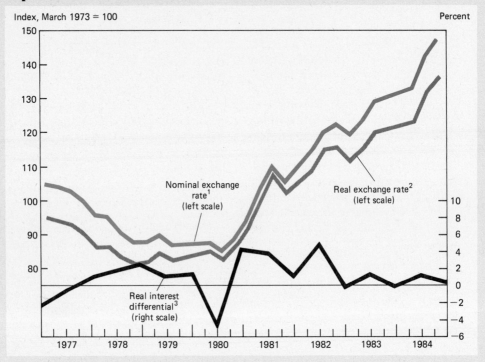

Index, March 1973 = 100         Percent

[1] Multilateral trade-weighted dollar.
[2] Nominal exchange rate adjusted by relative consumer prices.
[3] U.S. interest rate (3-month) minus trade-weighted average interest rate (also 3-month) for six industrial countries adjusted by corresponding OECD inflation forecasts.

SOURCE: *Economic Report of the President*, 1985, p. 104.

current account deficits in an industrialized nation has been regarded as a sign of economic weakness and a reason to expect that nation's currency to depreciate. The traditional view would argue that as U.S. imports get ever larger relative to exports (increasing the current account deficit) the demand for foreign currency by Americans would go up relative to the supply and the dollar would depreciate, as in Figure 20-2 for example.

However, since the dollar was appreci-

ating as the current account deficit increased over the 1980–1985 period, the supply of foreign currency must have been increasing relative to the demand for it—the supply curve of foreign currency was shifting rightward faster than the demand curve. The appreciating dollar made U.S. exports more expensive to foreigners while at the same time it made imports less expensive to Americans. This dampened foreign demand for U.S. exports and increased U.S. demand for imports. Hence it must have been the appreciation of the dollar that *caused* the current account deficit to increase.

### The Role of the Capital Account

But what caused the appreciation of the dollar, or equivalently, what caused the supply of foreign currency to increase relative to the demand for it? Recall that corresponding to the current account deficit there must be a matching capital account surplus. Foreigners must invest and lend more in the United States than Americans are investing and lending abroad. The increase in foreigners' desire to lend and invest in the United States by buying dollar securities (American bonds, stocks, and other debt claims and titles of ownership) caused the United States's capital account surplus to increase during the 1980–1985 period. This increased the supply of foreign currency (the demand for dollars) relative to demand for foreign currency (the supply of dollars) and caused the dollar to appreciate, which in turn caused the increase in the current account deficit.

### Why Foreign Demand for Dollar Securities Increased

Economists have generally identified four basic reasons why dollar securities became relatively more attractive investments than foreign assets during the 1980–1985 period.

1. *Higher real interest rates in the United States.* Starting in late 1979 U.S. monetary policy tightened significantly, causing a sharp increase in nominal interest rates and a subsequent fall in actual and expected inflation. Consequently U.S. real interest rates moved strongly upward, with a brief interruption in mid-1980, and

peaked in 1982. Though they fell somewhat after that, they still remained at relatively high levels. There was also a rise in real interest rates abroad, but because it was less pronounced a positive gap existed between U.S. and foreign real interest rates during most of the 1980–1985 period, as indicated in Figure P20–2. In addition, the Fed's commitment to pursuing an inflationary policy continued to reduce the perceived risk of future inflation. This, together with the positive real interest rate gap, increased the attractiveness of dollar securities.

2. *Higher after-tax rates of return on U.S. investments after 1981.* The Economic Recovery and Tax Act of 1981, together with the reduced rate of inflation, substantially reduced the effective tax rate on income earned on investments in plant and equipment. This increased the after-tax real rate of return on business investment in the United States and was reflected in higher real rates of return on dollar-dominated assets generally. At the same time, Europe's sluggish economic performance and high wage rates squeezed pre-tax profitability in Europe to levels that appear to have been well below those in the United States. Taken together, these developments also tended to make dollar securities more attractive relative to foreign securities.

3. *The U.S. government budget deficit.* Many economists argue that a principal cause of the high real rate of return on dollar securities has been, and will continue to be, the large federal government budget deficits. The budget deficit constitutes a large portion of the demand for funds provided by the net savings generated in the U.S. economy by households, businesses, pension funds, and state and local governments. The real rate of interest has had to rise to balance the supply and demand for these funds by dampen-

ing private investment and by attracting a capital inflow from abroad, as reflected in the balance of payments surplus on the capital account. During the 1980–1985 period the expanded U.S. budget deficit was accompanied by a monetary policy that curbed inflation. The increased budget deficits accompanied by a generally sound monetary policy brought the expected inflation rate down while raising the real interest rate.

4. *The strength of the U.S. economy.* The three factors listed above do not account for all of the increased attractiveness of dollar securities to foreigners. The fact that the dollar has appreciated steadily, while the real interest rate gap in favor of the dollar has narrowed since 1982, suggests other factors also contributed to the increased demand for dollar securities. The robust U.S. economic recovery from the 1982 recession (relative to the sluggish performance of the European economies), the sharp reduction of the U.S. inflation rate, and the increased after-tax profitability of U.S. businesses all contributed to more favorable longer-run prospects for the U.S. economy. All of these developments combined probably prompted additional demand for dollar securities based on confidence in the growing strength of the U.S. economy relative to many of the other industrialized economies.

### Questions

1. Explain why it is claimed that the behavior of the U.S. capital account, rather than that of the current account, caused the appreciation of the dollar during the 1980–1985 period.

2. Explain why foreigners found dollar securities so attractive during the 1980–1985 period.

## SUMMARY

**1.** International trade has a monetary aspect because trade between nations requires the exchange of one nation's currency for that of another. A nation's exports of goods, services, and financial obligations (IOUs) give rise to a demand for its currency and a supply of foreign currencies in the foreign exchange market. A nation's imports of goods, services, and financial obligations give rise to a supply of its currency and a demand for foreign currencies in the foreign exchange market.

**2.** A nation's balance of payments is an accounting statement that itemizes its total payments to other nations and the total payments it receives from other nations. This statement reflects the fact that total payments to other nations must be equal to (or balanced by) total payments received from other nations.

**3.** A nation has a balance of payments deficit when its government must draw on its official reserves, issue liquid claims (to other nations) on these reserves, or both, to finance an excess of payments to cover payments from other nations. A balance of payments surplus occurs when payments received exceed payments to other nations, so that the government receives official reserves and liquid claims from other nations to finance the difference.

**4.** The forces of supply and demand automatically adjust flexible, or floating, exchange rates to eliminate balance of payments deficits and surpluses. They do this by changing the relative attractiveness of goods, services, and assets between nations. Flexible exchange rates tend to adjust to reflect differential rates of inflation and changes in relative interest rate levels between nations.

**5.** Exchange rates can be fixed, or pegged,

only if governments intervene in foreign exchange markets to buy and sell currencies. Fixed exchange rates give rise to balance of payments deficits and surpluses. Under fixed exchange rates deficits can be eliminated either by currency devaluation or by pursuing a restrictive fiscal and monetary policy to curb total demand and income. Conversely, surpluses can be eliminated either by revaluation or by an expansionary fiscal and monetary policy. Devaluation and revaluation are often resisted because of political considerations.

**6.** Critics contend that in practice a fixed exchange rate system tends to be biased toward forcing contractionary fiscal and monetary policies on nations with overvalued currencies. Advocates of fixed exchange rates argue that the uncertainty about future levels of flexible exchange rates tends to put a damper on international trade. Advocates of flexible exchange rates respond that it is possible to hedge against much of this uncertainty by entering into futures contracts. Moreover, they note, fixed exchange rates are not immune to uncertainty—namely, uncertainty about currencies that are likely to be devalued to eliminate chronic balance of payments deficits.

**7.** The gold standard has provided a system of fixed exchange rates in the past. However, balance of payments adjustments under this system often require severe changes in employment, income, and prices, thus sacrificing domestic policy objectives to balance of payments equilibrium.

**8.** The Bretton Woods system provided the financial framework for international trade from 1944 to 1971. Under this system nations fixed their exchange rates in terms of the dollar, the key currency, which was convertible into gold at a fixed rate of exchange maintained by the United States. The International Monetary System (IMF) was established to supervise the system, to lend official reserves to nations with temporary payments deficits, and to decide when exchange rate adjustments were needed to correct chronic payments deficits. The system eventually foundered in 1971 due to chronic and rising U.S. payments deficits that led to growing concern about the dollar's continued convertibility into gold.

**9.** Since the demise of the Bretton Wood system, the international financial system has been a mixture of flexible exchange rates, managed floats, and continued attempts to fix some exchange rates in terms of the dollar.

## KEY TERMS AND CONCEPTS

balance of payments
balance of payments account
balance of payments deficit
balance of payments surplus
balance of trade
Bretton Woods system
currency appreciation
currency depreciation
currency devaluation
currency revaluation
exchange rate
flexible (or floating) exchange rate
foreign exchange market
gold standard
managed float
Special Drawing Rights (SDRs)

## QUESTIONS AND PROBLEMS

**1.** When a nation has a balance of payments deficit, would you say it is exporting or importing official reserves and liquid claims? Why?

**2.** Tell whether each of the following generates a demand for foreign currency (any currency other than dollars) or a supply of foreign currency on foreign exchange markets.

a. A German firm builds a plant in Hawaii.

b. A British firm transfers a million dollars from its bank account in a New York bank to its bank account in a London bank.

c. The U.S. government makes a foreign aid grant to the Philippines.

d. An American firm transports goods from the East Coast to the West Coast through the Panama Canal on a Liberian freighter.

e. Belgium has a balance of payments deficit in its transactions with the United States.

f. An American's French government bond matures.

3. Suppose you observe the following exchange rates: 5 French francs exchange for $1, 4 German marks exchange for $1, and 3 French francs exchange for 2 German marks.

a. Can you think of a way to make money out of this situation?

b. What would you expect to happen if exchange rates were flexible?

c. What would you expect to happen if exchange rates were fixed at these levels?

4. How would a nation's exchange rate likely be affected by each of the following, all other things remaining the same?

a. The nation's trading partners start to pursue relatively more expansionary monetary policies.

b. The nation increases its imports.

c. The nation experiences a decline in the growth of productivity relative to that of its trading partners, thus weakening its competitive position in the world economy.

d. The nation cuts its income taxes.

e. The nation has a recession.

f. The nation steps up its advertising about its tourist attractions.

5. Suppose Great Britain and the United States were the only two trading nations in the world. Suppose also that the exchange rate between pounds and dollars is fixed so that pounds are overvalued in terms of dollars. Furthermore, suppose Britain decides to let its currency float but the United States wants to keep the dollar pegged. Will Britain lose dollar reserves? What will the United States get for its efforts? Which country gets the "better deal" out of this situation and why?

6. Explain why exchange rates are fixed under a gold standard and describe how balance of payments adjustments take place. Explain why you never hear about balance of payments adjustment problems between Texas and Wisconsin, New York and Pennsylvania, or between any of the other states of the Union. How does balance of payments adjustment take place between the states? How has balance of payments adjustment occurred between inner city slums and suburbia?

7. Compare and contrast a gold standard with the Bretton Woods system. Given that both operate under a system of fixed exchange rates, why could there be persistent balance of payments deficits and surpluses under the Bretton Woods system but not under a gold standard?

# 21

# Comparative Economic Systems

AFTER READING THIS CHAPTER, YOU WILL BE ABLE TO:

1. List the four basic features of any economic system.

2. Describe capitalism, market socialism, and planned socialism in terms of their four basic features.

3. Outline the ideological differences among the three main variants of socialism: Communism, social democracy, and third world socialism.

4. Summarize the performance of socialist countries with regard to economic performance, liberty and individual freedom, quality of life, and equality.

5. Outline socialism's basic criticisms of capitalism and capitalism's responses to these criticisms.

6. Describe and contrast the economic systems of China and Yugoslavia as examples of planned and market socialism.

There is a wide variety of ways of organizing an economy to answer the basic questions of what and how much to produce, how to organize production, and for whom to produce. In this book we have focused almost exclusively on the mixed capitalist economy, where households and firms rely largely on markets to answer these questions, assisted by government intervention when it is considered necessary to improve upon the results. The United States, West Germany, Japan, and Canada are good examples of such economies.

But what about the rest of the world? The economic systems of many countries differ markedly from the mixed capitalist economies with which we are familiar. Moreover, these countries deal with the basic economic problem of scarcity—and the questions it poses—in a way that often reflects a quite different vision of the relationship between the individual and society. The various economic systems thus to a large extent reflect different political ideologies. A comparison of the relative merits of differing economic systems cannot avoid an examination of differing political ideologies.

In this chapter we will examine other types of economic systems and compare them with the mixed capitalist economy already more familiar to us. We will begin by considering the basic features that describe any economic system. This will be of help in our examination of the major classifications of economic systems. We will then consider the ways in which particular political ideologies and types of economic systems tend to be related. Finally, to illustrate how socialist systems have worked in practice, we will look briefly at the economies of China and Yugoslavia.

Before we begin, a word of caution is in order. Any attempt to classify the economic systems of different countries into broad categories, such as "communistic" or "socialistic" or "capitalistic," is bound to hide a great variety of differences between them. Such broad classifications are meant to identify economic systems only insofar as they may share, or not share, certain basic characteristics. However, countries may differ in a variety of ways not revealed by simple labels: property may be owned privately or by the state; decision making may be in the hands of a few or of many; decisions may be coordinated by the market or by a plan; incentives may be material, moral, or due to threats of force. These and other possible variations should be kept in mind when the economic systems of different countries are compared—even those that might be classified under the same broad label.

## DEFINING AND COMPARING ECONOMIC SYSTEMS

Most people would agree that the United States has a capitalistic economy and the Soviet Union a socialistic economy. But what do these labels mean? What do they say about the operation of an economic system? To find out, we will look at four basic features of economic systems and use them to develop some broad categories of systems. Later, we will see that these categories are more in the nature of idealizations than descriptions of actual economic systems.

### Basic Features of Economic Systems

When we speak of a country's economy, we mean its particular form of organization for the production, distribution, and consumption of goods and services by its citizens. We often refer to an economy as an *economic system* when we want to focus on its organizational features. Quite generally, *an* **economic system** *consists of the institutions, rules, and decision-making processes that a country uses to organize and allocate its scarce resources to produce and distribute goods and services.* A complete description of a country's economic system would require an understanding of the ways in which its institutions, organizations, laws, rules, values, traditions, beliefs, and basic political ideology affect economic behavior and outcomes.

Obviously, each country's economic system may differ from that of every other country in a number of ways. But do all economic systems have certain basic features that allow them to be classified into only two or three broad categories of systems? Does it make sense to speak of an economic system as being "capitalistic" or "socialistic"? We all know it is common practice to simplify in this way—in the news media and in casual and even learned discussions. It is, in fact, also reasonable. Economists often focus on four features of a country's economic system. Based on these four features, the country may be classified as representative of a basic type of economic system. These features are:

1. the decision-making process;
2. the mechanism for providing information and coordinating activities;
3. property rights; and
4. incentives to performance.

Some economists argue that there are other important features, such as a country's level of economic development. There is certainly room for debate. Nonetheless, it is generally recognized that the four features just listed are crucial to any description of an economic system. Moreover, the details of these four features often differ considerably from one country to another; the differences provide a basis for comparing the economic systems of various countries. In addition, similarities of features are useful in classifying economic systems according to broadly defined types, such as capitalistic or socialistic. Let us examine each feature more closely.

### Decision-Making Process: Centralized or Decentralized

Perhaps the most important characteristic of an economic system's decision-making process is its degree of centralization or decentralization. *Decision making is said to be centralized to the extent that the authority to make decisions is concentrated in the hands of a few at the upper levels of an economic system's organizational structure. Decision making is decentralized to the extent that such authority is spread among many at the lower levels of the organizational structure.*

Centralized economic decision making is characteristic of command, or planned, economic systems, in which government planning boards dictate how to organize production, what and how much to produce, and for whom. China and the Soviet Union and its East bloc satellites provide examples, to varying degrees, of centralized economic decision making. On the other hand, decentralized decision making is characteristic of economic systems in which decisions are made primarily by individual households and firms interacting through a network of markets, with limited government direction and interference. The United States, Japan, Canada, and the Western European countries provide examples of decentralized economic decision making.

Of course, the extent to which decision making is centralized or decentralized can vary widely. The decision-making process is completely (perfectly) centralized if decision-making authority rests solely in a single command unit that issues orders to all lower units in the economy. In less extreme cases, some decision-making authority is granted to subunits at different levels within the economy. As more decision-making authority is granted to lower economic units, the economy tends more toward decentralization. Finally, if all decision-making authority rests with the lowest subunits in the economic structure (with individual households and firms, say), independent of higher levels of authority, the decision-making process is completely decentralized. This is the other end of the spectrum from complete centralization. In sum, *an economic system can be characterized as centralized or decentralized according to the extent to which decision-making authority is distributed among the various units, subunits, and levels of the system's organizational structure.*

## Mechanism for Providing Information and Coordination: Plan or Market

In today's world, the two commonest mechanisms for providing information and coordinating decisions in economic systems are the plan and the market.

An economic *plan,* designed by a central planning board, is used in so-called **planned economies** to inform, direct, and coordinate the economic activities of subunits such as firms. Details may vary, but generally in a planned economy economic activity is guided by instructions devised by higher units and handed down to lower units in the organizational structure. A variety of incentives may be used to encourage or compel the subunits to operate according to instructions derived from the plan. Economies that are popularly called planned can in fact vary considerably. For example, the Soviet Union and Yugoslavia are planned economies. Yet planning is more centralized in the Soviet Union. Yugoslavia relies to a significant extent on a combination of planning and market mechanisms.

The *market* mechanism, the interaction of demand and supply on prices, provides information signals that direct subunits to make resource allocation decisions in a **market economy.** A network of markets thereby coordinates the activities of different decision-making units in the system. For example, households earn income by providing land, labor, and capital to the system, and with this income they generate demand in the marketplace to which firms respond in pursuit of profit. In other words, the subunits—firms and households—work through and respond to the market.

A central issue in the comparison of economic systems is the relative merits of the planning versus the market mechanism. The contrast is apparent in that a planned economy allocates resources through the instructions of planners, thereby replacing the market's role as an allocator of resources. It is commonly argued that in a market economy there is **consumer sovereignty,** which is exercised by consumer "votes" in the marketplace. That is, the basic decisions about what to produce (which products and services) and how much are dominated by consumers. By contrast, planners' preferences dominate in a planned economy, since the important decisions about what and how much to produce are made by planners.

In fact, complete consumer sovereignty in the market economy and complete planner dominance in the planned economy are extremes not typically observed in reality. Planners often feel compelled to consider consumer preferences (say for more tv sets as opposed to more tanks) at least to some degree, perhaps for political reasons or to promote morale or provide incentives. And in market economies, advertising and the market power of large corporations tend to reduce the degree to which consumer sovereignty actually dictates resource allocation. Moreover, in market economies governments typically have considerable influence over the mix of goods and services actually produced. For example, in the United States, federal, state, and local government expenditures account for roughly one-third of total spending in the economy.

## Property Rights: Who Owns What?

The nature of property ownership arrangements has traditionally been the main feature used to classify economic systems.

The popular image of socialism, and even more so of Communism, is that the state or government owns the means of production: land, raw materials, and capital. Socialists often argue that since the state represents its citizens, the people "collectively" own the means of production through the state. In the Soviet Union the government does indeed own all the principal means of production: factories, railways, airlines, raw materials, and so forth. But even the Soviet Union allows citizens some limited ownership of the means of production in areas such as agriculture, retail trade, and housing.

At the other extreme, the popular view of capitalism holds that citizens, individually and collectively (through partnerships and corporations), own the means of production. Yet even in the capitalistic United States, where private ownership is dominant, government owns the postal service, many local transit systems, public housing, some power production facilities (the Tennessee Valley Authority), public schools and universities, highways, libraries, national parks and forest preserves, airports, bridges, fire and police protection equipment, numerous public buildings, and the means for waging war.

Ownership patterns will differ from one economic system to another. For example, Great Britain does not have as much government ownership of industry as the Soviet Union, but it does have more than the United States. However, the most important point is that differences in ownership rights affect economic outcomes in complex ways. For instance, Soviet agricultural productivity is lower than that of the United States. It is often argued that this is because Soviet farm workers have less incentive to work state-owned collective farms to meet state quotas, than American farmers have to work their own farms to make a profit for themselves. Differences in ownership lead to differences in decision making, incentives, motivation, and goals, and these lead to differences in outcomes, such as the distribution of income.

### Incentives: Material or Moral

Another important feature of an economic system is the nature of the rewards and incentives that motivate people to work in the system. Capitalistic, market-oriented societies rely mainly on the monetary or material incentives provided by wages and profits. Such a system of *material incentives* promotes desirable behavior by giving a larger claim over material goods to those who perform better than others.

Socialist societies rely more on *moral in-*centives, which promote desirable behavior by appealing to the citizen's sense of responsibility to society. For example, a worker may be awarded a medal in the name of the state for outstanding performance on the job. Note that moral incentives, unlike monetary incentives, do not provide more productive citizens with greater command over material goods.

Nowadays the authorities in most socialistic economic systems seem to recognize that material incentives are needed, that people will not respond to moral incentives alone. The early idealism of the Communist Revolution in Russia held that the state would take "from each according to his ability" and give "to each according to his needs." But experience has taught that the hardworking and able are typically not willing to settle for the same rewards received by people of lesser motivation and talent. Attempts to reward all workers equally tend to dampen the motivation of the more able and potentially harder-working members of society.

## Classifications of Economic Systems

The four basic features may be used to distinguish a few broad classifications of economic systems. Suppose we consider three: capitalism, planned socialism, and market socialism. It is important to realize in this discussion that there is no general agreement on three as the appropriate number of classifications. For example, it might be argued that the classification "capitalism" could be further subdivided according to the extent of the role played by government.

Table 21–1 shows how our three classifications of economic systems are distinguished by particular combinations of the four features. Elaborating on the table, we may define these economic systems as follows.

*Capitalism.* Decision making is decentralized and is done by households and firms. The market mechanism provides information for decision making and coordinates economic activities. Perhaps the most frequently

TABLE 21-1 **A Classification of Economic Systems**

| | Decision-Making Process | Information and Coordination Mechanism | Property Rights | Incentives |
|---|---|---|---|---|
| Capitalism | Decentralized | Market | Mainly private | Mainly material |
| Market Socialism | Mainly decentralized | Mainly market | State or collective ownership or both | Material and moral |
| Planned Socialism | Mainly centralized | Mainly plan | Mainly state ownership | Material and moral |

cited characteristic of capitalism is private ownership of the factors of production. Material incentives such as wages and profits are the primary incentives.

*Market socialism.* Decision-making authority is mainly decentralized, with information and coordination provided largely by the market mechanism. Ownership of land and capital resides principally with the state. Economic units are motivated to achieve goals by both material and moral incentives.

*Planned socialism.* Decision-making authority is mainly centralized and economic activities are coordinated by a central plan. The factors of production are owned by the state. Economic units are motivated to achieve planned goals by both material and moral incentives.

No real-world economic system fits any one of these definitions exactly. The definitions merely describe what might be considered the most important characteristics of three generally recognized types of economic systems. We will consider real-world examples of planned socialism and market socialism later in this chapter.

---

*CHECKPOINT\* 21-1*

**Do you think there is any relationship between an economic system's property rights arrangements and its system of incentives? Explain.**

*\*Answers to all Checkpoints can be found at the back of the text.*

# SOCIALISM: VARIATIONS, RECORD, AND CAPITALIST RIVALRY

We noted at the outset that any economic system is, to a large extent, a reflection of a political ideology. Let's turn now to a consideration of the ideology of socialism, its general record of economic performance, and the pros and cons of the socialist and capitalist points of view.

There is no universal model of socialism. Socialism is an ideology that has been adopted in one form or another by a variety of countries ranging from Western-style democracies to repressive Communist dictatorships, from constitutional republics to hereditary monarchies. Despite this diversity, socialists of whatever stripe share several beliefs. One is the conviction that if the means of production remain under the complete control of private owners, workers will be exploited. It was Karl Marx (1818–1883) who originally made the accusation that capitalism turned labor into a commodity and thus exploited and dehumanized workers while enriching bourgeois owners. Another socialist principle is egalitarianism, the notion that all should share equally in the fruits of production. A closely related socialist belief is that people live for society, or, in a more extreme form, that the individual exists to serve the state—as opposed to the more capitalistic idea that the state exists to serve the individual.

## ECONOMIC THINKERS

### Karl Marx—1818–1883

Karl Marx combined his abilities as a philosopher, sociologist, historian, economist, and professional revolutionary to become the chief founder of revolutionary Communism. His criticisms of capitalism and prophecies of its downfall have inspired socialist movements and Communist revolutions throughout the world. Marx and his lifelong benefactor and collaborator Friedrich Engels published the *Communist Manifesto* in 1848, the most succinct statement of Marxist ideas, as well as the best-known declaration of the principles of the international Communist movement.

Marx's most complete and celebrated work is *Das Kapital,* the first volume of which was published in 1867; the second and third volumes were edited and published posthumously by Engels. In *Das Kapital* Marx described and analyzed what he considered to be the historically inevitable transition from capitalism to socialism. According to Marx, society's beliefs, laws, and ideologies reflect and are shaped by the material conditions of life and the material interests of different classes. Marx argued that the production process under capitalism inevitably gives rise to a division of labor that results in two classes—a ruling class, the capitalists who own the means of production, and an oppressed class, the workers who are exploited

by the capitalists. Indeed, Marx claimed that all history could be viewed as a struggle between the ruling and the working classes. Capitalism would be but one stage in that conflict.

Marx argued that private ownership of the means of production under capitalism was the heart of the class conflict. Moreover, he claimed that capitalism would experience severe periods of depression and inflation that, coupled with an increasing class consciousness among workers, would lead to capitalism's collapse. The collapse would take place when the *proletariat* (working class) revolted against the *bourgeoisie* (owners of the means of production, the capitalists). Then, Marx claimed, man would be truly free. The means of production would be publicly owned by the whole community, and there would be a classless society. Even the government, formerly used to oppress the working class, would become unnecessary and "wither away." In the new classless, Communist society, individuals would contribute "according to their ability" and take "according to their needs."

Many of Marx's prophecies have not come to pass. Communist revolutions have not occurred in the advanced capitalist societies, as Marx predicted, but rather in countries with less developed economies such as Russia (1917) and China (1949). Moreover, in advanced capitalist countries the distinction between the owners of the means of production and the working class has become less sharp as the growth of the modern corporation has opened business ownership to masses of small investors. In addition, increased upward and downward social and economic mobility in Western economies has lessened class consciousness. Finally, in the most advanced Communist countries, such as the Soviet Union, the government shows no signs of "withering away," nor can it be said that these societies are classless. Perhaps Marx's most enduring contribution is his perception of society as a process of continual change, an ongoing struggle for power between competing groups motivated by their particular material interests in the production process.

FOR FURTHER READING

Balinsky, Alexander. *Marx's Economics: Origins and Development.* Lexington, Mass.: Heath, 1970.

Heilbroner, Robert L. *Marxism: For and Against.* New York: Norton, 1980.

We will briefly consider the main political forms of socialism in today's world, the overall experience of countries living under socialism, and the most often heard socialist criticisms of capitalism.

## Socialism in Today's World

Although it may take on many forms, socialism in today's world is recognizable in three main political varieties: Communism, social democracy, and third world socialism. We emphasize that these are *political* classifications, as distinct from the two *economic* classifications of socialism—market socialism and planned socialism. Any one of the three political varieties of socialism may have an economic system that is either market socialism or planned socialism. For example, China and Yugoslavia are both classified politically as Communist countries. Yet the economic system of China generally would be classified as planned socialism, while that of Yugoslavia typically would be classified as market socialism.

### *Communism*

Sometimes called Marxism-Leninism, Communism is the form of socialism governing the Soviet Union and its East bloc satellites, as well as Albania, Cambodia, China, Cuba, Laos, Mongolia, North Korea, Vietnam, and Yugoslavia. Communism is the most totalitarian form of socialism. With a religious zeal, its adherents preach the necessity of class warfare. It calls for a dictatorship of the proletariat (the working class) and the concentration of near total power in a tightly structured party that supposedly represents the revolutionary masses. Communism's ultimate goal is a classless society in which there is no private property and the means of production are owned by the state.

### *Social Democracy*

Social democracy is the most liberal and flexible form of socialism. At various times in the postwar era, social democrats have controlled the governments of Austria, Belgium, Britain, Denmark, Finland, Luxembourg, the Netherlands, Norway, Portugal, and Sweden, to name only European examples. Social democracy involves the belief in gradual, peaceful means of reaching socialist goals, and it accepts a multiparty political system. Hence, social democrats have concentrated on removing what they regard as the hardships created by capitalist economies (such as unemployment and "unjust" wage and salary differences). They are less interested than Communists in restructuring societies according to some utopian blueprint. States ruled by social democrats are generally mixed economies, combining state ownership or direction of key industries with elements of free-enterprise competition and the market mechanism.

### *Third World Socialism*

The term *third world socialism* refers to the variety of socialist regimes that exist among the underdeveloped countries of the world. These include such different systems as the Islamic socialism of Algeria and Libya, the Baathist socialism of Syria and Iraq, and the communalism of tribal Africa. Despite the differences among third world socialist countries, they have several things in common. First, although these countries call themselves socialist, their beliefs may be rooted more in nationalism than in the tenets of traditional Marxism. Second, they reject capitalism, identifying it with imperialism and exploitation, largely because of their experience with the colonialism of capitalist countries. Third, they tend to discourage investment by foreign firms and pursue policies aimed at decreasing the economic role of private property.

## The Socialist Experience

What has been the overall experience of countries living under socialism? We can only summarize it briefly here, focusing on such issues as economic performance, the extent of liberty and respect for individual freedom, the general quality of life, and the extent to which socialist countries have achieved the equality of the classless society.

### Economic Performance

All socialist countries try to inject order into their economies through government controls or by use of central planning. All reject what they consider the wasteful disorder of the capitalist marketplace. Socialists believe that controls and central planning will give rise to increased output, a more equitable distribution of goods, and a greater concentration of resources in socially useful production.

*Communist States.* Communist states can point to many significant achievements, which they attribute to their Five-Year Plans and all-embracing command of industry and agriculture. The Soviet Union has made dramatic economic gains, transforming itself in 6 decades from a war-shattered economy in the earliest stages of industrialization into a military superpower that produces more steel, crude oil, and manganese than the United States. The Chinese Communists seem to be on a similar growth path, and appear to have banished the recurring famines that once plagued that country's vast population.

However, Communist economic systems are having some serious difficulties. Communist countries claim to have abolished unemployment, but it appears they have succeeded only in hiding it in the form of underemployment—in heavily overstaffed offices and factories, for example, where workers seldom can be fired for failing to produce, or where workers cannot be kept fully occupied with productive work. Often bureaucratic controls reduce efficiency and leave managers little leeway for innovation. Consumer goods are chronically scarce and typically shoddy. Rumors that a shop is about to receive a shipment of shoes, fresh fruit, or fish often cause long lines to form in Moscow, Warsaw,

Prague, Havana, and other Communist cities. Communist countries claim to be immune to inflation. But in fact inflation is merely hidden because wages, prices, and even the kinds of goods available are set by the state. For example, while the "official" price of a good can remain stable for years, the product may not be available except on the black market, where it sells at a much higher price.

One of the most troublesome problems in Communist countries is lagging agricultural output. Critics argue that agricultural productivity suffers because state ownership of farmland deadens the initiative of farm workers. Hence, despite heavy investment in farm machinery and irrigation systems, food productivity remains low.

Yugoslavia is the least rigidly controlled economy in Eastern Europe, and it seems to have the fewest economic problems among Communist states. Yugoslav enterprises outperform the state-owned plants of most other Communist countries. Many observers argue that this is because Yugoslav planning and management have been decentralized. In addition, hard work and quality output have been rewarded with wage increases and generous bonuses.

*Social Democracies.* Social democrats have mostly come to power in industrially advanced and politically democratic nations. Therefore their efforts to change existing systems—by nationalizing industries, for example—have been cautious. Social democrats have pressed toward their goal of greater income equality by levying steep progressive taxes on income (up to 98 percent in Britain, 72 percent in the Netherlands, and 85 percent in Sweden) and on capital gains, profits, and inheritances. The tax revenues have been used to provide a host of cradle-to-grave benefits, such as nationalized health care. This practice amounts to taking income from those with higher incomes and redistributing it in the form of goods and services to the rest of the citizenry.

However, there are increasing fears that these heavy taxes have begun to discourage initiative, innovation, and enterprise by reducing the material rewards from work. This shows up in several ways: increased worker absenteeism; the emigration of skilled professionals (such as doctors and engineers), managers, and entrepreneurs to countries with lower tax rates; and increased tax evasion through the use of barter, which leaves no record for snooping tax collectors.

Social democrats have also weakened some of the traditional rights of property ownership. For example, British and Dutch laws have made it increasingly difficult for management to fire workers.

*Third World Socialists.* Many third world countries have turned to socialism as much from necessity as ideology. Since few of their citizens were able to develop managerial and entrepreneurial skills under colonialism, central planning and socialism often seemed the only way to solve their economic problems once they became independent.

Most third world socialist countries have placed centralized controls on their economies and have nationalized manufacturing, mining, and agriculture. But due to poor management and, often, corruption, the results frequently have been disappointing. While socialist regimes may have aided economic growth in some instances, high population growth rates have made it difficult to increase living standards.

### Liberty and Individual Freedom

Socialists have routinely accused capitalism of wage slavery, and of worker exploitation and alienation. They have long claimed that socialism will end these and other forms of repression. However, aside from social democracy, the historical record suggests just the opposite.

Instead of greater liberty, Communism and third world socialism have invariably led to authoritarian one-party and even one-man rule. The Soviet constitution guarantees freedom of speech, but it is in practice not guaranteed at all. Serious critics of the re-

gime are harassed, imprisoned, exiled, and even threatened with execution. Workers' strikes are not allowed. All organs of information and communication are rigidly controlled and used for the purposes of the state. How do Communists justify such human rights violations? They usually argue that the situation is only temporary, that once true Communism is established the dictatorship of the proletariat will disappear and the individual will be truly free. Among some third world socialist countries, the record on liberty and respect for individual freedom is no better than that of Communist countries.

In contrast, the social-democratic governments of Western Europe and elsewhere have consistently shown respect for parliamentary processes and human rights. Nevertheless, certain developments in social democracies pose potentially worrisome threats to liberties. Expanding bureaucracies, spawned by ambitious economic and social programs, threaten to become much larger than those in nonsocialist states. Large bureaucracies represent large concentrations of power that can and often do restrict individual freedom and enterprise. Critics of socialism argue that it is surely more than coincidence that the only functioning democracies are the capitalist or mixed-economy countries, while, except for the social democracies, authoritarianism is a fact of life in every socialist country.

### General Quality of Life

State-provided social services are a hallmark of socialist regimes. Elaborate programs for improving health care and expanding educational facilities are typically top-priority items in socialist countries. Consequently, in most socialist states, infant mortality has dropped dramatically, life expectancy has risen, and illiteracy has been greatly reduced.

In China, the mass training of doctors, nurses, and paramedics and the establishment of rural health centers have nearly eliminated cholera, plague, and other diseases that had periodically ravaged the population for centuries. When Castro came to power in Cuba in 1959, nearly one-quarter of the population could not read or write. Since then, illiteracy has been reduced to less than 4 percent by compulsory primary education and an ambitious school construction program.

The essential human services provided by Communist states often match and sometimes top those of Western democracies. Illness seldom imposes heavy financial burdens on patients. Eastern European states offer free education, though the Communist parties have considerable control over who is admitted to the universities.

The social democracies have provided an extensive array of social services, often referred to collectively as the welfare state. For example, Swedish citizens are given annual allowances for each child, free tuition through college, free hospital care, sick pay equal to 90 percent of working wages, and a substantial retirement pension. The British Labour party has passed laws that provide maternity allowances, free family planning services, retirement pensions, income supplements, and health care that includes treatment for alcoholism and drug addiction. However, critics of the British health-care system point out that treatment is impersonal and that there are often long waits for admission to hospitals.

In Communist states, central planning commissions, not consumers, decide what will be produced and how much. As a result, desired consumer goods and services are often scarce. Central planning and government controls give rise to economic inefficiencies that cause bottlenecks in production and shortages of most consumer goods. These difficulties contribute to the corruption, black marketeering, bribery, and theft that are reported to be a considerable problem in Communist states. For example, bribery is a recognized way of avoiding a prolonged wait in buying a car. While medical care is supposed to be free, demand so exceeds supply in some Communist states that it is often necessary to bribe doctors or hospital administrators just to get a bed.

### Equality or a New Elite?

A cornerstone of socialist ideology is that capitalism gives rise to an unjust gulf between rich and poor, between the privileged and the downtrodden. Socialism makes a moral commitment to egalitarianism. Has the commitment been realized?

Communism seems to have spawned a kind of class distinction of its own. The new privileged class in Communist states consists of party officials, managers of state enterprises, ranking bureaucrats, and superstars from sports and the arts. This new class receives larger monetary rewards than other citizens. However, because Communist states are often short of certain kinds of goods, the comfortable life-style of the new class depends less on money than on their privileged access to scarce goods and services. In the Soviet Union, various grades of party officials have access to special stores selling imported and otherwise scarce goods at very low prices. Average Soviet citizens never see such a selection of goods in the stores where they must shop. Even supposedly classless China is not exempt from the new elitism. High-ranking Chinese officials have access to special shops, and their children have access to special schools.

Social democracies have pursued egalitarianism by using taxes to redistribute income and wealth. As we have already noted, the tax revenues from inheritance taxes and steeply progressive personal income taxes are used to provide all manner of medical, educational, and other social services to the general citizenry of social democracies.

### Socialist Criticisms of Capitalism and the Capitalist Response

Debates over the relative merits of socialism and capitalism are often more emotional than informative. Here we will briefly outline some of socialism's main criticisms of capitalism, along with responses from the capitalist point of view.

### Inequalities of Wealth and Income

Socialist critics of capitalism charge that it creates severe inequalities of wealth and extravagantly rewards success.

Capitalism's defenders respond that the inequality of wealth under the free-enterprise system is the unavoidable result of the rewards that must be offered to encourage hard work, risk taking, and genius. They are quick to argue that the equality of results desired by socialist reformers tends to discourage initiative and produce a stagnant society and that, in fact, there is inequality in socialist countries as well. Winston Churchill once put it this way: "The inherent vice of capitalism is the unequal sharing of blessings; the inherent virtue of socialism is the equal sharing of miseries."

Capitalist societies have acknowledged some socialist criticism, particularly that large differences in income can be a cause of serious social tensions. Progressive income taxes and social welfare programs are capitalism's way of providing some leveling of income. On the issue of income distribution, capitalism's defenders are quick to point out that Marx's predictions were off the mark. Marx predicted that capitalists would push workers deeper into poverty. But in fact capitalism has lifted the vast majority of workers into the middle class. Moreover, labor unions have given workers an effective counterforce to management power.

### Instability of Capitalist Economies

Communism claims that capitalism requires periodic depressions in order to keep workers poor and on the defensive.

The business cycle has always plagued capitalism. However, some defenders of capitalism (such as Joseph Schumpeter) have argued that recessions are often beneficial because they purge the system of excesses, poor products, and mismanaged companies. Moreover, such slumps have been less severe since World War II. In addition, unemployment insurance has greatly reduced the hardship of those thrown out of work.

### Assumptions About Human Nature

Socialists have argued that the uncertainty of the marketplace and the social flux associated with capitalism, coupled with the drive for profit, cause people to be overly competitive, warped, and aggressive.

Defenders of capitalism respond that while socialism assumes that people are cooperative and instinctively look out for one another, capitalism has never had any such illusions about human nature. Adam Smith argued that each individual is motivated strongly and primarily by what is in his or her best self-interest. Defenders of capitalism argue that the economic success of capitalist countries lies precisely in the way such an economic system harnesses the self-interest of the individual to promote the general good of all. Advocates of capitalism argue that socialism blunts the powerful force of individual self-interest by stressing equality of reward regardless of performance and by eliminating the private ownership of the means of production.

### The Mix of Goods in Capitalist Economies

Critics have charged that a capitalistic market system tends to value wasteful private consumption more than needed public services.

Capitalists respond that the types of goods produced by any economic system raise the fundamental question of who is to direct and dominate whom. Defenders of capitalism argue that the market system provides the most democratic answers. By voting in the marketplace, consumers decide what should be produced, rather than having government planners dictate what society should produce. Nevertheless, even the most capitalistic governments tamper with the market mechanism to some extent, if only to regulate the money supply, set tariffs and import duties, and levy taxes. However, while socialists see the state as the main engine of social change, capitalists view such interference as an unfortunate but necessary compromise with an ideal. But capitalism has had to recognize, to some extent, the demands for social justice advanced by socialism.

### Capitalism's Ultimate Defense

Advocates of capitalism argue that its ultimate justification is that it permits and promotes freedom. How? By reserving ownership of the means of production for the private citizen, not the state. Defenders of capitalism argue that freedom is not possible without economic freedom. In the words of Hilaire Belloc, British poet and essayist, "The control of the production of wealth is the control of human life itself." According to the defenders of capitalism, history suggests that the more the state attempts to control society, for whatever desirable end, the greater are the ultimate restrictions on individual freedom.

### A Spectrum of Real-World Economic Systems

We have noted before that any classification of economic systems, such as that in Table 21–1, is an oversimplification. Nonetheless, most economists agree that real-world economic systems can be characterized as lying along a spectrum between pure, market economy capitalism at one extreme and pure, centrally planned socialism at the other. At any rate, any debate over the pros and cons of capitalism versus socialism that tries to look at the evidence must necessarily construct such a spectrum.

An example is provided in Figure 21–1. The countries indicated are listed along the spectrum according to the degree to which their economic systems tend to be more like one of the extremes—pure, market economy capitalism on the left or pure, centrally planned socialism on the right. Listed beside each country is a number indicating its rank among all countries in the world according to a measure of the country's economic and social conditions.

---

### CHECKPOINT 21-2
**What are the main differences between Communism and social democracy?**

---

## TWO SOCIALIST COUNTRIES: CHINA AND YUGOSLAVIA

We will now look briefly at two socialist economies: that of China, which is an example of planned socialism, and that of Yugoslavia, an example of market socialism. Politically, these two countries adhere to Communism. The economic system of each will be characterized in terms of the four basic features that we examined at the outset of this chapter: the decision-making process, information and coordination mechanism, property rights, and incentives.

### China and Planned Socialism

When the Chinese Communist party came to power in 1949, China was an underdeveloped country with a population about four times larger than that of the United States, and a land mass only slightly greater than ours. There was significant population pressure on arable land and other resources. Per capita income was low. Starting with a predominantly rural, peasant economy, the Chinese Communists have used planned socialism to achieve a substantial degree of economic growth and development.

Rapid industrialization has been the primary objective of the Chinese Communist regime since the founding of the People's Republic of China by Mao Tse-tung in 1949. However, this objective has been pursued jointly with other goals, such as the reeducation of the populace to increase social consciousness and the subordination of the self to the group, the achievement of a more equal distribution of income, and the provision of some guaranteed minimum standard of living for the individual. These social goals have often conflicted with the main goal, rapid industrialization. And from time to time this conflict has resulted in abrupt shifts in policy when it was deemed important to shore up progress toward the social goals—usually following periods of sustained progress toward industrialization.

**FIGURE 21-1  A Spectrum of Economic Systems and a World Ranking of Selected Countries by Economic and Social Conditions**

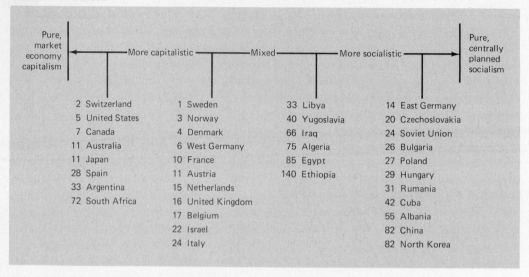

The countries shown here are listed along a spectrum according to the degree to which their economic systems tend to be more like pure, market economy capitalism at the one extreme or pure, centrally planned socialism at the other.

The number beside each country indicates its rank among all countries in the world according to a measure of the country's economic and social conditions. Rank is based on average ranks for gross national product per capita, education (encompassing public expenditures per capita, school-age population per teacher, percent school-age population in school, percent women in total university employment, and literacy rate), and health (encompassing public expenditures per capita, population per physician, population per hospital bed, infant mortality rate, and life expectancy).

SOURCE: Ruth Leger Sivard, *World Military and Social Expenditures,* World Priorities, Inc., Leesburg, Va., 1980.

## *Decision-Making Process*

Up until October 1984 all major industrial enterprises in China were under central control. In the autumn of 1984 the Chinese Communist party's Central Committee approved a landmark economic plan aimed at a gradual abandonment of Soviet-style central planning. Over the next several years, more than a million state enterprises and factories are to be cut loose from government planning and protection and will rise or fall on their own economic merit. It is too early to tell how this bold move toward market socialism will actually work, or how quickly it will be implemented. But much of Chinese industry was already decentralized, with control resting with authorities at the provincial and local levels. And the setting of prices was already largely decentralized to the provincial level. In the past both central and provincial authorities have allocated the most important producer goods, such as capital equipment.

The Chinese Communist party plays a large role in the decision-making process throughout the economic system and has often intervened directly in management. But the party's Central Committee communique of October 1984 states that: "From now on government departments at various levels will, in principle, not manage or operate enterprises directly." In sum, while the overall system seems basically a command system, there is a fair degree of freedom of action at local levels, coupled with some officially sanctioned use of the market mechanism.

The Soviet system of planned socialism served as the original model for the Chinese Communists. While there is considerable similarity between the organizational and administrative structures of the two countries, the differences suggest that there is more flexibility of organization and administration in China. In addition, small-scale firms, often using primitive techniques and the large supply of unskilled labor, are much commoner in China than in the Soviet Union. Moreover, in China there seems to be relatively greater freedom of action at local levels and more legal use of the market mechanism. The economic plan approved in 1984 indicates that China will definitely move even further away from the Soviet model of planned socialism.

### Information and Coordination Mechanism

The primary information and coordination mechanism in China has been the national economic plan. The Chinese planning structure, initiated in the early 1950s, was patterned after the Soviet model. Experience has led to subsequent modifications. The enterprise is the basic unit of production activity. A dual party-state administrative structure generates and implements a 5-year plan to guide both agricultural and industrial production. Plans are initially formulated by the State Planning Commission. The commission communicates with regional and enterprise officials through an industrial ministry system to arrive ultimately at a final working plan. Then after approval by the State Council (the highest administrative body, directed by the premier), the plan becomes law.

The process of generating a workable plan is complicated. The State Planning Commission specifies output targets—a list of goods and services to be produced during the plan period. Based on knowledge of the quantities of inputs (land, labor, and capital) required to produce a unit of output, the commission assigns inputs to the production of the various output targets. Obviously, the commission would like to produce as much as possible, but production is limited by the availability of inputs. If sufficient inputs are not available for a particular output target, then either the output target must be reduced or additional inputs must be allocated to that target. When all factor input allocations have been made, there must be an aggregate input balance for the whole economy, termed a *material balance*. That is, the sum of the amounts of all factor inputs needed to produce all output targets must equal the sum of all available factor inputs.

Using both central direction and local information, a material balance eventually is reached. There are difficulties in this process, however. Inevitably, the very complexity of the process, coupled with the usual unforeseeable "snafus" of any production activity, gives rise to imbalances and shortages, poor quality, and deviations of results from targets.

### Property Rights

State ownership of the means of production predominates in China. The transfer of ownership of economic units began almost immediately after the Chinese Communists seized control in 1949. During the land reform of 1950, the holdings of landlords and some of the holdings of the rich peasants were seized. Some land was distributed to landless laborers and poorer peasants. However, most of the land was used to establish large collective farms, or communes, owned by the state. The communes each comprised an average of almost 5,000 households. For capital as well, private ownership was largely replaced by state ownership. By 1956, ownership and control in industry, finance, agriculture, and various other production sectors rested with the government.

In 1978 China did an about-face on agricultural policy and began dismantling collectivized farming, restoring family farms and villages, and introducing production and free-market incentives to a rural population of 800 million. Production soared. The policy's success spawned the economic plan of 1984 aimed at applying some of the same types of reforms to the industrial sectors of the economy.

### Incentives

While the Soviet Union has served as a model for the Chinese Communists, the Chinese have tended to put more stress on moral incentives as opposed to material incentives. Indeed, ideological fervor has generally been more characteristic of the Chinese experience than of the Soviet. The Chinese have emphasized that the pursuit of social aims should accompany industrial progress. Chief among these aims is the development of a socially conscious citizenry guided by concern for the common good rather than for material possessions.

Yet material incentives do play a role in the Chinese economy, and inequality in the distribution of income does exist. Evidence suggests that there may be as much inequality of income in China as in the Soviet Union. Moreover, among the economic policy changes approved by the party's Central Committee in the bold initiative of 1984 was an expressed intent to tolerate larger income differentials and an endorsement of the idea that some people must be allowed to accumulate wealth and improve their standard of living before others.

Moral incentives in China take the form of ideological indoctrination and close administrative, even coercive, control. Such means are used to stimulate job performance as well as to transfer labor among firms, industries, and regions of the country.

On the income-equalizing side, most medical and educational services are free. In addition, China has an extensive social security system that provides a floor under every citizen's standard of living. Finally, compared to other Communist countries, the quality, variety, and availability of consumer goods in China is generally quite good.

## Yugoslavia and Market Socialism

A Communist regime led by Tito took control of Yugoslavia after World War II, accomplishing this feat without the assistance of the Soviet Union. From the end of the war until 1949, the Yugoslavs patterned their economy after the Soviet example of planned socialism. However, as a consequence of a falling out between Tito and Stalin in 1948, Yugoslavs undertook a critical reevaluation of their economic system. They concluded that it neglected consumer needs and was inefficient and overcentralized, and that the individual worker had no sense of meaningful involvement in the production process. Moreover, the collectivization of agriculture (the creation of state-owned farms) hampered agricultural productivity and was unpopular with farm workers.

These shortcomings led the Yugoslavs to remodel their economic system along the lines of market socialism. Since 1950 their system has combined management by workers with a relatively high degree of decentralization and reliance on the market mechanism.

### Decision-Making Process

Self-management of enterprises (firms) by workers is probably the most distinctive feature of the Yugoslav economic system. Worker self-management is based on the idea that workers (including white-collar employees) will run an enterprise well, even though they do not own it. In fact, they do have a financial interest in the enterprise, insofar as their wages are tied to its financial success or failure.

Within the individual enterprise, the highest governing body is the workers' council, which is elected by and responsible to all the enterprise's employees. The workers' council is responsible for the hiring (and firing) of an enterprise director, who runs the enterprise on a day-to-day basis. In addition, the workers' council has long-range policymaking responsibilities, such as setting wage rate differentials and establishing smaller decision-making units within the enterprise.

The enterprise is related to the rest of the economy much more by means of the market mechanism than by a Soviet-style command hierarchy. The enterprise director and workers' council develop an operating plan that determines what the enterprise will produce and, to a limited extent, the selling price. State control over prices has increased in recent years.

The state has maintained substantial control over the flow of bank loans to enterprises. The central banking system influences the flow of credit to coincide with regional or national objectives. In some instances the state uses rules to allocate enterprise income between investment and wages. This reflects state concern that worker-managed firms might allocate too much income to wages and not enough to investment in plant and equipment, which would retard Yugoslavia's economic growth.

The Yugoslav Communist party does not have the kind of centralized power of the Communist parties in China, the Soviet Union, and elsewhere in Eastern Europe. However, it is an important force in decision making, since many managers are party members. The labor unions that exist in Yugoslavia are also closely associated with the party. At the plant level they tend to handle worker grievances rather than wage bargaining with individual enterprises. On the national level they have on occasion fought for an increase in the portion of national income going to private consumption. From time to time there are strikes by workers against their own managements. Sometimes whole enterprises strike against the central authorities when there is discontent with the government's setting of taxes, control of prices, or management of investment funds, all of which affect the fortunes of the labor-managed enterprises.

## Information and Coordination Mechanism

Compared to the planned socialism of China or the Soviet Union, Yugoslavia has a relatively weak planning apparatus. Planned socialist economies impose compulsory plans from above. By contrast, under the market socialism of Yugoslavia, national plans originate with the enterprises—they are constructed "from the ground up." Enterprises declare their targets to planners, who aggregate these targets into a national plan. In 1976 a social-planning law was passed, requiring enterprises to draw up long-term plans committing themselves to output, wage, price, and investment targets. Enterprises that fail to meet the targets of their own plans are subject to fines, although there is some doubt about the actual significance of such penalties. Investment is the one area of the Yugoslav economy for which there is any significant centralized planning. Here the government exercises considerable influence over the flow of investment funds among the republics and provinces of Yugoslavia. Overall, however, the production and distribution of output is primarily a decentralized process consistent with the model of market socialism.

The extent to which markets have been allowed to operate free of government interference has varied over time. Until 1970, most enterprises set their own production schedules and selling prices. Exceptions were the product prices set by monopolists and near monopolists, which were negotiated with government authorities; ceiling prices on certain "strategic" goods, which were set by government; price supports on some agricultural products; and periodic price freezes on some or all goods. In the late 1960s, some 40 percent of prices were subject to some form of direct price control. However, since the mid-1970s this figure has risen to about 80 percent.

Since 1971 there has been more state control in the Yugoslav economic system. Much of this control represents a response to higher unemployment, increased inflation, and balance of payments problems—the same difficulties facing many capitalist economies. Nonetheless, worker self-management remains dominant, economic decisions still are made largely at the enterprise level, and planning is still done at the enterprise level.

### Property Rights

In Yugoslavia property rights reside mostly with the state. However, private ownership predominates in agriculture, where about 85 percent of arable land is in private hands. The only restriction on private farms is that they are not allowed to be larger than 24.7 acres. Outside of agriculture, there is private ownership in small-scale production and trade, although a private employer may employ no more than five persons (excepting family members). The assets of all other Yugoslav enterprises are held in trust for society by the workers who manage the enterprises. In other words, these assets are state owned.

### Incentives

Market socialism places much greater emphasis on material incentives than does planned socialism, where moral incentives are more important. In Yugoslavia a minimum annual wage is guaranteed to the workers in worker-managed enterprises. Wages in excess of the minimum may be paid if the enterprise performs well. Obviously, this provides workers with an incentive to operate the enterprise so as to maximize net income—the difference between revenues from sales and the costs of production. If an enterprise does not earn enough net income to cover the guaranteed minimum wages, then the workers are paid out of a reserve fund maintained for this purpose. If an enter-

prise's reserve fund is inadequate, the state must subsidize the minimum-wage payment.

Subject to limits set by law, each enterprise's workers' council determines the wage differentials that are to exist within their enterprise. These differentials are used to reward special employee contributions to the success of the enterprise. Because some enterprises are more successful than others, it is common for workers doing the same task in different enterprises to earn different wages. (Nevertheless, some evidence suggests that wage differentials are smaller in Yugoslavia than in most Western European countries.) Given such differentials, and given the freedom of worker mobility in Yugoslavia, workers obviously have an incentive to make their job choices based on the earning prospects of different enterprises. This enhances the efficiency of the Yugoslav economy, because labor tends to be allocated to those productive activities that use it most effectively.

Individual enterprises make their decisions about outputs, inputs, technology, and investments largely in response to the market incentives provided by prices. In turn, the activities of all enterprises are interrelated and coordinated primarily by the market mechanism. The market mechanism is not allowed to work unchecked, however. Under capitalism, continued losses by a firm usually put it out of business. In Yugoslavia, failing enterprises are typically kept afloat with help from local authorities and the banks. Moreover, Yugoslav authorities do not particularly encourage price competition. Antitrust-type laws are weak, and enterprises are allowed to collude through the formation of business associations.

The force of moral incentives and persuasion is represented by government officials and the Communist party. Although the Communist party in Yugoslavia does not have the centralized power of the parties in other Communist countries, it does have an important role in the Yugoslav economic system.

## CHECKPOINT 21-3
**Compare and contrast the economic systems of China and Yugoslavia in terms of the four criteria listed in Table 21-1.**

## SUMMARY

**1.** An economic system consists of the institutions, rules, and decision-making processes used to organize and allocate scarce resources to produce and distribute goods and services. Each country's economic system may differ from that of every other in a number of ways.

**2.** There are four basic features to any economic system: the process by which decisions are made, the mechanism for providing information and coordinating activities, the nature of property rights, and the types of incentives used to motivate performance. The details of these features may be used to compare and classify economic systems. One useful classification scheme identifies the following economic systems: capitalism, market socialism, and planned socialism.

**3.** Under capitalism, decision making is decentralized among households and firms; the market mechanism determines prices, which provide economic information and coordinate economic activity; the means of production are privately owned; and incentives are mainly material—prices and wages. Under market socialism, decision making is mainly decentralized, information and coordination are provided mainly by the market mechanism, assets are owned mainly by the state, and incentives are both material and moral. Under planned socialism, decision making is mainly centralized, information and coordination are provided mainly by plan, assets are predominantly owned by the state, and incentives are mainly moral.

**4.** There are three basic political variants of

socialism in today's world: Communism, social democracy, and third world socialism. Communism, the most totalitarian form of socialism, advocates class warfare, dictatorship by the proletariat, and the achievement of a classless society with state ownership of the means of production. Social democracy advocates gradual, peaceful means of reaching socialist goals in the context of a multiparty political system. Third world socialism consists mainly of a variety of socialist regimes among the underdeveloped countries; these tend to be nationalistic, to identify capitalism with imperialism, to subordinate the role of private property, and to discourage investment by foreign firms.

**5.** Communist regimes have made some dramatic economic gains, industrializing relatively backward economies and achieving notable economic growth. However, they tend to suffer from cumbersome bureaucracies, chronically scarce and shoddy consumer goods, lagging agricultural output, and bureaucratic controls that stifle efficiency and innovation. Social democracy, typically found in industrially advanced states, tends to concentrate on nationalizing existing industries and income redistribution through the levying of heavy taxes to finance elaborate social welfare programs. There is concern in social democracies that heavy taxation is discouraging initiative, innovation, and enterprise. Economic performance among third world socialist countries has been disappointing for the most part.

**6.** Communist and third world socialist regimes have shown little regard for liberty and individual freedom. Social democracies have consistently shown respect for individual freedom, although many see a potential threat in the growing concentration of power in large government bureaucracies.

**7.** The general quality of life, measured by such standards as availability of health care, educational opportunity, and cradle-to-grave social services, is impressive in most Communist and social-democratic countries. However, there are deficiencies as regards the general availability, variety, and quality of consumer goods in Communist countries.

**8.** Although socialist ideology advocates egalitarianism, Communist states have spawned an elite class of party officials, managers, ranking bureaucrats, and superstars in sports and the arts. This privileged class has access to otherwise scarce goods and services. Social democracies have promoted egalitarianism by redistributing income through taxation and the provision of all kinds of social services.

**9.** Socialism charges capitalism with creating inequalities of wealth and income; capitalism's defense is that this is the inevitable result of the rewards necessary to encourage enterprise and a dynamic economy. Communism charges that capitalism needs depressions to keep workers in line; capitalism responds that such episodes have been less severe since World War II, and that unemployment insurance has reduced the hardship of the unemployed. Socialism charges that capitalism makes people overly competitive and aggressive; capitalism responds that people are naturally motivated by self-interest and that capitalism's strength lies in the harnessing of such self-interest to promote the good of all. Socialism charges that capitalism promotes wasteful private consumption while shortchanging needed public services; capitalism responds that it provides more democratic answers to the question of the proper mix by allowing consumers to decide this question rather than planners. Capitalism's ultimate defense to all charges is that it best promotes freedom.

**10.** China has used planned socialism to achieve a substantial degree of economic growth and development. China's economic system is basically a command system, combined with a degree of freedom of action at local levels and some (officially permitted) use of the market mechanism. A national economic plan is the primary information and coordinating mechanism in China. State ownership of the means of production predominates. Moral incentives are heavily stressed through ideological indoctrination, administrative control, and even coercion. Material incentives are also used, particularly in agriculture.

**11.** Yugoslav market socialism is an attempt to improve on shortcomings in the Soviet model of planned socialism. A keystone of the Yugoslav system is the self-management of enterprises by workers. The enterprises are related to the rest of the economy by the market mechanism. A national plan is constructed by aggregating individual enterprise plans, but except for investment planning, there is little centralized planning. Except for agriculture and small enterprises, all property is held in trust for society by the workers who manage the enterprises. Material incentives in the form of wages and prices play a large role in Yugoslavia, although price controls, lax enforcement of antitrust-type laws, and government support of failing enterprises somewhat dampen competition and modify market forces.

## KEY TERMS AND CONCEPTS

consumer sovereignty
economic system
market economy
planned economy

## QUESTIONS AND PROBLEMS

**1.** What are the main differences between a capitalistic economic system and a socialistic economic system?

**2.** Socialism is often criticized for focusing too much on equality of results, such as a more equal distribution of income. It has been argued that equality of opportunity is more important for economic performance, and that there is a conflict between equality of results and equality of opportunity. Explain why you either agree or disagree with this point of view.

**3.** Do you think there is any relationship between an economic system's decision-making arrangements and the nature of its information and coordinating mechanism? Explain.

**4.** Some have claimed that socialism is a society based on cooperation instead of competition. What do you think an advocate of capitalism would say about the relationship between cooperation and competition?

**5.** Explain the nature of the relationship, if any, between an economic system's information and coordination mechanism and the nature of its system of incentives.

**6.** Yugoslav authorities have been concerned that the worker-managed enterprise might be too oriented to the short run. What is there about the incentive structure within such an enterprise that might justify this concern, and what are the implications for the economic performance of the Yugoslav economy?

**7.** Why is the concept of material balance important to the information and coordination mechanism used in China? What is the equivalent concept in a capitalistic economic system?

# Hints and Answers to Checkpoints

## CHAPTER 1

### Checkpoint 1-1

There is considerable leeway on what might be counted as correct in response to this question. Some statements in the news item have both positive and normative elements. What should be emphasized are the (potentially, at least) *verifiable* nature of the positive statements in the paragraph and the value-judgment nature of the normative statements. The use of "loaded language" as a prop for a shortage of factual statements should be noted.

### Checkpoint 1-2

The long gas lines could have been shortened—that is, the quantity of gasoline demanded could have been reduced—if the price of gas had been increased.

### Checkpoint 1-3

If the demand in the other city is less sensitive to changes in price, then the graph of its demand would be more vertical than the demand curve illustrated in Figure 1-3. This would show that a change in price would induce a smaller change in quantity demanded in the less sensitive city. Hence, the city whose demand is illustrated in Figure 1-3 would experience the greatest reduction in the quantity of electricity demanded, given an equal price change in the two cities.

### Checkpoint 1-4

Some examples of cause-and-effect confusion might include:

*People looking at the night sky for a longer time will see more shooting stars than people who look for a shorter time. But this does not mean that looking at the sky longer causes more shooting stars.*

*Ships can often be seen preparing to sail before high tide. But this does not mean that preparing to sail causes high tide.*

A football game crowd illustrates the fallacy of composition in this way: If one person stands up to watch the game, he or she will be able to see the game better. But this certainly does not remain true if everyone stands up.

## CHAPTER 2

### Checkpoint 2-1

The opportunity cost to Clyde of choosing combination $d$ instead of combination $c$ in Figure 2-1 is what Clyde must give up to move from combination $c$ to combination $d$, that is, 10 bushels of corn. Similarly, the opportunity cost of choosing $b$ instead of $d$ is what must be given up to move from $d$ to $b$, namely, 10 cords of wood. The opportunity cost of choosing $d$ instead of $b$ is the 20 bushels of corn that must be forgone in order to move from $b$ to $d$.

### Checkpoint 2-2

The cost of moving from $d$ to $c$ is 20,000 scrubbers, the cost of moving from $c$ to $b$ is 30,000 scrubbers, and the cost of moving from $d$ to $a$ is 100,000 scrubbers. Figure 2-2 can be used to illustrate the law of increasing costs as follows: The move from $e$ to $d$ gains 20 million bundles of other goods (including food) at a cost of 10,000 scrubbers, the move from $d$ to $c$ gains 20 million bundles at a cost of 20,000 scrubbers, the move from $c$ to $b$ gains 20 million bundles at a cost of 30,000 scrubbers, and the move from $b$ to $a$ gains 20 million bundles at a cost of 50,000 scrubbers. In each step, the 20 million bundles of other goods gained has a greater opportunity cost in terms of scrubbers, thus illustrating the law of increasing costs.

### Checkpoint 2-3

The questions of what to produce and for whom to produce are of a normative nature because they cannot be answered strictly by an appeal to the facts.

## Checkpoint 2-4

A pure market economy would select a point on the production possibilities frontier without any government intervention, using only the price signals generated in the marketplace to determine what quantity of scrubbers and bundles would be produced and purchased. If the public desired a different quantity of scrubbers than was currently being produced, its desires would cause changes in demand for scrubbers relative to other goods, and hence would cause changes in relative prices, profits, and production of scrubbers and bundles of other goods. In a command economy, the point on the production possibilities frontier would be mandated from above, with quotas for scrubbers being assigned from a central authority in the same manner as quotas for all other goods.

For both types of economies, greater industrial development would allow greater indulgence in the "luxury" of scrubbers. Less developed economies would probably consider food, shelter, and producer goods (capital goods) necessary to survival and development rather than scrubbers.

## CHAPTER 3

### Checkpoint 3-1

A coincidence of wants is lacking here. If trade were to be carried on at all, one of the people would have to accept an unwanted good and later trade for the wanted good. For example, since C wants fish and has wheat, C can travel to A's island, trade wheat for corn, and then travel to B's island and trade the corn for the fish C desires. Substantial transport time and costs are involved, even if C knows in advance what the supplies and wants of the other people are. If A, B, and C used money, C could travel to A's island and sell his wheat for money and then transport only the money to B's island to buy fish. Coincidence of wants would no longer necessitate someone transporting goods they did not want.

### Checkpoint 3-2

Gompers meant that a business that cannot operate at a profit is not operating efficiently. Since it wastes resources, it will eventually be driven out of business. The resulting loss of jobs will hurt working people. Also, a firm that is not able to operate at a profit cannot attract the investment capital necessary for growth and the creation of new jobs. While Marx saw capitalists' profits as a surplus value stolen from the working class, Gompers saw profits as a reward for wise management and entrepreneurship and as a return to attract financial capital.

### Checkpoint 3-3

The government's power to enforce contracts contributes to the development of markets by making the process of exchanging goods and services less risky. Government's power to enforce gives all parties to a contract added assurance of its fulfillment.

The postal service is not a public good because the exclusion principle applies: only those who pay for the service can have it. Furthermore, there is a private market incentive for providing such service. Parcel Post is an example of a mail service provided by a private firm.

The military draft may be thought of as a transfer of income from those who are drafted to those outside the military services, because the draftees are paid at less than the free-market wage for military labor services (if military wages were determined in a free market, there would be no shortage of military labor and the draft would be unnecessary). Also, since the draft does not discriminate in terms of wealth or income (at least in the absence of corruption), persons who would not enter military service even at the free-market wage are forced to serve. This too constitutes a redistribution of income.

In contrast to government agencies, private businesses that don't operate very efficiently are forced out of business by experiencing losses.

There are, of course, many pro and con arguments concerning the effect of limiting the number of terms a politician can remain in office. For example, one might argue that a politician who remains in office for many terms can set up a political machine that ensures reelection regardless of his or her responsiveness to public wishes. On the other side of the fence, one might argue that it is the threat of losing an election that forces politicians to be responsive to public desires. Thus, a politician who knows he or she is ineligible for reelection might be totally unresponsive to voters' wishes once in office. There are many other arguments that could be made for either side as well.

## CHAPTER 4

### Checkpoint 4-1

If the price of peas were to rise, this would shift the demand curve of lima beans to the right, since the two goods are substitutes, and more lima beans would be demanded at every price. If the price of pretzels were to fall, the demand curve for beer would shift to the right, since the two goods are complements. The demand curve for pretzels would remain unchanged, since we are talking about a change in the price of pretzels and this would result in a movement along the pretzel demand curve rather than a shift in the curve. If the price of hamburger buns were to go up, the demand curve for hamburgers would shift to the left, since these goods are complements, and less hamburger would now be demanded at every price.

### Checkpoint 4-2

If wages go up, then supplier costs go up and a higher price must be charged at each level of production. Hence the supply curve is shifted upward (alternatively, it can be said that at each purchase price, higher costs allow fewer units to be supplied, so that the supply curve shifts to the left). An improvement in technology, such as the improvement mentioned, will lower production costs and shift the supply curve to the right. If the price of lamb were to rise, some suppliers would begin to produce lamb instead of hamburger (since similar resources are used in producing either). This would cause a change in the supply of hamburger. Specifically, the supply curve of hamburger would shift leftward, reflecting the fact that a higher price would now have to be paid for resources that could otherwise be used to produce lamb.

Land is a resource potentially useful in both corn production and the factory production of CB radios. Suppose the land is being used in the production of corn, and an entrepreneur feels that it might be more profitably used in the production of CB radios. The entrepreneur can offer to buy the land at a price that reflects the potential profits in CB production. If this price is higher than what the farmer feels the land is worth in terms of expected potential profits from corn production, then the transaction will take place and the land will change uses.

### Checkpoint 4-3

This checkpoint deals with simultaneous changes in supply and demand. If the price of hot dogs should fall, it would affect the equilibrium price and quantity of hamburger on both the demand and supply sides of the market. On the demand side, hot dogs and hamburger are substitutes, and so the fall in the price of hot dogs would reduce the demand for hamburger. This would, other things held constant, reduce both the equilibrium price and the equilibrium quantity of hamburger. But on the supply side, the same resources can be used to produce both hamburger and hot dogs, so that if the price of hot dogs falls, suppliers will tend to produce more hamburger instead, shifting the supply curve of hamburger to the right. This would, other things being equal, tend to increase

equilibrium quantity and reduce equilibrium price. Therefore, equilibrium price will decrease, since both demand and supply influences push price downward. But we cannot say which way equilibrium quantity will go without knowing the relative sizes of the supply and demand influences, since they operate in opposite directions.

If hamburger bun prices fall, demand for hamburger will increase, since hamburger buns and hamburger are complementary goods. But if the cost of labor used in hamburger production falls, the supply of hamburger will increase at any given price; equilibrium quantity will tend to increase and equilibrium price will tend to decrease. Taken together with the increased demand, the net effect will be an increase in the market equilibrium quantity, with an indeterminate change in the equilibrium price.

If the price of electricity rises, then the demand for hamburger will fall, since these goods are complements. If the office rent for hamburger producers rises, then the supply of hamburger will decrease. A decrease in both demand and supply will decrease equilibrium quantity and have an indeterminate effect on equilibrium price.

If the only information that you were given was that the price of hamburger had risen, then you could not make any statement about what had happened to quantity, since it could have either risen or declined, depending on whether a shift occurred in supply or demand or both.

If consumers' income increased, then the demand for shoes would probably increase (assuming that shoes are a normal good). This would tend, *ceteris paribus*, to increase both the equilibrium price and the equilibrium quantity of shoes bought and sold. Since the equilibrium quantity actually decreased, some other factors must have caused a leftward shift in the supply curve, which more than offset any rightward shift in the demand curve.

## CHAPTER 5

### Checkpoint 5-1

Nationalization of certain businesses means that government now produces certain goods and services. This would be represented in the flow diagram of Figure 5–3 by the addition of a flow channel connecting government with the flow channel where goods and services are exchanged for money payments. Like the business sector, government would be producing and selling goods and services to households, and possibly to the business sector as well.

## Checkpoint 5-2

The sales commissions are included in GNP because although the goods being sold are not considered final goods produced in the current period, the service of selling represents current productive activity.

An increase in the proportion of working wives increases GNP. This is because housekeeping and child-rearing services performed by housewives are not included in GNP. When housewives move into the labor market and take paying jobs, their work activity is measured and included in GNP.

A sample table for bread could look like Table A-1.

## Checkpoint 5-3

The calculation procedure is the same as that in Table 5-2, except that the price index would be computed by dividing by $3, which is the price in year 2. The resulting real GNP figures would be year 1, $2,985; year 2, $3,300; year 3, $3,623; year 4, $3,999; and year 5, $4,397.

A given year's real GNP will be larger than its nominal GNP if it comes before the base year, and its real GNP will be smaller than its nominal GNP if it comes after the base year. This means that nominal GNP is "inflated" to arrive at real GNP before the base year, and it is "deflated" to arrive at real GNP after the base year.

## Checkpoint 5-4

Movement along a demand curve for an individual good corresponds to a change in the price of that good, the price of all other goods assumed constant. By contrast, movement along the economy's aggregate demand curve correponds to a change in the economy's price level, an average of the prices of all the goods and services that make up total output.

The aggregate demand curve has a negative slope because a higher price reduces the purchasing power of fixed-dollar assets, thereby reducing the purchasing power of consumer wealth, and causes consumers to cut back on the quantity of goods and services they demand.

## CHAPTER 6

### Checkpoint 6-1

A visual inspection of Figure 6-1, part a, gives the impression that the expansion phases of business cycles are a great deal longer than the recession phases because of the effect of economic growth. This impression is lessened in Figure 6-1, part b, which shows variations around the growth trend. The monthly seasonal adjustment factors for textbook sales would have to account for large seasonal bulges in sales in the beginning months of each semester, declining dramatically until the beginning of the next semester, with a smaller increase for the beginning of summer sessions.

### Checkpoint 6-2

(1) From a high to low degree of price reduction, they probably ranked: agricultural commodities, food products, leather, cement, textile products, petroleum, iron and steel, automobile tires, motor vehicles, and agricultural implements. (2) From a high to low degree of output reduction, they ranked the same way as in (1).

The shoe machine sales figures of column 4 would be larger and also exhibit larger changes. (From year 1 to year 6, respectively, the figures would be $2, $11, $23, $23, $14, and $2.) Higher

## TABLE A-1

| | Production Stage | Product | Sale Price of Product | | Cost of Intermediate Product | | Value Added (Wages, Interest, Rent, Profit) |
|---|---|---|---|---|---|---|---|
| Firm 1 | Wheat farm | Wheat | $.30 | — | $.00 | = | $.30 |
| Firm 2 | Flour mill | Flour | .40 | — | .30 | = | .10 |
| Firm 3 | Baker | Bread | .65 | — | .40 | = | .25 |
| Firm 4 | Grocery store | Retailing service | .75 | — | .65 | = | .10 |
| | | | | | | | $.75 (Final sale price = sum of value added) |

capital intensity seems to be associated with greater cyclical variation.

### Checkpoint 6-3
Based on Figure 6-4, parts b and c, the unemployment rate that is associated with achieving potential GNP is $4\frac{1}{2}$ to 5 percent.

### Checkpoint 6-4
An unanticipated deflation would redistribute wealth from debtors to creditors, because creditors would be paid back dollars that would buy more than the dollars they originally lent. Since debtors have not anticipated the fall in the general price level, they will not have protected themselves against the fact that their borrowings will have to be paid back with more purchasing power (dollars that buy more) than the purchasing power they originally borrowed. Had borrowers anticipated the deflation, they would have entered into the loan agreement at a lower interest rate than the one they in fact contracted for. It would have been lower by the amount of the rate of deflation. In this way borrowers would take account of the fact that they would have to pay back more valuable dollars than the ones they borrowed.

An unanticipated deflation would redistribute wealth from non-fixed-income groups to fixed-income groups. The fixed-income group would earn the same number of dollars, but these dollars would buy more as the price level fell. The non-fixed-income group would find their incomes falling right along with the general price level. Hence they would lose purchasing power relative to the fixed-income group.

Deflation essentially gives you money by giving each dollar you have more purchasing power.

The abrupt and dramatic increase in the rate of inflation in 1973 and 1974 may well have increased uncertainty about what the future rate of inflation would be. Fear of the consequences of unanticipated inflation may have made businesses and households more cautious about entering into loan agreements to finance investment and consumption spending. Hence further expansion in these expenditures was retarded, thus contributing to the recession.

## CHAPTER 7

### Checkpoint 7-1
Inventories accumulate when consumers do not buy as much as businesses expect them to at the time production plans were being made. This is not as desirable as increases in consumer expenditures because unanticipated increases in inventories mean goods are accumulating faster than they are being sold, and this will very likely lead to a cutback in production, output, and employment.

### Checkpoint 7-2
The double taxation of corporate profits tends to make retained earnings larger relative to the size of dividends. The owners of the corporation, the stockholders, can avoid the double taxation of their profits if the corporation holds the after-tax corporate profit (the profit left after payment of the corporate profit tax) in the form of retained earnings rather than paying it out in dividends which would then be subject to the income tax.

### Checkpoint 7-3
The transfer payments are financed out of tax revenues (indirect business taxes, corporate income taxes, personal taxes) and social security contributions.

## CHAPTER 8

### Checkpoint 8-1
The increase in the economy's aggregate demand would cause increases in demand in the many markets making up the economy. This would lead to price increases in these markets. Attempting to increase output in response, firms would increase their demand for labor. Since there is already full employment, wages would be bid up. Equilibrium would be restored with wages and prices at a higher level.

If the investment curve in Figure 8-1 shifts leftward and the interest rate for some reason cannot fall below $i_e$, then the savings-investment equality will break down and aggregate demand will fall (since the declining investment demand is a part of aggregate demand). The drop in the economy's aggregate demand will cause a leftward shift in the demand curves in the many markets making up the economy. Price and output will fall in these markets, and employers will be forced to lay off workers. This unemployment will cause wages to fall because unemployed labor will bid wages down in their attempts to find jobs. As long as the interest rate cannot fall below $i_e$, to equate saving and investment, wages and prices will continue to fall.

### Checkpoint 8-2
On Crusoe's island all saving and investment plans were made in one man's head. Hence, planned saving necessarily equaled planned investment. There could be no unemployment problem, since Crusoe was both the demander and

supplier of all labor, and the quantity supplied and demanded must always have been equal. Say's Law describes such an economy perfectly, since supply (the quantity that Crusoe was *willing* and able to supply) did in fact create its own demand (the quantity that Crusoe was willing and *able* to demand). In modern industrialized economies, supply does not necessarily create its own demand because the leakage caused by saving may not be matched by the injection of investment, since savers and investors are typically different people.

## Checkpoint 8-3

If interest rates decline, as the forecasters predict, then consumers will be encouraged to borrow more to finance consumption expenditures. Hence the consumption function will shift upward and the savings function will shift downward. In other words, when one of the "other things assumed constant" as we move along a fixed consumption function or saving function changes—in this case the interest rate—it causes these functions to shift.

## Checkpoint 8-4

An increase in the prices of new capital goods will cause the investment schedule to shift downward because the expected profit per dollar will be less. If labor contracts were successfully negotiated without strikes, this would reduce the uncertainty associated with future production and would make producers more willing to invest. This would in turn shift the investment schedule upward.

## Checkpoint 8-5

Examining the fourth row of Table 8–3, we can explain the various columns as follows. Based on past experience and expectations of the future, businesses expect total spending over the next period to occur at an annual rate of $800 billion (column 1). They produce $800 billion in goods and services and in the process generate exactly $800 billion in income (column 2). At this income level, consumer demand plus business demand gives a total expenditure of $900 billion (column 3). Since this dollar expenditure for goods is larger than the dollar value of goods actually produced in this period, business is forced to sell $100 billion out of inventories (column 4). Since sales have been larger than expected, businesses increase their expectation of sales for the next period and increase production accordingly. This makes total income rise (column 5).

## CHAPTER 9

## Checkpoint 9-1

Investment (realized) is always equal to saving because what consumers don't buy, businesses do buy—either as part of planned investment (at income levels below the equilibrium level) or as "purchases" to add to inventories (at income levels above the equilibrium level). Why is it sometimes said that "this is obvious because that part of output that is not consumed must go someplace"? Because total output not consumed by households must either end up in business inventories or be purchased by businesses.

## Checkpoint 9-2

In Figure 9–2, part a, the attempt by consumers to save less shifts their savings function downward, say from $S_1$ to $S_0$, but the resulting increase in total income leaves saving (the quantity actually saved) unchanged. In part b of the figure the downward shift in the saving function, from $S_1$ to $S_0$, actually results in an increase in the quantity saved.

As savers try to rebuild their savings, they will shift up their savings function and shift their consumption function downward. This will result in a decline in total output and income and will possibly result in layoffs for auto workers and steelworkers.

## Checkpoint 9-3

In order for the *APC* and the *MPC* to be equal at all levels of disposable income, the consumption function must be a straight line through the origin. In this case the *APS* and the *MPS* would also be equal at all levels of disposable income, and the saving function would be a straight line through the origin. The *APC* would increase and the *MPC* would remain unchanged if the consumption function shifted upward in parallel fashion.

## Checkpoint 9-4

If there was a $200 billion upward shift in the consumption function, the total expenditure curve in Figure 9–4, part a, would shift upward by $200 billion (note that this would look just like the shift in total expenditure caused by the $200 billion upward shift in the investment function). The equilibrium level of total income would increase to $1,400 billion. In part b of the figure, the saving function would shift downward by $200 billion, intersecting $I_0$ at the new equilibrium level of $1,400 billion.

If the *MPS* is $1/5$, then the *MPC* is $4/5$, as shown in Table A–2.

**TABLE A-2**

| Expenditure Round | Change in Income and Output | Change in Consumption | Change in Saving |
|---|---|---|---|
| First round | $100.00 | $ 80.00 | $ 20.00 |
| Second round | 80.00 | 64.00 | 16.00 |
| Third round | 64.00 | 51.20 | 12.80 |
| Fourth round | 51.20 | 40.96 | 10.24 |
| Fifth round | 40.96 | 32.77 | 8.19 |
| Rest of rounds | 163.84 | 131.07 | 32.77 |
| Totals | $500.00 | $400.00 | $100.00 |

Note that the shift in consumption is downward, so that all these changes are *decreases*. Graphically, the consumption function shifts downward by $100 and the saving function shifts upward by $100 billion. The final change in total output is a decrease of $500 billion. The slope of the consumption function (and the total demand schedule) is 4/5, and the slope of the saving function is 1/5.

The word *savings* is being used in the news item to refer to consumers' accumulated savings balances, which have been drawn on to enable consumers to "spend so heavily." In terms of a diagram like Figure 9–4, the upward shift of the consumption function has resulted in the increased total spending partly by a shift and partly by being "farther out" on the consumption function.

## CHAPTER 10

### Checkpoint 10-1

The $100 billion increase in government spending will raise total spending by $100 billion, which will increase equilibrium by $400 billion ($100 billion × 4, the multiplier) if it occurs by itself. The $100 billion increase in taxes will shift consumption down by $75 billion (= $MPC$ × $100 billion) which will tend to decrease equilibrium income by $300 billion. The net effect will be an increase in equilibrium income of $100 billion. Viewed on the injections-and-leakages side, the $100 billion increase in government spending will shift the $I + G$ line up by $100 billion, which tends to increase equilibrium income by $400 billion. The tax increase of $100 billion will have two effects: (1) it will shift savings downward by $25 billion (= $MPS$ × $100 billion) and (2) it

will shift the $S + T$ line up by the $100 billion increase in taxes (this shift will occur in the $S + T$ line, which includes the newly shifted saving function). These two effects on the $S$ and $T$ schedules will tend to decrease equilibrium income by $300 billion. The overall effect will therefore be an increase in equilibrium of $100 billion.

When the government takes a certain amount of income $\Delta T$ away from households in taxes, it spends all of it. If the money had been left in the hands of the households (not taxed away from them), the household would have spent only part of it. The part they would have spent would equal ($MPC$ × $\Delta T$). The net effect on total income equals $\Delta T(1/MPS) - (\Delta T)(MPC)(1/MPS)$, or $\Delta T(1/MPS)(1 - MPC)$. But since $1 - MPC = MPS$, this reduces to $\Delta T$, which equals $\Delta G$. Hence the balanced budget multiplier equals 1 no matter what the value of $MPS$ or $MPC$.

### Checkpoint 10-2

The $50-a-person rebate acts as a reduction in a lump-sum tax.

With a lump-sum tax, as is depicted in Figure 10–3, part a, taxes do not change with changes in GNP, so that increases or decreases in investment will have no effect on the state of balance of the budget.

With a proportional tax (Figure 10–3, part b), when investment increases and GNP increases (the economy is "heating up"), the tax revenues collected will increase. Since government spending is invariant, the budget will be pushed toward surplus. When investment decreases, tax revenues will decrease and the budget will be pushed toward deficit.

With a progressive tax (Figure 10–3, part c), the tax changes resulting from investment changes will be in the same directions as in the proportional tax case, but the magnitude of the changes toward surplus or toward deficit will be greater.

The automatic stabilization effect works by making the budget tend more toward surplus when the economy is "heating up" and by making the budget tend more toward deficit when the economy is "cooling off."

### Checkpoint 10-3
From 1971 to 1973 the actual level of GNP was fairly close to the level of potential GNP, and the cyclically adjusted budget concept seemed to work fairly well; the cyclically adjusted budget stayed almost in balance. From 1974 onward, however, substantial cyclically adjusted deficits seem to have failed to close the gap between actual and potential GNP, except briefly in 1979.

The effect of a cyclically adjusted deficit will be greater if the deficit is financed by printing money than it will be if it is financed by issuing bonds. If the cyclically adjusted budget is becoming less effective, this could be due in part to increased bond financing.

If a cyclically adjusted budget surplus is eliminated by holding funds from a budget surplus idle, the contractionary effect on GNP will be greater than if the funds are used to retire debt. However, if the cyclically adjusted budget is in surplus, the actual budget may not be in surplus. It is only when the actual budget is in surplus that funds can be held idle or used to retire debt, and the actual budget has not been in surplus since 1969.

### Checkpoint 10-4
Since half of the citizens would be holding the debt and receiving the interest payments on it, as the debt gets larger half of the citizens (the non-debt-holding citizens) would find themselves giving an ever larger share of their incomes in taxes to finance interest payments to the other half of the citizens holding debt. At some point the interest payments on the debt would involve such a large transfer of income from those without debt holdings to those holding the debt that political unrest would become serious. Certainly the government would be considered bankrupt when the interest payments became so large that the half of the population with no bonds was being taxed at 100 percent of their income to make interest payments to the other half of the population. No doubt there would be a tax rebellion (refusal to pay taxes) before this point was reached.

## CHAPTER 11

### Checkpoint 11-1
Changes in the price level change the purchasing power of consumers' fixed-dollar assets, hence the purchasing power of consumer wealth, thereby causing shifts in the total expenditure schedule that change the equilibrium level of real GNP. The inverse relationship between the price level and real GNP traced out in this fashion is the $AD$ curve.

For a given price level, any exogenous expenditure or tax rate change will cause the total expenditure schedule to shift and the equilibrium level of real GNP to change. Given the price level, the change in real GNP certainly can't be represented by movement along an $AD$ curve. Therefore it must be represented by a shift in the $AD$ curve.

From Chapter 10 we know that a $100 billion increase in government expenditures financed by a $100 billion increase in lump-sum taxes gives rise to a balanced budget multiplier equal to one. Therefore, for any given price level, real GNP will increase by $100 billion. Hence the $AD$ curve will shift rightward by $100 billion at each and every price level.

### Checkpoint 11-2
A decline in the price of imported oil would reduce the cost of energy which in turn would lower firms' costs of producing goods and services throughout the economy. Firms therefore will be willing to produce any level of output at a lower product price than was the case before the decline in the price of imported oil. Hence the $AS$ curve would shift downward.

Negative net investment during the Great Depression meant that the economy's capital stock was not even being maintained—that it was in fact shrinking. A shrinking and deteriorating capital stock reduces the economy's productive capacity and tends to increase the costs of production. This causes the $AS$ curve to shift upward and to the left.

### Checkpoint 11-3
If the $AS$ curve were more steeply sloped to the right of point $e_0$ in part b of Figure 11–6, then the price level would rise more and real GNP would rise less. The total expenditure schedule in part a of Figure 11–6 would shift downward from $E_1'$ to a position below $E_1$ so that the new equilibrium level of real GNP would be less than $y_1$.

In order for there to be no change in real GNP as a result of the simultaneous demand-pull and cost-push inflation, the leftward shift in the $AS$

curve and the rightward shift in the *AD* curve would have to be such that the intersection of the two curves continued to lie directly above the initial level of real GNP prevailing before the shifts occurred.

### Checkpoint 11-4

A strictly demand-side, or Keynesian, point of view would only recognize the leftward shift in the *AD* curve caused by an increase in marginal tax rates. The position of the *AS* curve would remain unchanged. However, the supply-side effects of the increase in marginal tax rates would tend to discourage work effort and reduce after-tax rates of return, thereby causing the *AS* curve to shift upward and leftward. Recognition of the leftward shift in the *AS* curve would mean that real GNP would fall further than is the case when only the leftward shift in the *AD* curve is taken into account. According to a strictly demand-side point of view, the price level would fall or remain unchanged (the latter if the demand curve shift occurred along the horizontal range of the *AS* curve). Taking account of supply-side effects, the price level could rise or fall depending on the relative sizes of the leftward shifts in the *AD* and *AS* curves, and their initial positions prior to the increase in the marginal tax rates.

Closing all tax loopholes most likely would increase the tax revenues collected for any given tax rate. Hence the Laffer curve in Figure 10-6 would be bowed further outward to the right.

## CHAPTER 12

### Checkpoint 12-1

The one that is easiest to carry. If aluminum has a higher value per pound, $10 worth of aluminum would be lighter to carry around. On the other hand, steel might be less bulky.

From high to low liquidity, the items would be ranked as follows: a $10 bill, a demand deposit, a Master Charge card, a $1,000 bill, a savings deposit, a $100,000 negotiable CD, a 90-day Treasury bill, a stamp collection, a lot in a suburb.

From high to low usefulness as a store of value, assuming a 10 percent rate of inflation: a lot in a suburb, a stamp collection, a 90-day Treasury bill, a $100,000 negotiable CD, a savings deposit, a $10 bill, a $1,000 bill, a demand deposit, a Master Charge card.

The statement "money is acceptable because it is acceptable" means that what gives money its value as a medium of exchange is the willingness of people to accept it in exchange for goods and services.

From Figure 12-1, it would appear that a dollar bill has not been a very good store of value, since a 1980 dollar bill would have bought $1/10$ of the market basket that a 1910 dollar bill would have bought (this ratio is obviously somewhat simplistic, since it abstracts from changes in the quality of goods and all the other problems associated with the measurement of price level over such a long period of time).

### Checkpoint 12-2

A bank note might be said to be an IOU because it is a piece of paper testifying to the bank's willingness to pay the bearer a given quantity of money that the bearer has deposited in the bank.

When currency is convertible into gold, there must be enough gold to redeem the currency. This means that the rate of growth of the supply of currency is limited to the rate of growth of the gold supply.

If people were to become less trusting of the soundness of banks, then they would be more likely to withdraw their money. Consequently banks would feel compelled to keep more reserves in their vaults. This would reduce their ability to create deposits through the making of loans. And this would reduce the upper limit to the economy's money supply.

If bankers were to become more cautious, then they would be less willing to make loans, and this would reduce the amount of IOUs on their balance sheets. If they made fewer loans for a given level of reserves, then the money supply would be smaller. This would make money conditions "tighter," and in the aggregate, people would spend less on goods and services.

### Checkpoint 12-3

The Federal Reserve System makes the money supply more elastic because the Fed is able to create reserves at a rate commensurate with growth in the level of economic activity.

The Fed is sometimes referred to as the lender of last resort, because a member bank can borrow reserves from its Federal Reserve bank if it finds itself in a credit squeeze due to sudden large withdrawals of deposits.

It is possible that deposit insurance is more effective than the member banks' borrowing privilege in preventing bank panics because bank panics are essentially crises of confidence, and the deposit insurance is a very effective confidence-building measure.

## CHAPTER 13

### Checkpoint 13-1

The commercial banks held larger excess reserves from 1933 to 1940 because many banks had failed when panics led depositors to withdraw their deposits in the 1929–1932 period, the early years of the Great Depression. Leery of such surges of withdrawals, banks that remained kept a large quantity of excess reserves on hand.

### Checkpoint 13-2

The resulting table is shown as Table A–3.

If a bank decided to hold all its excess reserves and make no new loans, it would stop the expansion process completely at that point. If at any point a depositor receiving one of the new loans took the entire value of his or her new loan out in cash, this would also put a stop to the expansion process.

If a bank's willingness to lend increases, the bank will keep fewer excess reserves as cautionary balances, and it will become more "loaned up." This will increase the money supply.

With a required reserve ratio of .25, the maximum effect of a $100 cash withdrawal is a decrease in the money supply of $400 (= $100 × [1/.25]). The withdrawal will have a minimum effect if the bank was holding excess reserves, since it can pay out the cash without calling in any of its investments. In that case, M1 will be unaffected, because the only demand deposit effect will be a decrease in your balance by $100, and this will be countered by the increase in the cash component of M1 by $100.

### Checkpoint 13-3

The existence of the discount window reduces the Fed's control over the money supply in the following sense. Suppose the Fed reduces the quantity of reserves in the banking system by conducting an open market sale. Member banks may offset this decrease in reserves by simply borrowing more reserves from the discount window. Hence the Fed's ability to control the quantity of reserves in the banking system, and thus the money supply, is compromised by the existence of the discount window.

The discount window gives the banking system some protection against an unnecessarily restrictive monetary policy. Again suppose the Fed conducts open market sales, thus reducing reserves. If this is an unnecessarily restrictive action, member banks can offset its effects by borrowing reserves at the discount window.

When the Fed raises the maximum interest that commercial banks can pay on time deposits, savers will be attracted away from "thrift" institutions such as the savings and loan associations that are the primary source of long-term mortgage loans used to finance residential construction. This will tend to restrict the amount of residential construction taking place in the economy. Lowering the Regulation Q ceiling will have the opposite effect.

### Checkpoint 13-4

An increase in money demand accompanied by a decrease in the money supply would have the greatest effect on the interest rate. This can be easily demonstrated by graphs similar to Figures

**TABLE A-3**

| Bank | New Reserves and Demand Deposits | Excess Reserves Equal to the Amount Bank Can Lend, Equal to the New Money Created | Required Reserves |
|---|---|---|---|
| A | $1,000 | $ 750 | $ 250 |
| B | 750 | 563 | 188 |
| C | 563 | 422 | 141 |
| D | 422 | 316 | 105 |
| E | 316 | 237 | 79 |
| F | 237 | 178 | 59 |
| G | 178 | 133 | 44 |
| H | 133 | 100 | 33 |
| All remaining banks | 401 | 301 | 100 |
| | $4,000 | $3,000 | $1,000 |

13–4 and 13–5. If people were to revise their notions of a normal level of the interest rate upward, the money demand curve would shift upward and money demand would be greater at every level of the interest rate—that is, money demand would increase. If people were to become more uncertain about their jobs, then they would tend to hold higher precautionary balances. This means that they would hold larger money balances at any given interest rate, and hence money demand would increase.

## CHAPTER 14

### Checkpoint 14-1

If the investment demand curve in part b of Figure 14–2 was made steeper, then the interest rate decrease resulting from the increase in money supply from $M_0$ to $M_1$ would cause investment spending to increase by less than before. If the money demand curve in part a of Figure 14–2 became steeper, then the shift in money supply from $M_0$ to $M_1$ would result in a larger decrease in the interest rate and hence a larger increase in investment spending. If money demand were more sensitive to a change in total income, then the increase in total income resulting from the money supply change in Figure 14–3 would be smaller than before. This is because the shift in money demand resulting from the change in total income tends to counteract the investment increase that results from the initial interest rate drop associated with movement along the money demand curve.

### Checkpoint 14-2

Stated by itself, the equation of exchange is true by definition. But if it is postulated that the velocity of money is inherently stable, then the equation of exchange becomes a theory linking changes in the money supply to changes in money GNP.

If the money demand curve becomes flat at some low level of the interest rate, then when the money supply is increased into the flat range, further increases in the money supply cause no changes in the interest rate, investment, or money GNP. If the money supply increases and there is no change in money GNP, then velocity must decrease in order for the equation of exchange to remain balanced.

## CHAPTER 15

### Checkpoint 15-1

In terms of Figure 15-1, the Fed sees the high level of government spending as pushing up aggregate demand so much that the inflationary zone of the aggregate supply curve has been entered. In terms of Figures 15–2 and 15–3, the Fed sees government spending as raising the interest rate because the increase in aggregate demand has increased precautionary and transactions demands for money and shifted money demand to the right. So while the committee seems to think that the Fed is causing high interest rates by keeping a tight rein on the money supply, the Fed thinks that the government's high spending is causing high interest rates and inflation.

If the Fed should accede to the Senate Budget Committee's wishes and take steps to lower the interest rate, it could use any of its three tools to increase reserves available to the banking system. This would shift the money supply curves in the top and bottom halves of Figure 15–2 to the right, decrease the interest rate, and increase investment spending. In the Keynesian view, a given money supply change would decrease interest rates and increase investment less than in the monetarist view. The increase in investment spending would increase total income but would move the economy farther into the inflationary zone on the supply curve illustrated in Figure 15–1. The increase in spending would also increase precautionary and transactions demands for money, which would tend to push the interest rate back up as money demand was shifted to the right. The net effect on total demand would be similar to that illustrated in Figure 15–3, with the change in government spending interpreted as a change in investment (caused by the original change in the money supply and the interest rate).

Greater discipline in fiscal policy would mean decreasing government spending. This would reverse the events pictured in Figure 15–3. Government spending would decrease and reduce total spending. The reduction in total spending would shift the money demand curve to the left, which would decrease the interest rate and increase investment, offsetting some of the original government-spending decline. The monetarists' view would have the offsetting change being larger than the Keynesian view. The leftward shift in the money demand curve due to the decrease in government spending is illustrated in Figure 15–2, which shows the larger offsetting change in investment predicted by the monetarist position. The net decrease in total spending and total income would ease the economy back out of the inflation zone of the aggregate supply curve illustrated in Figure 15–1, and the Fed would not be so concerned about the necessity of fighting inflation with a tight-money policy.

## Checkpoint 15-2

If there was a prolonged decrease in the price level, and there was an anticipated deflation, the money interest rate would be less than the real interest rate by an amount equal to the anticipated rate of deflation. Since borrowers would be paying back dollars that are worth more than the dollars they borrowed, they would demand compensation for this in the form of a lower money interest rate.

The interest rates shown in Figure 14–7, part a, tend to move with the rate of inflation shown in Figure 6–5, part a, because the anticipated rate of inflation is part of the money interest rate (money interest rate = real interest rate + anticipated rate of inflation).

## CHAPTER 16

### Checkpoint 16-1

If the Phillips curve were to rotate counterclockwise, then unemployment could be reduced with a smaller increase in inflation. If the economy could have a zero percent rate of inflation with 9 percent unemployment, then the Phillips curve would intersect the horizontal axis at 9 percent unemployment. It would also be twisted clockwise. If the Phillips curve represents a true menu of choices, then the choice of a point on the curve is a normative one, since it cannot be decided by an appeal to facts.

### Checkpoint 16-2

A Phillips curve might be put through the points 1976, 1977, and 1978. Another Phillips curve might also be passed through the cluster of points near the top of Figure 16-5, recognizing that inflationary expectations were most likely higher in that year than in 1979.

Short-run Phillips curves might well be shaped like those in Figure 16-4 based on the evidence for the years from 1961 through 1969, and 1976 through 1978 (see Figure 16-5). However, other years are not as suggestive of this shape.

### Checkpoint 16-3

The pattern of the data in Figure 16–2 suggests that the average level of the unemployment rate has increased over time. Certainly one possible explanation is the changing nature of the labor force we have discussed above. Another possibility is that there has been an increase in the natural rate of unemployment caused by the increasing variability of inflation, as hypothesized by Milton Friedman. Of course, both types of phenomena could jointly contribute to the apparent upward drift in the average level of the unemployment rate.

## CHAPTER 17

### Checkpoint 17-1

Wage and price controls can be said to operate "artificially" because they do not allow the market price-setting mechanism to determine price. Although prices can be held below those that would equate supply and demand (as illustrated in Figure 17–1) if there is a large enough enforcement effort, such controls do not eliminate the underlying demand and supply curves or prevent them from shifting while the controls are in effect. As soon as the controls are lifted, price will rise to the level that equates supply and demand, and this could be termed a "price explosion."

As soon as the congressional debate started, labor and business would rush to increase prices in an effort to set prices high enough so that they would not be hurt by the controls' effects. Since this would be an increase in wages and prices that was not caused by increases in total demand, it would constitute a cost-push type of inflation that would result in the aggregate supply curve being shifted upward. This would tend to increase prices and reduce output and employment. The Fed would have to combat the increased inflation by decreasing the money supply and hence reducing total demand. This would further decrease output and employment and send the economy into a recession.

### Checkpoint 17-2

Since tax cuts are always popular with the public at large, it is preferable from a political point of view to pass a number of discretionary tax-cut measures rather than pass a single tax-indexing measure that would automatically decrease taxes. Also, discretionary tax measures can be made to appear to political constituents as "nice guy" measures, whereas an indexing measure could be construed as a congressional admission that inflation is going to be long-lasting.

Government bond indexing could have an adverse effect on the private sector's ability to borrow because it would make government bonds a more attractive investment relative to private bonds.

Indexing could be thought of as the government's admission that inflation is going to last long enough to warrant such actions. Such an admission of a permanence to inflation is certainly politically undesirable. On the other hand, the lost tax revenues resulting from such indexing could give the government an incentive to reduce deficit spending and hence curb inflation.

## CHAPTER 18

### Checkpoint 18-1

The rule of 72 tells us that the rate of growth for the time period 1950 to 1981 is approximately 2.3 percent (= 72/31 years).

If the rate of growth of productivity is 1.5 percent and the "safe growth ceiling" is 3 percent, then the combined growth projected for the other three factors (population, percent of population in the labor force, and number of hours worked per laborer) must not exceed 1.5 percent.

Per capita real GNP in 1948 was approximately $3333 (= $500 billion/150 million) in 1972 dollars. Per capita GNP in 1980 was approximately $6,645.9 (= $1,480.7 billion/222.8 million) in 1972 dollars. This represents an increase in per capita GNP of about 90 percent.

### Checkpoint 18-2

Technically, an increase in any factor while other factors are held constant brings about diminishing returns for the increased factor. Historically, however, technical change and investment in human capital have tended to be the major sources of economic growth. This phenomenon would seem to suggest that technical change and investment in human capital are bound less by the law of diminishing returns than are the other factors. Hence, technical change and investment in human capital probably will have a larger impact on long-run growth than will increases in other factors of production.

## CHAPTER 19

### Checkpoint 19-1

If the economy's citizens decide to reduce the volume of goods and services they buy from abroad no matter what the level of GNP, then imports will decrease at all levels of GNP. This means that the $S + T + Imports$ line will shift downward, increasing the equilibrium level of GNP.

Although the leakages from imports exceed injections from exports, $1,400 billion is indeed the equilibrium value of GNP, because the total injections ($G + I + Exports$) are equal to the total leakages ($S + T + Imports$) at that point. This means that the injections from $I + G$ alone must exceed the leakages from $S + T$ alone by the same amount that leakages from imports exceed injections from exports.

The effect of positive (negative) net exports on the economy is similar to the effect of a government budget deficit (surplus) because they add to (subtract from) total spending and hence increase (decrease) equilibrium GNP through the multiplier effect. But note that the multiplier is different in an economy with imports and exports from the multiplier in an economy without them, because imports change the slope of the injections function.

### Checkpoint 19-2

Although the frontiersmen probably would be subject to increasing costs and hence would have nonlinear production possibility frontiers, this problem is illustrated most simply with linear production possibilities frontiers like those used in the text's Venezuela and United States example (Figure 19-2). If the two pioneers have differing abilities in the production of wood and wheat, then their production possibilities frontiers would have different slopes, reflecting different opportunity costs. Comparative advantage would lead to specialization and trade, giving rise to trading possibilities frontiers for the two frontiersmen that lie above the two production possibilities frontiers. This would allow both frontiersmen to have more of both goods than they would have in the absence of specialization and trade.

Although Florida can produce corn and the Midwest can produce citrus fruits, climatic differences give rise to a comparative advantage for Florida in citrus fruit production and for the Midwest in corn production—hence there is specialization and trade. Similarily, Appalachia specializes in coal production, whereas Texas specializes in oil production. The Gulf coastal region produces shrimp, and the Dakotas produce wheat. In each case, climate or resource endowments lead to a comparative advantage, which encourages specialization and trade. You should be able to list a number of similar examples.

### Checkpoint 19-3

The steelmakers are buying more foreign coke because it is available at a cheaper price than that charged by domestic coke producers. This difference could be due to a real comparative advantage for foreign coke producers, or it could be due to the fact that foreign producers are receiving government subsidies and are able to "dump" their coke in the U.S. market at less than production cost. If foreign coke producers do have a comparative advantage in coke production, then indeed U.S. steelmakers have less incentive to invest in more efficient coke ovens (this is true whether the comparative advantage is a real one or a "false" one due to dumping). This hurts the sales of domestic producers of coke ovens. Hence it is in their best interest to seek some protection (such as tariffs) from coke imports. Since it is very difficult to ascertain what the foreign coke production costs really are, the dumping claim might be very difficult to prove.

## CHAPTER 20

### Checkpoint 20-1
The French haircut is paid for with a U.S. payment to France and hence is a debit on the current account. The birthday present is a private unilateral transfer and by convention is entered as a credit item on the current account. A balancing debit entry is made under unilateral transfers. If you finance the Volkswagen domestically, then Volkswagen is paid "cash" for the car, and this constitutes a U.S. payment to Germany and is a merchandise import debit on the current account. If you buy the car and finance it with Volkswagen, then Volkswagen is "buying" your IOU for the amount of the purchase price, and this is a credit on the private capital account. As you pay off the loan, your payments will be debits on the private capital account. When the government buys French francs and finances the purchase with a liquid claim, this will be recorded as a credit item on the government's capital account because it is a payment received from France in exchange for the export of the U.S. government's IOU.

### Checkpoint 20-2
When one currency depreciates, it takes more of that currency to buy a unit of foreign currency. But of course this means that it takes less of the foreign currency to buy a unit of the first currency, and hence the foreign currency has appreciated.

The supply curve in Figure 20–1 is a demand curve for dollars in the sense that it is a schedule showing the quantity of francs that the French are willing and able to supply in exchange for dollars, which is the same thing as the quantity of dollars that the French are willing and able to purchase in exchange for francs. The demand curve in Figure 20–1 is a supply curve for dollars in the sense that it is a schedule showing the quantity of francs that Americans are willing and able to purchase in exchange for dollars, which is the same thing as the quantity of dollars that Americans are willing and able to supply in exchange for francs.

An American expansionary monetary policy will, *ceteris paribus*, increase the exchange rate of dollars for pounds (that is, it will take more dollars to buy a pound). This is because an expansionary monetary policy will increase money GNP in the United States and increase the demand for British imports. This will increase the demand for British currency to pay for these imports and will hence drive the equilibrium exchange rate upward when the demand curve for pounds shifts rightward.

A more restrictive British fiscal policy will, *ceteris paribus*, increase the exchange rate of dollars for pounds (that is, it will take more dollars to buy a pound). This is because a restrictive British fiscal policy will decrease GNP in Britain and decrease British demand for American exports. This will decrease the supply of British pounds in the foreign exchange market, since fewer pounds are needed to be exchanged for American dollars to pay for American goods. The supply curve for British pounds will decrease (shift leftward), and the equilibrium exchange rate of dollars for pounds will increase.

### Checkpoint 20-3
If a government wants to fix an exchange rate, it must be prepared to use its reserves to buy up the excess supply of currency at the fixed rate when the fixed rate is above the equilibrium and to supply the foreign market with currency equal to the excess demand when the fixed rate is below the equilibrium rate (this will increase its official reserves).

Balance of payments deficits and surpluses are inevitable under fixed exchange rates since as time passes, supply and demand curves in foreign exchange markets inevitably shift because of changing trade patterns and differing economic developments within each nation. Only occasionally will the equilibrium rate and the fixed rate happen to be equal—the rest of the time balance of payments deficits and surpluses will occur as the government has to intervene to maintain the fixed rate.

If a nation's currency was overvalued, then the fixed rate of exchange would be above the equilibrium rate and the nation would have to buy up the excess supply of currency continually at the fixed rate. This would continually draw down its official reserves. If the nation were to tighten its monetary policy, then its money GNP would decline and its demand for imports of foreign goods would decline. This would decrease the supply of its currency in foreign exchange markets and hence decrease the excess supply. This would decrease the drain on the nation's official reserves.

### Checkpoint 20-4
Since one of the costs of inflation to a nation is a depreciation of its currency relative to that of nations with less inflation, nations that had easy

monetary and fiscal policies would experience an increased balance of payments deficit. This is because the Bretton Woods system required a member nation to use its official reserves to prevent devaluation of its currency. Hence fiscal and monetary policies that encouraged inflation would cost a nation increased drains on its official reserves, and this would "impose a certain amount of fiscal and monetary discipline on governments," since they could not allow their official reserves to be drained continuously.

# CHAPTER 21

### Checkpoint 21-1
It seems to be characteristic of human behavior, at least in Western cultures, that the right to acquire and own property provides a strong incentive for people to work hard to achieve that end. Soviet experience with agricultural productivity on communes (large farms owned by the state) versus that on small plots that peasants are allowed to own individually appears to indicate that there is greater productivity where peasants own their own land. Both observation of human nature and evidence such as the Soviet experience suggest that property rights arrangements bear a close relationship to the system of incentives in an economy.

### Checkpoint 21-2
You should be able to answer this checkpoint by going over a previous section of this chapter ("Socialism: Variations, Record, and Capitalist Rivalry") and using that material to compare and contrast Communism and social democracy.

### Checkpoint 21-3
You should be able to answer this checkpoint by going over a previous section of this chapter ("Two Socialist Countries: China and Yugoslavia") and using that material to compare and contrast the economic systems of China and Yugoslavia. It would be useful to organize your answer in terms of the four features listed in Table 21-1.

# Glossary

## A

**absolute energy reserves** The world's total stocks of energy reserves, equal to the sum of proven reserves plus unproven reserves.

**accelerationist view** Holds that there is no stable long-run Phillips curve trade-off between the inflation rate and the unemployment rate, and that persistent attempts to stimulate aggregate demand to reduce the unemployment rate below the natural rate will cause an ever-increasing rate of inflation.

**accelerator principle** The relationship between changes in level of retail sales and the level of investment expenditures.

**aggregate demand curve (AD)** Shows the inverse relationship between the economy's total demand for output and the price level of that output.

**aggregate supply curve (AS)** Shows the amount of total output the economy's businesses will supply at different price levels.

**antidumping law** Law that sets a minimum price on an imported good such that if the import enters the country at a price below the minimum, the law triggers a government investigation of possible dumping.

**automatic stabilizers** Built-in features of the economy that operate continuously without human intervention to smooth out the peaks and troughs of business cycles.

**automatic transfer service (ATS)** A savings account from which funds are transferred automatically to the depositor's checking account to cover checks as they are drawn.

**average propensity to consume (APC)** The fraction or proportion of total income that is consumed.

**average propensity to save (APS)** The fraction or proportion of total income that is saved.

## B

**balanced budget** A budget in which total expenditures equal total tax revenues.

**balanced budget multiplier** The ratio of the amount of change in GNP to the change in government spending financed entirely by an increase in taxes; indicates that a simultaneous increase, or decrease, in government expenditures and taxes of a matched or balanced amount will result in an increase, or decrease, in GNP of the same amount.

**balance of payments** A nation's total payments to other nations must be equal to, or balanced by, the total payments received from other nations.

**balance of payments account** Record of all the payments made by a nation to other nations, as well as all the payments that it receives from other nations during the course of a year.

**balance of payments deficit** The excess of a nation's payments to other nations over the payments received from other nations, exclusive of government capital account transactions in official reserve assets; means that the government is reducing its holdings of official reserve assets or that the liquid claims of foreign governments against these reserves are increasing, or both.

**balance of payments surplus** Excess of payments received from other nations over the payments made to them, exclusive of government capital account transactions in official reserves and liquid claims; means that the government is increasing its holdings of official reserves or its holdings of liquid claims on the official reserve assets held by foreign governments, or both.

**balance of trade** The difference between merchandise exports and merchandise imports.

**bank note** Paper money issued by a commercial bank.

**barter economy** Trading goods directly for goods.

**bracket creep** A process whereby inflation pushes people into higher marginal tax brackets as their nominal income rises due to inflation, even when their real income remains unchanged; it causes the proportion of their personal income paid in taxes to increase.

**Bretton Woods system** System of fixed exchange rates in which only the dollar was directly convertible into gold at a fixed rate of exchange; all other currencies were indirectly convertible into gold by virtue of their convertibility into the dollar. Also called the *gold exchange system.*

**budget constraint** Straight line representing all possible combinations of goods that a consumer can purchase at given prices by spending a given-size budget. Also called *budget line.*

**budget deficit** Expenditures are greater than tax revenues.

**budget surplus** Expenditures are less than tax revenues.

**business cycles** The somewhat irregular but recurrent pattern of fluctuations in economic activity.

**business fluctuations** Recurring phenomena of increasing and decreasing unemployment associated with decreasing and increasing output. Also called *business cycles.*

## C

**capital consumption allowance** See *capital depreciation.*

**capital deepening** An increase in the stock of capital (machines, tools, buildings, highways, dams, and so forth) relative to the quantities of all other resources, including labor.

**capital depreciation** The wearing out of capital, often measured by its decline in value. Also called *capital consumption allowance.*

**capital gains taxes** Taxes levied on any gain one realizes from selling an asset at a price greater than the original purchase price.

**capitalism** Form of economic organization in which the means of production are privately owned and operated for profit and where freely operating markets coordinate the activities of consumers, businesses, and all suppliers of resources.

**certificate of deposit (CD)** Special type of time deposit that depositor agrees not to withdraw for a specified period of time, usually 3 months or more.

*ceteris paribus* Latin expression for "all other things remaining the same."

**closed economy** An economy that does not trade with other nations.

**coincidence of wants** The possibility of barter between two individuals that occurs when each has a good that the other wants.

**command economy** An economy in which the government answers the questions of how to organize production, what and how much to produce, and for whom to produce.

**commercial bank** Bank that can create money in the form of a demand deposit (checking account) by extending credit in the form of loans to businesses and households.

**comparative advantage** Theory holds that total world output is greatest when each good is produced by that nation which has the lower opportunity cost of producing the good—the nation is said to have a comparative advantage in that good.

**complementary good** A good that tends to be used jointly with another good.

**consent decree** Agreement with the Justice Department whereby a firm agrees to certain restrictions on the way it does business without being technically guilty of violating the law.

**consumer price index *(CPI)*** A commonly used and widely publicized measure of the general level of prices in the economy, constructed as a weighted average of the prices of a market basket of goods and services purchased by a typical urban worker's family.

**consumer sovereignty** The condition that exists when the basic decisions about what to produce (which products and services) and how much to produce are dominated by consumers acting individually or as households.

**consumption function** The relationship between the level of disposable income and the level of planned consumption.

**cost-push inflation** Inflation that occurs when suppliers of factors of production increase the prices at which they are willing to sell them.

**crowding out** The reduction in investment spending that can occur as a consequence of an expansionary fiscal policy.

**currency appreciation** A rise in the free-market value of a currency in terms of other currencies, with the result that fewer units of a currency will be required to buy a unit of a foreign currency.

**currency depreciation** A fall in the free-market value of a currency in terms of other currencies; means that more units of a currency will be required to buy a unit of a foreign currency.

**currency devaluation** A lowering of the level at which the price of a currency is fixed in terms of other currencies.

**currency revaluation** A rise in the level at which the price of a currency is fixed in terms of other currencies.

**cyclically adjusted budget** Equals the difference between the actual level of government spending and the level of tax revenue that would be collected if the economy were operating at a high-employment level of GNP.

## D

**deduction** Reasoning from generalizations to particular conclusions; going from theory to prediction.

**deflation** A general fall in prices that causes the value of a dollar measured in terms of its purchasing power to rise.

**demand curve** Graphic representation of the law of demand.

**demand deposit** A deposit from which funds may be withdrawn on demand and from which funds may be transferred to another party by means of a check.

**demand-pull inflation** Inflation that occurs because the economy's total demand for goods and services exceeds its capacity to supply them.

**demand schedule** Numerical tabulation of the quantitative relationship between quantity demanded and price.

**deposit multiplier** Assuming banks are fully loaned up, the multiplier is the reciprocal of the required reserve ratio.

**depository institution** A financial institution that can create money in the form of a checkable deposit (checking account) by extending credit in the form of loans to businesses and/or households.

**depreciation allowance** Funds set aside for the replacement of worn-out capital equipment.

**depression** An unusually severe recession.

**diminishing marginal rate of substitution** Characteristic of the behavior of the marginal rate of substitution along an indifference curve, reflecting the fact that the more of good B a consumer has *relative* to good A, the more of good B the consumer is willing to part with in order to get an additional unit of good A.

**direct relationship** Relationship between variables in which the value of each changes in the same way (both decrease or both increase).

**discount rate** The rate of interest that banks must pay to borrow from Federal Reserve banks.

**discount window** A teller's window, figuratively speaking, at a Federal Reserve bank where a bank may come to borrow money.

**disembodied technical change** Change that takes the form of new procedures or techniques for producing goods and services.

**disposable income (DI)** Personal income minus personal taxes.

**dumping** Selling a product in a foreign market at a price below the cost of producing the product.

## E

**economic efficiency** Using available resources to obtain the maximum possible output.

**economic growth** An outward shift in the production possibilities frontier caused by an increase in available resources and technological know-how.

**economic policy** Proposed method of dealing with a problem or problems posed by economic reality that is arrived at through the use of economic theory and analysis.

**economic problem** How to use scarce resources to best fulfill society's unlimited wants.

**economics** A social science concerned with the study of economies and the relationships among economies.

**economic system** The institutions, rules, and decision-making processes used to organize and allocate a nation's scarce resources to produce and distribute goods and services to its citizens.

**economic theory** A statement about the behavior of economic phenomena, often referred to as a law, principle, or model.

**economy** A particular system of organization for the production, distribution, and consumption of all things people use to obtain a standard of living.

**embodied technical change** Technological change that is embedded in the form of the capital good itself.

**employment tax credit** Program that allows firms to exclude from taxation an amount of income equal to some specified percent of the wages they pay labor, thereby effectively reducing the cost of labor and encouraging firms to hire more.

**equation of exchange** A relationship between the economy's money supply $M$, the money supply's velocity of circulation $V$, its price level $p$, and total real output $Q$; states that the total amount spent, $M \times V$, on final goods and services equals the total value of final goods and services produced, $p \times Q$—that is, $M \times V = p \times Q$.

**equilibrium income level** The level of total income that will be sustained once it is achieved. At equilibrium, the total income earned from production of the economy's total output corresponds to a level of total spending or demand just sufficient to purchase that total output.

**equilibrium price** Price at which market equilibrium is achieved.

**equilibrium quantity** Quantity of the good supplied and demanded at the point of market equilibrium.

**equity** The difference between a firm's total assets and its total liabilities.

**escalator clause** Clause in a labor contract that indexes wages to inflation by stipulating that wages must be periodically adjusted upward to keep pace with the rising cost of living.

**excess reserves** Total reserves minus required reserves.

**exchange rate** The price of foreign currency, or the amount of one currency that must be paid to obtain 1 unit of another currency.

**expansion** The upswing of a business cycle.

**expected rate of return** The amount of money a firm expects to earn per year on funds invested in a capital good, expressed as a percent of the funds invested.

**exports** The goods and services a nation produces and sells to other nations.

**export subsidy** Government payments to an export industry to cover part of the industry's costs of production.

### F

**factors of production** The inputs (land, labor, and capital) necessary to carry on production. Also called *economic resources.*

**fallacy of composition** Error in reasoning that assumes that what is true for the part is true for the whole.

**fallacy of division** Error in reasoning that assumes that what is true for the whole is true for its individual parts.

**fallacy of false cause** Error in reasoning that assumes one event is the cause of another event simply because it precedes the second event in time.

**fiat money** Money that is declared by the government to be legal tender—it is neither backed by nor convertible into gold or any other precious metal.

**financial intermediary** A business that acts as an intermediary by taking the funds of lenders and making them available to borrowers, receiving the difference between the interest it charges borrowers and the interest it pays lenders as payment for providing this service.

**financial markets** Markets that take the funds of savers and lend them to borrowers.

**fiscal policy** Government's efforts to use its spending, taxing, and debt-issuing authority to smooth out the business cycle and maintain full employment without inflation.

**fixed-dollar assets** Any kind of asset that guarantees a repayment of the initial dollar amount invested plus some stipulated rate of interest.

**flexible (or floating) exchange rate** Exchange rate freely determined by supply and demand in the foreign exchange market without government intervention.

**flow** A quantity per unit of time.

**foreign exchange market** Market in which exchange rates between different currencies are determined.

**fractional reserve banking** Managing a bank so that the amount of reserves on hand is equal to only a fraction of the amount of deposits.

### G

**general equilibrium analysis** Analysis of the adjustments a change in one market will cause in each and every other market.

**GNP gap** Potential GNP minus actual GNP, which is equal to the value of final goods and services not produced because there is unemployment.

**gold standard** A monetary system in which nations fix the rates of exchange between their currencies and gold and, hence, the exchange rates between their currencies.

**government budget** An itemized account of government expenditures and revenues over some period of time.

**gross national product (GNP)** The market value of all final goods and services produced by the economy during a year.

**gross private domestic investment** The total expenditures by business firms on new capital.

### H

**high-employment budget** Difference between the actual level of government spending and the level of tax revenue that would be collected if the economy were at a high-employment level of GNP.

### I

**ideology** Doctrine, opinion, or way of thinking.

**import quotas** Limitation on imports that specifies the maximum amount of a foreign-produced good that will be permitted into the country over a specified period of time.

**imports** The goods and services a nation purchases from other nations.

**indexing** Method of keeping the purchasing power of wages, taxes, and fixed-dollar, or nominal, assets constant by adjusting their dollar-denominated values to the change in the general price level.

**indifference curve** A graphical representation of an indifference schedule—the consumer gets the same level of satisfaction at any point along the curve.

**indifference map** All of an individual's indifference curves taken together.

**indifference schedule** A listing of all possible combinations of goods that give a consumer the same level of satisfaction.

**indirect business taxes** Sales and excise taxes and business property taxes.

**induction** Reasoning from particular facts and observations to generalizations.

**inferior good** A good that people typically want more of at lower income levels and less of at higher income levels.

**inflation** A rise in the general level of prices of all goods and services; this rise causes the purchasing power of a dollar to fall.

**interest rate, or interest** The price of borrowing money, or the price received for lending money, expressed as a percentage.

**inventory** A stock of unsold goods.

**inverse relationship** Relationship between variables in which the value of one increases as the value of the other decreases.

**involuntary unemployment** Occurs when workers willing to work at current wage rates are unable to find jobs.

## L

**labor force** All persons over the age of 16 who are employed plus all those actively looking for work.

**Laffer curve** Shows a relationship between the marginal tax rate and the amount of tax revenue the government receives. In particular, starting from a zero marginal tax rate, tax revenues rise as the rate is increased up to some point beyond which further increases in the marginal tax rate cause tax revenue to decline.

**laissez faire** ("let [people] do [as they choose]") The belief that people should be allowed to conduct their economic affairs without interference from the government.

**law of demand** Theory that the lower the price of a good, the greater will be the demand for it and, conversely, the higher the price, the smaller will be the demand.

**law of increasing costs** The cost per additional good obtained, measured in terms of the good sacrificed, rises due to the different productivity of resources when used in different production processes.

**law of supply** Theory that suppliers will supply larger quantities of a good at higher prices than they will at lower prices.

**liquidity** The degree to which any form of wealth is readily convertible into other goods and services; money is the most liquid form of wealth.

## M

**M1** Money defined as the sum of currency, demand deposits, and other checkable deposits.

**M2** Money defined as M1 plus money market fund shares plus savings and small time deposits that do not carry checklike privileges.

**M3** Money defined as M2 plus large negotiable CDs.

**macroeconomics** Branch of economic analysis that focuses on the workings of the whole economy or large sectors of it.

**managed float** Exchange rates subject to free-market forces modified by government intervention, but without any formal commitment to fix rates at specified levels. Also called *dirty float.*

**manpower programs** Job-training programs aimed at developing the job skills of the young and hard-core unemployed in order to increase their employability.

**marginal propensity to consume** *(MPC)* The fraction or proportion of any change in income that is consumed—equals the slope of the consumption function.

**marginal propensity to save** *(MPS)* Fraction or proportion of any change in income that is saved—equals the slope of the saving function.

**marginal rate of substitution** Rate at which the consumer is just willing to substitute one good for the other along an indifference curve.

**marginal tax rate** Indicates how much of an additional dollar of income, the marginal or last dollar earned, must be paid in taxes.

**margin requirement** The minimum percentage of a stock purchase that must be paid for with the purchaser's own funds, as legally set by the Fed.

**market** An area within which buyers and sellers of a particular good are in such close communication that the price of the good tends to be the same everywhere in the area.

**market demand curve**  The sum of all the individual demand curves for a good.

**market economy**  An economy in which the interaction of demand and supply on prices—the market mechanism—provides the information upon which firms and households make resource allocation decisions.

**market equilibrium**  Equilibrium established at the price where the quantity of the good buyers demand and purchase is just equal to the quantity suppliers supply and sell.

**microeconomics**  Branch of economic analysis that focuses on individual units or individual markets in the economy.

**mixed economy**  An economy in which what, how, and for whom to produce goods are determined partly by the operation of free markets and partly by government intervention.

**monetarism**  A school of thought that believes money is the main causal factor determining the level of economic activity.

**money**  Anything that is generally acceptable in trade as a medium of exchange and that also serves as a unit of account and a store of value.

**money GNP**  GNP measured in current prices or dollars.

**money interest rate**  The interest rate calculated in terms of units of money, not purchasing power over goods.

**money market fund share**  A depositlike interest-earning account at a money market mutual fund; typically it carries check writing privileges provided checks exceed some minimum amount.

**multiplier**  The number of times by which the change in total income exceeds the size of the expenditure change that brought it about.

### N

**national bank**  Commercial banks that are chartered by the federal government and are required by law to be members of the Federal Reserve System.

**national income (NI)**  Net national product minus indirect business taxes.

**nationalized industry**  An industry owned by the government.

**natural rate of unemployment**  The existence of frictional unemployment and a certain amount of structural unemployment constitutes a natural rate of unemployment towards which the economy automatically gravitates in the absence of other disturbances.

**near money**  Assets that are like money except that they can't be used as a medium of exchange, though they are readily convertible into currency or demand deposits.

**negotiable certificates of deposit**  CDs that are issued by commercial banks (usually in $100,000 denominations) and can be traded like bonds.

**negotiable order of withdrawal (NOW)**  Deposits at depository institutions from which the depositor may have funds transferred to a designated party by simply sending the depository institution a checklike form, the order of withdrawal.

**net exports**  The difference between the dollar value of the goods produced and sold to foreigners and the dollar value of the goods foreigners produce and sell to us.

**net national product (NNP)**  The dollar values of GNP minus capital depreciation or capital consumption allowance.

**net private domestic investment**  The increase (decrease) in the economy's capital stock.

**net worth**  See *equity*.

**new classical view**  Holds that systematic monetary and fiscal policy efforts to affect real variables in the economy, such as total output (real GNP) and the unemployment rate, will be ineffective because people can predict and anticipate such systematic actions according to rational expectations theory.

**normal good**  A good that people typically want more of as their income rises.

**normative statement**  A statement of what should or ought to be that cannot be supported or refuted by facts alone; a value judgment or opinion.

### O

**open economy**  An economy that trades with other nations.

**open market operations**  The Fed's buying and selling of government securities in the open market in which such securities are traded.

**opportunity cost**  The cost of a unit of a good measured in terms of the other goods that must be forgone in order to obtain it.

### P

**paradox of thrift**  If each household tries to save more, all households may end up saving and earning less.

**partial equilibrium analysis**  Analysis of a change in one market and its consequences for that market, and possibly a few others. All other markets are assumed to remain unchanged.

**peak** The uppermost point in the upswing (expansion) of a business cycle.

**per capita GNP** An economy's GNP divided by the size of its population.

**personal consumption** Household expenditures on goods and services.

**personal income (PI)** National income plus transfer payments minus corporate income taxes, undistributed corporate profits, and social security contributions.

**Phillips curve** An alleged relationship between the rate of inflation and the rate of unemployment suggesting that they tend to move in opposite directions to each other.

**planned economy** An economy in which an economic plan, designed by a central planning board, is used to inform, direct, and coordinate the activities of subunits such as firms.

**positive statement** A statement of what is, was, or will be that can be verified or refuted by looking at the facts.

**potential GNP** What GNP would be if the economy were "fully" employed.

**precautionary demand** The demand for money to cover unforeseen events or emergencies that require immediate expenditures.

**price** The exchange value of a good in terms of other goods, most often expressed as the amount of money people will pay for a unit of the good.

**price index** Ratio of current prices to prices in some base year.

**production possibilities frontier** A curve representing the maximum possible output combinations of goods for a fully employed economy.

**productivity** The efficiency with which each labor hour combines with the capital stock and the existing state of technology to produce output—often measured as output per labor hour.

**progressive tax** A tax that takes a *larger* percentage out of a high income than it does out of a low income.

**proportional tax** A tax that takes the same percentage of income no matter what the income level.

**proprietors' income** Income earned by the owners of unincorporated businesses.

**proven energy reserves** The quantities of oil, natural gas, and coal that producers are almost certain they can bring out of the ground given current energy prices and the state of mining and drilling technology.

**public assistance programs** Government programs aimed at providing help to dependent families, the sick, the handicapped, and the aged—those who for reasons largely beyond their control cannot work.

**public goods** Goods that will not be produced in private markets because there is no way for the producer to keep those who don't pay for the goods from using them—for example, a lighthouse beacon.

**pure market economy** An economy in which what, how, and for whom to produce goods is determined entirely by the operation of markets.

## Q

**quantity theory of money** Asserts that velocity, $V$, in the equation of exchange, $M \times V = p \times Q$, is stable and not just whatever number is necessary to make the equation true; therefore, changes in the money supply $M$ are asserted to cause proportional changes in money GNP, $p \times Q$.

## R

**rational expectations theory** Holds that people form their expectations about the future course of economic activity (wages, prices, employment, and so forth) on the basis of their knowledge, experience, and understanding of how the economy works (including the effects of systematic monetary and fiscal policy) and on all relevant economic data and information, and that they do not persist in making systematic mistakes when predicting future events.

**real GNP** GNP measured in terms of prices at which final goods and services are sold in some base year. Changes in real GNP are due only to changes in the quantity of final goods and services, not changes in price.

**realized investment** Intended investment minus any unintended inventory reduction or plus any unintended inventory addition.

**recession** A contraction, or slowing down, in the growth of economic activity.

**regressive tax** A tax that takes a smaller percentage out of a high income than it does out of a low income.

**required reserve ratio** The ratio of required reserves to the total amount of demand deposits.

**required reserves** Reserves that a bank is legally required to hold against demand deposits—equal to the required reserve ratio multiplied by the amount of demand deposits.

**reserves** Defined by law as cash held in the

bank's vault and the deposits of the bank at its district Federal Reserve bank.

**resource misallocation**   See *underemployment*.

**restrictive license**   Agreement under which the holder of a patent allows others to sell the product or use the process under restricted conditions (price limitations, quantity limitations, and so forth) stipulated in the license.

**retained earnings**   Money saved by businesses out of sales revenue.

## S

**saving function**   The relationship between the level of disposable income and the level of planned saving.

**Say's Law**   Supply creates its own demand.

**scarce**   Existing in a limited amount.

**scientific method**   Ongoing cycle of induction from observation to theory, followed by deduction from theory to prediction, and explanation and checking of predictions and explanations against new facts to see if theory is verified, refuted, or needs to be modified.

**seasonal variation**   Regular patterns in economic data associated with custom and weather over the course of the year.

**share draft**   An interest-earning demand-deposit-type checking account issued by federally insured credit unions.

**Special Drawing Rights (SDRs)**   Special accounts that the International Monetary Fund (IMF) creates for member nations, to be used as an official reserve to finance balance of payments deficits.

**specialization of labor**   System of production in which each worker performs only one task for which he or she is specifically trained.

**speculative demand**   The demand for money that arises from the anticipation that bond prices are more likely to fall than to rise.

**stagflation**   The existence of high rates of inflation and unemployment at the same time.

**state bank**   Commercial banks that are chartered by a state; they may join the Federal Reserve System if they wish.

**subsistence living level**   The minimum standard of living necessary to keep the population from declining—the death rate just equals the birthrate.

**substitute good**   A good that can be used in place of another good because it fulfills similar needs or desires.

**supply curve**   Graphic representation of the law of supply.

**supply schedule**   Numerical tabulation of the quantitative relationship between quantity supplied and price.

## T

**tariff (or duty)**   A tax on imports, most often calculated as a percent of the price charged for the good by the foreign supplier.

**tax-based income policy (TIP)**   Policies that use tax incentives to encourage compliance with wage guidelines; the carrot version of TIP rewards with tax credits (reductions in income taxes) those workers who keep their wage increases below the guideline rate for wage increases; the stick version of TIP punishes with tax penalties employers who grant wage increases in excess of the guideline rate for wage increases.

**technology**   The production methods used to combine resources of all kinds, including labor, to produce goods and services.

**terms of trade**   The ratio of exchange between an exported and an imported good.

**time deposit**   A deposit at a commercial bank that earns a fixed rate of interest and must be held a stipulated amount of time. Early withdrawal of funds is penalized, often by a loss of or a reduction in the interest rate earned.

**token coins**   Coins that contain an amount of metal (or other material) that is worth much less than the face value of the coin.

**trade credit**   Credit extended by one business to another business, allowing the latter to buy goods from the former without making immediate full payment by check or with currency. Serves as short-term medium of exchange though it is not a store of value like money.

**trading possibilities frontier**   Graphical representation of the choices that a nation has by specializing in the product in which it has a comparative advantage and trading (exporting) its specialty for the product in which it has a comparative disadvantage.

**transactions costs**   The costs associated with converting one asset into another asset—brokerage fees, telephone expense, time and effort, advertising cost, and so on.

**transactions demand**   Demand for money for its use as a medium of exchange to transact the purchase and sale of goods and services.

**transfer payments**   Payments characterized by the fact that the recipient is neither expected nor required to provide any contribution to GNP in return.

**Treasury bill**   A short-term government bond that matures either 1, 3, or 6 months after the day issued.

**trough** The lower turning point of a business cycle.

**U**

**unanticipated inflation** The amount of inflation that occurs that is unexpected.

**underemployment** A condition in which available resources are employed in tasks for which other resources are better suited or in which the best available technology is not used in a production process. Also called *resource misallocation*.

**unemployment** A condition in which available factors of production are idle; in reference to labor, unemployment is said to exist whenever workers are actively looking for a job but are unable to find one.

**unemployment compensation** Payments to workers who are involuntarily unemployed (they want work but can't find a job).

**V**

**value added** The difference at each stage of production between what the firm sells its product for and what it pays for all the materials it purchases to make the product.

**variable-dollar asset** An asset that has no guaranteed fixed-dollar value.

**velocity** The number of times a typical dollar of the money stock must go around the circular flow of money exchanged for final goods and services during a year.

**W**

**wage insurance** A guarantee that the government will repay labor for the purchasing power lost if consumer prices rise faster than the guideline rate for wages.

**wage-price controls** Government-specified rate of increase in wages and prices that it is illegal for business and labor to exceed—compliance is mandatory.

**wage-price guidelines** Government-specified rate of increase in wages and prices that business and labor are requested not to exceed—compliance is voluntary.

# Index

*Hi! Pelelik. Joust wanted to see if you would ever look in this book again - Especially this page. Love, McCaty 12-11-87 11:43 PJ*